FREDERICK LEONG, PH.D.
THE OHIO STATE UNIVERSITY
DEPARTMENT OF PSYCHOLOGY
142 TOWNSHEND HALL
1885 NEIL AVENUE MALL
COLUMBUS OHIO 43210-1222

SECOND EDITION

HUMAN BEHAVIOR IN GLOBAL PERSPECTIVE

An Introduction to Cross-Cultural Psychology

Marshall H. Segall
Syracuse University, USA

Pierre R. Dasen
University of Geneva, Switzerland

John W. Berry
Queens University, Canada

Ype H. Poortinga
Tilburg University, The Netherlands

Allyn and Bacon

Boston • London • Toronto • Sydney • Tokyo • Singapore

Vice-President and Editor-in-Chief, Social Sciences and Education: Sean W. Wakely
Series Editorial Assistant: Susan Hutchinson
Executive Marketing Manager: Joyce Nilsen
Manufacturing Buyer: Suzanne Lareau

Library of Congress Cataloging-in-Publication Data

Human behavior in global perspective : an introduction to cross-
    cultural psychology / Marshall H. Segall...[et al.].—2nd ed.
        p. cm.
    Includes bibliographical references and index.
    ISBN 0-205-18861-3 (pbk.)
    1. Ethnopsychology. 2. Human behavior. 3. Culture. 4. Social
psychology. I. Segall, Marshall H.
GN502.H86   1999
302—dc21   98-47786
                                               CIP

Printed in the United States of America
10 9 8 7 6 5 4 3 2 1   03 02 01 00 99

CONTENTS

PREFACE

Until recently, only a few cross-cultural psychology courses existed. Although psychology as a subject was thriving, it seemed to many psychologists that they were getting along well enough without cross-cultural courses, so their students received an insular, parochial education in psychology. Outside of North America and Europe, if any instruction in psychology existed, it consisted mostly of material that described the behavior of North Americans and Europeans. Thus, psychology left much to be desired everywhere.

A handful of psychologists felt strongly that cross-cultural psychology belonged in the undergraduate psychology curriculum in Europe and North America and that such courses could with good effect replace the Euro/American-centered courses that predominated elsewhere. But teaching materials for such courses were practically nonexistent. A need had to be met.

One response was a relatively brief text entitled *Cross-Cultural Psychology: Human Behavior in Global Perspective,* written by one of us (Segall) and published in 1979. Its goal, expressed in its preface, was "to demonstrate to undergraduate students—beginners and advanced psychology majors alike—that human behavior is both delightfully varied and satisfyingly orderly. That is, human behavior *can* be studied in a systematic, scientific fashion, but, to do justice to this subject, attention must be paid to diverse ecological and cultural settings in which human beings live."

The other three coauthors (Dasen, Berry, and Poortinga) of the present volume subscribed to the views expressed in the 1979 book and found it useful in their own teaching of cross-cultural psychology. All four of us discovered in our classrooms (in the United States, Canada, Switzerland, France, and the Netherlands), however, that there was much more that needed to be said about cross-cultural psychology.

When, from time to time, we would find ourselves together at cross-cultural psychology meetings, we would talk about the books that might be written. Then, at one such meeting (in Mexico, in 1984) we decided to join forces, using the 1979 book as a jumping-off place. We began to plan our project and soon discovered that it required two books.

This one, in its 1990 edition, was designed as an *introduction* to cross-cultural psychology. The present revision retains that intent. It can be used, we believe, in courses designed for students who have had no prior introduction to psychology. We expect that the book will be used that way in many parts of the world where it will serve new students of psychology better as an introduction to psychology than most books designed as general psychology texts.

This book can also be used effectively by students who have had some prior training in psychology. We expect that the book will be used mostly in courses that follow general psychology and social psychology. In such cases, a course built around this book extends the students' awareness of behavioral phenomena and challenges what they have previously been taught about psychological theory; this, because we cover material that students will probably not have encountered in their prior courses in psychology. When they add this material to what they already know, students are likely to feel a need to reassess and reinterpret what they know about human behavior. Instructors are likely to discover that by using this book they will have set the stage for some lively, engaging discussions with their students. Feedback from colleagues who used the 1990 edition assures us that this is the case.

Since the first edition of this book, the parochialism that long characterized undergraduate teaching in Europe and North America in most disciplines, including psychology, has given way to a more global perspective—a treatment of fundamental human concerns that acknowledges the increasing interdependence of the various regions of the world. In other parts of the world, where universities are newer and curricula still being developed, materials that pertain to local circumstances are needed for comparison and contrast with information regarding former colonial metropoles and other erstwhile "centers of power." From now on, educated persons everywhere need to cultivate a sense of their fellows everywhere—who we all are, what moves us, and how we cope, both similarly and differently, with the problems we face. There is a crucial role for psychology in this increasing effort to globalize knowledge and understanding.

Increasing numbers of psychologists have come to acknowledge that our discipline, to live up to the demands of this role, must be a cross-cultural psychology that is informed by the insights of several neighboring disciplines, preeminent among them anthropology. The four of us owe a debt to anthropology for pointing out to us the need to do research in societies other than our own. All of us have done fieldwork in several locations. So have many other psychologists, and it is the work of those who have occasionally behaved like anthropologists, for whom "the field" is their laboratory, that is featured in this book. Accordingly, the book might well be used in anthropology courses, for its contents will enrich traditional anthropological analyses by providing psychological data to be interpreted in varying ecocultural contexts.

Our other book, published in 1992 by Cambridge University Press, and nearing publication as a revised edition, deals with several topics not covered here. It also focuses more on how cross-cultural research and applications are done. Thus, it is intended primarily for more advanced students and, especially, students who might be considering careers in or related to cross-cultural psychology. We expect, therefore, that our other book might be used *after* this one wherever the curriculum contains a two-course sequence in cross-cultural psychology.

Each book, however, can stand alone. This one contains more than enough material for a semester-long course. We cover several basic psychological domains, including perception, cognition, and human development, and a number of issues of continuing concern to social psychologists, including matters relating to sex and gender, aggression, and intergroup relations. We deal also with various implications of the acculturative processes that are occurring everywhere in the world. Educational implications of cross-cultural research constitute a recurring theme. We deal also with a number of theoretical approaches and we touch on some methodological concerns, some of them unique to cross-cultural psychology.

Because the four of us were deeply involved in the production of the 1997 edition of the *Handbook of Cross-Cultural Psychology* (Berry as senior editor for all three volumes, with Poortinga, Dasen, and Segall serving as co-editors—along with colleagues Pandey, Saraswathi, and Kagitçibasi from India and Turkey—for volumes 1, 2, and 3, respectively), we benefited mightily from the work of dozens of colleagues who contributed chapters to the *Handbook*. Much of the updating of the field of cross-cultural psychology that is at the heart of this revision of *Human Behavior in Global Perspective* reflects what we four learned from interacting intensely with those colleagues.

As coauthors, we collectively stand behind the whole book but let it be known that our sometimes diverse perspectives, grounded in our own cultures (but probably influenced also by our stubborn natures), produced numerous debates and discussions about what to say, how to say it, who should write it, and how much to keep or discard. Disputes were settled by striving for consensus; no one of us had veto power.

Logistically, the writing of this book was a case study in high-tech word processing and electronic communication. Our computers were linked by electronic mail, and drafts flowed many times both ways across the Atlantic, somewhat haltingly during the work leading up to the 1990 edition, but with somewhat more sophistication during work on the present edition. But we never abandoned face-to-face communication; we also met from time to time over the past fifteen years, either in Syracuse, Kingston, Fribourg, Geneva, Strasbourg, or Dublin to carry on our debates and discussions. The nerve center for the enterprise was Syracuse, where Segall put it all together.

In the preparation of this revised edition, the four of us acknowledge the help of Sally Bennett Segall in Syracuse, Catherine Dasen in Geneva, and Najum Rashid in Kingston; useful comments from Linda Allal and Tania Ogay in Geneva; and input for some of the sections from Christophe and Hedwige Boesch, Patricia Greenfield, and Fabienne Tanon.

Marshall H. Segall
Pierre R. Dasen
John W. Berry
Ype H. Poortinga

1

THE SOCIOCULTURAL NATURE
OF HUMAN BEINGS

HOW TO COMPREHEND BEHAVIOR AND CULTURE

Human behavior *must* be viewed in the sociocultural context in which it occurs if we are truly to understand it. It is obvious that our behavior is fundamentally social, involving relationships with other people, reactions to their behavior, and engagement with innumerable products granted by those who preceded us. And although, like us, many other animal species are social, human beings are cultural as well. What does it mean to be *cultural?*

A Preliminary Definition of Culture

Culture, comprising diverse products of the behavior of many people, provides a relatively stable context for human development. Culture, in a very real sense, is "the man-made part of the environment" (Herskovits, 1948, p. 17). Our behavior occurs in, and is shaped and constrained by, environmental elements including those that are created by ourselves or other people. To say that culture shapes behavior is shorthand for "behavior is influenced by products of other persons' behavior." These products can be material objects, ideas, or social institutions. They are ubiquitous; everywhere we look, we can see them. So we need to acknowledge that culture always influences behavior (although we may not always be aware of it).

The room you might be in now is a "cultural product." It has a particular shape that reflects someone's architectural ideas and carpentry skills. If you are in Paris, London, Nairobi, or any other city, the room is most likely rectangular. (However, there are other places where the probability of your being in a rectangular room is very low. There are "non-carpentered" environments, about which more will be said later.) As you read this chapter, you might be sitting down, partly because some time ago some people designed and built "chairs." If you are sitting, this invention is shaping—in more ways than one—your behavior. (Again, however, there are places where the probability of your sitting would be much lower. There are, after all, societies without chairs.)

Chairs may be found in a "classroom," but some societies lack schools. That in some societies students gather in classrooms, facing teachers, reflects another kind of cultural product, an institution, called "schooling," which is a part of a formal educational system. It may have material aspects, including school buildings, and ideational ones like the notion that schooling should occupy a specific place and time, or the idea that individuals becoming "educated" should be evaluated and certified if deemed worthy. The institution of education also provides behavioral expectations for all who participate—a series of "roles" to be played. These include privileges that apply to "teachers" and responsibilities that "students" have to shoulder, and vice versa. As we will see in Chapter 3, "schooling" is now widespread in the world, but it is not universal. Some societies lack schools, but have developed alternative forms of formal education, and much of what is learned, in any society, is learned through informal education.

Much of our lives as human beings, then, involves responding to such cultural influences. But notice, just as culture shapes us, we shape culture. Recent anthropological writings (e.g., Shweder & Sullivan, 1990, 1993) have stressed the mutual influences of culture and psyche, each on the other, thus depicting an interactive relationship between individuals and their sociocultural surroundings. This perspective emphasizes that human beings are not passive recipients of cultural forces and that they themselves create the context in which their behavior is shaped (an idea clearly implied in Herskovits's (1948) definition of culture, cited above). According to Miller (1997), this focus makes salient the likelihood that psychological structures and, arguably, processes as well, will vary fundamentally in different cultural contexts. So, human beings shape culture and culture shapes the different functioning of human populations.

More Definitions of Culture

Culture is the key concept of anthropology. Like many key concepts (for example, *energy* in physics or *group* in sociology) culture is often ambiguously defined, yet used as if its meaning were clear. While definitions of *culture* abound (several useful ones appear in Box 1.1), they commonly point to some essential features of culture.

Culture, by almost any definition, includes behavioral products of others who preceded us. It indicates both substantial and abstract particulars with prior existence. Culture is already there as we begin life. It contains *values* that will be expressed and a *language* in which to express them. It contains *a way of life* that will be followed by most of us, and through most of our lifetimes we will unquestioningly assume that there is no better. Munroe and Munroe (1980) pointed out that "culture" is composed of numerous separable (but often correlated) factors, including subsistence patterns, social and political institutions, languages, rules governing

BOX 1.1   A Few Definitions of Culture

According to Ember and Ember (1985), culture encompasses the learned behaviors, beliefs, and attitudes that are characteristic of people in a particular society or population. They also defined it as "the shared customs of a society" (p. 166).

For one anthropologist of an earlier generation, White (1947), culture denotes all the symbolic behavior, especially language, that makes possible the transmission of wisdom, in the form of techniques for coping with the environment, from generation to generation. As White saw it, culture is continuous, cumulative, and progressive.

Moore and Lewis (1952) culled from diverse anthropological writings what they considered to be the essence of the concept. It is first of all an abstraction, in the sense that it is merely a convenient label for a very large category of phenomena. It designates knowledge, skills, and information that are learned. Further, it is social knowledge, in the sense that it is taught to and learned by many individuals and is thus shared. Because it tends to persist over generations, it is more or less adaptive. Finally, it tends to be integrated; that is to say, its contents tend to be mutually reinforcing. Given these characteristics of culture, it becomes simply the totality of whatever all people learn from each other.

In the same year, Kroeber and Kluckhohn (1952) reviewed as many as 164 definitions of culture found in the anthropological literature between 1871 and 1950. Their classification scheme and their own definition are summarized in Berry and colleagues (1992, pp. 165–166). A remarkable feature of their definition is that it places culture inside the head rather than outside: "The essential core of culture consists of…ideas and especially their attached values" (p. 181).

Barnlund and Araki (1985) offered a behavioristic definition, "Cultures have no existence except as they are manifest in the behavior of the people who constitute them. A culture is only an abstraction based on the commonalities displayed in the behavior of a given community of people" (p. 9). At the same time, culture is usually seen as superorganic (Kroeber, 1917), that is, it has an existence over and above individuals.

E. Boesch (1991) in his "symbolic action theory" states, "Culture is a field of action, whose contents range from objects made and used by human beings to institutions, ideas and myths. Being an action field, culture offers possibilities of, but by the same token stipulates conditions for, action…As an action field, culture not only induces and controls action, but is also continuously transformed by it; therefore, culture is as much a process as a structure" (p. 29).

Culture as process is stressed by Hutchins (cited in Cole, 1996, p. 129):

> [Culture] is a process and the 'things' that appear on listlike definitions of culture are residua of the process. Culture is an adaptive process that accumulates the partial solutions to frequently encountered problems…Culture is a human cognitive process that takes place both inside and outside the minds of people. It is the process in which our everyday cultural practices are enacted (Hutchins, 1995, p. 354).

For still other definitions of culture, see Chapter 7 in Berry, Poortinga, Segall, and Dasen (1992, pp. 165–168).

interpersonal relations, divisions of labor by sex, age, or ethnicity, population density, dwelling styles, and more.

Culture also includes music and art forms, as well as shared preferences, appetites, and aversions. It includes rules, norms, and standards. It shapes hopes and fears, beliefs and attitudes, convictions and doubts, at least to the extent that such are shared, taught, and transmitted among people.

Where Is Culture?

Some of these conceptualizations of culture appear to place it outside the individual. There are also treatments of culture that place it, metaphorically at least, inside the heads of many individuals. Thus, Geertz (1973) identified culture with "an historically transmitted pattern of meanings embodied in symbols" (p. 89). Culture provides meaning by creating significant categories, like social practices (e.g., marriage) and roles (e.g., bridegroom), as well as values, beliefs, and premises. These meanings move, in a sense, from head to head. As Shweder (1984) put it, to learn that "a pig is an animal not to eat" and "a mother's sister's husband is an 'uncle',...one must, somehow,...receive the 'frame' of understanding from others" (p. 49).

This "semiotic" approach implies a dialectic relationship between culture and individuals. As Miller (1997) shows, this approach underscores how culture not only shapes behavior, but is continuously reconstructed by individuals. They have some freedom of choice; they can select and accept some aspects of culture and reject others. Hence, culture is not completely homogeneous at the population level and, via this definition, culture differs from earlier structural definitions that spoke of "patterns of culture" (Benedict, 1946) or systems in which all parts are coherently linked. Geertz emphasizes culture's rather loose organization with the following simile: "[T]he elements of culture are not like a pile of sand and not like a spider's web. It's more like an octopus, a rather badly integrated creature" (Geertz, 1973, as quoted in Miller, 1997, p. 105).

Although the concept of culture may be an abstraction, it includes many real influences on human behavior; by employing the concept, we are able to categorize and explain many important differences in human behavior that in the past were erroneously attributed to ill-defined biological differences. If anthropologists had not invented culture, then psychologists would have had to, because the concept enables us to take into account the fact that the same stimuli are not equally probable in different places or at different times. The social and cultural context within which human development occurs varies widely over time and place. Children in Western Europe in the twenty-first century are unlikely to greet a parent by prostrating themselves and kissing her feet. A Ganda householder in his East African grass-thatched house is not likely to be confronted with a bowl of corn flakes for breakfast.[1]

---

[1]Because of cultural diffusion (see Chapter 10) all of these events could, in fact occur anywhere, if not today, tomorrow. Nevertheless, when this book was written, these events had differential probability of occurring in various parts of the world.

Culture and *society* are roughly coterminous; their meanings overlap. But society is one thing, and culture is another. A society is a "group of people who occupy a particular territory and speak a common language not generally understood by neighboring peoples" (Ember & Ember, 1996, p. 21). A society may or may not be a single nation, but every society *has* its own culture, and it is culture that shapes behavior differentially from society to society.

Culture is a label for all the many different features that vary from society to society and that comprise the independent variables (Segall, 1984) that psychologists must use in their research on human behavior. So, the discipline of psychology must be cross-cultural; we must study behavior as it develops differently in different contexts.

THE CENTRALITY OF LEARNING

Human beings acquire habits throughout life, continuously modifying behavior in response to environmental influences. This is the essence of the human potential.

Human behavior can best be understood as the product of learning, particularly learning that results from experiences with other people or with ideas, institutions, or other products of the behavior of other people. In short, we are largely what we are because of culturally based learning. You have learned how to behave in rooms designed, built, and furnished by others. You are probably clothed in garments of human design and production, which you learned to wear in response to certain social pressures, however nonconformist you believe yourself to be.

Our Capacity to Learn

A hallmark of human beings is our capacity to learn from others. Consider again a classroom, with thirty or so persons in the room, one of whom does most of the talking. How does it happen that the others spend so much time listening? There are obviously learned roles at work here, role expectations relating to school. Classroom behaviors reflect customs. They are the end result of experience in a particular culture, in which students learned to behave like students. Of course, if the example we had chosen here were that of a Quranic school, the students probably would have been talking aloud, simultaneously reciting different parts of the Quran, while the teacher listened silently.

Humans are both sociocultural and biological. Like other animals, we are first of all biological creatures. We have certain vital needs. Before anything else, our behavior must tend to enhance our probability of surviving; it must be functional in the sense that it answers our survival needs.

In fulfillment of these needs and in pursuit of a far more numerous set of unessential, but equally compelling, goals, we exercise our acquired skills and habits. Our sociocultural nature reflects a highly developed capacity to benefit from the lessons of experience, our own and our culture mates'. No other animal has this capacity to the same extent. No other animal has created whole systems of education. No other animal learns as much. As a result, we display many forms of behavior that are uniquely human, many of which are part of what we call *culture*. We have already recognized that we are both culture's creators and culture's creations. As the creation of culture, each person is the product of the twin processes of enculturation and socialization.

Enculturation and Socialization

From birth onward, all human beings learn to accommodate their behavior to that of others. Like other primates, we are subject to socialization. Much of our socialization involves formal education, which is a distinctly human institution, but a large part of it also occurs in nonformal settings. In addition, there is enculturation, which may require no education, either formal or informal. Even the most fundamental appreciation of the whys of human behavior demands that these processes be understood. The two concepts are clarified in the next two sections of this chapter.

Enculturation

Much of what we learn is learned without direct, deliberate teaching. We all learn particular ideas, concepts, and values, simply because of the differential availability in different places of what is to be learned, for example, what is music and what is noise. What we identify as music depends primarily on what is there, previously labeled as music, to be learned. Similarly, in every society a high percentage of the people would agree on what is worth standing up for, and not because there is a course in the curriculum on "supreme causes." Instead, such values are widely transmitted, both directly and indirectly, and are learned very well because they are hardly ever questioned. It is this kind of learning that we call "enculturation."

First employed by Herskovits (1948, pp. 39–42; 1955, pp. 326–329), the term *enculturation* refers to all of the learning that occurs in human life because of what is available to be learned. Whenever we learn by observation (cf. Bandura, 1971), any part of the content of our society—content that has been culturally shaped and limited during preceding generations—enculturation is occurring.

Although effects of enculturation are obvious to the social scientist, enculturated individuals are usually unaware of how much of what they do reflects the process. People are not likely to be aware of what was unavailable in the society to be learned. This leads to the apparent paradox that people who are most thoroughly enculturated are often the least aware of their culture's role in molding them.

Much of our learning involves both socialization and enculturation. Learning a language, for example, involves both. There is a certain amount of direct teaching of the language, as in grammar courses in elementary school. But a lot of the learning of language occurs (apparently) spontaneously, by children who, in monolingual societies, may assume that there is only one language to be learned.

Socialization

Child (1954) defined socialization as "the whole process by which an individual, born with behavioral potentialities of enormously wide range, is led to develop actual behavior which is confined within a much narrower range—the range of what is customary and acceptable for him according to the standards of his group" (p. 655).

This definition has the virtue of reminding us that all human beings are capable of a far greater repertory of behaviors than any single person ever exhibits. Each of us, because of the accident of birth, begins life in a particular social context, within which we learn to make certain responses and not others. The most dramatic illustration of this is our linguistic behavior. That one speaks one language rather than another, even though all languages are possible, aptly demonstrates this fact (cf. Bril & Lehalle, 1988; Mohanty & Perregaux, 1997). Less obviously, socialization also effectively narrows the range of responses each of us habitually makes in many other behavioral domains. The conditions under which we express emotions, and the ways in which we suppress them, are determined by socialization. Our reactions to authority figures, and their reactions to us, reflect the customs of the society into which we happened to be born. Many, if not all, of the behavioral differences that for centuries were attributed to "national character," such as British coolness and Latin abandon, are attributable to the differential reinforcement of certain responses and the effective elimination of others. Equally important, although less obvious, is the nonreinforcement of unwanted behavior. This, too, serves to lessen the probability of future occurrences of socially disapproved responses.

Although we are active creatures, able to choose within broad limits those with whom we come into contact, the probability of our behaving in certain ways is affected by them, at least by those who relate to us as "socialization agents." Anyone who possesses power relative to us can socialize us. Most often these agents include parents, teachers, and other elders, who are more knowledgeable in the ways of their society. Under certain circumstances, however, even age peers can effect socialization.

The process of socialization often involves conflict between the individual and socialization agents, as sometimes occurs between pupils and teachers. Not only are some responses likely to be punished, some may be blocked by the behavior of others in very subtle, but effective, ways. For example, socialization agents may withhold opportunities to behave in certain ways except at a time and place they consider appropriate. The socialization of feeding behavior during infancy involves this mechanism to a very great extent.

All socialization involves efforts by others to control behavior. Socialization, then, consists primarily of deliberate tutelage applied in an effort to produce "acceptable" behavior. The process, however, is not unidirectional. Individuals are not only influenced by their social environment, they also influence the latter; in fact, the two continuously influence each other (Camilleri & Malewska-Peyre, 1997). Particularly in societies that comprise many social groups, individuals can choose to some extent those to which they wish to belong, a point that will be stressed later, in Chapter 11.

With increased migration and mobility, individuals are not only socialized once, but are often resocialized differently during their life span (Valsiner & Lawrence, 1997).

Both processes, socialization and enculturation, result in behavioral similarities within societies and behavioral differences across societies. Both processes involve learning from other people how to behave. In the case of socialization, the learning involves teaching. In the case of enculturation, teaching is not necessary for the learning to take place. Because the term *enculturation* very neatly denotes the engagement of people in their culture, the term also serves well as a generic label for all human learning, encompassing socialization.

Finally, these processes are responsible for intergenerational learning that may result in "cultural transmission," a phenomenon that is "parallel" to, but different from, "biological transmission," as we shall see later in this chapter.

These, then, are some basic notions about the social and cultural context in which all human behavior is shaped and displayed. That our behavior has this contextual characteristic is largely a reflection of the fact that we are a species endowed with language and the ability to use it as well as other tools.

THE ESSENCE OF BEING HUMAN

What makes humans truly human, i.e., different from other animals? For a long time, it has been argued that the main distinguishing features were the use of language and tools, and, of course, the possession of culture in all its other respects as well. All of these arguments have been challenged in controversies involving comparisons between humans and chimpanzees and by recent research with rhesus monkeys.

Do Monkeys Count?

In a well-controlled laboratory experiment, Brannon and Terrace (1998) convincingly demonstrated that two rhesus monkeys, whom they called Rosencrantz and Macduff, after learning to choose in ascending order stimuli representing one, two, three, and four elements, could spontaneously do the same with stimuli representing five through nine elements. This ability to extrapolate an ordinal rule to novel numerosities is impressive. Is it counting? How is it related to the mastering of a language's integer list, which typically takes two years in very numerate cultures? It is not yet clear, but the evidence presented by Brannon and Terrace that some precultural phenomenon is involved in ordinal numerical understanding is impressive.

As Carey (1998) argued, "Until recently, the consensus was that the capacity to represent the positive integers was also the product of culture, dependent on the uniquely human capacity for language" (p. 641). Carey suggests that the feats performed by Rosencrantz and Macduff reflect an "analog magnitude" model for nonlinguistic numerical representation, a model in which number is represented by a continuous quantity. This model, according to Carey, is *not* the primary source of human symbolic number list representation, and we still do not know "the process by which explicit symbolic representations are constructed in the history of each culture and again by each child" (p. 642). But, we may be on the verge of understanding the nature of nonlinguistic representation of number. How the process or processes later interact with culturally based language learning could be a fruitful area of cross-cultural research with infants and children, research which would be informed by primate studies such as this one. Of course, we can't count on it.

Of Chimps and Humans

Present day chimpanzees (*Pantroglodytes*) and humans (*Homo sapiens sapiens*) have a lot in common; according to paleontology, they had a common ancestor as recently as 5.5 million years ago (Harris, 1993), and they now share more than 99 percent of their genes (King & Wilson, 1975). There are, of course, also major differences. For example, the comparatively small size of the chimpanzees' pharynx prevents them from making vowel sounds such as *i, u,* or *a,* which are essential in all human languages. Hence, research on chimpanzees' capacity to communicate has concentrated on sign language or the use of specially designed computer keyboards. Chimpanzees raised in captivity have been able to learn vocabularies of several hundred symbols. They can combine two of these to designate new objects or events, and to create the equivalent of short sentences. With extensive training, they can also learn to understand some spoken English, and can subsequently understand novel combinations of these words (Greenfield & Savage-Rumbaugh, 1990; Harris, 1993; Savage-Rumbaugh et al., 1993).

In wild chimpanzees in the Taï forest of Côte d'Ivoire, Boesch (1991a) has reported the use of drumming on buttressed trees to convey information on resting periods, on changes of travel direction, or on both of these combined. In an extensive observation of the drumming of one of the leading males, his drumming twice on the same tree within a short space of time (less than two minutes) meant that the group was to rest; drumming first on one tree and then on another indicated, via the orientation of the trees, the next direction he was proposing to take. By combining both messages, this chimp could propose both a rest and a subsequent change of direction; in this case he would drum twice on the same tree, and then once on another tree in the direction he was proposing to take, all within two minutes. Hence, even chimps that have not been encultured by humans can use some form of symbolic communication.

The research on symbolic communication in chimpanzees is impressive in view of the previous claims that only humans had language, but even the most astonishing performance remains far from the possibilities of human language. For example, only humans employ subjunctive and conditional grammatical forms to discuss possible events that might never have occurred!

Similarly, the use of tools has now been consistently documented in both captive and wild chimpanzees, but the complexity of the tools remains relatively limited in comparison to human toolmaking. For example, chimpanzees use sticks and grass stems to "fish" for termites or ants in their mounds; they can be observed to modify these objects—for example, stripping leaves from a stick—in an effort to make them into more useful tools (Goodall-van Lawick, 1971). Another example of this primitive form of toolmaking is the chewing of leaves to make them more absorbent and then putting them in hard-to-reach places to soak up rain water for drinking. Still another example is the use of branches and stones to crack nuts. In observations by Boesch and Boesch (1984), the choice of tool was found to be dependent on the hardness of the nutshell that they intended to crack.

Is Culture a Uniquely Human Property?

If neither language nor tool use is distinctly human, there remains the claim that humans are the only ones to possess culture. Is this so? The controversy is still raging. Tomasello, Kruger, and Ratner (1993) consider "cultural learning" as distinctly human. They summarized their position as follows:

Human beings evolved species-specific social-cognitive abilities to understand the psychological states of conspecifics in terms of their perceptions and intentions, their thoughts and beliefs, and their reflective thoughts and beliefs, which allowed them to take the perspective of others and to participate with them intersubjectively. These processes of social cognition then led humans to the species-specific ways of learning from one another that we call cultural learning, which then kicked off the evolutionary and historical processes that led to the species-specific form of social organization known as human cultures (p. 509).

According to Tomasello and colleagues, chimpanzees trained by humans can display imitative learning at about the level of two-year-old children. "With regard to instructed learning, it may be said quite simply that in their natural habitats chimpanzees do not actively instruct their young.... Chimpanzees cannot internalize instruction and use it to regulate their own behavior, in our view, because they cannot conceive of others as mental agents having thoughts and beliefs that may be contrasted with their own" (p. 505).

Not everyone agrees with Tomasello and colleagues' theory and their way of interpreting chimpanzee behavior. Boesch (1991b), for example, has observed two cases in which a mother chimpanzee was, according to him, making a clear demonstration of how to crack nuts. In the first case, the mother demonstrated repeatedly the correct positioning of the nut, while in the second case, the mother called Ricci, with her five-year-old daughter Nina sitting in front of her, "in a very deliberate manner, slowly rotated the hammer into the best position with which to pound the nut effectively. As if to emphasize the meaning of this movement, it took her a full minute to perform this simple rotation" (Boesch, 1991b, p. 532). When Ricci left,

Nina resumed the cracking, "now, by adopting the same hammer grip as her mother" (p. 532).

This incident seems clearly to involve a member of the older generation transmitting a skill to the younger generation through teaching. Remember that a main criterion of culture is its transmission from generation to generation. According to Parker and Mitchell (1994), "only chimpanzees and humans currently are known to engage in apprenticeship in tool-aided extractive foraging," while self-awareness (mirror self-recognition), symbol use, and imitation are also shared by gorillas and orangutans (having a common ancestor with humans 12 million years ago), and object permanence is found in all (New World and Old World) monkeys (with a common ancestor 35 million years ago) (see also Parker, 1996).

Another reason to view nutcracking behavior in wild chimpanzees as a cultural behavior, according to Boesch and colleagues (Boesch, 1996; Boesch, Marchesi, Fruth, & Joulian, 1994), is the fact that this behavior is restricted to a relatively small area in West Africa, with no ecological features (chimpanzee density, density of nut-producing trees, availability of anvils and hammers, etc.) explaining the irregular distribution.

Similarly, leaf-clipping occurs only in some groups and not in others; it has been observed to be practiced by all males, to remain constant over many years, but also to show modification in the context and function of use. "Thus, the three essential characteristics of human culture seem to be demonstrated by chimpanzees in leaf-clipping" (Boesch, 1995, p. 12). More generally, "new field data provide further support to the idea of chimpanzee culture in the sense that the behavioral differences observed seem not only independent of environmental variables, but also their function tends to follow social conventions that are learned by all group members and that may change over time" (Boesch, 1996, p. 426). Interestingly, in this case the behavior is considered cultural because of the very fact that it is *not* linked to ecology, and that it has "irregular and unpredictable distribution patterns similar to those of human culture" (Boesch et al., 1994, p. 325).

Still another approach is represented by McGrew, who sets eight conditions for recognizing cultural acts in other species.

Innovation	*New pattern is invented or modified*
Dissemination	*Pattern acquired by another from innovator*
Standardization	*Form of pattern is consistent and stylized*
Durability	*Pattern performed without presence of demonstrator*
Diffusion	*Pattern spreads from one group to another*
Tradition	*Pattern persists from innovator's generation to next one*
Non-subsistence	*Pattern transcends subsistence*
Naturalness	*Pattern shown in absence of direct human influence (McGrew, 1992, p. 77).*

After reviewing the evidence, McGrew concludes: "In summary, no single population of chimpanzees yet shows a single behavioural pattern which satisfies all eight conditions of culture. However, all conditions (except perhaps diffusion) are readily met by some chimpanzees in some cases" (p. 82). Hence, "Chimpanzees do not have human culture, material or otherwise. Similarly, even the simplest aspects of human culture are not those of apes, or other primates, mammals or vertebrates" (p. 230).

However, McGrew's criteria are very stringent. As Boesch (1996) remarks, the exclusion of food-oriented behaviors is particularly "difficult for a French person to understand!" (p. 405). And McGrew himself admits, "If the same data were reported in ethnological journals as cross-cultural comparisons of human beings, not an eyebrow would be raised" (p. 197).

The controversy obviously rests on the stringency of the criteria used to define *culture*. Whether chimpanzees have some mild form of it or not, human culture, without any doubt, stands alone in its complexity.

How this linguistically endowed, tool-using animal—the human being—has created and continues to create cultures is a fit and critically important object for study. So is the manner in which culture, in turn, molds the human individual. Cross-cultural psychology concerns itself with both of these overarching questions.

ANTHROPOLOGICAL PERSPECTIVES ON CULTURE

As we shall see frequently in later chapters, cross-cultural psychology finds both differences and similarities when it compares people from different societies. While some anthropologists emphasize mainly differences,[2] many others find it quite appropriate to compare cultures. When they do, they find that most phenomena of interest to any social scientist in any society exist in most others, but the form they take varies within certain limits, which can only be determined empirically by comparative research. Munroe and Munroe (1997) have reviewed many such studies, covering a wide range of phenomena. To cite one example derived from many ethnographies, they report that frequency of sexual intercourse varies from a maximum of three to five times daily to a culturally sanctioned total abstinence (e.g., for celibate priests, or for those practicing a postpartum period of sexual abstinence that can last up to five years).[3] But, in most societies for which we have data, the modal frequency is a long way from both the minimum and maximum, albeit closer to the minimum. (We will learn more about the role of culture in human sexual behavior in Chapter 8.)

---

[2]Extreme relativists and social constructivists question the very enterprise of cross-cultural comparison, because of the alleged "uniqueness" of each culture (e.g., Shweder & Sullivan, 1993).

[3]This extended five-year period of postpartum sexual abstinence, with no alternative sexual outlets, was reported by Heider (1976) for the Grand Valley Dani of Irian Jaya, with "no accompanying unhappiness or stress." It should be noted, however that about half of the Dani males are polygynous, which alleviates the hardship for them, if not for their wives.

Over a number of domains, Munroe and Munroe (1997) reveal that, while individual behavior is limited by biopsychological constraints, there is considerable cross-cultural variability. For interpersonal behaviors and institutional characteristics of societies as well, Munroe and Munroe (1997) acknowledge the important cultural variability but nevertheless emphasize the generality of behavioral domains and our ability to study them comparatively.

What to Make of Cultural Differences?

How should we think about the differences that characterize human groups, like the range of frequency in sexual intercourse we just mentioned? A basic perspective from which this book is written is that of cultural relativism (Herskovits, 1948), a view of the world in which the characteristic behaviors and the varying cultural contexts of human groups are described *but not evaluated.*[4] They are not considered better or worse, nor more or less civilized. Rather, every cultural system is seen as a solution to the problem of living that is workable in the particular conditions in which the culture evolved.

Along with cross-cultural psychology from its beginnings, the anthropological field dubbed "cultural psychology" offers, according to Miller (1997), "a relativistic view of cultural diversity as reflecting alternative yet equally adequate modes of understanding or forms of life." Because anthropologists adhere to the precept of cultural relativism, they consider each culture to be as valid as any other.

There is no one culture that is globally better or superior to another, but this does not mean that every aspect of culture is necessarily functional, or beyond criticism or public debate. As Morin and Kern (1993) have pointed out, "every culture has something *dys*functional.... One has to respect cultures, but they may well be inherently imperfect" (p. 124).

We will return to the issue of cultural relativism later, particularly in Chapter 10 on intergroup relations.

CULTURE AND BIOLOGY

What about Reflexes and Hormones?

A psychology that emphasizes culture must also include biological factors because there are, among other things, hormonally influenced behaviors and reflexive responses at the human level as well. These reflexes are mediated by lower centers

---

[4]The cultural relativist position is a necessary antidote to a prevailing tendency of people everywhere to evaluate their own culture (and, by extension themselves) as superior to others. This tendency, known as *ethnocentrism,* is something every one of us is likely to display in our own behavior and thinking (as we shall see in Chapter 10). Cultural relativism does not preclude holding one's own opinions and values.

of the human nervous system in a relatively simple way. A distinguishing feature of a reflex is stereotypy, or sameness. At the human level, reflexes account for a small proportion of our behavior, most of which involves the highest brain centers, notably the cortex. The result is that most human responses lack the characteristic stereotypy of a reflex. Similarly, while hormones are important in regulating human physiology, they do not completely control human behavior.

For example, sexual behavior, which surely involves hormones and reflexive reactions in mice and humans alike, becomes almost bewilderingly complex among human beings, whose cortical functions interact with their glandular secretions. Human mating behavior can hardly be described as reflexive. Partner preferences are a key feature of human sexual behavior. The bases of these preferences differ widely within societies, across societies, and over time. Our sexual behavior is affected by many rules, standards, values, and laws, with all of these controlling factors in a continuous process of change. One leading student of human sexuality, the sociologist Ira Reiss, whose work will be discussed more fully in Chapter 8, defined sexuality as "erotic and genital responses produced by the cultural scripts of a society" (Reiss, 1986, p. 37). To assert that human sexual behavior is determined by hormones or reflexes is to ignore a more complex reality.

There was a time in psychology when explanations of behavior were couched in terms of instincts. This is no longer the case. Neither instincts, reflexes, nor hormones can help us very much to understand human behavior. Clearly, then, we need an answer to the question of the nature of human beings that is very different from that provided by biological determinists. In the next section, we will clarify the often misunderstood notions of evolution and "race" and reveal how our sociocultural nature underlies nearly everything we do, wherever we may live and of whatever group we consider ourselves a part.

Our Sociocultural Nature

Our nature—the way we are—has evolved in ways reflecting both biological and cultural forces. Both sets of forces, operating respectively over long and short time periods, have made us alike in many ways and different in others. The differences inspired some of our predecessors to classify humans into groups popularly dubbed "races." Both evolution and the concept of "race" are widely, and badly, misunderstood, and these misunderstandings need to be confronted by anyone who truly wishes to understand what human nature really is. Here, we endeavor to make that clear.

Human Nature, as Popularly Misconceived
A popular meaning of Human Nature refers to a set of universally shared, unlearned tendencies, or instincts. Long ago, this instinctivistic version of Human Nature was evoked (and, in some quarters, still is) to "explain" any human behavior that was considered noteworthy. Among the Greek philosophers, Aristotle attributed the very

existence of societies to human beings' natural instinct to affiliate. Note that this notion reduces to "Humans affiliate because they have an instinct to affiliate." In a similar vein, centuries later, Adam Smith (1759) pointed to altruism as an intrinsic human quality. He explained our observed propensity to cooperate (sometimes) with our fellows: "How selfish soever man may be supposed, there are evidently some principles *in his nature* which interest him in the fortunes of others, and render their happiness necessary to him" (p. 1; italics ours).

Laypersons still invoke Human Nature to explain particular actions. The tendency for people to desire intensely that which is tabooed is a favorite popular example of "human nature." But a desire to please authority figures by doing what is prescribed and by not doing what is forbidden has also been attributed to that same Nature. Clearly, if a concept explains everything, even opposites, it in fact explains nothing!

Newer "Human Nature" arguments (e.g., Wilson & Herrnstein, 1985) continue a train that has a long history in twentieth-century psychology. Speculation about the nature of humans characterized early philosophical psychology. McDougall, in his pioneering social psychology textbook (1908) argued that instincts—like curiosity, self-assertion, submission, food seeking, mating, acquisitiveness, flight, repulsion, and parental feeling—are the basis of human behavior. Modern biologists concerned with human behavior have revived interest in genetically based behavioral potentials. Primatologists, especially, have called attention to numerous similarities between the behaviors of various monkeys and apes and those of humans, similarities that are consistent with the view that much of human behavior is rooted in evolutionary developments over millennia and that we share many biological characteristics with other animals.

Much of the behavior that has been studied by modern students of sociobiology[5] (see, for example, Wilson, 1975) is basic social behavior, such as courtship and mating, childrearing, and dominance and submission interactions. Some controversy surrounds sociobiology, especially when its findings are applied to very complex social issues. An example is the question of causes of behavioral differences between human males and females, which we will discuss in Chapter 8. And, even in more cautious applications of some of its findings, sociobiology seems to have resurrected the old, discredited instinct doctrine. It need not. Sociobiology, at its best, underscores the continuity of development of biologically related creatures while recognizing that no human behavior can be attributed solely to biological predispositions. That human behavior is profoundly affected by learning doesn't mean that biology isn't relevant; after all, the capacity to learn is itself a biologically rooted trait. It has evolved, as we will see very shortly, when we consider contemporary perspectives on human evolution.

---

[5]Sociobiology is a form of human ethology that explains human social behavior in an evolutionary framework on the basis of 'inclusive fitness': Each organism is supposed to behave so as to maximize its reproductive success. (For further details, see Berry et al., 1992.)

As the distinguished student of primate behavior S. L. Washburn (1978) put it:

I would be the first to agree that the full understanding of the behavior patterns of any species must include biology. But the more that learning is involved, the less there will be of any simple relation between basic biology and behavior. The laws of genetics are not the laws of learning. As a result of intelligence and speech, human beings provide the extreme example of highly varied behavior that is learned and executed by the same fundamental biology. Biology determines the basic need for food, but not the innumerable ways in which this need may be met.

Out of the present controversy, which, on a positive level, has stimulated renewed interest in human and animal behavior, a new interdisciplinary biologically and socially based behavioral science may emerge. But in applying biological thinking we must take care not to ignore history, sociology, and comparative studies. For if we do, we will be condemned to repeat the scientific errors of the past (p. 75).

One of those errors was an eighteenth- and nineteenth-century European idea about *social evolution,* a putative process from savagery through barbarism and so on until civilization was attained. European thinkers developed the notion of social evolution; they saw European societies, their own if not all of them, as personifying civilization. This outmoded idea will be discussed again in Chapters 3 and 10.

There is also some confusion about biological evolution as well. Some social scientists, in the course of arguing the primacy of culture in shaping human social behavior, have tended to treat human development as a process that could be understood without reference at all to biological evolution. It was as if evolution, to them, applied to the development of animal populations, but not to human ones.

Human Evolution
Recently, evolutionary perspectives within psychology have gained more prominence, with renewed interest in how theories of selection pressures (as are found in evolutionary biology, for example) serve to generate hypotheses about the functionality of human psychological processes.

In these newer evolutionary perspectives, which have been reviewed recently by Keller (1997) with a view toward their applicability to cross-cultural psychology, "the genetic endowment can no longer be misunderstood as expressing fixed, deterministic relationships between genes and behaviors" (p. 218). Instead, she cites the notion of "genetic preparedness," which suggests that the acquisition of particular behaviors via learning occurs in efficient ("low cost") ways in the interest of adaptiveness. The plasticity of human beings, our powerful ability to learn, is, in this perspective, not opposed to, or in contradiction with, biological influences, but in accord with them. Evolution, as originally conceptualized by Charles Darwin (1859) and as elaborated by many since Darwin (e.g., Dawkins, 1982; Voland, 1993) provides students of human behavior with the basis for thinking about the basic mechanisms that underlie the development of cultures and the shaping of the populations that reside in them.

Parallel Evolutionary Tracks: Biological and Cultural.   Boyd and Richerson (1985), while underscoring the fact that human beings are cultural organisms, account for human evolution in an essentially Darwinian manner. In their view, which we share, human evolution involves *both* genetic transmission and cultural transmission. These two processes are different in certain important respects, but they have parallel features.

Cultural transmission, a uniquely human process involving intergenerational learning (via teaching and imitation) has features that distinguish it from biological transmission. For example, in cultural transmission, individuals are influenced by people other than their biological parents, while in biological transmission only parents can be the source of influence. Thus, humans, and only humans, have "cultural parents" (for example, members of extended families, teachers, priests, and other influential people). Moreover, cultural evolution (unlike biological evolution) is not restricted to intergenerational influences. Ideas are transmitted within generations, too, so that it is even possible for older individuals to model their behavior after younger ones.

On the other hand, the two processes are, in important ways, analogous. Both proceed in interaction with environmental contingencies; both biological and cultural evolution involve changes that either become established or lost depending on how adaptive they are (or how well they "fit" the environment in which they first occurred).

This position is similar to that of Campbell (1965b) who argued that cultural evolution, like biological evolution, proceeds in a nonprescient manner (not predetermined, nor looking ahead to favorable outcomes) involving random variation and natural (environmental) selection. Similarly, Skinner (1974) described cultural change as a process involving selection by consequences. These insights set apart the positions of Boyd and Richerson, Campbell, and Skinner from that of many sociobiologists.

We, as cross-cultural psychologists, find the Boyd and Richerson "dual inheritance" theory to be a very fruitful approach. Dual inheritance theory shows that the nature *versus* nurture (or genetics *versus* culture) controversy is an inappropriate conceptualization of the relationship between biological and cultural forces. While they may have different outcomes, and involve different processes, they are parallel rather than competing forces. And, they interact with each other when applied to any particular individual human being.

RACE: CAN THIS TENACIOUS CONCEPT BE SUPPLANTED?

In the second half of the nineteenth century, through most of the twentieth, physical anthropologists (and nearly everybody else) categorized human groups in terms of "race" on the basis of visible physical characteristics, such as skin color, height, hair, and facial features. Their taxonomies usually included three to five categories such as, Negroid, Mongoloid, and Caucasoid, or "black, brown, yellow, red, and white." (Some early anthropologists suggested as many as 400 categories.)

At first glance, classifications like "white, black, brown, red, and yellow" seem obvious, a natural phenomenon, and linked to geography. None of us today would have any difficulty in distinguishing a native of Senegal from a native of the Netherlands. Nor would we have difficulty distinguishing a Chinese person from an Inuit person, nor guessing where they are from (although it would be harder to tell the Chinese from the Inuit if no cultural information such as clothing were available). In other words, some physical characteristics are correlated, and allow us to guess with a good probability where people (or their ancestors) came from.

However, these visible traits are not *highly* correlated with each other. The spatial distribution of skin color differs from the spatial distribution of hair form, which in turn is different from facial shapes, or any other visual characteristic.[6]

"Race" as a "scientific" category label served colonial times extremely well. Associating value judgments of superiority and inferiority with these physical characteristics, in relation to theories of cultural evolution that also prevailed at that time, allowed colonialists and slave owners to justify oppression and exploitation. Despite the end of slavery and colonialism, the concept of "races" is still popular, and has not disappeared entirely from school textbooks, dictionaries, and encyclopedias. In many countries in the world, there are even laws couched in terms of "race." While some time ago South Africa abolished its apartheid system, which was, of course, based on "race," in the United States, as this is being written, many states still prohibit adoption of children of one "race" by parents of another one!

Recent scientific evidence has shown that the reasons for human physical diversity are not as the early taxonomists put it. A consensus emerging among biologists (particularly population geneticists) and anthropologists is that "race" is not a useful biological concept at the human level. Harris (1993), for example, writes, "Indeed, the discrepancy between popular ideas about race and modern scientific principles of taxonomy and genetics is so great that many anthropologists want to eliminate the word *race* from anthropology textbooks altogether" (p. 83). In 1998, the executive board of the American Anthropology Association adopted and published an official statement noting that "human populations are not unambiguous, clearly demarcated, biologically distinct groups" (AAA, 1998, p. 3).

---

[6]Moreover, the spatial distribution of each of these separate traits, as well as others not listed here, is a gradual variation. Gradual variation of traits across space is known as *clinal.* One of the saddest incidents in the recent history of psychology occurred when Jefferson Fish, an American psychologist, in a letter to the *APA Monitor* in 1997 spoke about clinal variation, saying "Human physical variation is clinal, not racial." When his letter was published, the word *clinal* was edited to read *clinical,* not once, but on two separate occasions. Perhaps *clinal* is not on the psychologists' spell-check program or in their active vocabulary. (See Fish, 1997, 1998 for two chilling accounts (published without errors in anthropology journals) of how [many] psychologists think about "race.")

Many scientific books written for a larger public, both in English (Cavalli-Sforza & Bodmer, 1971; Cavalli-Sforza, Menozzi, & Piazza, 1994) and in French (Blondin, 1995; Cavalli-Sforza, 1996; Jacquard, 1978, 1983, 1987; Langaney, 1988) make it clear that human genetic diversity defies any simple classification. The same point has been made in an exhibition entitled "All of Us are Related, Each of Us is Unique" ("Tous Parents, Tous Différents," Langaney, Hubert Van Blijenburgh, and Sanchez-Mazas, 1992), shown so far in Paris, Geneva, Syracuse, New York, Bellingham, and Walla Walla, Washington.

These sources make it clear that external physical features previously used to distinguish "racial groups" do not constitute reliable genetic markers because they represent relatively recent (over the past 20,000 years) adaptations. Skin color and height, for example, are subject to rapid change (in genetic terms) in response to environmental conditions. Average height has changed by up to 2 centimeters within a single generation. Most Europeans of today would have a hard time wearing medieval European armor. The world distribution of skin color (before 1492 and the subsequent large-scale migrations), shows that darker skin characterized people living in the intertropical zones of all continents. In South India and Sri Lanka, for example, people who have otherwise "Caucasian" features are as dark as or darker than most Africans.

Skin color is a useful adaptation to exposure to the sun. Dark skin protects against the ultraviolet wavelength of sunlight, which can produce skin cancer. But sunshine also produces vitamin D, which plays a vital role in the absorption of calcium, and hence in bone growth and strength. Without it, people are prone to the crippling disease called *rickets*. In climates where there is limited solar radiation, such as in northern Europe, a light skin allows people to synthesize more vitamin D. "The particular color of a human population's skin therefore represents in large degree a trade-off between the hazards of too much versus too little solar radiation: acute sunburn and skin cancer on one hand, and rickets and osteomalacia on the other" (Harris, 1993, p. 94).

The crucial point about these variations is that they are not categorical but constitute a continuous dimension.[7] Variations along the skin color dimension, for example, are due to different concentrations of a single pigment, called *melanin*, in the skin. People can have more or less of this pigment, leading to a continuous scale from dark to light (or, in popular parlance, "black" to "white"), with so-called yellow skin somewhere in the middle toward the lighter end, and "red" being the color of blood seen through a transparent skin.

Is it impossible to classify people by skin color? Of course not; we *may* classify people however we want, by color of eyes, by height, by income, by religion, by

---

[7]The continuity of physical features and the fuzziness of boundaries between categories render an unambiguous classification impossible. The same argument could be applied to "culture," and indeed, labeling people as belonging to one culture or another is becoming more and more meaningless in today's increasing mix of populations. Cultural anthroplogy has often been severely criticized for freezing "cultures" in this way (see the previous discussion on definitions of culture in this chapter).

political party affiliation, and so on. It is also possible to classify human groups according to their average concentration of melanin. But why would we want to?

In Figure 1.1, we see twelve young men, their faces arrayed in a (rough) circle. The differences between any two adjacent faces are scarcely perceptible. Yet, one can probably locate on the circle what appear to be quintessential examples of "Black," "White," and other "races." But, note that each face flows, continuously, out of the others, so that what appear to be "prototypes" are nothing more than variations along a continuum, one without any end points!

Geneticists can now examine many more gene categories than the ones that determine *external* physical features; the best known of those that determine *internal* features are blood groups and the Human Leucocyte Antigen (HLA) system (because

Some of our physical differences give the impression that it is possible to divide us into races. But when these physical characteristics are subjected to detailed study, that cannot be concluded at all. Instead it becomes obvious that our physical diversity reflects continuous changes from one extreme to the other. To place any boundaries within this continuous diversity would be, therefore, completely arbitrary. Human diversity is in fact infinitely more complicated than the idea we have constructed of it. This is why attempts to make racial classifications that are typically made don't yield any coherent results; there is nothing scientific about "race."

FIGURE 1.1   The Illusion of Race.

It is an illusion that there are races. The diversity of human beings is so great and so complicated that it is impossible to classify the 5.8 billions of individuals into discrete "races."

Photographs taken from the exhibition "All of Us are Related. Each of Us is Unique" (*Tous Parents, Tous Différents*). Provided by J. L. Dubin and N. Hubert van Blyenburgh.

they have important implications for blood transfusion and the grafting of organs). These two also have important implications for our understanding of the diversity of human populations. Consider the following.

There are only four blood groups among all humans: A, B, AB, and O. Although there are geographical variations in the relative frequency of these groups (reflecting past migrations, and a process called *genetic drift*), the rules that govern blood transfusions are the same everywhere. If you are of blood group O, for example, you can give blood to all other groups, but can only receive blood from someone else of group O. This could be someone from the other side of the world, whose skin color and other external features are completely different from yours, while it could not be one of your own parents or siblings if they are of group A, B, or AB.

While there are only four blood groups, there are *many billion* possible combinations of genes in the HLA system. If human groupings based on these "hidden" genetic markers were treated as "races," the number would exceed the number of presently living humans! This is one of the reasons why the concept of "race" does not make sense at the human level. Genetically, humans are *all* different (with the exception of identical twins). And, as we are about to see, we are also all related.

Humans everywhere share a lot genetically. There is no gene that is specific to one particular human population and totally absent in any other. The genetic similarity between populations varies basically with geographic proximity, and reflects the history of population movements in the distant past. While scientists still disagree on the exact way in which this happened, the overwhelming evidence argues for a common origin of all humans. In other words, we are all one single species, called *Homo sapiens sapiens,* capable of interbreeding, and descendants, over approximately 5000 generations, of the same ancestors (Langaney et al., 1992).

Paleontology provides constantly changing theories, because so much depends on particular finds of fossils and bones, and some locations are better researched than others. Present evidence situates these common ancestors in the Middle East and Africa between 700,000 and 100,000 years ago. DNA research is also relevant. Recent research has shown Neanderthal DNA to be different from Human DNA, and it has therefore been convincingly shown that *Homo Sapiens Sapiens* (modern human beings) are not descended from the Neanderthals who lived in Europe and the Middle East between 120,000 and 30,000 B.P. (before present). Rather, we and the Neanderthals descended from a common ancestor. Homo Sapiens and Neanderthals may even have shared the same environment, and it is still not clear whether the Neanderthals were eliminated or absorbed. On the other hand, scientific evidence is strong that all human beings alive today have, as Stringer and McKie (1997) put it, an African origin. In their words, "Though modern humans may not look exactly alike, we are indeed all Africans under the skin" (p. 7). Box 1.2 provides more details on the question of when and where modern human beings first emerged.

Although many psychologists continue to treat "race" as a biological fact and continue to debate the nature of racial differences in behavior, a few voices can be heard decrying this repeated airing of what is essentially a meaningless question.

BOX 1.2   The Origin of Modern Human Beings

Paleoanthropologists and geneticists currently debate the locus and date of the beginnings of the passage from animal to human, but this debate takes place in the context of considerable consensus. Fossil evidence has long shown that man and the apes followed two lines of descent from a common ancestor, dating back 20 million years, with creatures more human than apelike appearing about 4.4 million years ago. Then, about 2 million years ago, in East Africa, there appeared *Homo habilis,* the first form to which the paleoanthropologists attach the label *Homo,* or "human." Later still, about a half million years ago, following some intermediate steps, there appeared *Homo sapiens,* of which there were two lines, one of which, Neanderthal, became extinct, and the other, *archaic sapiens,* the ancestors of true human beings, *Homo sapiens sapiens.*

After that, the plot gets complicated. As Pellegrini (1998) has made clear, the question of when and where genuine "modern humans" (*Homo sapiens sapiens*) was established as a species is a difficult one. Because a species is defined by the ability of all its members to interbreed (fecundity) and because bones provide no evidence concerning fecundity, other kinds of evidence, especially DNA evidence, must be relied on. That evidence allows two answers to the question of our origin.

One, called the "replacement model," relies on the DNA-inferred worldwide migration patterns of early Africans who appeared at most only 200,000 years ago. This model is supported by the theory of "African Eve" that was offered by Cann, Stoneking, and Wilson (1987), who used mitochondrial DNA techniques. The second is the candelabra or regional continuity model, which suggests that all homo sapiens resulted from parallel evolutions, on different continents, of populations of Homo erectus that had left Africa at least 700,000 years ago.

So, the origin of our species is far from resolved. Part of the debate, according to Pellegrini, is due to the fact that the methods of the geneticists, on the one hand, and those of the paleoanthropologists on the other, differ and are not well understood across the disciplines.

Yet, the most likely locus of our origins, as reflected in both models, is Africa.

One of the more dramatic challenges to this continuing error in the psychological literature appeared in *Psychology Today,* a semipopular magazine (Fish, 1995). There, complete with pictures, is a dramatic account of a two-generation family in which the daughter of a so-called African American woman and a so-called European American father is considered "black" in America. The young woman, whose boyfriend, a Brazilian, is darker-skinned than she, described herself as "black" while her boyfriend averred that he was not. The explanation lies in the fact that there is a folk taxonomy of race in the United States and a different folk taxonomy of race in Brazil. As Fish notes, "American racial categories are merely one of numerous, very culture-specific schemes for reducing uncertainty about how people should respond to other people" (p. 56).

If "race" does not exist as a biological fact, it is, as we have now seen, a compelling social construct. Since the illusion of "race" is so compelling and so widely held, we have to deal with the fact that many people think it is real and view the world *as if* it contained "races." When one adds to the belief in "race" the two further ideas that "races" are qualitatively different in terms of talent and capacity and that they should be treated differently, then we have the all-too-familiar attitude, "racism." Belief in the existence of "race," coupled with widely held beliefs in behavioral differences, is a powerful sociological phenomenon that we will examine in detail in subsequent chapters, particularly in Chapter 10, where we discuss intergroup relations.

Here we are also arguing that *merely* treating the social construct of "race" as if it were a biological reality is itself "racist" and should be resisted as vigorously as one resists "racial discrimination." It is important to keep in mind, from the very beginning of this text in cross-cultural psychology, that "race" itself has no foundation in human genetics.

THE POINT OF VIEW OF THIS BOOK

To the cross-cultural psychologist, cultures are seen both as products of past human behavior and as shapers of future human behavior. Thus, humans are producers of culture and, at the same time, our behavior is influenced by it. We have produced social environments that continually serve to bring about continuities and changes in lifestyles over time and uniformities and diversities in lifestyles over space. How human beings modify culture and how our cultures modify us is what cross-cultural psychology is all about. To all who would understand human behavior, to those who would predict it, and certainly to those who would seek consciously to modify it, knowledge of the network of interrelationships between culture and behavior is essential.

In this introduction to the scientific study of human behavior, we have learned that our subject matter can be understood only when viewed in its cultural context. Human behavior, we have found, is nearly always influenced by culture. There are culturally influenced differences in behavior and culturally influenced similarities, as well. But there are not "racial differences," except in the popular sense of that infelicitous phrase. To understand how we each become what we are, we must take account of the fact that our biological heritage interacts with our experiences, mediated largely through the processes of socialization and enculturation. Thus, a study of human behavior that ignores culture does so at great risk.

THE SCOPE OF THIS BOOK

In the following chapters on cross-cultural psychology, we intend to range rather widely over this rapidly developing field, to discuss its methodology, and to consider cultural influences on basic psychological processes. These include cognition and perception, the development and change of cognitive and affective behaviors, attitudes and values, sex, aggression, intergroup relations, intercultural contact and culture change, and intergroup relations. Although we will review many studies from diverse sources, we can only sample from the many hundreds that are available. The sample we have chosen to present comprises those studies that, for a variety of reasons, struck these four cross-cultural psychologists—two North Americans and two Europeans—as representative and most useful for undergraduate courses in psychology, education, anthropology, and other domains in which understanding human behavior is the primary goal.

What has been left out might fill another textbook. Readers of this book should understand that it aims to teach *about* cross-cultural psychology and not necessarily how to do it. That is the purpose of a related book entitled *Cross-Cultural Psychology: Research and Applications* (Berry, Poortinga, Segall, & Dasen, 1992).

Armed with the introduction to the field that this book aims to provide, the student should be prepared to move on to more sophisticated sources, such as the three-volume *Handbook of Cross-Cultural Psychology* (Berry et al., 1997) which repeatedly demonstrates that the laws governing human development are most likely to be discovered via systematic testing of hypotheses both within and across cultures.

Readers will note that the information contained herein comes primarily from professional publications, books, monographs, and, most often, scholarly journals. The latter appear periodically, so that the science of cross-cultural psychology is ever expanding. The serious student should consult recent issues of these journals. The journals, which are central to the field, include *Journal of Cross-Cultural Psychology, Cross-Cultural Research, International Journal of Psychology, Culture and Psychology, International Journal of Intercultural Relations,* and *Ethos.* The *Journal of Social Psychology,* under the editorship of Leonard Doob, one of the founders of cross-cultural psychology, has long encouraged cross-cultural research by giving it publication priority. Increasingly, cross-cultural studies can be found in other psychology journals as well. Knowing, then, that there is much more to cross-cultural psychology than can be covered in this introductory text, let us begin to learn about this rewarding approach to the study of human behavior. In the next chapter we will learn about the diverse approaches employed by cross-cultural psychologists and scholars in related disciplines and how these approaches attempt to address some of the difficulties of doing research outside of one's own backyard.

2

CROSS-CULTURAL RESEARCH: SCOPE AND METHODS

This book aims to teach *about* cross-cultural psychology and not necessarily how to do it. Nevertheless, in this chapter, as we survey the kinds of questions addressed in cross-cultural research, we will have to consider some of the advantages and difficulties of doing behavioral research cross-culturally and some solutions to the difficulties. You may not learn how to do research yourself, but you should certainly learn how to read critically the research done by others, enabling you to assess its validity and significance.

In this chapter, we will present our conceptual framework and some fundamental ideas about cross-cultural research methods.

A CONCEPTUAL FRAMEWORK FOR CROSS-CULTURAL PSYCHOLOGY

As we stated in Chapter 1, biological inheritance *by itself* explains little about human behavior. While behavior is in part a function of a multitude of inherited potentialities, *all* human behavior is shaped by experience. Human behavior, then, is a product of a complex interaction involving genetic and experiential factors, with both present and past experience weighted heavily in its ultimate determination. Our thinking on the relationship of ecology, culture, genetics, experience, and human behavior is illustrated in a conceptual framework presented in Figure 2.1. This framework links ecological and sociopolitical contexts with various psychological characteristics, and contains intervening process variables wherein both biological and cultural influences are transmitted from the context to the individual. Most, if not all, of the questions posed in cross-cultural psychology may be subsumed by Figure 2.1 and it will be instructive to return to it frequently and apply it to the topics in each chapter of this book.

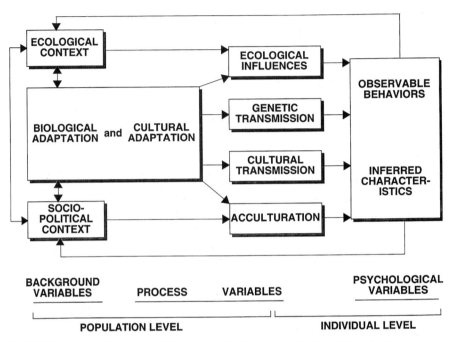

FIGURE 2.1   A Conceptual Framework for Cross-Cultural Psychology

The conceptual framework, which incorporates the diverse kinds of research done in cross-cultural psychology, was designed and modified by Berry (1971, 1976a, 1986). It is also the framework that guides the textbook that complements this one (Berry, Poortinga, Segall, & Dasen, 1992). The framework contains variables at the levels of populations and individuals. It includes background variables, process variables, and psychological outcomes. The background variables include two kinds of contexts, ecological and sociopolitical. These contexts constrain, pressure, and nurture cultural forms, which in turn shape behavior. Humans also change the ecological and sociopolitical contexts in which they live. This is signified by a general feedback loop, which also stands for particular feedbacks and reciprocal relations among other components in the framework.

Context Variables

The ecological context includes climatic and other natural factors—such as water supply, soil conditions, temperature, and terrain—that combine to influence, among other things, any society's food-production system. These natural conditions affect food-production techniques, which are clearly fundamental to the functioning of society. A decision to feed primarily on meat from large animals depends on their availability, which in turn depends on climate, water supply, type of ground cover, and the like. Herding as a way of producing food depends on the availability of conditions favorable to animal husbandry. Fishing demands that one live near water.

A convenient way to categorize different food-production systems is by degree of food accumulation, a variable investigated by Barry, Child, and Bacon (1959) in a study of childrearing patterns. At the low extreme are societies that pursue hunting and gathering as a primary feeding technique. Food is not stored for later consumption but is merely to be sought when needed. It is sometimes abundant and sometimes in short supply, but it is seldom accumulated. Societies at the high extreme include those that employ agriculture, accumulating food by producing, storing, and planting seeds. Such societies, particularly if they also raise animals, typically store much of their food for later needs. Animal-husbandry societies are very high in food accumulation, investing resources in meat on the hoof that may not be needed for months.

There are well-replicated anthropological observations (Barry et al., 1959; Hendrix, 1985) indicating that a society's degree of food accumulation is correlated with other characteristics. For example, high-food-accumulating societies, as well as technologically developed societies, tend to be sedentary and relatively dense in population. Low-food-accumulating societies tend to be composed of less dense, often migratory populations. (Later, in Chapter 8, we will see how degree of food accumulation relates to sexual division of labor and the ways men and women relate to each other.)

The history of human societies and of their interactions determines the sociopolitical context, which, of course, interacts both with the ecological context and with the process variables. Whether societies are rich or poor, how wealth, power, and influence are distributed among a society's members, and the degree of influence of a society on the world's geopolitical stage, are all aspects of the sociopolitical context. This, in combination with the ecological context, plays an important role in shaping human behavior. (Later, in Chapter 7, we will see how values, which influence behavior, are themselves shaped by the sociopolitical context. In Chapters 8, 9, and 10 as well, the importance of sociopolitical variables on interpersonal and intergroup behaviors will become quite evident.) While stability over time is an important feature of culture, it is never complete. Cultures change constantly, either because of endogenous innovations or through contact with other societies. In this dynamic process, it is sometimes difficult to differentiate what is due to invention and what is due to external influence, just as it is difficult to distinguish clearly an antecedent change in sociopolitical context and the processes of cultural adaptation and of acculturation. (Culture change and acculturation will be studied in detail in Chapter 11.)

Process Variables

The process variables at the population level include both cultural adaptation and biological adaptation. Cultural adaptations include all inventions that are adaptive to the pressures of ecology, taking into account the history of the sociopolitical context. Culture comprises all human institutions that in the long run help populations survive in a given ecological niche.[1] If, for example, the ecological context allows food accumulation (and hence a food surplus), which in turn is related to the probability of a society's being sedentary, that in turn will lead to a social and economic system that is compatible with being sedentary. A sedentary society is likely to have a different leadership system (one that is more hierarchical) from one that is migratory. That social system, in this sense, is "adaptive."

While, broadly speaking, culture can be seen as an adaptation to ecological and sociohistorical conditions, the relationship is far from deterministic and unidirectional. Miller (1997) notes that "the same social structural arrangements and ecological conditions may be associated with different cultural meanings and practices and that cultural meanings and practices are not exclusively functional in character" (p. 106). Furthermore, culture, as a system of representations and meanings, is an integral part of contextual variables that are not always predictable from the ecological and sociohistorical contexts. The notion of *symbolic culture* focuses on the fact that other factors aside from milieu, environment, and ecology introduce contextual differences: Factors such as conceptual frame, beliefs, and value systems shared by individuals in a given culture also enter into contextual differences. Hence, as we have seen in Chapter 1, culture can be defined either as context or as process or as both.

The second subcategory of process variables (biological adaptation) includes any response a population makes over many generations that is basically genetic. Such extremely long-term evolutionary changes are responsive to the press of ecology. Thus, genetic differences across subpopulations of human beings are treated in this framework as biological adaptations (usually in terms of physiology) to ecological pressure. These differences may show up, for example, as differential susceptibilities to certain diseases. These organismic differences do not reflect only genetic predispositions, of course. Health and nutritional status vary across populations far more because of cultural differences in diet and hygiene (ultimately linked to the sociopolitical context). But whatever their cause, they are differences in organismic status that reflect varying adaptations to ecological conditions.

These two subcategories of process (or adaptive) variables, biological and cultural, may also interact with one another. For example, cultural customs regarding food intake may reflect a society's experience in ages past with the positive and negative influences of a food, consequences that may have had a genetic basis. For example, the ability to digest milk depends on the production of the enzyme lactase that breaks down the lactose contained in the milk into the components glucose and galactose. Most adult mammals, including most adult humans, lose the ability to

---

[1]The concept of ecological niche reflects the constant interaction over time between a species and its environment.

digest unfermented milk. However, in populations whose subsistence depends on drinking large quantities of milk, a genetic adaptation allows the continued production of lactase. According to Harris (1993), this genetic adaptation was particularly useful when milk was also the primary source of calcium, as was the case of prehistoric northern Europeans: "This then accounts for the unusual ability of northern Europeans and their descendants to drink copious quantities of unfermented milk" (pp. 92–93). Many people in Asia, and some in Africa (mainly those who do not raise cattle), have a culturally sanctioned aversion to milk that is consistent with the lack of lactase production in adults. The complex of dietary practices of a population is part of that population's adaptation to its environment; this adaptation is both cultural and biological.

The link between the contextual and process variables at the population level and behavior, at the individual level, is provided by a series of process variables, some of which will be the main focus of this book. Some direct ecological influences will be illustrated in Chapter 4, when we study the effect of visual environments on perception. Generally speaking, however, they are mediated through culture. Genetic transmission is acknowledged in the framework because, as we have seen in Chapter 1, human evolution involves both biological and cultural transmission. The process variables that are of main interest to cross-cultural psychologists are cultural transmission and acculturation. Special attention will be paid to the former in Chapter 3, when we study enculturation and socialization, and childrearing practices (under the umbrella of another theoretical framework, the *developmental niche*), as well as informal and formal education. These processes are linked to contextual and cultural variables. For example, in any particular environment there are forces that make it likely that certain socialization practices are emphasized more than others, and population variables modulate fundamental interactive processes, orient parental behavior in one direction or another, and confer a specific style to communicative exchanges and communication in general (Rabain-Jamin, 1994).

The processes that are due to the contact between cultural groups, over time or space, are subsumed under the concept of *acculturation,* which will be studied specifically in Chapter 11, but are relevant to most topics covered in all other chapters.

Psychological Outcome Variables

These individual level variables include all measurable aspects of individual behavior that can be shown to be linked to ecological or adaptive variables or to both. Because in psychological research one often is concerned with presumed-to-exist characteristics (like personality traits, values, motives, abilities, and the like) that are inferred from observed behavior, such characteristics are also included in the model.

This framework is thus a conceptual system in which ecocultural forces are viewed as influencing human behavior, either directly or through the intervening adaptive variables, both cultural and biological. But the direction of relationship is not exclusively from ecology through culture to behavior. Obviously, individual behavior can also influence culture. Indeed, individual behavior can even influence ecology. People do go out and cut down the forest or divert water or use up natural resources. The framework, then, is a feedback system, or a network of relationships. Its ultimate usefulness lies in its calling attention to the possible relationships to look for among any combination of ecological, adaptive, and psychological variables. In this respect, the framework has heuristic value.

Related Disciplines

As noted in the conceptual framework, cross-cultural psychology spans both the population and individual levels. At both levels, other disciplines also study human behavior. At the population level, such disciplines as ecology, anthropology, sociology, linguistics, and biology study, describe, and analyze features of human groups. At the individual level, there is, of course, psychology, including its several branches of scientific inquiry, e.g., developmental, personality, cognition, perception, and social behavior, among others. Some of the disciplines at the population level tend to rely mostly on naturalistic observation (e.g., ethnographic anthropology), while psychology has long favored experimentation and other highly structured techniques, such as testing and the administration of closed-ended questionnaires, such as attitude scales. Cross-cultural psychology often endeavors to combine naturalistic observation with more structured techniques.

Of all the disciplines to which cross-cultural psychology relates, perhaps its closest relative is anthropology. Jahoda (1990) provides an interesting history of the long, not always harmonious, relationship between anthropology and psychology. Currently, as we approach the twenty-first century, comparative anthropology and cross-cultural psychology are quite close in many respects.[2]

These two disciplines together have influenced (and were influenced by) comparative research into abnormal behavior in an enterprise known as transcultural psychiatry. Cross-cultural research on psychopathology has shown that "abnormal" behaviors are differently perceived, defined, and explained in different societies. There are also differences in therapeutic techniques, as well as some provocative similarities, as regards some features of psychotherapy, whether provided by traditional healers or Western-trained psychiatrists. (See Tanaka-Matsumi and Draguns [1997] for a thorough treatment of psychopathology and psychotherapy in cross-cultural perspective.)

---

[2]The closely related disciplines are represented respectively by the Society for Cross-Cultural Research (SCCR) and the International Association for Cross-Cultural Psychology (IACCP); many individual scholars belong to both organizations. Many people (including sociologists, psychologists, and educators) interested in intercultural relations belong to l'Association pour la Recherche Interculturelle (ARIC), especially if they understand French. Social scientists interested in applied problems relating to intergroup relations and intercultural communication also find colleagues in these organizations.

A close kinship with sociology also exists. Within that field, the study of inter-group relations has long been a specialization. It is a field of keen interest within cross-cultural psychology as well. These related disciplines provide us some basic concepts that describe aspects of the context in which we live.

THE SOCIAL AND CULTURAL CONTEXT: BASIC CONCEPTS

Norms and Social Control

Norms are widely shared standards of conduct that control (within limits) the behavior of group members. Norms vary in degree of coerciveness; thus, *folkways* (e.g., stir your tea with a spoon, not your thumb) are merely conventional practices, while *mores* (avoid making sexual advances to a sibling) are considered obligatory for the maintenance of social order, and formal *laws* not only designate certain behaviors forbidden or, conversely, obligatory, but have sanctions attached to them. Most often these norms are phrased negatively, in the form of proscriptions (e.g., "Thou shalt not…", "It is illegal to…," etc.). Proscriptions in the realm of mores are sometimes termed *taboos,* a word that originated in Pacific Island societies and has become widely used by social scientists as well as by laypeople.

Social control is the enforcement of all norms, including folkways, mores, and laws. Socially acceptable behavior can be inculcated through enculturation and socialization. When these mechanisms fall short, further means of social control are available, embodied in enforcement agencies such as police, courts, the military and, in some societies, councils of elders and ecclesiastical authorities.

Social Structure

Societies vary in how they are structured or organized. The structure of a society is relevant to forms of social control employed in it. One dimension of structure concerns the degree of stratification of a society, which refers to possible forms of vertical hierarchies, wherein some persons are considered to be "higher" than others (and thus have power to control the behavior of others who are "lower"). Class and caste are examples of units of stratification. Some societies are more stratified than others.

All societies have one or another form of family structure. In cultural anthropology, there are five major areas of research dealing with issues of marriage, family, and kinship. These are, respectively, form of marriage, family type, residence pattern, descent rules, and kinship terminology. For students not familiar with these kinds of anthropological concerns, it would be very useful to consult an introductory anthropology text (e.g., Ember & Ember, 1996). A brief discussion of these four areas of concern appears in Box 2.1.

BOX 2.1   Basic Anthropological Dimensions of Variation in Societies[10]

1. *Form of marriage* can vary from monogamy (one husband–one wife) to polygyny (one husband–several wives) to polyandry (one wife–several husbands). These variations do not appear to be randomly distributed, but are consistently related to some other factors, for example, the male–female ratio (in societies with a high male mortality because of warfare, polygyny is more common).

2. *Family types* may be independent (child living with parent(s) in a separate household or extended by a blood tie, such as in a three-generational family. Extended families are more common in agricultural societies.

3. *Residence patterns* refer to the localities where newlyweds establish their homes. Patrilocal residence, where sons reside with or near their fathers after marriage and daughters go with their husbands, is characteristic of about two-thirds of all societies. Other residence patterns include matrilocal (daughters reside with or near their mothers and sons go with their wives, a form which is found in about 15 percent of societies), bilocal, where either of the two previous ones are possible, avunculocal, where the couple goes to live with or near the husband's maternal uncle, and neolocal, where they choose to live in a place different from their parents and family.

4. *Rules of descent* refer to ways in which people in a society trace their ancestry. The variations are fourfold: patrilineal, by far the most common (the father's side of the family); matrilineal (mother's side); bilateral (both sides); and ambilineal (one or the other, resulting in descent groups in a society showing both male and female genealogical links).

5. *Kinship* terminology consists of the ways that people refer to the categories of family relationships. A number of different systems have been discovered in various societies by anthropologists and these are usually named after one of the cultural groups employing them (viz., Omaha, Crow, Iroquois, Hawaiian, Eskimo, and Sudanese), which conveys little of their actual nature to the anthropologically uninitiated. The systems vary primarily in that kin that are lumped together in one system are separated in another, with a single term covering more cases in some systems than in others (e.g., "uncle" may refer to mother's brother, father's brother, mother's sister's husband, and father's sister's husband in some societies but not in others).

---

[10]See Chapter 11 in Ember and Ember (1996) for complete details of these societal variations.

All aspects of social structure, including some not discussed here, such as societal divisions of an economic kind, have important consequences for the behavior of individuals, because who we are, how we are related to people, and what stratum we find ourselves in, (in other words, the status we have ascribed to us or which we achieve) contributes to the amount of social influence we can exert on others or find applied by others to us.

Finally, social structures vary in cultural complexity. In some societies few status distinctions are made while in others there are many. Murdock (1967) distinguishes such variation in a two-variable system: (1) the number of political levels above the local community (e.g., regional, provincial, national) and (2) presence/absence of class distinctions. Related to this is another dimension of culture, looseness/tightness (Pelto, 1968). Small-sized communities with few different jobs ("simple" societies) tend to be tight, while large, multi-jobbed societies ("complex") tend to be loose.

Positions and Roles

The term *position* indicates where a person is in social space. One can occupy the position of daughter, mother, sister (in kin space), of employee, supervisor, and part-time music teacher (in occupational space), member, treasurer, and president-elect (in club space), citizen, party member and candidate (in political space), and so on. One person can occupy all of these positions in a lifetime, often simultaneously. Every person has several such positions. *Role* is the behavior that is prescribed, or expected, because one occupies a particular position. As relatives, workers, club members, and so on, our behavior in each case is guided by the role expectations held by others. Role expectations can take on a compelling, even obligatory, character, virtually controlling our behavior.

CROSS-CULTURAL PSYCHOLOGY'S PARADIGM: A BALANCED APPROACH

Cross-cultural psychologists try to determine how sociocultural variables influence human behavior. To do so, they sometimes focus on behavioral differences across cultures and sometimes on universal patterns of behavior. But the ultimate goal is always to discover how culture and individual behavior relate.

To reach this goal, cross-cultural psychologists, looking both to the science of psychology as it was carried out in most European and American universities during the twentieth century and to the discipline of anthropology as it developed over the same time span, are confronted by different general orientations, which vary between the extremes of *absolutism,* characteristic of much of traditional psychology, and *relativism,* characteristic of anthropology. Cross-cultural psychology is located between the two, borrowing some aspects of both. How the balanced approach of cross-cultural psychology relates to the absolutism–relativism dichotomy is spelled out in Box 2.2.

An Antecedent of the Eco-Cultural Framework: The Culture and Personality School

It is helpful to have an overall framework of ideas about possible relationships, such as the ecocultural framework. A framework like that suggests many possible ways

BOX 2.2   Absolutism and Relativism, and a Balanced Merger

Cultural relativism, a term advanced by the anthropologist Boas (1911) and expanded and disseminated by Herskovits (1948), was meant primarily to warn against invalid cross-cultural comparisons, flavored by ethnocentric value judgments. Berry, Poortinga, Segall, and Dasen (1992) appropriated the word *relativism* to designate one pole of a set of dichotomies, defined at the other end as characteristics of absolutism.

In this scheme, relativists are predisposed to give more weight to cultural factors than to biological ones. In contrast, absolutists would do the opposite. Relativists would attribute differences between groups mainly to cultural influences, while absolutists would seek other, noncultural factors to explain intergroup differences.

At the relativist extreme, there is typically little or no interest in intergroup similarities, while absolutists tend to expect there to be species-wide basic processes that produce many similarities, an expectation dramatically conveyed by the phrase, "the search for the psychic unity of mankind."

Absolutists would be prone to attempt context-free measurements, using standard psychological instruments, frequently making evaluative comparisons, and, as a consequence, open themselves up to the error of employing "imposed etics" (see Box 2.3) when working in societies other than their own. In contrast, relativists would lean toward strictly "emic" research, considering context-free concepts and their measurement to be impossible. They would try to avoid all comparisons, which, if made at all, would be as nonevaluative as possible.

Like most dichotomies, these are defined by extreme poles, and few scholars are found at either pole. However, for some years, one could find many European and U.S. experimental psychologists who stubbornly denied that cultural factors affected psychological processes and they proceeded to accumulate culture-bound findings that they believed to be universally valid for all of humankind. In parallel, some adherents of the cultural psychology movement place themselves sometimes quite close to the relativist pole, emphasizing that psychological processes and structures vary in such fundamental ways in different cultural contexts that they are beyond comparison, or nearly so. Or, they will suggest that culture should not be treated as existing outside individuals, where it can influence their behavior, but inside. (See Miller [1997] and Greenfield [1997] for two very thoughtful accounts of cultural psychology containing insightful discussions of methodological issues.)

Where are most cross-cultural psychologists on these dimensions defined in the extremes by absolutism and relativism? Somewhere in between, where they strike a balance, revealing an orientation that borrows from both of the poles. Cross-cultural psychologists expect both biological and cultural factors to influence human behavior, but, like relativists, assume that the role of culture in producing human variation both within and across groups (especially across groups) is substantial.

Like absolutists, cross-cultural psychologists allow for similarities due to species-wide basic processes, but consider their existence subject to empirical demonstration. When doing our research among different human groups, we adapt standard instruments to local conditions and make controlled, nonevaluative comparisons, employing "derived etics," as defined in Box 2.3.

in which individual behavior and various cultural variables interact with each other. Not surprisingly, preceding generations of students of culture and behavior, especially twentieth-century anthropologists interested in psychological theory, developed conceptual frameworks, too. One early framework was provided by the "culture and personality school."

The Culture and Personality School

For several decades, beginning in the 1930s, much anthropological research was guided by a formulation that asserted, as if it were self-evident, that culture and personality are interrelated. Influenced by a Freudian emphasis on early experience as a primary determinant of adult personality, anthropologists in this school of thought viewed culture as a set of conditions determining early experience and hence as a major shaper of personality. Following on field studies by Mead (1928) and Benedict (1946), Kardiner (1945) and Linton (1945) suggested that different societies develop different basic personality types.

According to the Kardiner and Linton formulation, because of socialization pressures, certain commonalties in individual development are produced within a society. This is not to say that everybody has the same personality; each total personality differs from every other total personality. But somehow at the core of each is something shared, some basic values and attitudes, and this they called *the projective system*. This was thought to be indirectly observable via projective tests (e.g., the Rorschach or Thematic Apperception Test [TAT]), developed initially in clinical settings as diagnostic devices in treating neurotic and psychotic individuals. The technique attracted the attention of anthropologists partly because the instruments seemed to lack culturally specific content and were presumably applicable in any cultural setting.

They were also linked conceptually with psychoanalysis, which in many respects constituted a novel and attractive way of understanding behavior. That psychoanalytic theory purported to be a universally applicable system for understanding human development also made it seem useful to students of non-Western cultures. From Freudian theory, many field workers were led to look for relations between childrearing practices and certain aspects of adult personality. Many studies spawned by this expectation yielded interesting empirical findings.

Like more modern conceptual frameworks (including the hologeistic [*worldwide*], correlational approach exemplified early on by Whiting and Child (1953) and continuing to the present, as well as the framework we employ in this volume, which derives somewhat from Whiting), the culture-and-personality approach carried the implication that there is a mutual relationship between social systems and personalities. As one anthropologist (Spiro, 1961) put it, in the culture and personality framework, a social system creates "the personality needs which, in turn, are satisfied by and motivate the operation of the social system" (p. 121). In other words, culture somehow induces people to want to behave in ways that sustain the culture. Every society has developed cultural norms and the devices by which its members come to conform to these norms. Much of that conformity is displayed willingly by individuals because they have internalized motives and role expectations that are compatible with the norms. To behave otherwise would be to court not only externally administered negative sanctions but also self-administered anxiety, an inevitable cost of nonconformity.

Shortcomings in Early Culture and Personality Research

How individuals internalize cultural norms is one of the most fundamental processes studied by cross-cultural psychology, under the headings of socialization, enculturation, childrearing, the formation of social identity, and similar topics. Within the early culture and personality framework, however, the process of norm internalization wasn't so much studied as merely assumed. Researchers set out to find core personalities, those personality characteristics that "had to be" shown by all members of a given society. And, with little or no concern for individual differences, cultural homogeneity was taken for granted. Zempleni (1972) criticized the postulate of homogeneity in the culture and personality approach, which he characterized, in French, as "le culturalisme," as well as the comparative approach of Whiting and others, which Zempleni viewed as an outgrowth of the culture and personality approach. A. F. C. Wallace (1961) also criticized the tendency of this school of anthropology to conceive of societies as culturally homogeneous and to expect individuals in them to share a uniform nuclear character. Wallace reminded us that there is much diversity not only across cultures but also within them.

As Wallace saw it, the "core personalities" produced by this research tradition were either abstractions gleaned from descriptions of individual personalities—with nonshared characteristics simply ignored—or, worse, merely deductions from cultural descriptions. Psychologists are more apt than anthropologists to expect individual differences, because an interest in such differences was predominant from the earliest days of modern psychology.

Another difficulty was the heavy dependence of culture and personality research on projective techniques. Numerous studies of national character and modal personality employed the Rorschach test and so ended up describing people in clinical terms.[3] Following a critique by Lindzey (1961), which concluded that the cross-cultural use of Rorschach tests was seriously methodologically flawed, the use of projective tests in cross-cultural research diminished and the search for modal personality ceased. Still, the basic notion that behaviors shared by members of a society

---

[3]A typical work is Cora Du Bois's *The People of Alor* (1944), which included the analysis (by a Swiss expert on the Rorschach test) of about fifty Rorschach protocols collected from the Alorese, an Indonesian island group. Her findings led the author to describe the core personality as characterized by fearfulness, suspicion, distrust, egocentricity, greed, shallowness of personal relations, lack of emotional responsiveness, but—suprisingly, perhaps, in light of the foregoing—"no evidence of neurotic conflict."

tend to be compatible with the society's values is reasonable. The expectation of finding functional relationships among elements of culture and aspects of behavior is embodied in the ecocultural framework that we employ in this book.

The Ecocultural Framework Revisited

The ecocultural framework suggests that we ought to examine in detail all aspects of human behavior and try to discover how and to what degree any is influenced (but not invariably *determined*) by the ecological and cultural contexts in which it occurs. We should also study the reverse process, whereby any innovative individual behavior reshapes culture and ecological relationships. And that is what contemporary cross-cultural psychologists, for the most part, are trying to do. But, as we are about to see, that is easier said than done.

METHODOLOGY IN CROSS-CULTURAL RESEARCH: SOME PROBLEMS AND SOME SOLUTIONS

Designing any study of human behavior to produce unambiguous findings is not easy, even when the study is done in the researcher's own society, where the psychologist knows the language, is knowledgeable about prevailing attitudes, is using measuring instruments of known reliability, and is able to detect subtle cues in the behavior of the respondents. Psychologists who work only in their own societies acknowledge that, despite these advantages, their research always carries the risk of invalidity. Imagine, then, the problems confronting cross-cultural psychologists.

First, they may not know the language well enough to read subtle cues familiar to insiders. In addition, theories, concepts, methods, and instruments developed in one society may not be applicable to the behaviors of individuals in any other society. For the very reason that psychologists do work in diverse cultures, because they are in some ways unique, they may confront fundamental problems of knowing what to observe, how to measure it, and how to make any sense at all out of what they have observed and measured! This is the fundamental paradox and dilemma of doing cross-cultural research.

Before we begin our review of problems faced by the cross-cultural researcher, we should note that research done in many societies, typically non-Western ones, is increasingly being done by scholars who themselves originate in those societies (or closely neighboring ones) and often these scholars deliberately seek indigenous psychological concepts and approaches (for example, Sinha, 1997). To some extent, the problems we are about to discuss are reduced in indigenous psychological research. But, as we will see later in this chapter, when we discuss interactions between investigators and the people they are studying, indigenous psychology does not eliminate all of the problems of method inherent in cross-cultural research.

Observation Problems

The primary observation problem in cross-cultural research is, simply, what to observe. That this is a problem may not at first be obvious (which, incidentally, compounds the problem!).

When the Same Thing Is Something Else!
Suppose you begin with an interest in aggressive behavior among adolescents in diverse cultures. Don't you and your colleagues on this project simply go to various cultures and observe adolescent aggression? Of course, but what kinds of behaviors are valid indexes of aggression? *Aggression,* after all, is only a name that we give to a class of behaviors, and even in our own societies we often are not sure which kinds of behaviors should be counted as aggression.

In cross-cultural research on interpersonal violence, Ember and Ember (1993, 1994b) avoid using the word *crime* because definitions of crime vary so widely from one society to another. In many societies, killing an infant intentionally is called a *homicide.* But in others, infanticide is an accepted practice. As we shall see again in Chapter 9, Minturn and Shashak (1982) found infanticide in 53 percent of the cases in their sample of mostly nonindustrial societies. Similarly, the killing of an adult means different things in different societies, again as we shall see in Chapter 9.

In many societies, wife-beating was (and is) not considered a crime. In many societies described by anthropologists, there are accounts of people's believing that a husband had the right to beat his wife for any "good" reason. In the United States today, where it is a "crime," policemen don't always take spousal abuse very seriously.

When psychologists leave their own culture, they may be confronted with behaviors that would be interpreted one way in their own society but quite differently in another. Thus, in a cross-cultural study it might be inappropriate to study the same behaviors in two or more different societies. We might, in fact, have to study different, but "functionally equivalent" behaviors in order to study the "same psychological phenomenon."

When at Some Level, It's All the Same
Although often overlooked in the search for cross-cultural differences, there *are* universal aspects of human behavior. Surely at some level of abstraction we are all alike, all human.[4] While aggressive behavior varies in form from place to place, some form of aggression occurs in all societies. Aggression is a cultural universal (Lonner, 1980; Segall, Ember, & Ember, 1997); how it is expressed is culturally specific.

The dangers inherent in the etic approach merit reemphasizing. Because cultures differ widely in the ways in which they express aggression, researchers seeking generalizations might still have to assess different behaviors in the various societies in which aggression was being studied. Because the researchers are, themselves,

---

[4]In the early twentieth century this position was called the "psychic unity of mankind" (Boas, 1911).

strongly rooted in and influenced by their own cultural backgrounds, there is the danger that they may be reflecting their own cultural biases when they select the behavior to observe. Researchers might erroneously choose a behavior that could only be considered an act of aggression in their own societies, but not in the ones currently being studied.

The Emic/Etic Distinction and Choice of Measuring Instruments

This distinction between culture-specific and universal behaviors is one version of what has come to be known in cross-cultural psychology as the *emic/etic* distinction. If there is a universal class of behavior, like aggression at a high level of abstraction, with a specific variety of aggressive behavior in several particular societies, we could decide whether to do emic or etic research. The emic approach, which is typical of much ethnographic anthropological research, emphasizes the uniqueness of every culture by focusing on culture-specific phenomena such as the behaviors, norms, values, customs, traditions, and so on that are characteristic of a particular society. Cross-cultural psychologists, on the other hand, are more apt to use an etic approach, seeking to identify universal behavioral categories, and then compare their diverse, culturally specific variants. To do research *across* cultures is to do etic research.

A researcher, seeking to make meaningful comparisons, may enter a society armed with an instrument that is inappropriate for application in that society. Following Berry (1969), we call that misapplication an "imposed etic." The emic/etic distinction, and the process of moving from an imposed etic, through an emic analysis, to a derived etic is described in detail in Box 2.3 and is graphically illustrated in Figure 2.2. This process helps in solving the problem of choosing and adapting measuring instruments.

An example of *avoiding* the imposed etic problem is rooted in indigenous psychology. In general, the danger of imposing the researcher's own cultural classification system onto the behaviors of another cultural group is greater when one deliberately seeks to make comparisons than when one works strictly emically, within a single culture. Emic researchers, such as ethnographers, typically utilize methods like participant observation, employment of local peoples to serve as informed observers, and local test construction in an attempt to tap a culture's own indigenous system of classification or what has also been termed "subjective culture" (Triandis, 1972).

One search for possible cultural universals began with a theory of human behavior that has its origins in East Asia (Chinese Cultural Connection, 1987). It started with concepts relating to values discernible in an emic analysis done in China; these were then used as a kind of derived etic in comparative studies, and this derived etic was contrasted with another that originated in a Western setting (Hofstede, 1980). We will discuss this approach in more detail in Chapter 7 on values.

Within the discipline of psychology, something called "intelligence" has been measured since at least the era of Binet. But how this was done traditionally, via

---

BOX 2.3   Emics and Etics, Imposed and Derived

The researcher, seeking to make meaningful comparisons, may enter a society armed with an instrument that is inappropriate for application in that society. Following Berry (1969), we call that misapplied instrument an "imposed etic."

The terms *emic* and *etic* were originally employed by the anthropologist Pike (1954) to reflect linguistic concepts differentiating phonemics (the study of sounds whose meaning-bearing roles are unique to a particular language) and phonetics (the study of universal sounds used in human language, their particular meanings aside). Later (1967), Pike suggested that *emic* and *etic* could designate different viewpoints for the study of behavior, noting that from an etic viewpoint one studies behavior from outside, and from an emic viewpoint one studies behavior from inside.

Berry (1969) agreed with Pike (1967) that comparative research must nearly always begin with an instrument or observation technique necessarily rooted in the researcher's own culture (hence, an emic for that culture) used as if it were an etic (brought in from outside, assumed to be valid in the alien culture and, hence, also assumed to be valid for comparison purposes). Berry called such an instrument an "imposed etic." Obviously, great risk attends the use of an imposed etic, because there would be no way of knowing whether it made any sense to use it in any culture other than its culture of origin.

Then, Berry advocated that the researcher working in the alien culture strive (through participant observation and other ethnographic methods) to grasp local points of view in an effort to attain emic knowledge. Then, bringing together the researcher's own emic, and the alien culture emic, and seeking the features that they have in common, the researcher might then emerge with what we can now call a "derived etic."

This process is graphically illustrated in Figure 2.2.

---

so-called intelligence tests, has long been controversial, even within the societies in which the tests were first developed (e.g., in France in Binet's case) and most widely used for individual classification and selection (e.g., the United States). Their validity (i.e., do they really measure *intelligence*) and their degree of culture-boundedness (i.e., do they work equally well for individuals in diverse cultures, or well for some, not at all for others) are important issues. These will be discussed in Chapter 5.

Quantifying Originally Qualitative Data

Cross-cultural research is at least implicitly comparative, and often explicitly so. If, when comparing, we want to say, at least, that there is more (or less) of some characteristic or trait in case *a* than in case *b*, then it is necessary to measure it, at least at the ordinal level of measurement. Whenever possible, we would like to work at a higher level of measurement, so that we could say how *much* more (or less) there is

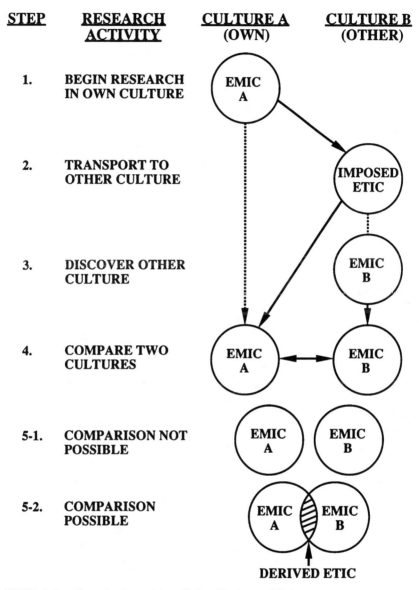

FIGURE 2.2   Steps in Operationalizing Emics and Etics

in *a* than in *b,* but we most often settle for ordinal comparisons. However, even ordinal comparisons are, by definition, quantitative.

But what if our original data come to us in the form of qualitative observations, as they often do, for example, when they are ethnographic reports provided by anthropologists who have written essentially emic, discursive, detailed reports of their observations in a particular society? Can we use such emic, qualitative data in etic, quantitative research?

The discipline of comparative anthropology employs a particular strategy, called *hologeistic research,* which does precisely that.

Hologeistic Research

Hologeistic research tests hypotheses on a worldwide sample of societies, most of them small-scale and usually constituting a single ethnic group resident in a specific locale. These samples are drawn from several hundreds of societies that have been described by a variety of scholars, many of them anthropologists, but some of them in other callings, such as missionaries and colonial civil servants, who took the time and had the interest to do descriptive fieldwork among the people with whom they were living and working. The resultant ethnographies have been painstakingly indexed by subject categories, and then assembled in a convenient format. This has resulted in a large collection called the Human Relations Area Files. This collection, known popularly as HRAF, exists in many libraries around the world, in various formats, including microfiche, paper, and, most usefully, electronic. In any of these formats, it can be searched by topic categories, so that in any given sample of ethnographies, all pages containing information on those categories can be easily found. In the electronic version of HRAF, one can also search by words in the texts, or one can search by HRAF categories *and* words.

A section of a single CD screen from the HRAF, showing numbers for the index categories, is reproduced in Figure 2.3. The screen shown here would appear in the course of searching by the topic "music" for all cultures, then selecting a particular culture (in this case Chinese Canadians, and finally selecting a particular author, in this case Hoe, Ban Seng). (See HRAF's home page [*http://www.yale.edu/hraf/home.htm*] for more information on how to use this rich database.)

To compare a sample on the variables of interest, the original descriptions must be encoded. This is a rather complex process by which numbers are substituted for the verbal descriptions. Multiple coders must be engaged in the effort and care must be taken to ensure intercoder reliability.

For example, if in a sample of many societies we are interested in where infants sleep (especially in what proximity to their parents), we would find the relevant categories or key words and note for these societies whether the child sleeps in the same bed with its mother and father or in a room separate from both mother and father (or other variations of "proximity to parents of infants during sleep" that might interest us). Based on what we find, we might very well be able to devise a scale for coding a variable called "proximity during sleep." The rules for assigning various levels of proximity would have to be made very explicit and the coders would have to become practiced in applying those rules. An example of a code for this variable, created by Barry and Paxson (1971) for a sample of 186 societies (of which 183 could be coded) is described in Box 2.4.

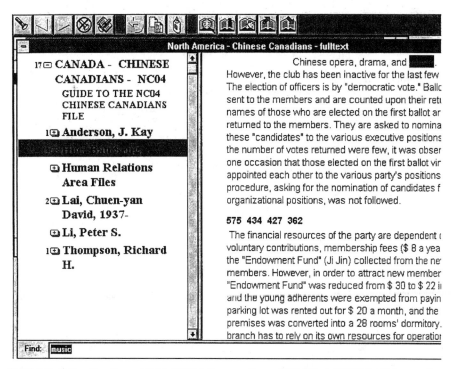

FIGURE 2.3 Section of CD-ROM Screen from HRAF: MUSIC, Chinese Canadians, Hoe Ban Seng

When a sample of societies has been coded on two variables, we can not only compare them on either variable, we can, more importantly, also test any hypothesis we might have about whether or not the variables are related to each other.[5] For example, if some theory suggested that societies living a mostly outdoors kind of life needed a more easily heard language than was needed in societies where daily life was spent mostly indoors, one could test such a theory, looking where the sample societies fall along both variables and testing the statistical significance of the relationship, as was done recently by Munroe, Munroe, and Winters (1996).

---

[5]These ethnographic materials pertaining to societies used in hologeistic research typically relate to only one or a few points in time. So, in hologeistic research, one examines relationships between presumed causes and effects synchronically, focusing on variables measured at a particular time in each case. It is assumed that regardless of different time focal points for sample cases, a significant result should obtain if there is a systematic relationship between measured variables. Unable to prove causation, this research strategy nevertheless provides a way to falsify hypotheses that have no predictive (and hence, presumably, no causal) value.

BOX 2.4   Proximity of Parents to Infant during Sleep, in a Sample of 183 Societies, as Coded by Barry and Paxson

Information on infant and parent sleeping arrangements could be described via a nine-part code for the 183 nonindustrialized societies for which relevant information was found in the ethnographies examined by Barry and Paxson (1971). Below, the distribution of codes is shown in tabular form.

(Incidentally, note that in this sample of societies, none were coded 1, which means that the arrangement common to many industrialized societies, in which the infant has its own room in the same house as its parents, is very rare, even nonexistent, in nonindustrialized societies).

Code	Meaning	N	%
1	Mother and father sleep in a separate room from infant	0	—
2–4	Mother sleeps in same room as infant but in different bed (father in another bed, or room, or house)	43	23.5
5	Mother and father sleep in same room as infant (bed unspecified)	62	34
6–8	Mother sleeps in same bed as infant (father in another bed, or room, or house)	56	30.5
9	Father and mother sleep in same bed as infant	22	12

Climate and Spoken Language Forms.   Munroe, Munroe, and Winters noted that all spoken languages have at least some syllables composed of a consonant followed by a vowel (CV, for short), for example, the English word *tuba* (CV–CV) and the Lugoli (spoken in western Kenya) word *gimisala* (CV–CV–CV–CV). While this form is dominant in some languages, it constitutes only a minority of the syllables used in others. The researchers tested the hypothesis that languages in which CV forms predominate would be found primarily in places where oral communicability over distance was highly desirable, as in societies where much of daily life is carried on outdoors, as in warmer climates.

They assigned fifty-three societies from the HRAF Probability Sample either to "warm to moderate" climates (temperatures not below 10 degrees Celsius for more than four months per year) or to "cold" climates (below 10 degrees for at least five months per year). They also assigned each society a CV score by dividing the number of CV syllables in each of a sample of words by the total number of syllables in each word, then adding together those ratios and dividing the sum by the total number of words. Then the societies were arrayed according to these two variables, CV score and climate (temperature). In Table 2.1, we present some of their results, which, as Munroe, Munroe, and Winters (1996) state, "indicate a striking association between temperature and CV score" (p. 71). Although the authors were clearly alert

TABLE 2.1   Numbers of Societies with High or Low CV Percentages in Warm/Moderate or Cold Climates*

	Climate	
	Warm/Moderate	Cold
CV percentages		
High (60 and up)	22	0
Low (59 and under)	18	13

*Summarized from complete data set in Munroe, Munroe, & Winters, 1996, pp. 72–73.

to alternative explanations of their findings, they concluded, "the argument that environmental factors like distance and noise will affect the oral communicability of messages seems prima facie a valid one" (p. 75).

Whenever the sample used is representative of the world's cultural units, the results of studies like that of Munroe and associates (1996) would be generalizable to human beings generally (hence, the term *hologeistic* which means 'whole world'). One popular way to ensure a representative sample is to employ the Standard Cross-Cultural Sample (described in detail by Murdock and White, 1969), which includes 186 mostly preindustrial societies distributed widely among cultural regions of the world or the HRAF Probability Sample, as was employed by Munroe and associates.

Happily, for many societies in the Standard Sample and in the HRAF more widely, many variables have already been coded (as we just saw for "proximity during sleep"), and these codes published, so that they are available for use by anyone who might wish to do a hologeistic study. Commonly, a new study involving a test of some hypotheses employs variables newly coded along with variables for which published codes already exist. Despite the fact that many societies in HRAF are small scale and were first described years ago,[6] comparisons across ethnographic cases have some advantages. Cultural variables, often merely assumed in cross-cultural psychology studies, can be explicitly isolated and tested for their predicted effects. Also, contemporary nation–states often contain many societies and therefore many cultures (e.g., more than fifty in China, and many in Nigeria). The results of a hologeistic study of "cultures" are more generalizable than those derived from a

---

[6]New cases are regularly added to the HRAF, including some contemporary multicultural societies. Recall that this whole process often begins with emic, ethnographic descriptions. Slightly ironically, we note that "outsiders" usually construct ethnographies, so they must always be inherently etic in part, with the outsider viewing the local culture in comparison, at least implicitly, with the ethnographer's own. Training in the techniques of ethnographic research encourages ethnographers to take an inside, or emic, view of the host culture.

narrower range of societies, such as modern nation–states. On the other hand, it is sometimes difficult to generalize to modern nation–states from a study done with only small-scale societies, simply because some of the very important conditions of life in modern nation–states (urbanicity, multiculturality, mass communications, etc.) simply do not exist in the small-scale societies. However, any hypothesis that receives support from a hologeistic study can subsequently be retested on a contemporary sample of societies, of whatever scale. Thus, the hologeistic, comparative anthropology strategy can be incorporated into cross-cultural psychology, which typically works with quantitative data, newly collected in, (obviously), contemporary societies. The two approaches are mutually complementary.[7]

Both approaches must also be concerned with sampling, but in different ways. In hologeistic research, the concern is with the representativeness of societies. In cross-cultural psychological research, it is with the representativeness of the individuals within societies, and the comparability of the resultant samples of societies. It is to the latter concern that we now turn our attention.

Sampling Problems

In all psychological research, even that carried out within a single society, we have to worry about the representativeness of a sample: to what population can findings be generalized. Whenever we compare samples, as we so often do in cross-cultural research, we have to worry also about their comparability. We'll deal with both of these problems here, in reverse order.

Obtaining Comparable Samples

There is an apparent paradox here. Whenever we do a cross-cultural study, we presumably want to work with samples that are different from each other. Yet we do want them to be comparable. How can they be both different and comparable at the same time? The point is, of course, that we want differences in some respects—for example, the degree of urbanicity (proportion of population living in cities) of two or more societies—and commonalties in other respects—for example, years of formal education—so we can investigate the hypothesized effect of some difference on people who do not differ on other pertinent variables.

Say we have a hypothesis about the effects of rural *versus* urban living on problem-solving ability. We might want to test this hypothesis by comparing a group of rural children with a group of urban children. We would want to "control for education" (try to compare groups that have had roughly equal amounts and kinds of schooling), because formal schooling provides training in problem-solving skills.

---

[7]A promising example of pooling HRAF societies into the contemporary nation–states of which they are a part, and assigning to those nation–states weighted scores reflecting the codes assigned to their constituent parts, has been developed by a team of researchers at the University of Zurich under the direction of Professor Müller (Müller, 1996).

But when we move from society to society, we find that age and years of schooling are highly correlated in some places but not in others. In this example, whereas urban-dwelling children who are, say, in their sixth year of schooling are likely to be within a year or two of twelve years of age, in rural societies they might represent a much wider range of ages, probably be higher in average age, and might be relatively rare people within their own societies. They would probably be richer, disproportionately male, and so on. So, when we hold one variable constant, we are almost inevitably confronted with variations along some unknown number of other variables.[8]

The aspect of the sampling problem that we have just discussed—the virtual impossibility of obtaining samples from more than one society that are truly comparable—is the major reason that Campbell warned (first in 1961 and again in 1972, with Raoul Naroll), that *all studies that consist solely of single-pair comparisons are uninterpretable.* The example Campbell used was Malinowski's material on Trobriand Island dreams compared with Freud's material on Viennese dreams. As we will see later in this chapter, this comparison demonstrated the need for cross-cultural testing of hypotheses spawned in a single culture. However, such a comparison could not definitively reveal the process underlying male adolescent hostility because between any two societies there are many differences that could constitute potential rival explanations. But, as Campbell pointed out, data collection need not be limited to a single pair of societies (Campbell, 1961, pp. 344–345).

Clearly, then, our sampling objective in any cross-cultural study must be to obtain a large number of societies (certainly more than two) that may be different in some respects (or we wouldn't be interested in them), but similar enough in other respects that they can be meaningfully compared. The objective is, of course, easier to state than to achieve. But it is always worth knowing what our objective is, if only to know how much any study falls short of achieving it.

Finding a Representative Sample

This sampling problem derives from the differential accessibility of individuals. Much intracultural psychological research, especially the vast majority of psychological experiments conducted in laboratories, employs student respondents who are invited, expected, and induced to volunteer. They are a kind of captive audience. As a result, accessibility is a minimal problem in such research (although representativeness is a major one).

In cross-cultural studies, locating, reaching, and inducing people to participate is difficult, time-consuming, and expensive. Consequently, there may well be subtle pressures on the researcher to recruit relatively accessible respondents. These are likely to be people on the beaten track (quite literally). They are likely to have had relatively high degrees of previous contact with outside cultures. They may be of

---

[8]Because age and years of schooling are differentially related to each other across cultures provides an advantage, in that these two variables, confounded in one society may be "unconfounded" in a cross-cultural research design. We will see some examples of this strategy in Chapter 4.

above average wealth and education and have linguistic skills or other characteristics that make them unrepresentative of the population they are (erroneously) taken to represent.

The accessibility problem in cross-cultural sampling has an interesting parallel in traditional ethnographic research. Sometimes an anthropologist employs a member of a society as an "informant" about the customs and institutions of that society. The informant must be someone with whom the anthropologist can communicate. People likely to apply for such a job are in some ways—linguistically, educationally, or otherwise—different from most in their own society. Informants, if members of the elite, would have a specialized, atypical knowledge about the society. As a result, what the anthropologist learns from the informant about the society may be true enough, but it may not be the most generally true set of facts that the anthropologist hoped to acquire. Thus, what is ultimately "known" about the culture—as in the records of the Human Relations Area Files, for example—would have been doubly filtered, through a foreign observer and an unrepresentative insider.

Although we have by no means exhausted the types of sampling problems confronting cross-cultural research,[9] enough has been said to make clear that it matters not only what we study and how we study it but also whom we study.

We have seen that observation problems and sampling problems present cross-cultural research with large hurdles to overcome. And there is still a third category of methodological problems that are particularly acute in cross-cultural research; it is to some of these that we now turn.

Researcher x Respondent Problems

Here we are concerned with threats to the validity of a study that derive from the *interaction* between the researcher and the people whose behavior is being studied. Obviously, people in other societies will be very different in many respects from a visiting researcher. (That is why, after all, one wants to study them.) Some intriguing methodological problems emerge from these differences.

For instance, there are likely to be serious impediments to communication, so serious that the respondents may misinterpret the task they are supposed to perform or the researcher may misinterpret the performance. There may be certain misperceptions by the respondents of the researcher's role and status, and these misperceptions may affect their performance in any variety of unknown ways. The respondents may be frightened, awed, cowed, or otherwise placed in some state of mind that will affect their motivation to perform. They may say or do whatever they think they have to in order to please, placate, or get away from someone they perceive as a tax collector, census enumerator, policeman, development project agent, or a potential source of income.

---

[9]See Lonner and Berry (1986) for more details on sampling in cross-cultural research.

Once again, if these difficulties are more prevalent in some societies than in others included in a single study, there will be the problem of differential meaningfulness of the behaviors observed in the societies. In some, the behaviors may be typical of what occurs when respondents are relaxed. In others, the behavior may be that which occurs when people are frightened out of their wits. Needless to say, comparability will have been threatened.

Because of such problems, cross-cultural psychologists disapprove of ill-planned, hastily arranged, brief incursions by researchers from industrialized nations into "exotic" non-Western societies. Such research practices, dubbed "safari research," are particularly prone to the problems recounted here.

These sorts of problems may be reduced when the researcher is a member of the same or a neighboring society as the people being studied. (Recall the discussion, above, on p. 37 of "indigenous psychology.") However, the higher status of the researcher, the fact that the researcher probably completed very high levels of university education, possibly abroad, makes the interaction between researcher and respondent problematic even in these instances. So, across the gamut from safari research to indigenous research, we must be wary of researcher–respondent interaction problems.

Minimizing Miscommunication

Suppose, as is so often the case in cross-cultural research, that respondents in one society perform a task one way and respondents in another society do it a different way. This is another way of saying that they give different responses and, if the responses are numerically graded, they earn different scores. We would like to be sure that such a difference across groups represents a "real" difference. But what if the two (or more) groups merely understood the tasks differently and were, in effect, performing what are, subjectively, different tasks?

Campbell (1964) dealt with this general problem by linking it to a concrete instance of a cross-cultural study of visual perception (Segall, Campbell, & Herskovits, 1966), which we will discuss in Chapter 4. For now it suffices to know that the study yielded significant differences among a large number of societies in the degree to which they seemed susceptible to a number of optical illusions. For example, in one society, respondents on average said that two lines appeared equal when one was actually eight percent longer; in another society, the average stated equality involved lines of which one was fifteen percent longer. Such differences were interpreted as evidence that these two groups were actually seeing things differently. But how can we tell when we are communicating well enough to know that people are indeed seeing things differently?

Campbell (1964) stated the problem: "Suppose that we parachuted an anthropologist and a test booklet into a totally isolated (society)...and that the anthropologist had first to learn the language without the help of an interpreter.... here is a problematic situation in which the cues and presumptions of communication need to be specified. It turns out that the anthropologist's main cue for achieved communication is similarity between the response of the other to a stimulus and the response that he himself would make. Disagreement turns out to be a sign of communication failure. How then can disagreement on an optical illusion test item be taken instead as a difference in perceiving the world?" (p. 317). The answer, again from Campbell (1964): "In essence, we could only observe differences in perception because these differences were small. Had any of our groups perceived in a radically different way from ourselves, we could not have determined that fact" (p. 325).

In the case of the Segall, Campbell, and Herskovits (1966) study, the problem was confronted in another way. This involved the use of four preliminary (or "comprehension check") stimuli. They were all prepared in such a way that, if the respondent did not respond exactly as the anthropologist would have, it could only be assumed that misunderstanding of the task was involved. For example, one such item was composed of a very short black line and a very long red line. The question asked was, "Which line is longer, the red or the black one?" If (as almost never happened) someone were to have said "black," it could not reasonably have been concluded that to that person the black line appeared longer. Rather, the conclusion would be that he had misunderstood one or a combination of the words *line, longer, black,* or *red,* or something else about what he or she was being asked to do.

Yet for the real test items, whatever responses were received were accepted at face value, because the preliminary items required comparisons of such extremely exaggerated line differences that anyone would find it incredible to interpret an incorrect response as indicating anything other than a failure of communication. Once it is shown that communication is not failing on the preliminary items, the assumption of achieved communication may then be confidently carried over to the test items.

Because nearly all people everywhere had behaved alike on the preliminary items, instances in which they did behave differently on the test items were taken as genuinely interesting and not merely artifacts of miscommunication. That the various groups in the study behaved similarly enough in certain respects made it possible to treat the differences that did show up as meaningful differences. As Campbell (1964) has put it, the preventive steps taken illustrate one important general principle:

> *Discrepancy can be noted and interpreted only against the background of an overwhelming proportion of non-discrepant fit, agreement, or pattern repetition. This principle is found in operation in knowledge processes as varied as binocular vision and astronomy. Again and again in science, the equivocal interpretations are available: separate entity* vs. *same entity changed, moved, or perceived from a different perspective. And in all such instances where the second interpretation occurs, it is made possible by the overwhelming bulk of stable non-changing background. Consider the reidentification of a single planet on successive nights, plus the inference that the planet migrates in an eccentric backtracking manner. Had Jupiter been the only star in the sky, this might never have been documented, cer-*

tainly not by a nomadic people. Had all the stars been planets, it would also have gone unascertained. Had the oscillations in the locations of the fixed stars been so great as to subtend several degrees of visual angle, the backtracking would not have been observed. It was the recurrent fixedness of 99.9 percent of the stars which made the wanderings of the few planets interpretable as such (p. 327).

Applying this principle to cross-cultural research, then, the dictum is obvious. Design the research in such a way that you ensure finding identical behaviors as well as different ones. For differences alone can only be ambiguous. A difference is interpretable only when embedded in a context of sameness.

One More Reason for Doing Psychological Research Cross-Culturally

One of the main goals of cross-cultural psychology is to test the generality of existing psychological knowledge and theories. A second goal is to discover psychological variations that are not present in a single social setting. While the first goal is akin to the search for psychological universals, the second leads to the documentation of diversity. These two goals are always complementary.

A further principle to be enunciated here is the *unconfounding function* of cross-cultural research. It is a principle about research strategy. The principle reflects the fact that, in any single culture, potentially causal factors for some behavior we wish to explain may coexist in a way that makes it impossible to disentangle them.

Suppose one is interested in cognitive skills, which could be acquired through learning in school, or, alternatively, simply develop as children grow and mature. In any society with nearly universal education, the variables "chronological age" and "years of schooling" are entangled (or, to use a technical term, *confounded*), while in societies where only some of the children go to school, these variables are independent of each other (thus, some eight-year-olds might be in the second year of primary school, many others not; at the same time, that amount of schooling might be characteristic of children of various ages, even some fifteen-year-olds). If one wanted to try to explain a particular kind of problem-solving performance that could be influenced by either years of schooling or chronological age (and one wished to know which of the two possible influences was more potent), it would be impossible to sort them out in a study done only in a city in Switzerland, for example, where age and schooling covary (i.e., are confounded). But in a rural sub-Saharan African setting, comparing children with the same degree of schooling but of various ages, and children of the same age with various degrees of schooling, would allow a determination of the importance of, respectively, age and schooling, for the problem-solving performance one wishes to understand.

When the famous Viennese psychiatrist, Freud, wanted to understand adolescent boys' hostility toward their fathers, he invented the so-called Oedipus complex, by which Freud attributed the hostility to sexual jealousy. (Like the character in the famous Greek tragedy who killed his father and made love to his mother, boys, Freud argued, love their mothers in a way that makes them resent their fathers' access to the boys' mothers' beds.) But in the society in which Freud worked (middle-class, patriarchal, Judeo-Christian, early twentieth-century Vienna), the role of mother's lover was confounded with the role of boy's disciplinarian, both played by the father, and both of which could lead to resentment on the boy's part. In some societies, like the Trobriand Island society studied by the anthropologist, Malinowski (1927), the roles are *unconfounded;* boys' fathers make love to the boys' mothers, but disciplining of boys is done by their maternal uncles (the mothers' brother). In that society, the target of hostility was found to be uncles, not fathers. So, limited to data from Vienna, we wouldn't know which role mattered (because fathers played both); with the Trobriand data in hand, we can suspect that what matters is not sexual jealousy, but resentment of discipline. A pioneer cross-cultural psychologist and one of general psychology's preeminent methodologists, Donald T. Campbell (1961), taught us this principle. Following Campbell, we argue that the unconfounding function alone justifies our arguing that psychologists should be obliged to test the generality of their theories and that the scientific study of human behavior requires that we employ a cross-cultural perspective.

CONCLUSION

We have presented enough in this chapter for you to understand, in a rather abstract fashion, what cross-cultural research covers and how it ought to be done. We have not, of course, discussed all the methodological issues that confront cross-cultural psychologists, nor have we discussed any in the detail that these issues require. Fortunately, such discussions are accessible (see, for example, Chapter 7 in Berry et al., [1992] and Berry, Portinga, & Pandey [1997]). However, you now should have an appreciation for problems of comparability and are ready to look at some research findings and begin to learn about some of the substantive issues that your newly acquired methodological sophistication should enable you to appreciate.

3

HUMAN DEVELOPMENT AND
INFORMAL EDUCATION

WHY STUDY DEVELOPMENTAL
PSYCHOLOGY CROSS-CULTURALLY?

Throughout its history, developmental psychology spawned many theories, all rooted in Western industrial society (North America and Europe, including the former USSR) and is, thus, to a certain degree, ethnocentric. The theories purport to be universal, despite their being based on observations and experiments involving a very narrow range of samples, usually children of a middle-class sociocultural background, studied in nurseries and schools. As in all branches of psychology, it is necessary to distinguish between what is in fact characteristic of human development everywhere and what is unique to a particular culture.

A cross-cultural approach to developmental psychology is relatively new but it has already yielded several texts and reference works. The reader may wish to delve more deeply into these than we will do in this chapter.[1]

This chapter presents an overall framework within which to study child development from a global perspective. While the chapter will not be organized by

---

[1]Particularly recommended are handbooks by Berry, Dasen, and Saraswathi (1997) and Munroe, Munroe, and Whiting (1981) and textbooks by Gardiner, Mutter, and Kosmitzki (1997), Munroe and Munroe (1975/1994b), and Bril and Lehalle (1988). Several other book-length treatments appeared (Bornstein, 1991; Lamb, Sternberg, Hwang, & Broberg, 1992; Super, 1987) as well as a series of volumes by Valsiner (1987, 1988, 1989a, 1989b). A few volumes specialize in infancy (Field, Sostek, Vietze, & Leiderman, 1981; Nugent, Lester, & Brazelton, 1989/1990) or adolescence (Esman, 1990; Schlegel & Barry, 1991), and a few volumes deal more specifically with human development in specific cultural areas, particularly Asia (Saraswathi & Dutta, 1988; Saraswathi & Kaur, 1993; Stevenson, Azuma, & Hakuta, 1986; Suvannathat, Bhanthumnavin, Bhuapirom, & Keats, 1985) and Africa (Nsamenang, 1992), or the "Majority World" in general (Kagitçibasi, 1996). Of interest also is a textbook of developmental psychology that is not cross-cultural as such, but takes culture seriously (Cole & Cole, 1996).

developmental periods, in the first part many examples will deal with infancy and childhood, and a section on adolescence and aging will come at the end. In this chapter we deal with the processes of cultural transmission, in particular enculturation, socialization and informal education. Other aspects of human development are taken up in subsequent chapters. In particular, in Chapter 5, we will pay close attention to the developmental theory of Piaget, and, in Chapter 6, to that of Vygotsky and the sociocultural school that it has inspired.

THE DEVELOPMENTAL NICHE

The theoretical framework of the developmental niche, proposed by Super and Harkness (1986, 1997; Harkness & Super, 1983, 1996) is a means for integrating findings from psychology and anthropology. Traditionally, developmental psychology tended to study the child out of sociocultural context, while cultural anthropology emphasized the context per se and the already socialized adult. The synthesis of these two approaches is to make the child in context the unit of analysis. This framework is illustrated in Figure 3.1.

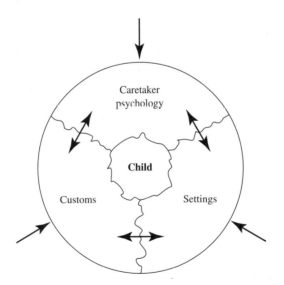

FIGURE 3.1   A Schematic Representation of the Developmental Niche

Reprinted with permission from Super, C. M., & Harkness, S. (1997). The cultural structuring of child development. In J. W. Berry, P. R. Dasen, & T. S. Saraswathi (Eds.), *Handbook of cross-cultural psychology, second edition. Vol. 2: Basic processes and human development* (pp. 1–39). Boston: Allyn & Bacon, Fig. 1.1, p. 26.

At the center of the developmental niche is the individual child, with his or her particular set of inherited dispositions, like temperament. Surrounding the child, there are three components or subsystems:

1. The settings, or physical and social contexts in which the child lives;
2. The customs, or culturally-determined rearing and educational practices;
3. The psychological characteristics of the caretakers, including the parental eth-
    notheories of child development.

Concerning the first component, B. Whiting (1980) noted that culture influences child development primarily by serving as a "provider of settings," that is, by furnishing the diverse contexts of daily life. For example, in rural Africa, babies are constantly exposed to the daily activities of the extended family by the simple fact that they are always present, and several different people interact with them. This is a very different setting from that of a baby who spends much of its time in a crib or a playpen, with only the mother as a caretaker. The social context formed by the people with whom the child interacts shapes social behavior, norms, and values. By the same token, certain characteristics of the social context are also strongly influenced by institutions (e.g., school).

The second component consists of the customs and mores that surround child care and prevailing educational practices. These vary enormously across societies. For example, different baby-carrying techniques determine the type and amount of bodily contact with the mother, and thus the habitual posture, both of which can influence motor development and perhaps even the personality of the child (cf. Berry, Poortinga, Segall, & Dasen, 1992; Bril & Lehalle, 1988).

The third component, the psychology of parents (or of other caretakers), includes the beliefs and values about the development of children, also called *parental ethnotheories*. Because they are usually not fully developed and conscious theories in the sense of a set of scientific laws, but are commonly shared in a social group, they might also be called social representations (Jodelet, 1989). These ethnotheories influence child development, in particular by determining contexts and training practices, but it also happens that parents do not always act according to the normative rules they convey verbally (Bril, Dasen, Krewer, & Sabatier, n.d.).

Some examples illustrating the components of the developmental niche are presented in Table 3.1. In the course of this chapter, several of these examples will be taken up and explained further.

The developmental niche is a system in which the component parts interact and function in coordinated fashion. Theoretically there is consonance among the elements of the niche, especially under conditions of stability in the society, but often there are also inconsistencies, especially under the impact of social change and acculturation. Moreover, it is an open system in which each component is linked with other aspects of the more general environment. For example, as Whiting (1981) has shown through holocultural research, the traditional mode of carrying a baby is

TABLE 3.1   Components of the Developmental Niche

1. SETTINGS/CONTEXTS:

PHYSICAL
- climate
- nutrition
- visual ecology
- objects, drawings, books
- size and organization of living space

etc.

SOCIAL
- family structure (nuclear, extended)
- multiple mothering
- children as caretakers
- prominence of father and mother
- multiple generations present
- size of peer group
- language(s) spoken

etc.

2. CUSTOMS/CHILDREARING PRACTICES
- carrying practices (arms, sling, crib)
- caretaking practices (handling, massage)
- postures
- stimulations
- sleeping routines
- eating schedules
- play
- chores, work
- informal and formal education

etc.

3. CARETAKER PSYCHOLOGY
- affective (emotional) orientations
- value systems (interdependence/independence)
- parental ethnotheories, cultural belief systems, social representations:
  - developmental theories (nature *versus* nurture)
  - religion (e.g., reincarnation)
  - developmental timetables
  - types of competencies expected
  - levels of skill mastery
  - evaluation procedures
  - final stage
  - definitions of *intelligence*

  etc.

linked to the climate; infants tend to be carried on the body when it is warm and in a crib (or equivalent contraption) when it is cold.

Super and Harkness (1986, 1997) explain that the organism and the developmental niche adapt to one another. As the individual adapts to its surroundings, the niche also adapts to the individual. Certain maturational changes in cognition and personality determine the expectations that adults have with respect to children of different ages. The developmental niche thus changes itself in the course of ontogenesis.

In the following sections, we will examine studies that deal with important aspects of the developmental niche. We will consider some aspects of the physical and social settings, then review in detail studies of everyday activities (in particular games played and chores carried out in the service of the family group). These provide both social and intellectual learning opportunities, and are, thus, part of informal education. This is a concept we will examine in some detail in a later section, contrasting it with formal education, or schooling. We will also examine various parental ethnotheories. Before we study these examples, we need to link the developmental niche to two other theoretical frameworks that are compatible with it.

The Ecocultural Framework

The ecocultural framework serves as the backbone to this book (cf. Fig. 2.1). The crucial link with the developmental niche is the box representing cultural transmission, which occurs mainly through the two processes of enculturation and socialization. Table 3.1 is an illustration of these processes.

Enculturation happens largely through the selection of contexts. Children learn what there is around them to be learned. But this selection of contexts is usually simply part of the cultural setup; it is not under the conscious control of parents. Consider the number of books available in a home, which is usually a function of the level of literacy and socioeconomic status of the parents: In more educated households, there are more books around. Some customs and childrearing practices are illustrative of enculturation, because they are mainly unconscious, while others are closer to socialization, because they are willingly chosen. For example, some parents purposefully buy "educational" children's books, or even an encyclopedia to help with schoolwork (more often, now, as a CD-ROM). In such a case we would speak of socialization rather than enculturation.

Child care practices are usually very homogeneous within a society: There is one, and only one, proper way of handling a baby, the one way that has been practiced over the generations, without any questions asked (or, in Euro-American society, the one advocated by the currently fashionable pediatrician, be it Spock or Brazelton). These practices, however, vary greatly between societies; a cross-cultural comparison is needed to become aware of the diversity. For example: "It's a sensible rule not to take a child into the parents' bed for any reason" is the advice given by Spock and Rothenberg (1992, p. 213, as quoted in Gardiner et al., 1997). Now recall

Box 2.4: The practice of cosleeping is routine in most of the world, including in present-day Japan, where children typically sleep with their parents until they are six or more. Putting a young infant to sleep in a separate room was seen by Mayan mothers as "tantamount to child neglect" (Morelli, Rogoff, Oppenheim, & Goldsmith, 1992, p. 608).

The third subsystem of the developmental niche is typical of socialization, because cultural belief systems represent conscious explanations or rationalizations for customs of childrearing. Hence, the developmental niche represents the whole spectrum between enculturation and socialization, and, as in the ecocultural framework, these processes are linked to culture, and ecological and sociopolitical contexts, on the one hand, and determine the child's behavioral development on the other. Acculturation and social change are processes that strongly influence the system, and genetic transmission is also recognized, particularly in terms of the child's temperament. It should be obvious that the two theoretical frameworks are fully compatible, even partly overlapping: The developmental niche is a refinement of part of the ecocultural framework, with particular attention to human development.

Ecological Systems Theory

The second theoretical framework that is close to that of the developmental niche is the one proposed by Urie Bronfenbrenner (1974, 1979, 1989, 1993) under the name of *ecological systems theory.* Bronfenbrenner's scheme is illustrated in Figure 3.2.

This framework also places the individual child in the middle, interacting actively (through bidirectional, reciprocal, influences) with the environment, structured in terms of the nested levels of the microsystem, the mesosystem, exosystem, and macrosystem. The microsystem represents the face-to-face interactions with the immediate, physical or social, surroundings. The way in which environment is experienced is important, rather than its objective qualities. The microsystem also includes, according to Bronfenbrenner (1993), institutions such as the day-care center, preschool or school, hospital, church, and so on. The mesosystem reflects the linkages between two or more of these settings. The exosystem comprises further such linkages with settings of which the individual is not a part, but that nevertheless exert an influence. The macrosystem is tantamount to "culture," in that it consists of such general aspects of society as its values, belief systems, and so on.

These two theoretical frameworks, the developmental niche and Bronfenbrenner's ecological systems theory, have much in common. Each of these frameworks makes it obvious that the developing individual cannot be isolated from the context, and that interactions are reciprocal, so that the proper unit of analysis is neither the individual out of context, nor the contexts in themselves, but the individual in context. Working with the theoretical framework of the developmental niche hence calls for the continuous cooperation of psychologists with other social scientists, particularly anthropologists.

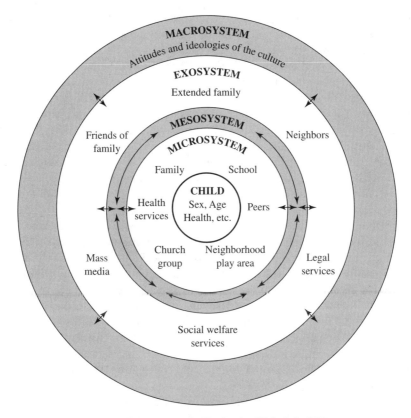

FIGURE 3.2   Bronfenbrenner's Ecological Model of Human Development

Reprinted with permission from Kopp, C. B., & Kaslow, J. B. (1982). *The child.* Reading, MA: Addison-Wesley, p. 648.

Physical and Social Settings

It is obvious to any world traveler that people speak different languages, dress differently, and eat strange but sometimes interesting food. It is just as obvious that the physical settings in which children grow up differ greatly. What is less obvious is how best to describe the impact of this diversity in settings on human development. Bril and Zack (1987) have used video recording to achieve such descriptions. They have, for example, compared three physical and social settings: French infants brought up in the home, in a day-care center, and Bambara infants in a rural setting in Mali. The home-based infants spend much of their time in a room filled with toys, alone or in the sole company of their mother, and possibly one other sibling. In the day-care center, they spend most of the time with dozens of playmates and several adult caretakers, and infants in a village in Mali partake of the daily life, full of noise and movement, of their mothers and sibling caretakers. As we will see below, these settings have a direct impact on childrearing practices.

Among the physical settings in Table 3.1, we have listed nutrition, but in most cases nutrition is not merely a function of food availability, but is controlled by social factors such as differential food distribution, and even aspects of mother–infant interactions (Dasen & Super, 1988). Visual ecology is also part of that list. It will be examined in the next chapter, when we review in some detail studies on the impact of visual ecology on perception. In fact, it is often difficult to separate physical from social settings, and from the practices that fit these settings. In any case, there are hardly any physical settings that are not culturally shaped.

Much research on the importance of various social settings comes from the six cultures study led by Beatrice and John Whiting. Whiting and Whiting (1975) organized the systematic ethnographic and psychological study of children in six cultures: Gusii in Nyansongo, Kenya; Mixtec Indians in Juxtlahuaca, Mexico; the villagers of Tarong on the Northwest coast of the Philippines; Taira in Okinawa (Japan); the Rajput in the village of Khalapur, in Uttar Pradesh, India; and Americans in Orchard Town, a suburban New England community in the United States. This major research project gave rise to several publications (from Minturn & Lambert, 1964, to Whiting & Edwards, 1988) and spurred much further research, summarized in the handbook edited by Munroe and colleagues (1981), and the textbook by Munroe and Munroe (1975/1994b).

This type of research often uses observation techniques that describe the daily behavior of children and the people they interact with, observations that may be quantified. Some of these techniques are described in Box 3.1.

Many interesting findings emerge from such studies. For example, Munroe and Munroe (1971) studied the effects of household density on infant socialization among the Logoli of Kenya. Infants in high-density households were held more often and attended to more quickly when they cried. On the other hand, the mother was less accessible to them: She was less often the baby's main caretaker, and was less often in close range, due to the greater economic responsibilities she bears in a large household.

Weisner and Gallimore (1977) reviewed the role of child caretakers in socialization. Child care is one of the most important tasks delegated to children by mothers with many offspring and a heavy workload. In Weisner's own observations among the Abaluyia of Kenya, girls at ages 6 to 8 were in the caretaker role about twice as often as boys (60 percent of the time *versus* 30 percent). Although older children were more often caretakers than younger children, girls aged 3 to 5 were in the caretaker role 34 percent of the time. Sex differences in social behavior may well result from such differential assignment to social settings (Whiting & Edwards, 1988).

BOX 3.1   Observational Techniques

Real-world observation and ethnographic description may be distorted by ethnocentric expectations. An example demonstrating this is the controversy raised by the work of Freeman (1983), whose description of adolescence in Samoa contrasts markedly with that given earlier by Mead (1928). Thus, it is well to develop precise and, if possible, quantitative measurement techniques. Bril (1983, 1984), for example, has studied the socialization process in detailed fashion by making precise, quantifiable observations. Using video recorders, which allowed computerized analyses of different bodily movements, Bril observed young Bambara girls in Mali learning the task of crushing millet. She demonstrated in an eloquent manner how the girls' gestures gradually come to resemble those of an adult model, with perfect conformity achieved by the age of 6 years.

The technique employed in the Six Cultures study (Whiting & Whiting, 1975), sometimes called continuous observation, required observers to familiarize themselves with and integrate themselves into the situation so as to become as unobtrusive as possible. Notes were made on children's behaviors as well as on their interactions with the physical and social environment during a predetermined period of time. These observations were distributed across entire days (but included only a single observation per day and per child). In order to standardize the analyses, Whiting and Whiting used only the first five minutes of the observations. In this manner, the research team was able to study 24 children between the ages of 3 and

10 in each cultural group, with a minimum of 15 continuous observations per child.

Another technique, developed by Munroe and Munroe (1971), is the method of spot-observations. This also requires the observer to be familiar both with the children to be observed and their surroundings, and, even better, to be a member of the same ethnic group. Children's behavior is sampled on a daily basis at different hours of the day. In the Munroe and Munroe (1971) study, spot-observations were made on a strict daily schedule and, in the case of school-going children, during nonschool hours. For each observation, the observer makes a written snapshot of the situation, noting where the child was located, whom the child was with, what it was doing, and so on. The observer may also question the child in order to learn, for example, whether the activity observed was demanded of the child by someone else and, if so, by whom. But this intervention in the flow of activity is minimal, in contrast to continuous observation techniques in which the intervention can modify the behavior being observed. Thus, spot-observation is a less "reactive" type of measurement. Reactivity of measurement is a concern in all science and, especially, social science. Whenever a measuring instrument is used, its mere presence may modify what is being measured. Obviously, the more reactive a measure, the less valid the observation.

Data using the technique of spot-observation have now been collected in a variety of societies using a more or less comparable schedule, and these raw data are available in computerized format through the HRAF.

The presence and role of grandparents change the childrearing setting to a large extent. Grandparents often have more time for focused interaction with the child because they are less pressed by subsistence tasks. Among the Gusii of Kenya, for example, the relationship between grandparents and children is warm and often jovial, while the father is seen by the child as a frightening and awesome person, who takes no part in child care, and is often away from home. When Gusii girls are 5 or 6 years old, they go to live and sleep at their grandmother's house (LeVine & LeVine, 1966, as summarized by Munroe & Munroe, 1975/1994b). As we will see in Chapter 8, the respective salience of the mother and of the father and, in particular, the father's (real or symbolic) absence, are influential aspects in the development of personality and in particular of sex-role identity.

The size and composition of peer groups is another feature that shows important cultural diversity. The custom of placing the child in a large same-age peer group, with most of the socialization done by an adult who is not part of the family, produces a special setting, and it may not be an optimal one for learning. In informal education, as we will see later in this chapter, most of the enculturation and socialization occurs through "horizontal transmission" (i.e., through peers [Berry et al., 1992, p. 18]). In particular, when peer groups comprise children of various ages, the younger ones learn a lot from the (even only slightly) older ones. This process is becoming popular as a deliberate teaching method. It has been, of course, one of the distinguishing features of youth groups such as scouts and in schools too small to have same-age classes, as in many rural areas.

In a holocultural study of adolescence, using ethnographic records on 186 societies, Schlegel and Barry (1991) found that adolescents the world over spend the majority of their time with same-sex adults.[2] This of course allows for role-modeling, and for an early incorporation of youths into adult society, features that alleviate the "problems" of adolescence. We will come back to the cross-cultural study of adolescence later in this chapter.

Language acquisition can be analyzed in terms of enculturation (i.e., the selection of a particular context). With the exception of mixed marriages, in which parents decide to each speak their own language to the child, there is usually no conscious choice of which language(s) are spoken around the baby. While infants are potentially able to learn any language, they become attuned early to pay attention to a particular set of sounds and acoustic distinctions. When they start speaking themselves, they practice only the relevant distinctions, to the point at which the pronunciation of some unusual syllables may become impossible (or at least very hard to learn) after the early teens.[3] Children who grow up in a plurilingual environment rapidly discriminate between the specific sounds of the languages they hear. Lan-

---

[2]There are a few exceptions, for example, when there are age groups related to initation, as among the Morans of the Masai of Kenya, or among Western adolescents in urban settings.

[3]Consider, for example, the click sounds current in some South African languages, as exemplified in some of Johnny Clegg's songs.

guage acquisition and bilingualism constitute an important and complex topic in cross-cultural research. (For a more detailed coverage, see Munroe and Munroe [1975/1994b], Berry et al., [1992], and Mohanty and Perregaux [1997]).

Customs: Childrearing Practices

Cross-cultural research on childrearing practices, both archival and field studies (such as the Six Cultures study), show how socialization practices are adaptive and linked to ecocultural dimensions such as food accumulation. Within these constraints, childrearing practices vary enormously. In some societies people believe that infants will be hurt if lifted by an arm, or if the head is not constantly supported; in contrast, a typical West African grandmother gives the baby a rather robust massage, during which she does not fear to lift it by pulling on an arm or shoulder, hold it up by the head, or stretch it by pulling on the hands and feet.

Bril and Sabatier (1986) and Bril and Zack (1989) analyzed the link between the diversity of settings and childrearing practices. Regarding the postures infants find themselves in, for example, French babies spend more than half of the day time in a horizontal (prone or supine) position until they are 6 to 7 months old (and still 30 percent at twelve months). In contrast, Bambara babies in Mali, after the age of 40 days, were found in a supine position in only 5 to 6 percent of the observation time (and never in a prone position). Most common for them is a semivertical or upright sitting position, either carried on the back or the side, or put down to sit. The time spent in body contact with a caregiver was estimated to be 93 percent at 2 months, decreasing slowly to 60 percent at 12 months. French babies reared at home were in body contact with the mother about 30 percent of the time throughout the first year, while the figure was 20 percent for those in a day-care center.

These different postures provide different types and amounts of stimulation. Bril and Zack (1989) report that the Bambara babies between 2 and 6 months of age were receiving vestibulo-kinesthetic stimulation[4] in 40 to 50 percent of the observation time, with only 10 percent for the French babies. After the age of 7 months, the stimulation increases for the French babies reared at home and decreases for the Bambara babies, so that the differences disappear by 12 months. The Bambara babies learn early to adjust to frequent changes in posture, and the caretakers monitor their manipulations as a function of the infant's developing motor abilities. "Mothers implicitly recognize the different developmental stages" (Bril & Sabatier, 1986, p. 452). There is congruence between the physical setting, the social setting, childrearing customs, and parents' social representation of development.

Childrearing practices also lead to different types of mother-infant communication, on the proximal/distal[5] dimension. When the baby is in constant body contact,

---

[4]Stimulation of the vestibular system in the innear ear, linked to movement.

[5]These words mean 'near' and 'far.'

communication can be nonverbal, while the baby who is put away in a crib has to broadcast its needs.

Research on sleeping routines shows diversity not only in where and with whom the child sleeps, shown in Box 2.4, but when and how long a child sleeps, as well as the bedtime routines. Some of these patterns are part of widely shared customs: Spanish children stay up all evening; children in Africa have no bedtime: they go to sleep whenever they choose (and sometimes in the middle of a noisy, dancing crowd). In Japan and China, they go to bed late and get up early because of home-work for school. Super and Harkness have organized a large-scale cross-cultural study to better document some of these routines. In Holland, for example, they found that parents insisted on long hours of sleep and regular bedtime routines (Super, Harkness, van Tijen, van der Vlugt, Fintelman, & Dijkstra, 1996). Dutch babies got on the average more sleep than babies in Cambridge, Massachusetts (two hours more at 6 months, down to twenty minutes in the fifth year), and went to bed regularly an hour earlier than their U.S. counterparts. As a presumed consequence, Dutch babies were calmer when awake than their U.S. counterparts (Super & Harkness, 1997).

According to Wolf, Lozoff, Latz, and Paludetto (1996):

How a child is allowed to fall asleep is one of the earliest forms of cultur-ally determined interaction with the child. Sleep practices are embedded in a set of childrearing behaviors that reflect values about what it means to be a 'good' parent and how the parents are to prepare the child for entry into the family and the community. A useful framework for interpreting cross-cultural differences is the varying emphases placed on autonomy ver-sus interrelatedness (p. 377).

Barry and Paxson (1971) found, among 119 societies drawn from the HRAF, none that expected children to fall asleep in their own beds and stay asleep all night isolated from the parents. Wolf and colleagues (1996) looked at bedtime practices in Japan, Italy and the United States. In the first two countries, regular all-night co-sleeping was found for respectively 58 percent and 42 percent of the mothers, as compared to 19 percent in the United States for white mothers. However, cosleeping was found for 58 percent of African American mothers.

Time Allocation Studies: Work and Play
The amount of time children spend in play, what type of toys they have and games they play, but also how much time they have to devote to work (chores to help the household)[6] deserve special attention in the study of enculturation and socialization

---

[6]Munroe, Munroe, and Shimmin (1984) operationally define work in these studies as "all instrumental activities judged to contribute to the maintenance of the household or to the well-being of its members" (p. 369). While production and maintenance activities (e.g., repair of objects, weaving, wage work) would be included in this definition, they hardly ever occurred in the studies reported here. The children's work consisted mainly of domestic chores and taking care of siblings.

processes. These are social occasions for learning not only skills, but also implicit values.

Observational techniques as described in Box 3.1 have been employed in the study of time allocation for work and play. Whiting and Whiting (1975) found that the relative proportions of these two kinds of activities varied across cultural groups. This difference was particularly striking between the Nyansongo children (Kenya), who devoted 41 percent of their time on average to work, and the U.S. American children (Orchard Town), who worked only 2 percent of the time. Munroe, Munroe, Michelson, Koel, Bolton, and Bolton (1983), in a spot-observation study of Kenyan (Kikuyu and Logoli), Peruvian, and U.S. children (aged 6 to 10 years) confirmed this: on average, outside of school hours, 5 percent work time for the U.S. children and 57 percent work time for the Kikuyu of Kenya (and 37 percent for the Logoli; 47 percent for the Canchinos in Peru).

The Whiting and Whiting (1975) study, while revealing important cultural differences, included only sedentary groups practicing agriculture, herding, or industrial production. There were no nomadic hunters, among whom adults typically spend relatively little time dealing with subsistence tasks (Sahlins, 1972) and who consequently demand very little from their children until about 9 years of age. This, of course, does not prevent children from imitating adults nor from participating in tasks if they wish (cf. Hamilton, 1981, for a study of Australian Aboriginal children). Draper (1976) found that !Kung San children between the ages of 4 and 9 years devote only 3 percent of their time to work tasks. Unfortunately, we have few quantitative observations for these kinds of populations.

Thus, the relation between cultural complexity and time devoted to work by children seems to be an inverse U-shaped one. Work time, for adults as well as for children, increases with the intensification of human control over the environment, rising to a maximum in agricultural societies with dense populations, and then diminishes with industrialization (Minge-Klevana, 1986; Munroe et al., 1983).

Furthermore, the demands made of children change with age. Whiting and Whiting (1975) asked parents to report how old children ought to be before they might comfortably be asked to perform particular tasks. Combining parental responses with direct observations, Whiting and Whiting determined the minimum age at which more than half of the children performed various tasks. The findings are displayed in Table 3.2. As these data show, certain societies not only expect more participation by children in chores, they require it at an earlier age. This was particularly striking for the Kenyan society, in which all the tasks included were performed by 3- to 4-year-old children.

The spot-observation technique allows an even more precise quantification of the time spent at work or play. In a study of Kipsigis[7] children up to 9 years of age, Harkness and Super (1983) found a rapid increase from infancy through 6 years of

---

[7]The Kipsigis are a Nilotic population in Kenya practicing animal husbandry and itinerant agriculture.

TABLE 3.2   Task Assignments: Youngest Age at which over Half the Children of a Given Age Group Were Reported or Observed Performing a Given Chore or Task.*

Chore or task	Nyansongo Kenya	Juxtlahuaca Mexico	Tarong Philippines	Taira Japan	Khalapur India	Orchard Town U.S.A.
Carrying wood and water	3–4	3–4	3–4	7–10	5–6	—
Preparing food	3–4	7–10	3–4	—	3–4	—
Gardening	3–4	7–10	7–10	—	—	—
Cleaning	3–4	5–6	3–4	3–4	5–6	3–4
Taking care of animals	3–4	3–4	5–6	7–10	7–10	—
Number of tasks performed by 3- to 4-year olds	5	2	3	1	1	1

* From Whiting and Whiting (1975), p. 94. Adapted with permission.

age in the time devoted to carrying out tasks in the service of the family group. From 15 percent at 2 years, the increments are approximately 10 percent each year, reaching 60 percent between 6 and 9 years. In contrast, the time devoted to play diminishes regularly from 40 percent at 2 years to only 8 percent at 8 to 9 years.

Similar studies have been conducted by Dasen (1988), using spot-observations with Kikuyu[8] and Baoulé[9] children. The observations were taken during school vacation times or outside school hours. The results are presented in Table 3.3. Young Kikuyu children have to devote about half of their out-of-school time to work, and work time continues to increase after age 7, with a concomitant decrease in play, and a strong sex difference. Kikuyu girls, from 10 years of age onward, have no more than 3 percent of the day time to play. Boys also work, but they also go off in peer groups more often, spending about half their time in work and half in play. The results of the 8- to 9-year-old Baoulé paralleled those of the Kikuyu children of the same age. Thus, among the Kikuyu and the Baoulé, a very sharp sex difference exists in the amount of time children spend working or playing. We will have more to say about sex differences below.

One might expect that a child who spends half of the out-of-school time working for the good of the social group would acquire not only the necessary job know-how, but also an appropriate value system. In a multivariate analysis of observed

---

[8]The Kikuyu are a Bantu group in Kenya, East Africa, a predominantly agricultural population who also do some herding.

[9]The Baoulé are an Akan group in Côte d'Ivoire, West Africa, engaged in subsistence agriculture, and producing coffee and cocoa as cash crops, in the context of a tropical forest.

TABLE 3.3 Percentage of Spot-Observations for which Kikuyu and Baoulé Children Play or Work

Age	Kikuyu					Baoulé
	5–7	8–9	10–11	12–16		8–9
Play:						
Boys	24	30	22	50		39
Girls	22	17	2	3		13
Work:						
Boys	45	48	70	50		42
Girls	50	60	70	80		70
N						
Boys	8	7	7	6	28	23
Girls	8	6	5	7	26	24
N spots						
Boys	268	228	221	188	905	672
Girls	220	168	151	216	755	738

From Dasen, 1988

social behavior of the children of six cultures (Whiting & Whiting, 1975), a dimension that emerged ranged from "nurturant–responsible" to "dependent–dominant." Those children who did more work were closer to the "nurturant–responsible" end, often offered affection or assistance, and made altruistic suggestions. In contrast, those at the "dependent–dominant" end sought attention or assistance and tended to make selfish suggestions.

Munroe, Munroe, and Shimmin (1984) confirmed this in a study of forty-eight 3- to 9-year-old children, employing the spot-observation method in four cultures: Logoli in Kenya, Newars in Nepal, Garifuna in Belize, and Samoans in the Pacific. The children more engaged in domestic and subsistence-related tasks displayed, even when not engaged in work, social behavior characterized by the following features: They made more altruistic suggestions, scolded the others and demanded assistance from them, and the others often obeyed them. Girls, who are often engaged with younger children, extend the behaviors they employ with them to other social situations. They often offer assistance or affection to people generally.

Differences between the Sexes.   As Munroe, Shimmin, and Munroe (1984) noted, societies differ considerably in the degree to which they distinguish between the sexes. Those that make a strong distinction have a tendency to involve girls from a very young age in subsistence activities, domestic tasks, and child-care, in fact, all the tasks that are typically defined as "feminine" in the society in question (see Ember, 1973). Very young boys are also likely to be induced to carry out these "feminine" tasks, especially if there is no older sister in the family, but the distinction between the sexes becomes quite clear-cut subsequently. In Dasen's (1988) study in Côte d'Ivoire, 8- to 9-year-old girls performed typically feminine activities in 53 percent of the cases, and masculine activities in only 4 percent; for the boys, typically masculine activities represented 25 percent, while feminine activities represented 16 percent. In Chapter 8, we will examine other sex differences in more detail.

Work and Child Labor.   A word of caution is appropriate at this stage about children at work. As noted above, in the research we have just examined in some detail, work consists of doing chores that contribute to the upkeep and well-being of the household. Children are given a useful role and an opportunity to learn many of the skills they will need as adults. In most cases, this type of work does not prevent them from attending school (although there may be other reasons for not going to school, and girls may sometimes be kept out of school to serve as child caretakers). Work in this context serves as a powerful and positive socialization practice.

There are other situations, far too many, in which children are being exploited at work (Bonnet, 1998; Schlemmer, 1996). This is usually the case when the subsistence is derived from the production of goods in semiindustrial or handicraft settings, such as the weaving of carpets (in East Asia), the production of shoes (in Portugal), mining (in Bolivia and other Latin American countries), or actual industrial settings (in the Pacific rim, and increasingly again in Europe). Often, girls are used as housemaids. The United Nations International Children's Fund (UNICEF) and the International Labor Organization (ILO) estimate that, of 1.15 billion children in the world, 200 million are subject to exploitation in child labor, and it is estimated that there will be 400 million of them by the year 2000, because the present world economic system tends to foster child exploitation, sometimes in situations that can only be called a modern form of slavery. These international organizations are now attempting to draw a line between child labor as a sometimes necessary contribution to the economy, and child exploitation, which should be abolished.

Even worse, children are currently reported to take part in armed conflicts in twenty-five countries in the world. In many countries, the army, whether governmental or rebel, recruit children by force. They are subjected to an indoctrination that is really socialization for violence.

Play and Games
The importance of play as a context for learning and socialization is obvious. It is integral to preschool teaching, but in many non-Western societies the value of play in formal schooling is contested because parents consider school a place to work and not to play (N'guessan, 1989). Under the pressure of social change, traditional games tend to disappear and to be replaced by television and commercially manufactured toys. Many researchers, sometimes sponsored by institutions such as UNICEF and OMEP (the World Organization for Pre-school Education), have inventoried traditional games, in Third World countries as well as in industrialized nations (e.g., Ivic & Marjonovic, 1986; Muralidharan, Khosla, Mian, & Kaur, 1981).

Games.   The ethnographic literature is rich in descriptions of games (e.g., Lancy, 1996). The HRAF can be used to study their worldwide distribution. An excellent summary of hologeistic studies of games may be found in Sutton-Smith and Roberts (1981), who distinguish between "games" and "play." The former, which have rules, in principle involve at least two parties (either individuals or groups) competing until a winner is declared. They further distinguish between three types of games:

1. Games of physical skill (e.g., racing, dart throwing);
2. Games of chance (the outcome is determined by a guess or a random event, e.g., roulette); and
3. Games of strategy (the outcome is determined by rational choices).

Games of skill are found in all societies. Games of chance, on the other hand, are frequent in societies in which economic or social uncertainty prevails, in particular in nomadic hunting–gathering societies. Chance games are usually absent or even forbidden in sedentary agricultural or animal husbandry societies, in which socialization is more authoritarian. In these societies, games of strategy that demand conformity to rules and planning prevail, values that are certainly important in societies practicing agriculture and/or animal husbandry.

Thus, there is a relationship between the type of subsistence economy and types of games, with each type reflecting different values. Chance games encourage becoming accustomed to risk, while knowing that everyone sooner or later will win. Not only are chance games particularly frequent in societies that traditionally live by hunting and gathering, such games prevail even as these societies modernize.

Games of strategy can be intellectually challenging and give rise to complex reasoning. Psychologists in the area of cognitive science and artificial intelligence have studied such games as chess or the tower of Hanoi. In Africa (as well as in parts of Indonesia and in the African diaspora in the Americas) there is a board game that takes slightly different forms, rules, and names in different locations (e.g., Mankala, Wari, Solo, Kalah, Awélé), but that shares a basic structure. Seeds or small stones are moved according to elaborate rules along two or four parallel lines of holes (in the ground or a piece of wood), and there are rules on how to capture seeds. The player who ends up with more than half of the seeds is the winner. Retschitzki (1990) studied the development of strategies in children (9 to 15 years), adults, and experts (in the national championship) in the Awélé game as played in Côte d'Ivoire. He videotaped games to allow frame-by-frame analysis, and devised specific tasks to test the participants' knowledge of the game and the level of their strategies and anticipations. The older children (13 to 15 years) who had a lot of practice with the game used complex strategies that involve the anticipation of several moves. Except for very specific skills (such as estimating the number of seeds in a game situation), there was no difference on a variety of cognitive tests between the better and medium players. As we shall see in Chapters 4 and 5, it is a common finding that cognitive skills, even at the higher levels of abstract reasoning, are often very situation-specific.

An interesting expansion of this research occurred when N'guessan (1992), a psychologist from Côte d'Ivoire working with Retschitski, studied the development of these strategies in Swiss children who were learning the Awélé game, of which they had no previous knowledge or experience. The problems encountered in learning the game, and the sequence in which strategies are acquired, were the same for the Swiss and the African children. This study is a nice illustration of the emic-imposed etic-derived etic research strategy described in Chapter 2. In this case the initial emic was African, and was imposed on Swiss subjects, a relatively rare reversal of circumstances in cross-cultural research. Another member of the same research team, Gottret (1996), studied the development of strategies in a popular board game in Bolivia called "fox and sheep." Bolivian children, at any given age level, showed more advanced strategies on this game than on "noughts-and-crosses" ("tick-tack-toe") with which they were less familiar. Such studies using local games are examples of research on "everyday cognition," a topic that we will examine in Chapter 6.

Make-Believe.   Make-believe permits novelty, creativity, and flexibility. It allows reversals of some power contingencies and the reversal of social control.[10] Whereas in games only the winner is "first," in playing make-believe, all can pretend to win. All can become what they are not, as when children pretend to be parents. Consider also the normative function of make-believe in enculturation. Children imitate and learn adult roles; make-believe facilitates the socialization of aggression, the learning of power tactics, and social interactions.

Whether make-believe serves primarily to encourage creativity or to maintain traditional values varies systematically across cultures (Sutton-Smith & Roberts, 1981). Unfortunately, we don't know of any detailed study of role-playing in hunting–gathering societies. In other traditional societies, however, with little work-role diversification, total conformity to adult roles seems to be the rule (Lancy, 1996). Dasen (1988) observed that Baoulé girls play domestic scenes in which they imitate the work that they will, before long, perform in reality. These include, for example, preparing a meal or a medicinal treatment, taking care of a doll (if not already responsible for the care of a real infant), fetching water or washing clothes, in short, all the maternal roles. Meanwhile, the boys imitate the agricultural jobs of their fathers, mimic the ritual dances, as well as practice those nontraditional occupations that are accessible to them, such as truck driving.

Media-influenced social change has augmented the number of adult roles that it is possible to imitate. In industrialized societies, children tend to role-play numerous roles (doctor, astronaut, cowboy, or Indian) including particular fictional ones (Superman, Goldorak, or Asterix)[11] that are highly unlikely to have any real corre-

---

[10]This is a reason why role-playing is often used in psychotherapy.

[11]Superman is a well-known comic strip character who first appeared in the United States of America in Action Comics in 1939 and has been the star of several motion pictures and television series. Goldorak is a hero in a television series produced in Japan. Asterix is a famous and well-traveled hero in French comic books.

spondence with future adult activities. The learning of a large number of potential roles, and learning to deal with unexpected novelty, probably stimulates flexibility, an important characteristic in societies undergoing rapid change.

Toy Construction.   Most societies provide children with relatively few commercial toys. In such cases (for example, in sub-Saharan Africa), not surprisingly, children make toys themselves. Toy cars are made from iron wire (if not available, of natural materials) by young boys all over Africa (Nsamenang, 1992). Lombard (1978) gave a detailed description of these constructions among the Baoulé: car models with easily recognizable trade names and steering devices that control movable wheels, bicycles, and little carts with wheels made from tree-nuts, spinning tops, and the like (See Figure 3.3).

These constructions express a remarkable creativity. Making these toys teaches children how to plan work, to organize tools and materials, to measure, and to conceive of objects in three-dimensional space, to mention only the cognitive features of the activity. In technologically developed societies, the toy-making industry tends to mass-produce single-purpose objects. These prepare the child to become a consumer and encourage possession, enhancing the importance of "to have" as opposed to "to do." Even commercially prepared building kits are now highly specialized; instead of generic blocks or elements with which one can create almost unlimited

FIGURE 3.3   Bicycle Constructed of Wire by a Zambian Boy

(Photo Patrik Dasen)

combinations, the toy store offers prefabricated fire engine, tank, or outer-space base kits, the elements of which can be assembled in only one way.

Even among the Baoulé, however, not everyone enjoys the potential creativity of toy-making. It is the boys, from about 10 years of age and up (and sometimes with the help of younger peers), who make the toys. Making toys constitutes about 10 percent of the play activities of 8- 9-year-old children (Dasen, 1988) but, already by this age, the difference between the sexes is quite sharp. In several African societies, toy-making is an activity reserved for boys; boys are also more apt than girls to be asked to assist in repairing a roof or fixing a chair.

Serpell (1979) asked Zambian boys familiar with wire constructions and second grade English primary schoolchildren to reproduce geometric forms using various materials. Using paper and pencil to reproduce the forms, the English children performed better than same-grade Zambians. When copying the models with iron wire, however, the Zambian children performed much better than the English. There were no differences between these groups when copying with clay or plasticine (materials equally familiar to both groups), nor via miming representations using hand gestures. This finding demonstrates the specificity of certain cognitive skills, or, as we shall see in the next chapter, the fact that children do not automatically apply certain cognitive competencies to all contexts.

Parental Ethnotheories

As part of cognitive anthropology, ethnoscience studies the ways in which different societies conceptualize aspects of the environment that correspond to different branches of science. Thus there is ethnomathematics (of which we will see some results in Chapter 6), ethnobotany, ethnomedicine, ethnoastronomy, and so on. Similarly, in what Bruner (1996) calls *folk psychology* and *folk pedagogy,* each society develops ideas about why people behave the way they do and how children grow up and become adults. Most often, these ideas have not been formalized, nor written down; sometimes they seem to emerge only as a researcher asks about them.[12]

Research on parental ethnotheories was presaged in the extensive studies of childrearing of the "culture and personality" school, epitomized by the work of Mar-

---

[12]Hence, the phrase "parental ethno*theories*" may be misleading. Parents have ideas about child development and they follow childrearing rules and routines, but most often these are implicit. Few parents have a "theory" in the sense of a systematically constituted set of concepts and relationships. Yet, sometimes with some prodding, people come up with an amazingly detailed set of ideas, usually (although not always) consistent with their childrearing practices and with the relevant cultural values. Sociologists use "social representations" in much the same way (Moscovici, 1982; Jodelet, 1989) as we use "parental ethnotheories." Goodnow (1981a/b, 1985), who did pioneering work in this area, speaks of everyday ideas, or parents' ideas. "Parental belief systems" is the title of an influential book edited by Sigel (1985; Sigel, McGillicuddy-De Lisi, & Goodnow, 1992, in the second edition). Harkness and Super (1996) have followed suit in calling their recent volume *Parents' cultural belief systems,* but in the text they often use the term *ethnotheories.*

garet Mead and Ruth Benedict. They, too, were interested in the way child development is conceptualized as part of a cultural system. The difference between earlier and contemporary research is mainly one of methodology: Researchers now use interviews and questionnaires as well as systematic observations with fairly large samples, and take into account intracultural variations in the parental beliefs. They also try to assess the extent to which the verbally expressed beliefs are actually reflected in cultural practices. The consistency of the belief/practices system has become a matter of empirical inquiry rather than a postulate.

Erny (1968, 1972a/b, 1981) summarized much ethnopsychological work on the African child, explaining how an African worldview and philosophy influences the way the child is perceived by the society. Similar information about West Africa in general, and the Nso of Cameroun in particular, is available in Nsamenang (1992; Nsamenang & Lamb, 1994). From the time of her pregnancy, the mother and the (future) child are the most highly valued assets of an extended family, understood as a "lineage" that includes not only the living family members but also the deceased ancestors (Rabain, 1979). The child, then, does not "belong" to the biological parents only, but to the whole community. This is reflected, for example, by the fact that anyone is allowed to ask a child for help in a chore, or to punish a child for a misbehavior, like not showing due respect to an elder.

The anthropologist Annette Hamilton (1981), who studied childrearing among Australian Aborigines, showed the influence of parental ethnotheories on childrearing practices. In her fieldwork, she took her own baby along, and hence could talk "mother to mother." Aborigines believe in a form of reincarnation in which the souls of the deceased stay in some sacred and secret location for some time, until one of them jumps into the womb of a woman passing nearby. Sometime after birth, the father, or a shaman, tries to determine who the child really is, and names it accordingly. A baby, being a respected ancestor, hence comes with a full-fledged personality that has to be respected. This ethnotheory is the opposite of one in which a neonate comes as an empty vessel that has to be filled up, shaped to conform to parents' wishes. Aboriginal childrearing is, correspondingly, exceedingly "laissez-faire." Children are not taught to obey, and they are always immediately given whatever they ask for, but they always have to share it with others.

Parental ethnotheories derive from the adults' observations of child development, just as their practices influence the latter. It is a circular system, in which it is difficult to detect cause and effect. For example, as we saw (earlier) in the research by Bril and her colleagues, the physical and social settings of the Bambara babies in Mali, as well as the postures they find themselves in, and the stimulations they receive because of child care practices, form such a system. When Bambara mothers were asked (by Zack & Bril, 1989) at what age babies should be able to sit alone, their answer was three months for boys, four months for girls. Three to four months is indeed the age at which Bambara babies are able to sit alone, as against the age of 7 months given by Western scales of psychomotor development (and the age of 6 months predicted by most French mothers in the interviews). As to the sex difference predicted by Bambara mothers, it does not seem factual, and is rather linked to Bambara cosmogony, which symbolically links the number 3 to anything male, and the number 4 to female. However, it would require more detailed observations to verify if Bambara mothers do not in effect train boys to sit earlier than they do girls. This early sitting is not linked, as was previously believed, to an overall African infant precocity, but is a motor skill specifically trained for in many African societies in which it is believed to be an important marker of child development (Super, 1981).

Survival *versus* Education

LeVine, Miller, and West (1988) proposed a theory of "socialization for survival" *versus* educational development. According to these authors, maternal interaction emphasizing close physical contact should occur in societies with the highest infant mortality and high birth rates.[13] The immediate perceived need is to protect infants. Education becomes more of a parental goal once the primary needs for survival have been met. This starts a self-reinforcing cycle, maternal education leading itself to a maternal interactive style that stresses children's learning and cognitive development.

This scheme explains the close infant–caretaker interactions described above in several examples (e.g., in Africa and among Australian Aborigines), the proximal *versus* distal communication style, and the perception of children as an economic asset *versus* one of economic liability. There is some support for this theory in LeVine's own previous research in Africa and elsewhere, and in a study of maternal behavior in Mexico (Tapia Uribe, LeVine, & LeVine, 1994); it has also been endorsed as a guiding framework by Greenfield and Cocking (1994) and by Lancy (1996). However, there is relatively little support for it in other studies. For example, Ho (1994) points out that, in Asian cultures, mothers and babies have a high degree of physical contact (cf. the Japanese cosleeping discussed above), even though survival is no longer a prime concern, and although academic achievement is among the most highly valued aspects of parental goals. Greenfield (1994) opines that LeVine and colleagues' scheme might hold for societies in Africa or among indigenous Mexicans where schooling is an imposition of colonial conquest, but not where scholarship has been part of society for a long time, as in Chinese and other Asian cultures.

Some aspects of LeVine's theory provide a convincing functional explanation for some childrearing practices. For example, in many societies in which infant mortality is (or was) high, neonates are not considered to be fully human individuals, presumably to guard against sorrow if they die. They are not buried in the same way as older children are, and are only given a name after several weeks (Hamilton, 1981; Nsamenang, 1992).

---

[13]Note the similarity of this theory to that of differential reproductive strategies in the field of sociobiology.

The Developmental Niche and Social Change

In both the theoretical framework of the developmental niche and ecological systems theory, it is obvious that we are dealing with open systems that change along with the sociohistorical circumstances. These are, as we have shown, part of the larger ecocultural framework. Nsamenang (1992), who devotes more than half of his book to Africa's sociocultural environment and historical roots, including the aftermath of the slave trade and colonization, to contextualize human development in Africa, shows that the developmental niche adapts to social change and acculturation, albeit sometimes with delay.

All societies always show some change, but to different degrees and at different rates. When the change is relatively slow, the enculturation and socialization processes also tend to be more homogeneous. "They have had the time to crystallize into an extended traditional heritage, usually respected to the point of being sacred" (Camilleri & Malewska-Peyre, 1997, p. 45). In societies that undergo rapid change, subgroups appear that do not share the same values and practices. "Knowledge of the culture at the level of the society is no longer sufficient to predict and interpret the representations of these subgroups, such as socio-economic subgroups" (Camilleri & Malewska-Peyre, 1997, p. 45). In this case, individuals often have more choice to select the subcultures they wish to belong to. In a way, they choose their own socialization, at the same time as socialization agents may change their models over time. When migration is involved, "individuals have to be ready for desocializations and successive resocializations in the course of their life span" (Camilleri & Malewska-Peyre, 1997, p. 46)

Western industrial countries are sometimes said to change rapidly, non-Western, "traditional" societies to change more slowly. This is quite untrue. If anything, social change is much more rapid in many situations in the quickly urbanizing "third world." This has been cogently pointed out by Sinha (1988), who analyzed how rapid social change in India is affecting the family and the socialization of children. In this case, the main feature is the unpredictability of the environment. The parents no longer know for which world to socialize their offspring, and conflicts between generations tend to appear.

Kagitçibasi (1998) stresses the fact that, in circumstances of rapid urbanization, industrialization, or Westernization, the traditional childrearing values and practices that were adaptive in the previous context are no longer functional:

> *Urban life styles make different demands on people, and some of the traditional values and habits may stop being functional. For example, with socio-economic development and the provision of other sources of old age support, an obedience orientation in childrearing, serving toward loyalty to the elderly, loses its function. Instead, autonomy of the growing child becomes functional in more specialized urban jobs requiring decision making (p. 485).*

How West African mothers adapt their child care practices when they emigrate and live in Paris has been documented by Rabain-Jamin (1994). Following up on her previous research in Senegal (Rabain, 1979), where she found that African caretakers never call on objects to mediate their relationships to babies, Rabain-Jamin (1994) observed French and immigrant African mother–baby dyads (10 and 15 months of age) in situations where objects were provided by the observer and placed on the floor. French mothers responded significantly more often to child-initiated object activity than African mothers, while the latter responded to a significantly higher percentage of messages that were unrelated to objects. In subsequent interviews, some African mothers criticized the use of educational toys.

> *By criticizing the 'tiring' toy, these African mothers, for whom, relative to Africa, Paris is a socially deprived context that makes the expression of fundamental social values more difficult to achieve, may be formulating a concern over the loss of communication that can be caused by solitary play where cognitive problems are thought to dominate, placing the child in a separate world.... It is clear that a culture that values the mastery of objects is more conducive to isolation (p. 157).*

The contrast between socialization for independence or for interdependence (akin to individualism/collectivism; cf. Chapter 7) is the major underlying scheme of the volume in which this study was reported (Greenfield and Cocking, 1994). A value orientation stressing interdependence was hypothesized to characterize the socialization practices and developmental goals of minority groups in the United States, Canada, and Europe, as opposed to the independence script characterizing the cultural roots of the latter host societies. The reason invoked for this is that the cultures of origin of these minority groups are supposed to be collectivistic. "When groups move from a homeland to a new country, the scripts move with them. They become a major source of continuity in the transition. Whether they are in conflict or harmony with the scripts of the new socio-cultural environment, the ancestral scripts influence the nature of adaptation to it" (Greenfield, 1994, p. 8). For this reason, this edited volume presents studies of socialization both in the cultures of origin, in the phase of migration, and in settled minority groups.

According to Ogbu (1994), the key to the impact of socialization styles on academic achievement lies in the different types of minority statuses, that is, voluntary immigrant minorities *versus* involuntary minorities (incorporated against their will through slavery, conquest, or colonization).[14] Refugees are a special case, and not part of the classification. Ogbu is a Nigerian anthropologist living in and studying U.S. society, and is therefore able to look at it both as an insider and as an outsider.

---

[14]For a similar distinction applied to the study of acculturation processes, see Chapter 11.

The voluntary minorities have what Ogbu (1994) calls a "primary" cultural dif-ference. They have made a choice, find that they are better off in the new land, but do not have to give up pride in their original culture.

Voluntary minorities strive to participate in the cultural frame of reference of the dominant group without fear of losing their own culture, language, or identity.... Because secondary cultural differences arise to enable minorities to deal with dominant-group members, they often become a part of bound-ary-maintaining mechanisms. For this reason, involuntary minorities have no desire to overcome the cultural (and language) differences because that would threaten their cultural or language identity (pp. 375–376).

The cultural frame of reference of involuntary minorities is oppositional; they consider Euro-American behaviors (such as speaking standard English) as inappro-priate for them. The perception of what is appropriate or inappropriate for them is emotionally charged, and is intimately bound up with their sense of social identity, self-worth, and security. These minorities consider the discrimination against them as more or less permanent and institutionalized, and not transient as for the voluntary immigrants. "Over generations of such treatment, they developed other ways of speaking, conceptualizing, and thinking, which have been demanded and enhanced by their menial and unskilled jobs and inferior education. Thus, involuntary minor-ities make a cognitive adaptation to their ecological niche, not an adaptation to a Euro-American ecological niche. The cognitive tasks posed by the two niches are different" (Ogbu, 1994, p. 380). Doing well on IQ tests and academic tasks at school historically did not bring to involuntary minorities the same rewards that these accomplishments brought to their Euro-American peers. They developed a deep dis-trust for the public schools, and the school's rules and practices are seen as imposi-tions, as "white" and therefore not acceptable to them.

While voluntary immigrants also experience and resent prejudice and discrimi-nation in school, they respond in ways that do not discourage them from doing well in school. According to Ogbu, the special problem of involuntary minorities arises from the nature of their own responses to their initial terms of incorporation into a dominating society and subsequent treatment, namely, their formation of a collective oppositional identity and oppositional cultural frame of reference.

"The situation creates a dilemma of choice for involuntary minority students: If a student believes and chooses the assimilation definition of schooling, he or she may indeed succeed academically but suffer peer criticism or ostracism, as well as suffer from 'affective dissonance' (Ogbu, 1994, p. 387). Minority students feel they have to choose between academic success and maintaining their identity. There are however "secondary strategies," such as "camouflaging," "clowning," or behaving differently in school and at home.

This analysis comes close to the one several French researchers describe for the North African second generation of immigrants in France, who also develop a number of more or less sophisticated "identity strategies" to cope with the constant devalorization they have to face from the dominant host society (Camilleri & Malewska-Peyre, 1997). At this point, we will turn to still another way to conceptualize the two processes of cultural transmission, enculturation and socialization, namely under the heading of *informal education.*

INFORMAL EDUCATION

In common parlance, the term *education* often connotes only what happens in schools. *Education* in this sense of the term includes relatively structured learning situations, with instruction provided at prearranged times and places by people who are specialists to some degree. We define *education* much more broadly as resulting from both enculturation and socialization. Education often proceeds informally in everyday situations, in response to momentary needs, and sometimes involves simply observation and imitation and other times active inculcation. So, many kinds of interactions are part of *education.* As Bruner (1996) remarks: "schooling is only one small part of how a culture inducts the young into its canonical ways. Indeed, schooling may even be at odds with a culture's other ways of inducting the young into the requirements of communal living" (p. ix). Moreover, formal educational institutions include not only schools, but also initiation ceremonies and instruction provided in age-grade societies and secret societies.

On the dimension from formal to informal, Ahmed (1983) distinguished the following categories of *education:*

1. Formal education or schooling;
2. Nonformal, or out-of-school education, which includes all educational programs aimed at those left out of formal education (very young children, the discards of the school system, young people in postprimary education, nonliterates, etc.);
3. Informal education, also called *traditional* or *parallel* education. In contrast with the first two, it is neither provided nor directed by governmental or nongovernmental institutions, but by parents, caretakers, peers, or other members of the community.

Schooling is a topic that we will mention only insofar as it relates to other issues. From a cross-cultural perspective, Serpell (1993) and Serpell and Hatano (1997) provide excellent coverage. The history of the exportation of Western-type schooling during colonial times has been what Serpell and Hatano (1997) have called a "hegemonic imposition." Julius Nyerere (1967), then president of Tanzania and formerly a teacher, was among the first to criticize Western-type schooling because of its lack of cultural relevance when it is exported to other settings such as Africa. Nyerere cited many attendant ill effects, such as fostering a generation gap, migration of rural populations to cities, reinforcing a social class structure, being out of tune with economic realities, and many more (see Erny, 1977; Mukene, 1988; Serpell, 1993). As Serpell and Hatano (1997) summarize the situation:

> *The entire design of public schooling in Africa tends to bear very little relevance to the demands of economically productive adult life in rural settings, where the vast majority of school-leavers will spend their lives. For most parents, teachers, and students in rural African schools, the primary definition of educational success remains extractive, luring students up and out of their community of origin along a staircase of progress toward increasingly alien cultural goals (p. 363).*

Serpell (1993), on the basis of his analysis of the Zambian school system, argues that the school should become a community resource, accountable to the local community rather than to the central authorities. In contrast, Kagitçibasi (1996), speaking from what she calls the "Majority World perspective," is afraid that these critiques of schooling may impede the implementation of policies to attain the UNESCO goal of "Education for All." This concern is especially compelling when structural adjustments imposed by the World Bank and the International Monetary Fund lead to a breakdown of public schooling in favor of privatization. Kagitçibasi points out the many positive effects of schooling, and especially of ECCE (early childhood care and education), notably in terms of health promotion and women's rights. In her defense of secular formal schooling, Kagitçibasi represents the opinion of many international agencies and education ministries. The critiques of schooling voiced by Serpell and others appear like a minority antidote against the majority's consensus. Without delving further into the debate, we at least agree with Kagitçibasi (1996, p. 115) when she writes: "Schooling promises to be a powerful instigator of societal development when it is rendered socially relevant and culturally appropriate."

Informal education is found not only in the Majority World. Everywhere, people learn most of what they know through informal education. Just like everyday cognition (cf. Chapter 6), informal education can be studied everywhere. When it is explicitly compared to Western schooling, in the situations of hegemonic imposition mentioned above, it is sometimes called *traditional education*.[15] There is an abundant literature on traditional education in many different societies, often dating back to the middle of the twentieth century and the culture and personality school. We can summarize this material by stating that traditional education, in contrast to traditional teaching, is in essence adapted to the local cultural system, which it tends to perpetuate.

---

[15]*Informal* and *traditional*, when applied to education, are almost synonyms. *Informal* has the disadvantage of suggesting that it is random, that it has no form; as we will see, this is far from true. *Traditional* has the disadvantage of implying that it is something of the past, to be relinquished. We will use both of these terms without these negative connotations.

Désalmand (1983) pointed out the major characteristics of traditional African education as compared to schooling, particularly the type of teaching that still prevails in many schools in Africa. Traditional education is provided everywhere, all the time, and by everyone (in contrast to occurring in a specialized place, at a specific time, with specialized personnel); it is closely tied to the environment, integrated with productive work, and addresses the needs of the society. It emphasizes cooperation rather than individual competition, and everyone is allowed to be successful at it (as opposed to the elitism of schools, with their selection and streaming roles). In traditional education, parents and elders play an important role, relations among participants are personalized, and occur in the local language. Traditional education has a broad character, and includes moral and spiritual aspects as well as physical education and manual labor. A similar typology elaborated by Greenfield and Lave (1979/1982) is presented in Table 3.4.

Greenfield and Lave (1979/1982) warn us that the contrast is not as clean in reality as suggested in Table 3.4. Any dichotomous typology is always an oversimplification, but can be a useful heuristic device (see also Désalmand [1983] for a similar but much more detailed typology). They point out that in instances in which informal education transmits specific, economically useful knowledge, particularly knowledge tied to crafts and occupations, informal education can include a very structured, albeit implicit, pedagogy. This was demonstrated in a study of weaving

TABLE 3.4   Some Idealized Characteristics of Informal and Formal Education.*

Informal Education

1. Embedded in daily life activities
2. Learner is responsible for obtaining knowledge and skill
3. Personal; relatives are appropriate teachers
4. Little or no explicit pedagogy or curriculum
5. Maintenance of continuity and traditions are values
6. Learning by observation and imitation
7. Teaching by demonstration
8. Motivated by social contribution of novices and their participation in adult sphere

Formal Education

1. Set apart from the context of everyday life
2. Teacher is responsible for imparting knowledge and skill
3. Impersonal; teachers should not be relatives
4. Explicit pedagogy and curriculum
5. Change and discontinuity are valued
6. Learning by verbal exchange, questioning
7. Teaching by verbal presentation of general principles
8. Less strong social motivation

* From Greenfield and Lave (1982), p.183. Reprinted with permission.

apprenticeship among Zinacanteco girls in Mexico (Childs & Greenfield, 1980). The same was found by Lave (Greenfield & Lave, 1979/1982), who studied the tailoring profession in Liberia, where master craftspersons formulated their verbal instructions in close correspondence with the productions of the students, constantly adapting to their needs. They organized the apprenticeship steps in order of ascending difficulty. Moreover, they employed scaffolding[16] to effect a progression within each step, allowing trial and error only in the beginning and if there was no risk of real loss. In these examples, informal education thus involved more than just observation and imitation. Verbal instruction on the part of the master was an integral part of the apprenticeship processes, at first in the form of orders, and later including confrontations and questions. The pupils, by contrast, spoke little and did not ask questions.

In most situations, formal teaching and informal education coexist. Officials often seek to supplant informal education by schooling. While in Western societies one of the roles of the school is social and cultural reproduction, school-based education in non-Western societies is often an agent of social change. This usually proceeds unidirectionally—toward a Western model—and is frequently called *modernization* or even *progress.* These are notions that we will examine critically in Chapter 11.

The Transmission of Know-How

Chamoux (1981, 1983, 1986), a French anthropologist, studied apprenticeship of different technical skills, including weaving, among the Nahua Indians of Mexico. She provided a typology of know-how ("savoir-faire," or skill) and its transmission that distinguishes between "incorporated know-how" and "the mastery of algorithms" (Chamoux, 1981). Incorporated know-how results from the personal, concrete experience of particular individuals or groups. One may have a certain skill, but be unable to describe it. It is therefore not easily transmitted by formal teaching. It is best acquired through apprenticeship, that is, participating in the activity.

Chamoux distinguished two kinds of incorporated know-how: general and particular. General know-how is transmitted to everyone, while particular know-how is transmitted only to certain individuals who become specialists. This distinction is illustrated with examples from a rural Nahua community. There, agriculture is "man's work," while cooking and weaving are "women's work." Nevertheless, Chamoux's observations revealed that women possess all the agricultural skills, although they normally don't use them. Similarly, the men know how to make tortillas (cornmeal pancakes) if circumstances require them to. In this context, agriculture and cooking

---

[16]*Scaffolding* is a kind of effective control of the learning process by adults. This Vygotskian term, as well as other technical terms referring to learning processes, will be explored further in Chapter 6.

are general know-hows. In contrast, weaving is an exclusively female activity that is taught specifically to girls.[17]

Chamoux (1981) further distinguished transmission of know-how by a master from transmission via a process of gradual *immersion*,[18] whereby the whole family or indeed the whole community assumes the role of teacher. Immersion occurs when there is a common cultural fund of gestures and activities that can frequently be observed and experienced.

This classification gives rise to the schema in Table 3.5, which includes the four logically possible combinations of types of know-how and modes of transmission. Chamoux provides examples of all four combinations in the daily life of the Nahuas. Note that the placement of the types of know-how into the four cells would differ from culture to culture: Butchering and meat processing, for example, is a particular know-how learned from experts in urban industrialized societies (Lave & Wenger, 1991), while it may be learned via immersion in some rural areas.

Among the Nahua, agricultural know-how is an example of general know-how, even if practiced only by Nahua men. Chamoux attributed this to incidental, or immersion learning during the early childhood years. In agricultural and domestic domains, children of both sexes can observe different skills being practiced just so long as they live with their parents in the village. What is observed is always a real activity, a productive one, and not some simulation or demonstration.

The distinction between what is openly available to be learned and what is hidden and needs specialized training has also been made by Lancy (1996) in comparing U.S. society to the Kpelle of Liberia:

> *Our [American or Western] childrearing procedures are adapted to the demands posed by an extremely complex and information-rich culture—a culture in which one can experience the failure of dropping out as early as 10. Much of what one needs to know in order to thrive in our society is, in*

---

[17]Chamoux reviewed the methodological problems inherent in empirical research on technical know-how. For incorporated know-how there could be competence without performance; in other words, one could know how but not do it. An outside observer can neither rely on the observation of practices alone (which might not reveal hidden competencies) nor on discourse alone (which often denies the distinction between competence and performance). Instead, the observer must attend to the division of tasks and performances according to social distinctions, sex, or specializations, as well as to the technical competencies that are not usually translated into actions. In fact, Chamoux insists on the fact that the technical know-how is inseparable from historical processes and social relationships. It is the latter that very much determine the transmission of know-how, and hence its division between social groups.

[18]Chamoux used the French word *imprégnation*, that means 'to be permeated,' 'to be saturated,' 'to soak up'; this is a neat metaphor for the process of enculturation, as distinguished from socialization. The immersion concept is close to that of "osmosis," used by Azuma (1994) to describe Japanese informal and to some extent formal learning. "This osmosis model also prevailed in the training of traditional arts and crafts of Japan. The master would not teach. Instead, the live-in disciples, called *uchideshis,* would "steal" the art, together with the professional living style and work ethic, while helping the master with his work and doing household chores" (p. 280).

TABLE 3.5   Know-How Transmission Modes among the Nahuas

	Via immersion	From a master
General know-how	Agriculture	Plowing, hunting
	Carrying loads	Embroidery
Particular know-how	Butchering	Weaving
	Meat processing	Music

effect, hidden in print material and specialized language. A part of Kpelle culture is also hidden; consequently, the society utilizes special procedures to enable individuals to gain access to it. [Mainly initiation.] However the amount that is hidden compared to that which is open is relatively small (p. 83).

Nahua Informal Education and Ethnotheories

Observing attentively is the most generally used learning method among the Nahuas. The only instructions provided to children by adults are to "watch carefully" and "concentrate." Rarely are verbal instructions employed and adults intervene only if the learner clearly fails to resolve a difficulty on his or her own. Trial-and-error learning is almost completely absent. There have been anecdotal reports that learning "strictly by observation" occurs frequently among Amerindians (Native Americans) and in Asia.[19] The topic of learning styles certainly merits further and systematic cross-cultural study.

In informal Nahua education, there are no formal steps or grades, no initiation ceremonies or rites of passage. No particular time is set aside for teaching. Because learning can take place, in effect, any time and anywhere, it is embedded in a great diversity of activities.

Among the Nahuas, pressure to learn is seldom applied. In childhood, the only chore is to carry burdens. Only during adolescence, when an "active" phase of apprenticeship begins and when it is time for a young person to become "responsible," does pressure to learn become obvious. Physical punishments may then be introduced, but they are rarely used. The usual negative sanction is laughter at the bizarre product, and the reward is verbal, such as a general call to all onlookers to admire the success. For the Nahuas, learning depends on the will of the apprentice

---

[19]Gardiner and colleagues (1997) quote an anecdote from Condon's (1984, p. 62) analysis of Japanese society. When asked what advice a senior Japanese executive would have for an incoming American manager, he replied: "I'd tell him not to do anything for the first six months." He continued: "I've seen a lot more problems caused by Americans trying to do things too quickly than waiting too long to act." In America, it is often said, "Don't just stand there, do something." In Japan, they say, "Don't just do something, stand there."

and not on that of the adult educator. Apprenticeship always involves real materials and full-sized products. The mark of success resides in the utility of the product. A potential for simulation exists in a few toys, but Nahua society does not value play.

Like Super and Harkness (1986), Chamoux (1986) grants importance to "indigenous theories of education," which she claims structure the pedagogical modalities in a coherent fashion. Chamoux's rendering of the Nahua parental ethnotheory is summarized in Box 3.2.

Guided Participation in Cultural Activity

Rogoff, Mistry, Göncü, and Mosier (1993) observed caregivers, usually mothers, and their toddlers in four different settings: Mayan Indians in a small town in Guatemala, a tribal village in India, and two middle-class urban neighborhoods, in Turkey and in the United States. They found both similarities across communities in the process of guided participation, the way caretakers structure children's participation in activities, and differences in how this occurs. In the first two communities, children were non-verbally encouraged to observe ongoing adult activities, but they were basically responsible for their own learning. In the two middle-class settings, mothers tended to structure explicitly their children's learning, used verbal interactions, and provided "lessons" removed from the context of ongoing activities. The middle-class mothers also

---

BOX 3.2   The Parental Ethnotheory of the Nahuas in Mexico

In the Nahuas's ethnotheory, the soul is not present from birth but gradually develops later. An individual has "soul levels," one of which is inborn and connotes character or destiny while another may be acquired through personal effort. The progressively acquired soul may also be lost, and it is the duty of the adults to conduct rites designed to ward off this possibility. Soul loss would be manifest in illness, or in a developmental retardation, which are never attributed to the childs constitution, but rather to external perturbations.

Entire portions of Nahua educational practices can be understood as deriving from this conception. The models of normal development are only guides to be sure that all goes well. Authoritarianism is an absurdity, since one can't influence stages.... Punishments cannot be contemplated except when the child has already acquired a good portion of his or her soul (or conscience). In brief, education can neither modify nor correct the process of acquisition of the soul. It can only make sure that this process is not hindered, and conserve what has already been acquired. It can also draw to the attention of the young their own maturation and the models to be followed. In a certain manner, it is the individual, the learner himself, who can best influence his own learning (Chamoux, 1986, p. 235; our translation).

tended to organize their schedule so as to separate adult activities from time devoted to interacting with children. In the two rural communities, adults shared their attention among a variety of activities, managing several tasks at the same time, including socializing with other adults and facilitating the children's involvement and learning.

The learning style of the middle-class mothers can be seen as a preparation for schooling. Rogoff and colleagues (1993), however, suggest that many school reforms move in the direction of group work in which the children become more responsible for their own learning. The teacher's role changes "from the inculcation of skills out of the context in which they are actually used to communicate or to solve problems to the practice of literate activities in the context of communicating and solving problems" (p. 160). This is close to Stevenson's (1994) portrait of the teacher in many Asian schools:

> *The East-Asian teacher acts as a knowledgeable guide. Indeed, the two characters in the Japanese term for teacher (sensei) mean "living or being before"—one who has had the experience and now can guide others through it. The teacher is not a lecturer but nevertheless knows what should be learned and the types of techniques that will lead children to learn. The teacher does not act as an authoritarian dispenser of knowledge and judge of what is correct but leads children to construct knowledge and evaluate the reliability of their own and other solutions (p. 320).*

Schooling and Apprenticeship

Medical School

Cador (1982) relied on his knowledge of medical school and practice and on testimony by masters responsible for advanced apprentices to contrast schooling and on-the-job training. He posits different cognitive functioning for each. The student (in school) learns to manipulate symbols, to derive general principles, but lacks access to concrete things that might be directly apprehended. School-based knowledge provides the ability to reason theoretically, to be able to explain how something works, rather than to make it work. The apprentice, on the other hand, and the professional craftsperson, work more by analogy, having learned "to read the facts." Their cognition always relates to practice and they are capable of extracting from reality abstract ideas without resorting to language.

Cador stated that a combination of the two modalities is necessary for the practice of medicine. In effect, a young doctor, about to begin a career, is almost obliged to relearn the profession. Cador attributes this to the extended period of study, the style of the examinations, and the increasingly high-tech nature of medicine. These features of medical education increase the barriers between physicians and patients.

In recent years, several medical schools have changed their teaching style, basing it on clinical problem solving through group work, and a constant flux from theory to practice and vice versa. Teacher training has also started to use this model.

The French Marsh-Sweepers

Geneviève Delbos, a rural sociologist, and Paul Jorion, an anthropologist, conducted research on the coastal populations of Brittany engaged in salt processing,[20] shellfish raising, and coastal fishing. In their book, *La transmission des savoirs* (1984), they reflect on how empirical knowledge is conveyed and contrast it to scientific and school-based knowledge.

In those activities where competence is acquired through experience, within the family structure, skills and empirical knowledge are transmitted to the next generation, not explicitly and willingly, but through participation in daily life and conversations about the work. Marsh-sweepers say precisely that when they state, "You are born there, so,…you know it" (Delbos & Jorion, 1984, p. 140, *our translation*). Also, empirical knowledge is transmitted as if it were an unquestionable truth.

> *The world teaches one to live, although it is not possible to attribute to it a specific educational action. From the whole environment knowledge wells up which can be received: to know how to do things, how to talk, how to live, all these are learned willy-nilly, discovered by oneself, but corrected if necessary. It's the very fact that these have been learned without having been taught that gives them the glow of evidence, and makes all other representations of the world impossible (Delbos & Jorion, 1984, p. 141).*

Informal education among the marsh-sweepers is described in more detail in Box 3.3.

Delbos and Jorion (1984) contrast practical knowledge with school-based knowledge and raise the question of transferability. While procedural knowledge is acquired on the job, and is, hence, necessarily specific, school knowledge is claimed to be general and even scientific. The authors conclude that,

> *things are not quite so simple. To the degree that school-based knowledge fails to be authentically theoretical and is often simply 'propositional,' it lacks plasticity and becomes tied to a specific context—the classroom—the only place where disjointed propositions have any legitimacy. Inversely, procedural knowledge, as a set of routine actions, is in fact transposable to other contexts. For as long as it constitutes an authentic experience of nature, of the material world, it is general and is easily transposed, through the process of analogy (p. 15).*

The marsh-sweepers think of school, as well as of training programs and institutionalized professional apprenticeship, as essentially useless. If the children go to a trade school, the parents often preferred to send them into the commercial section,

---

[20]Marsh-sweepers produce salt through the evaporation of sea water in marshes set up along the shore.

**BOX 3.3   Informal Education among French Marsh-Sweepers,
according to Delbos and Jorion (1984)**

In marsh-sweeper families, who also do a little farming and animal raising, children accompany the mother in all her work, and very quickly learn little jobs. In the swamps, they learn first to do little ancillary jobs that parents prefer not to do themselves because they take too much time. These include, for example, watching the rising tide and opening the floodgates. Then, little by little, the "ancillary" becomes the "complementary" for boys of about 10 years of age, thus allowing an increase in production. However, little girls do not participate in this. It is said, "It's too hard for her, and besides, it is not her place," except when an urgent helping hand is needed!

In the space of about five years, boys will practice successively all of the tasks that are performed in the swamps, reaching levels of expertise on each successive task, in an order determined by the elders. The latter claim to follow the order of increasing responsibility, and to give children only those tasks that carry no risk; in practice, this principle is breached in two ways: Risky tasks are occasionally authorized and, besides, other tasks with no material consequences are sometimes discouraged. For example, in order to free up a man, a boy may be entrusted to harness two horses to pull more than a ton of salt. By the same token, he is not allowed access to certain zones of the swamp except according to a progressive schedule, involving a symbolic hierarchy defined by concentric circles emanating from the exterior of the swamp toward the interior.

At no time do adults speak of teaching per se. Never does a father give an explanation. He only gives orders, asserts prohibitions, and swears. The boy finds himself involved in adult activities and holds his own in them, without anyone explicitly explaining the rules of the game. The child must discover via approximations, following the simple principle that if he doesn't get scolded, all is well. The notion that one can learn simply by copying others is not applicable here because never is it demanded that the child do the same things that adults do. Instead, the child must do other things and they must be done elsewhere. Mimicking would not work. Learning requires observation and deferred imitation, without demonstration and without verbal instruction.

---

where "at least they would learn something." They wouldn't learn to fish or how to care for a salt swamp, but the ritualized language of law and economics, and how to understand banking and administrative systems, and other means for avoiding being labelled as country bumpkins. "A schooled person knows how to juggle the account books, how to speak well, how to present a case, and how to get the advantage in the competition for grants and government subsidies" (Delbos & Jorion, 1984, p. 37).

What schooling provides, then, is more symbol than content; it provides the insignias of power. We will discuss the cognitive impact of schooling further in the next chapter, and will come back to the question of transfer of knowledge in Chapter 6.

Formal Aspects of Traditional Education

The term *formal education* usually means Western-style schooling and it is generally assumed that informal education predominates in nonindustrialized societies. To Strauss (1984), this typology is as false as it is ethnocentric (in more than one respect). Informal education not only occupies a significant role in industrialized societies, there are also some aspects of traditional education that are completely formal. Wagner (1983) calls these training systems "indigenous education, or "appropriate education" (1988a), by analogy to appropriate technology. They are characteristically well integrated in the life of a community, rooted in its history and religion, and make use of culturally adaptive practices.

In Europe, up to the Renaissance, all education was religiously based; only recently did education become secular and mandatory. All over the world, school systems linked to religious traditions (Buddhism, Confucianism, Hinduism, Islam, and Judaism) still exist. These parochial school systems have not been well studied and only recently has attention been brought back to them, as, for example, in studies of Quranic schools (Santerre, 1973; Santerre & Mercier-Tremblay, 1982; Wagner & Lofti, 1980; see also Serpell & Hatano, 1997).

Wagner (1988b) characterizes formal traditional education, with particular reference to Quranic schooling, as follows:

1. The schools are organized to pursue religious and other values of the society;
2. Memorization and mastery of sacred texts, sometimes written in foreign and non-spoken languages, are the principal objectives of the education. Recitation without comprehension is perfectly acceptable, especially early on in the educational experience;
3. Teaching, particularly for older children, often occurs in a two-person setting involving master and apprentice;
4. The master's role extends beyond transmitting knowledge in the school to impacting on the social life of the community as well;
5. The pupils are not grouped into classes by age; they progress through stages as a function of what they already know, there is no concept of academic failure;
6. Schoolmasters and pupils are most often males; this is particularly true in Islamic societies, where attendance by girls in Quranic schools is a recent phenomenon but one that is spreading.

Quranic schools take quite diverse forms in different countries, but now often tend to be preschools, or supplementary schools. The number of children attending Quranic schools worldwide is currently increasing.

Quranic schooling is often condemned in government circles as an impediment to development. Rote memorization (without comprehension and without critical thinking) is often criticized by educators. Is this justified? In longitudinal research in Morocco, Wagner and Spratt (1987) found that children who had completed

Quranic schooling before entering government schools performed better than children who had not had any preschooling. They suggest that traditional formal education has a definite contribution to make, given the needs of developing countries. Kagitçibasi (1996) strongly disagrees with this view. She voices the fear that Quranic education will compete with the modern secular school system and foster religious fundamentalism, undermining secularism. That may certainly be a reasonable fear in some circumstances, as in her own country, Turkey.

Kagitçibasi also raises an interesting issue of ethics. She disagrees with relativistic anthropologically oriented research, which finds certain practices appropriate for the Majority World that are not, or no longer, acceptable in the Minority World:

> *Again, we are faced with relativistic double standards. Religious education has declined in the world, especially in the industrialized West, and no one is proposing to return to it; but it is seen as 'appropriate' for the Third World (Muslim societies). Religious education cannot serve the functions of public schooling in promoting societal development, therefore it should not be considered as an alternative, but only as a supplementary form of education to universal schooling (1996, p. 113).*

Kagitçibasi also points out that the effects of Quranic schooling on cognitive development were found to be very limited and specific. Indeed, several projects, using techniques derived from the psychological laboratory, have examined the impact of Quranic schooling on performance in memory tasks (Wagner, 1978; Scribner & Cole, 1981). While great feats of memory might be expected from people who have learned by heart the entire Quran, the results of these studies have, in the main, not found any striking prowess. Only one kind of memorizing—serial incremental recall, whereby one keeps adding an element to a repeated series of related elements— showed any heightened performance in children schooled in the Quranic tradition. This is an issue we will come back to in Chapter 4.

We turn now to a consideration of life stages other than childhood.

ADOLESCENCE, LIFE SPAN, AND OLD AGE

Most of the research surveyed in this chapter has been concerned with infancy and childhood. Yet, in principle, the framework of the developmental niche is not restricted to child development, but could be applied throughout the life span.

Life Span Developmental Psychology

While there has been considerable interest in adolescence, as we shall see shortly, there is little cross-cultural psychological research on the later stages of life. The interesting domain of life span developmental psychology (Baltes & Baltes, 1990;

Baltes & Reese, 1984), in itself often sensitive to contexts like sociohistorical circum-stances, has not yet been taken up seriously by cross-cultural psychologists. Valsiner and Lawrence (1997) provide a review of the scant literature as well as their own model of a "co-constructivist account of life span development within culture" (p. 89).

Aging

We have to turn primarily to anthropologists to find descriptions of the culturally different ways of growing old (e.g., Amoss & Harrell, 1981; Myerhoff & Simic, 1978). In many societies, be it in Asia, Africa, or the Americas, the elderly are treated with respect and they keep a useful social role (for example, as we have seen, in childrearing). People from these cultural backgrounds often consider the way the elderly are treated in Western societies as absolutely barbaric. As aging becomes a phenomenon of major demographic and social importance in Western countries, more research, including cross-cultural research, is likely. And its results are sure to have social and political relevance.

Adolescence

Throughout the twentieth century, social scientists have debated whether adoles-cence is a biologically or a socially determined life stage. Adolescence has been described for a long time as a period during which the individual has to separate from the family, become autonomous, and rebel against adult norms and values. This picture of adolescence suggests inevitable psychological turmoil. Is adolescence really like this worldwide?

In the early years of this century, G. Stanley Hall, a developmental psychologist, described a period of turmoil, of "storm and stress," which he attributed to biology, to hormonal changes (Hall, 1916). This inevitability of internal turmoil, lability of mood, rebellion and problem behaviors, on the fringe of psychopathology, has been prominent in clinical psychology and in psychoanalytical writings.

As part of his battle against the eugenicist movement, Boas sent his twenty-three-year-old student, Margaret Mead, to Samoa in 1920 to study adolescent girls. To counter biological determinism, one single exception would be enough, a society in which there is a smooth transition from childhood to adulthood, without any storm and stress. Mead (1928) found just such a society. She reported, in short, that the sexual freedom allowed in Samoa during adolescence makes for a carefree time and a trouble-free integration into the adult community. Six decades later, Freeman (1983), on the basis of his own field observations, historical accounts, and content analysis of court cases, described Samoan society as puritan, guilt-ridden and vio-lent, and adolescence as a time of trouble!

How can two observers come to such diametrically opposite descriptions? Côté (1994) called this the biggest controversy in the social sciences and the issue is not yet resolved. While Côté's reconstruction comes out in favor of Mead, it may well be that she had been teased by her adolescent friends, who were embarrassed by the questions on such a taboo topic. In any case, her fundamental question remains: Which are the cultural contexts that best ensure a smooth transition from childhood to adulthood?

Social Adolescence as a Universal Stage

Schlegel and Barry (1991) examined the ethnographic information concerning adolescence in 175 societies. An adolescent social stage was found to be present in all societies examined; it usually starts right at puberty or just before, and there is an initiation ritual in 68 percent of the societies for boys (usually public) and 79 percent for girls (usually in the family circle). Adolescence is normally relatively brief, about 2 years for girls and 2 to 4 years for boys. It is longer when more training for adult roles is needed. The period is present even if there is no name for it. In many cases there is some nonlinguistic (visual) marking, like dress or hairstyle. Compared to adolescents in the Western world, adolescents in many societies are useful to their families and communities, and they are made to feel welcome in the adult community.

Regarding the very existence of an adolescent stage, some sociologists assume that adolescence as a stage did not exist until industrialization and extended schooling, which prolonged dependence on parents, created it (Friedenberg, 1973; Huerre, Pagan-Reymond, & Reymond, 1990). Adolescence may appear unnecessary in societies in which adult roles can be learned in childhood (such as foraging or horticultural societies) and would be reserved for complex societies in which adult roles take longer to be learned. Esman (1990), for example, writes:

> *The bulk of evidence supports the view that adolescence,* as we know it, *is a 'cultural invention'…a product of industrialization, of the need to extend the period of education and training for adult roles in the face of expanding technology, and the need…to keep young people out of the labor force in order to assure job opportunities for adults in times of scarcity (p. 16; emphasis added).*

Schlegel and Barry (1991) disagree. According to their holocultural study, social adolescence occurs in all societies. It is a time of social role learning and restructuring, marked by the ambivalence of maintaining some subordination while preparing for adulthood. Thus, some psychological discomfort (uncertainties, self-doubts, ambiguities in family attachments, etc.) is unavoidable, but neither pathology nor antisocial behavior need occur. "Social adolescence, then, is a response to the disjuncture between sexual reproductivity and full social maturity. It appears to be universal for boys; for girls, in the majority of societies, at least a short period of social adolescence intervenes between puberty and the full assumption of adult roles, usually after marriage" (p. 19).

After adolescence, if entry into full adulthood is delayed, there is an additional stage: "youth," during which various occupations and marriage partners can be tried out. A youth stage was found to be present in 25 percent of the societies for boys and 20 percent for girls. This is true of several societies in Africa that have age grades, such as the Masai or Samburu of Kenya, as well as of present-day Western society (Galland, 1991). In any case, behavioral reorganization may continue well into adulthood.

In summary, a picture emerges of adolescence as a universal stage with tensions being normal, even with some antisocial behavior expected (in 44 percent of societies for boys, 18 percent for girls), but it is not necessarily a "crisis." Fairly important differences exist between adolescents in Western societies and traditional ones, but not for the reasons described by Mead. If problems occur in Western or acculturating societies, they seem to be linked to the much longer adolescence and youth period, without a clear marking by ritual, no or little productive role or community participation, no childrearing duties, and distance from observing adult activities.

Rebelling against parents seems to be a necessary "developmental task" only if independence is highly valued. Trommsdorff (1989) has found that,

> *the expectations of German parents for their children reflected individualistic value preferences, and those of Japanese parents reflected collectivistic value preferences. Specifically, German parents expected their children to be independent, have conflicts with their parents, and learn through sanctions, and Japanese parents expected their children to be submissive, learn through imitation, and maintain harmonious relationships with their parents (p. 246).*

It should be noted that anthropological and cross-cultural studies of adolescence are adding weight to the statements of some of the major representatives of mainstream developmental psychology (e.g., Petersen, 1993), who speak of "debunking" the myths surrounding adolescence. On the question of adolescent adjustment *versus* turmoil, empirical studies in the United States started to document the absence of significant psychological difficulties in the majority of adolescents (Offer & Offer, 1975). Tumultuous growth seems to occur in only about 20 percent of U.S. adolescents, but relative calm prevails for the other 80 percent, and there is not much of a generation gap between adolescents and their parents.

Rapid Social Change

According to these recent perspectives, then, adolescence in Euro-American societies is not as problem-ridden as the popular stereotype would have it. What about adolescence in the Majority World? From the accounts we have, we can conclude that any serious problems, if they occur, are directly linked to rapid social change (Dasen, 1999), with the concomitant extension of adolescence and youth, without the institutions of social control provided by the traditional age-grades. Schooling increases the levels of aspiration, but these are rarely met, and youth is not given a productive role to play when entering adult society.

Most societies had developed effective ways for dealing with the transition from childhood to adulthood: An early introduction to adult roles and responsibilities, early marriage, or else age groups that provided an effective peer socialization and regulation of premarital sex insured a fairly smooth transition with few overt problems. Family continuity being the norm, adolescence did not include the developmental task of breaking away from the family, and the family continued to be the main support and social control institution.

According to some accounts, these community support systems are still functioning, both in rural and in urban areas, for example among the Ijo of Nigeria (Hollos & Leis, 1989). Other observers are not as optimistic (e.g., Worthman & Whiting, 1987; Bassitche, 1991; Delafosse, Fourasté, & Gbobouo, 1993). Still others castigate traditional society as authoritarian, preventing individual freedom, initiative, self-assertion, and creativity (Ho, 1994).

In any case, the option of returning to traditional institutions is not realistic, or is linked to fundamentalist policies. While it is not useful to lament the loss of the "good old times," the recognition of the benefits of some traditional values may help in preventing, softening, or slowing down some of the ill effects of too rapid social change. The question is how to deal with social change while avoiding some of its negative side effects. We will return to this question in Chapter 11.

CONCLUSION

We have seen in this chapter a sample of studies that place child development and education in its cultural context. The studies are all related to the concept of the developmental niche presented at the beginning of this chapter.

Instead of concentrating only on psychological development per se, cross-cultural developmental psychology takes into account the physical and social contexts in which this development takes place, as well as the relevant socialization practices and parental ethnotheories. In this manner, a coherent picture of human development is beginning to emerge.

In the next chapter, we turn to the cross-cultural study of cognitive processes, research that, while it may have involved children occasionally, is not specifically developmental in character. We will come back to some theories of child development in Chapters 5 and 6.

4

PERCEPTUAL AND
COGNITIVE PROCESSES

Cognition entails processes by which human beings deal with information. Obviously, everybody everywhere must process information, so there is a universal need for intellectual activities. This functional universality does not, of course, preclude cultural differences in the way these processes are implemented, in the contents that are being dealt with, in the contexts in which they are called into play, or in the more complex abilities that arise from a particular combination of basic cognitive processes. To specify the conditions under which these cultural variations arise is the goal of the cross-cultural study of cognition. That they are processes serving universal functions allows us to compare them across cultures.

What are these intellectual activities? First of all, we must process information coming from our sensory organs, so *perception* is one of these. Secondly, we all *categorize*. Attaching a single name to more than one object, such as calling several differently shaped objects (some soft, others hard) "chairs" is to categorize them, to treat them as exemplars of a particular category. The category itself may, however, be best represented by one particular type of chair that is taken as a standard or "prototype." Humans everywhere use prototypes to define categories, but these may depend on environmental factors and linguistic distinctions that vary across cultures. When we recognize and label a common attribute—for chairs, it is "sit-on-ability"— we are using our most important cognitive tool: language. Nouns are category labels. Because every language contains thing-names, people everywhere categorize. To decide whether distinct objects should receive the same label, they must be compared and judged as to the ways in which they might be equivalent or different.

People everywhere have to *remember* a large amount of information; otherwise they could not function. On the other hand, the kind of information they store, how they go about remembering it, and how much they are able to remember, may differ from one culture to another. It must also be obvious that people everywhere *solve problems* of various degrees of complexity. People everywhere are regularly confronted by all kinds of problems that they seek to solve.

While categorization, remembering, and solving problems fulfill universal needs, how they are carried out is dependent on cultural contexts. Because one of the major influences on all of these processes is formal education, the final section of this chapter will deal with the cognitive consequences of literacy and schooling.

PERCEPTION AND VISUAL ILLUSIONS

Cross-cultural psychologists have long wondered about both differences and uniformities in the most basic cognitive behavior of human beings, including the ways they perceive the physical world. While it is intuitively obvious that beliefs, attitudes, and values differ in striking ways across social classes, ethnic groups, religions, and nations (see Chapter 7), it may be much more surprising to find cultural differences in the way people perceive, say, two straight lines on a page!

We will look at a small proportion of perception research, dealing only with some opticogeometric illusions, focusing on a study by Segall, Campbell, and Herskovits (1966). There are extensive bodies of cross-cultural work on other aspects of perception, for example, pictorial depth perception and color perception. These are interesting issues in their own right and, incidentally, are not unrelated to the issue of illusion susceptibility. These other cross-cultural perception issues are discussed in Berry and colleagues (1992), Deregowski (1989), and Russell, Deregowski, and Kinnear (1997).

The differences to be reported here are differences in the *level* of susceptibility to visual illusions, not differences in kind. The processes that produce these visual illusions are found to be the same everywhere. And, the differences in susceptibility levels are relatively small. Still, the mere fact that differences exist at this level of basic perceptual activities is striking.

We will set the stage with some epistemological[1] concerns that have long been a part of Western philosophy.

To See Is to Discover Reality...or Is It?

The premise that the world is what it appears to be was challenged many centuries ago by Plato (circa 390 B.C.) in his famous parable of the cave (Republic 7). People are imprisoned in a cave, able to see only shadows projected on the back wall of the cave. Plato's point was that the prisoners will take these shadows for reality. If some

---

[1]Epistemology is the branch of philosophy concerned with knowledge. How do we know what the world is really like is an epistemological question.

of the prisoners are released and directly witness the objects and events that are casting the shadows, Plato said, the objects and events would appear less real than their reflections, or at least it would take time to adjust to the full reality. If they are taken back to the cave and try to convince the others that they merely see shadows, their fellow prisoners would not believe it.

Subsequently, Locke in 1690 and Berkeley in 1713 extended Plato's suggestion that the world, rather than appearing to us as it is, appears to us in ways determined by our prior experience. These two philosophers used a particularly compelling example: A single event generates two opposite impressions in the same observer at the same time! Box 4.1 provides a famous account of such a bizarre phenomenon, Berkeley's version, originally published in *Three Dialogues between Hylas and Philonous* (1713, p. 18).

In this dramatic experience—which, incidentally, can be repeated by anyone with three basins of water, one hot, one lukewarm, and one cold[2]—Berkeley demonstrates how the state of the observer contributes to his or her observation. Thus, he and other philosophers warn us against "naive realism." Given the way the world is filtered through our sense organs, it appears solid and real and constant, even when it isn't.

There are two main schools of thought on visual perception: nativism and empiricism. Nativists consider perceptual phenomena as revealing the structural demands of the human nervous system. They consider experience of minor import for perception. The empiricists say that the way we behave when looking at something reveals the importance of experience. Empiricist psychologists suggest that human beings regularly interpret cues and are easily misled by prior experience to be "phenomenal absolutists." Phenomenologically, the world seems to be perceived absolutely. But, the empiricists suggest, there is actually considerable relativity in our perceptions: The nature of any experience is relative to the state of the perceiver. Perception is not stimulus-determined. It is the product of experience in interaction with a stimulus.

Brunswik's Empiricist Theory: A Base for Cross-Cultural Research

Many psychologists during the early twentieth century who studied perception, known collectively as Gestalt psychologists, were nativists. Brunswik (1956) was an exception. From his point of view, perception involves transactions between the organism and the incoming sensations. Because most of these contribute to the survival of the organism, they are *functional,* or adaptive transactions. Perception helps

---

[2]Place one hand in the hot water and the other hand in the cold water. Keep them there for about three minutes, then plunge both into lukewarm water. You will be impressed, even though you know what to expect.

BOX 4.1   How Warm Is Hot; How Cool Is Cold?

Berkeley's seeming paradox is recounted as follows:

Philonous: Is it not an absurdity to think that the same thing should be at the same time both cold and warm?

Hylas: It is.

Philonous: Suppose now one of your hands was hot, the other cold, and that they are both at once put into the same vessel of water in an intermediate state: will not the water seem cold to one hand, and warm to the other?

Hylas: It will.

Philonous: Ought we not therefore by your principles to conclude it is really both cold and warm at the same time? That is, according to your own concession, to believe an absurdity?

Hylas: I confess it seems so.

---

the person get around in the world and prevents nasty accidents, like walking into walls. To Brunswik the perceived properties of an object are the combined product of the object and the perceiver, whose past experience plays a very important part.

Segall and colleagues (1966) studied optical illusions, such as the one shown in Figure 4.1, from a Brunswikian perspective. They argued that, if perception is influenced by learning, then there may well be ecological and cultural differences in perception, because people who grow up in different environments may learn to interpret cues differently.

To apply Brunswik's transactional functionalism to an explanation of optical illusions requires the hypothesis that an illusion taps a process that is functional in general but misleading in the particular instance. What makes the process misleading is the ecological unrepresentativeness of the situation: It is unlike the general run of situations to which the process is functionally adaptive. Thus, optical illusions may be thought of as providing atypical settings offering misleading cues.

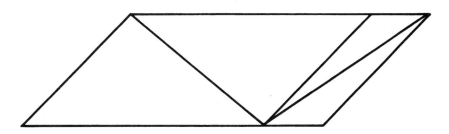

FIGURE 4.1   The Sander Parallelogram Illusion

Three Empiricist Hypotheses

From this position, Segall and his colleagues (1966) derived three specific hypotheses: (1) the carpentered world hypothesis, (2) front-horizontal foreshortening, and (3) symbolizing three dimensions in two. We will discuss each briefly.

The Carpentered World Hypothesis

This hypothesis applies to illusions like the Sander parallelogram, as shown in Figure 4.1. For this drawing, there is a tendency to judge the left diagonal as longer than it really is. This could result from a habit of perceiving a parallelogram drawn on a flat surface as a representation of a rectangular surface extended in space, forcing a judgment that *the distance* covered by the left diagonal is greater than *the distance* covered by the right diagonal. (In Figure 4.1, the left diagonal is actually longer than the right one.)

This judgment reflects a habit of inference that has ecological validity in highly carpentered environments. Many societies provide environments replete with rectangular objects. These objects, when projected on the retina, are represented by nonrectangular images. The tendency to interpret obtuse and acute angles in retinal images as deriving from rectangular objects is likely to be so pervasively reinforced in carpentered settings that the tendency becomes automatic and unconscious relatively early in life. By contrast, for those living where carpentered structures are a small portion of the visual environment, straight lines and precise right angles are a rarity. As a result, the inference habit of interpreting acute and obtuse angles as right angles extended in space would not be learned, at least not so well.

This line of reasoning may be applied also to the Müller-Lyer illusion shown in Figure 4.2.

People raised in a carpentered world would tend to perceive the Müller-Lyer figure as a representation of three-dimensional objects, extended in space. Here, the two main portions of the drawing represent two objects. For example, for the portion on the left, if the horizontal segment were perceived as the representation of, say, the edge of a box, it would be a front edge. For the portion on the right, if the horizontal segment were perceived as the edge of another box, it would be the back edge along the inside of the box. Hence, given two segments of the same length, the left-hand horizontal would "have to be" shorter than the drawing makes it out to be, while the right-hand horizontal would "have to be" longer.

FIGURE 4.2   The Müller-Lyer Illusion

Front-Horizontal Foreshortening
Lines in the horizontal plane that extend away from an observer appear to be more foreshortened than lines that cross the viewer's line of vision.

Picture a sidewalk one yard wide and marked off in squares one yard long. Consider first the square at your feet, then a square at some distance in front of you. In terms of retinal images (or extent on the surface of a photograph), whereas all dimensions of the square are reduced, in the one that is further away, the edges parallel to the line of regard are much more foreshortened.

Woodworth (1938) observed: "A short vertical line in a drawing may represent a relatively long horizontal line extending away from the observer. The horizontal–vertical illusion can be explained by supposing the vertical to represent such a foreshortened horizontal line" (p. 645). Such an inference habit would have varying validity in varying environments. For people living on flat plains with open vistas, there would be great ecological validity in interpreting vertical lines on the retina as long lines extending into the distance. The opposite would apply for canyon dwellers or rain forest dwellers, for whom vistas are constricted and who should be less susceptible, therefore, to the horizontal–vertical illusion than plain dwellers.

In Figure 4.3, the horizontal is actually longer than the vertical.

Symbolizing Three Dimensions in Two
Another dominant ecological factor relevant to the line illusions is the pervasive role of pictorial or graphic symbols on paper in some cultures. Although most of this symbolization is connected with the representation of language, it has also been used for an iconic representation of space. In European art, starting with the Renaissance, an increasingly dominant portion of such drawings has involved representing three-dimensional spatial arrays on the two-dimensional surfaces of paper, canvas, or wall, using a set of conventions such as perspective, relative object size, and overlap. It is

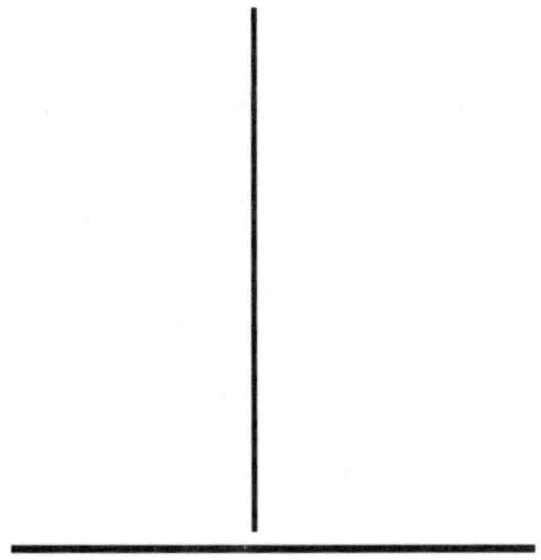

**FIGURE 4.3   The Horizontal–
Vertical Illusion**

hard for many people today to realize that this tradition of representing three dimensions in two also has the character of an arbitrary convention, because it is now so widespread, and represents the way our eyes (or cameras) see things. Nonetheless, it is a convention and, as such, it contributes to illusion susceptibility. The more experience we have with pictures, the more susceptible we will be to certain optical illusions, those that involve an element of depth perception.

To summarize the theoretical argument:

1. Optical illusions may happen because learned habits of inference are inappropriately applied.

2. In different physical and cultural environments, different habits of inference are likely to be acquired, reflecting differing ecological validities.

3. There is a learned tendency among people in carpentered environments to interpret nonrectangular figures as rectangular, to perceive the figures in perspective, and to interpret them as two-dimensional representations of three-dimensional objects. Such a tendency produces, or at least enhances, the Müller-Lyer illusion and the Sander parallelogram illusion. Because the tendency is assumed to have more ecological validity for people in carpentered environments, it is predicted that they will be more susceptible to these illusions than those who dwell in uncarpentered environments.

4. The horizontal–vertical illusion results from a tendency to counteract the foreshortening of lines extended into space away from a viewer. Because the tendency has more ecological validity for people living mostly outdoors in open, spacious environments, it is predicted that they will be more susceptible than people in urban environments, or, for example, rain forest or canyon dwellers.

5. Learning to interpret depth in representational drawings and in photographs should enhance these illusions.

Initial Support for the Empiricist Theory

Materials based on geometric illusions were prepared for standardized administration under varying field conditions. Over a six-year period, anthropologists and psychologists administered these tests to fourteen non-European samples of children and adults. The samples, most located in Africa, with one in the Philippines, ranged in size from 46 to 344. There were also three "European" groups: a sample ($N = 44$) of South Africans of European descent in Johannesburg, a North American (United States) undergraduate sample ($N = 30$), and a house-to-house sample ($N = 208$) in Evanston, Illinois. In all, data were collected from 1878 people.

The stimulus materials consisted of many items, each one a variation of particular illusions, including the Müller-Lyer, the Sander parallelogram, and two forms of the horizontal–vertical illusion. More details on the methods employed in the research are provided in Box 4.2.

Analysis of the choices made by people in the several samples, translated into points of subjective equality (or the average discrepancy at which two lines were

---

BOX 4.2   Methodological Details of the Illusion Research

As Campbell (1964) cogently argued, very large cultural differences in perception could not be distinguished from failures of communication.

For each illusion employed in the Segall, Campbell, and Herskovits study, the discrepancy in length of the segments to be compared varied from item to item. As each stimulus was shown, the respondent's task was simply to indicate the longer of two linear segments. If a respondent chose the usually exaggerated segment, this was scored as "an illusion-supported response." Each respondent received such a score on each illusion; each sample received a "mean number of illusion-supported responses" score on each

illusion. The higher the score, the greater the illusion susceptibility.

To minimize difficulties of communication, the linear segments to be compared were not connected to the other lines and were printed in different colors. Respondents could indicate choice by selecting one of two colors (saying "red" or "black") in response to the horizontal-vertical items and by indicating right or left for the other illusions. Another step taken to be sure that people in different samples understood the task was the administration of a short comprehension test requiring judgments similar to, but more obvious than, those demanded by the stimulus figures.

---

seen as equal), provided evidence of substantial cross-cultural differences. The results (including those of Gregor and McPherson, 1965) are summarized in Figures 4.4a and b.

When the samples were ranked according to mean susceptibility to the illusions, the rank orders varied across two classes of illusion. The Müller-Lyer and Sander parallelogram illusions composed one class (Figure 4.4a), the two horizontal–vertical illusions, another (Figure 4.4b). The pattern indicated not only overall cross-cultural differences in illusion susceptibility (with a range of about 20 percent between the lowest and highest mean), but differences in opposite directions for the two classes of illusions. On both the Müller-Lyer and Sander illusions the three "European" samples were more susceptible than non-European samples. On the two horizontal–vertical illusions, the European samples had relatively low scores, with many but not all of the non-European samples earning significantly larger mean scores. This outcome had been anticipated by the findings of W. H. R. Rivers (1901, 1905), a participant in the turn-of-the-century Cambridge expedition to the Torres Straits. But Rivers had been incapable of explaining the reasons for this pattern, because he was considering only great divide theories (see Box 4.3).

The cross-cultural differences in illusion susceptibility support the theory that attributes perceptual tendencies to ecologically valid inference habits, but it cannot be asserted that the data fit the theory perfectly. Also, support for the theory does not mean ruling out alternative hypotheses. The publication of Segall and colleagues' (1966) study spurred a large number of cross-cultural studies on illusion susceptibility

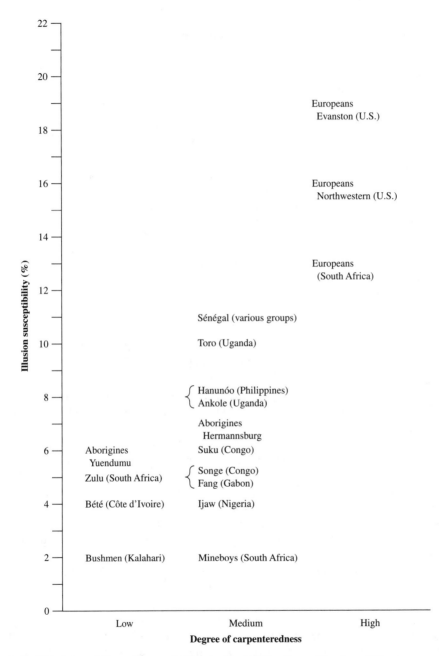

FIGURE 4.4a   Mean Susceptibility to the Müller-Lyer Illusion of Various Samples Classified According to Carpenteredness of the Environment.

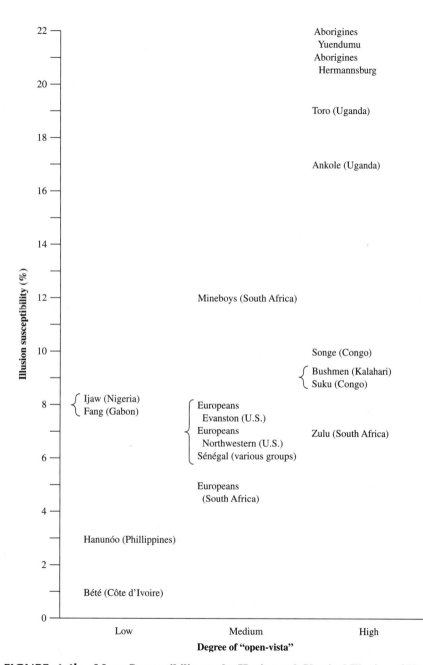

FIGURE 4.4b **Mean Susceptibility to the Horizontal–Vertical Illusion of Various Samples Classified According to Degree of "Open-Vista" in the Environment.**

BOX 4.3   Illusion Findings in the Cambridge Expedition

Rivers collected quantitative data using two geometrical illusions (the Müller-Lyer figure and the horizontal–vertical figure) among several samples in the Torres Straits islands (between Australia and Papua New Guinea) and in Southern India. For comparison purposes, data were also collected among English adults and children. Rivers (1901, 1905) reported that non-Western groups were more subject to the horizontal–vertical figure and less subject to the Müller-Lyer illusion than were English groups. Most provocative was the fact that differences between Western and non-Western people existed in both directions: The non-Western people were less subject to one illusion but more subject to another. Obviously, the failure to find differences consistent in direction eliminates any simple explanation of the existing differences.

One of those explanations, prevalent during the nineteenth century, held that, because "primitive" peoples were supposed to be less well endowed intellectually than "civilized" people, they should be more easily duped by illusions and therefore consistently more subject to them. Another hypothesis went just the other way: Because "primitive" peoples might develop simple perceptual skills more than complex intellectual ones, they might be less susceptible to illusions. None of these "great divide" theories could adequately account for Rivers's puzzling finding.

---

over more than a decade, some of which came out in support of one or more of the three empiricist hypotheses, and some that sought to challenge these with plausible alternatives. In the next section we will consider briefly a small number of these. More thorough reviews have been prepared by Deregowski (1980, 1989).

Age Trends in the Illusion Data: A Challenge to the Empiricists

The empiricist line of thinking has to predict—for carpentered world dwellers, at least—an increase in Müller-Lyer and Sander illusion susceptibility with age. But Segall and his colleagues found instead a general tendency for illusion susceptibility to decline with age. This age decline was found in their study for the Müller-Lyer and Sander illusions in nearly every society, and for the two horizontal–vertical illusions in about half of the samples.

Decline in illusion susceptibility with increasing age is a widely replicated phenomenon, at least for the Müller-Lyer and Sander illusions. It was first reported by Binet (1895/1965), and it was confirmed by Piaget (1969), who called these "primary" illusions. Piaget asserted that this kind of illusion decreases with age (or intellectual development) as children become increasingly able to make multiple glances that diminish the "Gestalt" of the compelling illusion. So-called secondary illusions, of which the L-shaped horizontal–vertical illusion is an example, are expected, according to Piaget, to increase with age.

To explain the failure of the data to reveal any increase—and, instead, mostly a decline—with age, it was suggested that the relevant learning that is theoretically assumed to produce susceptibility to illusions is achieved by early childhood (no later than age 6). Later, analytical skills are acquired that permit individuals to counteract the illusion effect. This "analytic sophistication" hypothesis is congruent with Piaget's perceptual activity theory, as well as with Witkin's differentiation theory.

Berry (1968) referred to the latter in a study comparing two samples of Canadian Inuit and two samples of Temne from Sierra Leone. In each location, the two samples differed in degree of acculturation and their environments differed in carpenteredness. Despite this difference in visual ecology, no difference was found on susceptibility to the Müller-Lyer illusion. Berry suggested that there could be a confounding of the hypothesized ecological and developmental determinants, because the samples with the more highly carpentered environments (predicting higher illusion) also had higher perceptual development (predicting lower illusion). The two influences could cancel each other out.

When he selected two subsamples of Inuit subjects matched on a measure of perceptual development (Kohs Blocks), they differed significantly in the direction expected from the ecological hypothesis. When he matched two subsamples of Temne on the individuals' history of living in carpentered environments, they differed in their mean score on Kohs Blocks, and the sample with the higher perceptual development also showed a significantly lower Müller-Lyer illusion. Thus, in both cases, when one of the factors was controlled through matching, the effect of the other factor became visible.

Dasen (1983a), in a study of visual illusion susceptibility and cognitive development in three samples of Australian children (two samples of Aborigines and one Anglo-Australian) yielded similar findings. The open vista factor was uncovered only when the results were plotted against a developmental score derived from Piagetian tasks, and not against chronological age.

A Rival Hypothesis

Despite this support for the ecological theory, a physiological hypothesis has also been considered. Silvar & Pollack (1967) argued that people with denser retinal pigmentation (e.g., dark-skinned people) have more difficulty detecting contours and that contour detection is involved in responding to illusions. Because the non-Western samples in the study by Segall and his associates were non-Europeans, Silvar and Pollack suggested that "race" might be responsible for what Segall and his colleagues had interpeted as cultural differences.

While some early support for the physiological hypothesis appeared in a few studies, it was effectively challenged by Stewart (1973; see Box 4.4).

BOX 4.4 Environment, not "Race," in Evanston and Zambia

Stewart (1973) correctly pointed out that Pollack's challenge to ecological theory underlines the need for a dual research strategy. First, one holds environmental carpenteredness constant while varying "race." Second, one tests across environments while holding "race" constant. In short, "race" and environment have to be unconfounded in order to assess their possible contributions to illusion susceptibility. To test across "race" with environment held constant, she administered the Müller-Lyer and Sander illusions to 60 black and 60 white schoolchildren, ranging in age from 6 to 17, and selected randomly from three schools in Evanston, Illinois. She found no significant difference in susceptibility between the two groups.

To test across environments with "race" constant, Stewart administered the same stimulus materials to Zambian school-aged children, again ranging in age from 6 to 17 and again with the sexes equally represented. In Zambia, however, the five levels sampled ranged widely from a group of unschooled Tonga children living in the very uncarpentered Zambezi Valley region to a group of middle-class children living in Zambia's cosmopolitan capital, Lusaka. A total of 432 Zambian subjects, all blacks, were tested. The major finding was that for both illusions, susceptibility rose with increases in the degree of carpenteredness. Stewart's overall findings are summarized in Figure 4.5.

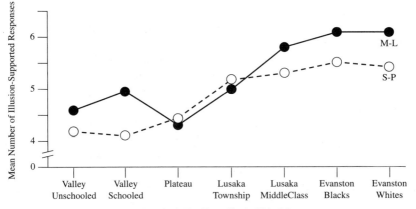

FIGURE 4.5 Mean Illusion-Supported Responses for the Müller-Lyer (M-L) and Sander Parallelogram (S-P) Illusions in Various Samples in Zambia and the U.S.A.

Clearly, susceptibility to both illusions increased with increasing carpenteredness of environment, whereas "race" mattered not at all. Stewart's research failed to replicate Silvar and Pollack's results, even though she varied "race" in the same geographical setting as they had, the Chicago metropolitan area. Her study's support for the ecological hypothesis is quite strong because she employed more than one illusion and got essentially the same findings with both. Moreover, she actually used a third instrument in Zambia—a miniature version of the Ames Distorted Room—and got similar results. Clearly, Stewart's research findings offer strong support for the empiricist point of view.

One More Study of Illusion Susceptibility

One of the studies that tested the "learned-habits-of-inference" position (Pollnac, 1977) was amusingly subtitled "Is the carpentered world hypothesis seaworthy?" This study in fact tested, not the carpentered world hypothesis, but the frontal-plane-foreshortening hypothesis. Employing a sample of twenty-one fishermen who work a very broad expanse of ocean along the Pacific coast of Costa Rica, Pollnac found that susceptibility to the inverted T form of the horizontal–vertical illusion was significantly related to years of fishing experience and to the degree of responsibility for navigation. The correlation between mere chronological age and susceptibility reduced to zero when it was controlled for by those two indices of experience in making survival-crucial judgments of distance and size.

Thus, Pollnac demonstrated that variance in illusion susceptibility, within such a small sample occupying a single ecological niche, is well accounted for by relevant experience.

Conclusions Regarding Illusion Susceptibility

The studies that have been reviewed and others that we did not mention here mostly support the interpretation that illusion susceptibility is a reflection of acquired habits of inference, habits that are ecologically valid ones. The alternative physiological hypothesis has not fared as well. It may be stated with confidence that people perceive in ways that are shaped by the inferences they have learned to make in order to function most effectively in the particular ecological settings in which they live. Although there has been very little if any further research on this topic in the last two decades, the research we have considered here confirms that we learn to perceive in the ways that we need to perceive. In that sense, environment and culture shape our perceptual habits.

CATEGORIZATION

Because the world consists of a virtually infinite number of discriminably different stimuli, an essential cognitive activity is the division of the environment into categories within which many nonidentical stimuli can be treated as equivalent. Are the principles of category formation culturally specific or are they universal? Research on color, form, and facial expressions provides some interesting answers.

Color

Various languages place boundaries between color names at different places along the visual spectrum.[3] However, according to Berlin and Kay (1969), if the physiology

---

[3]A more detailed treatment of the complex issue of color perception and naming can be found in Berry and associates (1992) and in Russell and associates (1997).

underlying color perception is panhuman, then, despite variations in color vocabulary, there should be agreement on "focal points" for color among speakers of different languages. Thus, there should be so-called focal colors that are more salient (i.e., that stand out among others and are more easily remembered), even when there is no basic color term to designate them (i.e., even if they are not more "codable").

However, codability and salience are confounded in English. Rosch (1977) designed a study to unconfound codability and salience, working in a culture in which the language contains only two color terms, "dark" and "light." She presented the Dani of West Irian (Indonesian New Guinea) with a color memory task, using focal and nonfocal colors. Because the Dani use only two basic color terms, all colors were (in their language) equally uncoded. The Dani provided an ideal opportunity to teach color names. The research question was: Would the Dani remember focal colors better than nonfocal ones?

The results of a recognition–memory task suggest that they do. Compared to the results of the same experiment conducted in the United States, the Dani had, on the average, a lower memory performance, which could have been due to various artifacts such as familiarity with the testing situation. However, the absolute level of performance is of no importance to the issue; the relevant finding here is that, in both cultures, focal colors were remembered more easily than nonfocal ones.[4]

Rosch (1977) tested the following hypothesis in an experiment that involved learning new codes in a paired associate task:

> *There are perceptually salient colors which more readily attract attention and are more easily remembered than other colors. When category names are learned, they tend to become attached first to the salient stimuli…, and by this means these natural prototype colors become the foci of organization for categories (pp. 10–11).*

In accord with Rosch's hypothesis, the focal-color name pairs were learned with fewer errors than the nonfocal-color name pairs, suggesting that perceptually focal (or "salient") colors are natural prototypes for the development and learning of color names.

Shapes

Color is not the only domain in which perceptually salient, natural prototypes appear to determine the focal points of categories. Perfect circles, squares, and equilateral triangles were found to be prototypes for the Dani despite the absence of a terminology for two-dimensional geometric forms.

---

[4]Note that, in this case, a study involving only two groups does yield interpretable results, because the researcher found a similarity rather than a difference.

Expressions of Emotion

Ekman (1973) found that facial expressions of emotion also form natural categories or prototypes. Ekman asserted that there are six basic human emotions (i.e., happiness, sadness, anger, fear, surprise, and disgust), and that each is associated with a specific set of facial muscle movements. When Ekman put together sets of pictures of "pure" expressions of the proposed basic emotions, these were judged correctly not only by Americans, Japanese, and South Americans, but also by the Fore and the Dani, two New Guinea groups with minimal contact with the facial expressions of other people. In this respect, Rosch makes the following methodological point:

> *Like color, universality was discovered in facial expressions of emotion only when an investigator thought to ask, not about all possible stimuli, but about the prototypes (best examples) of categories (Rosch, 1977, p. 17).*

On the other hand, cultural differences may occur in: (1) the elaboration of language codes for the categories, (2) the organization of categories into superordinated structures, (3) category boundaries, (4) the treatment of interprototype stimuli (such as blends of emotions), and (e) the rules for use of the categories (such as when and where emotion may be expressed). For a more detailed discussion of cross-cultural studies of emotion, see Mesquita, Frijda, and Scherer (1997).

Real Objects

Color, form, and the facial expression of emotion may all be structured in the same way because they are domains with a possible physiological basis. What about category formation in domains that do not have a physiological basis, like most common semantic categories (e.g., "chair")? Research within Euro-American culture has found that noun categories can be viewed as prototypes. That is, they define the category through an idea or image of the "best example."

The categorization of concrete objects may reflect the ecological structure of real-world attributes. So-called basic objects (e.g., chair) are the most inclusive level of categorization at which many attributes can be common to all members of the category; categories at higher or "superordinate" levels of abstraction (e.g., furniture) possess few attributes common to category members, while categories subordinate to the basic level share most attributes with other subordinate categories. The common motor movements evoked by objects, the similarity of shapes, and the ease with which an average shape is recognizable all determine the coding of categories in terms of prototypes.

The particular choice of prototypes that define categories should vary according to ecological cue validity (cf. the earlier section on visual perception); therefore the particular prototype that is chosen may or may not be the same in all cultures. What seems to be universal is the mechanism through which basic level categories are formed.

Equivalence Sorting

Discovering how people place objects into groups is another way to study categorization. Because categories can be defined by shared attributes, how these attributes are perceived or used may be assessable through tasks in which the people being studied have to sort pictures or objects into categories. Developmental trends in sorting behavior have been found: Younger children tend to judge objects as equivalent primarily on the basis of striking, superficial, or even incidental perceptual properties, such as color or number. Sorting by form is slightly more advanced, because it requires abstraction of features from the stimuli. Older children are likely to sort on the basis of such attributes as shared function (for a bicycle and a car: "to ride") or the nominal (taxonomic) label for it ("they are vehicles" or "transportation").

In studies done in some non-Western societies, especially in Africa, the subjects use form and functional sorting less than Western subjects. Arguing that free-sorting tests, as employed in the earlier studies, revealed only habits and not abilities, Evans and Segall (1969), working in Uganda, used a learning-to-sort task rather than a free-sorting task. They believed that a particular child might be able to sort by function but might never do so if merely asked to sort. If instructed to find the way the experimenter wanted her to sort, that same child might reveal some difficulty in discovering how to do it but might nevertheless come to do it.

This is exactly what was found. The number of years in school, rather than chronological age, was the critical factor relating to manifest ability to sort objects on the basis of shared function. Schooling enabled subjects to entertain more complicated hypotheses than color and to comprehend the function-sorting task more readily than the lesser educated children or the adults for whom schooling had been minimal and remote in time. This tendency to search for less obvious attributes of a stimulus is what schooling may instill in children. This was substantiated by a study done in Colombia (Evans, 1975), in which learning to sort on the basis of abstract qualities (functional or taxonomic as opposed to perceptual) was shown to be dependent on school grade level. Thus, functional sorting is at least partly a product of experience, of which schooling is a particularly influential kind. This experiment could not have been done within Euro-American culture, in which nearly all children are schooled and maturation and schooling are confounded, with age trends likely to be attributed to maturation, while in fact they result from experience.[5]

This effect of schooling cannot, however, be generalized. In a study among the Yupno of Papua New Guinea, Wassmann and Dasen (1994a) found that illiterate adults chose to sort mainly by function, while children, especially if schooled, and young adults, sorted mainly by color. The Yupno cultural model considers that all objects are either hot or cold, a highly abstract dimension that is not detectable by any visible feature. In this case, attention to the less obvious attribute was not pro-

---

[5]Recall the discussion, in Chapter 1, of the unconfounding function of cross-cultural research.

moted by schooling, but by traditional cultural knowledge, held more by the older generation, and especially by some expert old men.

Okonji (1971), who compared school-going children in a rural town in midwestern Nigeria with an age-comparable group of school-children in Glasgow, Scotland, found that the Nigerian children employed more accurate, inclusive, and superordinate bases for grouping objects than their Scottish counterparts (significantly so for those aged 11 to 12) when the objects to be sorted were more familiar to the Nigerian children than to the Scottish children. The Nigerian children performed overall at a level of conceptualization that at least equaled that of the Scottish sample. Okonji attributed the high performance of the Nigerian subjects to their familiarity with the objects. A similar point had been made by Price-Williams in 1962 and recurrently by others since (e.g., Serpell, 1976), although some studies have been reported in which familiarity with the testing materials had no influence (e.g., Dasen, 1984).

The different expectations of subjects and experimenter about the task may also be important. There is ample evidence from the domain of experimental anthropology (Cole, Gay, Glick, & Sharp, 1971; Cole & Scribner, 1974), to be reviewed below, that a change in the experimental context can elicit allegedly missing skills (Ciborowski, 1980).

The evidence from these and other studies is that the process of equivalence sorting occurs in much the same fashion among a wide variety of ethnic groups. Differences are found primarily among people who are tested with unfamiliar materials, who understand the task differently from what the experimenter means it to be, or who have not had certain types of experiences, such as schooling. What was once thought to be a difference across ethnic groups in the *capacity* to process information is better thought of as a reflection of the experiences people have, and of the cultural appropriateness of the way their skills are assessed. Given the right opportunities to learn to play the Euro-American psychologists' sorting games, people anywhere can come to play them well!

MEMORY

Is it possible that certain groups, especially people in nonliterate societies, have quantitatively *better* memories than people in societies in which much of the knowledge they want to retain is available in written form? Anecdotal evidence abounds that people with oral traditions have phenomenal memories. In contrast to the prevailing bias in Western/non-Western comparisons of cognitive skills, many observers, in tales of their travels to exotic lands, have reported remarkable mnemonic feats. Some serious students, perhaps influenced by these anecdotes, have argued that memory skills in preliterate societies develop differently from, if not better than, those in literate societies (e.g., Bartlett, 1932). They have noted that daily life in nonliterate societies places a premium on remembering details of the sort that in literate societies are a matter of bookkeeping or other forms of written record. Individuals in literate societies, because they can rely on memory banks such as telephone directories, history books, and computers, may have lost memory skills through lack of practice.

Some empirical evidence shows some superiority in memory among people reared in societies with a strong oral tradition. Ross and Millsom (1970), for example, suspected that the reliance on oral tradition that is characteristic of African societies might make Africans more likely to remember details in orally presented stories than a comparable group of people in the United States. Both groups were university students, one in Ghana and the other in New York. The researchers tested retention of the themes contained in several stories read aloud. They found that, in general, the Ghanaian students recalled the stories better than the New York students. The sole exception was one story told in seventeenth-century English. The Ghanaian performance was especially impressive, because they both heard and reproduced the stories in English, which to most of them was a second language. Generally speaking, there is evidence for better recall of stories consistent with people's own cultural knowledge (e.g., Harris, Schoen, & Hensley, 1992).

Cross-cultural studies of memory do not confirm an overall better performance in societies with an oral tradition (Wagner, 1981). Cole and his colleagues (see, for example, Cole, Gay, Glick, & Sharp, 1971; Cole & Scribner, 1974) reported a complex series of memory experiments with schooled and unschooled Kpelle in Liberia. In one experiment, Kpelle subjects heard and were then asked to recall the names of twenty common items, five each in four categories: food, clothing, tools, and utensils. They were given several trials. Compared with U.S. subjects, the Kpelle subjects remembered less and improved less over trials; there was little improvement with age; there was almost no clustering into semantic categories, a mnemonic skill current in U.S. children after the age of 10. Neither did the Kpelle groups seem to learn by "rote" (recalling the words in the order in which they are given). This surprising result prompted Scribner (1974) to propose that the categories employed were inappropriate for the Kpelle. When the subjects were allowed to use their own groupings, they used clustering in their recall, although more clustering did not always lead to better recall.

Cole and Scribner (1974) found that, when allowed to use their own categories, or when they employed certain aids to clustering the material to be remembered, the Kpelle subjects, particularly those with some schooling, were able to recall in a manner and to a degree comparable to U.S. subjects.

A major implication of this research was that the use of conceptual organization as a means to remembering was more likely to be characteristic of schooled persons. Cole and Scribner (1974) argued that schooling teaches people to remember aggregates of material that are not at first perceived as interrelated. People become practiced in learning new organizing principles, the acquisition of which then facilitates the remembering of instances that relate to the principle.

On the basis of research in Mexico and Morocco, Wagner (1981) concluded that the structure of memory (short-term memory capacity and forgetting rate) is universal, while the control processes (acquisition strategies, such as clustering and rehearsal, and retrieval strategies) are culturally influenced. Two experiments (short-term recall and recognition memory) were conducted in Morocco on a sample of 384 males, who differed in age (7 to 19 years), schooling, and urban–rural environment. Additional groups of subjects were tested to study possible culture-specific influences on mnemonics: pupils in Quranic schools (where the Quran is learned by rote through chanting) and rug sellers (because the experiment used the recall of oriental rug patterns).

The recency effect (the fact that the last items in a list are remembered best, a measure of short-term storage and hence a structural property of memory) was stable and relatively invariant across all populations studied, regardless of age, schooling, and environment. The primacy effect (the fact that the first items are remembered better, which is linked to verbal rehersal, a control process) developed with age only for schooled subjects, and to some degree in nonschooled children who lived in an urban setting. Thus, the hypothesis was supported.

Quranic students were originally thought to have special memory abilities, but in Wagner's experiments they remembered very little and made little use of memory strategies. In Liberia, Scribner and Cole (1981) found that Quranic students used mnemonics, but only when the task made use of serial ordering skills in so-called semantic incremental memory. Thus, the particular task used is a determinant of memory performance; there is no single, general memory skill but rather different specialized memory skills.

PROBLEM SOLVING

The drawing of inferences and the predicting of future events based on an analysis of past events—processes that often require postulating causal relationships—are forms of cognitive behavior characteristic of science. By Western values, scientific thinking represents the ultimate in intelligent behavior. To behave "scientifically" is, many believe, to perceive the world "as it really is."

Drawing causal inferences and discovering general principles on which valid predictions can be based are, of course, truly intellectual activities. They are often difficult to perform well, even with training. For centuries, scholars have struggled to provide guidelines for scientific thinking. The complex statistical techniques that help guard against perceiving relationships when none in fact exist, and the frequency with which such errors are nevertheless made, testify to the difficulty of scientific thinking. Yet, even in everyday life, logical analysis, predicting, and other scientific activities must occur.

Many people who hold Western values claim allegiance to scientific thinking. Some, maybe even in increasing numbers, argue that other modes of knowing—for example, intuition or mysticism—are also acceptable ways of understanding reality. Western culture has its share of poets, mystics, postmodernists, and others who insist that there is knowledge that cannot be penetrated by scientific inquiry, and insights that can be obtained by other means. Still, the scientific mode of knowledge seeking is most widely acclaimed. What is the case in non-Western societies? Is Piaget (1966) correct, for example, in assuming that all people tend toward formal–operational (scientific) thinking, but that non-Western people fall short of its achievement if they do not have a Western formal schooling at the secondary level? Might it be, as suggested by some of the "great divide" theories to be reviewed in Chapter 5, that such thinking is absent in nonschooled individuals? Is there some other mode so highly valued and practiced that it takes the place of science and serves as well or even better to reveal "knowledge"? Questions like these have prompted cross-cultural research, some of which we review here, and some in Chapters 5 and 6.

Inferential Reasoning

As Cole, Gay, Glick, and Sharp (1971) point out, it is difficult to get clear evidence of inferential reasoning by observing naturally occurring instances, which are always open to alternative interpretations. If a person sees a black cloud on the horizon and says it is going to rain, does she make an inference, or does she simply remember a common association? If that person says it is going to rain while using instruments to measure wind velocity and barometric pressure, does she make an inference? It is more likely, but not certain; she, too, may just have recalled an earlier experience. We need evidence that the person is using a *new* combination of previously learned elements. To be sure, we must study the inferential reasoning process in a new situation, where previous learning can be controlled by the experimenter, as in a laboratory.

Cole and associates (1971) presented their subjects in Liberia, nonliterate Kpelle adults and children, as well as schooled children and young adults, with an oblong box apparatus, divided into three parts (A, B, and C), each with its own door. In a training sequence, subjects were first taught that they could get a marble by opening door A only, and pushing the button in the middle of panel A. Then they were taught that they could get a ball bearing by pushing the button in panel C. Then, with doors A and C closed, candy (or some other reward) could be had by putting a marble (but not a ball bearing) into an appropriate opening on panel B. In the test sequence, subjects were told to do whatever necessary to get a candy. In other words, the problem had to be solved by combining two independently learned behaviors.

With U.S. children, there is a clear developmental trend: Young children (up to about 10 years) do not integrate the two segments of the problem, while older children do. Only 15 percent of the nonliterate Kpelle adults spontaneously solved the problem, fewer than the Liberian children (9- to 12-year-olds) of whom 30 percent succeeded, whether schooled or not. Schooling did have one influence: Only educated subjects were inclined to start working immediately with the strange apparatus. Among the nonliterate subjects, there were overt signs of fear. They would play with extraneous features of the apparatus, and then sit quietly, waiting for the experimenter to ask additional questions. With prompting, 60 percent to 80 percent of the subjects would end up solving the problem.

The researchers could have concluded that the Kpelle find it difficult to make simple inferences due to an incapacity for logical reasoning, but Cole and associates (1971) did not. Instead they designed a Kpelle version of the same problem, one that had the same logical structure but made use of familiar materials such as keys and match boxes. The additional experiments showed that the Kpelle, schooled or not, are quite able to use inferential reasoning, but only if the conditions are right. From 70 to 80 percent of the subjects (aged 7 through adulthood) solved the problem spontaneously and 90 percent solved it with a little prompting. It is this kind of finding that led Cole and his colleagues to the conclusion that the use of cognitive processes is context-specific.

Verbal Logical Reasoning

Logical reasoning can also be studied with verbal problems, such as syllogisms. Consider the syllogism:

> *All men are mortal;*
>
> *Socrates is a man;*
>
> *Therefore, Socrates is mortal.*

An early cross-cultural study with syllogisms was carried out in Uzbekistan and Kirghizistan (Central Asia) in the 1930s by Luria, but the report became available in Russian only in 1974, and in English another two years later (Luria, 1976). This was, in fact, a study of the consequences of social change. One group of subjects was composed of nonschooled, noncollectivized farmers, and the second of people from the same villages who were engaged in the collective planning of farm production, and had received about one year of literacy training. Luria found striking differences in the way these two groups responded to simple verbal syllogisms.

If the problems related to the concrete, practical experience of the villagers, they were not difficult to solve. But some contained unfamiliar content:

> *In the North, where there is snow all year, the bears are white;*
>
> *Novaya Zemlya is in the far North;*
>
> *What color are the bears there?*

Illiterate peasants typically said, "How should I know what color the bear was? I haven't been in the North. You should ask the people who have been there and seen them. We always speak only of what we see; we don't talk about what we haven't seen."

Luria (1976) concluded that the subjects in the two groups were using different reasoning processes; concrete or "graphico-functional" in the case of the illiterate group, abstract, or "hypothetico-deductive" for the collectivized, literate group. A relatively short-term sociohistorical change, he thought, was producing a completely new way of thinking. Consider his example of a student in a village school who had only a few months of schooling. This subject, he writes, clearly demonstrates the capacity to perform hypothetical, theoretical operations independently of his own practical personal experience. It is of considerable interest that this shift and the capacity to perform "theoretical" operations of formal discursive and logical thinking appear after relatively short-term school instruction. The significance of schooling lies not just in the acquisition of new knowledge, but in the creation of new motives and formal modes of discursive verbal and logical thinking divorced from immediate practical experience" (Luria, 1976, p. 133).[6]

An Estonian psychologist, Tulviste (1978), used syllogisms with thirty-five schoolchildren (aged 8 to 15 years) among the Nganassan, a formerly nomadic population living from hunting and raising reindeer in northern Eurasia. Ten syllogisms were presented, half with everyday content (e.g., "Saiba and Nakupté always drink tea together; Saiba drinks tea at 3 P.M.; Does Nakupté drink tea at 3 P.M. or not?), and half with school content (e.g., "All precious metals are rustfree; Molybdenum is a precious metal; Does molybdenum rust or not?"). The subjects were asked to explain their answers.

Like Scribner (1979), Tulviste called "theoretic" answers those in which the conclusion related explicitly to the premises; statements justifying the conclusion on the basis of what the subject knows or believes to be true, were classified "empiric." Syllogisms with school content were justified more often with theoretic explanations (in 59 out of 110 cases) than syllogisms with everyday premises (only 26 cases). Tulviste concluded:

Theoretic syllogistic reasoning…first appears in the sphere of school knowledge and only after that is also applied in the sphere of everyday knowledge. The results presented reveal that theoretic syllogistic reasoning is not a skill previously present in the subjects, which under the impact of formal education can be applied to new kinds of problems. Rather, it is a qualitatively new skill engendered by schooling, *which later on may be also applied to everday matters (1978, pp. 12–13).*

Like Luria and Vygotsky before him, Tulviste subscribes to a "great divide" theory: He considers theoretic reasoning as absent among traditional subjects. Theoretic reasoning, he claims, is an example of thinking in scientific concepts that first occurred in the social and cultural situation of ancient Greece, and from where, through schooling, it has come into different cultures and changed the thinking of people. As we shall see, not everyone agrees with this interpretation.

Syllogistic reasoning problems were also used in Liberia with Kpelle and Vai people, and among Mayan-speaking and Spanish-speaking, rural and semiurban,

---

[6]An alternative interpretation is that schooling may have had an actualizing effect. We will see in Chapter 5 that a short period of training is sometimes sufficient to actualize underlying concrete operational reasoning.

schooled and nonschooled, adult and child populations in Yucatan, Mexico (Cole et al., 1971; Cole & Scribner, 1974; Sharp, Cole, & Lave, 1978). The results were drawn together by Scribner (1979). Overall, the performance of "traditional" or "nonliterate" subjects was little better than chance. Within each culture, there was a large discrepancy in performance between schooled and nonschooled subjects; with schooling, there were only small cultural differences in performance. Figure 4.6, drawn from Cole (1996, p. 84), shows the relative frequency of theoretical responses as a function of respondents' age and years of schooling in the Yucatecan study (Sharp, Cole, & Lave, 1979). The inclusion of an adult sample with different levels of school experience enables the researcher to unconfound chronological age and schooling. The figure shows neatly that the use of theoretic answers increases exclusively as a function of years of schooling.

Do such results show that traditional, unschooled people do not reason logically? Or might it be that traditional people do not apply their logical skills to *verbal* material? Scribner rejected both of these hypotheses, illustrating logical reasoning by an illiterate Kpelle farmer with extracts from the following protocol:

Experimenter: If Sumo or Saki drink palm wine, the Town Chief gets vexed; Sumo is not drinking palm wine; Saki is drinking palm wine; Is the Town Chief vexed?

Subject: The Town Chief was not vexed on that day. The reason is that he doesn't love Sumo. Sumo's drinking gives people a hard time, that is why the Town Chief gets vexed. But when Saki drinks palm wine, he does not give a hard time to people,

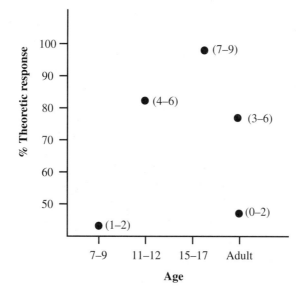

FIGURE 4.6 **Percentage of theoretic response to syllogistic reasoning problems as a function of age and years of education. Numbers in parentheses indicate years of education.**

he goes to lie down to sleep. At that rate people do not get vexed with him (Scribner, 1979, p. 8).

In this example, the reasoning follows logically from personal knowledge used by the subject, rather than from the evidence supplied in the premises. In other words, the illiterate subjects use information based on fact, belief, or opinion. While this is consonant with Luria's and Tulviste's observations, Scribner drew different implications from it. For her, the empiric mode enters the reasoning process

> *primarily as selector and editor of the 'evidence'. Personal knowledge and experience were used as 1) the criterion for acceptance or rejection of particular information conveyed in the premises, 2) the source of new information from which to derive a conclusion, 3) 'proof' or verification of a conclusion reached through use of problem information (1979, p. 14).*

When the illiterate subjects were asked to repeat the syllogisms after they were read, or to recall them after they had been solved, information was systematically omitted or transformed in such a way as to change the meaning of the problems, destroying their hypothetical status.

In other words, Scribner (1979), and Cole in the introduction to Luria's book (1976), interpret the empiric mode not as the absence of logical reasoning, but "the refusal to engage in the reasoning task at all, on the grounds that the problems presented are, *in principle,* unanswerable" (Scribner, 1979, p. 12; italics in original). Verbal logical problems are a special *genre,* a style of discourse, that is frequently used in school contexts, which explains why the theoretic mode is common among schooled subjects; the willingness to engage in this style does not reflect a different form of thought, but the habit of applying a common form of logical reasoning to a new context.

THE COGNITIVE CONSEQUENCES
OF LITERACY AND SCHOOLING

So far in our review, we have found schooling to be an important determinant of performance on sorting, memory, problem-solving, and syllogistic reasoning tasks. A broader array of studies on schooling and cognition (including the Piagetian ones that we will deal with in the next chapter), as reviewed by Gillet (1976), Nerlove and Snipper (1981), and Rogoff (1981), clearly shows varied, often substantial (but sometimes inconsistent), effects of schooling. Rogoff (1981) summarizes many findings in the following way:

> *Research suggests that schooled individuals have gained skills both in the use of graphic conventions to represent depth in two-dimensional stimuli and in the fine-grained analysis of two-dimensional patterns. They have increased facility in deliberately remembering disconnected bits of information, and spontaneously engage in strategies that provide greater orga-*

nization for the unrelated items. Schooled people are more likely to organize objects on a taxonomic basis, putting categorically similar objects together, whereas nonschooled people often use functional arrangements of objects that are used together. Schooled groups show greater facility in shifting to alternative dimensions of classification and in explaining the basis of their organization. Schooling appears to have no effect on rule learning nor on logical thought as long as the subject has understood the problem in the way the experimenter intended. Nonschooled subjects seem to prefer, however, to come to conclusions on the basis of experience rather than by relying on the information in the problem alone. The results of Piagetian tests are somewhat inconsistent, but they suggest that schooled children are more likely to show conservation and that schooling may be necessary for the solution of formal operational problems (p. 285).

There is some disagreement on the meaning of these results. Heuristically, we distinguish four alternative, although not necessarily competing, interpretations:

1. The first has it that schooling, and more particularly literacy,[7] produce new cognitive processes. This is how Luria (1976) and Tulviste (1978), and more generally the sociohistorical school influenced by Vygotsky, see it. Goody, Cole, and Scribner (1977), for example, wrote:

When an individual comes to master writing, the basic system underlying the nature of his mental processes is changed fundamentally as the external symbol system comes to mediate the organization of all of his basic intellectual operations (p. 298).

This is because writing is a double symbolic system: The letters stand for words that stand for ideas. Writing thus allows the decontextualization and formalization of thought; it promotes abstraction and critical thinking, or rationality. Literacy is here seen as one of the prerequisites of scientific reasoning.

2. The second interpretation claims that schooling promotes the application of existing processes to a large array of contexts, including new and unfamiliar ones (Bruner, 1966a; Gillet, 1976; Greenfield, 1972; Greenfield & Bruner, 1969; Scribner & Cole, 1973). Schooling emphasizes the searching for general rules, and is characterized by the use of verbal instruction out of context, free from immediate social contingencies. School learning is disconnected from everyday life, happens in an artificial context, usually with an adult who is not a family member. Schooled individuals are therefore more likely: (1) to use abstract principles; (2) to apply general rules to specific problems; and (3) to verbalize their actions and to explain the reasons for their behavior.

---

[7]We shall see in a little while how to distinguish between schooling and literacy.

3. A third interpretation attributes the empirical findings largely to experimental artifacts (Cole, Sharp, & Lave, 1976). The testing situations used, almost unavoidably, very much resemble the "hidden curriculum" of schools; for example, schooled individuals regularly interact with a strange adult, they dare to ask questions (instead of keeping respectfully silent), and are used to answering questions (even when they know that the adult already knows the answers). Schooled individuals are used to tackle strange tasks and to persist in searching for a solution. All these experiences are similar to the implicit demands of the research situations, and therefore the observed performances may have been enhanced artifically.

4. Lave (1977), considering that the skills learned in school are quite specific to the school situation, argued that these skills should therefore show up in schoollike experimental studies, but are likely to have little relevance for everyday life. We will take up this notion again in later chapters.

All four interpretations contain a germ of truth. The first one, however, seems to go somewhat beyond the facts and relates more explicitly to literacy, rather than schooling. Because literacy is typically attained through schooling, it is as difficult to study the respective effects of these two variables as it is to separate the effects of age and schooling in Western developmental studies. We now turn to this issue, relying on an excellent review by Akinnaso (1981).

Literacy or Schooling?

When considering the effects of literacy, we ought to distinguish its consequences for the individual from its impact on society as a whole. In fact, it is on the basis of a historical and anthropological analysis at the population level, comparing societies with or without writing (or, historically, the culture change when writing is invented or introduced), that Goody (1980) and his colleagues hypothesized the creation of new cognitive processes as a consequence of literacy.

Literacy is seen as a highly potent catalyst of cultural change (e.g., Goody & Watt, 1963; McLuhan, 1962; Olson, 1977). First of all, written language is different from speech. With the introduction of a writing system, the basic character of the storage and transmission of knowledge is changed. Transmission of information becomes possible beyond the limited circle of personal contacts, necessitating a more explicit, decontextualized form of language; writing also promotes the development of elaborate syntax. Written language cannot rely on the simultaneous transmission of information over other, paralinguistic channels, such as postures and gestures. In the words of Vygotsky (1962), "writing is speech without an interlocutor, addressed to an imaginary person or to no one in particular" (p. 99). The storage of information is no longer limited by human memory; knowledge becomes cumulative, even over generations, a basic condition for the development of science (Goody, 1968, 1977).

Historically, the invention of writing also allowed mass communication, and the spread of messianic religions based on a "revealed" holy text, the development of institutions such as bureaucracies, allowing the administration of large and complex political entities, and schools that help to perpetuate the system.

To study the effects of literacy on individual cognitive functioning, and to distinguish them from the effects of schooling, Scribner and Cole (1978, 1981; Cole, 1978, 1996) took advantage of a "natural experiment" among the Vai people in Liberia, some of whom are literate in their own script without ever having been to school. The Vai phonetic writing system consists of a syllabary of approximately 210 characters that are combined into a text without any separations between words. The script is used for writing letters and keeping personal records, and it is transmitted entirely outside of any institutional setting through individual tutoring among friends and relatives. Approximately 20 percent of Vai men are literate in Vai, 16 percent have attended Quranic schools, and are therefore more or less literate in Arabic, although that language is used only for religious purposes. Another 6 percent are literate in English, the official national language, that they have learned in Western-style schools. Vai women are generally not literate in any script.

Scribner and Cole compared the performance of Vai men who were literate in the various scripts, as well as that of nonliterates, on a variety of psychological tests, including classification (sorting), memory (free and incremental recall), and logical reasoning (syllogisms), as well as some tasks designed specifically for the project on the basis of an anthropological analysis of the skills involved in the use of each of the scripts.

The results showed consistent schooling effects on all but two of the tasks. The effects of the other types of literacies were much less systematic, indicating that literacy per se does not produce any general cognitive effect. Rather, the specific activities involved in the use of a particular script facilitated the development of closely related cognitive skills. For example, as we have already mentioned, Quranic schooling did not improve overall memory performance, but specifically incremental recall. Vai script literates performed well in a referential communication test, in which they had to describe a board game in its absence (but so did the schooled subjects). They also proved skillful at integrating auditory information (understanding sentences broken into syllables that were presented at a slow rate). When the sentences were presented word by word, they had no advantage over the other literates. This specific skill was attributed to the practice with a script without word or phrase division, in which reading implies strategies for integrating syllables into meaningful linguistic units.

Scribner and Cole provided no confirmation at all of Goody's hypothesis that literacy should produce new cognitive processes. Rather, certain forms of literacy promote very specific language processing and cognitive skills. On the other hand, the more general impact of schooling was confirmed once again. Note that even this very careful research design did not allow the researchers to distinguish clearly between the second and third interpretations mentioned above.

A partial replication of this study among the Cree of Northern Ontario was carried out by Berry and Bennett (1991). There, too, literacy was present in a form (a syllabic script) that is not associated with formal schooling. The Cree are functionally literate;

the script is less restricted than among the Vai because it is widely used by many people and for many purposes. However, it is restricted in the broader cultural senses noted by Scribner and Cole above. The results of this study also found no evidence for a general cognitive enhancement (assessed by an elaborated version of Raven's Progressive Matrices), but some evidence for abilities that involved the same mental operations (rotation and spatial tasks) that are important in using this particular script.

In the Berry and Bennett (1991) study, the interrelationships among test scores were examined, and all cognitive test performances were found to be positively intercorrelated. However, most of all they were found to be positively correlated with years of formal Western-style schooling, once again reminding us of the power of this acculturative influence.

Thus, in two studies on the effects of literacy, there is no evidence that a major shift in ways of thinking has taken place. The "watershed" view of the role of literacy in the course of human history thus has to be rejected, at least with respect to its effects on individual thought. Wagner (1993), in an extensive volume on literacy, comes to the same conclusion: "Today we know that the various communities of the contemporary world are so varied that simple dichotomies, such as literate versus illiterate, fail to capture the realities of the cultural practices that individuals engage in, whether schooled or unschooled" (p. 6).

However, the social and cultural consequences of literacy are not addressed by these studies, and Goody may be right as far as the sociohistorical part of his analyses is concerned: The invention of numbers, writing, later, of printing, and now the computer may have wide social and political consequences, even if the effects on individual cognitive processes cannot empirically be demonstrated.

EXPERIMENTAL ANTHROPOLOGY

We have discussed numerous studies conducted in many different parts of the world that dealt with diverse cognitive activities including classification, concept discovery, memory, logical thinking, and problem solving. Much of the research we have reviewed has been carried out, or has been inspired, by Michael Cole and his team, who concluded that "thus far there is no evidence for different *kinds* of reasoning processes such as the old classic theories alleged—we have no evidence for a 'primitive' logic" (Cole & Scribner, 1974, p. 170). And elsewhere (Cole et al., 1971): "Cultural differences in cognition reside more in the situations to which particular cognitive processes are applied than in the existence of a process in one cultural group and its absence in another" (p. 233).

This conclusion is based on a large array of studies by Cole's team, only a few of which have been sampled here, in what Cole was calling "experimental anthropology" (but that we acknowledge as an excellent example of cross-cultural psychology). This approach has also been called the "specific abilities" (Berry et al., 1992) or "specific skills" (Mishra, 1997) approach, and has been criticized for treating both

BOX 4.5 Estimating Amounts of Rice

The Kpelle have traditionally been upland rice farmers who sell surplus rice as a way to supplement their (very low) incomes. Upland rice farming is a marginal agricultural enterprise, and most villages experience what was called a "hungry time" in the two months between the end of their supply of food from the previous year and the harvesting of the new crop.

As might be expected from the centrality of this single crop to their survival, the Kpelle have a rich vocabulary for talking about rice. Of particular concern to us was the way in which they talked about amounts of rice because we had been told rather often that Kpelle "can't measure," and we wanted to test this in a domain of deep importance. John [Gay] discovered that their standard minimal measure for rice was a *kopi,* a tin can that holds one dry pint. Rice was also stored in *boke* (buckets), *tins* (tin cans), and *bags.* The kopi acted as a common unit of measure. It was said that there were twenty-four kopi to a bucket and forty-four to a tin, and that two buckets were equivalent to one tin. People claimed that there were just short of a hundred kopi to a *boro* (bag), which contained about two tins. The relationships between cups, buckets, tins, and bags are not exact by our standards, but they are close, and they reflect the use of a common metric, the cup.

We also learned that the transactions of buying and selling rice by the cup were slightly different in a crucial way. When a local trader bought rice, he used a kopi with the bottom pounded out to increase the volume in the container; when he sold rice, he used a kopi with a flat bottom. We surmised that this small margin of difference would make a big difference to people who refer to two months of the year as hungry time, so we decided to experiment on people's ability to estimate amounts of rice in a bowl, using the local measuring tool, the kopi.

Using these materials, we conducted a "backward" cross-cultural experiment, that is, an experiment modeled on our notion of Kpelle practices. The subjects in this case were eighty American working-class adults, twenty American schoolchildren aged 10 to 13, twenty Kpelle adults, and twenty Kpelle schoolchildren. Each subject was presented with four mixing bowls of equal size holding different amounts of rice (1½, 3, 4½, and 6 kopi), shown the tin to be used as the unit of measurement, and asked to estimate the number of tin cans (kopi) of rice in each bowl. Kpelle adults were extremely accurate at this task, averaging only one or two percent error. U.S. adults, on the other hand, overestimated the 1½-can amount by 30 percent and the 6-can amount by more than 100 percent. The U.S. schoolchildren were similar to the U.S. adults on the smallest amount and similar to the Kpelle schoolchildren for the other amounts.

These results supported our basic assumptions that people would develop cultural tools and associated cognitive skills in domains of life where such tools and skills were of central importance, as rice was central to Kpelle life. Whatever the cultural differences with respect to mathematics, a total lack of measurement concepts and skills was not one of them.

> In the rice estimation task we were able to create an experiment which incorporated not only local knowledge concerning content, such as the Kpelle system of units for amounts of rice, but also local procedures under which such estimates would be relevant: at markets one often encountered women selling rice from large bowls containing various amounts. Consequently, our task provided Kpelle people with both relevant content and relevant procedures.

The results mentioned in the text above are illustrated in Figure 4.7

(continued)

BOX 4.5   *Continued*

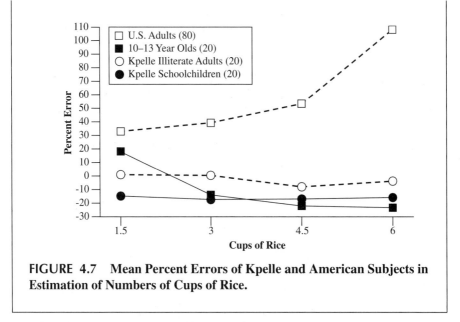

FIGURE 4.7   **Mean Percent Errors of Kpelle and American Subjects in Estimation of Numbers of Cups of Rice.**

Reproduced by permission from Cole (1996), pp. 75–76.

contexts and cognitive skills as if they were always fragmented, without any pattern or organization. Cognitive behavior appears as "context-bound"; it does not easily generalize across situations. For Jahoda (1980) this approach "appears to require extremely exhaustive and in practice almost endless exploration of quite specific pieces of behavior with no guarantee of a decisive outcome. This might not be necessary, if there were a workable 'theory of situations' at our disposal, but as Cole admits, there is none" (p. 126). In more recent writings, Cole has moderated the position somewhat. For example, he states that "skills and knowledge acquired in one setting often do appear in other settings under recognizably appropriate circumstances" (Laboratory of Comparative Human Cognition, 1983, p. 331). As we will see in Chapter 6, the debate about the transfer of cognitive skills continues to be heated.

Cole's (1996) retrospective assessment of the enterprise of experimental anthropology, and of cross-cultural psychology more generally, is rather scathing: "Its substantive offerings appear modest, and the evidence on which they are based is suspect" (p. 68). And further: "What we did not have was a systematic way of thinking about the relation between the psychological reality we created through our research practices and the psychological reality of people in their everyday practices" (p. 97). As we shall see in the following chapters, the sociohistorical approach stemming from Vygotsky's writings in general, and research on "everyday cognition" in particular (Chapter 6), are the current attempts to come closer to a culturally more sensitive (emic) study of culture and cognition.

Our own assessment of Cole's experimental anthropology is that it has been immensely useful in terms of methodology. Cole and his associates were always careful to start their research with an ethnographic study. What do people do in their daily lives that may be related to the cognitive skills under study? How could we design a task that is both relevant in its content and in its procedure? From the earliest research of Cole's team in Liberia (Gay & Cole, 1967), we still like the study in which participants were asked to estimate amounts of rice, using the local unit of a "cup." This is reproduced in Box 4.5 as summarized by Cole (1996, pp. 75–76).

CONCLUSION

In this chapter, we have come to understand human cognitive functioning as an active process dynamically influenced by cultural forces. All of us, everywhere, adapt to the world around us, using the same basic cognitive processes. Cultural diversity is marked in the way these processes are applied to specific contexts, depending on previous experience and current needs. Within any cultural setting, some individuals may be better equipped than others to apply their skills and strategies, and, across cultures, the preferred skills and strategies will vary. But everywhere, humans have found ways that work. The optimistic prediction, that we will continue to find new ways, as the old ways may prove less functional, is consistent with what we have seen.

Several of the studies we have reviewed in this chapter have been carried out quite some time ago, but it is still worthwhile knowing about them. Cross-cultural research on cognitive processes has accumulated a substantial body of knowledge, finally providing answers to some age-old questions. Of course we have not been able to mention all or even most of the ongoing research in this field. More information is available in review chapters (Liebing & Ohler, 1993; Mishra, 1997) and in a book edited by Altarriba (1993).

The point of departure for much of the research on cognition reported so far has been the use of tests, tasks, and experimental situations as they were first developed in Western psychology. This approach has its advantages, but it also has weaknesses: The kind of cognitive processes that are studied often bear little obvious relationship with daily life in the real world. In Chapter 6, we will examine a new trend common to both cross-cultural and mainstream psychology, namely the study of "everyday cognition" following the sociohistorical approach inspired by Vygotsky. First, however, we will turn, in Chapter 5, to the problems of studying competence and intelligence cross-culturally, and we will examine one of the classic theories of cognitive development, that of Jean Piaget, called "genetic epistemology."

5

ALTERNATIVE VIEWS ON HUMAN COMPETENCE: GENERAL INTELLIGENCE AND GENETIC EPISTEMOLOGY

Cognitive processes, which we covered in Chapter 3, involve general competence, often called *intelligence*. What constitutes intelligence has been debated endlessly in psychology. Adding a cross-cultural perspective complicates the picture further. Assuming that some people are more intelligent than others, psychologists have devised many methods in an attempt to measure individual differences in intelligence. Can this differential outlook be applied to social groups? Are some societies more intelligent than others?

In the late nineteenth and early twentieth century, most "scientists" as well as colonial administrators and lay people had an easy answer: Obviously, to them, Europeans were the most civilized and hence also the most intelligent! Social evolutionism was generally accepted. But some dissidents, like Lévy-Bruhl, claimed that there were differences not of quantity but of kind, and others, like Boas, argued for a "psychic unity of mankind." Europeans, from their earliest contacts with non-European societies, have felt a need to discover *how* non-Europeans think. They have long believed that "they, the primitives" don't think quite as rationally as "we, the civilized" do and that there is a form of thinking somehow adequately described as "primitive." To put it bluntly, many Westerners have thought that so-called primitive peoples are, simply, intellectually inferior.

Unfortunately, this is not an accident of history that has finally been expurgated. Some still believe in a "great divide" between "civilized" and "primitive." Many more reveal their implicit ethnocentrism by positing their own social group (often middle-class Western) as the standard against which others must "measure up." Even recent research in psychology and education, some of it cross-cultural, contains latent ethnocentric biases. Some ethnocentrism is almost inevitable, even in this chapter, because the very questions dealt with here are rooted in Eurocentric theorizing about cognition (Liebing & Ohler, 1993).

Ethnocentrism universally is a consequence of enculturation into any society, because each values its own ways of being and behaving. A positive feature of ethnocentrism is a sense of belonging; its negative aspects are derrogation and rejection of out-groups (Herskovits, 1948; Preiswerk & Perrot, 1975). Ethnocentrism is not unique to Europeans or Americans; it is pervasive worldwide, as we shall see in Chapter 10. However, here we are concerned with the particular manifestation of ethnocentrism wherein Europeans and Americans consider themselves to be intellectually superior to other groups.

Most cross-cultural research on cognition, as we have seen in the previous chapter, convincingly demonstrates the invalidity of the "superior, us versus inferior, them" worldview. The research shows that people in different cultural settings vary in the way they learn to solve problems and in the patterns of skills they acquire. Cultures vary in the salience attached to certain skills, in the combination of basic cognitive processes that are called on in any given context or in the order in which specific skills are acquired.

While abandoning the ethnocentric expectation of differences in the *levels* of cognitive activity, contemporary cross-cultural psychologists still expect *performance* differences on cognitive tasks and seek to understand how cognitive behavior in each setting is influenced by culturally-based experiences. We do not deny the existence of cultural differences in cognitive performance, but interpret them in the light of the cultural context in which people function. Some of our early predecessors failed to distinguish differences in performance from differences in competence, as we see from a brief history of research on culture and cognition.[1]

In this chapter, we start by examining some of these early debates, remnants of which are still with us. We then discuss the construct of "general intelligence," and the use of IQ tests to measure it. We will conclude that whatever "intelligence" is, we always rely on a particular sampling of skills to "measure" it. Therefore, the meaningful transfer of measuring scales across cultures is extremely difficult, often even impossible. Different societies consider varying sets of skills as constituting the general competence that would be translated as *intelligence*.

At the end of the chapter, we touch on the question of cultural differences in cognitive styles (but only lightly, because that topic is covered in more detail in

---

[1]The reader *Culture and Cognition,* edited by Berry and Dasen (1974) is still a handy source for historical material, as well as original studies in the field. See also Jahoda (1982, 1992; Jahoda & Krewer, 1997) for a detailed history of the intellectual forerunners of cross-cultural psychology, including the early influences on the cross-cultural study of intellectual performance.

Berry and colleagues, 1992). In more detail, we will consider the very influential theory of the development of intelligence formulated by Jean Piaget.

THE HISTORICAL LEGACY

Nineteenth-Century Social Evolutionism

After the publication of Darwin's *Origin of Species* (1859), the notion of unilinear social evolution was developed mainly by Tylor (1865), Spencer (1876), and Morgan (1877). It asserted that humanity had moved from savagery through barbarism to civilization via a series of stages, and that all social groups were subject to the same type of evolution, albeit at different speeds, with some societies being arrested at different levels along the way. The theory of social evolution suited the colonial imperialism of the time by "scientifically" justifying European conquest and domination.

In the social sciences, its influence was widespread. It also influenced Marxism to a large extent, especially via the writing of Engels. Much theory in developmental psychology reflects this evolutionary bias. Developmentalists have tended to think of development, *both* individual and social, as a kind of linear unfolding process. The development from childhood through adulthood was viewed as analogous to a development from "primitive" society to "civilization." The so-called recapitulation theory of Haeckel, namely, that "ontogeny recapitulates phylogeny," was a compelling model. Developmental psychologists such as Jean Piaget, Lev Vygotsky, Heinz Werner, and G. Stanley Hall (as well as Sigmund Freud and many others) were influenced by the dominant theory of social evolutionism, and occasionally assigned the "mental development" of non-Western peoples to a category that included children and mental patients.

Social evolutionism "justified" the racist view that non-Western peoples suffer from arrested development. If this idea were not so recurrently fashionable and if it were not reasserted by otherwise competent and respected scholars, it could be dismissed as ludicrous. But it is a very tenacious idea. Our inability to understand people from a different culture easily tends to be attributed to their "primitive," or childlike way of thinking.

Wilhelm Wundt and Franz Boas

Work in the philology tradition (essentially the comparative study of languages) gave rise in 1860 to the first cross-cultural journal, *Zeitschrift für Völkerpsychologie und Sprachwissenschaften,* edited by Steinthal and Lazarus, who were both linguists and psychologists. The term *Völkerpsychologie* had been introduced earlier in the nineteenth century by Wilhelm von Humboldt to refer to the study of what was later called *national character.* Wilhelm Wundt, in Leipzig, had established the first laboratory for experimental psychology in 1879, in which he studied elementary sensations and perception. To study what he called higher psychological functions, such as reasoning and language, Wundt argued for a second branch of psychology, calling it *Völkerpsychologie*. Under that name, he published a ten-volume opus between 1912 and 1921 (*Elements of Folk Psychology,* 1916, in English).

In the field of anthropology, Boas's *The Mind of Primitive Man* had just been published (in 1911). Both writers came out of a rigorous scientific background (Boas in physics and geography, and Wundt in linguistics, physiology, and experimental psychology), and both brought as much of this rigor as possible to the study of the "native mind." Surprisingly, perhaps, to the psychologist who often considers his experimental approach to be more rigorous than the anthropologist's field observational method, it is Boas's volume that is the clearer and less dated of the two. Boas asserted that "the possession of language, and the use of tools, and the power of reasoning" (pp. 96–97) distinguish humans from other animals. By implication, Boas may be said to consider that humans's uniqueness lies in their cognitive capacities rather than in their emotional or motivational life.

Wundt's translator ventured the opinion that "One may hazard the prophecy, that the final verdict of history will ascribe to his latest studies, those in folk psychology, a significance not inferior to that which is now generally conceded to the writings of his earlier years" (Wundt, 1916, p. vi). This prophecy turned out to be generally incorrect (Berry, 1983b; Danziger, 1983); much of Wundt's writing in this domain is not free of ethnocentrism, especially in his classification of cultures into four "ages": "Primitive Man," "The Totemic Age," "The Age of Heroes and Gods," and, finally, "The Development to Humanity."

For Wundt (1916), the intellectual capacities of "primitive man" had remained at a low level because of "the very meagre character of his external cultural possessions as well as his lack of any impulse to perfect these" (p. 110), but, like Boas, he declined to consider these to be intellectual *deficiencies:*

> *It is characteristic of primitive culture that it has failed to advance since immemorial times, and this accounts for the uniformity prevalent in widely separated regions of the earth. This, however, does not at all imply that within the narrow sphere that constitutes his world, the intelligence of primitive man is inferior to that of cultural man (p. 112).*

He concluded that:

> *The intellectual endowment of primitive man is in itself approximately equal to that of civilized man. Primitive man merely exercises his ability in a more restricted field; his horizon is essentially narrower because of his contentment under these limitations (p. 113).*

Wundt thus echoed the opinion of Boas that intellectual processes and competence are basically the same in "primitive" and "civilized" man. But the universality of thought processes soon came under attack from Lucien Lévy-Bruhl.

Lucien Lévy-Bruhl

The French sociologist Lévy-Bruhl (1910, 1922, 1949) characterized non-Western thought processes as "pre-logical." As was common in those days, Lévy-Bruhl did not do fieldwork himself, but relied mainly on the reports of travelers and missionaries. To Lévy-Bruhl, *pre*logical thought was not *a*logical, nor *anti*logical, nor even a reflection of a stage prior to logical thought, (despite the prefix *pre-*). Prelogical thought was characterized as a totally different worldview.

It is important to note that Lévy-Bruhl himself severely criticized the evolutionary views of Tylor and Frazer. Lévy-Bruhl used the word *primitive* because it was convenient and current at the time, but clearly stated that its usage as such was improper. If Lévy-Bruhl himself did not necessarily attach a lower value to the terms *pre-logical* and *primitive,* most of his readers did.

Prelogical thought, according to Lévy-Bruhl, was characterized by (1) the absence of a need to avoid contradiction, and (2) the "law of participation." To illustrate the first characteristic—the absence of a binary logic that does not admit contradiction—Lévy-Bruhl used an anecdote gleaned from a missionary's report. A South American Indian dreams that his neighbor is stealing one of his pumpkins. The next morning he searches for the neighbor and learns that he had been in a town some 150 kilometers distant for the past few days. For the Indian, however, this is not an alibi, and when the neighbor returns, he accuses him of the theft. According to Lévy-Bruhl, the Indian did not distinguish between dreaming and "reality," and he did not feel compelled to choose between incompatible alternatives.

Lévy-Bruhl's law of participation refers to an alleged confusion between human beings and objects or animals. In "totemic" societies, such as Australian Aborigines, people identify with a particular animal as their common ancestor in mythical times, performing rituals believed to ensure the continual existence of that particular species, and sometimes saying they "are" the animal. In Lévy-Bruhl's interpretation, they lack a clear sense of individual identity:[2]

> *Primitive mentality does not recognize an individual existence as such: individuals, human or otherwise, only exist inasmuch as they participate in their group and their ancestors.... To exist is to participate in a power, an essence, a mystical reality (1910, pp. 250–251; our translation).*

Many of Lévy-Bruhl's conclusions were based on the study of mystical or religious beliefs. This reflected the Zeitgeist of French sociology of his day, influenced by Durkheim, that considered the existence of social facts ("collective representations") as independent from individuals. Ignoring individual psychology, Lévy-Bruhl willingly inferred individual cognitive functions from collective representations. If

---

[2]Note that this issue is raised again in the current debate on individualism and collectivism (cf. Chapter 7).

logical thinking were assessed solely by examining Christian doctrine (e.g., a child born to a virgin), might it not, too, appear to be prelogical?

While Lévy-Bruhl (1910, p. 10) stated that "primitives perceive nothing in the same way as we do," he attributed this fundamental difference not to biology, but to environmental causes: "The social milieu which surrounds them differs from ours, and precisely because it is different, the external world they perceive differs from that which we apprehend" (p. 10). Lévy-Bruhl also described "primitive" mental activity as less differentiated, not purely intellectual, with emotional and motor elements always involved.

In a later work, published posthumously, Lévy-Bruhl (1949) reconsidered his positions somewhat, partly in response to severe attacks from anthropologists with field experience, including Boas and Malinowski. For example, he wrote "I should have said: primitives perceive nothing *exactly* in the same way as we do" (p. 245). He also acknowledged situational variability, admitting that the mystical orientation was not all pervasive, and that "primitive mentality, in everyday practical situations and in the technical domain, conforms to the laws of causality between phenomena observed sometimes with minute attention" (p. 244; our translation). However, he maintained, such thinking would become mystical, i.e., prelogical, in case of an accident or some other unusual event such as sickness.

The Psychic Unity of Mankind

The invention of the doctrine of the "psychic unity of mankind" is attributed to the nineteenth-century German scholars Adolf Bastian and Theodore Waitz, who stated that humanity as a whole shares a certain number of elementary ideas and concepts that account for the similarities in cultural traits that developed independently in widely different parts of the world (Jahoda, 1992). It was first stated in modern anthropology by Franz Boas (1911) and developed later by anthropologists such as Herskovits, Kroeber, Wallace, and Kluckhohn. In fact, it finds its origins in the eighteenth-century Enlightenment, in particular in the writings of Helvetius, Volney, and Turgot (Jahoda & Krewer, 1997).

The problem with this doctrine, according to Jahoda (1992), is that it has sometimes been associated with nineteenth-century cultural evolutionism as well as with its opponents. Among other interpretations of the phrase, one has it that, if psychological processes are postulated to be universal, it is unnecessary to carry out cross-cultural studies. In other words, the concept has been used in so many different ways as to have become useless. "Hence, we have the amazing paradox whereby one and the same principle is invoked by anthropologists who wish to claim that all that matters is culture, and by psychologists who want to argue that culture does not matter!" writes Jahoda (1992, p. 52)

In our understanding of the concept, universality cannot be postulated without empirical demonstration. As we have seen in the last chapter, and will find additional evidence in this one, the vast bulk of contemporary cross-cultural studies on intellectual performance seems to confirm Boas's early generalizations. However, claims for qualitative differences in thinking are continuing to be made, and are gaining new prominence with the advent of "cultural psychology."

Lévy-Bruhlian Revival and "Great Divide" Theories

Social evolutionism, as well as Lévy-Bruhl's theory, oversimplify and exaggerate contrasts, dividing the world into two parts: primitive and civilized. Several other such "great divide" theories have appeared since, and, indeed, keep appearing. For example, the British social anthropologist Evans-Pritchard (1971), although asserting that Lévy-Bruhl's conclusions about primitive mentality could no longer be accepted, bowed in the direction of a qualitative difference. He asserted that "much of the thought of primitive people [sic] is difficult, if not impossible, for us to understand" (p. 283). Lévi-Strauss (1962), while on the whole revealing the structural universality of mind, contrasts Western science with myth and sorcery; the "savage mind" is that of a "bricoleur," a jack-of-all-trades, using concrete signs instead of abstract concepts. Horton (1967a,b, 1982) similarly calls Western science an "open" system, as opposed to the "closed" African prescientific thought.

Despite the weakness of great divide theories, they keep turning up in different guises. A recent example is Bain's (1992) interesting attempt to analyze the reasons for the frequent misunderstandings that occur systematically in the communication between white and Australian Aboriginal communities, especially in economic affairs. According to Bain, Aboriginal society functions according to rules of *interaction* (authority and type of relationship based on kinship and friendship), while the dominant society distinguishes between personal interactions in the private sphere and rules of *transaction* (authority based on professional roles and expertise, formal rules of business relationships) in public affairs (business and employment, law, education). More generally, says Bain, the "thinking of preliterate peoples as contrasted with the thinking of literate, industrialised people" (p. 13) is concrete; it "remains no more than one step from what can be perceived through the senses" (p. 109). In other words it is based on observable fact, while Western thinking would be more abstract. The author is careful to point out that this is not a question of intellectual capacity, but an espistemological preference (possibly a cognitive style). Still, her analysis typifies great divide thinking.

The terms *primitive* and *civilized* having gone out of fashion, in more recent writings they are replaced by Western *versus* non-Western, or literate vs. illiterate, as we have seen in the last chapter. While it may occasionally be heuristically useful to build up such a contrasted typology, it always represents an oversimplification. The world is not that simple. Great divide theories are not restricted to the domain of human competence and cognition; a recent example in the study of values is the contrast between individualism and collectivism, which will be dealt with in Chapter 7.

GENERAL INTELLIGENCE

In a classic early study of social class and intelligence, Gordon (1923) studied a group of very poor people who eked out a livelihood on boats that plied the canals of England. The canal-boat children only irregularly attended school. Their lifestyle generated disdain on the part of members of the more affluent core culture. The canal-boat people were considered lazy and stupid, and their failure to behave like middle-class English was attributed to a basic lack of intelligence.

Gordon doubted that the canal-boat people's behavior reflected inherent deficiency in intelligence, so he set out to measure the IQ of the canal-boat children. Binet's IQ test had recently been translated into English. Using it, Gordon found an appallingly low average score equivalent to an IQ of 60. He also found a decline of IQ with age; the older the children, the "less intelligent" they appeared to be. Gordon was intrigued by this second finding because it suggested to him that their intellectual performance was subject to negative influences that accumulated with age. He concluded, then, that the children's test performances were more a reflection of the social and cultural conditions to which their canal-boat environment subjected them than a measure of their potential intellectual abilities.

The notion of *general intelligence* was elaborated by Spearman (1927), who pursued Galton's idea that there is an orderly mathematical relationship among all cognitive abilities: that is, they are positively intercorrelated. These positive correlations suggested to Spearman that there is a fundamental source of energy at work in all mental test performance, which he called *g* (for *general intelligence*).

Vernon (1969) proposed a hierarchical model that incorporates *g* and other factors, such as reasoning, verbal, figural, mathematical, and conceptual reasoning, at varying levels of increased specificity. In his empirical examinations of such a model cross-culturally, he claimed to find support for the existence of *g* and the other levels. Vernon (1969) called on Hebb's (1949) distinction between "Intelligence A" and "Intelligence B": The former is the genetic equipment and potentiality of the individual, while the latter is the result of its development through interaction with one's cultural environment (compare the *genotype–phenotype* distinction of geneticists). However, Vernon went further, introducing the notion of "Intelligence C," which he used to refer to the performance of an individual on a particular intelligence test. This distinction between intelligence B and C allows cross-cultural psychologists to consider the role of culture, because intelligence (B) may not be properly sampled or assessed by the test, yielding a performance (C) that does not represent the competence that is actually there. Numerous cultural factors (such as language, item content, motivation, and speed) may contribute to this discrepancy. It should be clear that testers are able only to obtain data that speak directly to intelligence C. Only by drawing inferences can researchers say something about Intelligence B, let alone Intelligence A.

For a long time (e.g., Maistriaux, 1955/1956; Porteus, 1937; Rushton, 1988) comparisons have been made of "Intelligence C" presuming them to be valid estimates of "Intelligence B," and then claims were made about fundamental differences in "Intelligence A" on this basis. Cross-cultural psychologists generally distance themselves from such faulty use of the "scientific" and comparative methods. The persistence of such comparisons may be explained only by a combination of ignorance of cross-cultural methods and of ethnocentrism on the part of such researchers. A rather extreme example of such racism in scientific disguise is given in Box 5.1.

Biesheuvel (1943) provided an early critique of this approach, distinguishing between mental competence and performance. Biesheuvel attributed differences between groups to the differential stimulation of the environment, and concluded:

> *Hence measures of intelligence, as indications of the power of mind, are strictly comparable only within homogeneous cultures. There is no possibility of comparing the ultimate intellectual capacity of different ethnic or cultural groups (Biesheuvel, 1959, p. 97).*

The Measurement of Intelligence

Just because a test is *called* an intelligence test does not guarantee that it is *measuring* intelligence. The point has been made by LeVine (1970, p. 581): "Standard intelligence tests measure [only] the current capacity of individuals to participate effectively in Western schools." Most psychologists accept this limitation on what an IQ test does. An IQ score is simply a shorthand expression for an individual's level of performance relative to other individuals on a sample of tasks chosen because they predict success in school and performance at the workplace quite well.

If we recall the history of IQ tests, we appreciate that they were originally meant to do *only* that. Binet constructed his test in response to a request from the Board of Education of Paris, which wanted to be able to detect in advance the children who were likely to fail. They asked for a test that would find those children who were unlikely to succeed in the school system. That's all the IQ test was designed to do. Despite the fact that people generally believe that IQ tests measure some internal quality called "intelligence," an IQ test is only a scholastic aptitude test.

That point is well known and widely accepted, at least by psychologists. But the second point, that an IQ test applied in a culture other than the one in which it was developed may not even measure scholastic aptitude, needs also to be understood. It is now well known that IQ tests are biased against those whose cultural background differs from that of the test's original normative sample. Early evidence of IQ tests' cultural bias in the United States was reviewed by Klineberg (1954). Studies had shown that, for Northern urban African Americans born in Southern rural settings, there was a positive correlation between length of time in the North and IQ scores. Clearly, the more exposure to the kind of culture in which the tests were first developed, the better the performance on the tests. As far back as 1927, Herskovits commented:

> *Environmental background, cultural as well as natural, plays a tremendous part in whatever manifestations of innate intelligence an individual may*

BOX 5.1   Racism in Scientific Disguise

In the latter part of the nineteenth century, racism was the accepted ideology even among scientists, whose statements were justifying the European exploitation of colonies. Sir Francis Galton had established a "classification of men according to their natural gifts," in which the Greeks were rated two grades above Englishmen, and African Negroes two grades below (Jahoda & Krewer, 1997). Claiming allegiance to Galton's "London School," Rushton (1895), in a book entitled *Race, evolution and behavior,* established a scheme in which he distinguished three main races: Orientals, Whites, and Blacks.

According to Rushton, the relative ranking of these races on many different variables produced a systematic pattern, in which Orientals came out on top, Blacks at the bottom, and Whites in-between. For example, endocranial volume, averaged over large samples, followed this sequence, and so did the intelligence that goes with brain size. Blacks were found to be precocious in various indices of maturation, Whites being intermediate, and Orientals showing a much slower maturation rate. At the same time, Blacks had the shortest life span and Orientals the longest. Along went modal personality, Blacks being more impulsive and aggressive, and Orientals calm and cautious. Blacks were also found to have a lower mental health, and a higher record of criminality.

Rushton explained this pattern through genetic differences that represent adaptations to evolutionary pressures. The first stages of *Homo sapiens,* he thought, had evolved in Africa, and Blacks remained at the level of "archaic sapiens" because of an undemanding warm climate; "modern sapiens" evolved when part of the population moved out of Africa into the Middle East, about 110,000 years ago, and the Caucasoid/Mongoloid split occurred 41,000 years ago, when part of that population moved into more demanding colder climates. "The Caucasoid and Mongoloid peoples who evolved in Eurasia were subjected to pressures for improved intelligence to deal with the problems of survival in the cold northern latitudes" (p. 228). Indeed, "the cognitive demands of manufacturing sophisticated tools and making fires, clothing, and shelters...would have selected for higher average intelligence levels than in the less cognitively demanding environment in sub-Saharan Africa" (p. 229). As Jahoda (1995) has shown, climate was considered as a main explanatory variable at that time, and still enjoys some currency today.

Comparing various species of animals and plants, biologists had established two types of "reproductive strategies." Some organisms produce a large number of offspring, but spend little effort in parental care (e.g., oysters, fish, and frogs), others take the opposite strategy of producing only a few young, sometimes only one or two, but taking good care of them, for example in terms of educational investment (great apes, humans). Rushton applied this scheme to his three races of humanity, claiming that, while they all clustered around the second type of strategy, Blacks were relatively closer to the first. Indeed, he claimed, Blacks have a higher breeding rate, but lower marital stability; they also show a higher rate of reproductive effort, shown by hormone levels, size of genitalia, and intercourse frequencies. They are sexually more permissive, and have higher rates of sexually transmitted diseases, all this in opposition to Orientals, who have the lowest, while Whites are intermediate.

Continued

BOX 5.1   *Continued*

This scheme makes perfectly good sense in terms of what is called "inclusive fitness," a combination of personal reproductive success and that of genetic relatives. According to this theory, "an organism is just a gene's way of making another gene.... Because certain gene combinations will be reproductively more successful than others in a particular environment, they will increase in relative number in the population. An organism's body and behavior are mechanisms by which genes maintain and replicate themselves more efficiently" (Rushton, 1895, p. 200).

* * *

The above account is an accurate summary of Rushton's theory, one of the most extreme forms of sociobiology. To tell the truth, only one single digit has to be changed; in fact, Rushton's book was published in 1995, not 1895!

There is no need for us to demonstrate here how Rushton's version of a great divide theory is, in our view, completely mistaken, and represents only racism in scientific disguise.

---

give us through...standardized tests.... Thus it has been found that the American Indians usually rate somewhat lower in psychological tests than whites, and that this holds true when the tests are of a nonlanguage variety, where the use of words is reduced to a minimum. But the consideration of the fact that the tests ordinarily used have been constructed by persons of a background different from that of the subjects is usually overlooked; and were there to be presented, for consideration as to what is wrong with a given picture, a six-clawed bear rather than a net-less tennis court, one wonders whether the city-dwelling white might not be at a loss rather than the Indians (p. 3).

Over the decades since Herskovits warned that intergroup differences in intelligence test scores might tell more about the tests than about the groups, attempts have been made to produce "culture-free" or "culture-fair" IQ tests, but none of these has been successful. Clearly, culturally mediated experience *always* interacts with test content to influence test performance.

By definition, a culture-*free* test would actually measure some inherent quality of human capacity equally well in all cultures (Frijda & Jahoda, 1966). There can be no such test. A test featuring a set of items that are equally unfamiliar to all possible people in all possible cultures, so everyone would have the same probability of passing the items, would be a culture-*fair* test. But this is a virtual impossibility. Alternatively, a culture-fair test could consist of multiple sets of items, modified for use in each culture to ensure that each version of the test would contain the same amount of familiarity. These would be culture-specific tests and members of each culture would have about the same probability of being able to deal with one version of it. Such culture-fair tests are possible in theory, but, in practice, they are difficult to construct.

The root of all measurement problems in cross-cultural research is the possibility that the same behaviors may have different meanings across cultures or that the same processes may have different overt manifestations. As a result, the "same" test, be it a psychometric one or another type of instrument, might be "different" when applied in different cultures. Therefore, the effort to devise culture-fair testing procedures will probably never be completely successful. The degree to which we are measuring the same thing in more than one culture, whether we are using the same or different test items, will always worry us.

In the long run, of course, we will acquire confidence that we are measuring truly comparable phenomena if we accumulate evidence that they relate to other variables in a predictable, understandable fashion. But, until such evidence has been accumulated, we cannot be sure of the comparability of what we are measuring when we apply a test—any test—in more than one culture. (A more technical treatment of these methodological problems, including the means to overcome test bias, is provided by Berry et al., 1992, and van de Vijver & Leung, 1997.)

The importance of this problem depends somewhat on the purpose for which performance scores in any test are accumulated and the interpretation made of those scores (Vernon, 1969). When we are not disposed to interpret performance differences as manifestations of inherent qualities of personality, the problem is less severe. An example is the use of an aptitude test to select workers who will require the least amount of training to perform a task. However, even here we might not get a valid assessment if the testing procedure itself somehow inhibits the people being tested from displaying their current skills. Moreover, the practice of using tests for selection purposes, enabling employers to discriminate against particular groups of potential employees, might be profoundly culturally unacceptable.

One factor that has not yet been mentioned is acculturation. Education (a frequent indicator of acculturation because it is usually formal Western-style schooling) has often been identified as having a role in the distribution of intelligence test scores; it is common to find "years of schooling" to be the single best predictor of test scores in many studies. The reason for finding a single factor in the analysis of cognitive test performance may not be within the person's cognitive apparatus, but due to a common experience of formal Western-style schooling.

Are There "Racial" Differences in Intelligence?

Differences in cognitive competence have sometimes been attributed to genetic ("racial") instead of cultural factors. The issue of so-called racial differences in IQ scores was hotly debated during the 1970s in the United States, giving rise to the "Jensen controversy" (Jensen, 1969, 1981), reaching also Britain (e.g., Eysenck, 1971) and France (Hebert, 1977). The debate was revived by Herrnstein and Murray's (1994) book *The Bell Curve,* leading to a renewed controversy (Fraser, 1995;

Jacoby & Glauberman, 1995), compounded as well by the most extreme commentator, Rushton (1995).

To raise the issue of the heritability of intelligence is a perfectly reasonable scientific question that should not be condemned for the sole reason that it is not politically correct. Unfortunately, the issue tends to take an ideological stance. Research on so-called racial differences in intelligence has a long and distressing history. Much of the discourse has been sloppy, irrational, politically motivated, and extremely costly in human terms. In multicultural societies where "whites" have been politically and economically dominant and "blacks" and other "nonwhites" have long been targets of discrimination, some of the most pernicious and inhumane discriminatory acts have been justified on the basis of the erroneous belief in "racial" differences in intelligence.

In the United States, for example, as Gould (1981) has compellingly recalled, biological determinism permeated not only popular belief but much of scientific thought, including the field of psychometrics; it went almost unchallenged up to the 1950s, and was used to justify eugenic policies. Gould's history of this sad chapter in psychological thinking provides critical accounts of studies that allegedly revealed cross-"racial" differences in brain size, in which the data were without doubt distorted by the biased expectations of the researchers. Gould also described programs of legally enforced sterilization operations performed without consent or even awareness on women who scored low on IQ tests. Gould's account of this program, legally mandated in at least one state in the United States as recently as 1972, illustrates dramatically the extreme implications that can flow from the naive belief that intelligence is biologically determined and that test performance accurately reflects it.

Herrnstein and Murray (1994) argue that in the United States, IQ is more highly correlated than socioeconomic status to a series of negative social outcomes, such as school failure, unemployment, poverty, welfare dependency, crime, unwed motherhood, and so on. This they interpret to mean that there is a "cognitive underclass" that is genetically determined, and hence immutable, out of reach of public policy for any improvement. The authors worry about "dysgenesis," the decline of average IQ by one or two points in each generation because of differential fertility rates between unprivileged and privileged women. "The case is strong that something worth worrying about is happening to the cognitive capacity of the country" they state (p. 364) in reference to the United States. They therefore suggest a number of policy changes, such as a more elitist educational system, giving up affirmative action, immigration laws stressing competency rather than what they call nepotistic rules (for the reunification of relatives), and denial of federal assistance for unwed mothers. These policy issues are certainly worthy of political debate, but it is a fallacy to claim a scientific justification for their implementation.

In the introduction to their book, Herrnstein and Murray review three conceptions of intelligence that they attribute to the factions of the "classicists" (those who believe in IQ tests, a large general factor of intellectual ability or *g,* and a 40 percent to 80 percent heritability of intelligence), the "revisionists" (Piaget, and those interested in processes of thought, such as Sternberg [1988] and his triarchic theory of intelligence), and the "radicals" (like Gardner [1983] and his multiple intelligences). Herrnstein and Murray opt for the first of these conceptions, and clearly state premises that they consider to be "beyond significant technical dispute" (p. 22), for example, that "properly administered IQ tests are not demonstrably biased against social, economic, ethnic, or racial groups" or that "IQ scores are stable, although not perfectly so, over much of a person's life" (p. 23).

In relation to these premises, Gould (1995) remarks:

> *Intelligence, in their [Herrnstein and Murray's] formulation, must be depictable as a single number, capable of ranking people in linear order, genetically based, and effectively immutable. If any of these premises are false, their entire argument collapses. For example, if all are true except immutability, then programs for early intervention in education might work to boost IQ permanently, just as a pair of eyeglasses may correct a genetic defect in vision. The central argument of The Bell Curve fails because most of the premises are false (pp. 12–13).*

That the premises are false is demonstrated with ample evidence by many contributions in the volume edited by Fraser (1995). For example, on the technical grounds of statistics, Gould (1995) as well as Gardner (1995) remark that the reported correlations are very weak, in the 0.2 to 0.4 range, so that they explain at the most 16 percent of the variance. Even accepting the authors' estimate of a 60 percent heritability of IQ, they argue, means that less than 10 percent of the variance can be attributed to genetics.

Wolfe (1995, p. 122) captures very well what is, in our view, the summary of the debate: "Herrnstein and Murray find a strong relationship between race and IQ, but neither race nor IQ are strong phenomena. A strong relationship between weak variables is a weak relationship."

Reasons for rejecting the genetic explanations are many, and were asserted a long time ago (e.g., Segall, 1976):

1. However much genetic factors may contribute to intellectual performance of people *within* any group, between-group differences may still be entirely produced by nongenetic factors. The point that between-group and within-group IQ heritability estimates are totally independent of each other was first made by Scarr-Salapatek (1971)—a compelling agricultural analogy:

> *Draw two random samples of seeds from the same genetically heterogeneous population. Plant one sample in uniformly good conditions, the other in uniformly poor conditions. The average height difference between the populations of plants will be entirely environmental although the individual differences...within each sample will be entirely genetic (p. 1286).*

2. IQ is more influenced by environmental factors among some groups than among others. In other words, the within-group heritability of IQ is not the same for all groups.

3. The environmental factors that are known to depress IQ scores are far more prevalent for groups with lower average scores.

4. Negative biasing factors inherent in the tests themselves apply far more to the very groups who have been maligned as "racially inferior" than to those who score high and prefer to think of all scores as revealing inherent capacity.

5. Recent research in genetics shows that interindividual variation in genes is much larger than intergroup variation (see Chapter 1).

The idea of a single measure such as an IQ implies the existence of a universal general intelligence. As Sternberg (1988) shows, the range of positions in this regard is wide, ranging from radical cultural relativism (Berry, 1972), through a variety of intermediate, more or less contextualist positions (such as LCHC, 1982), to the extreme biometric fundamentalism of Jensen (1988) and Eysenck (1988), "who hold that intelligence is the same thing from one culture to another, regardless of what difference there may be in customs and patterns of functioning. Eysenck, for example, would relate intelligence to *accuracy* of neuronal conduction, whereas Jensen would relate it to *speed* of neuronal conduction" (Sternberg, 1988, p. 63). In these absolutist positions, the construct, related to neuronal makeup, is universal, but individuals and groups differ quantitatively in the amount of intelligence. Contrary to this view, we conclude that the evidence is against intelligence as a single entity, but we also reject the view that intelligence consists of unrelated specific aptitudes. We prefer to think of groups of cognitive functions, constituting "cognitive styles," which relate to certain ecocultural variables.

Earlier in this book, we asserted that no behavior is determined solely by culture or solely by biology. The two major classes of behavioral determinants always operate in such an interactive manner that they are difficult to separate. For intelligence, as for any other human characteristic, biological factors provide a broad range of potential and the outer limits or constraints of that potential, but experience has much room to operate within those limits.

The main point is that biological determinism, whether in the IQ debate or in some of the sociobiology discussed in Box 5.1, attempts to explain complex behavior in simple, indeed simpleminded terms. Throughout this book, we will discover that a simple answer is almost always sure to be wrong; when we deal with human behavior, we must deal with complexity.

DEFICIENCY *VERSUS* DIFFERENCE INTERPRETATIONS OF COGNITIVE ACHIEVEMENT

It is beyond dispute that large differences in accomplishment exist between cultural groups, and between socioeconomic groups within complex industrial societies, in skills that are highly valued by the dominant cultures or subcultures: success in school, in speaking the dominant language "correctly," in competing for jobs, in gaining social status, recognition, and political power. But to interpret these achievement differences there are two competing models that have implications for strategies to be used (if any) for intervention. These two quite different worldviews can be labeled the "deficit or deficiency" model and the "difference" model, described by McShane and Berry (1988) as "D-models."

For the *deficit model,* McShane and Berry (1988) identified, in addition to the *genetic and physiological deficits* proposed by some, individual *deprivation* (poverty, poor nutrition, and health), cultural *disorganization* (a group-level version of deprivation in which whole cultural groups experience the deculturation and marginalization that will be discussed in Chapter 11), and *disruption* (or uprooting, leading to maladjustment and loss of coping skills). In contrast to these deficit explanations a number of *difference* models were identified that do not share the negative value-laden character of the deficit models. Instead, it is assumed that processes and levels of competence are widely shared across cultural groups; performance differences arise because of cultural or other differences in the way these underlying qualities are expressed.

Many cross-cultural psychologists (such as Vernon and Irvine) who espouse the general intelligence notion use a differentiated set of cultural experiences to account for variations in intelligence test performance. For Vernon (1969, p. 230), these factors include: perceptual and kinesthetic experience; varied stimulation (including play); "demanding" but "democratic" family climate; linguistic and conceptual stimulation (for example, books, travel); absence of magical beliefs; tolerance of nonconformity in the family; regular and prolonged schooling; positive self-concept; and broad cultural and other leisure interests that provide varied experience.

The Deficit Interpretation

Cole and Bruner (1971) were the first to seriously deal with the implications of the two approaches, followed by Howard and Scott (1981), as well as others (e.g., McShane, 1983). Here is how Cole and Bruner (1971) aptly summarized the most prevalent view of the source of ethnic and social class differences in intellectual performance, the "deficit hypothesis":

> *It rests on the assumption that a community under conditions of poverty...is a disorganized community, and this disorganization expresses itself in various forms of deficit. One widely agreed-upon source of deficit is mothering; the child of poverty is assumed to lack adequate parental attention. Given the illegitimacy rate in the urban ghetto, the most conspicuous 'deficit' is a missing father and, consequently, a missing father model. The mother is away at work or, in any case, less involved with raising her children than she should be by white middle-class standards. There is said*

to be less regularity, less mutuality in interaction with her. There are said to be specialized deficits in interaction as well—less guidance in goal seeking from the parents, less emphasis upon means and ends in maternal instruction, or less positive and more negative reinforcement.

More particularly, the deficit hypothesis has been applied to the symbolic and linguistic environment of the growing child. His or her linguistic community as portrayed in the early work of Basil Bernstein (1961), for example, is characterized by a restricted code, dealing more in the stereotype of interaction than in language that explains and elaborates on social and material events. The games that are played by poor children and to which they are exposed are less strategy-bound than those of more advantaged children; their homes are said to have a more confused noise background...and the certainty of the environment is sufficiently reduced so that children have difficulty in delaying reinforcement or in accepting verbal reinforcement instead of the real article (pp. 876–877).

The social science literature dealing with poverty-stricken populations and minority ethnic groups, especially in the United States, contains many such descriptions. "They imply failure or inability to behave in an appropriate way and so imply social and personal deficits" (Howard & Scott, 1981, p. 113). There are a host of characteristics that seem to occur together, that are part of a system, a subculture, sometimes described as the "culture of poverty" (Lewis, 1966). "It would be helpful to think of the subcultures of poverty as the zero point on a continuum which leads to the working class and middle class" (Lewis, 1969, p. 190, quoted in Howard & Scott, 1981, p. 116). In other words, the culture of poverty is defined only in negative terms, as what is lacking of the middle-class features, as "cultural deprivation."

Just as "primitive mentality" served as a rationalization of colonial domination, the "culture of poverty" concept and the deficiency model can serve to foster blame for economic deprivation on the poor themselves. "The poor are less intelligent—otherwise they wouldn't be poor—and they transmit their inferior genes to their offspring" is not an uncommon opinion that links the deficit hypothesis to theories of biological determinism such as those of Herrnstein and Murray (1994) and Rushton (1995).

Of course such a model also has implications for the choice of intervention policies: Because something is lacking, it has to be supplied from outside (like giving food to the malnourished); the deficits have to be compensated. The intervention models that match the deficit hypothesis are therefore "early stimulation" and "compensatory education." Early stimulation and compensatory education programs have both positive and negative features, just as the programs have both advocates and critics. Advocates stress the evidence that such programs (often preschool programs) often do provide the "headstart" that poorer children might not otherwise get. One class of critics, reflecting a genetic determination bias, argue that compensatory programs do not work because interventions cannot influence genetic differences. Another more subtle and compelling kind of criticism notes that, in the intellectual sphere, these models usually mean practice in middle-class standard language, practice in using abstractions, and sometimes providing a setting that allows self-initiated discovery. As Howard and Scott (1981) have phrased it:

> *Perhaps the ultimate conclusion to which one is drawn is that the deficiency perspective, by labeling people as incompetent, tends to generate remedial structures that perpetuate powerlessness and dependence, thereby validating the initial judgments (p. 147).*

While there had been a number of unfavorable early evaluations of Head Start and similar enrichment programs, more recent longitudinal research has shown significant and lasting positive effects. A summary of this research is provided by Kagitçibasi (1996), who also conducted her own Early Childhood Care and Education programs in Turkey. Both preschool-based programs and nonformal adult education programs showed wide-ranging significant effects.

The Difference Model

The proponents of the difference model criticize the way in which social science research with minority groups has been done, namely by starting with the "imposed etic" of the dominant group (McShane & Berry, 1988), and studying only the skills that are valued by the dominant subculture; using a methodology (such as psychometric tests) that has been developed in and for the dominant subculture may be inappropriate and may put minority groups at a disadvantage. They also claim that differences in aptitudes have been artificially exaggerated, that they are artifacts of testing, that they are more superficial than real, that is, at the level of "performance" rather than at the level of "competence" (in one of the formulations we shall come to later in this chapter), or in "content" rather than in "process."

> *The crux of the argument, when applied to the problem of 'cultural deprivation,' is that those groups ordinarily diagnosed as culturally deprived have the same underlying competence as those in the mainstream of the dominant culture, the differences in performance being accounted for by the situations and contexts in which the competence is expressed (Cole & Bruner, 1971/1974, p. 238).*

Alternatively, without denying that differences exist, one could interpret these in a nonevaluative fashion. Differences are just that: differences, not deficits. Then the researcher must look for those skills and values that the subculture chooses for itself, taking an emic approach. For example, Gallimore (1981) found in Hawaii that industriousness (for example school achievement) in Hawaiian American children is linked to the expressed need to affiliate with a social group rather than with individual competitiveness and achievement, as it is in Anglo-Americans. Cole and Bruner (1971) cited Labov (1970), who demonstrated that African American "ghetto language," if appropriately observed, displays the same grammatical competence as middle-class Standard English, but according to its own rules rather than being a deviation from the "norm."

The difference model may also be criticized. While the model itself may be correct in recognizing that minority groups have their own strengths, they are nevertheless confronted practically with a world in which only the behaviors valued by the dominant social group are rewarded by economic and status benefits: In practice, then, they must learn the tricks, or else remain marginal (and poor), and remedial programs are needed to help them learn those tricks. For example, de Lacey and Poole (1979) conclude a volume on the Australian situation in the following way: "In the pragmatic bread-and-butter world, the reality has to be faced: it is the Anglo-Australian majority that is likely, naturally enough, to call the linguistic and cultural tune. Let us be realistic enough to acknowledge this and to plan, educationally and socially, accordingly" (p. 390).

But a difference interpretation need not imply ignoring policies designed to secure a more equitable distribution of wealth. Quite the contrary, that the poor are poor or the minorities economically less successful is not questioned, but is attributable to the social organization of the complex society and its political structure, rather than to any inherent incompetence. Programs based on the difference model will therefore acknowledge the need for structural social changes. Without them, little will be accomplished. Some pluralistic societies are attempting to change their institutions (education, work legislation, health care, etc.) to diversify the value systems taken into account.

Such policies may also include the transfer of specific cognitive skills needed to cope with the demands of the dominant social environment. The most important aspect of programs of this kind is that they attempt to build on the group's own strengths, autonomy, and cultural identity. Becoming more competent in its own context allows the group to become more competent also in the dominant social environment (Feuerstein, 1980).

This examination of the plight of minority groups in complex societies may seem a digression. However, the study of ethnic groups, minority subcultures, immigrants, refugees, and so on is an integral part of cross-cultural psychology. Also, it will become obvious in subsequent chapters that the issues raised here are basically the same whether we deal with subcultures in larger societies or with different societies, because many cultural groups are at the periphery (the "third" world) in relation to a dominant and acculturating center. In each particular case, the historical context of dominant–minority group relations has to be taken into account, a topic we shall cover in greater detail in Chapter 10, on intercultural relations, and Chapter 11, on acculturation.

Culture-Specific Definitions of Intelligence

In this section, we will examine the "indigenous" or popular definitions of intelligence in different societies, or what we might call the "social representations of intelligence." This is an example of a parental ethnotheory of human development that we discussed in Chapter 3.

Bisilliat, Laya, Pierre, and Pidoux (1967) did the first study of this topic among the Djerma-Songhai in Niger in West Africa. They investigated the concept *lakkal,* a term that translates into English as intelligence, and that means simultaneously understanding, know-how, and social conformity. *Lakkal* is a gift of God, present at birth, but invisible before about age 7. In fact, parents do not use an age criterion; they say that *lakkal* should be there once the child knows how to count to ten. If children don't have *lakkal* by then, they never will, although a traditional healer can administer certain treatments to increase it. A child who has *lakkal* has a good understanding of many things, has a good memory, is obedient, does rapidly or even spontaneously what is expected, and displays respect toward elders. Thus, this concept has at least two dimensions, one of them concerning aptitude and know-how, and the other, social competence.

Among the Baganda (in Uganda, East Africa), Wober (1974) studied a similar term, *obugezi,* which refers equally to wisdom and to social skills. To Baganda villagers, *obugezi* is slow, stable, cautious, and friendly, while to school children and urban-dwelling Baganda in the capital city, Kampala, it has connotations similar to those of the English term *intelligence.*

Mundy-Castle (1974), in a theoretical article, distinguished two dimensions of an African definition of *intelligence,* technological and social; we would now say individualistic and collectivistic (see Chapter 7). In the Western world the first has been emphasized at the expense of the second, largely through the influence of writing. In Mundy-Castle's view, literacy allows an impersonal objectivity and the kind of analytic thinking that is the basis of technological development because it involves the manipulation of objects and control of the environment. Social intelligence, on the other hand, involves "being" more than "having," and interpersonal relations more than relations with objects. It is a dimension of intelligence that involves "the art of the soul," to which traditional education in Africa attached primary importance.

Mundy-Castle hypothesized that, in Africa, these two dimensions are integrated, with the technological integrated into the social dimension. For example, school-based knowledge would not be part of intelligence unless it could be put to practical use in the service of the social group rather than for individual gain. Mundy-Castle attributed the origin of this social intelligence to the socialization emphases present in this part of Africa during early childhood, particularly the way mothers interact with their babies through body contact, without involving objects as intermediaries (see also Rabain [1979; Rabain-Jamin, 1994], who confirms this observation). The social dimension of the African definition of intelligence is well confirmed by a large number of studies in Africa, reviewed by Berry (1984b), Dasen, Dembélé, Ettien, Kabran, Kamagaté, Koffi, and N'guessan (1985), and Serpell (1989, 1993); in the current fashion of contrasting individualism and collectivism (see Chapter 7), these social definitions are congruent with a collectivistic value system. A social dimension in the definition of intelligence also occurs in other parts of the world, for example among indigenous groups in North America (Berry & Bennett, 1991), in Malaysia (Gill & Keats, 1980), and China (Keats, 1982).

Serpell (1977, 1993) studied the social representations of intelligence among the Chewa of Zambia and constructed tests specifically for this population: imitating hand positions, copying a human figure with iron wire or with clay, a verbal comprehension test in Chi-Chewa; he also used a foreign, nonverbal psychometric test of general aptitude. There were no significant correlations between the results of these tests and adult evaluations of children's intelligence. Serpell concluded that these tests, because they consisted solely of cognitive aptitudes, did not measure what the Chewa themselves define as intelligence, cooperation and obedience.

In light of these results, we may hypothesize that there is no relationship between this African conception of intelligence and the results of Piagetian tests at the level of concrete operations (see last part of this chapter). Dasen and associates (1985; Dasen, 1984) set out to test this question by exploring the concept of *n'glouèlê* among the Baoulé in Côte d'Ivoire. As elsewhere in sub-Saharan Africa, this concept certainly has a social dimension to which the more technological or cognitive dimension is subordinate. The components of the definition of *n'glouèlê* are listed in Table 5.1.

Among the different components of this concept, the most frequently mentioned one is *ô ti kpa* or a willingness to help. Children have more *n'glouèlê* if they voluntarily offer services and carry their share of both domestic and agricultural tasks. This is not a question simply of obeying when an adult demands a service; the task has to be carried out well, spontaneously, and responsibly. For example, Baoulé adults describe a child who is *ô ti kpa* as "one who helps parents instead of playing with friends," "one who does the dishes and other chores without parents telling him or her to do so," or they might illustrate the concept with the following anecdote: "When I leave my daughter with her brothers in the village, and when she notices that the children are hungry she prepares porridge for them, and picks up her baby sister and puts her on her back when she cries."

As we have seen in Chapter 3, the importance of a readiness to carry out tasks in the service of the family and the community has been reported in several studies in Africa. Super (1983) provided the following example given by a Kipsigi woman in Kenya: "A girl who is *gnom* after eating sweeps the house because she knows it should be done. Then she washes the dishes, looks for vegetables, and takes good care of the baby" (p. 202).

Among the components that Dasen and colleagues (1985) consider "technological" is *I sa si n'glouèlê* (manual dexterity), which is translated literally as "the hands

TABLE 5.1   *N'glouèlê:* **Its Components and Their Meanings**

Social components	
O ti kpa	Obligingness, responsibility, initative, know-how, obedience, honesty
Agnyhiè	Politeness, obedience, respect
O si hidjo	To retell a story (or an event) with precision: verbal memory; to speak in a socially appropriate way Adults: to speak well in public, to know how to use proverbs
Angundan	To act like an adult Reflection, responsibility, memory Adults: wisdom
Technological components	
I gni ti klè klè	"The eyes follow everything" Observation, attention, fast learning, memory
O si floua	"To know papers" Literacy, school intelligence
I ti ti kpa	Memory (especially for school) To be lucky, to bring luck
I sa si n'glouèlê	Manual dexterity At school: writing and drawing

are intelligent." For the Baoulé, manual dexterity is not independent of the intellect, as sometimes seems to be the case in Western culture. *O si floua* (school-based intelligence) is a part of *n'glouèlê* only insofar as scholarly accomplishments are employed for the good of the group. On the whole, these facts confirm Mundy-Castle's (1974) hypothesis that different components of intelligence in Africa are integrated into a concept that includes both a social dimension and a technological dimension, with the latter subordinated to the former.

Some years later, a similar study was carried out by Schurmans and Dasen (1992; Fournier, Schurmans, & Dasen, 1995) in a small village in the Swiss Alps. The location was chosen because that area had remained fairly remote and traditional until recently, and, even nowadays, the people wear their traditional costume and speak their own language, an old form of French, called *patois.* While schooling occurs in French, and all the communication with the outside world is done in French, amongst themselves the villagers use the patois even with young children. Dairy farming is the main form of subsistence, along with tourism, and children are involved in the family enterprise with various chores. Schurmans and Dasen hypothesized that the parents involved in farming, being closer to the more traditional way of life, would provide a more social definition of intelligence than those employed in the modern sector.

The researchers first used interviews in French with parents, who were asked "How does one recognize, according to you, whether a child of about nine years is intelligent?" Some categories of answers that had not occurred in the previous research had to be added, such as "to stay modest" (which was classified as social) or "logical reasoning" (classified as technological), but, overall, the classification scheme derived from the study in Côte d'Ivoire could be used. All of the parents, whether farmers or not, whether young (defined in this project as 25 to 68 years) or old (75 and above), provided mainly technological definitions. This confirmed that they were following the common Western conception of intelligence (see Table 5.2).

However, when the informants were asked to sort cards, half of which presented social descriptions, the young farmers, and even more so the elderly people, shifted to choosing more social items. In other words, the card-sorting technique allowed them to express social representations more in tune with the traditional, collectivistic way of life. Two or three years later, some of the people were interviewed again, but in patois. For the younger people, whether they be farmers or not, this made no difference, but the elderly switched to a predominantly social definition of intelligence. The local language linked their social representations to the past.

As we have now seen, intelligence is not defined in the same way in different societies or even subgroups of a society. The Baoulé definition is very broad, and includes features that psychologists usually label as aspects of personality, so that the constructs are not comparable psychometrically. In any case, it would not come to our minds to measure the intelligence of the Swiss with a scale derived from Baoulé emics, just as we have refuted the appropriateness of using IQ tests to measure the intelligence of the Baoulé.

IQ tests are constructed on a purely empirical basis, as a collection of skills with little or no theoretical background; Binet himself defined intelligence as whatever

TABLE 5.2   Proportion of Social and Technological Definitions of Intelligence among the Baoulé of Côte d'Ivoire (Cdl) and in the Swiss Alps.

Location	Cdl	Alps	Alps	Alps	Alps	Alps	Alps
Language	Baoulé	French	French	French	Patois	Patois	Patois
Age	Young	Young	Young	Elderly	Young	Young	Elderly
Economy	Farming	Modern	Farming	Farming	Modern	Farming	Farming
Interviews							
Social	**63**	24	27	21	30	35	**65**
Technological	37	**76**	**73**	**79**	**70**	**65**	35
Card sorting							
Social	—	32	44	**52**	—	—	—
Technological	—	**68**	56	48	—	—	—
N	42	17	17	32	7	5	8

(Modified from Fournier, Schurmans, & Dasen, 1995).

his test measured. Piaget defines intelligence as the process of adaptation during ontogenesis, that is, during the individual's development. Would a definition of intelligence that has a strong theoretical base fare better in cross-cultural comparisons? It is to this question that we turn now.

GENETIC EPISTEMOLOGY

Like the approach of general intelligence, the theoretical contribution of Jean Piaget posits coherence among cognitive performances when various tasks are presented to an individual. Piaget (1936; 1947/1950) also claimed to study "intelligence," but defined it very differently from IQ. The formal name of this theory, Genetic Epistemology, reflects its fundamental paradigm: the study of the genesis of scientific thinking. For Piaget, the essence of genetic epistemology resides in studying both the history of science and the development of the individual human being (Piaget & Garcia, 1987). According to this view, adult reasoning is intelligible only insofar as we succeed in retracing its development. We cannot here provide a complete summary of this complex theory. To acquire the basics in Piagetian theory, the reader may consult one of the many introductions that have been written: Droz & Rahmy (1972), Ginsburg & Opper (1969), or the masters themselves, Piaget, 1970b, Piaget & Inhelder, 1966.

Four stages are proposed (each with its own underlying cognitive structure), appearing one after the other in a fixed sequence as a child develops (Piaget, 1972): sensorimotor, preoperational, concrete operational, and formal operational. At each stage, the cognitive structures incorporate those of the previous level. The two processes by which these changes take place are "assimilation" (the integration of new external elements) and "accommodation" (the adaptation of internal structures to external novelty).

In the sensorimotor stage (in the first two years of life) the baby deals with reality in basic ways through its sensory and motor activity. At the concrete operational stage (corresponding in Western industrialized settings approximately to primary school age) the child is able, in particular, to perform the "conservation" tasks (see Figure 5.1 below), implying the "reversibility" of thought. In between these two stages is the preoperational stage, during which the child is able to use symbols (e.g., language) and begins to organize its world of ideas. With the formal operational stage comes the capacity to carry out hypothetico-deductive reasoning and scientific thinking. While the performances on various tasks within a stage are thought to be related to each other, there is, nevertheless, some temporal sequencing (called "horizontal decalages") when the same structure gets applied to contents of different difficulty, for example, when conservation is applied to quantity before weight and to weight before volume.

With respect to factors that are antecedent to cognitive development, Piaget (1966) proposed four categories. First, *biological* factors lie at the root of the maturation of the nervous system and are unrelated (in Piaget's view) to social or cultural factors. Second are *equilibration* factors, involving the autoregulation that develops as the biological organism interacts with its physical environment; for Piaget, this factor is also universal, because everywhere there are objects to interact with (like stones or sticks that can be counted in different spatial arrays). Third are *social* factors, again ones that are common to all societies, because social interactions occur everywhere. Fourth are the *cultural transmission* factors that are variable across cultures, including education, customs, and institutions. According to Piaget, it is only these latter factors that account for cross-cultural variance, and Piaget paid only lip-service to these.[3] Thus Piaget produced a theory of the development of an "epistemic subject," an idealized, nonexistent individual, completely divorced from the social environment.

But Piaget was not alone in disregarding the sociocultural context. Most of the researchers studying cognition in the experimental psychology laboratory, be it concept formation or problem solving, or within the more recent paradigms of artificial intelligence and cognitive science, tend to study the individual in isolation from outside influences. Challenges to this predominant line of inquiry came from social psychologists from within Piaget's own school, such as Doise, Mugny, and Perret-Clermont (1975; Doise & Mugny, 1981; Perret-Clermont, 1979), who demonstrated the importance for cognitive development of interindividual interaction. Their work was, of course, informed by the sociohistorical school of Vygotsky (1978) and Luria (1976) that we will review in the next chapter.

Despite its reference to a single theory, and most often to a set of more or less standardized tasks, Piagetian psychology is not any longer a homogeneous research venture. The "orthodox" tradition tends to follow an absolutist orientation, taking the sequence of stages and the definition of the end state of development as the same everywhere and paying little attention to the cultural validity of the assessment contexts. Piaget himself posited the invariance of the theory, even though he paid lip service (Piaget, 1966) to the need for empirical, cross-cultural tests. In orthodox Piagetian theory no attempt is usually made to account for cultural differences. The theory deals with an "epistemic" subject that often has no counterpart in a "real" child. The stages are defined by unitary structures that lead to the expectation of overarching "developmental levels," not unlike "general intelligence."

Preiswerk (1976), in his essay on the implications of Piagetian theory for intercultural relations, raised the possibility that the theory contained inherent ethnocentric characteristics:

Does not the work of Piaget contain elements of thought deriving from rationalism, from universalism, from ethnocentrism, and from evolutionism, all elements that are central to the fashion in which the West understands other cultures? The first, rationalism, it appears to me, is very clearly a

---

[3]The single paragraph on factors of educational and cultural transmission, in Piaget's (1966) ten-pages-long paper, comprises only twelve lines.

fundamental aspect of Piaget's work. Belief in decentralized Reason and in objective science are the elements which can eventually make intercultural relations difficult. With respect to the three other problems, it is necessary to proceed with great care (p. 509).

An absolutist Piagetian approach has been criticized repeatedly, notably because the interpretation of cultural differences in terms of a standard developmental sequence may easily lead to value judgments in terms of "retardation" or "deficit" against an ethnocentric, middle-class Western norm (Cole & Scribner, 1977). However, Dasen, Berry, and Witkin (1979) have argued that it is not necessary to link developmental sequences to value judgments if an ecocultural framework is used as a guiding paradigm, because each adaptive context sets its own standards for development.

The Stage of Sensorimotor Intelligence

There have been relatively few cross-cultural studies relative to this stage (for a short review, see Berry et al., 1992). The most complete longitudinal study was carried out by Dasen, Inhelder, Lavallée, and Retschitzki (1978) among rural Baoulé in Côte d'Ivoire, aged 6 to 30 months. The results of this study demonstrated the universality of the sequence of the substages of sensorimotor intelligence. The Baoulé children showed exactly the same behavior as that observed by Piaget on his own three children, and as later described on larger samples in France with a more standardized scale (Casati & Lézine, 1968). The only difference that was found is that the Baoulé babies, who sat on their caretaker's lap for these examinations, would more often appeal to their mothers to solve the problems for them. To get an object that was out of reach, they would, for example, push the mother's arm towards the object. Dasen and colleagues (1978) also found that the Baoulé babies were in advance over the French norms on certain tasks (for example, using an instrument to attain an object or combining two objects), but there was no overall precocity.

The Stage of Concrete Operations

Concrete operational reasoning allows the child logically to resolve concrete problems (problems that involve manipulating real objects). This new-found logic follows a particular mathematical model ("grouping") and is characterized by, among other things, the construction of invariants ("conservation") and by "reversibility" (the ability to invert an operation mentally). The development of concrete operational thought relates to many different kinds of concepts, including number, measurement, space, and time; to mention only a few. The development of concrete operational thought is studied by means of standardized situations called *tasks* to distinguish them from psychometric tests (see, for example, Inhelder, Sinclair, & Bovet, 1974; Laurendeau & Pinard, 1968/1970; Longeot, 1974). These tasks are presented using a "clinical" method, involving semistructured interactive dialogue with the subject. The conceptual domains that have been most thoroughly studied are conservation, elementary logic, and space. That these are indeed separate *domains* has been confirmed by factor analytic studies employing many different tasks (Dasen, 1984; Lautrey, de Ribaupierre, & Rieben, 1986; Shayer, Demetriou, & Pervez, 1988). Within a single domain, the same structure may appear at different ages depending on the content to which it is applied.

Two characteristic Piagetian tasks, the conservation of liquids, and the spatial task of "horizontality" are illustrated respectively in Figures 5.1 and 5.2.

In the conservation of liquids task, the child is first presented with two identical glasses (A = B), filled to the same level. Then the liquid of one of these glasses is poured into a glass of a different shape, for example, thinner and higher (as in B" in Fig. 5.1), or broader (B'). The question is: "Is there still the same amount to drink?" (A = ? B' or B"). Concrete operational thought is evidenced if the child says something like "Yes, it is still the same, because the liquid is now higher but also narrower, and you could see it is still the same by pouring it back." At the preoperational level, the child concentrates on one single dimension of the display, and will say, for example "There is more in B" because the level of the water is higher."

In the "horizontality" task, a flask is presented upright, half filled with liquid (position A in Fig. 5.2). The child is then asked where the water level would be if the flask were tilted in various ways. The child is usually asked to provide an answer

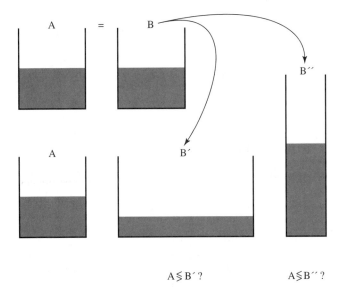

$A \lesseqgtr B' \,?$ $A \lesseqgtr B'' \,?$

FIGURE 5.1   A Piagetian Task in the Domain of Quantification: The Conservation of Liquids.

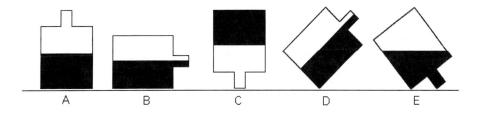

FIGURE 5.2   A Piagetian Task in the Domain of Spatial Concepts: Horizontality.

on outline drawings, and the bottle is actually displayed in the various positions, but hidden in a cloth bag.[4] According to Piaget's analysis of this task, the subject has to handle and combine two systems of coordinates, the one given by gravity (and the surface of the table), and the one internal to the bottle. The task is easier if the two systems correspond, such as when the flask is placed on its side (B), or upside down (C). The more difficult items are those in which the flask is tilted in an oblique position (D, E). At one particular substage, the child knows that the water does not stick to the bottom, but does not know in which way it moves (example D).

Cross-Cultural Tests
Since 1966, the year in which Piaget himself called for cross-cultural research in an article in the inaugural issue of the *International Journal of Psychology,* numerous studies have been conducted in different societies, inspired more or less accurately by Piagetian theory and using Piagetian tasks. Early results of these cross-cultural studies were summarized by Dasen (1972); subsequently, many other reviews on this topic have been published (see for example Dasen & Heron, 1981; LCHC, 1983; Mishra, 1997; Price-Williams, 1981).

One of the major problems is methodological. The behaviors observed when using Piagetian tasks, the children's responses, including the verbal explanations or "justifications" usually called for, contribute to the categorization by stages. Can this categorization be made in a reliable fashion in all cases and in all cultural contexts? As we saw earlier in this chapter, the transfer of a test, whether psychometric or Piagetian, is not simply a translation problem; it is possible that the experimental situation has different meanings for subjects in different societies. Does it have the meaning that the researcher intended it to have? Many discussions have dealt with cultural subtleties which, if not recognized and controlled, constitute a threat to

---

[4]The experiment can also be done without hiding the water level. The child is asked to observe "where the water is," and to show the water level with the hand or a pencil. It is striking to find (and an interesting lesson for science teachers) that children at the preoperational stage will still draw the water as if it stuck to the bottom of the flask. In other words, they draw what they know rather than what they see.

validity. Moreover, many empirical studies have dealt with the importance of the language in which the questioning takes place, with results varying according to circumstances: better performance in English than in the maternal language (Kelly & Philp, 1975), just the opposite (Nyiti, 1982), or no influence of language (Keats, 1985). Familiarity with content (Okonji, 1971; Price-Williams, 1962), or even the skill with which the clinical method is applied (Kamara & Easley, 1977) have also been noted as potential methodological concerns. Too many researchers treat Piagetian tasks as if they were standardized psychometric tests, sometimes even reducing the results to simple pass/fail scores (e.g., Irvine, 1983); another concern arises when Piagetian tasks are analyzed with parametric statistical methods that are inappropriate to the nominal or ordinal data[5] that result from Piagetian tasks. Furthermore, the importance of familiarity with the assessment situation is underscored by the fact that simply repeating a task at the end of a session can significantly change the obtained results; it would thus be appropriate to systematically accompany the tasks with training sessions (e.g., Dasen, Ngini, & Lavallée, 1979).

Despite these important methodological difficulties, researchers in numerous societies and cultures have, on the whole, been able to employ Piagetian stage categorizations without much difficulty, at least for tasks at the level of concrete operations. Some exceptions exist, but no more often in cross-cultural studies than in single culture studies. *Whenever people use concrete operational reasoning in a particular task, they display it similarly everywhere.*

Rhythms of Development

At what age are the different stages attained? Piaget considered this question of relatively little importance. He expected to find differences of one to two years as a consequence of variations in the degree of stimulation provided by various environments. Actually, cross-cultural studies have brought to light much larger differences, occasionally time lags of five to six years. Some members of a given population may even appear to lack concrete operational reasoning for a particular concept altogether. This is reflected in "asymptotic" developmental curves,[6] which level off at less than 100 percent operational responses after the age at which all individuals in Western samples have acquired the particular concept.

The meaning of these asymptotes was examined by Dasen and his colleagues (Dasen, 1982; Dasen, Lavallée, & Retschitzki, 1979; Dasen, Ngini, & Lavallée, 1979) by means of techniques involving training. The researchers were able to show that children 12 years and older (among the Inuit in Canada, Baoulé in Côte d'Ivoire, and

---

[5]*Nominal* and *ordinal* are terms that refer to the nature of the numbers employed in a set of scores. Nominal numbers indicate only that two things that bear different numbers are not the same. Ordinal numbers carry an additional meaning, *viz.,* that the thing with a higher number is *more* than the other (for example, that stage 3 occurs after stage 2). Many mathematical operations, including those used in parametric statistical tests, assume a higher level of meaning of numbers. Parametric statistics are those procedures based on the normal distribution (means and standard deviation); they require measurements to occur on an equal interval scale.

[6]The usual way to represent data relevant to rate of development is to plot, as a function of age, the proportions of people in the sample giving a concrete operational response. This yields a "developmental curve."

Kikuyu in Kenya) who did not *spontaneously* use concrete operational reasoning in a given task, nonetheless did so following a brief learning sequence, or when the task was presented a second time at the end of the testing sessions. The asymptote in the developmental curves is thus a "performance" phenomenon rather than one of "competence." In other words, these adolescents obviously could use concrete operations if they were incited to do so, but would not necessarily use them spontaneously.

The Existence of Culturally Unique Stages

Is it possible to have supplementary stages with respect to the sequence described by Piaget? A cautious response suggests itself. In effect, the finer the analysis, the better able we are to delineate more stages, without having to postulate so-called supplementary stages. A supplementary stage is therefore one that is needed only to account for results obtained in a certain culture, when that stage was not described by Piaget or others who studied Western children.

The possibility of culturally unique stages was first suggested by Bovet (1974) in a study of conservation of liquids among unschooled Algerian children. At 7 to 8 years of age, although they would say that the amounts to drink in the two containers (A and B') were "the same," they could not explain why. Bovet showed, in fact, that they were not paying any attention to the dimensions of the receptacles and were simply persisting in giving their initial answer. After a training session, which directed their attention to the container dimensions, they gave classic *non*conservation responses, as did the 9- to 10-year-olds without any prompting. This led Bovet to speak of "pseudo-conservation," a supplementary stage preceding nonconservation that had never before been described. Probably, part of the results of Dasen (1974) among the Australian Aborigines could also be explained this way, but this supplementary stage of pseudoconservation has never been formally replicated.

Saxe (1981, 1982) studied the construction of the concept of number among the Oksapmin of Papua New Guinea, who use a number system that employs the names of body parts (see Figure 5.3). When the Oksapmin count, they show each body part in turn, calling out its name, from the thumb of the right hand over the arms to the nose. Starting with the left eye, the body part names are preceded by the prefix *tan* to indicate that the count is now on the second half of the body. The count normally ends with the little finger on the left hand (27 in the decimal system). If they need to count further, they can continue back to the wrist of the second hand and progres back upward on the body.

Saxe observed the same stages in the development of number that are known to prevail for European and U.S. children. In particular, there is a stage in which the child knows how to count the elements within each of two sets, (for example, two groups of nine sweet potatoes each), but cannot use the results to make comparisons between the two. Depending on the spatial array of the potatoes, they may agree that while there are nine in each group, there are more on the side where they are spread out wider. Saxe also found this stage, which he called *premediational,* among the Oksapmin children, but at approximately 9 years of age as compared with 5 to 6 years for Euro-American children.

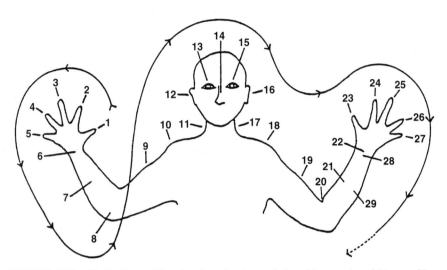

FIGURE 5.3   Body Parts Numbering System of the Oksapmin of Papua New Guinea. The Numerals Denote the Order of Occurrence of Body Parts in the Counting System.

Reproduced with permission from Saxe, 1981, p. 307. Copyright © The Society for Research in Child Development, Inc.

The Oksapmin number system presents a specific difficulty that is tied to the use of symmetrical parts of the body. Oksapmin children (even between 12 and 16 years of age) experience difficulty distinguishing between the cardinal values of two symmetrical parts (for example, they think that the left eye and the right eye have the same value), even after they no longer have difficulty with asymmetrical parts. Later, they become capable of completely dissociating number from its bodily equivalent, at which time they are able to resolve hypothetical problems ("And what if one began to count by the left thumb?"). There is, thus, for Oksapmin children, a supplementary step to get through that is tied to the peculiarities of their numerical system. However, this is the only demonstration of a culturally specific sequence of development that we know of, and it constitutes only a minor amendment to what has quite convincingly been revealed as a universal succession of stages. Other innovative features of Saxe's research in Papua New Guinea are illustrated in Box 5.2.

Before you read Box 5.2, stop and try to solve the simple addition of 8 + 6, or rather, "elbow" + "wrist" in the Oksapmin system. Remember that you are not allowed to use numerals (Figure 5.3 may be somewhat misleading in this respect, because it is labelled with arabic numerals), only body part names. Whether or not your answer is nose, you will be interested in comparing your strategy with those described in Figure 5.4.

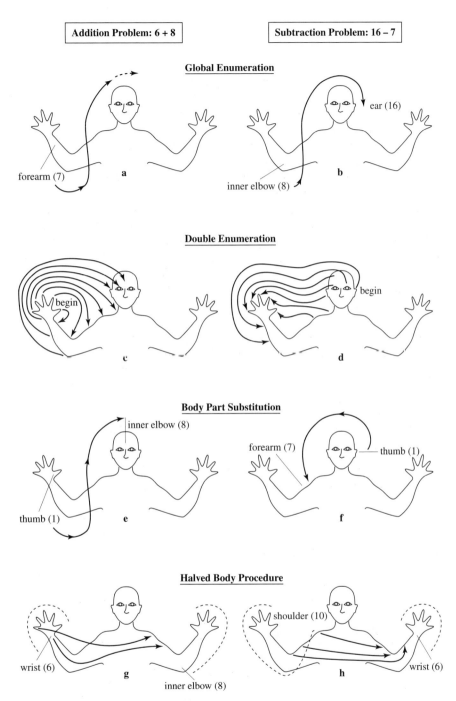

Addition Problem: 6 + 8

Subtraction Problem: 16 – 7

Global Enumeration

ear (16)

forearm (7)

a

b

inner elbow (8)

Double Enumeration

begin

begin

c

d

Body Part Substitution

inner elbow (8)

forearm (7)

thumb (1)

thumb (1)

e

f

Halved Body Procedure

shoulder (10)

wrist (6)

wrist (6)

g

h

inner elbow (8)

FIGURE 5.4   Four Body-Part Computational Strategies Used by the Oksapmin on the Addition and Subtraction Problems.

Reproduced with permission from Saxe, 1982, p. 589. Copyright © American Psychological Association, Inc.

BOX 5.2   Emic Piagetian Research in Papua New Guinea

One problem with cross-cultural Piagetian research is that, in most cases, the so-called Piagetian tasks were transported to the field with only minimal adaptations. Geoffrey Saxe's research among the Oksapmin of Papua New Guinea is an interesting exception to this rule. Beyond the study of counting and the construction of number, Saxe devised a number of situations that were derived from culturally specific features.

To study measurement, for example, and the conservation of length, he devised a series of tasks using locally made string bags. These bags are made in a number of sizes, and every Oksapmin after the age of 5 years, whether male or female, almost always carries one of these bags. String bags are measured in the course of production by inserting the arms into the bags; the length is reported using the same body parts as used in the numeration system (see Figure 5.3). An interesting feature of this system is that units are therefore not equivalent across individuals, because peoples' arms vary in size from one individual to another.

For the conservation of length, Saxe and Moylan (1982) used both the standard task (two sticks of equal length, 30 centimeters, were first aligned in parallel with their endpoints matching, and the subject was asked to ascertain that they were the same length; then one of the sticks was moved so that it extended about 10 centimeters beyond the other; the subject was then asked whether they were still the same length or whether one was longer) and a task using string bags, for which the subject was asked to put his or her arm into the bag as if to measure it. The measurement was marked on the arm with charcoal, and then the subject was asked to place the marked arm so that the hand

was midway along the length of the bag, with the arm parallel to the side of the bag, and the conservation of length question was asked.[11]

For both unschooled children (mean age 8 years) and school children (grade 2, mean age 11 years, and grade 6, mean age 14 years), the task format made little difference. The older children gave conservation answers 65 percent of the time on both tasks, significantly more than the younger children. Unschooled adults, however, gave only 40 percent conservation answers on the standard task, while they gave 97 percent such answers on the string bag conservation task. Saxe and Moylan (1982) interpreted these results as follows:

> School-related activities present children with an opportunity to elaborate the concept of conservation beyond the constraints of the traditional context. By gaining experience with new conventions of measurement and practice with a variety of activities which involve making inferences about length, schooled children, unlike traditional adults, may more readily structure an understanding of the conservation of length that is independent of particular conventions (p. 1247).

Another task involved comparing the measurements of two individuals of markedly different arm lengths. Four stories were told, one of which went as follows:

---

[11]Note that the two tasks are not absolutely equivalent, because an actual body part measurement was used in the second but not in the first task.

"A little girl made a string bag for her tall father. She measured it and it came to her forearm. When the father put the bag on his arm, did it come up to his forearm, or not? Where did it come to, and how did you know?"

The majority of the unschooled children believed that the string bag would come up to the same place on the recipient as the donor on all of the stories, whereas the majority of the unschooled adults demonstrated an understanding that there would be a discrepancy, and predicted the correct direction of the discrepancy on at least three of the four stories. The school children's performance was intermediate, and some children (25 percent to 30 percent) gave an interesting type of transitional response. They predicted that the bag would reach a higher point on the father's body because he had long arms. In these transitional responses, the subjects demonstrated, through their justifications, that they recognized the problem of the lack of equivalent units, but failed to understand the inverse relation.

The Oksapmin counting system was traditionally used only for counting objects (e.g., yams, pigs), and bartering involved a one-for-one or one-for-many exchange without any need for computation. Counting was always performed in the presence of objects (or possibly sticks to represent them). Currency was introduced to the Oksapmin region in the early sixties (and has changed on three occasions, from Australian shillings and pounds, to Australian dollars and cents, to PNG kina and toea). Young men often left for two-year stints of labor on coastal plantations, and established a small trade store when they returned. The first trade store was started in 1972, and, by the early eighties, there were more than 100 stores in the district.

Saxe (1982) took advantage of this ongoing social change to study the adaptation of the traditional counting system to the new requirements of purchasing goods in trade stores, which involves addition and subtraction. First of all, the Oksapmin adapted the system to the base structure of the early Australian currency system by counting shillings up to the inner elbow on the other side of the body (20 in the decimal system), and calling it one pound. Even with the current money, the same scheme can be used, because 10 toea coins are taken as a unit, and twenty of them correspond to the two-kina notes.

Saxe (1982) studied four groups of adults who had different levels of experience with the money economy: trade store owners; men who had returned from a period of work at a plantation, but did not own a store; young adults who had not left the area; and older adults who had only peripheral experience with the money economy. These subjects were asked to perform eight arithmetic problems involving the addition and subtraction of coins (such as $6 + 8$; $16 - 7$); in half of the problems, actual coins were used, while the other four problems were administered without coins present.

The various strategies used by the participants are illustrated in Figure 5.4. According to Saxe (1982, p. 588), "these four types are considered to be ordered as a developmental sequence; each subsequent one represents a more advanced solution than its predecessor."

The strategy of global enumeration consists of enumerating body parts to represent the first term, then continuing the count to represent the addition of the second term. For example, to add $6 + 8$, an individual might enumerate body parts for the first term from the thumb (1) to the wrist (6), then continue counting upward for the second term, stopping at an estimate of the correct answer. Because there is no method of keeping track of when the second term is completed, the result is typically incorrect.

Continued

BOX 5.2 *Continued*

In the second strategy, of double enu-meration, as the subject adds the second term, a record is kept by establishing physical one-to-one correspondences with the body parts starting with the thumb (1) and ending with the second term, in our example, until the subject reaches the cor-respondence between the inner elbow (8) and the nose (14). With this strategy, the result is usually correct, but the calcula-tions are slow and laborious.

The body part substitution procedure is similar, with one major exception: Rather than establishing physical one-to-one correspondences, one series is strictly verbal: The individual calls the forearm "thumb," the elbow "index," until the nose is called "elbow," which indicates that the addition is complete. This proce-dure is effective and fast, and represents a functional shift in the way body part names can refer to any body part to serve the purpose of calculation.

Finally, in what Saxe considers the most sophisticated strategy, the halved body procedure, subjects use each part of the body as a separate register up to the shoulder (10, the base of the present cur-rency system). For instance, to add 6 + 8, an individual would put 8 on one arm (el-bow) and 6 on the other (wrist), then trans-fer the 6th (wrist) and 5th (little finger) body parts from the second arm to the 9th (bicep) and 10th (shoulder) body parts of

the first arm. The solution would then be 1 kina (shoulder) and 40 toea (ring finger).

The last three of these procedures are considered "advanced" strategies for pre-senting the results in Figure 5.5. Because two problems of each type (addition *ver-sus* subtraction; with or without coins) were presented, the maximum score is 2. The graph represents the number of ad-vanced strategies used by the four groups of participants.

As can be seen in the graph, trade store owners use advanced strategies in every case, plantation returnees and young adults use them frequently, but more on problems when coins are present, while older adults never use these strategies without coins present. For individuals with less participation in the money econ-omy, this no doubt reflects the fact that, in the traditional use of the system, concrete objects are always present.

Saxe's research, its methods informed by Vygotsky and the sociocultural ap-proach (see Chapter 6), is an exciting con-firmation of Piaget's theory. The stages in the construction of concepts of number and measurement are remarkably similar to those described by Piaget, despite the fundamentally different counting system used in Papua New Guinea. We see here the sociogenesis of cognition through the analysis of newly emerging forms of arith-metic thought as social change occurs.

A Test of the Ecocultural Framework

As a test of the ecocultural framework (cf. Fig. 2.1) he was developing at the time, Berry (1976a) conducted a study that included seventeen societies, spread along the dimension of low- to high-food-accumulation; corresponding to one end of this dimension are hunting and food-gathering nomadic people, and to the other end sed-entary people practicing subsistence-level agriculture. Working within the frame-

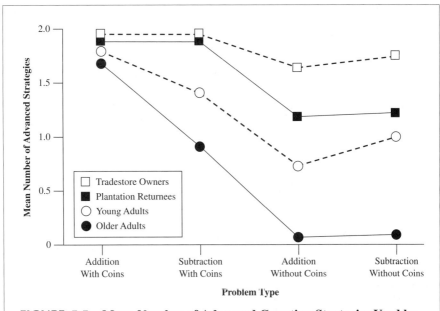

FIGURE 5.5 Mean Number of Advanced Counting Strategies Used by Subjects as a Function of Population Group and Problem Type.

Reproduced with permission from Saxe, 1982, p. 591. Copyright © American Psychological Association, Inc.

work of Witkin's theory of psychological differentiation (Witkin, Dyk, Faterson, Goodenough, & Karp, 1962; for a review of cross-cultural studies, see Berry et al., 1992), Berry found that the former develop higher levels of restructuring skills, indicating field independence, and higher levels of spatial skills than the latter. The hypothesis was that those skills were more useful to nomadic, hunting and gathering people than to sedentary agriculturalists. The link between the ecocultural contexts and the psychological outcomes was established using the concepts of enculturation and socialization practices during infancy and childhood.

Inspired by this study, Dasen (1975) predicted that the development of concrete operational reasoning in the domain of space would be particularly rapid in nomadic hunting and gathering societies because of the necessity to find one's bearings in an extended territory, while quantitative concepts (for example, conservation of quantity, of weight, and of volume) would be more valued and would develop more rapidly in sedentary agricultural societies, which must deal with harvested produce in several ways, including storage and exchange or sale of surplus. No systematic differences were predicted for tasks of elementary logic (seriation, reclassification, class inclusion).

These hypotheses were confirmed in the 1975 report that involved 6- to 15-year-old Australian Aboriginal (in two locations, Hermannsburg and Areyonga), Inuit (Cape Dorset, Canada), and Ebrié (Côte d'Ivoire) children. Later, the study was expanded to include a group of Baoulé children in Côte d'Ivoire (Kpouebo) and Kikuyu children in Kenya (Ngecha). The Inuit and Australian Aborigines were hunting and gathering nomadic people, the Ebrié relied on fishing and agriculture, and the other two groups (Baoulé and Kikuyu) were sedentary, agricultural people. The samples were not matched perfectly on acculturation: Ngecha was a periurban community near Nairobi, and therefore relatively acculturated. The Aborigines at Hermannsburg were slightly more acculturated than those at Areyonga, but both groups lived close to traditional customs on remote reserves in Central Australia. The results are illustrated in Figure 5.6 for two concrete operational tasks, conservation of liquid and the concept of horizontality (several other Piagetian tasks were used in the original study, yielding similar results).

In the conservation of liquids (graph a), the developmental curves obtained in Ngecha and Kpouebo show a relatively fast development of this concept (relatively close to the results of urban, Anglo children in Canberra, Australia), Ebrié (Adiopodoumé) following suit with a delay of two to three years. In contrast, the developmental curves of the three hunting and gathering nomadic groups show a much slower development of this concept, with so-called asymptotic development curves.[7] Note that all of these development curves represent performance (the first spontaneous answer on the task, without training), rather than competence. An assessment of competence (through training techniques) was performed for the Ngecha, Kpouebo, and Cape Dorset children; the competence curves for the first two are indistinguishable from the development curve obtained in Canberra; the competence development curve for Cape Dorset is no longer asymptotic, 100 percent conservation answers being reached at age 12.

For the horizontality task (graph b), a very rapid development is shown by the Inuit children, and a very slow development by the Ebrié (Adiopodoumé) and Baoulé (Kpouebo) children, with the other three groups showing intermediate rates of development. The relatively high level of acculturation for Ngecha against the lower level of acculturation for Areyonga and Hermannsburg are congruent with these results.

Overall, the results show important variations in the rates of development for these concepts, linked at least partly to the ecocultural dimension. Another way to look at these results is to compare the developmental curves in the two graphs for each group separately. The Inuit of Cape Dorset, for example, develop the spatial concept much more rapidly than the conservation of liquids. In reverse, for the

---

[7]The developmental curve for the Hermannsburg children has been corrected for the likely occurrence of pseudoconservation.

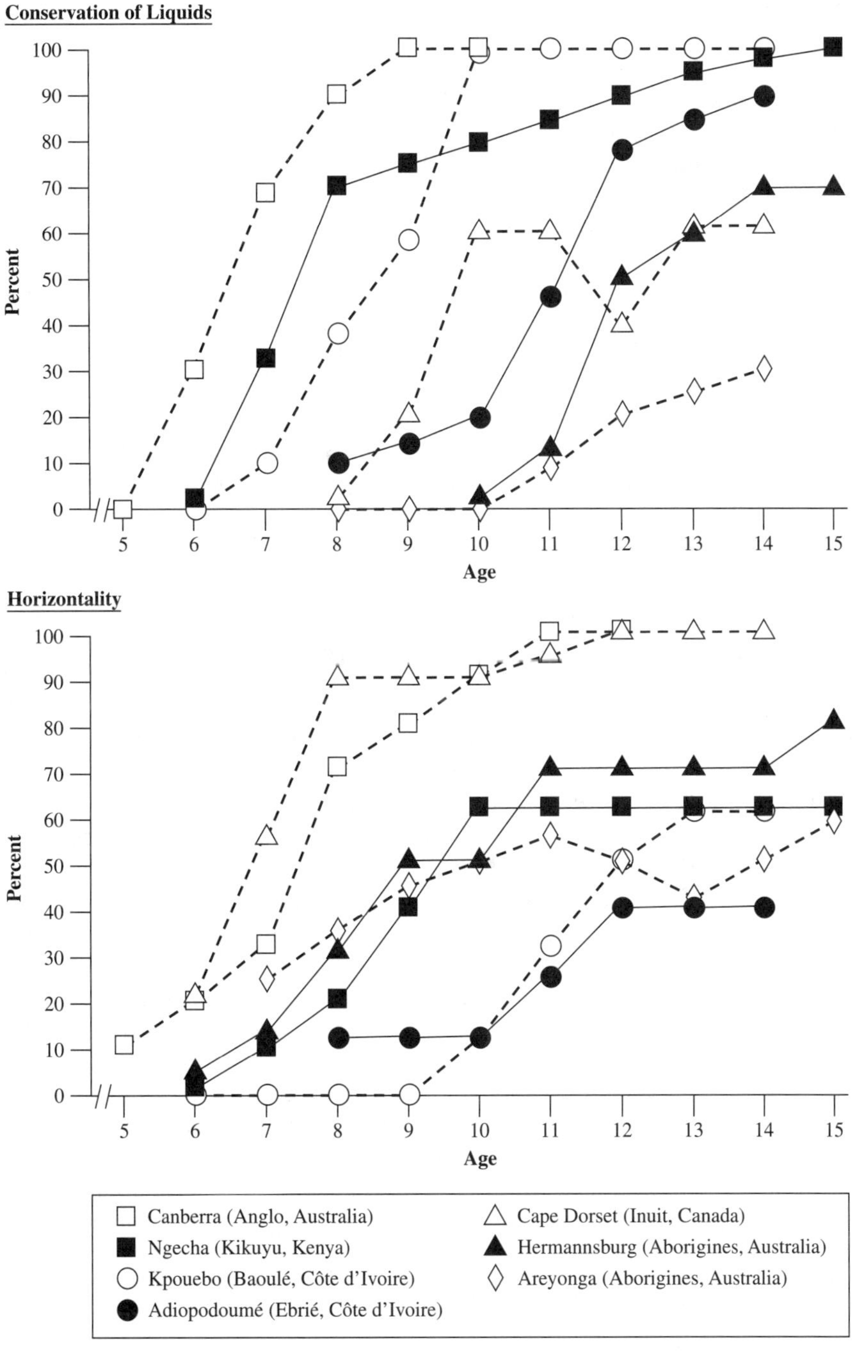

Conservation of Liquids

Horizontality

Legend:

☐ Canberra (Anglo, Australia) △ Cape Dorset (Inuit, Canada)

■ Ngecha (Kikuyu, Kenya) ▲ Hermannsburg (Aborigines, Australia)

○ Kpouebo (Baoulé, Côte d'Ivoire) ◇ Areyonga (Aborigines, Australia)

● Adiopodoumé (Ebrié, Côte d'Ivoire)

FIGURE 5.6 A Test of the Ecocultural Framework: Dasen's results on the Conservation of Liquids and the Horizontality Tasks.

Baoulé of Kpouebo, we see a much more rapid development of the concept related to quantification than of the spatial concept.[8]

These results contributed to challenging one element of Piagetian theory, namely the idea of domain consistency (*structure d'ensemble,* in French) according to which the development of different concepts belonging to the same stage unfolds concurrently. This is the impression that one gains in reading Piaget's work, because the development of each concept is described in terms of the same succession of substages, while in fact the studies were done in each case with different samples. When researchers presented a large number of tasks to the same sample, it appeared that heterogeneity was the rule, even among children in Western societies (Longeot, 1978; de Ribaupierre, Rieben, & Lautrey, 1985). The cultural differences are superimposed on an individual variability much more important than what had been initially anticipated. There is, nevertheless, a certain coherence in other respects in the development of concepts within a single domain; this has been shown by studies using factorial analyses (Dasen, 1984; Shayer, Demetriou, & Pervez, 1988), and by training studies, in which the learning of a concept generalizes mainly to other concepts in the same domain (Dasen, Ngini, & Lavallée, 1979; Inhelder et al., 1974).

Cross-cultural research using this paradigm has led to the conclusion that ecological and cultural factors do not influence the sequence of stages, but the rate at which they are attained. Cultural differences are expected to occur not only at the performance (surface) level for concepts that are culturally valued (that is, needed for adaptation in a particular ecocultural setting), but also at the competence (deep) level for concepts that are not valued.

In summary, if the hypothesis of an absolutely homogeneous and unidimensional development in all cultures has not been verified by empirical research, neither has the converse, a complete relativity of particular concepts, each specific to a particular cultural context. The empirical results allow us to opt for an intermediate solution, a simultaneous universality of hierarchical sequences and cultural variation in the timing of development. In other words, the sequence of stages is the same everywhere, only the timing varies. Dasen (1980, 1983b) has called this intermediate solution "local constructivism," illustrated by the metaphor "valleys of construction" suggested by Harris & Heelas (1979). This is in contrast both with the absolutist approach of orthodox Piagetian theory and extreme contextualism, which denies any structuralist construction and links between concepts.

Still another question is, What aspects of child development are most valued by the parents? Dasen and colleagues's (1985) study of *n'glouèlê,* reviewed earlier in this chapter, is relevant here. In the second part of their study, the researchers asked

---

[8]Posner and Baroody (1979) compared a group of Baoulé children to Dioula on the development of number concepts. The Dioula are merchants, and should therefore value quantification even more than agriculturalists. Indeed, the Dioula children showed a more rapid development of conservation of number than the Baoulé children.

47 sets of parents, each of whom had one child in the study, to designate, by citing some illustrative behaviors, which were the positive or negative aspects of *n'glouèlê* (and of its different components) that pertained to their own child. The correlations between parental judgments and the performance of the children on various conservation tasks and in elementary logic (seriation, class inclusion, reclassification) were, in general, close to zero. In the spatial domain, correlation coefficients with technological components of *n'glouèlê* ranged between –.40 and –.77, showing a very significant inverse statistical relationship. These results show the gap that exists between the Baoulé definition of intelligence and concrete operational reasoning. They are also in line with Dasen's (1975) hypothesis that spatial concepts are not highly valued in sedentary societies such as the Baoulé.

In this same study, correlations between parental judgments of *n'glouèlê* and "natural indicators" derived from spot-observations were also obtained. Dasen and colleagues (1985) found that "non-directed activity" correlated positively with parental judgments of *n'glouèlê,* particularly for girls. This latter indicator measured initiative and responsibility-taking in those situations in which children's behaviors are spontaneous and not demanded by an adult, and in which they are not under direct control of an adult or of an older child. These studies reveal a coherence between parental ethnotheories and the daily activities of children. In contrast, Piagetian tasks do not necessarily measure what is valued in societies that do not acknowledge scientific reasoning as the ultimate end of human development.

The Stage of Formal Operations

The conclusions that we have reached regarding the sequence and timing of stages of cognitive development apply to the stage of concrete operations. Piaget's theory concerning the stage of formal operations has been only partially confirmed, even in the Western, industrialized context. According to Piagetian theory, reasoning at the formal operational stage is no longer tied to the concrete, but can be applied to any, even hypothetical, content. Yet, research has shown that the majority of adolescents and adults in Western societies, even those schooled at the level of high school or university, do not reason in formal operational fashion except under certain conditions and in certain domains (particularly in their professional specialization). This led Piaget (1972) to revise his position by stating that all adults have the capacity for formal operational reasoning, but that this capacity would not reflect itself in performance except under favorable circumstances.

At the moment, not enough systematic information is available to confirm the universal applicability of Piaget's conclusion. Cross-cultural studies that have employed Piagetian tasks in the formal domain have all shown that schooling up to the secondary level is a necessary but not sufficient condition for success at these tasks (e.g., Laurendeau-Bendavid, 1977; Shea, 1985). That is not at all surprising, because these tasks (even when administered in noncurriculum-related situations) relate directly to physics, chemistry, or mathematics as they are taught in school.

This does not necessarily mean that cross-cultural studies that employ formal operational tasks are uninteresting or invalid, particularly if subjects are schooled. Keats (1985), for example, administered six tasks of formal operations to high school students 16- to 17 years of age and university students 20 to 24 years of age in Australia and also among Malays, Indians, and Chinese in Malaysia. Three of the tasks were administered in repeated fashion before and after a proportionality training session. The author concluded: "The effectiveness of the training program in removing initial differences between the groups suggests that although the initial testing did show differences in performance, these did not reflect differences in competence...Evidence of formal operational thinking was found for some subjects within all groups, but not for all subjects within any group" (pp. 316–317).

Tapé (1994) used three formal stage Piagetian tasks (the flexibility of rods, the pendulum, and permutations) in Côte d'Ivoire with secondary school pupils in urban and rural areas, and with illiterate adults. With the adults, he used group interviews, social situations that are culturally more appropriate than individual examinations; this part of the study produced the most interesting results. The adults would approach the problems in a wholistic fashion, clustering the dimensions into blocks of information, and imparting an order of importance to the relevant factors. For example, in the pendulum problem,[9] they asserted that the most important factor is the initial push, because without it there would be no movement at all. They also took everyday experience into account; for example, in the flexibility of rods task, they did not accept the problem as it was set by the experimenter, but claimed that the flexibility has to be tested over time. This, Tapé argued, results from the experience they have in using wooden rods for constructing traps.

Tapé concluded that there are two styles of thinking that become clearly distinguishable during adolescence, and that correspond to two ways of assigning meaning to nature. There is the experimental and analytical style that corresponds to formal logic, answers the question "how," and is designed to establish causal laws. Secondly, there is the "experiential" style that works through iconic or symbolic representation, and corresponds to a pragmatic or action-oriented logic; it answers the question "why," and is designed to search for the ends which might be served. According to Tapé, this second style corresponds to Bantu philosophy, is produced by informal education, and was obvious in the way the illiterate adults approached and solved the Piagetian tasks.

To study formal reasoning among nonschooled subjects, it would be best not to use experimental situations, because these often tend to be culturally inappropriate. Observing formal reasoning in everyday situations is practically impossible. The fact

---

[9]The problem is to discover which factors (length of string, weight of the pendulum, height from where it is released, etc.) determine the frequency of the pendulum swings. Similarly, in the flexibility of rods task, the problem is to discover which factors (type of material, shape, diameter, length, weight put on the end, etc.) determine whether metallic rods fixed at one end (like a diving board) will bend or not. In the permutations task, given a number of colored tokens, the subject has to figure out how many different groups of tokens can be set out, changing the order of the tokens systematically.

that a behavior is complex and abstract is not enough to make it formal in terms of Piagetian criteria, which demand that subjects perform the task themselves without help from others, that they consider all possible combinations, and hold all factors constant except the one under study, and that they be able to derive and verbalize a general law. Rarely are these criteria met outside of an experimental or school situation.

This problem is well illustrated in a most interesting study of Micronesian navigational skills (Gladwin, 1970), of which we will discuss only a small part.[10] The navigators use a highly abstract representation of the course the outrigger canoe is taking, in which a nonvisible reference island (real or imaginary), called the *etak* island, is passing through segments on the horizon identified by the rising and setting positions of stars (themselves often not visible, for example, during the day time). This representational system is obviously highly complex and abstract, but it is difficult to analyze it in terms of Piaget's "formal" operations.

Another part of the navigational skills, however, comes closer to the combinatorial thinking Piaget considers as formal reasoning. Apprentice navigators have to learn the direction in which to leave any particlar island in the archipelago to reach almost any other of the islands. There are more than twenty-six islands of which they learn, even if they have not actually visited them. The task is, obviously, a combinatorial task. When Gladwin presented expert navigators with the task of working out the number of combinations in which a set of four colored chips can be arranged, they were unable to solve the task. Young schooled Micronesians, on the other hand (who were not navigators), could handle the problem without much difficulty. The Piagetian part of Gladwin's research lacked the methodological precision psychologists are used to, but it is very telling in demonstrating the situational variability of formal operations.

As Shea (1985) rightly pointed out, it would be premature to conclude there is an absence of formal reasoning in certain societies based on the results of a few Piagetian tasks. Highly abstract thinking of some sort can often be found in traditional court cases (Jahoda, 1980) or land disputes (Hutchins, 1980), even if they are not strictly speaking "formal." A more tenable hypothesis, congruent with Tapé's (1994) analysis and with the idea of cognitive styles, might be that this particular form of reasoning—in effect, scientific reasoning—is not what is valued in all cultures. This at least is the opinion of Greenfield (1976), who proposed that it is necessary to follow the example of Piaget himself: first determine what the final stage is and then study its ontogenesis according to the particular value systems of each society.

Neo-Piagetian Approaches

A revival of structuralist approaches occurred at the end of the 1970s in an attempt to integrate both structural and contextual aspects. The new models look for structural

---

[10]For more information on traditional navigational skills, see also Hutchins (1983, 1993) and Lewis (1980).

invariants accounting for developmental changes or for commonalities across situations, while insisting on the necessity to take situational variables into account. These so-called neo-Piagetian theories have been developed by a number of authors, notably Case (1985), Fischer (1980); Fischer, Knight, & Van Parys, (1993), and Pascual-Leone (1980). In a special issue of the *International Journal of Psychology*, statements by most neo-Piagetians have been brought together, and Dasen and de Ribaupierre (1987) have assessed the potential of these theories for taking cultural variables (and individual differences) into account.

Neo-Piagetian models combine a Piagetian qualitative-structuralist framework (the existence of qualitatively different stages) with functional approaches; they draw heavily on Piaget's description of development, while refining it (by describing more stages and substages), but most of them reject the use of general logical structures such as those favored by Piaget. Some of the theories import contributions from information-processing approaches, such as minute task analyses and the concept of attentional capacity (or working memory). The latter plays an important role in most neo-Piagetian theories and corresponds to the quantitative aspects of individual development. Attentional capacity refers to the number of units of information that a subject can process simultaneously. For Case (1985), this quantitative mechanism is seen as coexisting with qualitative changes, whereas for Pascual-Leone (1980), *M-power* (the chronological increment in the number of elements that can be integrated) is seen as sufficient to account for the qualitative changes. As Dasen and de Ribaupierre (1987) point out, there have only been a few and partial cross-cultural replications of neo-Piagetian theories. The time lag between theory development and cross-cultural theory testing is possibly increased by the jargon and the technicalities that abound in this area of research.

CONCLUSION

In this chapter and the previous one, we found evidence of differences across cultural groups, differences in habitual strategies for classifying and for solving problems, differences in rates of progression through developmental stages, and variations in cognitive styles. Variations across groups in the way individuals interact with the world around them appear from early in life and tend to increase throughout the life span. These differences occur in the way basic cognitive processes are applied to particular contexts, rather than in the presence or absence of the processes. Despite these differences, then, there is an underlying universality of cognitive processes.

These conclusions are illustrated in Figure 5.7, in which the distinction is made clearly between the "deep" level of basic cognitive processes and structures, and the "surface" level of the diverse contexts and contents to which these processes are applied. Behavior can be observed at the surface level only, in terms of performance, that does not necessarily truly reflect the underlying competence. Competence is thus "actualized" in different ways, for example, made culturally relevant in partic-

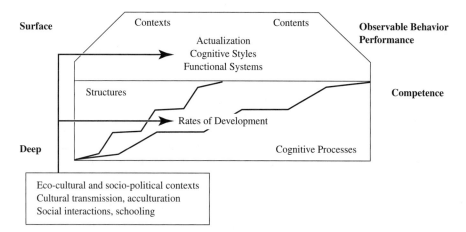

FIGURE 5.7   Summary Representation of the Development of Cognitive Competence and its Manifestation in Observable Behavior.

Adapted from Dasen, 1993.

ular contexts, or is expressed in different cognitive styles that reflect the predominant values. Cognitive structures are constructed in ontogeny in a stagelike pattern; the succession of these stages is universal, but cultural differences occur in the rates of development with chronological age. Both these rates of development, at the deep level, and the various aspects of performance at the surface, are influenced by the ecocultural and sociopolitical contexts, through process variables such as cultural transmission and acculturation (including such variables as social interactions, schooling, etc.).

In accordance with the ecocultural framework, the central theme that might help explain cross-cultural differences in cognitive performance is that the modes of knowing toward which development proceeds in any setting are those that are most valued and produced by the socialization practices that are emphasized there. These values and socialization emphases in turn reflect cultual adaptations to ecological and sociohistorical forces.

Individuals in all societies are heir to a culturally shaped way of conceptualizing the world and their relation to it. What is inherited through acculturation and socialization) tends to conserve the modes of knowing that have, over generations, permitted the society to survive in its particular habitat. This does not mean a static adherence to tradition. The ecocultural framework is inherently dynamic and underscores the fundamental flexibility of human beings. Implicit is the expectation that, as ecological or cultural forces change, so will the use of basic cognitive processes in the new contexts.

Therefore, any test of ability constructed in one cultural setting will, most probably, elicit relatively "poor" performances in some other culture. In general, we know this to be the case for Western intelligence tests applied to minorities within Western societies, and to populations outside of a Westernized, urban, industrial world. But working within the ecocultural framework, we need no longer accept the characterization of different performances by such persons as "poor."

We have come to recognize that the Western world's concept of intelligence is culture-bound, as are the tests that measure it. The Western definition of *intelligence,* and the tests that reflect it, relate primarily to academic performance. In other societies, the key concept will be whatever is valued, just as scientific reasoning is valued in some. But whatever kinds of behavior are seen as intelligent, those behaviors are likely to be found in good supply.

What we have also seen in this chapter is that the study of culture and cognition does not occur in a vacuum; it is related to historical trends in social science, each of which brings with it a particular frame of reference. We have claimed that it is important to be aware of these paradigms to better understand in what contexts the research findings have been obtained and can be interpreted. In the next chapter, we turn to another of these paradigms that is gaining in attention. Based on the theory of Lev Vygotsky, this is the sociohistorical school, best exemplified in the study of everyday cognition.

6

EVERYDAY COGNITION

Experimental anthropology (discussed in Chapter 4) has demonstrated how one can profitably adapt laboratory techniques to cross-cultural research, provided one first acquires profound ethnographic (emic) understanding. In experimental anthropology, one is never content simply to measure performance: Experimental procedures may first have to be modified to allow people to display their real cognitive competence. Yet, despite the care experimental anthropologists take to be culturally sensitive, the cognitive processes that they choose to study (such as memory and syllogistic reasoning) derive from interests inherent in Western psychology.

An even more emic methodology is to determine the cognitive processes that are involved in ongoing daily activities. In this case, the researcher will work in natural situations, as far as possible, with observational methods. These behaviors are sometimes so banal that, until very recently, they hardly attracted the attention of researchers. Everyday cognition research is concerned with the informal, oral, "traditional" or "popular" knowledge, meaning the knowledge of ordinary people (*jpfs,* or *just-plain-folks,* is a current acronym in this field), in contrast with school- or book-based, expert or scientific knowledge.

To maximize cultural validity in everyday cognition studies, experimental methods, if they are used at all, must be combined with natural observation to adapt them to the particular cultural milieu. While the loss of some experimental control is a cost, cultural validity is a worthwhile gain. What makes the research "cross-cultural" is the premise that culture has to be taken seriously. The research can be carried out in one location, or in many different locations. Researchers may seek situations that are rare in Western societies (e.g., children selling produce in the market, unschooled construction foremen), especially to unconfound variables, such as experience and schooling. But everyday cognition also occurs in cities and industrialized settings. Informal learning is a common phenomenon, even in complex and highly institutionalized societies. Research in this domain has been conducted in supermarkets, in factories, and in cocktail lounges (Rogoff & Lave, 1984). These studies have in common the researcher's departure from the laboratory in order to become involved in daily life settings.

First, we will deal briefly with two approaches that are at the root of the study of everyday cognition: the sociohistorical approach and cognitive anthropology or ethnoscience.

THE SOCIOHISTORICAL APPROACH: PIAGET *VERSUS* VYGOTSKY

As we saw in Chapter 5, "orthodox" Piagetian theory does not take culture seriously into account. Piaget (1966) himself, when discussing the factors that determine cognitive development, only paid lip service to the variable of educational and cultural transmission. He saw the individual's own activity as the major process of development and was of the opinion that this was universal, because, everywhere, the child had objects to interact with. These objects could also be people, and Piaget (1965, 1975) expected the same structures to develop from interactions with the physical and the social environments.

The importance of social interactions was taken seriously by some of Piaget's colleagues within the "Geneva school." Doise and his colleagues (Doise & Mugny, 1981/1984; Doise, Mugny, & Perret-Clermont, 1975; Doise & Palmonari, 1984; Perret-Clermont, 1979/1980) demonstrated how cognitive development is facilitated when the child is allowed to interact with peers over Piagetian tasks. The advantage gained through social interaction depends on various factors, such as the children's ages and cognitive stages, the nature of the "sociocognitive conflict" that is being created, and the subjects' understanding of the task and of the questions asked by the adult experimenters. Iannaccone and Perret-Clermont (1993) found that the performance on a Piagetian task, such as the conservation of number, depends on the setting (inside or outside of the classroom) and the "social marking" of the situation (whether the tester takes the role of a teacher or of a playmate). Schubauer-Leoni, Perret-Clermont, and Grossen (1992) conclude:

> *Both knowledge and cognitive competence are dependent on each interactor's representations of the role of his partner, of what knowledge is about, of the common task, and of the setting in which the encounter takes place. The shared representations are organized in terms of the tacit* social *contract.... [E]ach actualization of a competence, of an understanding or a knowledge takes a different meaning according to the setting (p. 76).*

Although this line of research has been conducted in single cultural contexts (Switzerland, Italy), without explicit reference to cross-cultural studies, its conclusions agree fully with what has been found in cross-cultural research. They also relate to a research tradition that comes from another well-known twentieth-century developmental psychologist, Lev Semyonovich Vygotsky (1896–1934).

The contributions of famous Soviet psychologists, like Luria, Leontiev, and Vygotsky, while not completely unknown in Western countries (cf. Piaget, 1956), have been only slowly translated into English, to a large extent thanks to the journal *Soviet Psychology* and the influence of Michael Cole. For example, one of Vygotsky's major works, *Thought and Language,* appeared in Russian in 1934, the year its author died of tuberculosis; an English translation was published only in 1962. Despite this late start, the influence of Vygotsky on Western psychology is presently much greater than that of Piaget (Schneuwly & Bronckart, 1985; Wertsch, 1985). This trend has crystallized in the founding of the Society for Socio-cultural Studies, and its biennial conferences (Wertsch, del Río, & Alvarez, 1995).

For Vygotsky, culture, and especially language, play a key role in cognitive development. The social and cultural contexts, particularly adults interacting with the child, provide whatever is to be learned, through the process of tutoring in the "zone of proximal development" (*zoped*). This represents the gap between what children can accomplish independently and when they are interacting with adults or more competent peers. Through a process called *scaffolding,* adults provide assistance just slightly beyond the child's current competence, stimulating development.

This idea is close to the role of cognitive conflict in Piaget's theory: There is an optimal discrepancy between the child's current knowledge and the new problem that leads to adaptation. If the discrepancy is too small, no learning is necessary; if it is too large, no learning is possible. The difference between the two theories is that for Vygotsky the zoped is provided by adults, while, for Piaget, development is generated by the child's own activities with respect to objects in the environment, or, later, in his or her own mind with respect to mental representations. Indeed, Piaget tended to see adult intervention, such as teaching, as unfortunate because it prevents children from discovering things by themselves.

In contrast to Piaget, Vygotsky asserts that there is always sociocultural mediation in individual development, with every function appearing twice: first at the "inter-mental" (or social) level, then at the "intra-mental" (or individually interiorized) level (Rogoff & Gardner, 1984; Wertsch, Minick, & Arns, 1984). "What originally had collective-cultural meaning in the inter-personal (or inter-mental) domain, under the guidance of socially defined interpretations of reality becomes intra-personal (intra-mental)" (Valsiner & Lawrence, 1997, p. 95). Hence, knowledge is always a social construction before it becomes individual. It is always contextualized, mediated by symbolic systems. In other words, culture provides tools (writing systems, schools, computers, and so on). "It is culture that provides the tools for organizing and understanding our worlds in communicable ways.... [L]earning and thinking are always *situated* in a cultural setting and always dependent upon the utilization of cultural resources" (Bruner, 1996, pp. 3–4; emphasis in original).

Vygotsky's sociohistorical framework adds still another dimension, that of phylogeny and cultural history, developed particularly clearly in Cole's (1996) "cultural psychology." This is a line of thinking that is not fundamentally different from Piaget's own interests in the history of science (Piaget, 1970a; Piaget & Garcia, 1987). Hence, while it is easy to oppose Vygotsky and Piaget, there are also some obvious overlaps, and the contrasts have sometimes been overstated. In the words of Tryphon and Vonèche (1996):

> *[T]he development of knowledge is not simply inside/out for Piaget and outside/in for Vygotsky. Both views combine intra-psychical and inter-psychical mechanisms. They both share actions as the starting block for further development. But they understand it differently. For Piaget, action is a natural event taking place in a natural environment. For Vygotsky it is a rich and meaningful human act constructed by history and society (pp. 8–9).*

While Vygotsky's theory has not been tested cross-culturally as Piaget's theory has, it has become influential in cross-cultural psychology, particularly through the work of Cole and his associates. The study of "everyday cognition" has grown largely out of this sociohistorical movement, at the same time as "cognition in context" (Laboratory of Comparative Human Cognition, 1983), "situated cognition" (Brown, Collins, & Duguid, 1989), "socially shared cognition" (Resnick, Levine, & Teasley, 1991), or "distributed cognition" (Salomon, 1993). According to these approaches, cognitive processes are not seen as exclusively individual central processors, but they are extended to peripheral tools and are situationally specific. Problem solving can even involve several individuals, because cognition is not necessarily situated "within the head" but is shared among people and settings. The "location" of cognition, inside or outside the individual, is a matter of much debate (Wassmann & Dasen, 1993).

ETHNOGRAPHY OF DAILY LIFE

Cultural anthropology has also contributed to the interest in everyday cognition. By its very nature, ethnography is the science of the everyday. But while it is common-place for anthropologists to describe in minute detail every twist and turn of whatever "exotic" people they have traveled far to study, we are surprised when researchers in industrialized societies use the same approach for the daily life that surrounds them. Augé (1986), for example, talks about traveling in the Paris subway. In another example from France, de Certeau (1980) describes and analyzes "popular culture" activities and the rituals of daily life in urban space. His colleague Giard (1980) provides a finely detailed description of everything involved in cooking (an important aspect of French society!), that includes customs and mores, but also individual knowledge and know-how, as well as the cognitive processes that support them:

> *As soon as one takes a close look at the process of culinary art, it becomes obvious that it demands a multiple memory. One must remember what one was taught, what movements witnessed, what textures felt, how thick a*

sauce should be.... It also requires a kind of intelligence that permits plan-
ning ahead. It is necessary to calculate assiduously both preparation and
cooking times and to integrate all the various sequences with each other....
        Each meal requires inventing a mini-strategy of substitution, whenever
a particular ingredient or utensil is not at hand.... Thus, to undertake the
art of cooking, to manipulate these mundane things, puts intelligence to
practical work. It must be a subtle kind of intelligence, full of nuances, of
on-the-spot innovations, an intelligence that is light-hearted and which can
be made out without clearly revealing itself. It is an intelligence of the most
ordinary kind (pp. 158–159; our translation).

Such reports are phenomenological. The language is more literary than scientific and the facts are "soft," qualitative, and difficult to verify. But given the research
goal, we welcome the richness of the observations. However, ethnology must do
more than describe and transcribe; the hidden meaning of the activities should be
revealed.

COGNITIVE ANTHROPOLOGY OR ETHNOSCIENCE

A slightly different approach is offered by cognitive anthropology or ethnoscience,
which seeks to build a model of an underlying cognitive structure from systematically gathered empirical facts. Pioneering work of this kind was described by Tyler
(1969) and more recent studies were covered in a critical and synthetic analysis by
Gardner (1985). This approach is also discussed by Berry and associates (1992),
Jahoda (1982), and Wassmann (1993).

Ethnoscientists try to work emically (i.e., using a society's own category system) to ascertain the cognitive principles by which the society's members apprehend
their world. Accordingly, ethnoscientists try to determine which aspects of the environment are considered important, what they are called, and how they are related
one to another. In effect, cognitive anthropology is an attempt to discover how each
culture creates order out of chaos.

According to Edgerton and Langness (1974, cited by Gardner, 1985, p. 246),
the goal of ethnoscience is "to write a set of rules for a culture which is so complete
that any outsider could use them to behave appropriately in that culture." This
amounts to extracting the "grammar" of a culture or its underlying structure. However, as with any generative grammar, the model might predict what is generally
appropriate in a culture but could not predict the behavior of any particular *individual* member of the society. The model must be able to explain all of the relevant
observations parsimoniously (i.e., with a minimum number of necessary principles).

How do ethnoscientists proceed? First, on the basis of their own observations
and intuitions, they choose a semantic domain that appears to be important in the
society being studied, such as kinship terms. Then all the lexical elements in this
domain (e.g., *mother, father, sister, nephew,* etc.) are collected. Next, the ethnologists

look for the dimensions or principles according to which it seems possible to organize those elements, such as sex, generation, linearity, and so on. In this manner, a "componential analysis" is completed, the results of which are usually reported in graphic form. A simple example with English language kinship terms, from Wallace and Atkins (1980), is provided in Table 6.1.

Considerable attention is paid to reliability in componential analysis. The likelihood that different ethnologists would obtain the same results is assessed routinely. But the method is plagued by several difficult methodological problems, all of which pose threats to its validity:

1. The information on which the analysis is based comes usually from privileged informants. Sometimes different informants each provide partial data. There is uncertainty as to whether everybody (or even anybody!) in the society actually employs the total model;
2. Interindividual variations are not often taken into account;
3. It is not clear whether the results of a componential analysis reflect a psychological reality. This problem is similar to that encountered in the study of artificial intelligence;
4. The models are based solely on linguistic facts. Nonverbal elements that might be important are missing.

Briefly, then, ethnoscience is the emic determination of domains that are generally treated scientifically. Accordingly, what it produces may properly be termed *ethno-botany, ethno-astronomy, ethno-medicine,* and the like. Because of its methodological difficulties, it is no longer widely practiced, but a combination with psychological methods attending to individual differences may enhance its potential (Wassmann & Dasen, 1994a/b). The relation of ethnoscience to everyday cognition

TABLE 6.1 English Language Kinship Terms

	c_1		c_2		c_3	
	a_1	a_2	a_1	a_2	a_1	a_2
b_1	grandmother	grandfather	uncle	aunt	cousin	
b_2	father	mother				
b_3	[ego]		brother	sister		
b_4	son	daughter	nephew	niece		
b_5	grandson	grandaughter				

is obvious because both try simultaneously to determine modes of popular thought and to derive the cognitive principles that underlie them.

To review: In emic research, we try to study a culture in order to see it as its own members do. Thus, research designed to show how a particular people classify experience, yielding the classification system they habitually employ, is a form of emic research known as ethnoscience (Dougherty, 1985; Gardner, 1985; Tyler, 1969). Ethnoscience is usually "ideographic": It describes how a particular group of people understand the world, what the elements are that are considered important, what they are called, and what relations exist among them, without attempting to compare this scheme to others. It is also "nomothetic," insofar as ethnoscience views all people in a culture as having the same cognitive categories.

It is, of course, also a perfectly legitimate question to ask how different cultures classify their world, and to produce some comparisons among the different schemes. In any case, total relativism would imply mutual ignorance. What needs emphasizing, however, is that any single culture's classification system should first be expressed in the terms employed indigenously.

The study of everyday cognition provides perfect ground for a combination of psychological and anthropological methods. The researcher is interested in cognitive processes as exemplified by the observable behavior of individuals, but as it occurs in the context of daily life and not on tests or tasks. Such an approach is not necessarily comparative. Many such observations have been carried out in single cultural contexts. Several studies to be reported below were carried out in Africa, India, or Brazil, particularly with children and adults who had no or limited schooling. Everyday cognition is usually conceived as "out of school" cognition.

EVERYDAY KNOWLEDGE OF ARITHMETIC

Many readers are likely to think of arithmetic as linked with schooling and literacy. We will now look at some studies demonstrating that the ability to read and write is by no means a prerequisite for arithmetic competence, and that illiterate persons can sometimes perform mentally very complex arithmetic calculations. Rosin (1973) described the kinds of calculations made by an illiterate peasant in Rajasthan (India). Box 6.1 provides an excerpt from this anecdotal but nevertheless instructive account.

It is fascinating to examine the (pre)historic development of number systems (Ifrah, 1985) and their diverse forms and usages in contemporary societies. Numbers were first invented in Mesopotamia about 5000 BP, and were used for accounting. The system was a combination of base 5 and 12, i.e., 60 and multiples of 60, a system that has left traces in our way of measuring time and angles. Nowadays, every society has a number system, albeit sometimes rudimentary. The Aranda, for example, an aboriginal group in central Australia, name only three numbers—1, 2, and 3—that they combine to express 4 and 5. Beyond 5, they say only "many" (Elkin, 1943). This no doubt reflects a cultural devaluing of quantification, a characteristic of nomadic hunter societies throughout the world. The production of a surplus

---

BOX 6.1   A Virtuoso Display of Everyday Arithmetic

Rosin (1973) made very detailed observations of some elaborate calculations by an illiterate peasant from Rajasthan (India), named Rupsingh (whose writing skill was limited to placing X on a document as a signature). Rosin accompanied Rupsingh to a goldsmith where they bought two gold medallions, each weighing 3¾ *tola*. A tola of gold costs 6¾ *roupees*. A roupee is equivalent to 16 *annas* or 100 *naya paisa*. The price for each medallion came to 25 roupees and 5 anna (or 25 roupees and 31 naya paisa). Rosin did the calculations twice in writing, once using fractions and once with decimals, and he got two different solutions. Because one of them corresponded to what the goldsmith asked, Rosin was prepared to pay it, but Rupsingh proposed instead that he verify the calculation himself to be sure that the goldsmith was not in error.

Rupsingh's strategy was to triple 6¾, then to find ¾ of 6¾, and to combine the results. This he did only by multiplication and division by two. He did addition by counting on his fingers (fifteen finger joints) and by memorizing the intermediate results each time. The calculation took him several hours spread over several days, after which he called his younger brother and his nephew, both of them schooled, and discovered that they had not yet solved the problem even with the use of paper and pencil.

This observation is anecdotal and limited to a single example. Nevertheless, this limitation is balanced by the richness and the detail of the description. You may want to test your mental calculation skills in solving the problem without using paper and pencil, or a calculator, of course!

---

among high-food-accumulation groups such as farmers and herders provides the motivation for the development of arithmetic, particularly where commerce is important.

Recall, from Chapter 5, the work of Saxe, who studied the body parts numbering system of the Oksapmin of Papua New Guinea. That illustrates the ethnographic diversity we can still find today, but it is rather exceptional. Most current number systems combine a base 5 (most probably derived from the five fingers) and a base 10 or 20 (two hands and two feet). Wassmann and Dasen (1994b) studied the number system of the Yupno, also in Papua New Guinea, which combines a base 5 and 20 with body parts counted from the head down the chest to end with the penis (33 in our count). The study looked at the social distribution of this knowledge (among the Yupno, only men were supposed to count, and only old men knew the full system) and interindividual variability (all men did not use exactly the same system).

Everyday Arithmetic and School-Based Arithmetic

The following questions will guide our comparison of everyday, informal arithmetic with its school-based counterpart:

1. Are the calculation strategies employed in the two situations the same or different?

2. How effective is everyday arithmetic and what are its limits?

A first group of studies was carried out mainly in Africa and in the United States by H. P. Ginsburg and colleagues (Ginsburg, 1982; Ginsburg & Russell, 1981; Posner & Baroody, 1979). These researchers found that knowledge of elementary arithmetic (including the conservation of number) can develop without schooling, particularly if children have opportunities to practice certain fundamental concepts in their everyday activities. A study of mental arithmetic among Dioula[1] children and adults (Ginsburg, Posner, & Russell, 1981) showed that nonschooled people make efficient use of regrouping (breaking addends into more manageable units that can then be added), which shows that they are implicitly using decomposition, associativity, and commutativity. In this study, nonschooled adults did not make any more errors than schooled adults (this was not so for children). But Petitto and Ginsburg (1982), in another study of mental calculation among illiterate Dioula, tested subjects on all four arithmetic operations (addition, subtraction, multiplication, and division) and found that informal arithmetic skills have their limits. This study is described in Box 6.2.

Other research in West Africa by different teams included that of Reed and Lave (1979), who demonstrated how computational errors made by Vai tailors in Liberia could be explained by features of their number system. The Vai system uses the base 5 in combination with the base 20. Schooled subjects tended to use the decimal system or to combine it with the Vai system. They made errors of place (i.e., being wrong by a factor of 10 or 100), while nonschooled subjects either made smaller errors (being wrong by 5, 10, or 20 units) or simply proceeded by approximation. Reed and Lave distinguished two classes of strategies for performing arithmetic operations: (1) those that deal with *quantities,* in *oral* arithmetic, using strategies such as counting on fingers, manipulating pebbles, or using an abacus; (2) strategies using number names, school-based algorithms designed for the manipulation of *symbols* and using a *written* numerical representation. In other words, everyday arithmetic calls on heuristic procedures, while conventional algorithms are taught in schools. Reed and Lave (1979) found that reasoning by quantities often led to more correct solutions than reasoning by symbols.

Brenner (1985) also worked among the Vai in Liberia, addressing the question of the efficiency of combining school-based algorithms with traditional methods. Brenner's study was based on observations of pupils (preschool, first and fourth grade primary) in four Liberian schools, to whom he presented an arithmetic test covering all four operations. Observations in the marketplace of the everyday arithmetic of tailors and carpenters revealed that everyday calculations involved diverse

---

[1]The Dioula can be found throughout West Africa; they are often merchants. This study took place in Côte d'Ivoire.

BOX 6.2   How Limited Are Informal Arithmetic Strategies?

The participants in Petitto and Ginsburg's (1982) experiment were 20 nonschooled Dioula adults, either tailors or cloth merchants, as well as 14 U.S. students. The problems given to them consisted of eight pairs of mental calculations related to each other by reciprocity (e.g., 90 + 35 and 125 − 90; 100 × 6, and 6 × 100).

For addition and subtraction (treated as inverse addition), the subjects used regrouping without any difficulty, thus applying implicitly the principles of associativity and commutativity. The results were nearly always precisely correct.

For multiplication, a problem like 100 × 6 presented practically no difficulty. It is expressed in Dioula by "100 added six times" and is solved effectively by successive addition. In contrast, the reciprocal, 6 × 100 or "6 added one hundred times," becomes a practically unsolvable problem and commutativity is not in general recognized.

Division is done by looking for a corresponding multiplication (or successive additions), sometimes employing approximations. For example, 300 ÷ 3 is easily solved by adding 100 three times (and noting that this equals 300). For a problem like 300 ÷ 100, some subjects first chose a small number like 2, added it one hundred times, and then tried another number until they found the solution.

The limitation of informal strategies in comparison with school-based algorithms is thus very real. All calculations are reduced to addition and the number position is not used, despite the existence of a base 10 in the Dioula number system. But this limitation is probably of very little functional importance in the ongoing life of Dioula merchants because the problems they have to solve never involve such large multipliers or divisors.

---

strategies, including breaking down a problem into the simplest possible units, counting concrete objects, reducing multiplication to addition, and the like. In class and on the test, nearly all the pupils (97 percent) used a combination of Vai and school-based strategies. This combined method appeared to be very powerful; those who used the greatest variety of combinations of school-based methods and different Vai techniques did best on the test. The Vai teachers apparently accepted the use of diverse arithmetic methods.

Perhaps the most productive group of researchers in the area of everyday arithmetic was situated for many years in Recife, Brazil. They designed a large number of studies that can be found summarized in a book entitled *Street mathematics and school mathematics* (Nunes, Schliemann, & Carraher, 1993) and in a chapter on everyday cognition in the *Handbook of cross-cultural psychology* (Schliemann, Carraher, & Ceci, 1997). These studies demonstrated, in particular, that nearly illiterate adults can use proportional reasoning (considered in Piaget's theory to require reasoning at the stage of formal operations) within the confines of their professional practice, for example, foremen working with scales on blueprints, or fishermen calculating the price and ratio of processed to unprocessed seafood.

One of the neatest uses of an everyday situation, in our view, is when these researchers observed children who were selling fruit in a market. While the children solved fairly complex calculations correctly in *this* situation, the same children, in school, solved only half of the same calculations correctly. Extracts from this research are provided in Box 6.3.

Applying these results to formal education practices, the Brazilian authors suggested that arithmetic be taught, at least in the beginning, in contexts that have practical significance, thereby taking advantage of the arithmetic knowledge children have already picked up in their daily activities. Then teachers could gradually add more powerful algorithms instead of trying to teach them first. The heuristic procedures are often quite complex and call for a surprisingly high level of skill in manipulating numbers. Furthermore, they vary among individuals and across problems. In contrast, school algorithms are general tools that are supposed to be applicable to many different situations, but, in fact, are often not used out of the school's context.

Several other studies of everyday cognition were carried out in and around Recife, Brazil, involving people in a variety of trades, including farm hands, cooks, and lottery bookies (Schliemann, Carraher, & Ceci, 1997). For example, Saxe (1991) provides a detailed study of candy sellers, children between 6 and 15 years with various degrees of schooling (from no school to seventh grade) who buy candy wholesale and then retail it on the street. The study was carried out at a time when inflation was very high, so that prices had to be adjusted continuously. It is particularly rich in describing the intricacies of the practice and its embeddedness in social conventions (the monetary system) and social interactions. Schooled nonsellers were also included. A summary of this research, and of the way it fits together with other of his studies, is provided by Saxe (1994), described in Box 6.4.

Arithmetic in the Supermarket

As mentioned above, in industrial societies, practical know-how and problem-solving skills (often requiring arithmetic calculations) are often brought to bear in everyday situations in which we can study the degree to which subjects use school-based skills or other more specific strategies.

The everyday situations studied in North America include calculations made by shoppers in a supermarket (Lave, Murtaugh, & de la Rocha, 1984; Murtaugh, 1985), computations made by weight watchers following a strict diet (de la Rocha, 1985), and problem solving in an industrial dairy (Scribner, 1984). These studies all revealed competencies that often exceed purely school-based techniques in efficiency and accuracy. The basic difference between the two types of situations is that, in practical settings, subjects must frame the question themselves, deriving it from a meaningful reality. They have to be able to simplify the problem and to be satisfied with a functionally acceptable approximation.

Lave (1988) and her colleagues (Lave, Murtaugh, & de La Rocha, 1984; Murtaugh, 1985) systematically observed twenty-four adults shopping in a supermarket,

BOX 6.3   Oral and Written Arithmetic

Carraher, Carraher, and Schliemann (1985) observed some schooled children in Recife in Brazil who also worked as sellers in the market. In the practical market setting, the children solved correctly 98 percent of some relatively complicated problems. For example, they solved the problem 35 × 10 as follows: 3 × 35 = 105; 105 + 105 + 105 + 35 = 350. In the school situation, the same children solved equivalent calculations correctly 74 percent of the time if presented in problem form, but only 37 percent of the time when presented in the form of numerical calculations.

The authors employed Reed and Lave's (1979) formulation to distinguish heuristic arithmetic procedures from school-based algorithms. This distinction is illustrated by the following example of an observation with a 12-year-old child:

Solve: 4 coconuts at 35 centavos each (4 × 35):

(1) Market situation: "3 coconuts cost 105" (here the child is using his knowledge of a frequent fact) "plus 30, that makes 135 and 1 coconut costs 35, and that makes 140."

(2) School setting: "4 × 5 = 20; I write down 0, and I carry the 2; 2 + 3 = 5; 5 × 4 = 20. I attach the 0 to the 20, and so the answer is 200."

The child in the market situation proceeded by successive addition, using an already memorized quantity (105) and decomposition (35 = 30 + 5). In the school situation, by contrast, the child tried to use the multiplication algorithm, but erred because he added the 10's before multiplying them. From all the evidence, it appears that the child learned a routine without understanding it, and wasn't surprised by an erroneous result because it didn't represent anything in terms of money.

In a follow-up study, Carraher, Carraher, and Schliemann (1987) gave some arithmetic problems to 16 children, aged 8 to 13 years, in the third primary grade in Recife. These problems included all four operations and each in three different situations. In one, the child took the role of grocer and the experimenter was the customer; real objects were available. The same calculations were presented in the form of meaningful problems and as written calculation exercises. The three series of 10 problems were administered by the same experimenter in a systematically varied order.

The authors discovered that the children tended more to use oral, heuristic procedures in the first two situations, and school-based algorithms in the third. On the whole, the oral procedures led to more correct responses than the written procedures. This was clearly so for subtraction, multiplication, and division (on the average, 65 to 75 percent correct responses with oral procedures, and 40 to 44 percent for written procedures). Thus it was not so much the formality or nonformality of the situation that mattered, but the choice of procedures.

The oral procedures rested on decomposition and/or regrouping, which allowed working with quantities that are easier to manipulate and then be part of a calculation of an iterative nature, such as successive additions or successive divisions by 2.

More details of such studies can be found in Nunes, Schliemann, and Carraher (1993).

BOX 6.4   Saxe's Practice-Based Framework

The theoretical "practice-based" framework that Saxe has developed consists of three interacting components. The first component, "emergent goals," is geared for understanding the dynamics of goal formation. These goals emerge in everyday practices, and interact with artifacts (e.g., currency), activity structures (e.g., the routines of making a purchase), social interactions (with sales clerks, peers, and customers), and the individual's prior understandings (e.g., of counting). Candy sellers go through a cyclic activity structure of buying wholesale, preparing smaller lots of candy, selling them, and preparing a new purchase. One of the main emerging goals is markup from wholesale to retail price. This is dealt with according to conventions and artifacts (using Cr$500 and Cr$1000 notes), according to prior understandings (e.g., the concept of profit), and in social interactions.

The second component, "form–function shifts," deals with the different cultural forms the child is appropriating during ontogeny to accomplish emergent goals, and which cognitive functions these

forms are serving. For example, all sellers made use of a price ratio convention (e.g., three candy bars for Cr$1000), but the use of this convention shifts considerably between a 6-year-old who is told what to charge, and an older seller who uses several ratios in "what-if" computations to determine the wholesale price that would give him a good profit.

Third, the "interplay across practices" is the component concerned with transfer: "In what way do cognitive forms elaborated in one practice become appropriated and specialized to accomplish new functions in others?" (Saxe, 1994, p. 149). For example, do sellers who also go to school make use of their street mathematics to solve computational problems in class?

Differences between sellers and nonsellers were most pronounced at grade 2 level: more than a threefold difference in the number of problems solved correctly by sellers, and five times more adequate regrouping strategies. Starting with grade 3, however, nonsellers and schooled sellers acquire more adequate algorithmic forms such as multiplication.

---

following them and asking them to explain their various selections and to describe the kinds of calculations they needed to perform. Rather complex calculations were required because products were packaged in nonmetric sizes (involving numbers like 24, 32, and 64, for example, in ounce- and pound-denominated weights) and often lacked unit price markings.

Of a total of 803 purchases, 312 required an explicit decision, either based on brand preferences (reflecting habits, tastes, and advertisements) or taking into account such factors as package size in relation to family size. In addition to these kinds of decisions, 213 calculations were performed. In 30 percent of these cases, "best buy" calculations were performed. Of these, 16 involved simply using unit prices that were provided on the packages. In the other 49 cases, the buyers rarely tried to determine the precise unit cost, but simply multiplied the price of one item to compare it roughly with another of equal weight. They tried to find out simply which was more advantageous (but not by how much) and often employed simplification and approximation. Exact calculations were performed in only 5 percent of the cases.

Still, the calculations performed led to correct choices 98 percent of the time, even though the same people who participated in the supermarket study solved, on the average, only 59 percent of the items on an arithmetic test. However, unlike the Brazilian study described in Box 6.3, the problems presented were not the same in both situations.

The authors concluded that, in everyday situations, one has not only to *solve* problems but to *frame* them as well. This must be done in practical terms, and often requires simplifying the problem. "Problem-formation and problem-solving are very likely to be integral parts of a single process in many real-world environments" (Murtaugh, 1985, p. 192).

Newman, Griffin, and Cole (1984) also noted that in everyday situations, people first have to define a problem before being able to solve it. Moreover, these real-life situations typically involve social interaction. In contrast, in psychological laboratory situations, the task is usually defined by the experimenter while the subject (often an isolated individual) attempts to solve the problem alone. Classroom situations tend to fall somewhere between these two extremes.

To summarize: everyday arithmetic has both strengths and weaknesses. Because the strategies employed are so varied, everyday arithmetic often leads to more correct solutions than school-derived algorithms. These strategies often involve decomposition and regrouping, which are based on principles of associativity and commutativity. On the other hand, the reciprocity of two operations is not always recognized. The four basic operations are, in general, reduced to successive addition. This under scores the limits of everyday arithmetic, particularly with large numbers.

The characteristics of everyday arithmetic most often demonstrated are:

1. Quantities are manipulated more often than symbols;
2. Problems are redefined in order to simplify them;
3. Solutions tend to be idiosyncratic; they vary both across individuals and across problems.

EVERYDAY SPACE AND GEOMETRY

While the topic of arithmetic has received the most attention in the area of everyday cognition, space and geometry have been covered as well. A part of the relevant literature has been reviewed by Dasen and Bossel-Lagos (1989), and we will mention here only a small selection of other studies. Pinxten, van Dooren, and Harvey (1983) have provided an analysis of Navajo space, based largely on linguistic material.

Gerdes (1988b) provided a detailed analysis of sand drawings that are a traditional practice among the Tchokwe of Angola. Some examples of these are provided in Figure 6.1. The drawing always starts with a set of dots arranged into an orthogonal net of equidistant points, in fact, a coordinate system. The pattern is then drawn in a smooth motion using this grid as a background. Gerdes analyzes these drawings as the expression of geometric algorithms that give rise to more or less complex mathematical formulae. For example, the drawings in Figure 6.1 can illustrate the "Pythagorean triplet," $3^2 + 4^2 = 5^2$. The drawing starts with two superposed grids, one of 4×4 points and one of 3×3 points; the solution 5×5 can be derived through several motifs, very old designs that appear already on rockpaintings in the Upper Zambeze region.

Gerdes (1988a) similarly uses everyday activities (such as weaving leaves into a traditional fish traps) for what he calls "the unfreezing of culturally frozen mathematics" (p. 153). The geometrical principles underlying the artisan's practice can thus be revealed. Introducing such activities into the classroom, or in teacher training, demonstrates to the pupils and their teachers that geometrical thinking is not alien to the local cultural heritage. Incorporating such "indigenous mathematics" or "ethnomathematics" into the curriculum should help to build effective bridges to universal "world mathematics," defined as the union of all "ethnomathematics" (Gerdes, 1988b). Much effort is presently geared to adapting educational curricula to indigenous cultures (Teasdale, 1994). For example, Harris (1991) has studied the contexts for teaching and learning about space (as well as time and money) among Australian Aboriginal children; mathematics and science curricula, and the language needed for these, now exist for the Maori of New Zealand (Barton, Fairhall, & Trinick, 1995).

Saxe and Gearhart (1990) studied the development of topological concepts in unschooled straw weavers (5 to 15 years of age) in rural communities in Brazil's Northeast, and observed carefully how expert weavers demonstrate the process to novices. Weavers were more able to construct homeomorphic patterns for novel weaves than age-matched nonweavers, but performed poorly on tasks that required them to verbalize how to weave known patterns. They represented their knowledge in topological action schemes (e.g., folding under, pushing through, separating), and

FIGURE 6.1 **Tchokwe Sand Drawings.**

Reprinted with permission from Gerdes, P. (1988b). On possible uses of traditional Angolan sand drawings in the mathematics classroom. *Educational Studies in Mathematics, 19,* 3–22.

this knowledge was found to be conceptual. The authors conclude: "Evidently, speech is not the only form that enables the individual to appropriate and restructure knowledge generated in one context to solve problems in others" (p. 257).

Saxe and Gearhart (1990) conclude that the straw weavers' knowledge is transferable from one situation to another. Much debate has occurred on this question of transfer and generalization of everyday cognition.

TRANSFER AND GENERALIZATION

Is everyday knowledge transferable to new situations? Is it generalizable[2] or is it inextricably tied to the contexts in which it was learned?

In Chapters 4 and 5, we touched on the specificity *versus* interdependence controversy with respect to cognitive mechanisms (see also Mishra, 1997). We noted that Cole and his colleagues adopted an extreme contextualist viewpoint whereby each aptitude is treated as independent of the others yet tied to the context in which it is functional (LCHC, 1983). They would expect a minimum of transfer from one context to another. At the other extreme are researchers (often using factor analysis) who postulate the existence of a very general aptitude (the *g* factor), a position similar to that of orthodox Piagetian theory, in which a certain homogeneity of behaviors within any given stage was assumed, and easy transfer was expected.

A third alternative is intermediate and is exemplified by "local constructivism" (Harris & Heelas, 1979; Dasen, 1983b) and "cognitive styles" (Berry, 1984b), both of which postulate a functional connection between contexts and cognitive domains. Transfer would be expected within but not across domains.

Research reviewed in the previous chapters clearly favors this third alternative. In the research Dasen and his colleagues carried out using Piagetian training techniques (Dasen, Ngini, & Lavallée, 1979), transfer occurred regularly within each domain (within the spatial domain, or between different conservation tasks, but not between space and conservation nor vice versa). Some cognitive styles may be in themselves more or less conducive to transfer. For example Sylvia Scribner's (1979) "empiric style," or Tapé Gozé's (1994) "experiential style" (see Chapters 4 and 5), both describe a mode of thinking that is attached to experienced reality and refuses to deal with conjecture. In schools, much of the training entails dealing with

---

[2]Experimental psychologists study transfer by measuring the effects of prior learning on performance. Learning is a cumulative process. The more information acquired, the greater the probability that new learning experiences will be affected by prior experiences. An adult never learns anything entirely from scratch; even when confronting unknown tasks, accumulated information and habits are involved. Piéron (1957) offered the following definition: "[T]here is transfer when the progress obtained in the course of learning a certain form of activity involves an improvement in the performance of a different, more or less related, activity" (p. 370). If there is a strong effect on relatively far-removed tasks, one speaks of generalization rather than of transfer.

topics that are not related to everyday experience, which explains why schooling seems to have such a widespread effect on cognitive skills. Hence, one may expect school-related learning to be easily generalizable, while everyday knowledge would be restricted to the contexts in which it is functional. Is such a conclusion really warranted?

Conceptual and Procedural Knowledge

Hatano (1982) subscribed to the above-mentioned conclusion in introducing a contrast between "procedural skills" and "conceptual knowledge." The former are routine procedures for rapidly and efficiently solving problems in a specific context. They are efficient only if external constraints do not change. Procedural skills are often specific to a society and go unquestioned; they are institutionalized and are considered necessarily "the best" method. For example, Hatano points to the Asian cultural tradition of counting with an abacus, internalized for the purposes of mental counting in the form of an extremely efficient "mental abacus" (e.g., Stigler, 1984). The performance by some experts is astonishing, calculations involving fifteen numbers, sometimes performed more rapidly than on an electronic calculator! On the basis of earlier work, however, Hatano suggested that this procedural skill does not transfer to other forms of calculation, such as those with numbers to the base 10 or those requiring comprehension of the remainder principle. Neither did it transfer to problems requiring the memorization of information other than numbers.

It thus appears that procedural skill transfer is limited when unaccompanied by conceptual knowledge. Conceptual knowledge involves the mental representation of a procedure's meaning, an understanding of why and how it works, and some notion of what its variations might be. Transfer, and, hence, flexibility, adaptiveness, and innovation, are possible only with this kind of understanding. Conceptual knowledge will be more easily acquired if external constraints change, if the situation demands procedural variations, if procedural skill is put into some doubt (either by the user or by others), and if the user is encouraged to *think about* the procedure rather than *execute* it as rapidly as possible.

Most instances of everyday cognition are of the procedural kind. Insofar as people live in a stable cultural setting, procedural skill is enough to ensure production. The culture provides the procedural model, but only rarely is this accompanied by an explanation for its use.

In conclusion, we assume that though practice in most culture-specific procedural skills tends to produce routine experts, with developed special processes involved in their performance, it usually doesn't facilitate development of the corresponding conceptual knowledge, nor competence under a new set of constraints even in the same domain (Hatano, 1982, p. 17).

Weaving in Various Cultural Contexts

Greenfield and Childs (1977), in a study of the learning of weaving among young Zinacanteco (Mexico) girls (also discussed in Childs & Greenfield, 1980 and Greenfield & Lave, 1979, 1982) explored the cognitive effects of weaving on the representation of patterns similar to those that are used in traditional fabrics (always involving alternating red and white bands of varying width). The two tasks employed in this study involved, (1) copying two familiar figures with sticks of colored wood, and (2) completing six incomplete figures, varying both in complexity and familiarity, also with wooden sticks. The subjects, between 13 and 18 years of age, included 9 nonschooled female weavers and 18 nonweaving boys, half of them schooled, the others not.

In the first task, the girls used the sticks as if they were threads, while the nonschooled boys dealt with the figure as a whole. The girls were thus able to transfer their practical knowledge to a different material. But the schooled boys were also proceeding analytically. The authors explained the boys' performance not as a consequence of familiarity with the figures but of a general ability acquired in school to move from one content to another.

On the second kind of task, which involved a problem that is truly novel with respect to traditional weaving, one could have reasonably expected to find good performance only among the schooled boys. In fact, it was all the boys, schooled or not, who outperformed the weaving girls. The authors explained this result as a gender role phenomenon, related to the fact that, in this society, boys are the predominant participants in the money economy, and make frequent trips to urban centers, where they have ample opportunity to see a great variety of fabrics.

The lack of generalization from weaving to these test situations demonstrates the specificity of this kind of know-how, at least in cultural contexts in which innovation is not valued. In effect, the Zinacantecos, at the time of this study, used to weave only two or three designs and did not consider variations. Later in this chapter, we will see that social change in this village went along with changes in the weaving practice and in the way weaving is learned.

Among many other studies of weaving in traditional settings (Chamoux, 1981; Coy, 1989; Rogoff, 1986, 1990), Rogoff and Gauvain (1984) examined the transfer of this skill among adult Navajo women. Weaving skill was the best predictor of performance on a task resembling weaving (continuing a woven pattern) but not for other tasks (continuing a pattern with pipe cleaners, or in a multiple-choice format). Schooling contributed little, and on the multiple-choice task, only age was a significant predictor. In this context, experience with the multiple-choice format seems to have come through other activities (such as getting a driver's license) rather than through schooling. The overall conclusion was that transfer was rather limited both for everyday skills and for schooling.

Different conclusions come from a study of the generalization of schooling and weaving skills among Dioula young men in Côte d'Ivoire (Tanon, 1994). The study included weavers and nonweavers, both schooled and unschooled. The training of young boys as weavers starts at 10 to 12 years. Scaffolding is used for the beginning of the practice, the setup of the warp, and the production of the first large cloths, in which mistakes would be difficult to correct and, hence, have economical consequences. Trial and error is used in the weaving of more complex patterns or innovative designs that can be easily corrected if noticed immediately. At the beginning, boys slide into the father's loom during his absence, and try to weave. When the father returns and notices it, he asks around "Who sat to weave on my loom?" and he corrects the mistakes. This little game goes on until the father no longer notices any difference in the weaving. At that time, the boy receives his own loom, and the apprenticeship continues. Among the Dioula, the invention of new patterns is highly valued, the weavers are organized in a cooperative, and are active in selling their products, especially to tourists.

Tanon devised two tasks of planning skills, one involving pattern matching based on either traditional or commercial cloths, and one involving the loading and unloading of passengers and luggage in a small bus (taxi van). Loading had to be done taking into consideration the order in which the passengers would disembark at various stops. Both weaving and schooling had significant effects on planning skills in both tasks and the schooled weavers had the best performance overall. On the taxi van task, the weavers did better than the nonweavers, in particular in carrying the planning task to the end. In this case, the control procedures that allow planning, stressed in strip weaving, transferred to a new task, unrelated to weaving.

Transfer of Formal Operations in Brazil

A series of studies carried out in Recife, Brazil (Nunes, Schliemann, & Carraher, 1993) demonstrates transfer in combinatorial and proportional reasoning among minimally schooled adults, who use it in the practice of their craft. Brazilian foremen, observed on building sites, are capable of calculating proportions by using the scales of their plans. They are also able to transfer their knowledge to the utilization of unfamiliar scales (for example, 1/40 and 1/33.3, while they normally use 1/20, 1/50, or 1/100). In this study, 60 percent of the subjects gave evidence of transfer by using their knowledge in a flexible manner, independently of their degree of schooling (which varied from zero to eleven years). A similar result was found with fishermen, who were accustomed to using proportional reasoning for price calculation and for estimating the proportions of processed to unprocessed fish and shellfish. The problems given to them required that they invert the normal procedures: They had to calculate the unit price from the price of a large amount or calculate the amount of fish that had to be caught in order to obtain a given weight of filets. Again, performance was not correlated with amount of prior schooling (which varied from one to nine years). Daily experience with betting in a number lottery was another practice that favored this kind of reasoning to some extent, and also showed transfer from an everyday situation to the solution of new problems. Nunes, Schliemann, and Carraher (1993) conclude from this whole set of studies that everyday activities foster the development of transferable, flexible knowledge, which is conceptual and not merely procedural.

Conclusion Regarding Transfer

What can we conclude from the various studies of transfer of everyday cognition? We seem to have a contradiction between a series of studies showing that everyday cognitions are most often tied to the context in which they are usually applied, and other research that does show evidence of transfer. Schliemann, Carraher, and Ceci (1997) conclude that "everyday activities do promote the development of conceptual knowledge rather than only procedural knowledge for specific problems. As such, knowledge acquired in specific everyday activities does transfer to other activities, but this is more likely to occur for those subjects who also benefited from school instruction" (p. 202).

For those studies that did not find transfer, the test situations were often artificial (e.g., "weaving" with wood sticks or pipe cleaners, choosing designs in a multiple-choice format) and were therefore inherently strange. Might not transfer be more easily demonstrated in situations that are new but, at the same time, not so foreign, such as those used in the Recife studies? As regards knowledge acquired in formal schooling, even if it is more generalizable than everyday cognition, it, too, has limits and is, in a certain sense, contextualized. Increasingly, school (and the laboratory) is seen as simply another context for learning, with its own specific cognitive outcomes. School knowledge can also be closely linked to the conditions in which it was acquired, the types of settings, interactions, and tools allowed or required (learning to write with or without a word processor).

The whole issue of transfer is a complex one, which goes well beyond cross-cultural psychology and the scope of this book. Detterman (1994) doubts whether it exists at all: "There is no good evidence that people produce significant amounts of transfer or that they can be taught to do so" (p. 17). Also, the framework of situated learning and cognition calls into question the very paradigm of transfer research (Greeno, Smith, & Moore, 1994). Lave (1988) sees transfer as a research question specifically linked to a positivist stance that treats culture and cognition as separate entities. She proposes instead to study the "continuity in activity across settings" (p. 186), with a focus not on cognitive processes but on the social organization of activity settings. The question becomes how activities relate to each other, and how people move from one activity setting to another (Rogoff, 1996, as quoted by Miller, 1997). We shall return to this position in the final section of this chapter.

LEARNING AND TEACHING PROCESSES

What are the learning or instructional processes that are associated with everyday situations? And, are some of them more conducive to transfer than others? Are there cultural differences in learning styles?

Greenfield and Lave (1979, 1982) distinguished three types of processes: (1) trial and error, (2) shaping, and (3) scaffolding. In the trial-and-error process, learners are confronted by a new situation constituting a conflict with what they already know. They have to try different approaches, and usually succeed only after making successive adjustments. According to Piaget, this process should lead to conceptual knowledge. In this type of learning, motivation is seen as internal to the learner. Conflict and making errors are seen as positive features, leading to progress.

Shaping is a process in which the learner's responses are controlled by a teacher, who organizes problems according to a sequence of small steps designed, as much as possible, to avoid errors. Correct responses are reinforced by external rewards. Much of schooling, and particularly programmed learning, is of this type.

Learning by scaffolding also involves an adult, and also tries to avoid errors, but the whole problem (too difficult to be managed by the novice alone) is presented immediately in its entirety. The expert provides support to the novice, furnishing information and intervening, even taking the apprentice's place, when some step appears to be too difficult. Scaffolding therefore involves continuously assessing the ability level of the learner. The expert's intervention diminishes in the course of the apprenticeship until it is no longer needed. Scaffolding allows the novice eventually to do alone what at the beginning could be done only with help from the expert. Thus, scaffolding is an instructional process that always involves social interaction. This model illustrates Vygotsky's concept of a "zone of proximal development."

Figure 6.2 depicts these different learning and teaching processes, combining elements from Chamoux (1981), Greenfield (1984), and Strauss (1984). On the left side of Figure 6.2 are the mechanisms that tend to predominate in informal education (observation, imitation) and on the right side those of formal education (trial and error). But the processes do not divide cleanly across the informal–formal dichotomy. Chanting is characteristic of formal, traditional education, such as religious schooling. The distinction between well-defined and ill-defined procedures (Strauss, 1984) does not imply a value judgment, but derives from studies on artificial intelligence and problem solving. Well-defined procedures are those in which the necessary information is fully laid out, and the steps to be taken and the goals to be attained are completely specified, while in ill-defined procedures the learner is confronted with uncertainty, which requires proceeding by trial and error. Cultural differences with respect to these learning processes consist primarily of the degree to which they predominate in any particular setting, and not in the presence or absence of any one process. The differential frequency of settings itself characterizes different societies.

The prevalence of some learning processes also depends on their respective economic implications. In their study of weaving apprenticeship among the Zinacantecan girls in Mexico (and also Lave's study of the tailors in Liberia), Greenfield and Lave (1979, 1982) found that the masters "use scaffolded intervention to achieve developmental sequencing within chunks. This results in relatively errorless learning under circumstances where errors would cause considerable economic harm to the teacher's household" (p. 207).

Greenfield (1984) proposed that the concept of learning by scaffolding characterizes especially those situations in which the economic stakes are high. By contrast, when cost doesn't matter, as in many school-based situations, trial-and-error

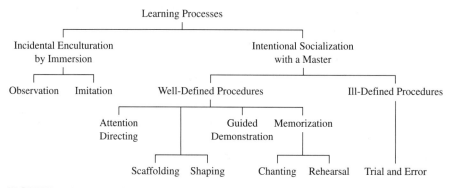

FIGURE 6.2   Learning and Teaching Processes in Formal and Informal Education.

learning is more common. Shaping can be combined with either of the other learning processes. Learning by observation, shaping, and especially scaffolding, is congruent with a value system oriented toward the maintenance of traditional ways. In contrast, trial-and-error learning is found when innovation is valued more.

These predictions were confirmed in a long-term longitudinal study when Greenfield (1996, 1998) returned to the same Zinacantec Maya community in Mexico twenty-one years after her initial study of weaving apprenticeship. The girls had become mothers, who in turn had daughters who were learning to weave. But the learning processes, Greenfield found, had changed substantially in many families: Girls were often learning much more by themselves, by trial and error, only calling for help when they deemed it necessary. Mothers were often busy with their own work, and were not providing any direct scaffolding.

This change in learning processes went along with extensive social change. In the intervening years, the community had started transport companies and developed much more frequent contacts with the town of San Cristobal, and even contacts with Mexico City for the first time. Woven artifacts produced in the village were being sold there, both to foreign and Mexican tourists. Although still based on the traditional patterns, they were now made of commercially produced thread of many different colors, and the women were competing in inventing new styles of decorations or copying them from books. Errorless learning had become less essential, because thread had become cheaper. The changes in weaving apprenticeship from more scaffolded to more independent trial-and-error learning was concentrated in families in which mothers and daughters were more involved in textile-related commerce (Greenfield, Maynard, and Childs, 1997).

Greenfield's (1996) "major theoretical proposition is that not only do cultures change over historical time, but the very processes of cultural learning and cultural transmission also change. More specifically, a somewhat different set of learning processes are highlighted when cultures are in a more stable state, compared with when they are in a more dynamic state" (p. 239).

THE SOCIOCULTURAL PARADIGM

As a relatively recent outgrowth of Vygotsky's theory, and in line with "cultural psychology" (Greenfield, 1997; Miller, 1997), the study of everyday cognition has shifted from an attention to cognitive and learning processes to the study of "social practices." According to this school, it is "reasonable to avoid the assumption of a boundary between the mind and the environment" (Super & Harkness, 1997, pp. 10–11). As Miller (1997) summarizes the position: "One of the striking theoretical shifts in research from a sociocultural perspective is the move away from a focus on psychological processes as internal to individuals to a focus on their embodiment in the context of social interactions and engagement with cultural tools" (p. 92).

Together with this theoretical shift, a new vocabulary and a whole set of new concepts have to be addressed. For example, Lave and Wenger (1991) introduced the concept of "legitimate peripheral participation" (LPP) as an approach to the study of learning, particularly in the form of apprenticeship. In LPP, newcomers start with getting a view of the whole enterprise, but are not asked to perform the whole task: They are given small tasks, usually at the end of a process line. Motivation stems from the opportunity to move toward fuller participation. There is not necessarily a master–apprentice relationship, because most learning can occur in interactions with other learners or peers. "Engaging in practice, rather than being its object, may well be a *condition* for the effectiveness of learning" (p. 93).

In LPP, newcomers gradually become practitioners, and then old-timers: members of the community of practitioners, with a new identity. In this process, they learn "who is involved, what they do, what everyday life is like, how masters talk, walk, work, and generally conduct their lives…and what learners need to learn to become full practitioners" (Lave & Wenger, 1991, p. 95). Note the similarity of this account to previous reports on informal education, such as those of Chamoux (1986) and Delbos and Jorion (1984) discussed in Chapter 3.

As an illustration, the authors use, in addition to Lave's own study of tailors in Liberia, four ethnographic studies of apprenticeship carried out by other researchers who do not refer to the LPP paradigm themselves: midwives in Yucatan, US navy quartermasters, butchers in US supermarkets, and members of Alcoholics Anonymous.

While the concept of LPP is certainly very useful to describe the sociocultural context in which apprenticeship occurs, "everyday cognition" has almost completely disappeared from the analysis. We are left with a description of social experience that is difficult to relate to more precise studies of learning. The authors seem to take a stand against psychological approaches, instead of seeing psychological and anthropological approaches as being complementary at different levels of description.

Rogoff's (1990, 1995) "guided participation" is a concept that does not suffer from this drawback. It refers to the interactions between people, often a child and an adult, as they jointly participate in a culturally valued activity. The guidance refers to "the direction offered by cultural and social values, as well as social partners" (Rogoff, 1995, p. 142). It can be seen as a generalization of the scaffolding metaphor, or more generally speaking, a dynamic, interactive view of the process of socialization. Participation includes observation, pointing to the fact that children can be very active in attending to what they watch. Rogoff (1995) calls "participatory appropriation" the individual change that occurs through involvement in interpersonal activity. Apprenticeship refers to a culturally organized activity at the institutional level. The three processes (participatory appropriation, guided participation, and apprenticeship) always occur together, but distinguishing them helps to focus on three levels: personal, interpersonal, and institutional.

These general processes are deemed to be universal, but with wide cultural variations in the styles of interaction with children, and especially in the goals of development (Rogoff, 1990). This is illustrated by several cross-cultural studies. For example, Rogoff, Mistry, Göncü, and Mosier (1993) examined how toddlers and their caregivers from four cultural communities (a Mayan Indian town in Guatemala, a middle-class urban group in the United States, a tribal village in India, and a middle-class urban neighborhood in Turkey) collaborate in shared activities. A key cultural difference was found to entail who is responsible for learning, depending on the cultural variation in the segregation of children from adult activities of their community and in emphasis on formal schooling.

Middle-class mothers seem to prepare their children for schooling: They structure learning situations, and actively encourage language learning; bookreading and pretend-play are considered important. In the two rural communities, caretakers do not have to organize special learning situations; children soon manage full participation in the activities of the community. They become keen observers, and skilled participants.

Keen observation through sharing attention among complex ongoing events was more apparent in Guatemala and in India than in the two middle-class communities, in which children are more segregated from adult activities. A summary of the contrast between the models of learning in Guatemala and in a middle-class European-American community, based on Rogoff (1994), is provided in Box 6.5.

Another study by Rogoff and her colleagues (Rogoff, 1995; Rogoff, Baker-Sennett, Lacasa, & Goldsmith, 1995) involved observing troops of 10- and 11-year-old girl scouts in the United States in their activity of preparing, selling, and delivering cookies as a fund-raising project. Like much of the research in the area of everyday cognition, Rogoff's contribution illustrates the strategy of combining studies carried out in one single cultural setting with cross-cultural, comparative work.

BOX 6.5 Models of Teaching and Learning in Guatemala and in the United States

Rogoff and her colleagues (1993) made home visits with middle-class families in the United States (Salt Lake City) and with Mayan families in Guatemala. They included an interview about daily routines and childrearing practices as well as videotapes of the interactions between the toddlers and caregivers in problem-solving situations, namely operating interesting novel objects and getting toddler arms through shirt sleeves.

Rogoff (1994) summarized the characteristics of Mayan toddler–caregiver interactions in the following way:

In the problem-solving activities, the Mayan toddlers and their caregivers contributed to the direction of the activity, with mutuality. The toddlers were very responsible for observing and provided leadership in problem-solving, while the caregivers oriented the children to the activity, made suggestions and alertly monitored the toddlers' activities, and provided sensitive assistance when the toddlers needed help. The caregivers did not direct the toddlers' activities by providing adult-run lessons or insisting on a certain way that an activity be done. Rather, they provided orientation and suggestions and generally maintained themselves in readiness to assist the child's direction of activity, while they simultaneously engaged with the group (not exclusively with the child). The toddlers observed and participated in the activities of the group even if they were also engaged in a separate activity, with embeddedness in group activities, rather than simply solo or dyadic engagements (p. 215).

In the Mayan community, children learn through participation in mature activities of the community. They are not segregated from observing and participating in community events and adults seldom create specialized learning situations for children such as lessons or adult–child play. Mayan children are involved as participants rather than the targets of specialized instruction segregated from ongoing activities.

In contrast, European-American caregivers often took charge of problem solving in ways that can be regarded as adult-run. They often directed the toddlers' activities, tried to motivate the child's involvement and to manage the toddler's attention. They organized didactic lessons (e.g., on vocabulary) and sometimes insisted on a certain way that an activity be done. The caregivers' efforts to organize the toddlers' problem solving occurred only when the toddler was the main focus of adult attention. If the caregiver attended to adult activities, her efforts with the toddler usually ceased.

Rogoff comments on the difficulties that European-American researchers had to understand the learning and interactions of the Mayan toddlers and caregivers. On viewing videotaped interactions of the Mayan interactions, they often could not see the shared involvement of both the toddler and the caregiver, and the supportive role of the Mayan caregivers, because they focused on the caregivers' simultaneous involvement with other ongoing activities. Because they focused on the conversation between the mother and another adult, for example, they assumed

Continued

BOX 6.5 *Continued*

that the mother was doing nothing with the child. Only if prompted to ignore the adult conversation and focus on the mother's involvement with the child did they see that she was simultaneously communicating with and assisting the child in a fluent way.

Rogoff (1994, p. 216) found that "European-American coders often require extensive training to be able to see meaning in richly structured group activities and in simultaneous and subtle communication in several modalities. Coders of other backgrounds (e.g., Navajo, Mayan, Japanese-American, East Indian) seem to see the group-oriented attention and communication as common sense, without training."

Rogoff (1994) also comments on social change, and on the way in which the formal (school) learning style ends up influencing informal interactions:

> When the Mayan children reach school, they meet a different philosophy of learning, in which teachers utilize the 'recitation' script that has been common in European and U.S. education for decades. The teachers focus on dictating to the children and quizzing them on what they

have learned with teacher as one side of the adult-run communication dyad and students (en masse or singly) as the other side. This encounter between different models is contributing to some changes in caregivers' practices. Mothers of the Mayan toddlers studied by Rogoff [and colleagues] (1993) who had spent more than six years in school spoke to their toddlers in ways consistent with the adult-run model of schooling: they were more likely to try to motivate the toddlers' involvement with mock excitement and to give lessons. However, their alert involvement with the child's direction of the activity and readiness to support the toddlers' efforts did not differ from that of the less-schooled Mayan mothers. When middle-class European-American children reach school, they ordinarily encounter a model of learning that resembles that used in their homes, with teachers giving lessons and quizzing children's knowledge, and discouraging children from learning from each other (p. 217).

CONCLUSION

Research on everyday cognition is a relatively new field of enquiry that illustrates well the interdisciplinary nature of cross-cultural psychology. It is an attempt to study cognition in its sociocultural context, that is, culturally relevant cognition. Through the emphasis on specific contexts, the particularities of knowledge in action may have been overemphasized, as well as the lack of transfer to new problems. Further research should look for the common threads across situations, and develop a stronger theory of settings.

At the present time, we witness an almost complete incompatibility between the more extreme versions of sociocultural theory and mainstream cognitive psychology, in particular research in artificial intelligence and cognitive science. Locating cognition completely outside of the individual to the extent of denying the very existence of cognitive processes seems to be as one-sided an approach as denying any importance to context and culture. In the future, after some swings of the pendulum, we will no doubt find that these competing paradigms are at least complementary, and we may even expect some convergence.

7

BELIEFS, MOTIVES, AND VALUES

WHY STUDY VALUES CROSS-CULTURALLY?

If we wish to know what beliefs any group of people hold and what motivates them ("What makes them tick?" as the saying goes) it would help to be familiar with their culture's values and priorities. Individual motives and beliefs often reflect a culture's values.

An examination of others' values may reveal attractive alternatives to our own, encouraging us perhaps to enrich our lives by reconsidering our values. Moreover, to study the values of many cultures is to search not only for fundamental cultural differences but also—possibly even more importantly—for overarching values that subsume them. The discovery of possibly "universal values" could reveal shared human characteristics.

What Are Values and How Do They Relate to Culture?

General precepts of a whole society, implying rules and standards for its members' conduct, values express the society's moral and ethical guidelines. Hence, values are reflected in the beliefs, attitudes, and behaviors of everybody, at least to some degree. As expressed by individuals, in however uniquely a manner, values are a quintessential topic for cross-cultural psychology.

In their review of cross-cultural research on values, Smith and Schwartz (1997) suggest that the set of value priorities that prevail in any society constitutes perhaps the most central element in its culture. Values are conceptualized by Smith and Schwartz (1997) as cultural variables that mediate between ecocultural variables on the one hand and behavioral variables on the other. Thus, values would be located right at the heart of the ecocultural model we employ in this book.

To extend this metaphor, values are reflected in heartfelt beliefs. While values are characteristics of the cultures of societies, they enter into the psychological makeup of individual human beings. If *filial piety* were a cultural value in a particular society (as it is identified in China and in other societies influenced by Confucian doctrines), then we would expect many individuals affected by that culture to care deeply for their parents. When activated by individuals, values become infused with feeling, as Schwartz and Bilskey (1987) suggested. Relatively abstract, values transcend situations and provide standards for evaluating specific behaviors, both before and after they occur. They may refer to goals and behaviors considered appropriate for achieving them.

How Do We Know Values Are There?

In popular discourse, there is widespread reference to values. One hears of family values, values pertaining to human rights, fairness, the sanctity of human life, and so on, often with the implication that these values are universal, inalienable, and immutable. Are there universal values? Do we find any values *everywhere*? More fundamentally, how do we find them *anywhere*?

It is not easy to study values because they are never directly observable; they may only be inferred from behavior.[1] Yet, as some philosophers of science teach us, if we can "measure" values, there are such things.[2] At least, once measured, they exist as theoretical constructs. And psychologists and other social scientists have indeed measured values (but only indirectly) at both the cultural and individual levels. As we shall see, some of the measurement efforts have had built-in problems, and there have been some difficulties, both conceptual and operational, in keeping the two levels of analysis—cultural and individual—separate. But there is a long history of measurement of values that continues to the present.

Sources of Values

In general, values derive in a societal context from diverse social and economic forces that evolve historically. Values are taught, preached, and argued in political arenas, in religious organizations, in schools, and in family settings. The mechanisms of socialization and enculturation are obviously involved, but so are business and—its hand-maiden—advertising in so-called free market economies. More particularly,

---

[1]The reader may object that values can be found directly by reading the books, holy and civil, that constitute the canon of any society. But, for our present purposes, all such books are considered products of the behaviors of individuals, albeit some of whom are long gone.

[2]A cultural value, rooted in the Western tradition of logical positivism, infuses this notion that the valid "existence" of a concept is evidenced by its measurability.

some of the value domains we focus on in this chapter have been linked to particular forces of this general kind in various theories and models. A clear case in point is achievement motivation and a less clear one is individualism/collectivism. We will deal with both of these in turn.

We will try to explain the mechanisms by which the beliefs and motives of individuals seem to reflect their culture's values, and the underlying ecocultural forces which might shape them.[3] With respect to this concern, *socialization* is the mediating link between ecocultural forces and beliefs rooted in cultural values. This is illustrated by a classic cross-cultural study concerning shared beliefs on what we might do that could make us ill, and what we ought to do to make us better, with which we begin our review of research on values.

CULTURALLY-INFLUENCED BELIEFS ABOUT ILLNESS -

Freudian hypotheses, sharpened so that they might be subjected to empirical examination, were tested by Whiting and Child (1953) in their classic study of relationships between child-training emphases and adult belief systems. The Freudian concept that attracted their attention was *fixation,* or, as Freud originally viewed it, arrested development at one or another putative stage of psychosexual development. Freud had argued that fixation could result either from "overindulgence" *or* frustration. Thus, a child might become orally fixated as a result of an extremely permissive feeding schedule *or* as a result of a too rigid one. Whiting and Child, acutely aware of the contrasting effects of reward (indulgence) and nonreward (frustration), found it desirable to modify Freud's fixation notion by postulating opposing effects of indulgence and frustration.

Hence, they introduced the two concepts of positive fixation and negative fixation. They argued that the former—a product of indulgence—should lead to a positive evaluation of relevant behaviors. The latter, in contrast, should lead to a negative evaluation. In adulthood, then, behaviors like those that had been subjected to much reward during childhood would be strong and accompanied by positive feelings. But behaviors associated with earlier punishments should be anxiety provoking and otherwise accompanied by negative feelings.

Although these assumed mechanisms occur at the individual level, the authors actually tested their modification of Freudian theory at the societal level of analysis.

---

[3]Values in some definitions are treated as held both by individuals and by groups; that is, values could be defined as orientations toward what is considred desirable or preferable by social groups and individuals. Values, not directly observable, could be defined as the "deep structure" of attitudes and beliefs. In this chapter, we first distinguish values and motives, the former being held by groups and the latter by individuals. Values and motives in turn are distinguished from attitudes and beliefs. Attitudes have traditionally been defined in social psychology as learned predispositions held by individuals (favorable or unfavorable) toward various objects, persons, groups, and so on. When related to attitudes, beliefs are their cognitive elements.

They reasoned that positive or negative aspects of shared belief systems would reflect, respectively, childhood indulgence or severity of socialization of behaviors related to the beliefs. They investigated belief systems concerning the suspected causes of illnesses and their preferred therapies, assuming that what a society modally tends to believe makes one ill is a good index of anxiety surrounding certain activities, whereas what the society tends to believe can cure illness is an index of behaviors that evoke positive feelings. Thus, Whiting and Child had to predict that, in societies in which feeding training (oral socialization) is strict and severe, oral activities would be likely to appear in the belief system as an illness-causation factor. But in a society in which children are orally indulged, oral activity would more likely be viewed as therapeutic.

Using data from the Human Relations Area Files, the authors found much stronger evidence for negative fixation than for positive fixation. And the predicted correlations between aspects of child training and illness belief varied in magnitude for the various behavioral arenas studied. The strongest relationships involved severe and sudden weaning and oral explanations for illness (Whiting & Child, 1953). Their study stands as a pioneer example of a cross-cultural approach to the study of shared beliefs.[4]

Next, we examine a popular approach to the study of shared values, an approach that seeks to classify societies as high or low on dimensions thought to be universal. These include "need to achieve" and "individualism/collectivism."

MEASUREMENT OF VALUES

Earlier Approaches to Measurement of Values

Although social scientists, such as the anthropologist Kluckhohn (1956), generally advocated the comparison of values as a mode of comparing cultures, values have been assessed mostly at the individual level via structured questionnaires. Typically, individual respondents are asked to indicate their degree of endorsement of particular values, represented by words or phrases that refer to a goal.

Kluckhohn and Strodtbeck (1961) employed five philosophical issues: human nature as good or evil; past, present, or future time perspective; linearity–collaterality–individualism; being–becoming–doing; and the relation of humankind to nature. For each issue, the researchers formulated several detailed positions that might be preferred. In interviews done in the United States, respondents ranked these positions, thereby indicating their value priorities.

---

[4]A somewhat fuller account of this classic cross-cultural study of childrearing and adult beliefs may be found in Berry and associates (1992).

Rokeach's (1973) technique asks individual respondents to rank two comprehensive lists of eighteen values according to their personal relative importance.[5] Thus, values are operationalized as guiding principles for individuals. Although Rokeach's values are clearly individually held, the rank orders of values in different cultural groups have often been compared both within the United States and across nations. For example, Rokeach (1973) compared student rankings of values in Australia, Canada, Israel, and the United States. Feather (1986) did the same in Australia, Papua New Guinea, and China. These studies found both similarities and differences across samples.

Students of human groups have long categorized societies, often into as few as two types, sometimes viewed as opposites (e.g., *Gemeinschaft versus Gesellschaft* [Tonnies, 1887/1957], *high and low Achievement motivation* [McClelland, 1958, 1961, 1971] and *Individualism/Collectivism* [Hofstede, 1980; Triandis, 1995]). Efforts to measure some of these bipolar dimensions of cultural values have been creative, even ingenious. For example, achievement motivation levels of whole societies have been inferred from their literary and artistic products. These scores could then be "validated" by assessing their correlations with various other measures, such as social indicators of economic activity, which a theory suggested ought to be related to levels of achievement motivation.[6]

What is Achievement Motivation?

N_{ach},[7] a value at the cultural level, is a motive at the individual level. Because "motives" per se are not directly observable, they have to be inferred from some kind of behavior. Psychologists have invented a number of indirect verbal techniques for eliciting behavior from individuals whose motives they want to study. Among these are projective techniques like the Thematic Apperception Test (TAT), in which relatively ambiguous pictures are displayed to respondents who are instructed to tell the stories that the pictures suggest to them.

Imagine a TAT picture of a shadowy figure holding aloft a misty object shaped somewhat like a figure eight. Responding to this, a person tells a story about a young man who practices the violin six hours a day in anticipation of his concert debut before a wildly cheering audience and enthralled music critics. One might infer that this person attaches high importance to individual achievement, particularly if most other people who are shown the same picture tell stories that lack such themes.

---

[5]Rokeach thought that the specific values fell along two dimensions—personal-to-social values and moral-to-competence values—each including eighteen separate values. Subsequent research tended not to support this two-factor structure, however.

[6]This sort of validation is known in the science of statistics as *construct validation.*

[7]This is the symbol for achievement motivation, or "need to achieve" that was used by McClelland and others when research on this construct was in fashion.

The Measurement of Achievement Motivation ⁃

McClelland invented the concept "achievement motivation" in the United States in the 1950s. To assess it, he used pictures that potentially elicit stories about striving to meet standards of excellence. The fantasy productions elicited by TAT cards were found to be consistent and correlated with achievement-oriented behavior in the real world (Atkinson, 1958), such as indexes of persistence, the willingness to take risks, and the pursuit of difficult-to-attain goals.

At the social level, McClelland content-analyzed fantasy productions (popular stories) of various societies in order to assess their levels of N_{ach}. For a number of contemporary nations, McClelland (1961) used children's readers from about 1925 as the source of collective fantasy from which N_{ach} was assessed. Earlier, Child, Storm, and Veroff (1958) had related achievement themes in folktales of various societies to socialization practices in those societies. Zimet, Wiberg, and Blom (1971) did a multitheme content analysis of primers employed contemporaneously in thirteen (mostly industrialized) nations in another attempt to gain insight into some of the values that are stressed in socialization. In what was perhaps the most fanciful measurement technique, ceramic designs were used as the source of inferences about achievement motivation, McClelland studied designs on ancient Greek pots. Later we will see a study that showed how variations in these designs correlated with different historical periods.

Most often, culture level scores for values are aggregated from individual level scores involving verbal behavior. Thus, when LeVine (1966) contrasted three Nigerian societies' (Yoruba, Ibo, and Hausa) levels of achievement motivation, he based his societal scores on content analyses of many individual boys' reports of dreams. LeVine found differences in dream content across three samples, using McClelland's scoring scheme for N_{ach}. These differences were interpretable on the basis of ethnographic and sociological descriptions of the three Nigerian societies. (See Box 7.1, for more details.)

What Produces the Need to Achieve? ⁃

Weber (1904) attributed to Protestantism the sociopsychological impetus for the capitalist spirit that arose in some European countries from the seventeenth through the nineteenth centuries. From this thesis, McClelland (1971) fashioned a more general argument. He asserted that the key factor in instilling achievement motivation in significant members of a population is the existence of a religious, or ideological, belief. This belief holds, according to McClelland, that one's own group is superior to groups that invest more authority in institutions rather than individuals. Many analyses of groups differing in characteristic levels of N_{ach} have resulted in findings that are consistent with this argument.

McClelland and his colleagues searched for experiential antecedents of different levels of this motive. Focusing on differences in childhood experience within U.S. culture, they found that males who scored high on N_{ach} were products of homes in

BOX 7.1   Nigerian Dreams –

LeVine (1966) collected dream reports from secondary school boys in Nigeria. The boys were either Hausa (the predominantly Muslim tribe from northern Nigeria), Yoruba (the politically dominant, relatively Westernized tribe from western Nigeria), or Ibo (the economically dominant, also relatively Westernized tribe from eastern Nigeria, the part of the country that temporarily seceded from Nigeria just a few years after LeVine's study to form the short-lived nation of Biafra).

LeVine's method for obtaining N_{ach} scores was to ask individuals for a report of a recent or recurring dream and to score the obtained reports just as if they were stories told after viewing a TAT card. The stimulus employed—the request to tell a story—is far more likely to be culture-free than a TAT card, which, however ambiguous, contains some content that is potentially misinterpretable. So LeVine's data-collection method is worthy of emulation in future cross-cultural studies of achievement motivation. The fact that a given dream report may be fictional would matter not at all, because a fantasy production would have been elicited with a minimum of stimulus direction.

With blind scoring of the dream reports, the Ibo sample outscored both the Yoruba and the Hausa (especially the latter) on achievement motivation. Ibo performance in this regard fit well their actual achievements as an ethnic group in this large, developing nation. Their reputation as hardworking, money-saving in-dividuals, who wandered over all parts of Nigeria, earning the envy and enmity of local people who competed too little or too late for the same jobs, has spread well beyond Nigeria. That Ibo schoolboys should outscore their Hausa and Yoruba peers on N_{ach} corresponds to much of what is known about the three ethnic groups. LeVine sought reasons, both social and psychological, for the apparent acquisition of different levels of N_{ach} by the three groups of boys. Analysis of the anthropological and historical facts pertaining to the three societies led LeVine to a "status mobility" hypothesis, referring to differences among the three societies in their traditional socioeconomic, and related political, practices. At one extreme was the Hausas' centralized and hierarchical system, within which authority trickled down through subservient layers. Power tended to be inherited, although it might shift as the result of warfare. Class status was relatively unchanging, so that a young man not well born might hope to improve his lot only by choosing to serve a powerful leader. At the other extreme, Ibo society was quite decentralized, with a variety of activities leading to wealth and, hence, local power, provided they were viewed as well performed. Such contrasting possibilities for status mobility would result in differences in values held by parents, which, in turn, would lead to differing childrearing practices and, finally, to personality differences along several dimensions including achievement motivation.

which mothers had been warm and encouraging and fathers nonauthoritarian. Males who scored low had, during childhood, been dominated by respect-demanding, authoritarian fathers (Rosen & D'Andrade, 1959).

The research was extended to other societies in order to determine whether similar patterns of antecedents could be found in non-American settings. Working in

Brazil, Rosen (1962) found that families with highly authoritarian fathers tended to produce sons with relatively low levels of N_{ach}. In Turkey, a society in which the typical father tends to be very authoritarian, even with adult sons, Bradburn (1963) found that individuals who had grown up relatively independent of their fathers scored relatively high on N_{ach}. Rosen's and Bradburn's findings confirmed the existence of similar patterns of antecedents to N_{ach} in at least three different societies.

Correlates of Achievement Motivation

Assuming that, on the average, Turkish fathers are more authoritarian than U.S. fathers, Bradburn predicted—and found—lower mean scores on N_{ach} for a Turkish sample of individuals participating in a management-training program than for a sample of U.S. graduate students.

For a sample of contemporary nations in which McClelland (1961) used children's readers from about 1925 to assess N_{ach}, he used gain in electric power consumption from about 1925 to 1950 as indicative of economic growth. McClelland found that the N_{ach} predicted the increase in consumption.

McClelland (1971) found folktale scores to be related to societal-level entrepreneurial activity as predicted by his theory of entrepreneurship's dependence on a critical mass of high achievement motivated people in any society. Testing the notion that a society needs high need achievers before it can develop economically, McClelland reported, "Of the twenty-two cultures whose stories were high in N_{ach}, 74 percent were observed to have at least some men engaged as full-time entrepreneurs, whereas for the twenty-three tribes below average in N_{ach}, only 35 percent contained any full-time entrepreneurs..." (p. 8).[8]

Beshai (1972), working in Egypt, assessed the magnitude of themes relating to N_{ach} in stories produced during three recent historical periods—the 1920s, the mid-1950s, and the late 1960s. He found a significant increase in N_{ach} imagery from the earliest to the latest period. He also discovered the overall incidence of N_{ach} imagery in Egypt to be lower than that reported for the United States and some developing nations, a fact he attributed to the traditional Muslim ethic of egalitarianism and success within the confines of group sanctions. The increase from 1920 to 1970, however, he attributed to the Western-influenced industrial development now under way in Egypt.

Berlew (cited in McClelland, 1961, 1971) analyzed Greek literary documents from three distinct historical periods, one of growth, one of climax, and one of decline economically. Berlew found achievement themes to have peaked well before the economic growth peaked and to have declined in advance of the economic decline. A similar finding for fifteenth- through nineteenth-century England, based on street ballads and other literary products and relating the times at which achieve-

---

[8]Readers might have noticed the ethnocentrism implicit in the wording, whereby groups high on achievement motivation are referred to as *cultures* while those that are low are called *tribes*. Recall our earlier discussion of great divide theories.

ment themes were high to temporal fluctuations in coal imports, was reported by Bradburn and Berlew (1961). Both studies support the proposition that some sufficiently high level of N_{ach} needs to exist in a society as a prerequisite for economic growth.

Inspired by a finding that male U.S. college students with high N_{ach} doodled in more orderly fashion than those with low N_{ach} scores (Aronson, 1958), the McClelland team found that on the basis of designs on ancient Greek pots they could also predict the waxing and waning of Greek economic activity (McClelland, 1971, p. 9). Davies (1969) found the same for the Minoan civilization.

However, Finison (1976), who focused on industrialized nations, found no correlation between N_{ach} in 1950 and growth in electrical production between then and 1971. Finison also reported a negative correlation between N_{ach} and national income growth. This failure to replicate McClelland's earlier work casts doubt on his model of development, on its applicability to the time period studied by Finison, or on the measures employed. (As usual, negative results are ambiguous.)

In recent years, attention to achievement motivation has waned. A strikingly good likeness of it, however, resides in the currently popular notion of individualism/collectivism. A highly motivated, high achievement-oriented person would probably be, in today's jargon, an individualist rather than a collectivist.

Individualism/Collectivism

Because all human beings are parts of social entities (families, clans, ethnic groups, societies, etc.), it is universally true that we are all individuals *within* collectivities. It must also be universally the case that there is a tension between our individualism and our collectivism, a tension that is resolved differentially both for individuals and for societies. That is, some societies tend to be more collectivistic than other societies and, within any society, some individuals tend to be more collectivistic than others.

Notions about individualism/collectivism (I/C) have been replete in the social sciences and the humanities (especially philosophy) for many centuries, dating back to ancient Greece. In a recent history of the concept (Kagitçibasi, 1997), collectivism as a theme was noted in Plato's *Republic,* and individualism was linked to the emergence of private property in England by the thirteenth century, and again as an economic idea in Hobbes, Smith, and Bentham in the seventeenth and eighteenth centuries. By the nineteenth century, the concepts entered German social science as *Gesellschaft* and *Gemeinschaft* (Tonnies, 1887/1957, p. 350). Elsewhere in Europe, individualism was stressed by Descartes, collectivism by Rousseau. Hegel and Marx were also influential proponents of forms of collectivism.

The linked concepts individualism/collectivism as cultural values seemingly burst on the scene in cross-cultural psychology in 1980, with the publication of Hofstede's questionnaire study of workplace attitudes and values among 117,000 IBM employees in some fifty nations scattered across three regions (Hofstede, 1980).[9] In

---

[9]Factor analysis based on country mean scores yielded four factors—individualism, power distance, masculinity, and uncertainty avoidance. Subsequent research reveals little interest in the latter three and high interest in individualism/collectivism.

a later publication, Hofstede stated (1991), "Individualism stands for a society in which the ties between individuals are loose; everyone is expected to look after himself or herself and his or her immediate family only," and "collectivism stands for a society in which people from birth onwards are integrated into strong, cohesive in-groups, which throughout people's lifetime continue to protect them in exchange for unquestioning loyalty" (pp. 260–261).

Kagitçibasi (1997) in her thorough review of I/C research, including Hofstede's (1991) discussion, noted that Hofstede's three questionnaire items associated with individualism stressed having a job that gives one sufficient time for personal or family life; having freedom to adapt one's own approach to the job; and having challenging work to do (providing a personal sense of accomplishment). Those associated with collectivism stressed having training opportunities; having good physical working conditions; and having the possibility of fully using skills and abilities on the job.

Despite threads of collectivism in European history, Kagitçibasi (1997) is one among many contemporary students of these concepts to suggest that there prevails "an individualistic ethos in the western world" (p. 4). On the other hand, "the majority of humankind share at least some aspects of collectivism" (p. 5). Collectivism, she suggests, finds its underpinnings in fifth century B.C. Confucian teachings in China, as well as in the teachings of Taoism, Buddhism, Hinduism, and Shintoism in the Far East, and Judaism, Christianity, and Islam in the Middle East, (although individualism got a big boost from the Protestant Reformation in Europe).

Triandis and colleagues launched a cross-cultural research program focused on this value dimension, a program that was recently summarized in a book (Triandis, 1995) that covers the essential ideas inherent in the Individualism/Collectivism construct.

From Hofstede's 1980 study through Triandis's 1995 update, nations have been labeled as individualistic or collectivistic societies, but the labeling has varied somewhat as other dimensions of variation (e.g., "horizontality/verticality" (Rokeach, 1973), "tightness/looseness" (Pelto, 1968), and "uncertainty avoidance" (Gudykunst, 1995) were added to I/C in efforts to refine the assignment of nations. Because we worry a lot about stereotyping nations, we are not here including a table showing these assignments. However, to provide the flavor of these characterizations, we note that, as of 1995, Triandis (1995, p. 104) displayed a cluster of nations that he placed near the high end of "individualism" and just to the weak side of "uncertainty avoidance." Triandis has also classified prewar Japan as "vertical collectivistic" but contemporary Japan as shifting toward horizontal collectivism, with "the younger generation…moving both in the horizontal direction and toward individualism" (1995, p. 89).[10]

---

[10]In much research, comparisons of samples of people in the United States and Japan are treated as if these comparisons constitute contrasts between individualistic and collectivistic societies, and obtained differences in the selected behavior are then sometimes *attributed* to individualism/collectivism, as if they were "causes" of the obtained differences. We shall make clear later in this chapter that we deplore this practice because it epitomizes circular reasoning.

Hofstede's ground-breaking research (1980), which led to an almost unquestioning acceptance of Individualism/Collectivism as a basic contrast *between societies,* was, as we have seen, based on individuals' scores. Nation scores were actually composites of individual scores. Focusing on work-related values, Hofstede found the value of individualism to be less characteristic in the less industrialized nations.

Triandis (1983) dealt with individualism and collectivism as two poles of a dimension along which societies might vary. Hui and Triandis (1984) produced a scale to measure individualism/collectivism, which Hsu (1981) had suggested was a salient difference between Americans and Chinese. Collectivism, as defined by this scale, involves being concerned with others, considering the implications for others of one's decisions, and the sharing of material resources.

Triandis popularized I/C in cross-cultural psychology by suggesting that the construct had similar meaning across cultures. Hui and Triandis (1984) conceptualized collectivism as "concern" (for others) and asked a total of eighty-one psychologists and anthropologists in many parts of the world to indicate how an individualist (idiocentrist) and a collectivist (allocentrist) would respond to seven questions tapping aspects of this concern. The data showed some consensus in the construal of collectivism as subordination of individual goals to the goals of the collective. Triandis (1990, p. 113) concluded that the defining attributes of idiocentrism are distance from in-groups and emotional detachment and competition, while the defining attributes of allocentrism are family integrity and solidarity.

Allocentric students in the United States were found to be low on anomie, alienation, and loneliness; they report that they receive greater social support of better quality and value most cooperation, equality, and honesty. Idiocentric students, in contrast, value a comfortable life, competition, pleasure, and social recognition (Triandis, Leung, Villareal, & Clack, 1985). Subordination of in-group goals to personal goals was found to be the most important aspect of U.S. individualism (Triandis, Villareal, Asai, & Lucca, 1988). On the other hand, the later findings of Triandis and his colleagues that "individualism is the opposite of authoritarianism" (Gelfand, Triandis, & Chan, 1996, p. 408) suggest that idiocentrics (individualists) ought to "behave in ways that are contrary to those high in authoritarianism" (p. 408). If so, they might be rather civic-minded, because authoritarians have been shown (Peterson, Doty, & Winter, 1993) to endorse punishment of AIDS victims, express more hostility toward the environmental movement than toward polluters, consider homeless people "lazy," and disapprove of diversity in universities!

Antecedents of Individualism/Collectivism

Most political philosophies in the West, from the late eighteenth century onward, like that of John Locke, which stressed freedom for individuals, must surely have encouraged the value "individualism." In the West, the two major eighteenth century revolutions (U.S. and French) fostered it, too. In the mid nineteenth century observations of U.S. society by de Tocqueville, the nonaristocratic emphases of the new democracy were treated as contributors to individualism. And, as was also the case for achievement motivation (see previous discussion), Protestantism has been cited by many observers (e.g., Dumont, 1983) as another antecedent of individualism. Concepts like individualism have long been discussed by various Francophone scholars as characteristic of Western peoples; a recent example is in the work of Cohen-Emerique (1991).

In contrast, various non-Western philosophies, religions, and political ideologies have been pointed to, at least by Westerners, as likely sources of collectivism. Among these are Confucianism, totalitarian governments, and social systems in which religion is doctrinaire and intertwined with the conduct of civil affairs. In these respects, however, collectivism as a concept blends fuzzily with authoritarianism.

What makes a society more I than C, and vice versa? Among the antecedents of collectivism cited by Triandis (1995) are cultural homogeneity, high population density, isolation from other groups, and the perception of external threat.[11] In contrast, I factors reflect cultural complexity, affluence, modernity, and, at the individual level, education, maleness, urbanism, social class, and social and geographic mobility. All these I factors are more common as societies modernize, so, as we have already seen, with modernization, individuals and their societies become more individualistic.

Corrclates (Consequences?) of I/C

Among the social–psychological differences that Triandis (1995) tentatively attributes to I/C are the following: "In collectivist cultures conflict is more likely to be intergroup, with ethnicity, language, religion, or race as the boundaries of conflict" (p. 111) and "Russian and Japanese physicians are less likely to tell a patient that she has cancer than are American doctors" (p. 117). Later in this chapter, we will consider whether it is necessary, or even desirable, to make such attributions.

Individualism/Collectivism and Distributive Justice. The question of what is fair is likely to come up in any society whenever resources have to be allocated. The resources may be positive, such as a financial reward, or negative, such as a salary cut or a tax levy. Which allocation principle seems most fair may depend on whether a positive or negative resource is being contemplated. Thus, cultural norms might favor assigning a positive resource to the most productive people (an equity principle) while protecting poor people from a negative resource (a need principle). Moreover, because the norms that govern resource allocation are cultural norms, definitions of fairness might well vary from culture to culture.

The values of shared work and shared rewards may reflect collectivism. After Hui (1984) showed that collectivism was more likely to be valued by Chinese college students than by U.S. college students, Hui and Triandis (1984) conducted a

---

[11]Later, in Chapter 9, on aggression, and in Chapter 10, on intergroup relations, we will see how a theory of ethnocentrism suggests that the perception of external threat can increase in-group solidarity and patriotism, a form of collectivism.

scenario study both in Hong Kong and in Illinois (United States), wherein students allocated money to themselves and to partners. In such studies, alternative principles of reward allocation are possible, most notably "equity" (reward based on quality of performance), "equality" (equal rewards to all regardless of performance), and "need" (unequal rewards reflecting differential needs). Hui and Triandis found that the Chinese students were more equality oriented and more other-serving than their U.S. counterparts.

In a study done in India and the United States, (Berman, Murphy-Berman, & Singh, 1985), students of psychology at universities in both nations considered twelve hypothetical distribution problems (presented as vignettes written in English and Hindi, with back-translation to make them as similar as possible), half of which involved positive distributions and half negative, with target people either an excellent worker who was economically comfortable or an average worker in economic need.

Respondents in both samples had to decide whether to distribute the resource ($200 or its purchasing power equivalent in rupees, described as a bonus in the positive instance and as a pay cut in the negative one) in one of five ways: (1) all to the needy person, none to the meritorious one, (2) ¾ and ¼, (3) ½ and ½, (4) ¼ and ¾, and (5) none to the needy, all to the meritorious person.

Classifying the first two responses as a "need" decision, the middle one as an "equality" decision, and the last two as an "equity" decision, the psychologists found that for the U.S. respondents, "equity" was the most popular decision when there was a positive resource (a bonus) to distribute (49 percent, with 16 percent saying "need"), while for the Indian respondents, "need" was the most popular decision (52 percent, with only 16 percent saying "equity"). When a pay cut was the resource in question, both samples of respondents favored need but this decision preference was more marked for the Indians (65 percent made the need decision for allocating negative resources compared to 41 percent of the U.S. respondents). Clearly, for the Indian sample, need was the preferred mode of assigning distributive justice; in contrast, for the U.S. sample, while need mattered when taking resources away, merit prevailed when assigning rewards.

Both the Indians and the U.S. respondents chose the need principle more often when taking away than when giving (65 percent *versus* 52 percent for the Indians, 41 percent *versus* 16 percent for the U.S. people). Despite other cultural differences in concepts of distributive justice, both cultures distinguish between what is fair when giving and what is fair when taking away.

The overall tendency of the Indians to favor need over merit is attributable to the fact that "need is so much more visible and such a salient part of the Indian experience" (Berman et al., 1985, p. 63). An alternative suggestion focuses on the fact that the Indians were less sensitive to merit, because in India family background and social status, including caste, are often more important in determining how one is evaluated than one's achievements. Either or both of these interpretations account for the pattern of findings and reflect a more general argument that concepts of distributive justice are influenced by norms rooted in the economic and social characteristics of societies.[12]

Leung and Bond (1984) suggested that in collectivistic cultures "equality and need rather than equity [merit] will be more influential in reward allocation" (p. 5), but they expected this relationship to hold only when the target person is an in-group member. They found support for their hypothesis that Chinese subjects would allocate more equitably than U.S. subjects with out-group members. When the experimenters manipulated the group membership of the recipient, the input of the allocator, and the allocation principle, they found that, "compared with American subjects, Chinese subjects liked an allocator who divided the group reward equally with an in-group member more, and regarded such an allocation as fairer" (p. 793).

Even Western cultural groups (thought to be individualistic in the I/C research paradigm) may differ among themselves in what they believe is fair. Tornblom and Foa (1983) detected some differences between Sweden, West Germany, and the United States in reward allocation.

Problems in Assessing "Consequences" of Individualism/Collectivism

Are the social–psychological differences between societies that are putatively individualistic or collectivistic somehow the *result* of I/C? It has become almost fashionable to design a cross-cultural study by arranging to collect data on a particular instrument in two societies, selected on the basis of their putative standing on the I/C dimension, and then to explain any difference that might obtain as a consequence of that standing. While there are some very respectable studies of this type (e.g., Smith & Bond, 1993), there are also some weak ones, as the fashion shades over into a fad.

Social Loafing and Social Striving.   Does the typical contribution of individuals in a work-sharing situation vary between so-called individualistic and collectivistic cultures? Laboratory studies done in the United States found that people exert greater effort in a group when they work individually than when individual outputs of each member are not visible (Latané, Williams, & Harkins, 1979); Latané & Nida, 1981). Termed *social loafing,* the phenomenon has also been reported in Thailand (Latané, 1981), India (Weiner, Pandey, & Latané, 1981), Malaysia (Ward, 1982) and Japan (Williams, Williams, Kawana, & Latané, 1984).

Given similar findings in several cultures, "social loafing" would appear to be potentially a universal feature of social behavior. However, Gabrenya, Latané, and Wang (1983) found that graduate students in China worked even harder in groups. Gabrenya, Wang, and Latané (1985) did a study in Taiwan and Florida (United States) with school children. No cultural difference in social loafing occurred for six graders,

---

[12]This study was a comparison between only two groups; as such, interpretations of the obtained differences in behavior remain ambiguous.

but for ninth graders, the U.S. children loafed more than did the Chinese, who actually displayed social striving. Thus, persons in some societies (collectivists?) seem to care about how their group will be judged. Rather than loaf, they strive even harder and perform even better. But, are the differences reported here really a consequence of I/C? We need to pursue this question further.

Intergroup Relations.   Triandis (1995) suggests many consequences of I/C for intergroup relations. For example, "In collectivist cultures conflict is more likely to be intergroup, with ethnicity, language, religion, or race as the boundaries of conflicts" (p. 111) and "Prejudice and discrimination will be high among vertical collectivists, followed by vertical individualists, followed by horizontal collectivists, and will be low among horizontal individualists" (p. 127).

In a chapter that reviews cross-cultural research on intergroup relations, Gudykunst and Bond (1997) note that many researchers have linked the cultural variability dimension of collectivism/individualism (C/I) to intergroup behavior. This research typically contrasts a Western society, presumably high in I, with an Asian culture, presumed to be high in C.[13]

Much of this research involves the assumption that people in C cultures would interact more frequently, more widely, more deeply and more positively with in-group members than would members of I cultures (see Wheeler, Reis, & Bond, 1989), the processes of mutual influence, harmony enhancement, and in-group favoritism should also be stronger in C cultures than in I cultures. Gudykunst and Bond (1997) argue that in C cultures people would be more biased in favor of their in-group than people in I cultures. Al-Zahrani and Kaplowitz (1993) found that the more allocentric Saudis showed more intergroup bias and out-group derogation in their attributions than did more idiocentric U.S. people.

On the other hand, there is some evidence that individuals from C societies treat out-group members quite fairly, more so than do I individuals. Following the Leung and Bond (1984) study of distribution of rewards in I and C samples, Leung (1988) found that members of C cultures use the equity norm with out-group members more than members of I cultures. Gudykunst and Bond (1997) opine that the use of the equity norm with out-groups in C cultures, however, would be less likely where there are hostile relations between the groups.

Because single core ethnic groups predominate in some C cultures, social identities are likely to be more important in C cultures than in I cultures. Gabrenya and Wang (1983) found that a sample of Chinese used more group-based self-descriptions than a U.S. sample. Similarly, Bochner (1994) found that collectivists in Malaysia produce more group and fewer individual self-descriptions than individualists in Australia and Britain.

Self-disclosure is a related matter. Gudykunst, Gao, Schmidt, Nishida, Bond, Leung, Wang, and Barraclough (1992) found more self-disclosure with in-group

---

[13]Singelis (1994) has warned that these findings may be elaborating a distinctively Asian variant of collectivism.

members than with out-group members in two Chinese samples (Hong Kong and Taiwan) than in Australian, Japanese, and U.S. samples. There was, in fact, no difference in in-group and out-group self-disclosure in the Australian and U.S. samples.

Gudykunst (1995) presents a number of axioms pertaining to changes in intergroup communication patterns as individuals become more or less collectivistic. To cite only one example, "an increase in collectivism will be associated with an increase in the degree [that] social identities influence behavior when interacting with strangers" (p. 46). The entire set of axioms is worth consulting by anyone contemplating research on ways individualism/collectivism might influence intergroup relations (also see Chapter 10 in this volume).

Triandis's Modification of I/C Theory

While cultures are thought by many to be either individualistic or collectivistic, Triandis (1995) does not consider I and C as highly correlated dimensions. Rather, a particular society can be high or low on both (1995, p. 82). As mentioned earlier, Gelfand, Triandis, and Chan (1996) obtained results from a study in which thirty-eight U.S. university undergraduates judged the similarity of ideas reflective of individualism, collectivism, and authoritarianism). These results showed that, for these people, at least, individualism and collectivism are perceived as independent of each other, and that individualism is conceived as the opposite of authoritarianism.[14] So, I and C are not poles of a single dimension.

Moreover, there are two subsets of both I and C, called *vertical* and *horizontal,* (derived from Rokeach's [1973] values typology [see above] that dealt with political systems and related ideas of freedom and equality). There is also "looseness–tightness" (Pelto, 1968) and cultural complexity, which Triandis suggests "may be the most important dimension that discriminates among cultures" (1995, p. 57). These dimensions interact with I/C to create a multidimensional classification scheme for societies.

To make matters even more complex, in every society whether collectivistic–vertical and loose or individualistic–horizontal and tight, there are *both* individualists and collectivists (which Triandis would rather call *idiocentrics* and *allocentrics*). For Triandis to label a society "collectivistic," a majority of its members would have to be allocentrics; to be called an individualistic culture, the reverse.

Gudykunst and Bond (1997) argued that, because it is individuals, not cultures, who behave, we must clearly move toward measuring I/C at the level of individual persons (see also Singelis & Brown, [1995]). One of several available questionnaires that might be used to measure I/C was published by Gudykunst (1995); you will find it in Box 7.2 and you may use it to assess your own individualistic or collectivistic

---

[14]"Authoritarianism" (Adorno, Frenkel-Brunswik, Levinson, & Sanford, 1950) is typically treated as a set of social attitudes, or an orientation toward society, characterized by obedience toward authority figures, approval of punishment for those who deviate from social norms, and high adherence to social conventions and customs. With respect to the adherence element, authoritarianism is like collectivism; in other respects, it is different.

BOX 7.2   Assessing a Person's I/C Tendencies[16]

Indicate the degree to which the value reflected in each phrase is important to you:
1 = opposed to my values; 2 = not important to me; 3 = somewhat important to me; 4 = important to me; 5 = very important to me.

_____ 1. Obtaining pleasure or sensual gratification
_____ 2. Preserving the welfare of others
_____ 3. Being successful by demonstrating my individual competency
_____ 4. Restraining my behavior if it is going to harms others
_____ 5. Being dependent in thought and action
_____ 6. Having safety and stability of people with whom I identify
_____ 7. Obtaining status and prestige
_____ 8. Having harmony in my relations with others
_____ 9. Having an exciting and challenging life

_____10. Accepting cultural and religious traditions
_____11. Being recognized for my individual work
_____12. Avoiding the violation of social norms
_____13. Leading a comfortable life
_____14. Living in a stable society
_____15. Being logical in my approach to work
_____16. Being polite to others
_____17. Being ambitious
_____18. Being self-controlled
_____19. Being able to choose what I do
_____20. Enhancing the welfare of others

Your individualism score is the sum of your responses to the odd-numbered items; your collectivism score is the sum of your responses to the even-numbered items. Your scores on each can range from 0 to 50.

---

[16]Based on Gudykunst (1995).

tendencies. Triandis shares the view that different measurement techniques must be used for I/C at the societal and individual levels, and he provides details on such techniques in an appendix to his book (Triandis, 1995).

PROBLEMS INVOLVED IN ASSESSING CULTURAL VALUES

At the societal level, as we have seen, I/C is treated as if it were a value, because it refers to a general orientation of a whole society. At the individual level of analysis, I/C (or allocentrism/idiocentrism) refers to tendencies of people who live within the societies. Thus, as different level concepts, they require different kinds of measurement. Measures of I/C at the individual level, for example, have been derived from work by Markus and Kitayama (1991) who distinguish one notion of self as "an entity containing significant dispositional attributes" from self as "interdependent with the surrounding context" (p. 225). The first notion is more I than the second.

The distinction between levels of analysis is often not attended to, presenting a risk of "circularity" (Berry, 1992b) by correlating scores at two levels when they were not independently measured. While a society may be shown to have a particular value, individuals in that society may not all share it to the same degree. Some may pay it mere lip service; others may devoutly subscribe to it. Still others may vigorously reject it.

In complex, multicultural societies, there may be whole groups of people for whom a particular societal value seems a mockery, because of that group's history of being left out. Sometimes, values are encouraged by one or another elite group in a society, fostered only at the verbal level, as abstractions, when they in fact hardly exist in reality for many people.

The mass media in a society may play a role in creating illusory values that, nevertheless, may serve as sources of dreams for some (inspiring hard work, conformity to the rules, all in the hope of "making it," with some actually doing so) and a source of bitterness for others because the dream is, for them, so elusive.

Cultural level values may have both positive and negative implications, sometimes for the same persons, but often for different ones. Thus, the Hollywood-fostered image of the privately owned, single-family dwelling, surrounded by a white picket fence implied a goal that was attractive to many, but once achieved, (*if* achieved), was likely a far better deal for the husbands who *came home* through the fence gate than it was for the nurturant wife–mother who was always *at home* to greet him.

For these and other reasons, we should keep as distinct as possible cultural values and individual motives and beliefs. They are not the same thing and they must therefore be measured independently of each other.

A Critique of the I/C Research Movement

Psychological concepts, especially of the "values" variety seem to have their moments in the sun. The concepts "achievement motivation" and "traditionalism/ modernism," featured in the first edition (1990) of this book because of their prominence at the time, have faded from view.[15] When they shone, those concepts, too, were used to explain many observed cross-cultural differences, probably too many. Individualism/collectivism has replaced those faded concepts in several ways, even explaining today what one or the other of them explained yesterday. So, while I/C is a very useful heuristic device, we must caution against believing that every

---

[15]In this edition, we include a discussion of achievement motivation in this chapter because we think it is instructive to do so, despite its waning use. Also, we will refer (albeit only briefly) to traditionalism/ modernism in Chapter 11 (Acculturation).

cross-cultural difference it purports to explain is really explained by it. We agree with Gudykunst and Bond (1997) who conclude, "Cultures *can* be characterized by their degree of 'C–I'" (p. 123; our italics). We welcome it as a heuristic. As such, it inspires much research (see Smith & Bond, 1993), the findings of which, we reiterate, should be accepted as phenomena still awaiting definitive explanation.

Investing too much explanatory power in I/C is a real risk. The concepts have such powerful heuristic value that we may be tempted to explain differences between groups labeled I or C and to assume not only that that's what they are, and that's what matters, but whatever else the groups are doesn't matter. For example, what about the powerful potential of economic forces, political ideologies, and religious and ethnic fundamentalisms to influence behavior patterns in nearly every society? For some societies, such forces are so strong that their position on the I/C dimension may be a relatively trivial fact. This point is argued more fully in Box 7.3.

Another difficulty is that individualism and collectivism are value-laden terms, suggesting different things to different people. So, it is not always easy to know what the concepts mean, as actually used by some writers. At the extremes, both individualism and collectivism imply behaviors that are probably not very functional, and, hence, the societies labeled either I or C are evaluated negatively. For example, for some critics, extreme individualism shades easily into selfishness, egocentrism, and a lack of social concern. In these respects, quintessential, stereotypical "American individualism" has often been criticized. At the other extreme, collectivism merges with blind obedience to authority, lack of individual creativity and initiative, and a stifling of people's true selves.

By the same token, both individualism and collectivism include what many observers view with approval. Thus, de Tocqueville, in the 1830s, was impressed by the volunteerism that he saw as characteristic of U.S. individualism. And who would not applaud the community spirit that is often displayed in collective enterprises like the kibbutzim that characterized the pioneering days of the state of Israel?

Finally, is this concept really applicable to all societies? At first glance, it appears to be, but, then again, it may not be. Ever since Hofstede (1980) reported a correlation of .82 between societal-level individualism and levels of economic development, individualism has been imbued with the potential to cause economic achievements (and, by extension, collectivism is potentially viewed as impeding it). However, it is common to treat Asian societies generally as collectivistic and those extremely successful Asian societies on the Pacific Rim (up to the late 1990s, when economic difficulties befell Japan, Indonesia, and other victims of "the Asian flu") constitute problem cases for this argument. Are these societies, in fact, not so collectivist after all, or is the link between individualism and economic growth more tenuous than some have argued?

A careful effort at measuring I/C, undertaken by a group of scholars known as The Chinese Culture Connection (1987), leads to an interesting answer. The study, described in considerable detail in Box 7.4, looked for overlap between values described by Hofstede and values generated by a study done in Chinese settings.

BOX 7.3 How Not to Do Research on Individualism/Collectivism

Imagine a paper entitled "The Impact of National Culture (Individualism/Collectivism) on Management Style in Hong Kong and Chicago." During the 1990s, such papers flooded into psychology journal editors' offices, but they seldom merited publication because they typically violated several methodological principles. First, and foremost, they ignore Campbell's dictum that a comparison between only two samples is inherently uninterpretable. The two samples employed in such studies usually differ from each other in so many ways that there is no way of telling which of them might be relevant to the difference in performance on the instrument administered to both of them. While the author(s) might attribute the difference to that most overused dichotomy of the past fifteen years in cross-cultural psychology—Individualism/Collectivism—there is seldom no justifiable reason for doing so. There are always numerous plausible alternative hypotheses. The following are just a few real examples found in papers submitted to us for review by various journal editors.

1. Differences in languages spoken, which is particularly problematic when the measuring instrument is, as it often is, administered in English. Even when both samples are fluent in English, according to the authors, only one sample is likely to be composed of native speakers of English; the other uses English as a second (or third, or whatever) language. Their different responses to the instrument (administered in English) could reflect differences in understanding it, both quantitative and qualitative, across the two samples.

2. Measuring instruments often employed a unidirectional response scale (thus, all items were worded in the same direction, from strongly approve to strongly disapprove, from left to right). If one sample was more likely to respond positively, regardless of item content, while the other was more likely to respond negatively (again, independently of item content), either or both of those response biases (yea-saying and nay-saying) could produce the obtained difference in scores across the two samples.

3. Samples are typically composed of some specialized group, e.g., "advanced students of management," that in neither society could be taken as representative samples of their "national cultures." Also, the title might promise that the paper will reveal "the impact" of the national culture on…whatever. It does no such thing. There is nothing about how either of the two "national cultures" might *impact.* There is seldom even a discussion, fanciful or otherwise, about how the alleged individualism of one society and the alleged collectivism of the other might shape students in the putatively more collectivistic culture differently from their counterparts in the putatively more individualistic one.

In cross-cultural psychology it is trivially easy to obtain a difference in scores on any instrument between any two samples; it is difficult to know what, if anything, to make of it. Just because somebody has labeled these two societies as falling at different places along the (hypothetical) dimension of individualism and collectivism is no justification for concluding that the difference was "caused by" the labels. The two societies likely differ from each other in so many ways other than I/C (e.g., language, history, wealth, size, diversity, climate, social structure, political ideology, and so on).

Continued

BOX 7.3 *Continued*

As Segall and Kagitçibasi (1997) commented, with respect to the frequent tendency to attribute any behavioral difference between a sample from China and a sample from the United States to individualism/collectivism, "China and the United States are vastly different from each other in terms of several socioeconomic variables, including, and especially, level and distribution of wealth" (p. xxxiv). As just one concrete index of this great disparity in wealth, they noted that the United States, where one third of all the world's cars in the late 1990s were registered, was a country in which three out of four households had at least two cars. Most significantly, every 1.7 persons (including children and the elderly) owned a car. In stark contrast, in China, as of the late 1990s, there was one car per 18,000 persons.

Much overlap was found. The research described in Box 7.4 also suggests that we must not be too quick to attribute causal status to individualism/collectivism.

Is Individualism a Postmodern Value?

As we have already seen in this section on "reflections of values," the relationship between values on the one hand and social, economic, and political phenomena on the other is very complex. Surely the latter can have an impact on the former, but the reverse can also be true. However, when the two covary (that is, when they both change), it is usually impossible to determine the direction of causality, or even if the relationship is a causal one. Consider, for example, a recent discussion of changing values that appear to have accompanied widespread changes in many societies from "modernization" to "postmodernism."

Lecomte (1998) cites Inglehart's (1995) notion that values reflect certain waves of cultural, political, and economic changes having to do with modernization and postmodernism, with shifts from the one to the other over the latter decades of the twentieth century. During the first wave (modernization, which included urbanization, professional specialization, and the development of the mass media, among other features) economic development and scientific and technological discoveries were considered as "good" and as signs of progress. In short, they were values. Now, in contrast with much of human history during which most people experienced poverty, people today react to relatively elevated levels of economic security experienced during their youth and feel more masters of their own fate. They are postmaterialist, or postmodernists, who value nonmaterial aspects of life because they realize that their economic gains have not greatly influenced their sense of well-being.

According to Inglehart, in postmodern societies, the emphasis is on individualistic preoccupations, such as leisure activities and emotional relationships of love and friendship. Authority, whether of state or church, is rejected in favor of personal, individualistic wants. Ingelhart presents survey data that reveal that people are losing

BOX 7.4   Chinese Values and the Search for Psychological Universals

In Chapter 2, in Box 2.1, we presented one method for cross-cultural comparisons involving derived etics. Bond (1986) suggests a method of uncovering cultural universals that takes as its starting point an emic theory of human behavior with roots in an Eastern culture, China. Most psychological theories of human behavior and most of the instruments that have been developed to test those theories have grown out of distinctly Western cultural belief systems. Bond argues that, given the 4,000-year recorded history of Chinese civilization and its pervasive cultural influence on all of East Asia, China provides an equally valid alternative place to begin the search for cultural universals.

Bond's approach emphasizes cultural diversity as a means of getting at universals. He proposes beginning simultaneously with two distinctly different emic views of human behavior (one Eastern and one Western) and, within their respective cultural settings (in his study, China and West Germany), deliberately developing tests that have a strong cultural bias. After testing each theory in a wide variety of cultural settings, the resultant test scores for those cultural groups on items that are common to both samples are correlated. If, despite the strong emic biases in the two tests, those scores correlate, then, according to Bond, that would strongly suggest the existence of some cultural universal.

Bond used this method, which he calls "teasing etics out of emics," in a study of human values in which he compared results from a Chinese Value Survey (CVS), developed with the cooperation of Chinese social scientists in Hong Kong, with results from Hofstede's (1980) international survey of work-related values. The Chinese survey was deliberately ethno-centric in its construction, selecting for its forty test items only those values that Bond deemed relevant and pertinent to Chinese culture. Colleagues in twenty-two countries administered the CVS, in the appropriate local language, to homogeneous bodies of students who were fairly comparable in terms of the academic standards of their institutions. Data were analyzed at the cultural level and a factor analysis yielded four factors (values loading > .55) named CVS I (Integration), CVS II (Confucian Work Dynamism), CVS III (Human-Heartedness), and CVS IV (Moral Discipline). Each of the twenty-two cultural groups was then ranked according to where they fell on scales for each of these four factors.

Countries that were common to both Bond's and Hofstede's studies (N=20) were then compared, revealing correlations among the CVS factors and Hofstede's four dimensions of Power Distance (PD), Uncertainty Avoidance (UA), Individualism (IDV), and Masculinity (MAS). Specifically, a significant correlation was found between Hofstede's PD and IDV (which together correlate negatively) and CVS I and CVS IV. A significant correlation was also found between Hofstede's MAS and CVS III. Finally, CVS II was found to be unrelated to any of Hofstede's dimensions.

Bond and his colleagues argue that, because Power Distance, Individualism, Integration, and Moral Discipline all cluster together in a second-order factor analysis, these four dimensions all tap into a single complex universal construct. Because the dimensions are all concerned with the dichotomy between self-seeking behavior and the maintenance of group harmony, the construct can be named "collectivism."

Continued

BOX 7.4   *Continued*

A second universal emerged from the strong positive correlation between Masculinity and Human-Heartedness. This construct focuses on the opposition between "masculine" or "task-centered" considerations and a "feminine," "human-hearted" view. This construct differentiates between Eastern and Western cultures, with Chinese or Eastern values falling decidedly more on the "feminine" end of the dimension.

One construct has a distinctly "Oriental flavor." Confucian Work Dynamism was the only Chinese value that did not correlate with any of Hofstede's Western work values. It seems to be an emic value that is peculiar to Eastern cultures, with the Five economic Dragons of Taiwan,

Hong Kong, Japan, South Korea, and Singapore falling at the top end of this dimension. Furthermore, a high positive correlation (r = .72) was found between this construct and Gross National Product, offering strong support for the "post-Confucian Hypothesis," which attributes the amazing economic growth and development of modern Oriental cultures to their strong heritage of Confucian social philosophy. The emergence of this emic, which Hofstede's survey was unable to tap, also points up the importance of developing indigenous theories and instruments in non-Western cultures in order to get at those unique ways of being that the foreign eye may miss altogether.

---

interest in government and in political parties. He also finds that, while postmodern societies may have either authoritarian or democratic regimes, there is a strong tendency toward democratization that is correlated with postmodernism. In the realm of occupations, postmodernists tend to seek jobs in which the work is interesting, rather than well-paid. But not everyone agrees that postmodernism brings these value changes so clearly.

Brooks and Manza (1994) argue that in societies that might be considered as "becoming postmodern" more often than not one finds a mix of materialistic and postmaterialistic values in the same people. They even found that young Germans, Americans, and Dutch respondents held less "postmodern" views than their parents on certain points. They also contested Inglehart's thesis that postmodernists reject the state and political parties, particularly insofar as those institutions seem concerned with matters of social justice and the environment. Perhaps it is too early to tell if new values are appearing as a reflection of the emergence of postmodern societies.

OTHER VALUE DOMAINS

Schwartz's Value Domains

The influence of I/C classifying shows in a theory of human values (Schwartz & Bilsky, 1990) that identifies value domains. Some domains, like "enjoyment," "achievement," and "self-direction" are thought to serve individual interests, while "prosocial, restrictive conformity" and "security" serve collective interests.

Schwartz (1992; 1994a, 1994b) and Schwartz and Bilsky (1987, 1990) studied ten types of values that were conceived of as motivations reflected in organismic needs, social motives, and social institutional demands: Universalism, Benevolence, Tradition, Conformity, Security, Power, Achievement, Hedonism, Stimulation, and Self-Direction. Many of these were derived from the Rokeach Value Survey (1973); others were added.

In a theory of the universal psychological content and structure of human values, Schwartz and Bilsky (1990) argue that the interests served by value domains can be individualistic, collectivistic, or mixed. Some so-called value domains (e.g., enjoyment, achievement, and self-direction) serve individual interests, while others (e.g., prosocial, restrictive conformity, and security) serve collective interests, with the value domain of maturity serving mixed interests. Schwartz (1992, 1994a/b) criticized the I/C dichotomy for omitting some possibly universal goals and values that do not serve merely the in-group, such as equality for all, social justice, a world at peace, and preserving the natural environment.

There are other value domains that have attracted some attention from cross-cultural psychologists. Albeit not postmodern values, cooperativeness, morality, and politeness are three examples of values.

Cooperativeness and Competitiveness

Whether one person strives with or against another in circumstances in which limited resources are being sought is probably determined by a complex of factors, including scarcity of the resources in question and the prevailing cultural norms that govern such potentially competitive situations.

When in Doubt—if American—Compete

Cooperation and competition have been studied in the United States with variations of the so-called Prisoner's Dilemma game (Luce & Raifa, 1957). Each of two players must choose one of two moves, with the rewards on each trial contingent on four possible joint choices. If one player chooses the move that offers the maximum possible personal payoff, the payoff will occur only if the other player simultaneously chooses the move with the lesser payoff. If both players simultaneously choose the maximum possible payoff move, they will both, in effect, be penalized by gaining less (or losing more) than they would have if both had chosen the lesser payoff move (in which case they would each have received a moderate reward).

It would be to both players' advantage consistently to make the lesser payoff move. Any rational player would do so, provided he or she expected the other player to do the same, rather than expecting the other player to take advantage of his or her good will. If players tend to make the lesser payoff move, it would constitute evidence of mutual trust, mutual expectation of cooperation, and a shared predisposition to cooperate. The general finding in U.S. studies, however, has been that competitive responses (choosing the maximum possible payoff move) predominate.

This tendency is found over a wide variety of payoff arrangements and with players of diverse personality profiles (and of both sexes). Even though a confederate of the experimenter may shame a real player into cooperating by doing so consistently, competition prevails even when a confederate makes a high proportion of cooperative responses. It is possible, of course, that there are other shared values that influence behavior in situations that are epitomized by this game, such as "fairness" or "reluctance to take advantage" of another.

When Game-Playing Values Conflict ·

A study by Oskamp and Perlman (1966) illustrates how conflicting values might interact. Male college students in the United States played a thirty-trial game with cash payoffs. The players were paired on the basis of degree of friendship: Pairs were either best friends, acquaintances, nonacquaintances, or mutually disliked persons, as determined earlier by sociometric questioning. The study was done in both a liberal arts college and a business training school.

In the former setting, best-friend pairs made an average of 22 cooperative responses; acquaintances, 20, nonacquaintances, 14, and mutually disliked pairs, 11. Clearly, liberal arts students' cooperativeness was enhanced by the closeness of their relationship. By contrast, best-friend pairs in the business school averaged only 6 cooperative responses, while all other kinds of pairs made about 14! Thus, while friendship encouraged cooperation among the liberal arts students, it had just the opposite effect among the business school students.

In an atmosphere like that of a U.S. business school or in other countries where free-market capitalism is spreading, competitiveness may be so highly valued (and justified as leading to some greater good such as economic progress) that competitive behavior will emerge, especially when a player is interacting with a person whose approval he or she seeks and respects. It seems that a good businessman, like a good poker player, may actually enhance the bond that exists between himself and a good friend by taking advantage of him! Within traditional, rural, subsistence-level societies, what do we find?

Are There Links with Degree of Food Accumulation? --

Because low-food-accumulating societies (hunting, fishing, and gathering groups that are nomadic rather than sedentary) stress training for achievement, self-reliance, and independence, such societies might value individual competitiveness. However, low-food-accumulating societies are often more egalitarian, and individual competition is strongly discouraged in such settings, so we still have a lot to learn about the ecocultural conditions that are correlated with cooperation/competition.

We can cite some very indirect evidence that involvement in *high*-food-accumulation activities leads to lowered individual initiative. Whiting and Whiting (1971) compared herdboys of between 5 and 11 years of age in the Kisii district of Kenya (and in some other societies in which herding is an important subsistence activity) with nonherding Gusii schoolboys. They found that the herdboys (1) were more frequently told what to do by their mothers, (2) were more frequently punished for disobedience, (3) more frequently issued commands and "responsible suggestions" to their peers, and (4) were less often boastful or otherwise likely to call attention to themselves. In short, prosocial behavior was more prevalent among boys assigned the traditional task of caring for the valuable accumulated food that meat on the hoof constitutes in Kisii society than among boys who spent their days in Western-style schools where, according to Whiting and Whiting, "each individual is out for himself and his goal is individual achievement" (1971, p. 36). This study leaves us still unsure about any possible relationship with competitiveness, however.

Morality and Ethics

Cross-cultural relativists might expect there to be cultural differences in moral judgments. Nevertheless, because every scholar's own enculturation included moral training, with little early warning that different morals might exist elsewhere, it is difficult to be objective about morality in cultures other than one's own. Despite these difficulties, there is a rich cross-cultural literature on moral judgments and related behaviors.

Traditionally subjects of philosophy, morality, and ethics may also be studied by focusing on what individuals actually say or do about situations that pose dilemmas because of conflicting values. Psychological morality may be studied developmentally by examining changes in solutions to moral dilemmas as people grow older and presumably learn their culture's values. A developmental approach to the study of morality is exemplified by some of Piaget's work (1932) and by the work of Kohlberg (Kohlberg, 1969a, 1969b, 1970). These two psychologists offered stage theories of moral development that could be taken as possible models of the universal unfolding of morality.

These models have been compared with the developmental trends revealed by empirical research, much of it done by the models' authors themselves. Various standardized tests of behavior in situations that pose dilemmas have been administered, and differences in response as a function of age compared across cultures. Such research can test the universality of the stage theories. It can demonstrate similar adult-level definitions of morality, accompanied by different rates of progress over age toward the incorporation of that definition in actual behavior, or one might find different definitions of morality, as was demonstrated by Mundy-Castle and Bundy (1988).

We might expect all societies to recognize behavior that serves others (rather than self-serving behavior) as morally desirable. In one manner or another, a central concern of childrearing in any society should be to instill in children this concern for others. But societies also teach respect for authority, obedience, and some self-aggrandizing behaviors (for example, individual achievement), such that competing behavioral tendencies are likely to emerge among individuals in any society. And, as societies become more individualistic, as Triandis (1995) suggests that most, in fact, are, then self-serving behavior might be expected to become more common. The particular mix of competing behaviors is likely to vary from society to society. Hence, the prevailing moral dilemmas and their characteristic modes of solution are also likely to vary across societies.

For the most part the available research relating to this argument is descriptive, revealing similarities or differences in moral behavior across a small number of societies, with minimal efforts to explain those similarities or differences. Bloom (1977) administered questionnaires to French and U.S. university students and to a sample of adult residents in Hong Kong in order to test Kohlberg's postulated link between "moral autonomy" (meant to denote a readiness to differentiate between a conventional and a personal standard of morality) and "social humanism," or a readiness to give priority to human welfare. Bloom found instead that in all three cultural settings these two potentially competing values were independent of each other. In all three societies, while many persons were high scorers on only one or the other, some persons scored high on both dimensions.

In Israel, the kibbutz ideology was shown to be related to moral reasoning (Fuchs, Eisenberg, Herz-Lazarowitz, & Shrabany, 1986; Snarey, Reimer, & Kohlberg, 1985). It may well be the case that the Kohlbergian model of moral development applies mostly, if not exclusively, to urban, middle-class groups, as Snarey and colleagues (1985) suggested, and involves a gender bias, as Gilligan (1982) asserted.

Studies that go beyond attempts to measure moral beliefs or attitudes would be welcome, such as cross-cultural replications of field experiments in helping behavior. (See, for example, Feldman [1971] for a report of real-life tests of honesty conducted in the streets, shops, and taxis of Boston, Paris, and Athens.)

Compliments: Is "Being Polite" the Same Behavior Everywhere?

People everywhere probably enjoy being complimented, but the conditions under which compliments are welcomed and perceived as such (rather than as unwelcomed flattery) vary, because cultural norms govern their use.

Barnlund and Araki (1985) studied the relative frequency of compliments, their topical themes, the preferred manner of expressing them, and their relationship to the status of the givers and receivers of compliments in Japan and the United States. They found that: (1) compliments occur with far greater frequency in the United States than in Japan; (2) in Japan, there is a wider variety of themes than in the United States; (3) U.S. people employ a wider variety of adjectives and more superlatives than the Japanese; (4) U.S. people are more likely to accept compliments; and (5) Japanese are more likely to employ compliments in interactions with nonintimates, whereas people in the United States are more likely to do so with close friends.

There were also similarities. In both societies, females were more often recipients and givers of compliments and, in both societies, nearly everyone studied reported "feeling good" about receiving and giving compliments. Although it is not demanded by the data, the authors considered this pattern of findings as consistent with individualism/collectivism differences between Japan and the United States. "A society founded on the group rather than the individual, that stresses harmonious relations, is not likely to encourage comparisons that inherently weaken group membership" (Barnlund & Araki, 1985, p. 25). Presumably, the authors consider complimenting a form of interpersonal comparison, and they also consider I/C to have considerable explanatory value for a behavioral difference across these two societies, Japan and the United States.

SOME CONCLUDING OBSERVATIONS

In this chapter we have described variations in values and motives. We found few relationships for which a particular explanation must be favored, although most point to socialization as the mediating link between ccocultural forces and human values.

Perhaps the single best generalization that can be made from the material reviewed in this chapter is that in any society there is likely to be a meaningful relationship between child-training emphases and adult behavior. This generalization has guided research from Whiting and Child's study in the early 1950s. It is clear that ecological and economic factors are also important, so that our generalization is probably best expressed in these terms: Children are likely to be induced to behave in ways compatible with adult roles that they will have to assume, with those roles in turn reflective of socioeconomic complexity and social organization. This generalization applies to nearly everything we have covered in the present chapter.

Because most studies were done by Western-trained cross-cultural psychologists, ironically much cross-cultural research on human values may be fundamentally culture-bound. Future cross-cultural research on values should be of a systematic, hypothesis-testing kind. It should focus attention on ecological and economic variables, childrearing, child behavior, and adult behavior and should seek interrelationships among all of these. It should also be informed by non-Western ideas about values. Conducted in such a manner, the research is likely to succeed in filling in many details, as yet unrecorded, of the network of relationships expressed in this now well-supported generalization.

We also wonder about how cross-cultural psychologists choose their topics when they study values. We have seen ample evidence in this chapter that much research seems driven by grand schemes invented by our colleagues (so-called paradigms) about value dimensions. Do we, as well, look at the real worlds around us for topics to study? Where, for example, is research on the value of consumption of material goods, which seems to be spreading around the world, or the high value placed on "entertainment," which includes performances for vast audiences by highly paid musicians, actors, and professional athletes? Perhaps we don't study these "values" because entertainers are better known (and surely better paid) than we are, and we can't afford the material goods that they and others who emulate them do. By decrying these values and resenting those who hold them, are we denying their very existence?

In any case, motives, beliefs, and values are nowhere static. As ecological systems and social structures change, we might expect the associated childrearing systems and the behavioral dispositions they instill to change also. The degree to which this is so and the intergenerational conflicts this might induce are issues which we will examine in detail in Chapter 11, where we will consider cultural change.

But first we must deal with some very important matters concerning sex (Chapter 8), aggression (Chapter 9), and intergroup relations (Chapter 10).

8

MALES AND FEMALES AND THE RELATIONS BETWEEN THEM

WHY STUDY SEX AND GENDER CROSS-CULTURALLY? -

We devote a whole chapter to matters relating to sex—including differences between the sexes in behavior, the development and change of gender roles, and relations between the sexes—because none of these issues can be understood without taking into account the ways in which cultural variables impact on them. While sex itself (i.e., membership in one or the other physiological/anatomical subgroups of human-kind, male or female) is biologically determined, behaviors that are characteristic of the two sexes (masculine and feminine behaviors) are not biologically determined. We must consider the accumulating evidence that, while males and females differ in some ways everywhere, they don't always differ in the same ways or to the same degree. Men and women are also behaviorally similar in some respects everywhere. And, as we shall see, there are also similarities across cultures in sex differences.

The mere fact that behavioral differences between the sexes are not *identical* in every society is enough to suggest that culture plays a role in shaping sex differ-ences. Social scientists have found sex differences more intriguing than the cross-sex similarities, in part because how the differences are explained has potential social significance.

It is tempting to interpret the variation across cultures in behavioral differences between the sexes as evidence that nurture, and not nature, is responsible for them. However, Ember (1981) warned that "the available evidence does not warrant any strong conclusions" (p. 531), because biological sex and differences in experiences dif-ferentially available to men and women are always confounded. The fact that they are confounded in different ways in different cultures could give cross-cultural research a theory-testing role. To date, however, little systematic theory-testing has been done. Nevertheless, we will advance some theoretical ideas in this chapter.

We will also present selections from a burgeoning empirical research literature. Sex and gender as a research domain has attracted much attention in recent decades, as shown by the proliferation of gender studies programs in universities in several countries, and by numerous publications. As cross-culturalists, we point particularly to a chapter by Best and Williams (1997), which provides a comprehensive review of topics including gender roles and stereotypes, relationships between men and women, the roles of biology and socialization, and theories of gender-role development.

Sex and Gender Distinguished

While *sex* is biological, *gender* is psycho-sociocultural. *Gender* refers to the meanings attached to being male or female, as reflected in social statuses, roles, and attitudes regarding the sexes. When we speak of gender, we have in mind such issues as: (1) gender role (culturally rooted definitions or prescriptions of male and female behaviors, e.g., division of labor by sex), (2) gender identity[1] (how one perceives oneself with respect to sex and gender roles), and (3) sex-role ideology (sex stereotypes, the attitudes governing relations between the two sexes, and their relative statuses). Such matters are not inherently biological; they are, in fact, inherently cultural.

For example, sex-role ideologies vary across cultures. In most societies, there is a power differential in favor of males, but the extent and nature of this differential is not the same everywhere. In some societies, the power differential is large and relatively stable, while in others it is breaking down. (Moreover, in a few societies, it has always been virtually nonexistent.) Later in this chapter we will examine in some detail cross-cultural similarities and differences in sex-role ideology.

Moreover, all of these things—gender roles, gender identity, and sex-role ideology—are intertwined. For example, the way the two sexes characteristically behave and define themselves is partly a cause of, and partly a result of, the way they relate to each other. With changes in the role of women come changes in behavior of both sexes. Because each and every part of this complex set of facts is influenced by culture, so is the whole set.

Accordingly, gender must be studied from a cross-cultural perspective. Some recent efforts to develop instruments to measure gender identity, as described in Box 8.1, point in this direction.

PSYCHOLOGICAL DIFFERENCES
BETWEEN THE SEXES

Before embarking on this section, it is well to consider a cautionary comment from Best and Williams (1997): "It is important to remember that human males and

---

[1]In the psychological literature, gender identity has sometimes been termed "sex role orientation."

BOX 8.1   Can Gender Identity Be Measured Cross-Culturally?

Interest in gender identity (or a broader concept used by Best and Williams (1997), viz., masculinity/femininity of self-concepts) has been spurred by the availability of instruments to measure it, such as the Sex-Role Inventory developed initially in the United States by Bem (1974). Essentially, such an instrument measures the degree to which individuals identify themselves as masculine, feminine, or androgynous (i.e., having both male and female sex-typed traits). Using the Bem Scale with university students of both sexes in the United States and Israel, Maloney, Wilkof, & Dambrot (1981) found that, while the two female samples were similar in their degree of femininity, the males differed across the two societies; Israeli men were less sex-typed (less masculine) than the U.S. men. If we assume that the Bem Scale is equivalent in the United States and Israel, these results suggest that Israeli culture provides experiences that shape male identities differently than in the United States.

Some researchers have developed translations and revisions of the Bem Scale for use in particular areas of the world, for example, the Spanish language Latin American Sex Role Inventory (Kaschak & Sharrat, 1983). Others (e.g., Diaz-Loving, Diaz-Guerrero, Helmreich, & Spence, 1981; Kranau, Green, & Valencia-Weber, 1982; Soto & Shaver, 1982) have employed similar scales for use with Hispanic peoples.

As Best and Williams (1997) point out, "researchers have taken different approaches: identifying self-descriptive questionnaire items differentially endorsed by men and women (California Personality Inventory femininity scale; Gough, 1952), examining frequency of endorsement of characteristics considered socially desirable in one gender or the other (Bem, 1974; Spence and Helmreich, 1978), or determining characteristics more frequently associated with one gender or the other without reference to social desirability (Williams and Best, 1990b)."

Illustrative of an imposed etic approach is the administration in Brazil by Spence and Helmreich of the Personal Attributes Questionnaire (PAQ), originally based on studies conducted in the United States (Spence & Helmreich, 1978). It was found that Brazilian men, unlike U.S. men, had higher femininity scores than masculinity scores. But, the items in this scale had been defined as *female* and *male* in the United States. In Brazil, or any other country for that matter, what is considered male or female may differ in some respects from the U.S. norms. So there is clearly a problem with employing translated scales verbatim. A better approach is that of Williams and Best (1990b) who employed culture-specific measures of masculinity/femininity in fourteen countries. With this more emic (or derived etic) approach, men in all countries scored more masculine than women.

---

females are only slightly variant members of the same species; women and men are much more similar than they are different, whether one is speaking biologically or psychologically" (p. 166).

We agree that it is all too easy to magnify the importance of any man–woman behavioral difference. One probably does so unconsciously, for example, whenever one speaks of the "opposite" sex! (See Tavris, 1992, for a lively book-length treatment of popular misinterpretations of sex differences.) However different their behaviors may appear at first glance, men and women in fact have highly similar biological and psychological natures. On the other hand, there *are* psychological differences. We must know what they are, we must assess their range and magnitude, and we must endeavor to understand their etiology.

As Tavris (1996) rightly points out, many apparent "sex differences" in behavior are really due to other variables that happen to be correlated with gender. She provides three telling examples of this important caveat:

1. In the United States, women are more likely than men to assert that they believe in horoscopes and psychics. Does this mean that women are more gullible than men? More spiritual than men? Neither, says Tavris. Controlling for math and science courses taken, this "gender gap" disappears. Tavris asserts, "What appears to be a gender gap is in fact a science gap" (p. A23).

2. U.S. women are less likely than U.S. men to express anger directly. Is this because women are less aggressive or sneakier? Again, Tavris rejects both of these explanations, noting that status must be taken into account. "Both sexes tend to be indirect and manipulative when they are angry at someone who has more power than they have...and both sexes are equally likely to lose their tempers with people who have less power than they have.... What appears to be a gender gap is really a power gap" (p. A23).

3. At a late stage in the 1996 presidential election campaign in the United States, there was much talk of another so-called gender gap, with a typical poll result showing women favoring the Democratic Party candidate (President Clinton) over the Republican candidate (Senator Dole) by 61 percent to 33 percent, while men favored the Democrat by only 49 percent to 42 percent.[2] Tavris notes, however, "both sexes choose the candidate they agree with, by a large margin.... women are more likely to agree with Bill Clinton *(whose party traditionally favors nurturing and aiding people in need)* than Bob Dole *(whose party traditionally opposes government programs like welfare and health care)*" (p. A23; parenthetic clauses not in original). Why do women tend more to agree with the Democratic Party views? Tavris says "experience." She explains, "More women than men today worry that they or their children might need a safety net if they lose a job, lose a partner, or lose their health. More women than men are taking care of aging, infirm parents. Many more single mothers than single fathers are raising children on their own." So, Tavris concludes, "The gender gap, then, is largely an experience gap."

Later in this chapter, we will consider a pair of carefully done experiments that together demonstrate once more how difficult it is sometimes to make sense out of these differences. (See below, the discussion of "women's fear of success.")

---

[2] These do not add to 100 percent because there were undecided voters in both groups.

Sex and Culture as They Relate to Cognition -

Do males and females have different cognitive skills? In the United States, where the testing of cognitive aptitudes for selection into educational programs and jobs is a culturally sanctioned practice, that affects multitudes every year, differences between the sexes in performance on tests of verbal and quantitative skills have regularly been reported. The nature and magnitude of the differences has changed over time, but males sometimes earn higher average scores on some tests than females, and vice versa on others. Irvine (1983), reviewing studies done over the years in various African countries, noted frequent, but not entirely consistent, sex differences, favoring males, in performance on tests that employ figural test items (like Kohs Blocks and the Ravens Progressive Matrices).

In most if not all cultures, task assignments to the two sexes reflect beliefs that the assignments are appropriate because they reflect inherent sex differences in skills. But surely, the opposite is possible, that the division of labor by sex sets up social forces leading to differential socialization of the sexes during childhood, as a result of which they learn different skills to different degrees. Consider, for example, what we know about sex and cognitive style.

Sex Differences in Cognitive Style -

Research on cognitive style (the manner in which people characteristically approach analytic problems)[3] in the United States revealed robust and reliable sex differences in degree of psychological differentiation. Males are more field-independent, at least by adolescence. Cross-cultural studies have partly confirmed the U.S. findings but have also produced other findings that throw light on the mechanisms that probably produced the sex differences first noted in the United States.

Employing three perceptual-cognitive tests (the Embedded Figures test, Kohs Blocks, and a visual discrimination task) in seventeen societies, Berry (1976b) found a considerable cross-cultural variation in sex differences on these tasks that was correlated with degree of food accumulation.

Van Leeuwen (1978) reviewed thirty studies done outside the United States, employing various measures of psychological differentiation. When significant sex differences were found, they were nearly always in the direction of males' earning scores closer to the differentiated end of the scale. Although this clear trend is consistent with a hypothesis of universality of sex differences, Van Leeuwen, like Berry before her, properly noted that the variation in the magnitude of the sex differences was more intriguing. An effort to explain this variation—from minimal to large—might reveal the social and cultural forces that impinge on

---

[3]Witkin (1978) referred to cognitive style as including a dimension called "psychological differentiation," with individuals varying along this dimension from "field-dependent" to "field-independent." This distinction refers to tendencies to be either responsive to contextual cues or more likely to ignore them. (See Berry et al., 1992, pp. 124–129, for a full exposition of these concepts.)

psychological differentiation generally—that is, for individuals regardless of sex—as well as an understanding of the sex differences.

Van Leeuwen adapted the ecological framework to encompass the findings from a number of the studies reviewed, including all those done in non-Western societies engaged primarily in subsistence-level economic ʾactivities.

Van Leeuwen's Theoretical Approach: An Application of the Ecological Framework. ˙ This application of Berry's (1966, 1971) framework points to economic conditions in subsistence-level societies that can produce sex differences in psychological differentiation through socialization practices that may differentially influence the two sexes.

The framework includes the idea that the degree of food accumulation in a subsistence-level society will influence its level of psychological differentiation. It is in low-food-accumulating societies like the Inuits' that the environment demands very sharp perceptual articulation for survival. Berry's framework and Van Leeuwen's use of it are consistent with earlier work done by Herbert Barry and colleagues (see, for example, Barry, Child, & Bacon, 1959). These studies showed that socialization for obedience and responsibility was stressed in high-food-accumulating societies, while socialization for achievement, self-reliance, and general independence was more likely to be stressed in low-food-accumulating societies.

Taking into account the findings of Barry and his associates, Berry's ecological hypothesis, and some additional information (to be described below at appropriate points in the argument), Van Leeuwen (1978) formulated her argument as follows: "The relatively greater freedom of women in more nomadic hunting-gathering societies will result in lesser sex differences in performance on differentiation tasks, whereas the restrictiveness of agricultural groups will produce greater sex differences in performance" (p. 96).

It is, in fact, low-food-accumulating groups, for example, Inuits, Australian Aborigines, and some Canadian Indian groups, that show minimal or even no sex differences in psychological differentiation. And high-food-accumulating groups, for example, the Temne, Ibo, Zulu in Africa, and Maori in New Zealand, show significant sex differences.

Barry, Bacon, and Child (1957) found that high-food-accumulating societies, as indexed by the cultivation of grain crops and the domestication of large animals, emphasized the compliance training of girls. Barry, Child, and Bacon (1959) also found that, in cultures where nurturance, obedience, and responsibility training are stressed (high-food-accumulating societies), they are stressed more strongly for girls.

Thus, Van Leeuwen's use of the framework is consistent with reliable correlations between degree of food accumulation and magnitude of sex differences in psychological differentiation. The balance of her argument is more theoretical and is concerned with possible mechanisms for these empirical relationships. Among them are the following:

1. In every society, men have greater physical strength and women are the child-bearers; this led to a specialization of labor by sex in large-grain-crop or large-animal-subsistence societies. Family-maintenance tasks were relegated to women, and, hence, compliance, dutifulness, and nurturance are stressed for girls.

2. Greater role specialization in sedentary groups led to a more exclusively female preoccupation with child-related activities. Hence, girls receive more training in social sensitivity (a characteristic of the so-called undifferentiated cognitive style).

3. The low role diversity in hunting and gathering groups led to a higher valuation of women's activities. In sedentary, agricultural groups, in which women's roles are more numerous and diffuse,[4] the role of women is more apt to be regarded with contempt (possibly feigned). Male activities are more apt to be accorded inflated prestige, and male adults tend to scorn participation in childrearing activities. All of these contribute to a preponderance of maternal childrearing, considerable paternal absence, and measures to keep women "under control." Maternal dominance and father absence contribute to an undifferentiated cognitive style in general, and the control of women contributes to the even less differentiated cognitive style characteristic of women in such societies.

Any or all of these mechanisms can account for variations in degree of sex differences in psychological differentiation in essentially subsistence-level societies. For "Western or Westernized societies," Van Leeuwen notes, variations in sex differences may reflect such variables as degree of obedience, conformity, family and religious loyalty, and mother salience in early childhood. Once again, those societies that stress such socialization practices stress them more for girls than for boys. Hence, she postulates a "social conformity model" to encompass the pattern of sex differences found in studies done in industrialized societies. This is consistent with and incorporable within the ecological model.

In both subsistence-level societies and societies in which food-getting is less of a preoccupation, the socialization practices that tend toward compliance and conformity, and that contribute to greater field dependence, are applied more to females than to males. Thus, variations across societies in the degree of sex differences in cognitive style result in part from differential socialization with regard to compliance. Cross-cultural differences (regardless of sex) in cognitive style are also a partial product of varying degrees of compliance training. Van Leeuwen's application of the ecological model shows how cognitive style is shaped by culture, via socialization, with socialization in turn at least partly shaped by ecological and economic factors.

---

[4]In such societies, it is not uncommon for women to care for children, do the daily weeding, cook, clean, brew beer, fetch firewood and water, wash clothes, and so on.

Anxiety, Self-esteem, Accomplishments, and Gender

Best and Williams (1997) reviewed research on self-reports of anxiety and self-esteem by "boys and girls." In Sweden and Hungary girls report greater anxiety in response to hypothetical anxiety-provoking situations than boys, but not in Japan (Magnusson & Stattin, 1978). With respect to self-esteem, boys perceive themselves to be more competent than girls (van Dongen-Melman, Koot, & Verhulst, 1993), and girls are less satisfied with being girls than boys are with being boys (Burns & Homel, 1986). However, girls' dissatisfaction does not seem to manifest itself in consistently lower self-esteem than boys' (Calhoun & Sethi, 1987). Girls in Nepal, the Philippines, and Australia thought less of their physical abilities and mathematical competence than did boys, while in Australia and Nigeria, girls felt more competent in reading (Watkins & Akande, 1992; Watkins, Hattie, & Regmi, 1994; Watkins, Lam, & Regmi, 1991). Still, Nigerian boys believed themselves more intelligent than did girls (Olowu, 1985). So, as noted by Best and Williams (1997), sex differences in anxiety and self-esteem are not altogether consistent, but in the preponderance of studies noted here, girls suffer more than boys with respect to self-images.

Achievements and Attitudes toward Success

When research on achievement motivation was popular (see Chapter 7 for a review of this research tradition), most of it was done with males. What little had been done with females yielded either inconsistent findings or some provocative facts about females' achievement motivation that made them appear strikingly less optimistic about achievement than males. Then, in the late 1960s, Horner launched a research program with U.S. university students, dealing, she believed, with women's attitudes toward success. The outcome was striking. Women behaved very differently from men, in ways we are about to discover. Horner interpreted her findings to mean that these women, of above average intelligence and education, reared and living in one of the most achievement-oriented societies in the world, were typically burdened by strong fears of success!

Horner's Research Design and Findings. Horner (1969) administered a standard stimulus, analogous to a TAT picture but in the form of a start of a story, to be completed as one saw fit. The start read "After first-term finals, Anne found herself at the top of her medical school class." Stories were scored as expressing a success/fear disposition if they contained any references to negative consequences of doing well. Of the ninety stories obtained from the women, fifty-nine contained such references.

The fears expressed in the fifty-nine stories were varied in content. They included expectations of social rejection: "She will be a proud and successful, but alas a very lonely doctor." They also included doubts about femininity: "Anne no longer feels so certain that she wants to be a doctor. She is worried about herself and wonders if perhaps she isn't normal." Some of the stories revealed what appears to be an attempt at denying the very possibility of success: "It was luck that Anne came out on top because she didn't want to go to medical school anyway" (Horner, 1969, pp. 36, 38).

Horner's findings are all the more striking when contrasted with the behavior of a control group of eighty-eight male university students who responded to an identical stimulus sentence, except that the subject was "John." Among these eighty-eight stories, only eight could be scored as containing fear-of-success themes.

An African Replication of the Horner Study.   In Africa, Fleming (1975) obtained similar findings for Kenyan women. One hundred twenty-three University of Nairobi students (44 females and 79 males) and 143 secondary school students (87 females and 56 males) wrote stories to Horner's cue sentence concerning success in medical school. As in Horner's study, the sex of the actor and the sex of the respondent were the same. Although the frequency with which both sexes cited negative consequences for success was lower than in the U.S. studies, it was substantially higher for females than for males, especially among the secondary school students. In the university student sample, 36 percent of the stories about females contained negative imagery, whereas 20 percent of the male stories did. In the secondary school sample, 41 percent of the female stories did, while this was true of only 9 percent of the male stories.

Fleming also administered a female-success cue to fifty-one male university students; of these, 31 percent produced negative stories. This latter finding is quite thought-provoking; we shall better understand it when we examine a study by Monahan, Kuhn, and Shaver (1974).

A Clarification of the "Fear of Success" Argument.   The ambiguity in Horner's findings needs to be noted. It is not clear whether the women were expressing (by negative consequence stories) an internalized fear of success or merely a cultural stereotype that surrounds female achievement. In other words, were Horner's female subjects projecting their own motives on Anne or reacting to Anne in the way their culture had taught them to respond to a woman occupying a heretofore male-dominated role? These are, of course, closely related phenomena, but it is worth the effort to distinguish them, if possible.

Monahan and associates (1974) made just such an effort. They used younger subjects than Horner had studied; they employed 120 sixth- through eleventh-grade students in a middle-class urban school, of whom 52 were boys and 68 girls. Far more important, they modified Horner's research design by assigning the "Anne" story to both male and female respondents. Similarly, they gave the "John" story to two additional groups of respondents, one male and the other female.

Monahan and colleagues reasoned that, if negative consequence responses occurred only, or predominantly, among female respondents and to either the John or Anne cue sentence, this would be strong evidence for an internalized motive among females. But if only the Anne cue sentence elicited negative consequence responses from both males and females, this would be evidence that the stereotypes surrounding women's achievements are negative and are learned and accepted by both sexes.

The Monahan team first found that a majority of the female respondents (51 percent) confronted by the Anne cue told stories with negative content, but only 21 percent of the male respondents who were given the John cue did so. This finding replicated Horner, and was similar to Fleming's main finding.

Monahan and colleagues' most important finding, however, was that for *both* sexes of respondents, the Anne cue elicited a higher proportion of negative stories. Coupling that finding with the fact that boys responded to the Anne cue even more negatively than the girls did, the authors properly concluded that *the sex of the actor in the cue was a more critical variable than the sex of the respondent.* The cultural stereotype hypothesis had to be favored as an interpretation of the reaction-to-success phenomenon.

Horner's (1969) study and the clarification provided by the later studies together showed that attitudes toward success are contaminated by attitudes toward the sexes. While success for males is generally viewed as a positive goal, success for females is not an unqualified good. At least for people who hold a traditional, sexist orientation, female success in a traditionally male role is viewed negatively. People who have adopted a less sex-linked sense of role demands (who do not perceive one sex or another as more qualified for a particular occupation) should view success for females in "male" roles more positively.

Gender Roles: Some Characteristically Masculine and Feminine Behaviors

Besides differing in cognitive behaviors, males and females differ in additional ways, some of which involve values, attitudes and other behaviors of social significance. These behaviors tend to be shaped by social norms, or behavioral expectations.

With few exceptions anywhere in the world, males are more likely than females to initiate sexual activity. Males are more likely to be physically aggressive. Males are more likely to express dominance over females, rather than vice versa; females are more likely to conform, defer, comply, and otherwise submit to an authority figure of either sex, but especially to a male.

These generalizations derive from many publications, including several from the The Six Cultures Study (Whiting, 1963; Whiting & Edwards, 1973; Whiting & Whiting, 1975). Of course, there are many individuals of both sexes whose behavior departs from these roles and the anthropological literature contains examples of whole societies in which the role differences are generally smaller than as described here.[5]

---

[5]For a thorough review of empirical research findings on differences as well as similarities between the sexes in social behaviors such as aggression, conformity, and helping, see Eagly (1987). In her book, Eagly argues that sex differences reflect primarily gender role differences, or what she calls "the differing social positions of women and men" (p. 9). For a discussion of how research findings on sex differences and similarities can be affected by political contexts, see Eagly (1995).

Whiting and Edwards (1973) report observations of children of both sexes in two age groups (3 to 6 years and 7 to 11 years) in Okinawa, India, the Philippines, Mexico, Kenya, and New England. Among the behavior classes for which boys generally outscored girls in these six diverse societies were (1) expressing dominance, (2) responding aggressively to aggressive instigations, and (3) manifesting aggression both physically and verbally. Girls outscored boys on two subclasses of dependency: "seeking help" and "seeking or offering physical contact," but not on a third subclass, "seeking attention," which was found to be mostly a male form of dependency. A female superiority in nurturance was found, but only among the 7- to 11-year-olds.

The tasks assigned to girls provided the best predictor of the degree to which girls exceeded boys in displaying "feminine" behavior. For example, in the Kenyan society, some child care and other domestic tasks are assigned to boys, and in the New England town, tasks assigned to girls are not exclusively stereotypically feminine ones; in these two societies, sex differences in behavior were smaller or less frequent than in the others (Whiting & Edwards, 1973).

DIFFERING SOCIALIZATION FOR BOYS AND GIRLS: WHY AND WITH WHAT CONSEQUENCES?

Consider what we have seen already in this chapter about sex differences and what anthropologists tell us about division of labor by sex. You might well conclude, as did Munroe and Munroe (1975, p. 116), that (1) there are modal sex differences in behavior in every society, and (2) every society has some division of labor by sex. These two phenomena, besides being universal, are also probably interrelated in a functional way. Let us now see how.

Earlier, we learned that Barry, Bacon, and Child (1957) had found rather consistent differences in the way many societies discriminate between the sexes in childhood-socialization emphases. A later publication by the same team of cross-cultural psychologists (Barry, Bacon, & Child, 1967) was based on ratings of reports in the Human Relations Area Files for forty-five societies. The team reported sex differences in every society in nurturance, responsibility, and obedience (with females displaying more of those classes of behavior) and in self-reliance, achievement, and independence (with males displaying more of those).

The correspondence between sex differences in socialization emphases and sex differences in behavior is virtually perfect. That the two sexes behave in ways they are taught to behave is, of course, not surprising, but it still raises some interesting questions. For example, have all these societies observed different inborn behavioral tendencies in males and females and shaped their socialization practices to reinforce such biologically determined tendencies? Or are societies' socialization practices merely influenced by certain physical differences between males and females, with those practices responsible for behavioral differences?

Risking oversimplification, we can summarize the picture of sex differences in behavior that is presented by anthropology and cross-cultural psychology as showing males to be more self-assertive, achieving, and dominant and females to be more socially responsive, passive, and submissive. How best might this be explained?

Economic and Biological Roots ⇀

One key to the explanation is the fact that the behavioral differences just summarized, although nearly universal and almost never reversed, range in magnitude from quite large down to virtually nil. A satisfactory explanation, then, will account for both the universality of direction of difference and the variation in magnitude of the difference.

Such an explanation takes into account economic factors—including division of labor by sex—and socialization practices. Key contributors to this explanation have been Barry, Bacon, and Child (1957), Barry, Child, and Bacon (1959), and Van Leeuwen (1978). Their arguments were reviewed at the beginning of this chapter in the context of a discussion of sex differences in field-independence–dependence, but they can now be amplified and generalized.

The argument begins with an early anthropological finding (Murdock, 1937) that a division of labor by sex is universal (or nearly so) and quite consistent in content. For example, food preparation is done predominantly by females in nearly all societies. Childrearing is usually the responsibility of females. Sometimes it is shared, but in no society is it the modal practice for males to assume the responsibility themselves. Although there are many cross-cultural variations in the content of sexual division of labor, there are, once again, hardly ever significant reversals.

Barry, Bacon, and Child (1957) suggested that this consistent pattern of sex-role differentiation during adulthood represents a set of solutions that societies have invented to deal with what were, for subsistence-level societies, practical problems. These problems are viewed as arising from biologically based physical differences (and not behavioral ones) between the sexes, especially the female's lesser overall physical strength and—most of all—her childbearing function. Different economic roles for males and females, with the latter consigned mostly to close-to-home activities, would have been a functional response.

It is likely that differential socialization of the two sexes evolved as a means for preparing children to assume their sex-linked adult roles. Then, the behavioral differences are a product of different socialization emphases, with those in turn reflective of, and appropriate training for, different adult activities.

Consistent with this argument is Barry, Child, and Bacon's (1959) finding that large differentiation between the sexes in socialization tends to occur more often in societies with "an economy that places a high premium on superior strength, and superior development of motor skills requiring strength" (p. 330). Also consistent with the argument is the finding that—if sexual differentiation occurs during socialization—girls nearly always receive more training in nurturance, obedience, and responsibility than boys and less in assertiveness, achievement, and independence (Barry, Child, & Bacon, 1959).

The ecological framework expands the argument so that it can accommodate numerous details about the subsistence mode and variations in degree of sex differences in behavior. Thus, in sedentary, high-food-accumulating societies, not only are females subjected to more training to be nurturant and compliant, but the degree of the difference between the sexes' training is also very high. In low-food-accumulating societies, such as gathering or hunting societies, there will be less division of labor by sex and little need for either sex to be trained to be compliant. Often in such societies (at least in gathering societies, if not hunting ones, as we will see shortly), women's contributions to the basic subsistence activity are integral to it. Hence, women's work is valued by the men, who are then not inclined to denigrate women or to insist on subservience from them.

Some related findings have been reported by Schlegel and Barry (1986) that expand our understanding of some of the consequences of division of labor by sex. One way in which division of labor by sex varies across cultures is in the degree to which women contribute to subsistence, or food-getting activities. This varies, depending on the activity. For example, if food is gathered, women's participation is usually high; in 11 of 14 gathering societies for which ethnographic reports were coded by Schlegel and Barry (1986), women were high contributors. By contrast, in only 2 of 16 hunting societies did women make a high contribution. (Schlegel and Barry defined high contribution as any percentage above the mean contribution for their entire sample of 186 nonindustrial societies, which was about 35 percent.)

Proportions of societies with above-average contributions by females for other types of subsistence were as follows: fishing, .29, animal husbandry, .46, incipient agriculture, .77, extensive agriculture, .72, and intensive agriculture, .33. Thus, women are more apt to contribute relatively highly to subsistence when the main activity is either gathering or agriculture other than intensive agriculture, and less highly where the activity is animal husbandry, intensive agriculture, fishing, or hunting (Schlegel & Barry, 1986, p. 144).[6]

Does this variation in the subsistence role played by women have any consequences? Schlegel and Barry (1986) found that it did, indeed, on such aspects of social life as sexual and marital relations, pregnancy norms, certain childrearing practices, values accorded to females, and the amount of personal freedom enjoyed by them. Associated with high female contributions to subsistence were: (1) polygyny, (2) bridewealth (gifts from the groom to the bride's family), (3) exogamy

---

[6]These findings differ somewhat from what was reported above when we discussed van Leeuwen's findings and those of Barry, Child, and Bacon pertaining to valuation of females and subsistence type. There, in the context of research on psychological differentiation, we learned that low-food-accumulation societies tended to value women more; here, somewhat the opposite. Because the various studies differed from each other in methodological and procedural ways, we cannot resolve this apparent contradiction, but it may well be that valuation of females relates to subsistence type in a curvilinear manner.

(going outside the immediate society for mates), (4) long postpartum sex taboos (which results in fewer and more widely spaced pregnancies), (5) more industrious-ness-training for girls, (6) higher valuation of females, (7) more permissiveness with respect to premarital sexuality, and (8) lower probability of rape.

Schlegel and Barry (1986) thus found that two sets of cultural features—adaptive and attitudinal—are associated with female contribution to subsistence. Where women play a relatively large subsistence role, the adaptive features of polygyny, exogamy, brideprice, birth control, and work orientation training for girls prevail. And under these same conditions (high contribution by females to subsistence), females are relatively highly valued, allowed freedoms, and are generally less likely to be perceived as objects for male sexual and reproductive needs.

Needless to say, the behavior of women varies across societies as a consequence of their role in subsistence activities. So, women not only behave differently from men, both men and women behave differently in different societies, and the two sexes relate to each other differently in different societies.

Thus, females do indeed have some behavioral dispositions that are different from those of males. But, thanks primarily to cross-cultural research, it is clear that these sex differences are the product of cultural forces, operating through socializa-tion practices and reflective of ecological factors. Both the consistencies in the cross-cultural data and the variations from society to society help us to understand how cultural values have been defined differently for the two sexes and how individuals come to behave in accord with them.

GENDER IDENTITY: SELF-PERCEPTIONS OF MEN AND WOMEN ACROSS CULTURES

Masculine and Feminine Stereotypes -

Whatever the real differences in behavior between the sexes may be, there are widely shared beliefs about those differences. As Williams and Best (1982/1990a) have shown, children in many Western countries (for example, France, Germany, Norway, the Neth-erlands, Italy, and the United States) and some non-Western nations as well (e.g., Malaysia, Nigeria, and Peru),[7] behave very similarly in the way they differentially ascribe patterns of traits to men and women. These consensual stereotypes, although held even by 5-year-old children, were more pervasively shared among 8-year-olds. Generally, with Norway and Germany as exceptions, children of each sex knew their own sex stereotype better than that of the other sex. These differences aside, the most striking finding of this project is the prevalence across cultures of sex stereotypes.[8]

---

[7]These were the only non-Western nations included in this report.

[8]Stereotypes about the two sexes, like any other stereotypes, may of course include beliefs about real differences.

Findings from many studies of stereotypes conducted by an international group of researchers cooperating in a thirty-two-country project have been reviewed and integrated by Williams and Best (1990a). As part of this project, university students in twenty-seven countries were presented with a list of 300 adjectives and were asked to indicate whether, in their culture, each adjective was more frequently associated with men, more frequently associated with women, or not differentially associated by gender. These frequencies were converted to an M percent score, with high values indicating items that were highly associated with men.

Correlation coefficients computed for M percent scores between pairs of countries across all 300 items indicated a substantial degree of agreement concerning the psychological characteristics differentially associated with men and with women. Male and female stereotypes were the most different in the Netherlands, Finland, Norway, and Germany and least different in Scotland, Bolivia, and Venezuela. Taking a different look at these same data, Best and Williams (1997) note that stereotypes of men and women were more different in Protestant than in Catholic countries and the difference was greater also in more developed countries.

Across all countries, dominance, autonomy, aggression, exhibition, and achievement were associated with men, while nurturance, succorance, deference, and abasement were associated with women. In all countries the male stereotype items were (as described by Best and Williams, 1997, p. 170) "more active and stronger" than the female stereotype items. The male stereotype was judged more positively in some countries (e.g., Japan, South Africa, Nigeria) while the female stereotype was more favorably viewed in others (e.g., Italy, Peru, Australia). These findings, Best and Williams (1997) suggest, support a general pancultural sex stereotype.

Turning from stereotypes to self-perceptions, in another (1989) study, Williams and Best found that the self-perceptions of men and women were less stereotypical in more economically and socially developed countries. Indeed, the most interesting of all their findings relate to sex role ideology.

SEX ROLE IDEOLOGY: CULTURE AND MALE–FEMALE RELATIONSHIPS

How do people in different parts of the world believe that men and women should relate to each other? Williams and Best (1990b) did a fourteen-country study of sex-role ideology. University students responded to the thirty-item Kalin Sex Role Ideology (SRI) measure (Kalin & Tilby, 1978); e.g., "The husband should be regarded as the legal representative of the family group in all matters of law"). National groups were scored along a dimension of "modern/traditional." European countries (the Netherlands, Germany, Finland, England, Italy) were the most "modern," the United States was in the middle, and African and Asian countries (Nigeria, Pakistan, India, Japan, Malaysia) were most "traditional." Generally, women had more "modern" views than men, but not in all countries (e.g., Malaysia and Pakistan departed from this general tendency). However, there was high correspondence between men's and women's scores in a given country with a correlation of .95 for men and women across the fourteen countries. In this particular study, overall, the effect of culture was greater than the effect of sex.

Both men's and women's SRI scores were related to economic–social development; that is, sex-role ideology tended to be more modern in more developed countries. Sex-role ideology also was more modern in more heavily Christian countries, in more urbanized countries, and in countries in the high latitudes (i.e., relatively far from the equator).

In several studies, the sex-role ideologies of students (and other people) in Western and non-Western countries have been compared. For example, Trommsdorff and Iwawaki (1989) found German adolescents to be less traditional than Japanese adolescents. (Unfortunately, as we noted in Chapter 2, studies that involve a comparison of only two groups are impossible to interpret. This is one of those and the alert reader will spot some others in this review.)

While many studies show some cross-cultural differences for both males and females combined, a male–female difference is rather consistently found across cultures. (In other words, there is, generally speaking, a culture by sex interaction, with the sex difference often more striking than the culture difference, as in the following examples.) Chinese American university students have more conservative views than Caucasian Americans, but women in both groups are more liberal than men (Chia, Moore, Lam, Chuang, & Cheng, 1994). Also, Indian students expressed more traditional sex-role ideology than U.S. students, but women in both groups were more modern than were men (Agarwal & Lester, 1992; Rao & Rao, 1985) when asked what qualities women in their culture should and should not possess. Furnham and Karani (1985) found cross-cultural similarity among English Christians, Indian Hindus, and Indian Zoroastrians in sex-role ideology, particularly among females.

In an Arab Israeli community, young females opposed the imposition of social constraints on women more than their male counterparts, but both expressed strong traditionally conservative attitudes regarding the Islamic code of protecting female honor and chastity (Rapoport, Lomski-Feder, & Masalha, 1989). Seginer, Karayanni, and Mar'i (1990) found that Jews, females, and older adolescents in Israel expressed more liberal views toward women's roles than did Arabs, males, and younger adolescents.

Suzuki (1991a) reported that U.S. women have more "modern," egalitarian attitudes than Japanese women though Japanese women's attitudes have become more egalitarian and individualistic over the past two decades, with sex-role ideology related to education and professional managerial work among both Japanese and U.S. women (Suzuki, 1991b). Best and Williams (1997) also found studies showing that female college students in Japan, Slovenia, and the United States are less conservative than men, with Japanese students the most conservative of the three groups (Morinaga, Frieze, & Ferligoj, 1993).

Gibbons, Stiles, and Shkodriani (1991) studied sex-role ideology among adolescents from forty-six different countries attending schools in the Netherlands. Students from less wealthy countries had more traditional attitudes than students from wealthier countries, and, once again, girls generally responded less conservatively than boys. Summarizing studies such as these, Best and Williams (1997) opine that it is not surprising that males generally have more conservative sex-role ideologies because "in most countries males benefit in terms of status and privileges from more traditional male-dominant orientations" (p. 168).

Changing Sex-Role Ideology

In wealthier countries, where higher proportions of women are gainfully employed and where women attend universities in relatively high numbers, ideology regarding the status of women is also more egalitarian. In such countries, Williams and Best (1989) found that men and women perceive themselves in a more similar fashion.

As sexual equality ideals spread, behavioral differences may diminish and so may the prevailing sex stereotypes. There is evidence that the ideology of sexual equality is spreading, but it is still more acceptable to females than to males. In most countries in the Williams and Best (1989) study, the women subjects were more liberal than the men. Similarly, Kalin, Heusser, and Edmonds (1982) found that females were more egalitarian than males in Canada, England, and Ireland. Whether the prevailing ideologies in these three countries were more egalitarian than in the past was not addressed by this study. Scher, Nevo, and Beit-Hallahmi (1979) also found Israeli female students to be more egalitarian than their male counterparts, while Israeli respondents of both sexes were more egalitarian than their U.S. counterparts. Israeli males in particular were more likely to endorse sexual equality than U.S. males.

Furnham and Karani (1985) compared the attitudes toward women of three different religious groups (Hindus and Parsis in India, and British Christians). They found that men in all three groups were more conservative than women in their attitudes toward sexual equality. Regardless of religion or culture, men in this study were more likely than women to believe in a just world (i.e., to believe that one gets what one deserves), and these beliefs were related to their conservative sex-role attitudes. Women, on the other hand, attributed more to chance and to powerful others (i.e., an external locus of control), and held more unjust world beliefs. These results suggest that the persistence of sex stereotypes may be closely linked with a cross-cultural power differential that accords one sex more privileges and power than the other. Whether men support or resist changing women's roles may in part reflect the extent to which they experience this power differential as unfair and are willing to give up some of the privileges and controls that greater male prestige has afforded them in the past.

Many social scientists interested in changing sex roles assume that male–female equality and societal modernization are closely linked. Indeed, as Williams and Best revealed, changes in the roles of women in a given society may be one indicator of that society's level of economic development. In many societies, as such development proceeds, traditional patriarchal patterns of female seclusion and male dominance are gradually replaced by women's greater civil equality and political participation.

A study by Biri, Pendleton, and Garland (1987) focused on men's attitudes toward changing women's roles in a society, Libya, where the effects of development on the family and society were becoming increasingly evident, particularly as more and more Libyan women sought gainful employment outside of the home. The Biri and colleagues study is discussed in more detail in Box 8.2.

BOX 8.2   Men's Attitudes toward Changing Women's Roles in Libya -

In the United States, sex roles are related to age, education, socioeconomic status, and religion. Biri, Pendleton, and Garland (1987) searched for a relationship among these characteristics in Libyan men and their attitudes toward women's changing roles.

Biri and associates defined "traditional" attitudes as "those which encourage male dominance and a subservient role for women within the home and discourage women's participation in political and economic activities outside of the home," and "modern" attitudes as "those which encourage women's participation in decision making within the home as well as their active participation in political and economic activities outside the home" (p. 297). The social characteristics on which their study focused were age, education, socioeconomic background (urban *versus* rural), religiosity, social status, mother's employment, and family type (extended *versus* nuclear).

They hypothesized that men most likely to hold "modern" attitudes would be ones with an urban background, who grew up in a nuclear family with a mother who worked outside the home, who are young, highly educated (high school or above), of high social status (as measured by family income), and without a strong commit-

ment to religion. Interviews were conducted (in Arabic) with 200 Libyan men in Tripoli, using scales of attitudes toward (1) division of labor within the household, (2) women's participation in family decision making, (3) women's political participation, and (4) women's participation in the labor force.

The results confirm the investigators' hypotheses concerning age, education, and mother's employment. That is, young educated men whose mothers worked outside the home generally showed more modern attitudes toward all four dependent variables. However, contrary to the investigators' hypotheses, they found that men who came from extended families showed more modern attitudes toward division of labor at home and toward women's participation in family decision making than did men from nuclear families.

The authors explained that high social status, though not an influential variable by itself, is closely linked with educational level. Furthermore, in Libya, those families with higher incomes have better access to educational opportunities, and these families are most likely to be extended families. Thus, the modern attitudes of Libyan men from extended families seem to be a function of the higher educational level of those men.

Toward Equality of the Sexes ﹨

Awareness of a movement for equality of the sexes probably exists worldwide, as indicated by the 1985 international conference held in Nairobi to mark the end of the United Nations' Decade of Women and subsequent meetings, both worldwide and regional. Still, it is probably no accident that the movement for equality of the sexes took root and flourished effectively in industrial nations, in which division of labor by sex is not nearly so functional as it is in predominantly subsistence-level societies. Modern technology has produced numerous laborsaving devices, which make possible unprecedented leisure time and make differences in physical strength between the sexes virtually irrelevant. Males who tend to be principally employed outside the home, in fact, have many hours available each day to spend at home. Hence, they are available to perform domestic tasks, including childrearing. Similarly, women in modern societies are no longer so tied to such tasks. Furthermore, family-planning technology, very pervasively employed in industrial societies but not yet very widely accepted elsewhere, has drastically reduced the time and attention that must be devoted to infant care, traditionally the most time-consuming and restricting activity of female adults.

Hence, it is no surprise that in industrial societies sexual differentiation during childhood socialization is minimal (Barry, Bacon, & Child, 1957) or that sex differences in behavior among children are minimal (Whiting & Edwards, 1973). A visitor from Mars dropping into most nonindustrialized nations would have little difficulty detecting the existence of two sexes (how could she fail to note differences in hairstyles, dress, and so on?). But if the visitor arrived in some U.S. or European university classroom, utter confusion might result. If warned in advance to look for men and women, the visitor might expect the men to be the short-haired ones wearing blue jeans and using four-letter expletives! These and other once-reliable sex-distinguishing characteristics would mislead our visitor as often as they would help. Clearly, a degree of gender homogenization has emerged, albeit with constraints and countertendencies.

In these same societies where a blurring of sex differences in childrearing and in behavior has begun, inequality of economic opportunity remains as an anachronism. Not surprisingly, these societies have seen the emergence of feminist movements as an inevitable response to that inconsistency. No such inconsistency characterizes mostly subsistence-level societies. Where tradition prevails, adult roles remain sex-linked, and socialization practices include clear and effective efforts to produce behavioral differences between the sexes that are for the most part accepted as normal, natural, and appropriate.

Of particular interest in this regard are those nonindustrial societies in which certain cultural facts may contribute to an unanticipated blurring of sexual distinctions. For example, because in most societies both boys and girls are reared primarily by female caretakers, there is the likelihood that young boys will have available adult role models who are preponderantly female. Practices that enhance the probability of maternal predominance in rearing include polygyny, exclusive mother–child sleeping arrangements, and matrilocal residence patterns, all of which enhance father absence and reduce male salience. If these societies also accord social dominance to adult males (as is clearly the case in high-food-accumulating, subsistence-level societies), they are further very likely to have severe male initiation ceremonies during adolescence, including circumcision (Burton & Whiting, 1961; Harrington, 1968; Whiting, 1962).

A persuasive interpretation of the cross-cultural correlation between low male salience during infancy and male initiation ceremonies during later childhood is that the ceremonies represent an institutional response designed to overcome cross-sex identification tendencies in young males.

Munroe and Munroe (1975) provided a thorough review of studies bearing on cross-sex identification and other societal responses to it. These responses include the *couvade* ("male pseudopregnancy," an institutionalized set of practices whereby an expectant father is treated like an expectant mother) and still other institutions that permit males to display "feminine" behaviors in societies that do not structurally emphasize maleness. Munroe and Munroe (1988) reiterated that the couvade was more apt to be present in societies in which mothers and their infants sleep together and in societies with a high frequency of matrilocal residence. On the other hand, when societies are scored on "defensive masculinity" (a concept similar to Broude's notion of hypermasculinity (1983), which will be discussed below), the couvade is found disproportionately often in societies that are low on this variable. (In Chapter 9, which deals with culture and aggression, we will discuss some other implications of cross-sex identification.)

Societies differ in the value attached to the maintenance of differences between the sexes. Some sex distinction is universal, but the content of the distinction—as well as its perceived desirability—vary across cultures. With the spread of feminist ideology, in many societies gender-role boundaries are actively being blurred. In others, they are being reinforced, and in still others there is conflict between pressures to diminish them and institutional practices that reinforce them. How and to what degree societies struggle against, tolerate, or even celebrate sex distinctions reflects the perceived functionality of adult division of labor by sex. Where the economic system functions more smoothly with such a division of labor, acceptance of long-standing sexual inequalities is likely. Where a sexual division of labor is largely irrelevant to the economic system (as is probably the case in postindustrial societies), sharp distinctions between male and female roles become less functional and sexual equality is more apt to be accepted as a societal norm.

It might also be the case that little boys and little girls will increasingly be treated alike. But for the moment, as we saw in an earlier section of this chapter, there remain some sharp differences in socialization for males and females.

A SOCIOCULTURAL THEORY OF HUMAN SEXUALITY

Now we turn our attention to sexual behavior itself, surely a critically important aspect of interpersonal relations. Our perspective on human sexuality emphasizes that it, too, has social and cultural meanings.

In his book, *Journey into sexuality: An exploratory voyage,* sociologist Ira Reiss (1986) examined cross-culturally patterns of sexual behavior, relying heavily on anthropological data from the Human Relations Area Files. Interpreting these data, Reiss offered a view of human sexuality that sees sexual practices and customs as linked to other features of a society such as kinship patterns and power structures.

For Reiss, human sexuality practices follow "shared cultural scripts" that promote specific types of sexual behavior while discouraging others. All groups attach great importance to sexual scripts, but these vary greatly between ethnic groups, social classes, age groups, and societies. All societies have the need to regulate sexual behavior in some way, so the existence of sexual scripts constitutes a cultural universal.

Whether sexual scripts restrict and control sexual behavior or encourage sexual promiscuity (and both kinds can be found), it is these sexual scripts, and not biological stimuli, that determine what people find erotically arousing. Thus, according to Reiss, sexual arousal is a learned response to social and cultural stimuli. Of course, sexual arousal has biological underpinnings, so it might be more accurate to say that sexual arousal is a product of an interaction between biological forces and what Reiss has termed "sexual scripts."

To explain why certain sexual scripts exist in some societies but not in others, Reiss examined cross-cultural patterns of sexual activity as they relate to specific social systems. He found sexual practices to be closely linked with the kinship system, power structure, and ideological beliefs of a given society. Based on these findings, Reiss proposed a sociological theory of human sexuality that understands these links as initially stemming from the potential of sexual bonding to create lasting human relationships and a support system that will provide for the needs of the newborn infant. From these kinship ties, a pattern of task assignment emerges that is typically based on gender. These gender-based task assignments, as we saw earlier in this chapter, are the basis for a power structure favoring men, both within the kinship system and in the wider society. However, where women's kinship ties are strong, such as in matrilineal societies, female power is also likely to be greater and women will experience less sexual abuse. The greater the power of one sex, the greater that sex's ability to control sexuality and define sexual scripts.

In Reiss's view, members of the more powerful sex not only secure control of major social institutions, they can also shape gender roles in ways that accord themselves greater sexual privilege. Thus, the sexual scripts and erotic preferences of a given culture may reflect a power differential that favors one sex (typically males) over the other.

As noted above, relations between the sexes are influenced by gender roles, gender identity, and sex-role ideology. Broude (1983) explored cross-culturally the relationship between these variables and male–female interaction, utilizing coded data for approximately 200 societies in the Human Relations Area Files.[9] Prior research

---

[9]Broude used 201 societies listed in the Standard Cross-Cultural Sample, which is a portion of the societies listed in the HRAF.

(e.g., Whiting & Whiting, 1975) had suggested that male sex-role ideology and gender identity (labeled *hypermasculinity* by Broude) may be related to both the quality of sexual relationships and nonsexual intimacy. Broude expected that heightened masculinity (as indicated by such cultural features as "male boasting" and a double standard governing extramarital sex) would be reflected in (1) sexual hostility, (2) repressive attitudes toward female sexuality, (3) less sexual intimacy, and (4) greater husband–wife aloofness.

Seeking evidence for such relationships, Broude included three categories of variables in her study: measures of hypermasculinity (e.g., male boasting), of sexual intimacy (e.g., frequency of extramarital and premarital sex), and of nonsexual intimacy or husband–wife aloofness (e.g., the extent to which husbands and wives eat, room, and spend leisure time together). Various patterns of intercorrelations emerged, leading Broude to several conclusions, including the following.

First, Broude did not find that hypermasculinity relates to sexual intimacy or marital aloofness to the extent that the earlier literature had suggested. However, Broude's various indices of hypermasculinity did correlate highly amongst themselves.

Second, although Broude reported that hypermasculinity was not directly related to degree of cross-sex intimacy, her findings suggest that male self-concepts and attitudes toward women and sex influence certain behaviors affecting marital stability. That is, where the frequency of extramarital sex is high for men but low for women (i.e., the double standard), marriages are more likely to end in divorce. Conversely, where women have some degree of premarital sexual experience (i.e., where attitudes toward female sexuality are less repressive), marriages tend to be more stable.

Broude suggested that male behaviors such as boasting, sexual hostility, and marital infidelity may best be understood as attempts by men to overcompensate for underlying insecurities about their masculinity. These findings replicate an earlier study by Broude (1980) in which she found the extramarital double standard to be significantly related to boasting, machismo, men's houses, segregation of the sexes in chore assignments, and father absence, all components of the pattern of male protest behavior. The works of Reiss (1986) and Broude (1980, 1983), which deal primarily with sexual behavior, dramatically suggest that even one of the most biological acts human beings perform is enmeshed in culture.

CONCLUSION

Our discussion of cultural differences in values, attitudes, and behavior relating to the sexes has revealed a considerable amount of consistency around the world in the ways in which the sexes differ from each other in characteristic behaviors and in the ways that socialization practices instill those behaviors.

These consistencies are probably linked to division of labor by sex, so that if adult sex roles remain stable, so will socialization practices and behavioral differences. However, there is reason to believe that the division of labor by sex, gender roles, and related sex-role ideologies are changing and, as they change, so might socialization practices and the behaviors that characterize the two sexes. Still, in the world today, there are some tenacious differences between the sexes in behavior. One of these is aggression, to which we turn in the next chapter.

9

CULTURE AND AGGRESSION

HOW IS AGGRESSION RELATED TO CULTURE?

One of the sex differences noted in the last chapter is that, on the average around the world, males quite consistently commit more aggressive acts than do females. This is probably a cultural universal. Later in this chapter, we shall examine this sex difference very closely because it may be crucial to our understanding of aggression per se. We must first put aside sex differences and ask some fundamental questions about aggression and culture.

Do we find aggression everywhere to the same degree, or do societies vary in their typical levels of aggression? If they vary, is the variation systematically related to certain aspects of culture? Do these relationships reveal how aggression is both caused and controlled? Until we can answer these cross-cultural questions, we cannot claim to understand human aggression.

Aggression and violence are so pervasive throughout the world that aggression appears to be a particularly compelling example of a human universal. Our species, *homo sapiens,* truly capable of heartfelt deeds of love, nurturance, caring, and altruism, can also commit heartbreaking acts of violence. It seems that many of us can do *both* great good and unspeakable evil. By the same token, some of us are, characteristically, kind, while others are more consistently cruel. Even whole societies strike us as relatively pacific, and others as warlike. How do these contrasting capacities to be helpful and hurtful play out in different societies? What is the role of culture in this story of good and evil?

Insights from Literature and the Arts

Many of the most enduring literary works produced in diverse societies attest to the ubiquitousness of aggressive acts through all of recorded time. Illustrations of aggression even appear in prehistoric rock paintings (Woodhouse, 1987). Many literary works attest also to stirring acts of self-sacrifice and kindness.

Another, less venerable, "literature," that of the social sciences, comprising empirical research in many settings and employing diverse methods of inquiry, confirms the picture created by the great novels, plays, and epic poems that have come down to us through the ages: in every society, we are capable of violence ranging from the putatively glorious to the apparently senseless.

Literary artists at their best surpass social scientists in conveying the emotions, the hatred, the ugliness, the pain, and the suffering that accompany aggression and violence. Descriptions in literature may rival reality in their vividness and, when violence is presented theatrically—on the stage and, more importantly, on the screen—the effect on the audience may be sickening, arousing, or cathartic. But while such artistic, ideographic, literature describes, depicts, and recreates, it seldom explains with the force of empirical data dispassionately analyzed. Although artists may explicate a fictional perpetrator's motivations and other contributing factors, the artist's inferences may not stand up to the light of nomothetic social scientific inquiry.

Insights from Cross-Cultural Psychology and Comparative Anthropology

To explain human aggression, social scientists collect data both within and across societies, and organize their findings into testable theories about its etiology and control. In this chapter, we note intersocietal variation in characteristic levels of aggression and ask how this variation is systematically related to cultural variables. The goal of cross-cultural research on aggression is to understand why human beings, in whatever society, sometimes and under certain conditions, behave aggressively, which is to say, behave in ways that inflict harm on other people. For many social scientists, this goal serves another: to control and prevent aggression.

In explicit pursuit of that goal, Goldstein and Segall (1983) provided broad geographic coverage (sixteen modern nation–states from various regions of the world, including Holland, Israel, Italy, France, Ireland, Hungary, China, Japan, Finland, India, Brazil, Germany, Peru, Turkey, Nigeria, Hawaii and the United States), but for only some were cultural antecedents and consequences of aggression dealt with. Most of the chapters stood alone, describing rather than comparing across societies.

A more comprehensive review (Segall, Ember, & Ember, 1997) presented both psychological and anthropological data and theory pertaining to aggression, crime, and warfare. Parts of that *Handbook* chapter influence the present chapter and other parts contribute to Chapter 10 on intergroup relations.

The Many Varieties of Aggression

What is aggression? Tentatively, we define it as any action by one or more persons that intentionally inflicts harm on one or more other persons. (We return to this definition below, on p. 257.) This broad definition covers, so to speak, a multitude of sins. The perpetrators and victims of an aggressive act may be unknown to each other, or may have a history of personal competition and conflict. They may even be intimates, such as lovers, spouses, parents and offspring. In any society, particular violent acts may be negatively sanctioned (as in "criminal" violence), tolerated (as in playful jostling by children), encouraged (as in some forms of organized "sport"), or even positively sanctioned by law (as in capital punishment). The acts may be premeditated or impulsive; they may be followed by rejoicing or remorse. They may go relatively unnoticed or they may unleash vengeful acts no less violent than the actions to which they are a reaction.

Matters of emic and etic definitions of aggressive acts must concern us, of course. See, for example, the problems discussed in Box 9.1.

Then there is aggression and violence *between and among* societies, both smaller ones popularly referred to as *tribes* (but preferably called ethnic groups), and very much larger and more powerful ones, more recent arrivals on the scene, called *nation–states*. Intergroup relations, much of the time harmonious, often involve intergroup conflicts, which all too often evolve into full-blown warfare. In this chapter, however, our attention will be directed mostly to interpersonal violent acts. (Intergroup relations will be discussed in Chapter 10.)

Not only are they varied in these respects, in some places aggressive acts may hardly ever occur. Is there a society in which aggression *never* occurs? Probably not, despite occasional, unsubstantiated claims to the contrary, typically in journalistic accounts of a "discovery" of a pacific society, heretofore unknown to anthropology. On the other hand, as has cogently been argued (e.g., Montagu, 1976) and amply shown by research reviewed below, there is considerable variation across cultures in the nature and magnitude of aggressive interpersonal behavior. This cross-cultural variation may provide the key to understanding the causes of aggression and possible ways to control it.

Aggression, Power, and Status

Many seemingly "aggressive" behaviors might better be thought of as attempts to exercise social control via coercion, according to an argument by Tedeschi and colleagues (Tedeschi, Gaes, & Rivera, 1977; Tedeschi & Melburg, 1983; Tedeschi, Smith, & Brown, 1974). If coercive acts are considered unjustified and committed with an intent to harm their target, they are likely to be judged "aggressive," but similar acts, when committed by an acknowledged superior toward a subordinate, might well be seen as legitimate exercise of authority and not as aggression. Because societies vary in the extent to which subordinates accept their lower status (Hofstede, 1980) cross-cultural differences in the judgment of the aggressiveness of coercive acts may be anticipated.

This line of reasoning led Bond, Wan, Leung, and Giacalone (1985) to predict that Chinese students in Hong Kong and U.S. students in Albany, New York would

BOX 9.1   Cultural Variations in Meanings

When speaking of aggression, violence, and crime as they are manifested in various societies, the terms themselves are problematic. In their hologeistic research on "interpersonal violence" (mainly focusing on homicide and assault), C. R. Ember and M. Ember (1993, 1994a,b) talk about violence behaviorally; thus, they avoid using the word *crime* because definitions of *crime* vary so widely from one society to another. In many societies, killing an infant intentionally is called a "homicide." But in others, including many societies described in the Human Relations Area Files (HRAF), infanticide is an accepted practice. Minturn and Shashak (1982) found infanticide in 53 percent of the cases in their sample of mostly nonindustrial societies. They suggest that infanticide is best defined as "terminal abortion," because the reasons given for it are very similar to those given for abortion (e.g., illegitimacy, excess children). An infanticide almost always occurs before the ceremony that socially marks or announces a birth. So, when a society socially recognizes a new person (before, at, or after birth) is related to whether or not infanticide is considered a crime.

Similarly, the killing of an adult means different things in different societies, depending generally on the adult's origin. For example, among the Kapauku of New Guinea, punishment for killing a person varied according to whether or not the killing occurred within the polity ("village" or "tribe"); intention did not count. Killing within the village and the *confederacy* (comprising a few villages) was punishable; outside those political units killing was not punishable because it was "war" (Pospisil 1958, as referred to in Ember & Ember, 1993).

Because the biggest political unit in many societies is the band or village, it is not surprising that killing a person is interpreted differently in different societies. In most industrialized nations, killing in the context of war is considered to be legiti-

mate because those who are targeted for killing belong to another polity. Further, in these societies, execution may be considered legitimate not just because of what the "criminal" did, or because justice is administered by constituted authority, but because murderers (and traitors, too) put themselves "outside the law," which would otherwise protect their right to live.

In most societies known to anthropology, the killing of some people is considered a "crime." But some acts called crimes in some societies have no analogs in others. In a society with no concept of private property in land, the concept of trespass may not have any meaning (see Rudmin, 1992). In societies in which physical punishment is considered an appropriate form of discipline, severe beatings of a family member will not be considered assault if they are administered by someone who is considered to have that right.

For example, in many societies, wife-beating was (and is) not considered a crime. In the United States today, where it is a "crime," newspaper accounts often note that police officers don't always take spousal abuse very seriously. In his hologeistic study of family violence, Levinson (1989) examined the relative frequency of wife-beating in societies in which it is considered appropriate and in which it is not. There are many accounts of people's believing, in many societies, that a husband had the right to beat his wife for any reason.

When meanings vary, it is difficult to use a term like *crime* in a cross-cultural study. In anthropological discourse, the cultural or local meaning is the emic meaning. But the emic meaning may be too difficult to discover in an ethnographic document, precluding easy hologeistic comparison. So we usually define variables in etic or observable terms and try to measure the frequency of killing a person or of wife-beating, rather than the "meaning" inherent in terms like *murder* and *assault*.

respond differently to verbal insults delivered by a superior to a subordinate, with the Chinese students (whose culture, in Hofstede's terms [1980, 1983] is character-ized by relatively high "power distance") less apt to characterize the insults as aggressive acts. Bond and associates' (1985) research is described in Box 9.2.

This brief review of some relevant studies suggests that systematic cross-cultural analysis of socialization practices, ecocultural antecedents, institutionalized expressions of aggression, and other potentially related variables is necessary if we are to under-stand aggression.

To understand why human beings sometimes behave aggressively is to detect those factors in the natural and man-made environments that influence our behavior in more or less adaptive ways. That we do aggress in differing degrees, in different ways, and for different reasons is clear. Nevertheless, these individual and societal differences possibly reflect some universally applicable principles concerning aggression's causes. So cross-cultural research should help us discern them. An anal-ysis of differences across cultures should also enable us to find the general principles underlying the differences.

BOX 9.2   Are Insults Aggressive Acts?

Bond, Wan, Leung, and Giacalone (1985) presented male undergraduates in both Hong Kong and Albany, New York with a scenario in which a manager in a company board meeting insults either a superior or a subordinate either within or outside his own department and had the undergradu-ates rate both the legitimacy of the insult and the personality of the insulter. These ratings were obtained both as unstructured responses (free responses describing ac-tions that should be taken before the next meeting and characterizations of the in-sulter's behavior) and as structured re-sponses to a sixteen-item bipolar rating scale.

Bond and colleagues expected that, be-cause Chinese culture is more collectivis-tic than U.S. culture, Hong Kong students would differentiate more between in-group and out-group sources of insults, negatively sanctioning in-group insulters more than out-group insulters to a greater

extent than would the students in New York. The hypothesis that markers of sta-tus and group membership would be more influential in determining the response of the higher power distance/higher collec-tivism Chinese students was confirmed. For example, for the Chinese students, the high status, in-group insulter was per-ceived as less unlikable and his acts as less illegitimate than the U.S. graduates per-ceived them. However, the prediction that, among the Chinese, insults from in-group members would be disparaged more than those from out-group members was not confirmed. In this high collectiv-ist society, it appeared that insults within the group are acceptable while insults di-rected beyond the group are not. Most im-portantly, however, among the Chinese subjects in this study, insults from a high-er to lower status member of a group are not seen as aggressive but rather as justi-fied, legitimate, and acceptable.

Before we undertake an analysis of cross-cultural variations in aggression, we need first to consider a few preliminary generalizations about aggression that hold across most, if not all, cultures. Donald Campbell (1975) saw belief in the pervasiveness of aggression as a cultural universal. In Campbell's view, people everywhere expect aggression to occur often; this expectation probably reflects a belief that somehow to aggress is simply to express "human nature." Also universally, Campbell noted, cultures have developed traditions (ethical, religious, political, etc.) to *control* aggression. Therefore, some combination of ideas about the cause of aggression and what needs to be done about it may be found in any society.

There are, however, cultural variations in the content of these ideas concerning cause and control of aggression. Whatever their content, they are not without subtle but significant consequences. For example, in most contemporary Western industrialized societies, prevailing political ideologies regarding individual freedom (Skinner, 1971) and individualism more generally (Triandis, 1995) can derail efforts to control aggression by reinforcing popular beliefs in negative implications of "repressing" aggression. By the same token, beliefs in the efficacy of punishment lead to practices that inadvertently encourage aggression. Punishment of aggression, as most psychologists have long been aware, does not usually have its intended effect. Thus, beliefs about aggression in any society influence the level of aggression itself.

The story is even more complex because the real antecedents of aggressive behavior are numerous. They are both ecological and structural. They include the probability of conflict over resources, the probability of frustrations of various kinds, norms governing conflict resolution, childrearing emphases, and the kinds of behaviors displayed by people who might serve as models to be emulated. All of these antecedents, as well as others, exist in every culture but they vary in kind across cultures.

A CONCEPTUAL FRAMEWORK FOR AGGRESSION RESEARCH

The way diverse variables interact to influence aggressive behavior is shown in diagrammatic form in Figure 9.1, where we see many possible contributing factors that bear on an individual's likelihood of behaving aggressively. The diagram illustrates possible links between ecocultural forces, socialization practices, individual experiences, and individual behavioral dispositions when people find themselves in situations in which frustrations need to be overcome or conflicts need to be resolved.

Definitions

Terms in the diagram, including *aggression* itself, need defining, because they have diverse meanings in popular discourse.

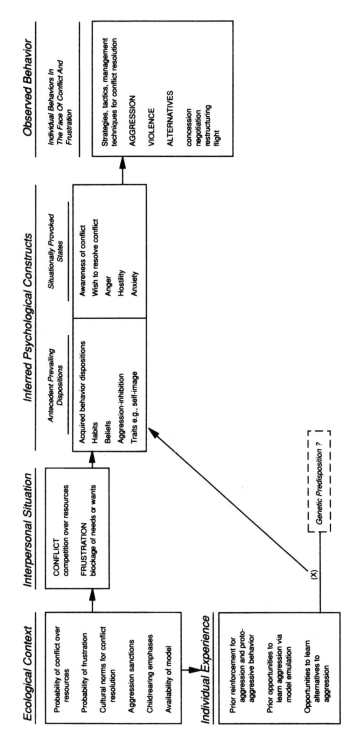

FIGURE 9.1 A Conceptual Framework for the Study of Aggression

We define *aggression* in much the same way as did Dollard, Doob, Miller, Mowrer, and Sears (1939), who described it as "a sequence of behavior, the goal response of which is the injury to the person toward whom it is directed." Implicit in this classic definition is that the "injury" may be physical or psychological and that the "response" is an overt manifestation of an inferred behavioral disposition, which probably includes an intention to harm.[1]

By *conflict* we mean any situation involving a disagreement about the allocation of resources, with the participants in the conflict motivated somehow to resolve it.

Frustration, often a feature of a conflict, is defined as a barrier to satisfaction of a need or want. Frustration can lead to anger or hostility (to be defined forthwith) and can increase the probability of aggression.

Anger is an inferred state of an individual denoting a feeling that often accompanies conflict or frustration. A short-lived state, anger is usually provoked by the behavior of another person, toward whom it is directed (although it may be displaced onto others).

Hostility is a longer-lived state, inferred from behavior, usually less intense than anger, and frequently directed diffusely to a collective target, as in cases of enduring ethnic hostility. It is often shared by many people, who learn hostility by emulating others, as when one group of people feel hostile toward a group of "foreigners" whom they have never met.

In these definitions, we deliberately stress aggression's overt behavioral quality in order to avoid unnecessary problems that surround notions of behavioral intent. Particularly when dealing with aggression in a cross-cultural context, inferring correctly the intent that may underlie a particular aggressive act is very problematic.

By recognizing that anger and hostility are never directly observed, but only inferred from observed aggression, we emphasize that not all aggressive acts are caused by anger or hostility. Aggression occasionally reflects other motives, such as a felt need to appear "manly," possibly more so in some cultures than in others.

We also wish to distinguish aggression *as a class of behavior* from the popular, quasi-psychiatric notion of "aggression" *as a drive or an instinct,* the blockage of which might result in some psychic harm.[2]

Aggression's Multiple Causes

Now that the meaning of the key terms in the diagram has been made clear, its central theme should be obvious. *Aggressive behavior is a product of cultural influences,*

---

[1]Some readers will no doubt detect the behavioristic tone of this definition. Although the language of behaviorism has almost disappeared from contemporary psychological discourse, we retain it here to honor those scholars who made pioneering contributions to the study of aggression. Besides, their definition still makes good sense.

[2]*Aggression,* as defined here, is also to be distinguished from *assertiveness,* with which (in popular U.S. English usage and perhaps in other languages as well) it is often confused. The difference between aggression and assertiveness is that assertiveness need not inflict harm, while aggression, by definition, always does. Thus, while one can readily approve of assertiveness, it is difficult ever to applaud aggression.

acting largely through culturally-mediated childhood experiences. Our framework also acknowledges the possibility that some genetically based dispositions, products of human biological evolution, interact with experience-based dispositions to produce aggression as one of several reactions to frustration or as a conflict-resolution strategy. But we do not label these genetic dispositions "instincts" and we use question marks in the diagram to indicate that we do not know the precise nature of these genetic factors.

That aggression is pervasive—possibly even universal—does not require that we consider it instinctive. Other biological factors, especially hormonal ones, must be taken into account. They, combined with various cultural forces, are common enough to contribute to aggression everywhere.

The Biological Bases of Aggression

All behavior has a biological basis; aggressive behavior is no exception. For aggression at the human level, there is much that is known about the implication of genes and hormones, like androgen or testosterone. Other biological factors may also play a role, like hypoglycemia, found by Bolton (1973, 1984) to be linked with homicide among the Qolla, an Amerindian society living in the Andes. Booth (1993) reported a relationship in the United States between testosterone and deviance in adulthood, and Constantino (1993) discussed testosterone and aggression in problem boys, also in the United States. In studies of male sexual behavior and aggression, of which Loosen (1994) is an example, hormones and gonadal function are implicated.

The only question to be asked about the role of biology in aggression is: *To what extent* does it explain aggression? The cross-cultural evidence, which is previewed by the conceptual framework in Figure 9.1, makes it clear that only by *combining biological factors with cultural ones* can the documented variations across cultures, across genders, and even across age groups in aggression be understood.

If some social scientists in the past gave short shrift to biological factors implicated in the story of human aggression, it may partly have been a reaction to the unjustified public acceptance in many societies of biological-deterministic accounts of human aggression, earlier by instinct theorists (e.g., Ardrey, 1966; Lorenz, 1963), and, later, by some sociobiologists (e.g., Wilson & Herrnstein, 1985), who conceived of criminal behavior as reflecting "criminality," a syndrome of traits reflecting genetic and biopsychological variables that predispose certain individuals to become "criminal.") And, there is Rushton (1995), whom we cited in Chapter 5 only to show that books are still published that link "race" to "traits." In this particularly glaring example of absurd, racist biologizing, Rushton explains "lawabidingness" as "racially determined" among such unreal categories as "Mongoloids," "Caucasoids," and "Negroids."[3]

---

[3]The pernicious social and political implication of biological–deterministic arguments like this suffices to make us wary, but to rebut such arguments convincingly, we need to disseminate the findings of cross-cultural research more widely than has thus far been the case.

These absurdities aside, biological factors, including (but not only) genetic ones, surely predispose individuals to react in certain ways to particular experiences they might have in their lifetimes.

Our Biologically-Based Ability to Learn

One relevant biological fact is that every individual, in every society, starts life with a limited set of behaviors. Infants cannot signal their needs and wants by complex verbalizations such as, "Mother, please, may I have my thirst quenched and my bottom cleaned?" Later, of course, they learn to utter such requests, in whatever language and according to whatever rules of polite discourse prevail in their linguistic community. In the beginning, however, all of us are limited to intense, diffuse, thrashings about, accompanied by loud crying and hard-to-interpret struggling. Such infantile behavior has been dubbed "proto-aggressive" (Segall, 1976, p. 201) because it resembles in certain respects what later emerges as *bona fide* aggressive behavior. This so-called proto-aggressive behavior is subject to partial reinforcement by often bewildered parents, who sometimes inadvertently wait until the behavior they are rewarding is very intense indeed. Thus, for all of us, our "infantile" efforts to get what we need or want acquire considerable strength as early-learned dispositions for response to frustrations. For some of us, such behavior remains highly probable even later in life; for most of us, it is replaced, thanks to parenting and other forms of socialization, by more acceptable modes of communication. Various social learning theories that stress the importance of socialization (e.g., Bandura, 1980; Berkowitz, 1989; Dollard et al., 1939; and Freud, in some but not all of his discussions of aggression) also help explain the pervasiveness of aggression by revealing how experience interacts with biology.

Hormones

Other biological factors, particularly hormonal ones, stand out when we confront sex differences in aggression. However, even sex differences in aggression cannot be attributed solely to biological factors in any simple, direct way. So we will move now to a consideration of other factors with which biological ones surely interact. We will do this in the context of a review of sex differences, better called, for reasons that will become apparent, "gender differences."

CROSS-CULTURAL STUDIES OF GENDER DIFFERENCES IN AGGRESSION

Some biologically oriented students of aggression have found it tempting to conclude from the empirically documented differences between males and females in aggressive behavior that the keys to understanding them are genetic and hormonal, pure and simple. What do we know, *cross-culturally,* about these differences, and how are they best to be interpreted?

On the average around the world, males quite consistently display more aggression than do females. Carol Ember (1981) noted, "the most consistent and most documented cross-cultural difference in interpersonal behavior appears to be that boys exhibit more aggression (than girls) after age 3 or so" (p. 551). This is true in the United States (Maccoby & Jacklin, 1974, 1980), and among children in the several societies studied in the Six Cultures study (Whiting & Edwards, 1973; Whiting & Whiting, 1975) during which observations were made in Kenya (Nyansongo), Mexico (Juxtlahuaca), Philippines (Tarong), India (Khalapur), Okinawa (Taira), and the United States (Orchard Town). Other observations, again showing the sex differences, were reported from Kenya (Luo) by Ember (1973), from an Israeli kibbutz by Spiro (1965), and among the !Kung in southwestern Africa by Blurton-Jones and Konner (1973). In fourteen societies for which ethnographic reports on aggression by young children (2 to 6 years old) were examined by Rohner (1976), either males clearly out-aggressed females or no difference was detectable. Natural observations conducted in a four-culture project (Munroe & Munroe, 1994a) among the Logoli (Kenya), Garifuna (Belize), Newars (India), and Samoans (American Samoa) found that countering aggression with aggression was significantly higher in 7- to 11-year-old boys than in comparable aged girls. They also found that boys in all four cultures show more overall aggression than do girls.

With regard to antisocial behavior, the findings are similar. Bacon, Child, and Barry (1963) showed that males commit the preponderance of "criminal acts" in forty-eight nonindustrialized societies. Similarly, in large industrialized societies, the United States, for example, the best predictor of fluctuations in published "crime rates" has long been the proportion of the population composed of adolescent males. In the mid-1990s, a decline in the 14- to 24-year-old male cohort in the United States was paralleled by a decline in violent crimes.

This correlation between sex and aggression exists across most societies, and is accompanied by a relation between age and aggression.

Gender Modified by Age

Schlegel and Barry (1991) report, in a study using the Standard Cross-Cultural Sample, "For boys but not for girls, adolescence tends to be the stage during which antisocial behavior most often occurs, if it occurs at all" (p. 39). Turning to large-scale contemporary societies, Goldstein (1983) singles out a particular age group, 18- to 24-year-olds, as the perpetrators of most crimes in the United States. In Japan, from 1966 through 1979, 14- to 24-year-olds outnumbered 25- to 39-year-olds by almost 4 to 1 in arrests (Goldstein & Ibaraki, 1983, p. 317). In other industrialized societies, Newman's (1979) profile of the most typical violent individuals shows they are 15- to 30-year-old males, with lower socioeconomic status, living in urban areas, and disproportionately likely to be members of an ethnic group that is low in the social hierarchy in the country. Naroll's (1983) "Juvenile Criminal Ratios" for forty-two industrialized societies showed that at least a quarter and as many as half of *all reported crimes* were committed by adolescent males (Naroll, 1983, p. 389).

Cross-culturally, homicide, a relatively rare aggression, is higher in the twenties than earlier ages. Its relationship to age is probably curvilinear, with declines later in life (Daly & Wilson, 1988, p. 169). For aggravated assault, a more common form in the United States, data cited by Lore and Schultz (1993) show a peak at age 21 with a gradual decline thereafter, falling to 50 percent of the 21-year-olds' rate by age 36. Daly and Wilson show that males are by far responsible for most of the lethal violence cross-culturally. Daly and Wilson (1988, pp. 147–148) present comparisons of the proportion of homicides in which the perpetrator and victim were the same sex for twenty-two different societies. The smallest ratio of male–male homicide to female–female was 11 to 1! The numbers underrepresent the proportion of homicides committed by men if we add male–female homicides, many of which seem to occur over issues of sexual jealousy or male resentment of females perceived to have spurned them.[4]

Thus we have cross-cultural evidence that males perform most aggressive acts and are most apt to do so as they move toward adulthood. What should we make of this?

Biological Explanations of Gender Differences

One kind of biological explanation of the gender–age difference in aggression is that the hormone androgen may be implicated in producing more aggression (cf. Benton, 1992). The second is that aggression in males may be functional and is part of a reproductive strategy favored by natural selection.

Androgen (testosterone)

Mazur (1985) linked testosterone to male adolescent dominance-seeking behavior: "As young primate males pass through adolescence, they often become more assertive with posturing and strutting that may be labeled "macho" in human terms.... These changes may be a consequence of the massive increase in testosterone production that occurs during puberty" (p. 383). Mazur (1985) concluded, however, that dominance and aggression are not inextricably linked. He suggested that we must distinguish dominance behavior from aggressive behavior, especially in humans, "who often assert their dominance without any intent to cause injury" (p. 382). Whether dominance-striving by male adolescents includes aggressive acts probably depends, in the end, on cultural norms. In this view, culture acts on an organism already primed for the sex difference.

Mazur also noted that "violent threat and attack is discouraged in most modern societies as a mode of allocating status, but it is still common among certain subgroups, such as adolescent males, where there are culturally specific norms that govern fights" (1985, p. 390).

---

[4]In mid-1998, as this chapter was being written, newspaper accounts in the United States reviewing "serial murders" (the killing of several people in succession over some period of time by the same perpetrator) reported that they "nearly always" involve male killers and female victims.

Reports presented at the 1995 annual meeting of the (American) Endocrine Society led a prominent science writer, Natalie Angier, to state, "As it turns out, testosterone may not be the dread 'hormone of aggression' that researchers and the popular imagination have long had it (1995, p. A1). She concluded: "Considered together, the new work underscores how primitive is scientists' understanding of the effects of hormones on human and even animal behavior" (p. C3).

Social Explanations for Sex Differences

Near the end of the preceding section on potential biological explanations for gender differences in aggression, we used the phrase "training for aggressiveness." This implies that social learning plays a role. What evidence is there for social learning as a cause of sex differences? Are males taught, or otherwise learn, to be more aggressive? Are females taught to inhibit and control their aggression more? Are both phenomena implicated in the story?

There are, in fact, many documented differences in the ways boys and girls are treated. Cross-culturally, where there *are* reported gender differences in socialization, boys receive more pressure than girls to be aggressive (Barry, Josephson, Lauer, & Marshall, 1976; C. R. Ember, 1981). However, these socialization pressure differences are far from universal; many societies in these studies show no obvious differences in *socialization* for aggression of boys and girls. Learning, however, may take place through much more subtle mechanisms, such as differential chore assignment, the encouragement of games, the rough or gentle handling of a child, or parental attention, among other differences. Children also learn from other children. Given gender-role differences, boys and girls will acquire different behavioral expectations. Indeed, by the age of four or five in the United States, girls and boys generally have very clear and different gender stereotypes and, as we saw in Chapter 8, there is similar evidence from other industrialized and developing nations (Best & Williams, 1997).

In a study conducted in Kenya, C. R. Ember (1973) found that boys assigned girls' work (e.g., baby-sitting, household chores) were significantly less aggressive than other boys, even when not doing chores. These boys, who did less "girls' work" than girls did, were intermediate in aggression between other boys and girls. Self-selection was not apparently at issue because the assignment of girls' work to boys was determined by the absence of an older sister in the home. The Six Cultures project (Whiting & Whiting, 1975) revealed that the presence of peers tends to evoke aggressive and sociable behavior, while being around adults seems to eliminate aggressive behavior. Schlegel and Barry (1991) report similar findings for adolescents (see below).

Given this evidence of the potential for differential social learning by boys and girls of aggressive behavior, we remain cautious about the degree to which social learning accounts for the gender differences in actual aggressive behavior. However, based on the few studies that were designed to test the effects of subtle socialization (such as the role of task assignment, toys, rough play with parents, time allowed with large groups of peers) on the development of aggressive behaviors, it is pretty obvious that males are somehow induced far more than females to behave aggressively in most societies in the world.

Differential Inculcation of Aggression: Some Evidence

One good source of evidence for the foregoing conclusion emerges from the efforts of Schlegel and Barry (1991), who examined many patterns of variables pertaining to adolescent males and females in a hologeistic study employing the Standard Cross-Cultural Sample of 186 societies (Murdock & White, 1969). In one part of their study, Schlegel and Barry examined anew the issue of differences across the sexes in inculcation of various traits. Using an 11-point scale, they found a less than one point difference across the sexes on inculcation of most traits, including obedience, sexual expression, sexual restraint, conformity, trust, responsibility, and achievement. In short, males and females were given essentially the same degree of encouragement in these domains. In the context of this general absence of sex difference, however, there were greater differences across the sexes in inculcation of aggressiveness, self-reliance, and competitiveness, "with boys receiving higher mean scores in all cases" (Schlegel & Barry, 1991, p. 41). Another part of their study dealt with family structure and antisocial behavior including violence. Some findings include "an association between violence and a lesser degree of early contact with both the mother and the father than usual for the sample" (p. 155) and, "extensive involvement with adults seems to dampen boys' aggressiveness" (p. 163).[5]

Recall, however, that Barry and associates (1976), who found a sex difference on the average over 150 societies—more inculcation of aggression for boys than for girls—found it to be significant in only one out of five of these societies. In the others it was either very small or nonexistent. So we cannot account for the cross-cultural consistency in greater male aggressive behavior *solely* on the basis of differences in inculcation of aggression. Other factors must be implicated in the phenomenon of greater aggressive behaviors among males than merely their hormones or the fact that generally they are subjected to more inculcation of aggression than are females. It is to these other factors that we now turn.

A Combined Biocultural Model

Earlier, we suggested that, whatever biological mechanisms are involved in gender differences in aggression, they probably interact with cultural mechanisms. Furthermore, we have just asserted that these cultural mechanisms must be more complex than inculcation alone. We now suggest that they include (1) division of labor by

---

[5]The latter finding involved a comparison between various family types. In families in which the ratio of adults to children is higher, there was found to be lower inculcation of aggression for boys.

sex, (2) gender identity, and (3) aggressive behavior that serves a gender-marking function.

Division of Labor by Sex

Every society has some division of labor by sex. Barry, Bacon, and Child (1957) suggested that the division of labor by sex sets the stage for differentiation between the sexes in socialization emphases and that this differentiation in turn functions as a means for preparing children to assume their sex-linked adult roles.

The clearest (and most nearly universal) of all sex-linked adult roles is childrearing itself. During socialization, females are taught traits that are compatible with childrearing and are later encouraged to assume that role. Males are taught other traits during childhood, like independence, and encouraged later to assume roles (e.g., food-getting) that are largely incompatible with childrearing. Consequently, females do most of the childrearing in most societies and virtually all of it in some.

Whatever the reasons for this, young males in most societies have a somewhat restricted opportunity to observe adult males at home because their fathers tend to be nonparticipants in childrearing. To the extent that gender-role learning involves modeling (or learning by observation), boys will have restricted opportunity to acquire a masculine identity early in life. Not surprisingly, father absence is most marked in societies with the sharpest division of labor by sex. Thus, precisely in those societies in which the two sexes are expected to have the most distinct gender identities, young males have restricted opportunity to acquire their masculine identity by emulation of male models.

Cross-Gender Identity

In societies with a particularly distinct division of labor by sex, there is, therefore, a likelihood that young males will acquire a cross-sex identity. How ironic this is, considering that in societies in which there is a relatively sharp gender-role distinctiveness, the role of women is often regarded with contempt by males, whose own activities are accorded higher prestige. Consider the pressure that adult males in such societies must face to avoid behaving "in womanly fashion." Yet their sons, we are here suggesting, are likely, initially during childhood, to acquire a predominantly female identity.

Gender-Marking Aggression

The Bacon, Child, and Barry (1963) study of crime (discussed previously), which showed that males commit the preponderance of crimes in most societies, also revealed that aggressive crimes, such as assaults, rapes, and murders, were more apt to occur in societies that provided exclusive mother–child sleeping arrangements, which prevail, of course, in societies in which fathers are not active participants in childrearing. Bacon and colleagues related this finding to the idea of "cross-sex identity" that had been introduced earlier (Whiting, Kluckhohn, Anthony, & Hartley, 1958) as a likely problem to be found in "low-male-salience" societies. Applying this idea to crime, Bacon and associates offered the hypothesis that aggressive crimes are part of a defense reaction against initial feminine identification in males.[6]

Extending the Bacon and colleagues' hypothesis, the anthropologist. B. Whiting (1965) suggested that males reared primarily by females would be more susceptible to envy of powerful adult males, but could not become like them until escaping somehow from the early influence of their mothers. In her field notes, Whiting found two societies, Khalapur in India and Nyasongo in Kenya, to be particularly interesting. In both of these societies, husbands and wives do not regularly eat, sleep, work, or relax together. Both societies are characterized by considerable father absence and higher male prestige. Both have a tradition of extolling warriors and cattle raiders, and, most importantly, both have high rates of physical assault and homicide. Whiting linked the young males' status envy to what she called "protest masculinity." What do societies that produce this identity conflict do about it?

Making Men out of Boys

The identity conflict designated by Whiting would obviously constitute a problem for societies that encourage sharply distinguished gender roles. In some such societies, the problem is dealt with in an institutionalized manner, for example, by male initiation ceremonies. Severe male initiation ceremonies at puberty, often including tests of endurance and manliness, were found by J. W. M. Whiting and associates (1958) to be correlated with exclusive mother–son sleeping arrangements and post-partum sex taboos, both indices of father absence. The interpretation of this finding that is pertinent to our present discussion is that such ceremonies serve the function of stamping in masculinity for boys who need it due to inadequate opportunity to acquire it in childhood.

What happens, however, in societies that have this identity conflict but lack the initiation ceremony? We suggest that, in societies that have the preconditions requiring a stamping-in of masculinity, but that do not achieve this via initiation ceremonies or other institutionalized practices, adolescent males will try on their own to assert their masculinity.

Compensatory Machoism

One way for males to assert their masculinity might well be to behave aggressively. If a society is one in which aggressiveness and such allied traits as fortitude and courage are an integral part of the definition of *manliness,* boys approaching manhood will wish to display these characteristics. They may have been taught and encouraged to behave this way but, as we have seen, in addition to whatever inculcation may have occurred during childhood, a sharply defined division of labor by sex can set the stage for the boys' need to acquire these behaviors and traits during

---

[6]Long ago, a similar hypothesis was hinted at by students of crime and delinquency in the United States (see, for example, Glueck & Glueck, 1950; Rohrer & Edmonson, 1960).

adolescence. This sharply defined division of labor by sex, with childrearing assigned primarily or even exclusively to mothers, results in relative father absence during the boys' childhood. That in turn leads to cross-sex identity during childhood that has to be undone by displays of the "manly" behaviors and traits, notably fortitude, courage, and aggression.

We call the resultant aggression *compensatory machoism* to underscore that it is rooted not in anger but in a felt need to escape from womanliness and to mark one's masculine gender.[7] In other words, such aggression has the function of displaying that the actor is behaving like an adult male, in accord with that society's definition of the masculine gender. This theory of "compensatory machoism" (Segall, 1988; Segall & Knaack, 1989) is only a theory. What support can be found for it?

Empirical Studies of Father Absence and Aggression ˎ

Studies conducted in the United States suggest that juvenile delinquents (usually boys) are more likely than nondelinquents to come from broken homes, with the father absent for much of the time the boy is growing up (Burton & Whiting, 1961; Munroe, Munroe, & Whiting, 1981). The conclusion often drawn is that father absence somehow increases the likelihood of delinquency and adult forms of physical violence. However, other conditions associated with broken homes in the United States (not father absence by itself) may be the real causes of delinquency. Therefore, as B. B. Whiting (1965) noted, it is necessary to investigate situations in which father absence does not occur in concert with other possible causal factors, in order to avoid confounding with those other factors. Clearly, cross-cultural research provides appropriate opportunities.

We stated above that in many societies with an appreciable incidence of polygyny, children often grow up in a "mother–child" household; the father eats and sleeps separately most of the time (in a nearby house, in a men's house, or in a distant town where he works for wages) and is hardly ever around the child. Does the "father absence" explanation of delinquency and violence fit such societies? The answer apparently is yes. We have also already seen that societies in which children are reared in mother–child households, where the father spends little or no time in child care, tend to have more physical violence by males (Bacon et al., 1963).

Earlier we suggested that the need for the stamping-in of masculinity is, in societies with initiation ceremonies, taken care of by the initiation institution and that, in societies without, adolescent males may be expected to assert their masculinity on their own. One might therefore expect more warfare or other forms of aggression

---

[7]This concept, compensatory machoism, is clearly derived from Whiting's notion of "protest masculinity." Both concepts are concerned with attempts to resolve cross-sex identity problems. Compensatory machoism further specifies that these attempts will include aggression by adolescent males, especially in societies lacking gender-marking rituals.

in societies that fit this pattern. However, C. R. Ember and M. Ember (1994b) identified ten conditions of socialization that theoretically would make expressions of masculinity more likely and only two of the ten (infrequent interaction of fathers and infants, and a long postpartum sex taboo) significantly, but weakly, predicted warfare frequency. With respect to homicide and assault, only one out of ten was significant (mother sleeps closer to baby than to father). These observations suggest that "protest masculinity" or "compensatory machoism" is a cause neither of war nor of homicide/assault.

Still, it may contribute to other forms of interpersonal aggression, particularly as displayed by insecure male adolescents. Schlegel and Barry (1991), in their hologeistic study of adolescence, found that boys' contact with men was inversely related to aggressiveness, but to a nonstatistically significant degree. However, there is a trend toward an association between high inculcation of aggression in adolescence and infrequent contact with the father in childhood.

Schlegel and Barry suggest that "this association supports the position that aggression can be a form of masculine protest, engaged in by boys as a way of asserting a masculinity about which they are in doubt. Their weakness of masculine identity results from an absent or uninvolved father in childhood" (1991, p. 164). While more research is clearly needed before the notion of "protest masculinity" or "compensatory machoism" can claim convincing empirical support, it seems to us to account well for much of what we know about aggressive behavior in young males.

Delinquency Revisited

In the preceding section, we developed a theory of adolescent male aggression that was partly inspired by the fact that father absence is a frequent characteristic of so-called juvenile delinquents. There are alternative theories. For example, Kaplan (1980) provides a theory of such deviant behavior, developed primarily in the light of circumstances in the United States. The theory implies that low self-esteem, rooted in such experiences as parental and peer rejection, perceived lack of competence and school failure, predisposes young people to engage in delinquent behavior. Such behavior conceivably involves actions that serve a self-enhancing function, despite being deviant from normative patterns. Leung and Drasgow (1986) examined relationships between self-esteem and self-reported delinquent behavior in three groups totaling over 12,000 male youths, aged 14 to 21 years (designated in the study as Whites, Blacks, and Hispanics) in a U.S. national survey and found: (1) significantly lower self-esteem among the Hispanics (with no difference between the other two groups), (2) significantly higher frequency of self-reported delinquent behavior among Whites (again with no difference between the other two groups), and (3) the kind of relationship predicted by Kaplan (1980), a negative relationship between self-esteem and self-reported delinquency *only* for Whites. The authors suggest the intriguing possibility that in the United States, in Black and Hispanic cultures, for whatever reasons, people may not consider various acts that are defined as delinquent by Whites as counter-normative or worthy of disapproval and indignation.

Camilleri and Malewska-Peyre (1997) provide a thought-provoking discussion of the disproportionately high numbers of Arab immigrants in French prisons, which might be explainable as a reflection of discrimination within the criminal justice system in France (and in French society generally), or, simply, attributable to higher rates of criminal (including aggressive and violent) behavior in the immigrant population. Camilleri and Malewska-Peyre have concluded that both explanations hold, but that they are linked, with discrimination causing "negative identity" (or low self-esteem) in the immigrant group, which in turn induces criminal behavior. This line of argument is consistent with the analyses by Leung and Drasgow (1986) and Kaplan (1980) of delinquent behavior in groups discriminated against in the United States.

Other Cultural Contributions to Aggression

Effects of the Mass Media

Wherever in the world the mass media, especially television and cinema, now extend—and that's practically everywhere, and still spreading—audiences of viewers, including children, are exposed frequently to fictionalized violence. For several decades, a debate has raged over its impact, with media producers in the main arguing that there is either no effect, a insignificantly small effect, or even a cathartic effect on viewers, while social scientists repeatedly have documented negative effects (incitement to aggress among some, especially younger viewers, following a viewing experience). The social science research in the United States has been done experimentally in laboratories, and correlationally in field studies, some of them very large-scale and long-term. Based on the results of those studies, the question seems not to be "*If* media violence spawns aggression" but "*How?*" Geen (1983) offered four hypotheses for the relationship between mass media violence and aggressive behavior: (1) elicitation of aggressive impulses, (2) modeling, (3) desensitization, and (4) changes in attitudes and beliefs about aggression. Heusmann (1983) came to similar conclusions, updating a classic study authorized a decade earlier by the United States Surgeon General's Office. We turn now to that study and others that followed.

Eron, along with Heusmann and other colleagues, were responsible for two longitudinal studies of the long-term effects among U.S. children of their early childhood television viewing. Both showed long-term effects, with early viewing correlated positively with later aggressing.[8] Following the second U.S. study, replications occurred in Finland, Poland, Australia, the Netherlands, and Israel. These

---

[8]Eron and associates (1987) and others who have done longitudinal research in the United States also show that children who behave in antisocial ways tend to become adults with many problems, including alcoholism, criminality, and a history of violent acts. This is quite apart from, but in addition to, the effects of television viewing.

were summarized in Eron and Heusmann (1984), where it is made clear that the oft-replicated U.S. finding (that violence in the media contributes to aggression in the real world) is a phenomenon common to several nations.

However, the effects are not independent of viewer characteristics. Heusmann, Lagerspetz, and Eron (1984) found both in Finland and the United States that boys are more affected by television viewing than girls, but the girls who happened to be among the very aggressive children were those who preferred boys' activities.

Another of the Heusmann and colleagues' (1984) findings was that viewing violence and aggressivity had bidirectional effects: each could lead to the other. More aggressive children are drawn to more violent shows, which could contribute to a maintenance or enhancement of their aggressive behaviors. It thus appears that, around the world, fictional and real violence are interrelated.

Societal Reactions to Aggressive Behavior

There are, as one might expect, individual differences in attitudes about aggression, both across and within cultures. The same aggressive acts may be approved by some people and strongly condemned by others. Whole groups, too, (such as ethnic groups or socioeconomic groups) may vary in their judgments of aggressive acts. For example, when aggression is commited as a political act, one group's "freedom fighters" may be seen by another group as "terrorists." Some groups have no moral objection to police actions that the target groups consider examples of "police brutality" (Kahn, 1972).

Recent cross-cultural research concerns attitudes toward and reactions to acts of aggression. A number of studies focus on punishment, which may well be the most popularly supported type of attempted aggression control, despite its being consistently deplored by child development scholars (e.g., Kurz, 1991; McCord, 1991; Weiss, 1992). Some of these cross-cultural studies in recent years have dealt with childrearing practices, especially discipline. Some cross-national studies found differences (e.g., Conroy, Hess, Azuma, & Kashiwagi, 1980), comparing Japanese and U.S. maternal strategies), but because so many variables are confounded with parental discipline in a two-nation comparison, not much can be concluded from such studies. According to Schlegel and Barry (1991), "Generally lower permissiveness toward infants and children is associated with adolescent misbehavior, particularly physical aggression" (p. 154), and "Severe punishment also characterizes the societies in which violence is expected of at least some adolescent boys" (p. 155). They also commented: "Unsurprisingly, antisocial behavior occurs among adolescents when it occurs among adults.... Adolescent violence, a physically impulsive form (of antisocial behavior) is likely to be found along with adult sexual license, also physically impulsive" (p. 154).

One interesting cross-national study, albeit with only two nations involved, was reported by Pinto, Folkers, and Sines (1991), who administered culturally appropriate, comparable questionnaires dealing with children's behaviors and various responses elicited by them to 681 mothers of school-aged children in a Middle Western part of the United States and to 419 mothers in the cities of Bangalore and Mangalore in India. In these rather contrasting settings, some striking similarities in patterns of findings occurred: In both settings, there was a significant sex difference in reported aggression while measures of parental rejection (reminiscent of the work of Rohner, 1975) and rejection by peers outside the home were both positively correlated with aggression for children of both sexes. Parental affection was negatively correlated with children's aggression, again both in the United States and India, and for both sexes.

Numerous within-country studies of diverse ethnic groups have also been reported. Lambert (1987) studied Canadian parents of Italian, Greek, Japanese, Portuguese, and Anglo origins, and found no large differences in parental disciplinary techniques. Spiro and Swartz (1994) interviewed sixty mothers of preschool children in various clinic settings in Cape Town, of "African," "Malay," and "White" ethnicity, about various "behavior problems." There was no difference in general frequencies of problems across the three groups, but there was a significant difference in tendency for Malay mothers to be very concerned with temper tantrums, which the authors explained as possibly "due to the premium on discipline, in keeping with Muslim tradition, that is characteristic of Malay homes..." (p. 348). Also worth noting is the authors' observation that, while many African and White mothers ignored "conduct disorders," "Malay mothers physically punished the child" (p. 349).

Of course, in such studies as those reviewed earlier, the precise "cultural" factors responsible for a given level of aggressive behavior by parents or by their children can seldom be specified. Indeed, in many such studies, economic disadvantage (rather than "cultural value" factors) may be in play. There are numerous examples of studies relating aggression to disadvantaged circumstances in the United States. Bernard (1990) discusses subcultural differences in criminal behavior in these terms; Keenan (1994) focuses on the low-income status of aggressive toddlers; and Skinner (1992) links economic hardship to adolescent aggression. Young (1991), among other students of Native Americans, finds poverty related to aggression within this group. So, we must be vigilant about studies in which apparent ethnic group differences may be confounded with socioeconomic group differences. In all such studies, either ethnicity or social class may contain, as "packaged variables," factors that contribute to aggression.

Related to parental reactions to children's aggression and other "bad behavior" is the prevailing set of attitudes toward aggressive acts committed by adults. One relevant variable may be whether the aggression appears to be validly provoked (with the "validity" a function of a cultural value system). After reviewing numerous U.S. laboratory experiments in which various kinds of aversive events increased aggressiveness, Carlson and Miller (1988) concluded that social provocation increased aggressive responding (of a retaliatory nature) to a very high degree. In Western cultures, then, according to Carlson and Miller, the "dominant response" to an insult or a criticism is "to counteraggress" (p. 157).

Some research done in Europe shows that, in some settings at least, different kinds of aggression are differently assessed. In Finland, Lagerspetz and Westman (1980) found that eighty-three adult subjects were more likely to approve of aggressive acts motivated by altruism than by self-interest, and suggested that in European culture the presence or absence of provocation shapes a people's attitude toward aggression. With it, approval is likely; without, there is disapproval.

In Poland and Finland, Fraczek (1985) inventoried approval/disapproval of various kinds of aggressive acts among sixty-four extramural university students of both genders, about 30 years old, and found for both samples that violent aggressive behaviors to benefit others or for self-defense were the most approved kinds. Generally, however, the Polish sample gave higher approval to more violent forms of aggression than did the Finnish sample. The author attributed these attitudes to various "socialization experiences." Fraczek cited legal codes suggesting that Polish society is highly punitive and approves of severe punishment. Notable is the fact that Poland uses capital punishment, which Finland long ago abandoned. (Paradoxically, however, Finland was cited by Lore and Schultz [1993] as having the highest murder rate in Europe. This is difficult to reconcile with Fraczek's argument.)

The studies reviewed in this section support the view that there are cultural differences in aggressive behaviors of both children and adults and in various circumstances surrounding them.

Capital Punishment

The prevalent myth about aggression—that punishment is an effective control—takes the form in some parts of the world of a belief that capital punishment deters the crimes to which it is applied as a threat (Young, 1992). Where this belief prevails, (for example, in the United States, one of the very few industrialized nations in the world that still allows executions) all available evidence, consisting primarily of a positive correlation between murder rates and numbers of executions, rather than the negative correlation that a deterrence theory requires, points in the very opposite direction.

Ellsworth and Gross (1994) note that U.S. support for the death penalty has steadily increased from 1966, to reach record highs in the mid 1990s. Worse, they add, "Factual information (e.g., about deterrence and discrimination) is generally irrelevant to people's attitudes, and they are aware that this is so" (p. 19).

Lore and Schultz (1993) studied many forms of aggression, including homicide, assault, forcible rapes, warfare, wife-beating, childhood violence, and others. They argued that these tend to vary together across societies. They reason that this is so because of varying cultural "convictions about the potential effectiveness and desirability of controlling aggression" (p. 16). Applying this idea to the United States, they state that most people hold "antiquated views about the nature of human violence" and are convinced that aggression cannot be controlled. This conviction is attributed to a prior belief in the "naturalness" of aggressive "drives" and "instincts," concepts fostered, they say, by influential works by Lorenz (1963) and "the pervasive influence in the United States of Freudian psychology" (p. 17).

We are in accord with the Lore and Schultz argument. We suggest that theories dominated by such concepts as instinct and drive enjoy continuing popularity only because of the justification they offer both to perpetrators of aggression; ("I couldn't help myself") and for an ideology that precludes social programs that promise prevention, in favor of punitive policies (p. 267).

The supposed effect of capital punishment may be relevant in this context. In the United States (but not in most of Europe) it is commonly believed that would-be murderers are deterred by the prospect of capital punishment. Yet cross-national research suggests otherwise. Instead of increasing after capital punishment is abolished, murder rates generally go down (Archer & Gartner, 1984, pp. 118–139). Why? Perhaps capital punishment, which of course is homicide committed on behalf of society, legitimizes violence.

CONCLUSION

In this chapter, we presented a framework for studying human aggression cross-culturally. The several studies we described that we believe fit into this framework make it clear that we cannot understand human aggression without viewing it from a cross-cultural perspective. While biology is surely implicated, it is dangerously incorrect to conclude that aggression is simply instinctive. Our biology interacts with our culturally shaped experiences to lead us to react to frustration, to assert dominance, and to attempt to resolve conflicts in a wide variety of ways.

We saw in this chapter that societies vary in their characteristic levels of aggression. We saw, too, that individuals vary in their aggressive habits. A pan-species generalization concerning individual variation is that male adolescents tend to be the kinds of individuals who aggress the most. Because the evidence reviewed in this chapter does not support the view that it is inevitable that male adolescents will aggress, there is hope that the pervasive amount of aggression that presently characterizes the world may be reduced, but only if we become more knowledgeable about the experiential factors, rooted in culture, that presently encourage so many people to aggress.

10

INTERCULTURAL RELATIONS IN A SHRINKING WORLD

FROM PAROCHIALISM TOWARD GLOBAL CONSCIOUSNESS?

Views of Earth from outer space underscore that all of us who inhabit this globe share a single fate. Resource depletion, environmental degradation, and discrepancies in economic well-being can be confronted effectively only if viewed as worldwide challenges. Yet a "consciousness of kind" tenaciously persists, fueling a loyalty to ethnic or national segments. Even though the most pressing problems confronting humankind may be global in scope, most people identify primarily with relatively small groups.

For many, perhaps, this seems the only way they can imagine themselves to have the power to react against stronger, but vaguely defined, forces that constrain them from realizing a quality of life to which they aspire. So, for many, the world remains divided into Us and Them.

Why most people relate most positively to their own cultural groups has been implicit in all the previous chapters. As we have already seen, our views of the world, our values, and our lifestyles are largely conditioned by our particular cultures. Much cultural content is internalized by each of us; we are, in a sense, our own cultures. That we identify with our particular cultural groups, as reflected in our nationalities, religions, or so-called "races," is therefore not surprising and, as we shall see in this chapter, this tendency is, in many respects, quite functional.

For all their functionality, however, parochial tendencies, we shall argue, will have to be reduced in favor of a more global approach to enhancing the survivability of our species, to bring about an improvement in the quality of life for all people, wherever in the world they might live. The global approach that we advocate in this chapter is not to be identified with, we take pains to clarify, the late twentieth-century version of a "global economy," which has been an attempt to allow untrammeled "market forces" to shape the human future. This is easily characterized as a form of neocapitalist expansion, aided and abetted by a Western cultural set of institutions (like the World Bank and the International Monetary Fund)—a movement that so far has exacerbated, rather than reduced, the gap between rich and poor everywhere. Rather, we envision a global understanding, in the most profound sense, of the common humanity of all people. Such understanding entails a respect for the potential innovativeness that can be derived from attention to solutions inherent in cultural diversity, and a commitment to pursuing a balanced set of policies that honor valuable cultural differences while attacking invidious differences in status and well-being. Underlying our discussion of intergroup relations is the belief that to encourage the blossoming of a global identity is *not* to disparage cultural differences, or even people's various senses of cultural identity. However, it *is* to discourage harmful, often deadly, competitive conflict between them.

To start this discussion, however, we will first examine psychological ties that bind individuals to the smaller groups to which they belong and from which they derive much of their sense of self. The first of these is the probably universal tendency to identify oneself partly in terms of one's group memberships. Gudykunst and Bond (1997) summarized some relevant theory pertaining to social identity. The following discussion is based in part on their treatment of the subject.

Social Identity

Everyone has an identity; this is self-evident. But, we are less apt usually to be aware that each of us has several identities in addition to our unique sense of self, and that these derive from different kinds of social categories to which we belong, including familial, occupational, national, religious, and ethnic groups, among others. Many of these are nested: one can be, simultaneously, Parisian, French, and European, while some are cross-cutting, like female, heterosexual, and Jewish.

In addition, others may deal with our multiple identities differently from the way we deal with them ourselves. Bourhis and Leyens (1994) attribute the following comment to Albert Einstein.

> *If the theory of relativity is found to be correct, the Germans may claim that I am German, the Swiss that I am a Swiss citizen, and the French that I am a great man of science. But, if the theory is found to be false, the French are likely to say that I am Swiss, the Swiss that I am German, and the Germans...that I am a Jew. (p. 1; our translation from French to English).*

However multidimensional their social identities, whenever individuals engage in intergroup behavior, their behavior is usually driven by some one or other of their social identities and the way these are evaluated in a particular intergroup context.

The European social psychologist, Henri Tajfel, in a number of empirical and theoretical works produced with various colleagues (e.g., Tajfel, 1978; Tajfel, Jaspers, & Fraser, 1984; Tajfel and Turner, 1979) developed a social identity theory (SIT). The central concept of this theory is that a part of everyone's self-concept "derives from his knowledge of his membership of a social group (or groups) together with the value and emotional significance attached to that membership" (Tajfel, 1978, p. 63). To the extent that a person recognizes his or her membership(s), social identity comes into play in a variety of ways. One very important one, according to this theory, is that people take personal satisfaction from belonging to groups that are distinct and have positive features. In a sense, this is an outside-in kind of *social* psychological theory, with group-level phenomena shaping individual-level cognition, attitudes, and feelings.

A fundamental cognitive process involved in the phenomena of social identity is categorization of the world, a process that applies not only to the physical world, but to the social world as well. According to social identity theory, people are classified into groups in order to create a sense of orderliness and a locus for self within that orderly structure. Of course, for most of us, that structure has a history that precedes our arrival in the world. We are born into it and gradually learn "who we are" in its terms.[1]

If one's group is perceived to be well off in at least certain respects and highly regarded and properly treated by members of other groups, then one feels good about belonging to it and is strongly inclined to defend it. Of course, many people belong to groups that are disadvantaged in ways obvious to their own members (and, often, but not always, to others as well). While discounting or denying membership in such groups might be coping mechanisms for some individuals under such circumstances, there are also many ways of enhancing the value of belonging to a disadvantaged group, as, for example, by attempting to improve the group's relative status. So, belonging to a disadvantaged group can be a valued part of one's identity, provided there is a perception of some movement toward an improvement in the lot of the group.

Just how well off one's group is requires, said Tajfel, a social comparison process that can either confirm a positive social identity or one that requires change. If the latter, the theory suggests, there will be motivation to create social changes that make the comparison more favorable.

Taylor and Moghaddam (1987, p. 78) neatly summarized social identity theory by noting that it addresses such questions as why individuals desire to be members of distinct groups that have high status, and how they will endeavor to change unsatisfactory situations via various strategies designed to improve their group's status.

---

[1]By early childhood, most of us have pretty much learned it. While some people during adolescence or young adulthood move away from these socially imposed classification-based identities, many people never unlearn the classification scheme or the identity derived from it.

For our present purposes, we cite this theory here to underscore one of the fundamental reasons for individuals to identify themselves parochially: to enhance one's own feeling of distinctiveness and value.

Social identity theory (SIT) deals with people's motivations to maintain or change their group memberships and their relations with other groups. Motives like these could lead to making one or another of these social identities particularly salient at some particular moment, in some particular setting. A basic premise of SIT is that in order to have a positive self-concept, individuals *want* to belong to groups that have high status. According to Tajfel (1978), individuals compare their own groups to others' groups on dimensions that they value. Then, they develop positive social identities if they perceive their groups as higher on the valued dimensions but negative social identities if and when they perceive their groups as lower. Negative social identities are unpleasant, so individuals may be motivated, according to SIT, to change the intergroup situation in an effort to develop positive identities, including identifying with high status groups, working to bring about social change through vigorous but peaceful means, or by encouraging revolution!

According to this view, individuals, particularly when interacting with others, select from among their available identities. Thus, they might categorize themselves and others in terms of gender rather than nationality, particularly if the first is shared and the second is not. When they categorize themselves, they tend to assign positive traits to the in-group. This "in-group bias" tends to involve negative interpersonal attraction toward out-group members (Turner, Shaver, & Hogg, 1983). We are about to see that ethnocentrism theory makes a similar prediction.

Although it originated in a European setting, SIT might, nevertheless, generalize to other cultures. In India, Majeed and Ghosh (1982) found differential evaluations of self, in-group, and out-groups in High Caste, Muslims, and Scheduled Caste members; Ghosh and Huq (1985) obtained similar findings for Hindu and Muslim groups in India and Bangladesh. SIT is consistent with the the data from Eastern Africa reported by Brewer and Campbell (1976) and data from New Zealand reported by Wetherell (1982).

In the Wetherell study, both Europeans and Polynesians in New Zealand showed the in-group bias, but the Polynesians moderated their discrimination toward the out-group more than Europeans. This finding suggests that the Polynesians, who, like other putatively collectivistic cultures, are supposed to use different norms for in-group and out-group members, use the equity norm with out-group members more than do people in putatively individualistic cultures, at least when there are not hostile relations between groups.

At first glance inconsistent with SIT, but in fact compatible with it, are findings from Hong Kong. Bond and Hewstone (1988) found that British high school students in Hong Kong attached more importance to social identity and intergroup differentiation than did Chinese high school students, probably because social differentiation in Hong Kong is relatively muted as a reflection of Chinese tendencies to avoid conflict, a point argued by Gudykunst and Bond (1997, p. 127).

A second approach to understanding why individuals (in most if not all societies) cling to an identity that results in an "us/them" view of the world is ethnocentrism theory.

Ethnocentrism

A core concept that helps us to understand the tenacity of group identity, with consequent in-group and out-group attitudes, is ethnocentrism, first employed in an analysis of individuals' links with their own and neighboring groups by William Graham Sumner (1906) in his classic sociological treatise, *Folkways*. The concept embraces both positive feelings toward one's own group (the in-group), (or the we-group, in Sumner's terminology) and negative feelings toward others (out-groups). Indeed, in Sumner's insightful theorizing, each feeds on the other.

> *The relation of comradeship and peace in the we-group and that of hostility and war toward others-groups are correlative to each other. The exigencies of war with outsiders are what make peace inside, lest internal discord should weaken the we-group for war. These exigencies also make government and law in the in-group, in order to prevent quarrels and enforce discipline.... Ethnocentrism is the technical name for this view of things in which one's own group is the center of everything, and all others are scaled and rated with reference to it.... Each group nourishes its own pride and vanity, boasts itself superior, exalts its own divinities, and looks with contempt on outsiders. Each group thinks its own folkways [the contemporary equivalent is customs] the only right ones, and if it observes that other groups have other folkways, these excite its scorn (pp. 12–13).*

Sumner postulated a universal syndrome of behavioral dispositions in which positive links with the in-group are reinforced by negative attitudes and behaviors toward out-groups. Later we will consider the degree to which our social identities do indeed imply negative attitudes and behaviors toward groups other than our own, as suggested by ethnocentrism theory.

Next, however, we consider "primordial" groups and nationalism, two ideas that are examples of the ways group identities can be made to assume very significant meanings and importance.

"Primordial" Groups

In Chapter 1, we discussed the tenacity of beliefs in "races," allegedly distinct, separate categories of human beings, differentially endowed, and far less closely related to each other than they are in reality. Similar to this fallacious view of humankind is another, built around a notion of "primordial groups," whereby almost any identifiable ethnic group can believe itself to have ancient roots. It might have a mythic origin, expressed in folktales, both oral and written, that speak of a destiny wedded to a particular geography, with a God-given right to that part of the earth. Such "primordial" groups often speak of a centuries-old history of competitive, if not warlike, relations with certain neighboring groups, with whom generations-old scores remain still to be settled. However, human history has had so many twists and turns, in fact, that it is highly unlikely that any contemporary groups are truly "primordial." Still, many behave as if they were. Reasons for so doing often have much to do with contemporary politics. For example, political leaders may find it convenient to evoke or fan beliefs in the primordial nature of their citizenry, which provides them with justification for lashing out against their "ancient enemies." This phenomenon, some observers have noted, is present in the conflicts in the Balkans, in Northern Ireland, in Israel/Palestine, and in Rwanda, to cite only four examples from the 1990s.

Psychological Concomitants of Nationalism

The nation–state is a relatively new form of political organization, with a history spanning only a few centuries in some parts of the world and only a few decades in many others. Yet, psychologically speaking, national identity is very salient for many people, and for some it is paramount. People even go to war to defend a nation, and think of it as if it were rooted in some ancient past, a special type of "primordial group."

Today, most people in the world tend to think of their nationalities as one of the fundamental aspects of their identity. Nationalism is an ideology that provides justification for the existence of a nation–state, a definition of its particular population, and a prescription of the relationship of its included individuals to that state (Kelman, 1976).

During much of the twentieth century, and at an accelerating pace following the end of World War II, many new nations were created out of former colonial possessions of major European and Asian powers. This led to a process known as "nation-building," which is described in Box 10.1. As suggested there, even citizens of relatively new nations can be nationalistic. Moreover, despite some differences in overcoming "tribal" identities, they can become even more nationalistic than citizens of older nations, for whom national pride often loses its importance as the nation's status in the world is otherwise established.

IMPLICATIONS OF VARIOUS KINDS OF ETHNOCENTRISM

From primordialism, nationalism, and other such "isms" does it necessarily follow that we must relate negatively to groups other than our own? Must we live in a world characterized by "in-groups" and "out-groups"? Inherent in Sumner's "ethnocentrism" is a discouraging answer to this question. Research into individuals' relations

BOX 10.1 Nation-Building

Within some recently created, ethnically diverse nation–states, a set of ethnic groups is considered a nation only because it constitutes the citizenry of the state, not because the population is an interrelated group of people aware of their interrelationship. In such nation–states, a psychological process of nation-building must go on. Two pioneer cross-cultural psychologists studied this process many years ago.

As Doob (1962) pointed out, Africa contains approximately 700 traditional societies integrated into approximately 50 nations. For citizens to function effectively in such nations requires the acquisition of behaviors different from those that led to adaptive functioning as members of small traditional societies in which they were linked by kinship, language, and common lifestyles. Moreover, "the mere existence of common cultural elements among members of a collectivity is not enough to define them as a nation. They must also have the consciousness that these common elements represent special bonds that tie them to one another" (Kelman, 1976, pp. 9–10).

In any recently established nation, which is typically less real psychologically than the smaller ethnic groups it comprises, "it is most difficult to create a sense of loyalty to the nation and an iden-

tification with it" (Doob, 1962, p. 152). Such feelings exist within each "tribe" or "ethnie," where coethnics easily identify with each other. Nation-building, as a sociopolitical process, merely begins with the declaration of national independence. It also requires a psychological process that must take place in the minds of many individuals. Less obvious perhaps than the political and economic aspects of nation-building, its psychological components are nevertheless fundamental. A nation is not merely a geopolitical fact; it is also a state of mind. Yet, once a nation exists, a sense of national identity can very quickly become very salient for individual citizens, a sense that might well include feelings of rivalry with neighboring nations.

More recently, the attention of some political scientists has shifted from nation-building to the problem of the creation of supranational identities, as in the European Union. Perhaps the psychological problems inherent in this process of union-building are similar to those described years ago by Doob and Kelman for nascent nations. On the other hand, we must now be at least equally concerned with the tenacity of certain "nationalisms" as we once were with the difficulties of nation-building.

with in-groups and out-groups, informed by ethnocentrism theory, can illuminate the magnitude of the problem and may even facilitate the difficult process of enhancing global consciousness.

Research Inspired by Ethnocentrism Theory

The classic study of ethnocentrism was done by Brewer and Campbell (1976) in Eastern Africa where scores of traditional societies were brought together into three nation–states, which, prior to their attainment of national independence in the mid-twentieth century, had been colonial constructions. As such, they had rather arbitrary boundaries, created, as it happened, by negotiations among the colonial powers. (Consequently, some of the ethnic groups involved found themselves straddling boundaries. For example, the Masai were split into two groups, one dwelling in Kenya, the other in Tanzania.)

The Brewer and Campbell study was designed to test hypotheses concerning the characteristics of out-groups that are most likely to be targets of hostility and the role of proximity and cultural similarity in shaping attitudes toward out-groups. There were also hypotheses about the content of stereotypes that are likely to develop for particular in-group/out-group pairs, and the significance of contact between groups as a determinant of mutual perceptions and attitudes. These were derived from Sumner's (1906) theory of ethnocentrism.[2]

Data were collected in 1965 among thirty East African societies, ten each in Uganda, Kenya, and Tanzania, with fifty individuals questioned in each society by a native speaker. Respondents were queried about their own group and thirteen others, nine living within their country and four from neighboring countries.

The interview contained (1) questions relating to social distance (Bogardus, 1925), for example, "Would you willingly agree to become related to a —— by marriage?"[3] (2) questions on familiarity, for example, "Do you know any ——? Do you speak their language?" (3) open-ended questions eliciting "good" and "bad" traits about thirteen out-groups; (4) a structured list of traits to be assigned to the one group that the respondent thought each trait fit best; and (5) direct questions seeking the most liked, the most disliked, and the most and least similar out-group.

Although the study was completed a quarter-century before this chapter was written, the findings provide the best available information on the dynamics of intergroup attraction and perception yet assembled. They permit us to consider the fundamental features of intergroup relations, as they exist in one part of the world, and perhaps elsewhere. Of course, whether the processes uncovered in this Eastern Afri-

---

[2]Other theories of intergroup relations provide more hypotheses. In a systematic compilation, LeVine and Campbell (1972) listed 331 testable propositions, including 253 correlational hypotheses derived from Sumner. Many refer to attitudes and behaviors that, in a strict reading of Sumner, would be thought to be universally present and interrelated.

[3]Their four-item scale of social distance was of interest in its own right. In most of the thirty societies the items "scaled" in the following order: (1) willingness to share a meal with; (2) willingness to work with; (3) willingness to have as a neighbor; and (4) willingness to become related by marriage. In these East African societies the least degree of intimacy, subjectively speaking, is offered by sharing a meal and the most by permitting intermarriage. That the items scaled means that an individual who named an out-group in response to the intermarriage social distance item probably named that group in response to the three other items. If a group was named in response to only three items, it was probably to the items other than the intermarriage one. Most individuals followed this orderly pattern of responding to the four-item set, so that the scale proved to be highly reliable and valid. Furthermore, this measure of social distance correlated highly with both liking and familiarity, adding further credence to the social distance measure as an index of intergroup affect.

can study will be found anywhere else in the world remains an open question until studies like the Brewer and Campbell one are done elsewhere.

Affect between Groups ⌐

Brewer and Campbell found, over all thirty societies, that measures of liking for particular groups, of social distance assigned to them, and of familiarity toward them were highly interrelated. Liking correlated .63 with social distance and .54 with familiarity and social distance correlated .77 with familiarity. This pattern of intercorrelations justifies a single underlying dimension of intergroup affect, described by the authors as "desirability of close interpersonal relations."

Brewer and Campbell asked what characteristics of out-groups seemed to determine scores on this index of intergroup attraction. The scores covaried mostly with opportunity for contact with out-group members. High scores (that is, low social distance and high liking and familiarity were most likely to be assigned to groups that were similar in culture and language to the in-group and that enjoyed geographic proximity to it. Most individuals in any group felt closest to those groups that were nearer, better known, and culturally most like their own group.

Highest positive affect was attached to groups with whom traditionally there had been much contact. Even when overt conflict had recently occurred between two "familiar" groups, the psychological distance was relatively small and the mutual attraction high.

Another variable was the perceived (and actual) level of modernity of particular out-groups. Groups perceived as "backward" were generally assigned high social distance and were otherwise treated as unattractive. High-status groups, such as the economically favored Chagga of Tanzania, Baganda of Uganda, and Kikuyu of Kenya, toward all of whom respect was high, were found to earn particularly high or low attractiveness scores depending on their cultural similarity to a particular in-group. Brewer and Campbell suggested that high-status groups may serve either as "models of a desired status" or as "visible targets for resentment" (or both). "Modern" groups will be emulated and found attractive if they are culturally similar but resented and rejected if not, underscoring once more the overriding importance of similarity.

Within each in-group, while there were individual differences relating to education and urbanization, the norms of attractiveness toward out-groups were found to be widely shared. This suggests that attitudes toward out-groups are acquired through socialization and enculturation early in life and are relatively immune to subsequent individual experience.

The Reciprocity of Intergroup Affect ⌐

It was generally found that, if group X liked group Y, group Y liked group X. Intergroup attraction, and lack thereof, were usually reciprocated. This follows from what we have already learned. Because attraction appears to be determined primarily by cultural similarity, similar groups will be attracted to each other and dissimilar ones will find each other relatively unattractive. The empirical finding of reciprocity also suggests that a group that feels negative toward another group is not necessarily being perverse or hostile in a willy-nilly fashion. It is likely to be the target of similar feelings directed toward it from that other group. It is further likely to find "justification" for its own negative feelings toward that group in its "mistreatment of us." The mutuality of negative intergroup affect thus makes the negative affect virtually self-reinforcing and, hence, rather tenacious. This pattern shows up widely, including in multiethnic societies like Canada (see, for example, Berry & Kalin [1979] and Kalin & Berry [1995]). There, additional evidence may be found that if group *a* manifests dislike for group *b*, group *b* can justify its dislike of group *a* on that very basis. And, of course, vice versa.

The Brewer and Campbell findings reveal a process in which cultural similarity (both perceived and actual) generates in any given pair of groups shared, reciprocated feelings—positive for similar groups, negative for dissimilar ones. Considerable research concerning groups whose language and ethnicity differ in status, reported by Giles and colleagues (e.g., Giles, 1977; Giles & Johnson, 1987; Giles & Robinson, 1990) and by Clément and colleagues (e.g., Clément, 1984; Clément & Noels, 1994) suggests that, for groups unequal in power, feelings toward each other will *not* be very positive. Such groups, of course, are not similar to each other, so, once again, the variable of perceived similarity seems to account for the quality of feelings between groups.

An intriguing implication of this process may be that to reduce intergroup negative affect would require movement toward a mutual perception of increasing similarity. A perception of this sort could be brought about either by changes in the behavior of both groups—each toward the model provided by the other—or by a reduction in the power gap between them.[4] As long as either perceives the other as different, it will not like the other, the other will reciprocate the dislike, and the affect will remain negative. Thus, cultural contact and modernization might improve intergroup relations. These processes tend to produce cultural homogenization. We shall return to this speculative point later in this chapter.

Intergroup Perceptions

Although one might expect liked groups to be perceived as possessing mostly positive traits and disliked groups negative ones, the facts are apparently not that simple. The contents of intergroup perceptions, unlike intergroup attraction, could not be represented by a single dimension of "acceptability/rejection." Brewer and Campbell

---

[4]In this regard, it is interesting to think about changes in relations between the so-called superpowers, the Soviet Union and the United States, over the periods of the "Cold War," through détente, beyond the fall of the Berlin Wall in 1989, and on to cooperative explorations of space in the 1990s. Increased friendship and perceptions of enhanced similarity seem to have gone hand-in-hand. At the same time, of course, one could argue that these two groups didn't find friendship until one of them lost much of its ability to menace the other, so that they actually became less like each other than they had been when they were enemies. In this chapter's section on stereotypes, there is a discussion of mirror-images that once characterized the United States and the Soviet Union.

needed three dimensions to account for intergroup perceptions, which they labeled trust/conflict, attraction/repulsion, and admiration/disrespect. On this three-dimensional map, the distance between any two groups varied, depending on which dimension was salient at the time.

Sumner's (1906) model of intergroup perceptions, "convergent ethnocentrism," must be altered. Whereas Sumner held that each in-group and its allies would be perceived as positive in all respects, Brewer and Campbell found this to be true only when "all bases of distinction between 'us' and 'them' are highly correlated" (1976, p. 144). Sumner's model applies when (1) contact opportunities are low, (2) environmental survival threats require extremely high internal cooperation and in-group loyalty, or (3) ethnic discrimination is legally or otherwise encouraged. In the absence of such conditions, which is most often the case, there is "flexibility in adapting patterns of alliance to correspond to differing functional requirements" (p. 145).

Contact was also related to the content of intergroup perceptions. For individuals with little or no familiarity with an out-group, the perceptions of it tended to be more simplistic, consistent, and based largely on reputational stereotypes. Individuals better acquainted with an out-group held more idiosyncratic, less consistent—but not necessarily more positive—perceptions.

Perceptions of the In-Group Itself
The aspect of Sumner's theory that was most clearly supported concerns high self-regard: "Each group nourishes its own pride and vanity, boasts itself superior, exalts its own divinities" (1906, p. 13). Negative perception of out-groups is not universal, but positive perception of in-groups may well be. Brewer and Campbell found that all in-groups in their study rated themselves more favorably than they were rated by others. Specifically, "The facet of ethnocentrism that comes closest to universality is the tendency to regard own group members as more honorable and trustworthy than others" (1976, p. 143).

Positive self-regard was maximal for groups granted either high or low respect by other groups, and it somewhat diminished among moderately respected groups. That especially low- and high-status groups should hold themselves in such high self-regard led the authors to hypothesize that these Sumnerian ethnocentric feelings may reflect "high self-esteem associated with achievement and positive regard from others, or a defensive self-esteem associated with rejection and/or threat" (p. 143).

Generalizations from the East African Study

The findings from the Brewer and Campbell study allow us to hypothesize that:

1. People generally like their own groups best and perceive them in a most positive light;

2. The degree of attraction felt toward other groups is fundamentally a cultural fact, internalized by individuals early in life;

3. Intergroup attractiveness tends to be reciprocal;

4. Intergroup attraction depends on opportunity for intergroup contact, which, in turn, reflects cultural similarity and proximity;

5. Out-groups perceived as "backward" are generally unattractive, whereas groups perceived as "advanced" enjoy high attractiveness if they are culturally similar to the in-group of the perceiver;[5]

6. Out-group perceptions cannot be predicted solely on the basis of attractiveness (trustworthiness and achievement also matter); and

7. Opportunity for contact relates to intergroup perceptions but in a complex manner: The perceptions tend to be stereotyped for individuals with little opportunity for contact, but varied and idiosyncratic among individuals who know more about the out-groups in question.

All of this is more or less consistent with Sumner's ethnocentrism theory, "more" regarding in-group perceptions and intergroup attraction, "less" with regard to intergroup perception. The importance of intercultural similarity was clearly shown by this study.

These findings, involving thirty distinct ethnic groups, need, of course, to be replicated in other parts of the world. Until they are, we can only tentatively conclude that intergroup attraction and perception are products of cultural similarity and status, with the former more important than the latter.

Additional Insights from Other Cross-Cultural Studies

Cultural Variations in Content of an In-Group Concept
Asserting that "each culture cuts the pie of experience differently," (or has its own "subjective culture"), Triandis has explored the likelihood that definitions of an in-group member will vary from culture to culture. Triandis, Vassiliou, and Nassiakou (1968) described the Greek definition of the in-group as more personal in character than a U.S. one; the former includes family members, friends, and even foreign tourists, but not people one doesn't know, even if they happen to be Greek. In contrast, people in the U.S. do not typically consider "non-American" tourists part of the in-group, but all "Americans," even those unknown personally, are usually included.[6]

This is not to say that conationality doesn't matter to Greeks. In an earlier study (Triandis & Triandis, 1962), a part of which focused on norms governing social distance, while people in the United States emphasized "race" to a degree not present in Greece, the Greeks emphasized religion and nationality.

---

[5]An exception to this generalization may be seen in the tendency of people in "advanced" societies to admire "simpler" societies for their alleged simplicity and exoticism.

[6]Of course, there is ethnocentrism involved here, too, in a rather complex way. Thus, from a U.S. perspective, the term *American* often does not include Canadians, Mexicans, Guatemalans, and so on.

The detailed content of in-group definitions and the guidelines of behavior toward people so defined vary across cultures. A relationship that is considered intimate in one culture and available only to a highly valued in-group member may, therefore, be considered more casual in another culture and available to a larger category of people (Triandis, 1975). The kissing of each other's cheeks, by two acquaintances, even if only casually acquainted, is an example of such behavior. It is frequent in much of Europe and only recently found with any frequency in the United States.

How Do We Speak of Out-Groups?

Vallerand (1994, p. 719) cites a comment that was frequently circulated in Europe during the past decade as the European Union was taking shape. Tongue in cheek, we cite it here in Box 10.2 to introduce our (more serious) discussion of stereotyping.

A *stereotype* has been defined as "a cognitive structure containing the perceiver's knowledge and beliefs about a social group and its members" (Hamilton, Sherman, & Ruvolo (1990, p. 36). Gudykunst and Bond (1997, p. 129) refer to stereotypes as "packages of beliefs about typical members of groups." Stereotypes, put very simply, are beliefs that may be widely shared, not necessarily well-grounded in reality, but likely to influence the way people are perceived and the way the holder of the stereotype is predisposed to interact with them should the opportunity arise.[7]

In Sumner's view, because out-groups are usually treated badly, verbal descriptions of them should be dominated by negatively valued characteristics to legitimize the hostility. To make an out-group appear deserving of animosity, one might even invent negative characteristics. Such invention, however, is seldom necessary, because one can always find some difference in "their" behavior as compared with "ours," and because ours is moral and good, theirs "must be" immoral and bad. Because, as we have seen, not every out-group is held at a large social distance, Sumner's view is exaggerated. Not every out-group will be characterized by negative stereotypes. But such stereotyping is common, particularly with relatively unknown and culturally different groups.

BOX 10.2   Heaven and Hell: A European View

Heaven is where the police are British, the chefs French, the mechanics German, the lovers Italian,...and it is all organized by the Swiss.

Hell is where the police are German, the chefs British, the mechanics French, the lovers Swiss,...and it is all organized by the Italians.

---

[7]Stereotypes can reflect and, at the same time, reinforce "prejudice," which is any tendency to evaluate others unfairly, and "discrimination," which consists of unfair actions vis-à-vis others. Prejudice and discrimination are key parts of the vicious cycle of negative intergroup relations.

Ethnocentrism theory also predicts that stereotyping will be a mutual, reciprocal process between any two groups aware of each other. The stereotypes may reflect real, noticed, and acknowledged differences in modal behavior patterns, with the differences described in positive terms for each in-group and in negative terms for each out-group. Because every language is rich in both positive and negative adjectives, it is usually possible to treat any noticed difference between them and us in our favor. On the one hand, if they appear typically to work harder than we do, we can describe them as "compulsive." They, in turn, can describe us as "lazy." If, on the other hand, we work harder than they do, we can describe ourselves as "industrious," and they can describe themselves as "relaxed." Finally, the theory predicts a tendency to exaggerate the degree to which any negative trait is possessed by out-group members, attributing it to all or most. These ideas lead to a set of expectations about the content of stereotypes; Gudykunst and Bond (1997, pp. 129–131) discuss the role of stereotyping in setting up intergroup expectations.

Empirical Studies of Stereotyping

People not only choose identities for us, as in the Einstein comment above, they also attribute characteristics to us, viewing us simply as members of the identified group to which they assign us. These categorical attributions are, ipso facto, stereotypical. Taylor and Moghaddam (1987) consider stereotyping as a process central to social psychology and relevant to all theories dealing with intergroup behavior. What does empirical research show in this regard? In some studies, at least, the facts are more complicated than theory leads one to expect.

Katz and Braly (1933) did the classic study in the United States with college students, (nearly all of them from the dominant White Anglo-Saxon core culture that was disproportionately enrolled in U.S. colleges and universities at that time) who selected terms from an adjective checklist and assigned them to numerous out-groups, some known, some not. The Katz and Braly findings were dominated by much agreement in the assignment of negative traits to any but the core-cultural White Protestant in-group. By 1971 a review of the literature spanning more than four decades (Cauthen, Robinson, & Krauss, 1971) could conclude that in the United States the content of stereotypes remained very stable, with most groups described in much the same way they had been described by Katz and Braly's respondents. Another consistency in findings was that individuals who are members of groups stereotyped by others accept at least part of the stereotype as characteristic of their own group, if not of themselves personally.

Rothbart and Taylor (1992) underscore another important feature of stereotypes, that the social categories employed are usually perceived as *natural* categories, and not, as they usually are in fact, social constructions. In a telling instance of this phenomenon, Paulis (1994) provides examples of how parents who had adopted a child from a different, often distant society, albeit at a very early age, so that the child could have virtually no influence from his culture of origin, base certain behavioral expectations on a misplaced respect for the child's so-called deep-seated nature.

(Recall our discussion, in Chapter 1, of the potent illusions of "race" and, in the present chapter, of "primordial" groups.)

Mirror-Image Stereotypes.   Earlier, we discussed reciprocity in intergroup affect. Similarly, a parallelism in stereotypes is often found. Particularly when two groups are in a state of conflict, each tends to hold a view of the other that contrasts markedly with the view each holds of itself. Bronfenbrenner (1961) documented this for the United States and the Soviet Union at a time when the Cold War was intense, and he called the phenomenon the "mirror-image hypothesis." Haque (1973) applied the Katz and Braly technique with Indian and Pakistani respondents and found another example of this kind of parallelism. Specifically, both the Indians and Pakistanis tended to describe themselves as peaceloving, trustworthy, religious, kind, idealistic, democratic, and hospitable. And both described the other as cruel, threatening, selfish, warmongering, greedy, and cheating. It may be that the mirror-image phenomenon is stronger when two groups are in a heightened state of intergroup tension.

Not So Cut and Dried in Hawaii. ↳ In Hawaii, Kurokawa (1971) administered an 84-item checklist to 100 "White," 100 "Black," and 100 Japanese American respondents (adults, college students, and schoolchildren), who were to select five terms that best applied to each of those ethnic groups. There was high agreement among the three samples that Whites are materialistic and pleasure loving; Blacks, musical, aggressive, and straightforward; and Japanese Americans, industrious, ambitious, loyal to family, and quiet. To this extent, this study, like many others, showed that some existing stereotypes are "acknowledged" by the people being stereotyped.

On the other hand, Kurokawa derived a hypothesis from Katz and Braly (1933) that the dominant Whites would be endowed primarily with positive traits, whereas both minority groups would be ascribed predominantly negative traits. The hypothesis was not fully supported. So, on the basis of this study, we must conclude that, in some settings at least, positive traits are assigned to minority groups. Does this finding reflect the fact that Hawaii is a very multi-ethnic setting? Are Hawaiians, of whatever ethnicity, less likely to use "good/bad" dichotomous characterizations because they know each other so well because of regular contact?

The Influence of Contact on Stereotypes. ↷   Contact may influence the clarity and valence (positive/negative) of stereotypes. Triandis and Vassiliou (1967), working in Greece with both Greek respondents and U.S. citizens living there, found trait attributions of Greeks and U.S. citizens that could be compared with attributions made by people living in their own country and having little contact with nationals of the other country. They found that Anglos living in Greece had clearer stereotypes of Greeks than did those who had little contact with Greeks. Also, the U.S. respondents were more likely to describe the Greeks as similar to themselves if they were living in Greece and thus enjoying contact. But the same did not hold for Greek respondents, for whom contact with U.S. citizens did not correlate with higher clarity or increased "correspondence" of stereotypes.

However, Reigrotski and Anderson (1959), in a report of a multinational study of stereotyping, showed that both clarity and content of national stereotypes may be determined by international contact. Respondents from nations that enjoy much contact with other nations were found to be less likely to bias their own-group descriptions in a favorable direction, more likely to attribute favorable characteristics to members of other nations, and more likely to describe their own group in ways that corresponded with descriptions provided by outsiders.

There may well be circumstances under which sociopolitical factors matter more than contact. Following the Nigerian civil war, Ogunlade (1971) had one hundred university students from western Nigeria assign ten adjectives from a list of sixty-three to each of ten national groups (Americans, Russians, French, Chinese, and so forth), some of which had supported the federal Nigerian government (as did most people in western Nigeria) and some of which had been supporters of the secessionist Biafrans. Quite clearly, the nations that supported the federal side were described predominantly by positive adjectives, whereas the reverse was true for nations thought to have supported the rebels.

In a study by Nichols and McAndrew (1984) that also examined the effects of contact on stereotyping, rather small groups of college students (forty-seven Americans in the United States who had never lived abroad, nineteen others from the United States studying in Spain, eighteen Spaniards with whom the second group of Americans were costudents, and fourteen Malaysian students attending the American liberal arts college from which the American student samples were drawn) chose polar adjectives to describe their conationals and the other two groups. While the U.S. citizens who were studying at home revealed the most negative view of others (including members of their own group), the Americans in Spain did not share this outlook on the world. Whether this was a consequence of studying abroad or a reflection of a preexisting disposition that also led them to study abroad is, of course, not clear. Generally, however, the strongest trend in the data relating to contact was that respondents with more intercultural contact expressed stronger stereotypes with more confidence, including negative ones. A curious qualification to this was that guests (Malaysians studying in the United States and Americans in Spain) perceived their hosts as relatively friendly, while the host groups (Americans in the United States and Spaniards in Madrid) perceived their guests as relatively unfriendly. Might this finding suggest that people in a less powerful position, like students abroad, look more kindly on more powerful others, in this case, their hosts?

Corneille (1994) discusses intergroup contact as a mode of conflict resolution. In this paper, published in French, one can find a thorough review of studies relevant to the hypothesis that some kinds of intergroup contact increase mutual understanding and reduce intergroup conflict. Some kinds of contact, of course, do very little in this respect, beyond reinforcing already existing stereotypes.

The Role of Power in Intergroup Perceptions. Do groups that are discrepant in power deal differently with stereotypes and other kinds of group perceptions? Lindgren and Tebcherani (1971) argued that relative power influences the accuracy of intergroup perceptions, suggesting that relatively low-power groups would be more sensitive to, more aware of, and more accepting of a more powerful group's views of themselves than vice versa. On a measure of empathy in which Arab and U.S. male students at the American University in Beirut described themselves and a "typical" member of the other group, Arab students described the typical American more as the U.S. students described themselves than vice versa. So, perhaps more powerful groups are simply more accurately described, and less apt to be stereotyped. However, the authors acknowledged that this finding could also be accounted for by a tendency of the Americans to be more open and self-revealing, thus giving more accurate self-descriptions and permitting the Arab observers to predict better how the Americans would describe themselves.

The Role of Causal Attributions in Intergroup Perceptions.   As we have been reminded in our earlier discussions of human cognitive processes the world over (in Chapters 3 through 6 of this book), people everywhere seek to make sense out of the world in which they live. Confronted by events, over most of which they have little or no control, they are often motivated at least to try to discern their causes. Why did such and such an event happen? A judgment about the cause of any event is often based in a review of prior events, classified as similar ones. If the event is an act by a person one knows, for example, attributing cause to that event might well be based in a review of that person's prior acts, and what is known about the causes of those prior acts.

Causal attributions for acts performed by individuals have long been of interest to psychologists (e.g., Heider, 1958; Kelley, 1973). Earlier research in the domain of interpersonal perception dealt with the question of why an individual might focus on one kind of cause rather than another. Some causal attributions could be quite reasonable, based, as suggested above, on known facts about the acting individual's past patterns of behavior. On the other hand, the attributions could well be irrational. One well-known example of an irrational tendency came to be known as the "self-serving bias," which involved making an attribution that would serve to enhance one's own ego. Concretely, one could manifest the self-serving bias by taking credit for one's own successes and/or denying responsibility for one's own failures. Similarly and conversely, one could attribute an other person's success to external forces while assigning responsibility to that person for his or her failures. Ross (1977) subsumed this process under the "*fundamental* attribution error," stressing that for self, one would typically overestimate internal causes and underestimate external ones, with the reverse for other people.

Pettigrew (1978, 1979) extended this idea to intergroup attributions, for which he spoke of the *ultimate* attribution error. In Pettigrew's analysis, when confronted by socially desirable behaviors performed by members of their own, positively valued group, the tendency would be to emphasize internal, positive traits as the causes of that behavior; similarly, good behavior, when performed by members of an out-group, would be attributed to external, situational factors and vice versa: Bad behavior by in-group members would tend to be attributed to external factors, while the same bad behavior by out-group members would be attributed to their internal traits and dispositions.

These ideas about attributions fit well with what we learned earlier about stereotypes, because negative stereotypes applied to out-groups and positive stereotypes applied to one's own group would facilitate the kinds of attributions we have just reviewed.

ETHNIC CONFLICT

Among ethnic groups within a society, as well as across societies, there is sometimes harmony but sometimes tension, even hostility and overt conflict. Here we shall say a few words about interethnic relations when they go sour, as they so often seem to do. Presently, the world seems subject to both centrifugal and centripetal forces, with perhaps both in mutual, reciprocal reaction. Just as regional economic and political supranational organizations grow and strengthen (e.g., the European Union and the former General Agreement of Tariffs and Trade, now the World Trade Organization), some *intra*national groups, some so small as to be viewed, popularly, as "tribes," are defining themselves as nations. Many are seeking independent-nation status, a quest that often leads to warfare with the larger nation, or other parts thereof, with which it was affiliated. These groups are characterized by the language they speak, or the religion they profess, or a revisionist history of prior national glory, and they are victimized by, or themselves aggress against, groups who speak different languages, worship different gods or the same ones in different ways. And people are raped, hung, shot, bombarded, and otherwise debased. Ironically, however, despite the salience of journalistic accounts of shocking events in Rwanda, Northern Ireland, the former Yugoslavia (to mention only a few of the world's most turbulent trouble spots), there is not a lot of recent cross-cultural psychological research on violent conflict to report here. But can we find applicable principles in the research that was done years ago?

Ethnic Prejudice: An Individual or Group-Level Phenomenon?

Prejudice and Authoritarianism
Data from South Africa during the era of apartheid and from the southern United States before desegregation, although gathered a half-century ago, are still relevant to the issue of the relationship between prejudice and certain personality traits that might predispose some individuals to be more prejudiced than others.

Adorno, Frenkel-Brunswik, Levinson, and Sanford (1950) had found prejudice and authoritarianism (approving of rigid moral standards, strong policing, and the like) to be correlated in the United States. Generally, throughout the country, individuals who scored high on measures of authoritarianism tended to express high degrees of prejudice against "minority groups," such as "Negroes" and "Jews."

This led some theorists to argue that prejudice is an outward manifestation of a personality syndrome, indexed by scores on the authoritarianism measure, the F-scale. Pettigrew (1959, 1960) challenged this notion, at least for settings in which discrimination is sanctioned, e.g., southern states in the United States and South Africa. In these settings, Pettigrew found what he termed "other-directed" prejudice, behavior that is best understood as conformity with prevailing norms. In his U.S. study, Pettigrew (1959) found that manifest prejudice against Blacks by Whites was not correlated with F-scale scores any more highly than in other regions. But it was correlated highly with such measures of generalized tendency to conform as regularity of church attendance. Nor was anti-Black prejudice correlated with anti-Semitism in that setting, as authoritarianism theory would predict (and is, more generally speaking, the case in other parts of the United States).

In South Africa, where sanctions against Blacks were even more rigid than in the southern United States during the 1950s, Pettigrew (1960) again found that anti-Black prejudice was not highly correlated with F-scale scores. Lambley (1973) confirmed Pettigrew's findings with a sample of 190 White undergraduates taking introductory psychology at an English-speaking university in South Africa. He found only moderate positive correlations between authoritarianism and anti-Black prejudice, between authoritarianism and social distance, and between prejudice and social distance. Also working among English-speaking Whites in South Africa and using similar measures, Orpen (1971) found no significant correlations among the measures. Orpen's study was done in a setting where, as he put it, "the prevailing cultural norms explicitly sanction prejudiced ideas" (p. 301) and where individuals are encouraged to be intolerant, irrespective of personality.

Thus, under certain conditions, individual differences in degree of ethnic prejudice pale in significance in comparison with group-wide, almost universally shared attitudes toward out-groups. As with "authoritarianism," the trait "dogmatism" sometimes fails to predict prejudice, as we are about to see.

Prejudice and Dogmatism

Another personality dimension that, in the United States at least, sometimes correlated with ethnic prejudice is dogmatism, as measured by Rokeach (1960). This hypothetical personality trait is meant to characterize an individual whose cognitive processes tend to be "rigid" and who, thus, might be expected to be prone to simplistic, stereotypic thinking and to other symptoms of prejudice. Orpen and Rookledge (1972) administered Rokeach's Dogmatism Scale, a measure of anti-Black prejudice, and a social distance scale to seventy-two White English-speaking secondary school students of urban, middle-class background in South Africa, while

Apartheid was still in effect. They found that only about 5 percent of the variance in prejudice in this sample could be accounted for by individual differences in dogmatism. Instead, political party preference predicted prejudice, with respondents who preferred South Africa's White-supremacist party scoring more anti-Black on both the prejudice and social distance scales than respondents who preferred either of two integrationist parties, even though party preference was not related to dogmatism scores. Once again we see that, in settings characterized by sanctioned discrimination and other norms that encourage prejudice, sociocultural factors outweigh personality factors in shaping individual intergroup attitudes.

Conflict Theories

Theories of interethnic conflicts, their causes and variables that affect the probability of their occurrence, may be found in Boucher, Landis, and Clark (1987). Geographical/cultural coverage in this edited volume includes the United States (American Indians, Hawaii, Puerto Rico, and the state of Mississippi), Asia and Oceania (Sri Lanka, Hong Kong, China, Malaysia, the Philippines, the Solomon Islands, and New Zealand), and a single example from Europe (Basque). A volume edited by Giliomee and Gagiano (1990) focused on three long-term conflicts, those in South Africa, Israel, and Northern Ireland. As suggested earlier in this chapter, theoretical ideas that are useful in analyzing these and other conflicts include ethnocentrism, realistic group conflict theory, and social identity theory. This is apparent again in the following brief discussion of the most extremely negative form of intergroup conflict, warfare.

Warfare

War is, of course, an aggregate form of aggression, often institutionalized, and committed in the name of a geopolitical entity. So, we first consider ecocultural level influences that have been identified by scholars working at the group-level of analysis. For example, cross-culturally, in the kinds of societies described in the Human Relations Area Files, a high frequency of warfare is strongly predicted by resource unpredictability (Ember & Ember, 1992). In the contemporary world of large and small nation–states, many other causes of warfare may be discerned, including conflicts over territory and interethnic (including interreligious) rivalries, like those that characterized Northern Ireland, ex-Yugoslavia, and the Arab–Israeli conflicts.

There are, however, apparently competing views of the causes of warfare and its relationship to other forms of violence that occur within societies, some of which were discussed in Chapter 9, as manifestations of individual aggression. In this section, we will ask how warfare relates to individual aggression, if at all.

Does War Produce Internal Violence or Reduce It?
Warfare, or socially organized aggression between communities and larger territorial units, is related to many other forms of aggression, including more warlike sports,

severe punishment for wrongdoing, and family violence. Many cross-cultural and cross-national results also suggest that rates of violent interpersonal behavior increase as a result of war. Socialization for aggression may be the mechanism linking war to other forms of aggression as societies that engage in war try to rear boys to be unambivalent warriors and inadvertently encourage other forms of aggression.

That war is associated with higher rates of interpersonal violence is one of the most replicated findings to emerge from cross-national and hologeistic studies. However, this may be a particular aspect of the more general fact that many kinds of aggression go together, that some cultures are more violent generally than others.

Ember and Ember (1994a) point to socialization for aggression (i.e., encouragement of aggression) in boys as the linkage between some forms of interpersonal violence (homicide/assault) and war. They suggest that "war mainly causes socialization for aggression" (p. 621) because parents will want their sons to be courageous warriors. Once people learn to kill an enemy, they may find it easier to hurt or kill anyone. Thus, socialization for aggression inadvertently "causes high rates of interpersonal aggression" (p. 621 and 643).

However, to complicate matters, a Sumnerian view, advocated by Campbell, predicts that participation in a war (an intergroup event) will *reduce* intragroup violence and some findings, such as the decline in civilian violence in some countries during warfare, can be cited to support this view as well.

Campbell, beginning in 1965 and continuing into the 1990s, developed a position regarding intergroup conflict that is rooted in both the social and biological sciences. A brief exposition here will, we trust, encourage our readers to consult the Campbell papers on intergroup conflict; they are, in our opinion, profoundly significant.

Campbell (1965a), rejected "psychologizing in the explanation of intergroup conflict" (p. 286) and espoused a theory (pp. 287–291) that began with the straightforward assertion, "real conflict of group interests causes intergroup conflict" (pp. 287–288). Campbell attributed perception of threat to *real* threat, as may be found in "the presence of hostile, threatening, and competitive outgroup neighbors" (p. 288).

The Sumnerian dictum, "The exigencies of war with outsiders are what make peace inside, lest internal discord would weaken the we-group for war" (Sumner, 1906, p. 12), was cited by Campbell as the source of "the most recurrent and explicit proposition of this theory, namely that real threat causes ingroup solidarity" (p. 288). A thorough exposition of this dictum, buttressed with many citations and empirical research, may be found in LeVine and Campbell (1972, p. 31 onward). This notion clearly implies that the relationship between interpersonal aggression *within* a society and its participation in a war is negative, not positive.

It remains possible that both the Ember and Ember argument and the Campbell argument are correct. The former may deal primarily with internal violence following an external war, while the latter may deal mostly with the internal conditions of a society when it is confronting an external enemy.

Consistent with the Campbell argument, Landau and Beit-Hallahmi (1983) report that, in Israel, *during* war, rates of civilian aggression go down, primarily, they argue, because of an increase in numbers mobilized and a strong sense of solidarity among the remaining civilians. Nevertheless, they argue that there is no "cathartic" effect of war, and that war "may be an instigator of individual aggression toward ingroup targets" (p. 279).

The Relationship Between War and Subsequent Internal Violence.   Consistent with the Ember and Ember argument, Lore and Shultz (1993) addressed a number of public policy options that would, in their view, affect levels of aggression, in either direction. In one example, they cited nation–state efforts to legitimize violence toward "enemies" during wartime as possible provocation for postwar aggression by its citizens, an idea that they acknowledge was broached as early as the Renaissance by Erasmus (1975/1514) and was tested by Archer and Gartner (1967, 1984), who reported, among other findings, more increases in homicide rates in the first five postwar years in nations that had engaged in war than in nations not involved. More-over, the phenomenon occurred for victors and vanquished alike. An interpretation of this finding is that a country legitimizes violence during wartime. If it is permis-sible to kill enemies during wartime, inhibitions against killing may have conse-quently been relaxed, in turn causing homicide rates to go up.

That war legitimizes violence is also consistent with historical data provided by Gurr (1989, pp. 47–48). Although there seems to be a long-term downtrend in crime in Western countries, which, viewed optimistically, implies some emphasis on humanistic values and the nonviolent achievement of goals, people may behave and feel otherwise during (and immediately after) wartime. In the United States, for example, surges in violent crime rates occurred during the 1860s and 1870s (during and after the Civil War), after World War I, after World War II, and during and after the Vietnam War.

Hologeistic research results (Eckhardt, 1973; Ember & Ember, 1994b; Russell, 1972) are consistent with the cross-national results. War in the smaller, traditional societies is also associated with many kinds of aggression. Societies with more war tend to have more warlike sports (Sipes, 1973), beliefs in malevolent magic (Palmer, 1970; Sipes & Robertson, 1975), and severe punishment for all kinds of crime (Palmer, 1970; Sipes & Robertson, 1975). Violent feuding is associated with war between polities (Otterbein & Otterbein, 1965); family violence is associated with other kinds of violent conflict resolution (Levinson, 1989), including war (Erchak, 1994; Erchak & Rosenfeld, 1994); and some societies (at least among small-scale societies) are generally more violent than others (Ross, 1985). Ember and Ember (1992), in their examination of 186 mostly preindustrial societies showed that, while war involving such societies appears to be caused mostly by a fear of nature (assessed in their research as threat of resource unpredictability), it may also be par-tially a result of fear of others (assessed as socialization for mistrust). Whether or not war is causally central to all forms of violence is still an unanswered question, but we have certainly seen one set of results (Ember & Ember, 1994a) suggesting that war is a correlate of homicide and assault within the participating societies.

SOME CONCLUSIONS AND
TENTATIVE PRESCRIPTIONS

We have seen in this chapter that there are several theories about intergroup relations and many studies inspired by them. As befits an introductory textbook, we have not here gone into great detail on these theories. Taylor and Moghaddam (1987) and Gudykunst and Bond (1997) summarize major theoretical approaches, including realistic conflict theory, ethnocentrism theory, and social identity theory (Tajfel, 1978, 1982). An excellent account of social identity theory may be found in Lorenzi-Cioldi and Doise (1994) and another excellent compilation of theoretical ideas in Capozza and Volpato (1990). Bourhis and Leyens (1994) have edited a comprehensive volume that reviews, in French, the literatures pertaining to stereotypes, discrimination, and intergroup relations.

A central theme in this chapter has been the pervasiveness of ethnocentrism. Although, as Sumner suggests, ethnocentrism is difficult to overcome, as multinational entities like the European Union proliferate and as global environmental problems compound, we may have to become more than loyal members of our own societies. To avoid impending ecological catastrophes, more of us must learn to transcend our own cultures. We must develop, at a minimum, empathy with others. We might even be capable of identifying with the whole human race as enthusiastically as we presently do with our own tribes.

Our review of cross-cultural studies of intergroup relations has not been exhaustive, but contains enough to permit conclusions and tentative suggestions about how intergroup relations might be improved. What surely stands out is the importance of perceived similarity and of opportunities for equal status contact in enhancing intergroup attraction and diminishing intergroup social distance. Also, however much psychological factors (e.g., authoritarianism, dogmatism, etc.) may influence intergroup relations, behavior toward out-groups is subject to institutionalized norms and other forms of social control.

We have also seen that in-group identification and intergroup distance tend to be dynamically related parts of a whole syndrome of ethnocentric behaviors, much as Sumner argued in 1906. The cultural identity of any in-group can be recognized as socially functional in that it provides a psychological home base and a sense of belonging. By the same token, when individuals locate themselves in a relatively small collectivity that has meaning as an in-group, they can probably also identify comfortably with a larger collectivity that includes the smaller one.

But ethnic group identification also has a potential for divisiveness and alienation from other groups. From the Brewer and Campbell (1976) study and from the other cross-cultural studies we reviewed, we can draw consistent conclusions. People everywhere hold their own group in highest regard, and social distance increases as perceived similarity diminishes. Likability of other groups is correlated with cultural similarity, proximity, and opportunity for contact.

If these findings tentatively answer the question "Why do we persist in behaving ethnocentrically?" a prescription for breaking down the barriers to a more global consciousness follows clearly. Ways must be found and efforts expended to increase equal status contacts and to maximize the probability of experiences that will demonstrate and accentuate similarities, rather than differences.

But, of course, equal status contacts are not very likely between groups of unequal status! Katz and Taylor (1988) provide a booklength compilation of papers revealing the complexity of the situation in the United States, where debate still prevails among social scientists regarding the efficacy of desegregation efforts and affirmative action programs. It is not at all clear that these efforts have had the anticipated positive outcome. More equitable distribution of opportunities is probably a prerequisite for equal status contacts. The relatively deprived (groups within multiethnic societies and economically less developed nations) must be assisted in their efforts to "close the gap." As this happens, they will become less deprived and, as a consequence, more similar. When, for example, more similar levels of economic well-being and more similar lifestyles come into play, an awareness of our similarities will be enhanced. Until that happens, underprivileged groups will continue to be perceived as different, and hence less good, thereby "deserving" to be held at large degrees of social distance.

Of course, this is not always possible. Impermeable boundaries often confront members of minority groups who wish to assimilate more into a multicultural society. In settings where ethnic discrimination is institutionally sanctioned, one of the effects of that discrimination, of course, is to accentuate and even exacerbate economic, social, and cultural differences. So, in such settings political and legal changes may be necessary.[8]

Laws that force groups to remain separate from, and hence different from, their neighbors must be replaced by laws that force the opposite. Experience has shown that initial opposition to such reversals in the law is soon replaced by acceptance of them, just as Pettigrew's concept of the other-directed nature of much prejudice would suggest. Leadership of an enlightened nature must accompany such legal changes, of course.

Management of Conflict

In the domain of management of interethnic conflict, perhaps the most interesting and worthwhile category of research, inspired by the Ghandians, is called "Peace

---

[8]Taylor and Moghaddam (1987) studied multicultural policies in countries where minorities are manifesting enhanced efforts to improve their status. Berry (1984a) provides a discussion of multicultural policy in Canada; ideas derived from this policy are developed in Chapter 11 of the present volume.

Studies," or "Studies in Nonviolent Conflict Resolution." Many successes (as well as many failures) have been recorded by researchers in this tradition, which includes some earlier applied research by cross-cultural psychologists such as Doob (1981) and Kelman (1965). Mostly nonpsychologists, however, have been responsible for the more recent efforts in this regard. The sociologist Kriesberg (1993) describes in a cogent argument psychological forces (e.g., identity) that contribute to intercommunal conflicts, as well as ways to prevent them from developing or escalating. Political scientists Gurr and Harff (1994) discuss post-Cold War international politics, covering numerous ethnic conflicts occurring in the context of "the changing world order," with some particular attention to Kurds in Europe and Asia Minor, Miskitos in Latin America, Chinese in Malaysia, and various immigrant minorities in Europe, and review a number of "measures that may enable policymakers to anticipate and restrain ethno-political conflicts" (p. 151). These have to do with efforts to convince governments to reduce oppressive policies and to de-emphasize ethnic discrimination.

Gurr (1993) mentions 233 "politically active" communal groups, describes ethnic tensions on several continents, and assesses various strategies for reducing ethnic conflict. A good comparative politics approach to the study of interethnic conflict may be found in Giliomee and Gagiano (1990) who call for "acceptable accommodations" in these cases. McGarry and O'Leary (1993), whose own disciplines include history, political science, and public administration, provide in another edited volume case studies of ethnic conflicts, and their diverse forms of management, in Canada, the former Soviet Union, India, Malaysia, Northern Ireland, Burundi, ex-Yugoslavia, Spain, South Africa, Fiji, and Belgium.

Hope?

It was suggested at the outset of this chapter that parochial loyalties are tenacious and not easily modified. Yet they will have to change if we are to contend with our global survival problems. It was also suggested that cross-cultural research into intergroup relations can both illuminate the magnitude of this difficulty and offer some guidelines for dealing with it. The research we have reviewed has served both those functions. What we have seen is the potency of cultural forces in shaping human behavior. It is cultural identity that binds individuals to their own groups; it is cultural similarity that permits those same individuals to accept and interact with people from other groups. Just as people within groups can de-emphasize existing differences and instead emphasize what they have in common with other individuals, so they can do with other groups.

This will require a quantum leap in goodwill, accompanied by enlightened leadership and social policy that provide the requisite economic and normative settings in which such goodwill can flourish. In 1998, we may have seen a real-world example of this in the tentative agreements between Catholic and Protestant communities in Ireland concerning the seemingly intractable conflict involving the status of Northern Ireland.

Perhaps a new global identity can grow, one to which an increasingly large portion of humankind will relate. But even this need not destroy local loyalties, allegiances, and identifications based on small, traditional cultures. Appreciation of cultural diversity must prevail, for cultural homogenization is unlikely ever to come about, nor do many wish it to. A blend of acceptance of differences in the context of awareness of similarities is much to be preferred over the cultural parochialism and ethnocentrism from which we continue to suffer.

Camilleri (1993) conceived of a state of intercultural relations in which the legitimacy of all participant cultures is honored and emergent common values are encouraged, thereby permitting the emergence of a new collective group, with a kind of association contract in effect. In such a situation, a member group would not necessarily have to be similar, in an assimilationist manner, in order to be accepted in the overall group. This idealistic view of one of Europe's preeminent intercultural theorists is certainly consistent with other hopes expressed here, as we conclude this chapter of cross-cultural insights relevant to intergroup relations.

11

ACCULTURATION

Much of this book has been devoted to showing how cultural factors play an important role in the development and display of behavior. One central line of argument has been that human populations are adapted to their ecological settings, and that we can account for psychological differences and similarities across groups by taking these ecological and cultural factors into account.

A second line of argument was introduced in Chapter 2 in a preliminary description of the ecocultural framework: The sociopolitical and historical context of a group also potentially influences the development and display of human behavior, through the process of *acculturation.* This process parallels that of *cultural transmission,* which was described earlier as comprising the dual phenomena of *enculturation* and *socialization.* In the case of acculturation the sociopolitical context influences the individual from *outside* one's own culture, whereas enculturation and socialization are sources of influence from *within* one's culture. Another way to understand this distinction is to think about acculturation as a *second* set of cultural influences on an individual, while enculturation and socialization constitute the *first* set, beginning from a person's birth.

A fundamental question posed in this chapter is: If culture is such a profound factor in shaping an individual's behavior, what happens psychologically when someone comes into contact with, and experiences a second culture? One possible answer is that people continue pretty much as they were, guided by their initial socialization and enculturation; another possibility is that people change their behavior quickly and easily, in adaptation to the new culture. In fact both possibilities occur rarely. In this chapter we will see that people change in numerous ways, and with a great deal of variation from individual to individual. The pattern of change is complex, but a considerable amount of research has shown that the changes appear to follow some basic psychological principles. We will be presenting an outline of some of these basic principles, and then consider how they might be applied to immigrants and other groups who are experiencing acculturation.

CULTURE CHANGE

Cultures are constantly changing, and so the ways in which individuals behave are also likely to change in order for them to adapt. In fact, it is possible to use the study of the relationship between culture change and the accompanying psychological changes as a dynamic test of culture–behavior relationships. How people adapt to changes that are underway in their cultural setting, however, is not only of academic interest. The pace and extent of change in the "developing world" poses a serious challenge to millions of people in their daily lives.

Before focusing on acculturation, it is useful to examine those aspects of culture change that come about as a result of *internal* forces. Some of those forces are features of the *society* itself, such as social innovation and invention, population explosion, resource overutilization, ethnic or religious conflict, differential group access to power or wealth, and the presence of institutions that no longer meet the needs of the people living in a society. All of these factors are likely to contribute to social instability, sometimes leading to social change, which in turn requires individuals to then adapt psychologically.

Other sources of change are *psychological* features of individuals that may contribute to change in the society, and thence spread to psychological changes to others in the population. These psychological features are themselves likely to be the result of cultural conditions, bringing us to the conclusion that there is a highly interactive relationship between the population and individual levels of understanding culture change.

For many years (approximately 1960 to 1980) two psychological factors involved in culture change were intensively studied: These are *achievement motivation* and *individual modernity*. While no longer of major current interest, they provide a useful background to the study of acculturation because of the kinds of theory and method that they used.

Achievement Motivation

As we saw in Chapter 7, McClelland (1961) argued that a society must have a sufficiently high level of N_{Ach} for economic development characteristic of modern industrial society to take place. He initiated a program of research, resulting in considerable support for his contention. Early findings showed successful entrepreneurs to have been high in N_{Ach} years before their business success was noted (see, for example, McClelland, 1965). McClelland then predicted that any society should develop economically to the degree that it possesses people with high N_{Ach}.

McClelland found support for his proposition that a high level of achievement motivation precedes economic growth. The data, derived from analyses of such diverse collective products as literature and ceramics, at least suggest that the production of achievement themes does precede economic growth, in some places at some times. Whether high levels of achievement need are either necessary or sufficient is not so clear (in an elaboration of McClelland's theory, Pareek [1968] suggested a somewhat more general paradigm in which development is the result of achievement motivation plus a concern for others).

Individual Modernity

Although there are many different approaches to this concept, the work of Inkeles and Smith (1974) is, perhaps, the most important. They considered that individuals possess a "syndrome of individual modernity" composed of a number of values and behavioral tendencies, including: (1) openness to new experience; (2) the assertion of increasing independence from the authority of traditional figures, and a shift of allegiance to leaders of government, public affairs, trade unions, cooperatives, and the like; (3) belief in the efficacy of science and medicine and abandonment of passivity and fatalism in the face of life's difficulties; (4) ambition for oneself and one's children to achieve high occupational and educational goals; (5) preferences for punctuality and an interest in carefully planning one's affairs in advance; (6) strong interest and an active participation in civic and community affairs and local politics; and (7) a striving to keep up with the news and a preference for national and international news.

In their view (Inkeles & Smith, 1974), these psychological qualities are both the *result* of social factors (such as education, urban experience, mass media exposure, and consumer goods owned), and are *predictive* of social change (when widely distributed in a population), toward increased modernization.

Research on both the achievement and modernity approaches to social change has largely come to a halt, in part because the concepts are considered ethnocentric (e.g., Mazrui, 1968). As we will see in the next section, the processes of change are more complex and do not inevitably lead to modernization or westernization.

ACCULTURATION

The classic definition of *acculturation* was presented by Redfield, Linton, and Herskovits (1936): "Acculturation comprehends those phenomena which result when groups of individuals having different cultures come into continuous first-hand contact with subsequent changes in the original culture patterns of either or both groups" (p. 149). While *acculturation* is a neutral term in principle (that is, change may take place in either or both groups), in practice acculturation tends to induce more change in one of the groups (termed the *acculturating group* in Figure 11.1) than in the other (termed the dominant *culture*).

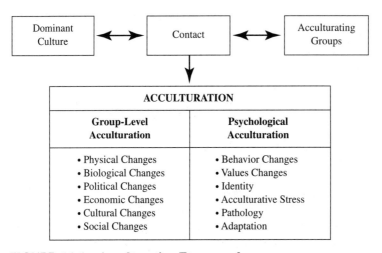

FIGURE 11.1   Acculturation Framework.

A distinction has been made by Graves (1967) between acculturation as a collective or group-level phenomenon and *psychological acculturation.* In the former (and original level of the concept), acculturation is a change in the culture of the group (on the lower left in Figure 11.1); in the latter, acculturation is a change in the psychology of the individual (on the lower right in Figure 11.1). This distinction between the set of cultural variables that influence the individual on the one hand, and the psychological outcomes of these influences, on the other, is important in order to examine the systematic relationships between these two sets of variables. Moreover, in the study of acculturation we need to attend to this distinction because not all individuals participate to the same extent in the general acculturation being experienced by their group. While the general changes may be profound in the group, individuals may vary greatly in the degree to which they participate in these community changes.

The concept of acculturation has become widely used in cross-cultural psychology and has also been the subject of criticism. One difficulty has been the gradual erosion of the original meaning of the concept (as outlined above) so that it became synonymous with only one possible outcome of acculturation. The concept came to mean only *assimilation* (absorption of the acculturating group by the dominant society), even though, in the original definition, this outcome was identified as just one of the many possible varieties of acculturation.

In addition to the concept of acculturation, there is another notion that has become widely used, mainly among Francophone scholars: *interculturation* (see Camilleri and Malewska-Peyre, 1997). This concept is defined as "the set of processes by which individuals and groups interact when they identify themselves as culturally distinct" (Clanet, 1990, p. 70). A more extended description of this approach emerged from recent conference discussions (Bouvy et al., 1994): *interculturation* "refers to the construction of cultural diversity in the context of intercultural contacts…Intercultural psychology has a specific research field (intercultural encounters), a specific research objective (cultural distinctiveness), and a specific mechanism ("interculturation", i.e., the formation of a new culture on the basis of these encounters)" (p. 2).

There are evident similarities between the acculturation and interculturation approaches, and it is often difficult in practice to distinguish the research done or the conclusions drawn from the two approaches. One distinguishing feature, however, is the interest in the formation of new cultures in the interculturation, more than in the acculturation, approach. Given these rather broad similarities, this chapter will employ the term *acculturation* to refer to the general processes and outcomes (both cultural and psychological) of cultural contact.

Plural Societies

Often, during the process of acculturation, societies become *culturally plural.* That is, people of many cultural backgrounds come to live together in a diverse society. In many cases they form cultural groups that are not equal in power (numerical, economic or political). These power differences have given rise to popular and social science terms such as *mainstream, minority, ethnic group,* and so forth. While recognizing the unequal influences and changes that exist during acculturation, we employ the term *cultural group* to refer to all groups, and the terms *dominant* and *acculturating* (or *nondominant*) to refer to their relative power when such a difference exists and is relevant to the discussion. In this way, we attempt to avoid a host of political and social assumptions that have distorted much of the work on psychological acculturation. Principally, we are concerned with the widespread view that "minorities" are inevitably (or should be in the process of) becoming part of the "mainstream" culture. While this does occur in many plural societies, it does not always occur, and in some cases it is resisted by either or both the dominant and nondominant cultural groups, resulting in the continuing cultural diversity of so many contemporary societies. In this way, our concepts and measures allow us to avoid prejudging this issue.

Acculturating Groups

Many kinds of cultural groups may exist in plural societies and their variety is primarily due to three factors: *mobility, voluntariness,* and *permanence* (see Figure 11.2). Some groups are in contact because they have migrated to a new location (e.g., immigrants and refugees), while others have had the new culture brought to them

MOBILITY	VOLUNTARINESS OF CONTACT	
	Voluntary	**Involuntary**
Sedentary	Ethnocultural Groups	Indigenous Peoples
Migrant **permanent** **temporary**	Immigrants Sojourners	Refugees Asylum Seekers

FIGURE 11.2   Types of Acculturating Groups.

(e.g., indigenous peoples). Second, some have entered into the acculturation process voluntarily (e.g., immigrants) while others experience acculturation without having sought it out (e.g., refugees, indigenous peoples). And third among those who have migrated, some are relatively permanently settled into the process (e.g., immigrants), while for others the situation is a temporary one (e.g., sojourners, such as international students and guest workers, or asylum seekers who may eventually be deported).

These three factors, when interacting as in Figure 11.2, correspond to six relatively independent kinds of acculturating peoples. Despite substantial variations in the life circumstances of these acculturating groups, and despite the large variation in cultural groups that experience acculturation, there is evidence that the psychological processes that operate during acculturation are essentially the same for all groups (Berry, 1990a); that is, it is possible to adopt a *universalistic* perspective on acculturation as well as on other behaviors. A framework that attempts to show these commonalities will be presented later (in Figure 11.4).

The *classification* of acculturating peoples into these six categories results from the identification of the three factors found to be important in the literature, and may have worldwide validity. However, the *labeling* of the six categories with the names used in Figure 11.2 is probably culturally-biased, based on terms used, and assumptions commonly made, in the societies where much of the work on acculturation has taken place. The colonized and immigrant-receiving countries of Australia, Canada, and the United States have been the most common settings for acculturation studies, and the terms used in Figure 11.2 reflect this state of affairs. Alternative terms, for example, for Europe or India, would have to be found when using such a framework there, even though the three underlying dimensions are likely to be valid everywhere.

A related issue is the allocation of specific cultural groups to the appropriate category. In some cases, a particular cultural group may fall in a number of categories. For example, people of Chinese origin in Australia or of Indonesian origin in the Netherlands could belong to five of the six categories (all except Indigenous). More problematic would be deciding whether, in Europe, Sami, Basque, and Breton people are Indigenous peoples or ethnic groups. However, the important question for the psychological study of acculturation is not so much the label, or even the precise category, but where individuals and their groups are in relation to the three underlying dimensions.

PSYCHOLOGICAL ACCULTURATION

Acculturation Strategies

In all plural societies, cultural groups and their individual members, in both the dominant and nondominant situations, must deal with the issue of *how* to acculturate. Strategies with respect to two major issues are usually worked out by groups and individuals in their daily encounters with each other. These issues are: *cultural maintenance* (to what extent are cultural identity and characteristics considered to be important, and their maintenance striven for); and *contact and participation* (to what extent should they become involved in other cultural groups, or remain primarily among themselves).

When these two underlying issues are considered simultaneously, a conceptual framework (Figure 11.3) is generated that posits four acculturation strategies. These two issues can be responded to on attitudinal dimensions, represented by bipolar arrows. For purposes of presentation, generally positive or negative ("yes" or "no" responses) to these issues intersect to define four strategies. These strategies carry different names, depending on which group (the dominant or nondominant) is being considered. From the point of view of nondominant groups, when individuals do not wish to maintain their cultural identity and seek daily interaction with other cultures, the Assimilation strategy is defined. In contrast, when individuals place a value on holding onto their original culture, and, at the same time, wish to avoid interaction with others, then the Separation alternative is defined. When there is an interest in both maintaining one's original culture, while having daily interactions with other groups, Integration is the option; here, there is some degree of cultural integrity maintained, while at the same time seeking to participate as an integral part of the larger social network. Finally, when there is little possibility or interest in cultural maintenance (often for reasons of enforced cultural loss), and little interest in having relations with others (often for reasons of exclusion or discrimination), then Margin-alization is defined.

The presentation above was not only from the point of view of the nondominant group, but it was also based on the assumption that such groups and their individual members have the freedom to choose how they want to acculturate. This, of course, is not always the case (Berry, 1974). When the dominant group enforces certain forms of acculturation, or constrains the choices of nondominant groups or individuals, then other terms need to be used. Most clearly, people may sometimes choose the Separation option; but when it is required of them by the dominant society, the situation is one of *Segregation.* Similarly, when people choose to Assimilate, the notion of the *Melting Pot* may be appropriate; but when forced to do so, it becomes more like a *Pressure Cooker.* In the case of Marginalization, people rarely choose such an option; rather they usually become marginalized as a result of attempts at forced assimilation (Pressure Cooker) combined with forced exclusion (Segregation); thus, no other term seems to be required beyond the single notion of Marginalization.

Integration can only be "freely" chosen and successfully pursued by nondomi-nant groups when the dominant society is open and inclusive in its orientation toward cultural diversity. Thus, a *mutual accommodation* is required for Integration to be attained, involving the acceptance by both groups of the right of all groups to

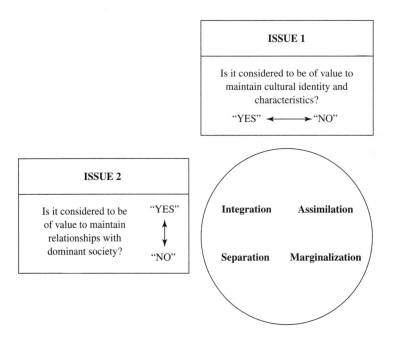

FIGURE 11.3   Acculturation Strategies.

live as culturally different peoples. This strategy requires nondominant groups to accept the basic values of the larger society, while at the same time the dominant group must be prepared to adapt national institutions to better meet the needs of all groups now living together in the plural society.

Obviously, the Integration strategy can only be pursued in societies that are explicitly *multicultural,* in which certain psychological preconditions are established (Berry & Kalin, 1995). These preconditions are: the widespread acceptance of the value to a society of cultural diversity (i.e., the presence of a positive "multicultural ideology"); relatively low levels of prejudice (i.e., minimal ethnocentrism, racism, and discrimination); positive mutual attitudes among cultural groups (i.e., no specific intergroup hatreds); and a sense of attachment to, or identification with, the larger society by all groups (Kalin & Berry, 1995).

Just as obviously, Integration (and Separation) can only be pursued when other members of one's ethnocultural group share in the wish to maintain the group's cultural heritage. In this sense, these two strategies are "collective," while assimilation is more "individualistic" (Lalonde & Cameron, 1993; Moghaddam, 1988). Other constraints on one's choice of acculturation strategy have also been noted. For example, those whose physical features set them apart from the society of settlement (e.g., Koreans in Canada or Turks in Germany) may experience prejudice and discrimination, and thus may be reluctant to pursue assimilation or integration (Berry, Kim, Power, Young, & Bujaki, 1989). Such attitudes can also be assessed among members of the larger society, to discover how they think ethnocultural group members *should* acculturate (Berry, 1974; Bourhis, Moise, Perrault, & Senécal, 1997).

Individuals and groups may hold varying *attitudes* toward these four ways of acculturating, and their actual *behaviors* may vary correspondingly. Together, these attitudes and behaviors comprise what we have called *acculturation strategies* (Berry, 1990a). Attitudes toward (preferences for) these four alternatives have been measured in numerous studies (reviewed in Berry et al., 1989). National policies and programs may also be analyzed in terms of these four approaches (Berry, 1990b). Some policies are clearly assimilationist, expecting all immigrant and ethnocultural groups to become like those in the dominant society; others are integrationist, willing (even pleased) to accept all groups on their own cultural terms. Yet others have pursued segregationist policies, and others have sought the marginalization of unwanted groups.

Other terms than those used here have been proposed by acculturation researchers (e.g., Gordon, 1964). In particular, the term *bicultural* has been employed to refer to acculturation that involves the individual simultaneously in the two cultures that are in contact (Cameron & Lalonde, 1994; LaFromboise, Coleman, & Gerton, 1993; Padilla, 1994; Szapocznik & Kurtines, 1993). This concept corresponds closely to the Integration strategy as defined here. Similarly, Gordon (1964) refers to two forms of incorporation: cultural assimilation and structural assimilation. In our terms, when both forms occur, complete assimilation is likely to result. However, when structural assimilation is present (a high degree of contact and participation), combined with a low degree of cultural assimilation (a high degree of cultural maintenance), then an outcome similar to Integration is likely.

Three other issues require commentary before proceeding, because preferences for one acculturation strategy over others are known to vary, depending on context and time period. First, although there is usually, in any particular setting, an overall coherent preference for one particular strategy, there can also be variation according to where one is acting: In more private spheres or domains (such as the home, the extended family, the ethnic community) more cultural maintenance may be sought than in more public spheres (such as the workplace, or in politics), and there may be less intergroup contact sought in private spheres than in the more public ones. Second, the broader national context may affect acculturation strategies, such that, in explicitly multicultural societies, individuals may seek to match their personal preference for integration with pluralist policies; or in assimilationist societies, acculturation may be easiest by adopting an assimilation strategy for oneself. That is, individuals may well be constrained in their choice of strategy, even to the point at which there is a very limited role for personal preference. Third, there is evidence that, during the course of development (and even in later life), individuals explore various strategies, eventually settling on one that is more useful and satisfying than the others. However, as far as is known, there is no set sequence or age at which different strategies are used.

Psychological Outcomes

It has been previously thought that acculturation inevitably brings social and psychological problems. However, such a negative view and broad generalization no longer appear to be valid. The social and psychological outcomes are now known to be highly variable. Three main points of view can be identified in acculturation research, each suggesting a different level of difficulty for the individual. The first is one that considers psychological changes to be rather easy to accomplish; this approach has been referred to variously as "behavioral shifts" by Berry (1980), "culture learning" by Brislin, Landis, and Brandt (1983), and "social skills" acquisition by Furnham and Bochner (1986). Here, psychological adaptations to acculturation are considered to be a matter of learning a new behavioral repertoire that is appropriate for the new cultural context. This also requires some "culture shedding" (Berry, 1992a) to occur (the *un*learning of aspects of one's previous repertoire that are no longer appropriate); and it may be accompanied by some "culture conflict" (in which incompatible behaviors create difficulties for the individual and have to be sorted out).

In cases where conflict exists, then, a second point of view is likely to prevail; here individuals may experience "culture shock" (Oberg, 1960) or "acculturative stress" (Berry, 1970; Berry, Kim, Minde, & Mok, 1987) if they cannot easily change their repertoire. While the "culture shock" concept is older and has wide popular acceptance, the "acculturative stress" conceptualization is preferable for three reasons. One is that it is closely linked to psychological models of stress (e.g., Lazarus & Folkman, 1984) as a response to environmental stressors (which, in the present case, reside in the experience of acculturation), and thus has some theoretical foundation. The second is that "shock" implies only negative experiences of contact and the outcomes of contact (cf. the "shell shock" notion popular earlier as a psychological outcome of war experiences). In most cases, only moderate difficulties are experienced (such as psychosomatic problems) because other psychological processes (such as problem appraisal and coping strategies) are usually available to the acculturating individual. Third, the sources of the problems that do arise are not cultural, but intercultural, residing in the process of acculturation, rather than in one particular culture.

Finally, when major difficulties are experienced, then the "psychopathology" or "mental disease" perspective is most appropriate (Malzberg & Lee, 1956; Murphy, 1965; World Health Organization, 1991). Here, changes in the cultural context exceed the individual's capacity to cope, because of the magnitude, speed, or some other aspect of the change, leading to serious psychological disturbances, such as clinical depression, and incapacitating anxiety (Berry & Kim, 1988).

Adaptation

In its most general sense, *adaptation* refers to changes that take place in individuals or groups in response to environmental demands. These adaptations can occur immediately, or they can be extended over the longer term. Short-term changes during acculturation are sometimes negative and often disruptive in character. However, for most acculturating individuals, after a period of time, some long-term adaptation to the new cultural context usually takes place. Depending on a variety of factors, these adaptations can take many different forms. Sometimes there is increased "fit" between the acculturating individual and the new context (e.g., when the assimilation or integration strategies are pursued, and when attitudes in the dominant society are accepting of the acculturating individual and group). Sometimes, however, a "fit" is not achieved (as in separation/segregation and marginalization) and the groups settle into a pattern of conflict, with resultant acculturative stress or psychopathology.

In the recent literature on psychological adaptation to acculturation, a distinction has been drawn between *psychological* and *sociocultural* adaptation (Searle & Ward, 1990). The first refers to a set of internal psychological outcomes including a clear sense of personal and cultural identity, good mental health, and the achievement of personal satisfaction in the new cultural context; the second is a set of external psychological outcomes that link individuals to their new context, including their ability to deal with daily problems, particularly in the areas of family life, work, and school. Although these two forms of adaptation are usually related empirically, there are two reasons for keeping them conceptually distinct. One is that factors predicting these two types of adaptation are often different (Ward, 1995). It is usually psychological characteristics of acculturating individuals that influence psychological adaptation, while it is features of the contact situation that influence sociocultural adaptation. The other is that psychological adaptation may best be analyzed within the context of the stress and psychopathology approaches, while sociocultural adaptation is more closely linked to the social skills framework (Ward & Kennedy, 1993a). That is, psychological adaptation may involve psychological disturbance, while sociocultural adaptation is often a matter of changing one's behavior and acquiring new ones.

AN ACCULTURATION FRAMEWORK

The complex findings on acculturation have been the subject of numerous conceptual frameworks; these have attempted to systematize the process of acculturation and to illustrate the main factors that affect an individual's adaptation. In Figure 11.4, one such framework (Berry, 1992a) is presented (see also Berry, Trimble, & Olmedo, 1986; Rogler, 1994).

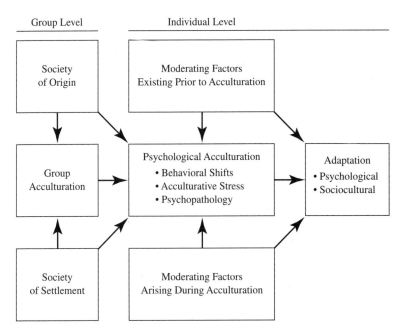

FIGURE 11.4   A Framework for Acculturation Research.

On the left are shown group- or cultural-level phenomena, which are mainly *situational* variables; to the right are individual- or psychological-level phenomena, which are predominantly *personal* variables. Along the top are features that exist prior to acculturation taking place, while along the bottom are those that arise during the process of acculturation. Through the middle of the framework are the main cultural and psychological acculturation phenomena. These flow from left to right beginning with the cultural groups in contact bringing about changes in many of the features of group life (e.g., political, economic, social structures), then affecting the individual who is experiencing acculturation (resulting in a number of possible changes, including behavioral shifts, acculturative stress, and psychopathology), leading finally to a person's adaptation (both psychological and sociocultural).

Contemporary work on acculturation has revealed that this central flow is highly variable. The nature of a person's psychological acculturation and eventual adaptation depends on specific features of the group-level factors (on the left) and of the moderating influence of individual factors that are prior to, or arise during, acculturation (at the top and bottom). It should be noted here that the terms used in Figure 11.4 are those that are more appropriate to immigrants and refugees than to the other kinds of acculturating groups that were identified in Figure 11.1. For example, if Indigenous Peoples were the acculturating group, their "precontact culture" would be examined rather than Society of Origin, and the Colonizing Society would be studied rather than the Society of Settlement or Society of Residence.

The main point of the framework is to show the key variables that should be attended to when studying psychological acculturation. Any study that ignores any of these broad classes of variables will be incomplete, and be unable to comprehend individuals who are experiencing acculturation. For example, research that does not attend to the cultural and psychological characteristics that the focal individuals bring to the process, merely characterizing them by name (e.g., as Vietnamese, or Somali, or even less helpfully as "minorities" or "immigrants"), cannot hope to understand their acculturation or adaptation. Similarly, research that ignores key features of the dominant society (such as its demography, immigration policies, and attitudes towards immigrants) is also incomplete. However, it is important to note that there is no single study that has incorporated or verified all aspects of the framework in Figure 11.4. It is a composite framework, assembling concepts and findings from numerous smaller scale studies.

To expand on Figure 11.4, Table 11.1 provides a listing of these broad classes of variables that can be found in the literature, using the case of Immigrants. Examples employing other groups and phenomena could serve the purpose equally well. Indeed, given our earlier expressed view that many of the phenomena are shared across acculturating groups, the list of factors affecting acculturation in Table 11.1 may be taken as a more general guide, one that is relevant to most acculturating groups and phenomena. To exemplify, Table 11.1 presents the

TABLE 11.1   Factors Affecting Acculturation

Variable	*Specific features*
	Society of Origin
	Ethnographic characteristics (e.g., language, religion, values)
	Political situation (e.g., conflict, civil war, repression)
	Economic conditions (e.g., poverty, disparity, famine)
	Demographic factors (e.g., crowding, population explosion)
	Society of Settlement
	Immigration history (longstanding *vs.* recent)
	Immigration policy (intentional *vs.* accidental)
	Attitudes toward immigration (favorable–unfavorable)
	Attitudes toward specific groups (favorable–unfavorable)
	Social support (availability, usefulness)
	Group Acculturation
	Changes in acculturating group (e.g., physical, biological, economic, social, and cultural)
	Psychological Acculturation
Behavioral Shifts	Culture learning (e.g., language, food, dress, social norms)
	Culture shedding (e.g., changing social norms, gender attitudes)
	Culture conflict (e.g., incompatibility, intergroup difficulties)
Acculturative Stress	Problem appraisal
	Stressors
	Stress phenomena (e.g., psychological, psychosomatic, anxiety)
Psychopathology	Problems
	Crises
	Pathological phenomena (e.g., depression, schizophrenia)
Psychological Adaptation	Self-esteem
	Identity consolidation
	Well-being/satisfaction
Sociocultural Adaptation	Cultural knowledge, social skills
	Interpersonal and intergroup relations
	Family and community relations
	Moderating Factors Prior to Acculturation
	Demographic (e.g., age, gender, education)
	Cultural (e.g., language, religion, distance)
	Economic (e.g., status)
	Personal (e.g., health, prior knowledge)
	Migration motivation (e.g., push *vs.* pull)
	Expectations (e.g., excessive *vs.* realistic)
	Moderating Factors Arising During Acculturation
	Acculturation strategies (Assimilation, Integration, Separation, Marginalization)
	Contact/participation
	Cultural maintenance
	Social support (appraisal and use)
	Coping strategies and resources
	Prejudice and discrimination

situational and personal factors that are now widely believed to influence psychological acculturation.

Society of Origin

To begin, a complete understanding of acculturation would need to include a fairly comprehensive knowledge of the two societal contexts: that of origin and that of settlement. In the society of origin, the cultural characteristics that accompany individuals into the acculturation process need description, in part to understand (literally) where the person is coming from, and in part to establish cultural features for comparison with the society of settlement as a basis for estimating an important factor to be discussed later, that of *cultural distance.* The combination of political, economic, and demographic conditions being faced by individuals in their society of origin also needs to be studied as a basis for understanding the degree of *voluntariness* in the *migration motivation* of acculturating individuals. Recent arguments by Richmond (1993) suggest that migrants can be ranged on a continuum between *reactive* and *proactive,* with the former being motivated by factors that are constraining or exclusionary, and generally negative in character, while the latter are motivated by factors that are facilitating or enabling, and generally positive in character. These contrasting factors have also been referred to as *push/pull* factors in the earlier literature on migration motivation.

Society of Settlement

In the society of settlement, a number of factors have importance. First there are the general orientations a society and its citizens have toward immigration and pluralism. Some have been built by immigration over the centuries, and this process may be a continuing one, guided by a deliberate immigration policy. In such cases, citizens know and accept this, often with pride (as in the phrase "we are all immigrants here"); but some individuals, of course, resent immigration and immigrants. The important issue to understand for the process of acculturation is both the historical and attitudinal situation faced by migrants in the society of settlement. Similarly, some societies are accepting of cultural pluralism resulting from immigration, taking steps to support the continuation of cultural diversity as a shared communal resource; this position is one that has been termed *multiculturalism,* and corresponds to the Integration strategy in Figure 11.3. Others seek to eliminate diversity through policies and programs of Assimilation, while others attempt to Segregate or Marginalize diverse populations in their societies. Murphy (1965) has argued that societies supportive of cultural pluralism (that is, with a positive multicultural ideology; Berry & Kalin, 1995) provide a more positive settlement context for two reasons: (1) They are less likely to enforce cultural change (assimilation) or exclusion (segregation and marginalization) on immigrants, and (2) they are more likely to provide social support both from the institutions of the larger society (e.g., culturally sensitive health care and multicultural curricula in schools), and from the continuing and evolving ethnocultural communities that usually make up pluralistic societies. However, even where pluralism is accepted, there are variations in the relative acceptance of specific cultural, racial, and religious groups (e.g., Berry & Kalin, 1995). Those groups that are less well accepted experience hostility, rejection and discrimination, one factor that is predictive of poor long-term adaptation (Beiser, Barwick, & Berry, 1988).

Group-Level Acculturation

With respect to group-level acculturation, whether in migrant or sedentary acculturating communities, ethnocultural groups usually change substantially as a result of living with two sets of cultural influences. Physical changes are often profound, frequently involving urbanization and increased population density. Biological changes include new dietary intake and exposure to new diseases, both of which have implications for the health status of the whole group. Economic changes can involve a general loss of status or new employment opportunities for the group. Social changes range from disrupted communities to new and important friendships. Finally, cultural changes (which are at the core of the notion of acculturation) range from relatively superficial changes in what is eaten or worn, to deeper ones involving language shifts, religious conversions, and fundamental alterations to value systems.

Turning to the moderating factors in Table 11.1, for policy reasons it is useful to distinguish between those factors that exist before major acculturation (and, hence, which cannot be much changed by public policies in the society of settlement) and those that may arise during the process of acculturation (and which are controllable, to some extent). These moderating factors attach both to groups and to individuals; these situational and individual factors are often intertwined. All these moderating variables are both risk factors and protective factors, depending on their degree or level, and many of them interact in complex ways. Because they influence the course of events along the central line in Figure 11.4 (from group acculturation to eventual long-term adaptation), they will be discussed following presentation of this course of events.

Psychological-Level Acculturation

The central line in Figure 11.4 is highly variable, not only because of these moderating risk and protective factors, but also because of the three different conceptualizations (behavioral shifts, acculturative stress, and psychopathology). There are five main events taking place over the course of acculturation. The first event is the *experience* of having to deal with two cultures in contact, and having to participate to various extents in both of them. Second, individuals consider the *meaning* of these experiences, evaluating and appraising them as a source of difficulty (i.e., as stressors) or as benign, sometimes even as opportunities.

The outcome of appraisal is variable across the three approaches: When acculturation experiences are judged to pose no problem for the individual, changes are likely to be easy and *behavioral shifts* will follow smoothly. This process encompasses three subprocesses: *cultural shedding; culture learning;* and *culture conflict* (discussed previously).

When greater levels of conflict are experienced, and the experiences are judged to be problematic, but controllable and surmountable, then the *acculturative stress* paradigm is the appropriate conceptualization. In this case, individuals understand that they are facing problems resulting from intercultural contact that cannot be dealt with easily or quickly by simply adjusting or assimilating to them. Drawing on the broader stress and adaptation paradigms (e.g., Lazarus & Folkman, 1984), this approach advocates the study of the process of how individuals deal with acculturative problems on first encountering them and over time. Any or all of the acculturation strategies may be tried out in attempting to deal with them, in combination with other coping strategies (discussed shortly).

When acculturation experiences overwhelm the individual, creating problems that cannot be controlled or surmounted, then the *psychopathology* paradigm is the appropriate one. In this case, there is little success in dealing with acculturation, sometimes resulting in withdrawal (separation), but sometimes involving culture shedding without culture learning (resulting in marginalization).

Third, as we have noted, individuals engage in activities that attempt to deal or cope with the experiences that are appraised as problematic. Lazarus and Folkman (1984) have worked extensively with the process of coping, within which two major functions are discerned: problem-focused coping (attempting to change the problem), and emotion-focused coping (attempting to regulate the emotions associated with the problem). More recently, Endler and Parker (1990) have identified a third: avoidance-oriented coping.

These analyses of coping may or may not be valid cross-culturally. Aldwin (1994) and Lazarus (1991) suggest that cross-cultural variations are likely to be present in these distinctions, and in which ones are preferred. One key distinction, made by Diaz-Guerrero (1979), is between *active* and *passive* coping. The former seeks to alter the situation, and hence may be similar to problem-focused coping. Passive coping reflects patience and self-modification, which does not appear to relate to either emotion-focused or avoidance-oriented coping, but does resemble the integration and assimilation acculturation strategies. These strategies are likely to be successful only if the dominant society has positive attitudes toward, and is willing to accept, members of the acculturating groups. If attitudes are hostile, the passive coping strategy may well lead to unacceptable levels of exclusion or domination.

The fourth event is a complex set of immediate effects, including physiological and emotional reactions, coming closest to the notion of *stress,* as a "reaction to conditions of living" (Lazarus, 1990, p. 5). In terms of the three conceptual approaches, when behavioral shifts have taken place, and without difficulty, stress is likely to be minimal and personal consequences are generally positive. When acculturative problems (stressors) have been successfully coped with, stress will be similarly low and the immediate effects positive; but when stressors are not completely surmounted, stress will be higher and effects more negative. And when acculturative problems have been overwhelming, and have not been successfully dealt with, immediate effects will be substantially negative and stress levels debilitating, including personal crises, and, commonly, anxiety and depression.

The last of the five main activities to be considered is the long-term *adaptation* that may be achieved. As we saw earlier, adaptation refers to the relatively stable changes that take place in an individual or group in response to environmental demands. Moreover, adaptation may or may not improve the "fit" between individuals and their environments. It is thus not a term that necessarily implies that individuals or groups change to become more like their environments, but may involve resistance and attempts to change their environments or move away from them altogether. In this usage, adaptation is an outcome that may or may not be positive in valence (meaning only *well*-adapted). It is in the bipolar sense that the concept of adaptation is used here. In this framework, long-term adaptation to acculturation is highly variable ranging from well to poorly adapted, even nonadapted, varying from a situation in which individuals can manage their new lives very well, to one in which they are unable to carry on in the new society.

We are now in a position to consider the *moderating factors* that exist *prior to* and those that *arise during* the process of acculturation.

Factors Existing Prior to Acculturation

Individuals begin the acculturation process with a number of personal characteristics of both a demographic and social nature (see Table 11.1). In particular, one's age has a known relationship to the way acculturation will proceed. When acculturation starts early (prior to entry into primary school), the process is generally smooth. The reasons for this are not clear; perhaps full enculturation into one's parents' culture is not sufficiently advanced to require much culture shedding or create any serious culture conflict, or perhaps personal flexibility and adaptability are maximal during these early years. However, youth do often experience substantial problems (Aronowitz, 1992; Beiser et al., 1988; Ghuman, 1991; Sam & Berry, 1995) particularly during adolescence. It is possible that conflicts between demands of parents and peers are maximal at this period, or that the problems of life transitions between childhood and adulthood are compounded by cultural transitions. For example, developmental issues of identity come to the fore at this time (Phinney, 1990) and interact with questions of ethnic identity, multiplying the questions about who one really is.

If acculturation begins in later life (on retirement, or when older parents migrate to join their adult offspring under family reunification programs) there appears to be increased risk (Beiser et al., 1988). Perhaps the same factors of enculturation and adaptability suggested for children are also at work here: A whole life in one cultural setting cannot easily be ignored when attempting to live in a new one.

Gender has variable influence on the acculturation process. There is substantial evidence that females may be more at risk for problems than males (Beiser et al., 1988; Carballo, 1994). However, this generalization itself probably depends on the relative status and differential treatment of females in the two cultures: Where there is a substantial difference, attempts by females to take on new roles available in the society of settlement may bring them into conflict with their heritage culture (Naidoo, 1992; Naidoo & Davis, 1988), placing them at risk.

Education appears as a consistent factor associated with positive adaptations: Higher education is predictive of lower stress. A number of reasons have been suggested for this relationship. First, education is a personal resource in itself: Problem analysis and problem solving are usually instilled by formal education and likely contribute to better adaptation. Second, education is a correlate of other resources, such as income, occupational status, and support networks, all of which are themselves protective factors (see below). Third, for many migrants, education may attune them to features of the society into which they settle; it is a kind of preacculturation to the language, history, values, and norms of the new culture.

Related to education is one's place in the economic world. Although high status (like education) is a resource, a common experience for migrants is a combination of status loss and limited status mobility. One's "departure status" is frequently higher than one's "entry status"; credentials (educational and work experience) are frequently devalued on arrival (Cumming, Lee, & Oreopoulos, 1989), due to ignorance and/or prejudice in the society of settlement, leading to status loss and the risk of stress. For similar reasons, the usual main goal of migration (upward status mobility) is thwarted, leading again to risk for various disorders, such as depression (Beiser, Johnson, & Turner, 1993). In a sense, these problems lie in personal qualities brought to the acculturation process, but they also reside in the interaction between the migrant and the institutions of the society of settlement; hence, problems of status loss and limited mobility can be addressed during the course of acculturation.

Cultural distance, too, lies not uniquely in the background of the acculturating individual but in the dissimilarity between the two cultures in contact. The general and consistent finding is that the greater the cultural differences, the less positive is the adaptation. This is the case for sojourners and immigrants (Ward & Kennedy, 1992; Ward & Searle, 1991) and for indigenous people (Berry, 1976a). Greater cultural distance implies the need for greater culture shedding and culture learning, and per-haps induces greater culture conflict.

Personal factors have been shown to affect the course of acculturation. In the personality domain, a number of traits have been proposed as both risk and protec-tive factors, including locus of control, introversion/extraversion, and dogmatism. However, consistent findings have been rare, possibly because, once again, it is not so much the trait by itself but its "fit" with the new cultural setting that matters. Kealey (1989) has advocated such a person x situation approach to studying sojourner adaptation.

One finding (Schmitz, 1994), among a group of immigrants to Germany, is that stress reaction styles are related to a person's preferred acculturation strategy: The Approach style was positively related to a preference for Assimilation, Avoidance to Separation, Flexible to Integration, and Psychopathology to Marginalization.

Reasons for migrating have long been studied using the concepts of *push/pull motivations* and *expectations.* As we noted earlier, Richmond (1993) has proposed that a reactive–proactive continuum of migration motivation be substituted, in which push motives (including involuntary or forced migration and negative expectations) characterize the reactive end of the dimension, while pull motives (including volun-tary migration and positive expectations) cluster at the proactive end. Such a single dimension allows for more concise conceptualization and ease of empirical analysis. Viewing previous research in this light permits some generalizations about the rela-tionship between motives and stress and adaptation. For example, Kim (1988) found that, as usual, those with high "push" motivation had more adaptation problems. However, those with high "pull" motivation had almost as great a number of prob-lems. It appears that those who are reactive are more at risk, but so too are those who are highly proactive; it is likely that these latter migrants had excessively high (even unrealistic) expectations about their life in the new society, which were not met, leading to greater stress.

Factors Arising during Acculturation

It is now clear that the *phase* of acculturation needs to be taken into account if stress and adaptation are to be understood. That is, how long a person has been experienc-ing acculturation strongly affects the kind and extent of problems. The classical description of positive adaptation in relation to time has been in terms of a U-curve. Conversely, acculturation problems have been described as following an inverted U: Only a few problems are present early, followed by more serious problems later, and finally a more positive long-term adaptation. However, there is little empirical evi-dence for such a standard course, nor for fixed times (in terms of months or years) when such variations will occur. Church (1982) has concluded that support for the U-curve is "weak, inconclusive and overgeneralized" (p. 542), although there are occasional longitudinal studies suggesting fluctuations in stress over time (Beiser, 1994; Hurh & Kim, 1990; Ward & Kennedy, 1995; Zheng & Berry, 1991).

An alternative to a fixed, stagelike conceptualization of the relationship between length of acculturation and problems experienced is to consider the specific nature of the experiences and problems as they change over time (e.g., initially learning a language, obtaining employment and housing, followed by establishing social relationships and recreational opportunities) and their relationship to the personal resources of the migrant and to opportunities in the society of settlement. This approach emphasizes the high degree of variability to be expected over the time course from initial contact to eventual long-term adaptation.

Acculturation strategies have been shown to have substantial relationships with positive adaptation: Integration is usually the most successful; marginalization is the least; and assimilation and separation strategies are intermediate. This pattern has been found in virtually every study, and is present for all types of acculturating groups (Berry, 1990a; Berry & Sam, 1997). Why this should be so, however, is not clear. In one interpretation, the integration strategy incorporates many of the other protective factors: a willingness for mutual accommodation (the presence of mutual positive attitudes and absence of prejudice and discrimination); involvement in two cultural communities (having two social support systems); and being flexible in personality. In sharp contrast, marginalization involves rejection by the dominant society combined with own-culture loss; this means the presence of hostility and much reduced social support. Assimilation involves own-culture shedding (even though it may be voluntary), and separation involves rejection of the dominant culture (perhaps reciprocated by it). In the simplest version of this explanation, in terms of Figure 11.3, Integration involves two positive orientations, Marginalization involves two negative ones, while Assimilation and Separation involve one positive and one negative relationship.

Another possible reason for the finding that Integration is the most adaptive strategy is that most studies of the relationship between acculturation strategies and adaptation have been carried out in multicultural societies. That is, there could be benefits to persons matching their acculturation strategies to that generally advocated and accepted in the larger society. However, in recent studies in societies that are more Melting Pot or Assimilationist in orientation, the Integration strategy remained the most adaptive (and conversely Marginalization was the least adaptive) strategy. For example, this was the case among Indian immigrants to the United States (Krishnan & Berry, 1992) and Third World immigrant youth in Norway (Sam & Berry, 1995). Schmitz (1992), working with a variety of immigrant groups in Germany, concluded that "The findings suggest that integration seems to be the most effective strategy if we take long term health and well-being as indicators" (p.368).

Related to acculturation strategies are the coping strategies discussed earlier. Some empirical evidence supports the relationship between coping and acculturation strategies. For example, in the same study Schmitz (1992) found, using the three coping styles identified by Endler and Parker (1990), that Integration is positively correlated with task orientation, Segregation is positively correlated with emotion and avoidance orientation, and Assimilation is positively correlated with both task and emotion orientation, but negatively with avoidance orientation. And, as we have just noted, these strategies were related to health outcomes for immigrants to Germany.

In the field of psychological well-being generally, the variable of social support has been widely studied (Lin, Dean, & Ensel, 1986). Its role in adaptation to acculturation has also been supported (Furnham & Alibhai, 1985; Furnham & Shiekh, 1993; Jayasuriya, Sang, & Fielding, 1992; Vega & Rumbaut, 1991). For some, links to one's heritage culture (with conationals) are associated with lower stress (Vega et al., 1991; Ward & Kennedy, 1993b), for others links to members of the society of settlement are more helpful, particularly if relationships match one's expectations (Berry & Kostorcik, 1990). But in most studies, supportive relationships with both cultures are most predictive of successful adaptation (Berry et al., 1987; Kealey, 1989). This latter finding corresponds to observations made earlier about the advantages of the integration strategy.

It has been widely reported that the experience of prejudice and discrimination has a significant negative effect on a person's well-being (Halpern, 1993). In groups experiencing acculturation this can be an added risk factor (Beiser et al., 1988). Murphy (1965) has argued that such prejudice is likely to be less prevalent in culturally plural societies, but it is by no means absent (Berry & Kalin, 1995). Indeed, Fernando (1993) has designated racism as the most serious problem and risk factor facing immigrants and their mental health.

SOME POSSIBLE APPLICATIONS

Research in the domains of immigration, acculturation, and adaptation, as outlined in this chapter, has provided some rather consistent and potentially applicable findings. This consistency is remarkable, because acculturation is one of the most complex areas of research in cross-cultural psychology. It is complex, in part, because the process involves more than one culture, in two distinct senses: Acculturation phenomena result from contact between two or more cultures; research on acculturation has to be comparative (like all cross-cultural psychology) in order to understand variations in psychological outcomes that are the result of cultural variations in the two groups in contact. This complexity has made the reviewing of the field both difficult and selective. The framing of the field (in Figures 11.1–11.4 and Table 11.1) was an attempt to provide a structure that could identify the main features of acculturation phenomena (the "skeleton"), and into which illustrative studies could be inserted (bits of "flesh"). The questions naturally arise: To what extent are these findings generalizable to other cultures? What still needs to be accomplished in order to apply them?

The empirical studies available do seem to point to some consistent findings. First, psychological acculturation is influenced by numerous group-level factors in the society of origin and in the society of settlement, and by the interaction between them. What led the acculturating group to begin the process (whether voluntary, whether on their own lands or elsewhere) appears to be an important source of variation in outcome. However, other factors have also been identified as contributing: national acculturation policies and attitudes in the dominant society, cultural distance, social support, and economic status. These population-level variables seem to be important in many studies, across many societies. However, their relative contributions will likely vary according to the specific acculturative context being considered. That is, they may be examples of a set of *universal* factors, ones that operate everywhere, but whose specific influence will vary in relation to features of the particular cultures in contact.

Still needed are systematic comparative studies that will take these population-level factors into account in a research design (see Berry et al., 1987, for such a proposed design). For example, a single acculturating group (e.g., Chinese) who experience acculturation as members of refugee, immigrant, sojourner, and ethnocultural groups, could be studied in societies with assimilationist, integrationist, and separationist policies. Within these settings, variations in ethnic attitudes and social support could be incorporated. Up until now, we have had to rely mostly upon sporadic ("one shot") studies of single acculturating groups, in single societies of settlement, with no control for other possibly important factors contributing to psychological acculturation.

Second, psychological acculturation is influenced by numerous individual-level factors. In particular, the integrationist or bicultural acculturation strategy appears to be a consistent predictor of more positive outcomes than the three alternatives of assimilation, separation, or, especially, marginalization. The availability and success of such a dual adaptation strategy, of course, depends on the willingness of the dominant society to allow it, and the wish of coethnics to pursue it. Thus, there is an apparent interaction between population-level and individual-level factors in contributing to psychological adaptations. But even in societies that tend toward assimilation policies, there was evidence that immigrants and ethnocultural group members generally prefer integration, and, when they do, they tend to make more positive adaptations. Whether such a finding is valid for all groups acculturating to all dominant societies is an important question for researchers, policy makers, and those involved in counseling acculturating individuals. Once again, systematic comparative studies are essential to answer this question.

Third, how are the personal outcomes of the acculturation process to be interpreted? Are they a matter of acquiring essential social skills (making some rather easy behavioral shifts), of coping with stressors in order to avoid acculturative stress, or of succumbing to problems so serious that psychopathology will result? There is evidence that all three conceptualizations are valid, but that they may constitute a sequence or hierarchy of outcomes: If sufficient behavioral shifts (involving new culture learning and former culture shedding) do not occur, stressors may appear in the daily intercultural encounters that require appraisal and coping in order to prevent acculturative stress. If these difficulties prove to be insurmountable, then psychopathologies may result. Because of the differing theoretical approaches taken by different researchers in their studies, it has not been possible to draw such a conclusion from any one study. What is required are large-scale, longitudinal studies, carried out comparatively, in which all three approaches are combined. In the meantime, it is possible to say on the basis of this review that most acculturating individuals make rather positive adaptations (there is not widespread psychopathology in evidence), but that the acculturative transition is not always an easy one (changing one's culture presents challenges that are not easy to overcome). Acculturation is a risk, but risk is not destiny (Beiser et al., 1988).

Because virtually all of the factors identified in this chapter are under human control, they should be amenable to change, guided by informed policy and program development. The contribution by cross-cultural psychologists to understanding these factors has been substantial, but much work remains to be done, both with respect to research and to communicating our findings and conclusions to acculturation policy and program developers, and to acculturating groups and individuals themselves. Policy and program implications from these findings are rather clear. While there is little that can be done in the societies of origin, some programs involving predeparture counseling and training, as well as realistic goal-setting are possible in many cases.

Most action can be taken, and most successes can be realized in the society of settlement. Foremost is the development of national policies that neither force culture shedding (assimilation) nor ghettoization (segregation), or some combination of them (leading to marginalization). Instead a policy balancing act between these alternatives (the policy option termed "Integration" here) can be sought (Berry, 1984a, 1991).

Second, public education and social legislation can promote an appreciation of the benefits of pluralism, and of the societal and personal costs of prejudice and discrimination to everyone. National studies of knowledge about and attitudes toward multiculturalism and specific ethnocultural groups among all residents can assist in monitoring progress toward these goals (Berry & Kalin, 1995).

At the individual level, the protective benefits of cultural maintenance and social support can also be disseminated through ethnocultural community interaction, thereby reducing the stresses associated with assimilation. At the same time, the benefits of seeking to participate in the national institutions (educational, work, judicial) to the extent desired can reduce the stresses associated with separation. And advocacy of both can be conveyed to acculturating individuals, accompanied by information about the dangers of marginalization that are likely when neither cultural maintenance nor participation in the larger society are achieved.

Perhaps most important is the advocacy of the view that acculturation involves *mutual accommodation* (*Integration* as defined here). Although there are obvious costs to both sides, (e.g., changing school curricula and health services by the dominant society, and shedding some aspects of their culture that are not adaptive by the acculturating group), the costs of *not* adopting integrationist policies are likely to be even greater, especially if marginalization is the end result. People without a sense of themselves (a cultural identity of their own), and who feel rejected by others (facing daily experiences of prejudice and discrimination), exact significant costs on their own and the dominant societies.

Less negatively, the benefits of pluralism, maintained in part through Integration, are numerous. Diversity in society is one of the spices of life, as well as providing competitive advantages in international diplomacy and trade. Perhaps most important is that, from a social systems perspective, cultural diversity enhances society's adaptability: Alternatives are present in the social system from which to draw when attempting to meet changing circumstances, due to changes in a society's ecological, or political context, whether arriving from within or outside a society.

12

CONCLUSIONS

ON THE IMPORTANCE OF THE SOCIOCULTURAL CONTEXT

We asserted in Chapter 1 that, to understand human behavior, it must be viewed in the sociocultural context in which it occurs. Having examined a variety of psychological topics, we can now ask whether we have demonstrated the validity of this assertion. By revisiting the Ecocultural Framework employed in this book, we can better appreciate how attending to the sociocultural context was repeatedly shown to be essential to the discipline of psychology.

The Ecocultural Framework Revisited

Illustrated in Figure 2.1 in Chapter 2, the ecocultural framework encompasses the processes of socialization and enculturation, to which we refer repeatedly in this book, as well as the concept of developmental niche, which we used in describing how early childhood development is environmentally influenced. In addition, the framework includes the process of acculturation, which was treated in detail in Chapter 11.

The framework reminds us that culture (or the "man-made" part of the environment) is not all that matters. So does the natural environment, which shapes human behavior both indirectly (that is, through culture) and directly, as when ecological factors relate to biological characteristics of populations.

The framework suggests that ecology influences cognitive behavior indirectly in ways illustrated in several chapters. The work linking the ecocultural context (degree of food accumulation) to cognitive style and cognitive development is particularly illustrative of the connections that are explicit in the framework. Berry's research on Witkin's psychological differentiation also illustrates the dynamic inter-

324

action between theory building and empirical research. While Berry's (1966) initial research design was based on an early version of the ecocultural framework, it evolved as a consequence of empirical findings into the version used in this book. While it was once thought that Witkin's theory might be universal (Berry, 1976a; Witkin & Berry, 1975), it is now obvious that a cultural adaptation of the theory is needed (Berry, van de Koppel, Sénéchal, Annis, Bahuchet, Cavalli-Sforza, & Witkin, 1987; Mishra, Sinha, & Berry, 1996). This requires more research on the socialization practices that mediate the influence of group-level variables on individual cognitive functioning.

The same observation holds for cultural differences in the development of concrete operations (Piaget, 1966) in the domains of quantification and space, reviewed in Chapter 5. Future research needs to document more fully the developmental niche, i.e., the social contexts, the childrearing practices, and the parental ethnotheories, that are relevant to cognitive development. We covered some of the research that provides this kind of documentation, but clearly more such research is needed.

A research program that covers all aspects of the sequence portrayed in the ecocultural framework is still lacking. Only Berry's long-term research program on psychological differentiation with individual subjects comes close to a complete design, although, as noted above, the socialization component requires more research.

In Chapter 3, we related the ecocultural framework to the ideas inherent in the developmental niche and showed how both physical and social settings influence childrearing patterns. Starting with climate as the ecological constraint, Whiting (1981) was able to show that infant-carrying practices are related to the mean temperature during the coldest months of the year. Carrying infants in cradles predominates in cold climates, carrying them on the body (using arms, a sling, or a piece of clothing) is significantly more frequent in warm climates. The latter carrying technique is linked to other childrearing practices, such as the sleeping arrangement (the infant sleeps near the mother at night), the postpartum taboo (the rule of avoiding sexual intercourse for some months after the birth of a child), and late weaning, all of which contribute to a close infant–mother body contact and the predominance of female role models. We also saw in Chapter 9 how these features of childrearing practices may lead to a feminine sex identity, which, under some circumstances, may lead to problematic compensatory aggressive behavior in boys and young men.

That ecological factors, both natural and human-made, influence the fundamental ways in which people everywhere perceive the world in which they live was revealed in some detail in Chapter 4, in the section on differences in susceptibility to visual illusions. In the same chapter, we saw that our very basic cognitive processes also vary in many ways across cultures, in a manner consistent with predictions subsumed by the ecocultural framework. These processes include categorization, memory, and problem solving. With respect to these cognitive activities, it is cultural factors, such as literacy and schooling, that seem to play the major role in the way these processes develop and are used.

In Chapter 5, in which we dealt with intelligence and its development through childhood, the ecocultural framework helped us to understand that differences in manifest abilities reflect ecocultural differences in ways that make people's particular modes of expressing intelligence appropriate to the settings in which they grow up. Many details of this phenomenon were presented in Chapter 6, in which we attended to the everyday ways in which people cope with mundane challenges, like calculating prices while selling in markets or shopping in supermarkets.

From Chapter 7 onward, we studied the social, historical, economic, and political forces (all included in the ecocultural framework) that are linked to various aspects of human social behavior. In Chapter 7, diverse attitudes, beliefs, and value systems were shown to vary across cultures not randomly, but in ways that make sense given the cultural setting in which they developed. In this chapter, we reviewed a series of research paradigms that characterized cross-cultural research on motives and values over the past several decades, including achievement motivation and individualism/collectivism (among others) and found it possible to incorporate them into our ecocultural framework.

Chapter 8 dealt with matters of sex and gender, noting many behavioral differences that were related to differential socialization, which in turn was related to varying biological and social (including economic) roots. Our ways of expressing our sexual identity, even our ways of engaging in sexual behavior, were shown to be embedded in a sociocultural context, as our framework led us to expect.

Aggression was shown in Chapter 9 to be better understood by viewing it in its sociocultural context, rather than as something that flows, as if through some instinctual hydraulic system, from inside the organism. The many cultural forces that operate either to encourage or impede aggressive behavior, including the content of the mass media, prevailing societal sanctions for aggression (including, and especially, punishments), and the availability of various kinds of role models, are the kinds of variables pointed to in the ecocultural framework.

Chapter 10 led us through a discussion of intergroup behavior, including its most negative aspects, violent conflict and warfare. There we found that a central theme in the analysis of intergroup relations, namely, the tendency of peoples everywhere to be ethnocentric, is itself understandable as a reflection of the universal phenomena of socialization, and therefore subject to change via the manipulation of social and political variables, many of them potentially under the control of the leadership of any society.

The topic of acculturation was covered in Chapter 11, in which it was treated as a second set of cultural influences on individuals exposed to the sociopolitical context that prevails in a culture other than their culture of origin, whenever they come into contact with another culture. In that chapter, the acculturation process was shown to be parallel to the cultural transmission process, comprising enculturation and socialization, which were highlighted in the ecocultural framework.

Thus, over eleven chapters, as we ranged widely from topic to topic, the ecocultural framework was employed to assist us in explicating empirical findings and theoretical notions that characterize contemporary research in cross-cultural psychology. This booklength effort will have succeeded if readers now recognize that all human populations are, generally speaking, adapted to their ecological settings and that we can account for psychological differences and similarities across groups only by taking these ecological and cultural factors into account. As rapid social change or acculturation takes place, this adaptation may be temporarily disrupted, but even this phenomenon can be understood by viewing the ecocultural framework as a dynamic system.

As Berry (1995) stressed: "It is essential to note that the term *ecological* refers to interactions between populations and features of the environment, rather than to a unidirectional determinism (from environment to culture)" (p. 375). Jahoda (1995) showed that the framework has strong roots in the history of Western thought from the Enlightenment onward, but he acknowledges that it is "a general framework cast in the form of a fairly complex model with feedback loops. It would of course be idle to pretend that such a sophisticated model, taking explicit account of interactions, had any direct predecessors" (pp. 14–15). Taking into account the newer definitions of culture, as reviewed in Chapter 1, in which there is a "coconstruction" between culture and mind, it is indeed the feedback loops that need to be further documented.

This book, it should now be obvious, advocates that all social scientists, psychologists especially, take culture seriously into account when attempting to understand human behavior. This has been a self-evident proposition to all whose work is covered in this introductory text on cross-cultural psychology and its many constituent parts—cultural psychology, ethnopsychology, societal psychology, and *la psychologie interculturelle*—and the closely related disciplines of psychological anthropology and comparative anthropology.

CROSS-CULTURAL PSYCHOLOGY VIS-À-VIS GENERAL PSYCHOLOGY

Cross-cultural psychology is unabashedly muticultural and maximally inclusive. In contrast, psychology in general continues to ignore culture as a source of influence on human behavior, and still takes little account of theories or data from other than Euro-American cultures. Recently, however, several introductory psychology texts made solid attempts to rectify this situation (Sternberg, 1995; Wade & Tavris, 1996; Westen, 1996) and we anticipate more of the same in the new millennium (as ethnocentrically measured on the Western, Christian calendar).

Cross-cultural psychology, as our discussions of methodology tried to show, comprises many ways of studying culture as an important context for human psychological development and behavior. Cultural psychology offers one approach for focusing on culture as integral to all psychological functioning, with culture and psychology viewed as "mutually constitutive phenomena" (Miller, 1997). Cross-cultural psychology consists mostly of diverse forms of comparative research (often explicitly and always at least implicitly) in order to discern the influence of various cultural factors, many of them related to ethnicity, on those forms of development and behavior. Recalling the famous early definition of culture by the anthropologist Herskovits "Culture is the man-made part of the environment" (Herskovits, 1948, p. 17), cross-cultural researchers occasionally seek as well the influence of individuals' behavior on ever-changing culture. When doing so, the independent and dependent variables are interchanged; their status is reversible, depending on the design of any particular study.

We have consistently argued in this book that a comparative research enterprise is *difficult* partly because all psychologists necessarily carry their own culturally-based perspectives with them when studying in other cultures. In its early days, cross-cultural psychology was marked by some conceptual and methodological weaknesses; for example, there was, far too often, a naive application of Euro-American theoretical notions to research conducted in other settings. During much of its history, cross-cultural psychology's typical research project consisted of taking a favorite test to some exotic place, comparing the obtained results with those of the homeland "norms," and thereby "discovering a cultural difference" that either remained unexplained or was fitted with some post hoc interpretations selected uncritically from among many uncontrolled alternatives. Often, in a vague and circular fashion, the difference was merely attributed to "culture." We have reiterated in this textbook that this "imposed *etic*" approach was doomed to yield uninterpretable "cross-cultural" differences. This "safari-style" research was typically carried out by psychologists from Western countries on leave from their home universities, doing short-term fieldwork, or through correspondence with a colleague in a foreign country. As this book will have made plain, we do not advocate this kind of research and we believe that enhanced publication standards will eliminate it.

Although more sophisticated aspects of cross-cultural methodology are dealt with in Berry and colleagues (1992, soon to appear in a revised second edition), and in Berry and associates (1997), throughout this book we pointed out questions of method in connection with particular studies. But we lacked enough space to describe, for every study, exactly how it was carried out. All of the included studies, in our judgment, contribute valuable knowledge, but not all of them are beyond criticism. Indeed, cross-cultural research is so difficult to carry out that there almost always remains some point of contention, some uncontrolled variable, or some doubt because the study was done with a small number of subjects, or no other researcher has attempted to replicate it. In other words, cross-cultural research tends to be "soft," in comparison with the "hard" data of experimental psychology. General psychology sometimes simply ignores cross-cultural psychology because of this characteristic. We think that this is a mistake. Alternative methods always have trade-offs. We are ready to weigh experimental control against the advantages to be gained from greater external validity, the possibility of increasing the variance in a crucial variable, or the ability to unconfound variables that are always linked in single societies. We are not saying that methodological rigor is unimportant; we are saying that one cannot always have it both ways, and that one occasionally has to make a choice, for example between experimental control and external validity. Although we have not tried in this book to teach how to do cross-cultural research, we hope to have enabled students to assess cross-cultural studies critically.

Theoretical Orientations within Cross-Cultural Psychology

We suggested here that someday a universal psychology might emerge but, we now emphasize, universality can never be assumed in advance. Every psychological theory that pretends to describe a general law should be put to empirical cross-cultural test. We are particularly concerned about the time lag between developing theories in general psychology and putting them to this cross-cultural test. While this has been done extensively for some theories, such as Piaget's, many of the more recent theories in the domain of cognition (those related to cognitive science and artificial intelligence) or in social psychology, claim to be universal without any attempt to demonstrate it. Even socioculturally oriented theories (neo-Piagetian, Vygotskyan) are often not systematically taken out of their initial Euro-American context.

In the francophone tradition of "intercultural" research, the emphasis is so much on studying only migrants in multicultural societies that comparative cross-cultural studies are almost completely neglected. Theories like Camilleri's "identity strategies" (Camilleri & Malewska-Peyre, 1997) are implicitly claimed to be generalizable, but are based almost exclusively on research with North African migrants in France, a rather specific social and political context (Dasen & Ogay, n.d.). Similarly, Berry's acculturation processes reviewed in Chapter 11 have been developed mainly on the basis of research in Canada and the United States, and have only recently started to be adapted to other contexts such as Europe (Berry & Sam, 1997). Hence, even research within a cross-cultural approach needs more extensive comparative replication.

Early in this text, we reviewed polar theoretical orientations in cross-cultural psychology—absolutism and relativism—and noted that few cross-cultural psychologists are at either pole. We saw that most strike a balance, borrowing from both poles. Cross-cultural psychologists expect both biological and cultural factors to influence human behavior, but, like relativists, assume that the role of culture in producing human variation both within and across groups (especially across groups) is substantial. We allow for similarities due to specieswide basic processes, as the absolutists stress, but consider the existence of specieswide processes subject to empirical demonstration. This kind of "universalism" assumes that basic human characteristics are common to all members of the species, and that culture influences the development and display of them.

PRACTICAL IMPLICATIONS OF CROSS-CULTURAL RESEARCH

We saw in this text that, beyond its historical links with general psychology, cross-cultural psychology has influences originating in anthropology, sociology, history, and political science, among others. As social scientists, willing to settle for truth in context, both historical and cultural context, cross-cultural psychologists take the world as it is and the people in it, as they are or, at least, as they perceive them to be, while trying not to express culturally rooted value judgments. In the process, they endeavor to give all human beings the respect and understanding they deserve. While following, in this respect, anthropology's basic principle of cultural relativism, cross-cultural psychologists need not deny their own attitudes and values and those of their own society. Also, they may well seek to place their research explicitly in a political context, in which they wish to serve the people they are studying.

Because cross-cultural psychologists often do research in settings where human problems are so dramatically visible, they can hardly pursue only "pure" science. Even in technologically developed nations we are often confronted by an uneven distribution, across ethnic groups, of well-being on the one hand and various kinds of distress on the other. So cross-cultural psychology lends itself not merely to discussions of scholarly findings but to their social implications as well.

In the present text, for example, we saw that there are differences between identifiable groups in performance in many different domains, including in some classical measures of "intellectual competence," but we showed the inherent faults of such measures, and we called attention to the many other variables that correlate both with membership in the various groups compared (e.g., income and wealth) and with performance. Accordingly, cross-cultural psychology can support in a compelling way policies that are designed to enhance the equality of opportunity and oppose vigorously the use of test measures as selection devices into experiences that prepare people for subsequent opportunities to improve their lot in life.

Cross-cultural research on gender that we reviewed in Chapter 8 has also resulted in socially applicable findings. There we showed the core finding to be the cultural embeddedness of all gender-related phenomena, from sex differences in behavior to relations between the sexes. Understanding traditional gender roles as rooted in economic, religious, political, and other cultural forces, does not support the continuation of any policies or programs that permit discrimination against either one of the sexes. Also, a form of behavior that is so unforgivably common in many societies—spouse battering, rape, and male bullying of females—might be reduced were we better able to articulate the relationship of such behaviors to culturally based "common wisdom" concerning how men ought to behave toward women. In this respect, as was shown elsewhere in this book as well, the vicious cycle of beliefs in superiority and inferiority, and the use of such beliefs to justify continuing discriminatory practices, might be broken were we to break the stranglehold of outmoded beliefs about the basis of differences between groups.

Intergroup relations is arguably the single most important domain in which cross-cultural psychology has important ideas, theories, and facts to contribute, many of which were covered in Chapter 10. Our primary contribution to efforts to deal with the twentieth-century record of holocaust, genocide, interethnic warfare and terrorism (a history that promises to continue well into the twenty-first century), is a generalization, perhaps our highest order generalization, namely, the notion that culture is the primary shaper and molder of everyone's behavior. In the very beginning of this book, in Chapter 1, we underscored our conviction that differences traditionally attributed to "race," which by definition makes those differences seem biologically determined and hence immutable, are now known to be cultural and hence changeable by policies that attempt to eliminate disadvantages suffered to date by various cultural groups. These are the very groups that we traditionally have thought of as "races," differentially blessed or damned by their nature to be among the haves or among the have-nots. If cross-cultural psychology should chip away at this prevailing misconception of human diversity rooted in "race," our discipline will have made a very significant social contribution.

SUMMARY AND FUTURE DIRECTIONS

We have covered a lot of territory in this book, the main point of which has been that "culture" and all that it implies with respect to human development, thought, and behavior should be central, not peripheral, in psychological theory and research. As noted by Segall, Lonner, and Berry (1998), cross-cultural psychology has become an increasingly important part of modern psychology. Fortunately, over roughly the past thirty years, many books, journals, and scholarly organizations have come to take culture seriously.

Standing out is the three-volume second edition of the *Handbook of Cross-Cultural Psychology* (Berry et al., 1997), which informed much of the present text. The scope of the cross-cultural effort in psychology is also reflected in the dozens of other recent books in the field (e.g., Berry et al., 1992; Gardiner, Mutter, & Kosmitzki, 1997; Matsumoto, 1996; and Smith & Bond, 1993, 1994).

Among several scholarly and professional organizations, within and adjacent to psychology, with an international or cross-cultural focus, the International Association for Cross-Cultural Psychology (IACCP) remains at the center of the enterprise's growth and development. Since its inaugural meeting in Hong Kong in 1972, IACCP has held international congresses every two years and a host of regional congresses in nearly every part of the world. To celebrate its twenty-fifth anniversary, IACCP held its first ever international congress to take place in the United States, in 1998, on the campus of Western Washington University in Bellingham, Washington. Some 350 scholars from over 50 nations attended.

Looking to the Future of Cross-Cultural Psychology

We have tried to show in this book that we need cross-cultural research that is carried out with a profound knowledge of the cultural context, a cross-cultural psychology that spends as much effort on specifying the (independent) cultural variables as it does attending to the (dependent) psychological outcome measures. Such a research program usually requires extensive and long-term fieldwork, and an interdisciplinary approach between anthropologists and psychologists. We have covered in this volume several such large-scale efforts by expatriate psychologists. Such major research efforts needed extensive funding and this is more difficult to secure than it was during some earlier periods. For this reason, as well as others linked to the ethics and politics of cross-cultural research, we anticipate the following trends:

1. There will be less research carried out by itinerant expatriates, and more research carried out by psychologists working in their own societies. The Western psychologists who used to travel afar will spend more time studying cultural subgroups within their own society; massive migration movements and the development of multicultural societies favor this trend. Increasingly, there are psychologists in all parts of the world able to carry out research within their own cultural framework. For some time, psychologists in third world universities have tended to copy the models they had learned during their studies in the West. It takes courage to slough off the leading paradigms in scientific psychology, even if they are obviously inappropriate to a culturally sensitive psychology. In recent years, however, several research programs have developed more appropriate paradigms. A few examples of research by psychologists working in their own lands on problems of local relevance and with concepts and instruments rooted in their own cultures have been included in this book. The future, we hope, will provide many more examples.

2. Thanks in part to the ability to communicate internationally via the Internet, there will be more truly collaborative research efforts between psychologists of different countries. These would not be limited to projects designed, funded, and directed from the West, and therefore dominated by the Western researcher, but research designed and carried out by partners of equal status and power. In the meantime, there will still be Ph.D. students from non-Western countries studying at Western institutions and carrying out their fieldwork in their own society. This form of research can be very valuable, if only the supervisors are at least informed in cross-cultural psychology.

3. As a consequence of the trends outlined above, cross-cultural research is likely to become more applied. On the one hand, funding for so-called pure research is becoming tighter, and on the other hand many researchers, and especially those working within their own societies, are becoming more aware of the importance of contributing to the solutions of major social problems that have local manifestations. Psychology in general, and cross-cultural psychology in particular, have not yet realized their potential in this respect, and are still likely to be ignored by policy makers. This is, we think, due to two reasons: (1) the public image of psychology as a helping profession is linked to clinical psychology or psychoanalysis, or as a technique restricted to testing; (2) the ignorance of most of mainstream psychology of the social and cultural variables that impinge on individual behavior and that would make scientific psychology more relevant to social policy. The cross-cultural approach, as a scientific method, should help to improve the image and the impact of psychology.

These three trends combined should influence the future of cross-cultural psychology in the following ways: There will be a movement away from a mainly theory-testing discipline. Research will tend to focus more on single societies, while still taking sociocultural variables seriously, either by comparing subgroups or through studying individual differences and correlates rather than relying on means across samples. Research will also become more truly interdisciplinary, combining biological, sociological, anthropological, and psychological methods and paradigms.

Cross-cultural psychology has grown into a thriving intellectual enterprise *circa* 2000. This leads us to conclude this introductory text with a paradox: Cross-cultural psychology will be shown to have succeeded when it disappears. For, when the whole field of psychology becomes truly international and genuinely intercultural, in other words, when it becomes truly a science of *human* behavior, cross-cultural psychology will have achieved its aims and become redundant. This introductory textbook has tried to move us a bit closer to that paradoxical achievement.

BIBLIOGRAPHY

Adorno, T., Frenkel-Brunswik, E., Levinson, D., & Sanford, R. N. (1950). *The authoritarian personality.* New York: Harper.

Agarwal, K. S., & Lester, D. (1992). A study of perception of women by Indian and American students. In Y. K. S. Iwawaki & K. Leung (Eds.), *Innovations in cross-cultural psychology* (pp. 123–134). Amsterdam: Swets & Zeitlinger.

Ahmed, M. (1983). Le non-formel et les questions critiques de l'éducation. *Perspectives, 13,* 37–47.

Akinnaso, F. (1981). The consequences of literacy in pragmatic and theoretical perspectives. *Anthropology and Education Quarterly, 12,* 163–200.

Aldwin, C. (1994). *Stress, coping and development.* New York: Guilford.

Altarriba, J. (Ed.). (1993). *Cognition and culture: A cross-cultural approach to cognitive psychology.* Amsterdam: Elsevier Science.

Al-Zahrani, S. S. A., & Kaplowitz, S. A. (1993). Attributional biases in individualistic and collectivistic cultures. *Social Psychology Quarterly, 56,* 223–233.

Amoss, P. T., & Harrell, S. (Eds.). (1981). *Other ways of growing old: Anthropological perpectives.* Stanford: Stanford University Press.

American Anthropology Association (1998). AAA statement on "race." *Anthropology Newsletter, 39,* 3.

Angier, N. (1995). Does testosterone equal aggression? Maybe not. *New York Times,* June 20, 1995, pp. A1–C3.

Archer, D., & Gartner, R. (1967). Violent acts and violent times: A comparative approach to postwar homicide rates. *American Sociological Review, 41,* 937–963.

Archer, D., & Gartner, R. (1984). *Violence and crime in cross-national perspective.* New Haven: Yale University Press.

Ardrey, R. (1966). *The territorial imperative.* New York: Atheneum.

Aronowitz, M. (1992). Adjustment of immigrant children as a function of parental attitudes to change. *International Migration Review, 26,* 86–110.

Aronson, E. (1958). The need for achievement as measured in graphic expression. In J. W. Atkinson (Ed.), *Motives in fantasy, action, and society* (pp. 249–265). Princeton, NJ: Van Nostrand.

Atkinson, J. W. (Ed.). (1958). *Motives in fantasy, action, and society.* Princeton, N.J.: Van Nostrand.

Augé, M. (1986). *Un ethnologue dans le métro.* Paris: Hachette.

Azuma, H. (1994). Two modes of cognitive socialization in Japan and the United States. In P. Greenfield & R. Cocking (Eds.), *Cross-cultural roots of minority child development* (pp. 275–284). Hillsdale, NJ: Lawrence Erlbaum.

Bacon, M. K., Child, I. L., & Barry, H. I. (1963). A cross-cultural study of correlates of crime. *Journal of Abnormal and Social Psychology, 66,* 291–300.

Bain, M. S. (1992). *The Aboriginal-white encounter. Towards better communication.* Darwin: Summer Institute of Linguistics, Australian Aborigines and Islanders Branch.

Baltes, P. B., & Baltes, M. M. (Eds.). (1990). *Successful aging: Perspectives from the behavioral sciences.* Cambridge: Cambridge University Press.

Baltes, P. B., & Reese, H. W. (1984). The lifespan perspective in developmental psychology. In M. H. Bornstein & M. E. Lamb (Eds.), *Developmental psychology: An advanced textbook* (pp. 493–531). Hillsdale, NJ: Erlbaum.

Bandura, A. (1971). *Social learning theory.* New York: General Learning Press.

Bandura, A. (1980). The social learning theory of aggression. In R. A. Falk & S. S. Kim (Eds.), *The war system: An interdisciplinary approach.* Boulder: Westview (originally 1973).

Barnlund, D. C., & Araki, S. (1985). Intercultural encounters: The management of compliments by Japanese and Americans. *Journal of Cross-Cultural Psychology, 16,* 9–26.

Barry, H. III, Bacon, M. K., & Child, I. L. (1957). A cross-cultural survey of some sex differences in socialization. *Journal of Abnormal and Social Psychology, 55,* 327–332.

Barry, H. III, Bacon, M. K., & Child, I. L. (1967). Definitions, ratings and bibliographic sources of child-training practices of 110 cultures. In C. S. Ford (Ed.), *Cross-cultural approaches.* New Haven, CT: HRAF Press.

Barry, H. III, Child, I. L., & Bacon, M. K. (1959). Relation of child training to subsistence economy. *American Anthropologist, 61,* 51–63.

Barry, H. III, Josephson, L., Lauer, E., & Marshall, C. (1976). Traits inculcated in childhood: Cross-cultural codes V. *Ethnology, 15,* 83–114.

Barry H. III, & Paxson, L. M. (1971). Infancy and early childhood: cross-cultural codes. *Ethnology, 10,* 466–508.

Bartlett, F. C. (1932). *Remembering.* Cambridge: Cambridge University Press.

Barton, B., Fairhall, U., & Trinick, T. (1995). Whakatupu reo tatai: History of the development of Maori mathematics vocabulary. In A. Jones, A. Begg, B. Bell, F. Biddulph, M. Carr, J. McChesney, E. McKinley, & J. Young Loveridge (Eds.), *Science and Mathematics Education Papers— 1995* (pp. 144–160). Hamilton, New Zealand: University of Waikato, Centre

for Science, Mathematics and Technology Education Research.

Bassitche, A. (1991). L'inadaptation juvénile dans Abidjan et ses environs: Les jeunes dits caractériels du Centre éducatif de la Zone 4. *Cahiers de Sociologie Economique et Culturelle (16),* 85–130.

Beiser, M. (1994). *Longitudinal study of Vietnamese refugee adaptation.* Toronto: Clarke Institute of Psychiatry.

Beiser, M., Barwick, C., & Berry, J. W. (1988). *Mental health issues affecting immigrants and refugees.* Ottawa: Health and Welfare Canada.

Beiser, M., Johnson, P., & Turner, J. (1993). Unemployment, underemployment and depressive affect among Southeast Asian refugees. *Psychological Medicine, 23,* 731–743.

Bem, S. L. (1974). The measurement of psychological androgeny. *Journal of Consulting and Clinical Psychology, 42,* 155–162.

Benedict, R. (1946). *The chrysanthemum and the sword.* Boston: Houghton Mifflin.

Benton, D. (1992). Hormones and human aggression. In K. Bjorkqvist & P. Niemela (Eds.), *Of mice and women: Aspects of female aggression* (pp. 37–48). San Diego, CA: Academic Press.

Berkowitz, L. (1989). Frustration-aggression hypothesis: Examination and reformulation. *Psycholgical Bulletin, 106,* 59–73.

Berlin, B., & Kay, P. (1969). *Basic color terms: Their universality and evolution.* Berkeley: University of California Press.

Berman, J. J., Murphy-Berman, V., & Singh, P. (1985). Cross-cultural similarities and differences in perceptions of fairness. *Journal of Cross-Cultural Psychology, 16,* 55–67.

Bernard, T. J. (1990). Angry aggression among the "truly disadvantaged." *Criminology, 28,* 73–96.

Bernstein, B. (1961). Social class and linguistic development: A theory of social learning. In A. H. Halsey, J. Floud, & C. A. Anderson (Eds.), *Education, economy and society* (pp. 288–314). New York: Free Press.

Berry, J. W. (1966). Temne and Eskimo perceptual skills. *International Journal of Psychology, 1,* 207–229.

Berry, J. W. (1968). Ecology, perceptual development and the Müller-Lyer illusion. *British Journal of Psychology, 59,* 205–210.

Berry, J. W. (1969). On cross-cultural comparability. *International Journal of Psychology, 4,* 119–128.

Berry, J. W. (1970). Marginality, stress and ethnic identification in an acculturated Aboriginal community. *Journal of Cross-Cultural Psychology, 1,* 239–252.

Berry, J. W. (1971). Ecological and cultural factors in spatial perceptual development. *Canadian Journal of Behavioural Science, 3,* 324–336.

Berry, J. W. (1972). Radical cultural relativism and the concept of intelligence. In L. J. Cronbach & P. J. D. Drenth (Eds.), *Mental tests and cultural adaptation* (pp. 77–88). The Hague: Mouton.

Berry, J. W. (1974). Psychological aspects of cultural pluralism: Unity and identity reconsidered. *Topics in Culture Learning, 2,* 17–22.

Berry, J. W. (1976a). *Human ecology and cognitive style: Comparative studies in cultural and psychological adaptation.* New York: Sage/Halstead/Wiley.

Berry, J. W. (1976b). Sex differences in behaviour and cultural complexity. *Indian Journal of Psychology, 51,* 89–97.

Berry, J. W. (1980). Social and cultural change. In H. C. Triandis & R. Brislin (Eds.), *Handbook of cross-cultural psychology,* Vol. 5, *Social,* (pp. 211–279). Boston: Allyn & Bacon.

Berry, J. W. (1983a). The sociogenesis of social sciences: An analysis of the cultural relativity of social psychology. In B. Bain (Ed.), *The sociogenesis of language and human conduct* (pp. 449–454). New York: Plenum.

Berry, J. W. (1983b). Wundt's Völkerpsychologie and the comparative study of human behavior. In G. Eckhardt & L. Sprung (Eds.), *In Memoriam: W. Wundt* (pp. 92–100). Berlin: Deutscher Verlag der Wissenschaften.

Berry, J. W. (1984a). Multicultural policy in Canada: A social psychological analysis. *Canadian Journal of Behavioral Science, 16,* 353–370.

Berry, J. W. (1984b). Towards a universal psychology of cognitive competence. *International Journal of Psychology, 19,* 335–361.

Berry, J. W. (1986). The comparative study of cognitive abilities: A summary. In S. E. Newstead, S. H. Irvine, & P. L. Dann (Eds.), *Human assessment: Cognition and motivation* (pp. 57–74). Dordrecht, Netherlands: Martinus Nijhoff.

Berry, J. W. (1990a). Psychology of acculturation. In J. Berman (Ed.), *Cross-cultural perspectives: Nebraska symposium on motivation* (pp. 201–234). Lincoln: University of Nebraska Press.

Berry, J. W. (1990b). The role of psychology in ethnic studies. *Canadian Ethnic Studies, 22,* 8–21.

Berry, J. W. (1991). Understanding and managing multiculturalism. *Journal of Psychology and Developing Societies, 3,* 17–49.

Berry, J. W. (1992a). Acculturation and adaptation in a new society. *International Migration, 30,* 69–85.

Berry, J. W. (1992b). *The cross-cultural study of values: The Jack Horner strategy and alternative approaches.* Paper presented at the Antecedents and consequences of value priorities: Cross-cultural perspectives, July 19–24, 1992. 25th International Congress of Psychology, Brussels.

Berry, J. W. (1994). *Aboriginal cultural identity: Its relation to social and psychological health.* Ottawa: Royal Commission on Aboriginal Peoples.

Berry, J. W. (1995). The descendents of a model. *Culture and Psychology, 1*(3), 373–380.

Berry, J. W., & Bennett, J. A. (1991). *Cree syllabic literacy: Cultural context and psychological consequences.* Tilburg: Tilburg University Press.

Berry, J. W., & Dasen, P. R. (Eds.). (1974). *Culture and cognition: Readings in cross-cultural psychology.* London: Methuen.

Berry, J. W., Dasen, P. R., & Saraswathi, T. S. (Eds.). (1997). *Handbook of cross-cultural psychology, second edition.* Vol. 2, *Basic processes and human development.* Boston, MA: Allyn & Bacon.

Berry, J. W., & Kalin, R. (1979). Reciprocity of inter-ethnic attitudes in a multicultural society. *International Journal of Internatinal Relations, 3,* 99–112.

Berry, J. W., & Kalin, R. (1995). Multicultural and ethnic attitudes in Canada. *Canadian Journal of Behavioral Science, 27,* 301–320.

Berry, J. W., & Kim, U. (1988). Acculturation and mental health. In P. R. Dasen, J. W. Berry,

& N. Sartorius (Eds.), *Health and cross-cultural psychology: Towards applications* (pp. 207–238). Newbury Park, CA: Sage.

Berry, J. W., Kim, U., Minde, T., & Mok, D. (1987). Comparative studies of acculturative stress. *International Migration Review, 21,* 491–511.

Berry, J. W., Kim, U., Power, S., Young, M., & Bujaki, M. (1989). Accculturation attitudes in plural societies. *Applied Psychology, 38,* 185–206.

Berry, J. W., & Kostorcik, N. (1990). Psychological adaptation of Malaysian students in Canada. In A. H. Othman & W. R. A. Rahman (Eds), *Psychology and socioeconomic development.* Bangi: Penerbit Universiti Kebangsaan Malaysia.

Berry, J. W., & Lonner W. J. (Eds.). (1975). *Applied cross-cultural psychology.* Amsterdam: Swets & Zeitlinger.

Berry, J. W., Poortinga, Y. H., & Pandey, J. (Eds.). (1997). *Handbook of cross-cultural psychology,* Vol. 1. *Theory and method* (2nd ed.). Boston, MA: Allyn & Bacon.

Berry, J. W., Poortinga, Y. H., Pandey, J., Dasen, P. R., Saraswathi, T. S., Segall, M. H., & Kagitçibasi, C. (Eds.). (1997). *Handbook of cross-cultural psychology* (2nd ed.). Boston, MA: Allyn & Bacon.

Berry, J. W., Poortinga, Y. H., Segall, M. H., & Dasen, P. R. (1992). *Cross-cultural psychology: Research and applications.* New York and Cambridge: Cambridge University Press.

Berry, J. W., Segall, M. H., & Kagitçibasi, C. (Eds.). (1997). *Handbook of cross-cultural psychology.* Vol. 3, *Social behavior and applications.* Boston: Allyn & Bacon.

Berry, J. W., & Sam, D. (1997). Acculturation and adaptation. In J. W. Berry, M. H. Segall, & C. Kagitçibasi (Eds.), *Handbook of cross-cultural psychology,* Vol. 3, *Social behavior and applications.* Boston: Allyn & Bacon.

Berry, J. W., Trimble, J., & Olmedo, E. (1986). The assessment of acculturation. In W. J. Lonner & J. W. Berry (Eds.), *Field methods in cross-cultural research.* Newbury Park, CA: Sage.

Berry, J. W., van de Koppel, J. M. H., Sénéchal, C., Annis, R. C., Bahuchet, S., Cavalli-Sforza, L. L., & Witkin, H. A. (1987). *On the edge of the forest: Cultural adaptation and cognitive development in Central Africa.* Lisse: Swets & Zeitlinger.

Beshai, J. A. (1972). Content analysis of Egyptian stories. *Journal of Social Psychology, 87,* 197–203.

Best, D., & Williams, J. E. (1997). Sex, gender, and culture. In J. W. Berry, M. H. Segall, & C. Kagitçibasi (Eds.), *Handbook of cross-cultural psychology,* Vol. 3, *Social behavior and applications* (pp. 163–212). Boston, MA: Allyn & Bacon.

Biesheuvel, S. (1943). *African intelligence.* Johannesburg: South African Institute of Race Relations.

Biesheuvel, S. (1959). The nature of intelligence: Some practical implications of its measurement. *Psygram, 1*(6), 78–80. (Reprinted in J. W. Berry & P. R. Dasen, Eds., *Culture and Cognition.* London: Methuen, 1974, pp. 221–224.).

Binet, A. (1965). The measurement of visual illusions in children. (Originally published in French, 1895). *Perceptual and Motor Skills, 20,* 917–930.

Biri, E. W., Pendleton, B. F. G., & Garland, T. N. (1987). Correlates of men's attitudes toward women's roles in Libya. *International Journal of Intercultural Relations, 11,* 295–312.

Bisilliat, J., Laya, D., Pierre, E., & Pidoux, C. (1967). La notion de lakkal dans la culture Djerma-Songhai. *Psychopathologie Africaine, 3,* 207–264.

Blondin, D. (1995). *Les deux espèces humaines: Autopsie du racisme ordinaire.* Paris: L'Harmattan.

Bloom, A. H. (1977). Two dimensions of moral reasoning: Social principledness and social humanism in cross-cultural perspective. *Journal of Social Psychology, 101,* 29–44.

Blurton-Jones, N. G., & Konner, M. (1973). Sex differences in behavior of London and Bushman children. In R. P. Michael & J. H. Crook (Eds.), *Comparative ecology and behaviour of primates* (pp. 690–750). London: Academic Press.

Boas, F. (1911). *The mind of primitive man.* New York: Macmillan.

Bochner, S. (1994). Cross-cultural differences in self-concept. *Journal of Cross-Cultural Psychology, 25,* 273–283.

Boesch, C. (1991a). Symbolic communication in wild chimpanzees? *Human Evolution, 6,* 81–90.

Boesch, C. (1991b). Teaching in wild chimpanzees. *Animal Behavior, 41,* 530–532.

Boesch, C. (1995). Innovation in wild chimpanzees (Pan troglodytes). *International Journal of Primatology, 16,* 1–16.

Boesch, C. (1996). Three approaches for assessing chimpanzee culture. In A. Russon, K. Bard, & S. Parcker (Eds.), *Reaching into thought.* (pp. 404–429) Cambridge, England: Cambridge University Press.

Boesch, C., & Boesch, H. (1984). Mental maps in wild chimpanzees: An analysis of hammer transports for nut cracking. *Primates, 25,* 160–170.

Boesch, C., Marchesi, N., Fruth, B., & Joulian, F. (1994). Is nut cracking in wild chimpanzees a cultural behavior? *Journal of Human Evolution, 26,* 325–338.

Boesch, E. E. (1991). *Symbolic action theory for cultural psychology.* Berlin: Springer.

Bogardus, E. S. (1925). Measuring social distance. *Journal of Applied Sociology, 9,* 299–308.

Bolton, R. (1973). Aggression and hypoglycemia among the Qolla: A study in psychobiological anthropology. *Ethnology, 12,* 227–257.

Bolton, R. (1984). The hypoglycemia-aggression hypothesis: Debate versus research. *Current Anthropology, 25,* 1–53.

Bond, M. H. (1986). (Ed.). *The psychology of the Chinese people.* Hong Kong: Oxford University Press.

Bond, M. H., & Hewstone, M. (1988). Social identity theory and the perception of intergroup relations in Hong Kong. *International Journal of Psychology, 12,* 153–170.

Bond, M. H., Wan, K.-C., Leung, K., & Giacalone, R. A. (1985). How are responses to verbal insult related to cultural collectivism and power distance? *Journal of Cross-Cultural Psychology, 16,* 111–127.

Bonnet, M. (1998). *Regards sur les enfants travailleurs.* Lausanne: Editions Page deux, CETIM.

Booth, A. (1993). The influence of testosterone on deviance in adulthood: Assessing and explaining the relationship. *Criminology, 31,* 93–117.

Bornstein, M. H. (1991). *Cultural approaches to parenting.* Hillsdale, NJ: Lawrence Erlbaum.

Boucher, J., Landis, D., & Clark, K. A. (Eds.). (1987). *Ethnic conflict: International perspectives.* Newbury Park, CA: Sage.

Bourhis, R. Y., & Leyens, J.-P. (Eds.). (1994). *Stéréotypes, discrimination et relations intergroupes.* Liege: Mardaga.

Bourhis, R. Y., Moïse, L. C., Perreault, S., & Senécal, S. (1997). Towards an interactive acculturation model: A social psychological approach. *International Journal of Psychology, 32*(6), 369–386.

Bouvy, A.-M., van de Vijver, F., Boski, P., & Schmitz, P. (Eds.). (1994). *Journeys into cross-cultural psychology.* Amsterdam: Swets & Zeitlinger.

Bovet, M. (1974). Cognitive processes among illiterate children and adults. In J. W. Berry & P. R. Dasen (Eds.), *Culture and cognition* (pp. 311–334). London: Methuen.

Boyd, R., & Richerson, J. (1985). *Culture and the evolutionary process.* Chicago: University of Chicago Press.

Bradburn, N. M. (1963). N achievement and father dominance in Turkey. *Journal of Abnormal and Social Psychology, 67,* 464–468.

Bradburn, N. M., & Berlew, D. E. (1961). Need for achievement and English economic growth. *Economic Development and Cultural Change, 10,* 8–20.

Brannon, E. M., & Terrace, H. S. (1998). Ordering of the numerosities 1 to 9 by monkeys. *Science, 282,* 746–749.

Brenner, M. E. (1985). The practice of arithmetic in Liberian schools. *Anthropology and Education Quarterly, 16,* 177–186.

Brewer, M. B., & Campbell, D. T. (1976). *Ethnocentrism and intergroup attitudes.* New York: Wiley.

Bril, B. (1983). Analyse d'un geste de percussion perpendiculaire lancée: La mouture du mil dans un village bambara (Dugurakoro-Mali). *Geste & Image, no. 3,* 97–118.

Bril, B. (1984). Description du geste technique: Quelles méthodes? *Techniques & Culture, 3,* 81–96.

Bril, B., Dasen, P. R., Krewer, B., & Sabatier, C. (Eds.). (n.d.). *Ethnothéories parentales et représentations de l'enfant et de l'adolescent: Une perspective culturelle comparative.* Paris: L'Harmattan, forthcoming.

Bril, B., & Lehalle, H. (1988). *Le développe-ment psychologique est-il universel? Ap-proches interculturelles.* Paris: Presses Universitaires de France.

Bril, B., & Sabatier, C. (1986). The cultural context of motor development: Postural manipulations in the daily life of Bambara babies (Mali). *International Journal of Behavioural Development, 9,* 439–453.

Bril, B., & Zack, M. (1987). *Motricité au quo-tidien: de la naissance à la marche, Paris–Dugurakoro.* Video film, 53 min. Paris: Centre d'Etudes des Processus Cognitifs et du Langage, Ecole des Hautes Etudes en Sciences Sociales.

Bril, B., & Zack, M. (1989). Analyse compara-tive de l' "emploi du temps postural" de la naissance à la marche. In J. Retschitzki, M. Bossel-Lagos, & P. R. Dasen (Eds.), *La recherche interculturelle* (pp. 18–30). Paris: L'Harmattan.

Brislin, R. (1990). (Ed). *Applied cross-cultural psychology.* Newbury Park, CA: Sage.

Brislin, R., Landis, D., & Brandt, M. (1983). Conceptualizations of intercultural be-havior and training. In D. Landis & R. Brislin (Eds.), *Handbook of intercultural training* (Vol. 1, pp. 1–35). New York: Pergamon.

Bronfenbrenner, U. (1961). The mirror image in Soviet-American relations: A social psychological report. *Journal of Social Is-sues, 17,* 45–56.

Bronfenbrenner, U. (1974). Developmental re-search, public policy, and the ecology of childhood. *Child Development, 45,* 1–5.

Bronfenbrenner, U. (1979). *The ecology of hu-man development.* Cambridge, MA: Har-vard University Press.

Bronfenbrenner, U. (1989). Ecological systems theory. *Annals of Child Development, 6,* 185–246.

Bronfenbrenner, U. (1993). The ecology of cog-nitive development: Research models and fugitive findings. In R. Wozniak & K. W. Fischer (Eds.), *Development in context* (pp. 3–44). Hillsdale, NJ: Lawrence Erlbaum.

Brooks, C., & Manza, J. (1994). Do changing values explain the new politics? A critical assessment of the postmaterialist thesis. *Sociological Quarterly, 35,* 541–570.

Broude, G. (1980). Extramarital sex norms in cross-cultural perspective. *Behavior Sci-ence Research, 15,* 181–218

Broude, G. (1983). Male-female relationships in cross-cultural perspective: A study of sex and intimacy. *Behavior Science Research, 18,* 154–181.

Brown, J. S., Collins, A., & Duguid, P. (1989). Situated cognition and the culture of learning. *Educational Researcher, 18,* 32–42.

Bruner, J. S. (1966). On cognitive growth. In J. S. Bruner, R. R. Olver, & P. M. Green-field (Eds.), *Studies in cognitive growth* (pp. 1–67). New York: Wiley.

Bruner, J. S. (1996). *The culture of education.* Cambridge, MA: Harvard University Press.

Brunswik, E. (1956). *Perception and the repre-sentative design of psychological experi-ments.* Berkeley, CA: University of California Press.

Burns, A., & Homel, R. (1986). Sex role satis-faction among Australian children: Some sex, age, and cultural group comparisons. *Psychology of Women Quarterly, 10,* 285–296.

Burton, R. V., & Whiting, J. W. M. (1961). The absent father and cross-sex identity. *Merrill-Palmer Quarterly, 7,* 85–95.

Cador, L. (1982). *Etudiant ou apprenti.* Paris: Presses Universitaires de France.

Calhoun, Jr., G., & Sethi, R. (1987). The self-esteem of pupils from India, the United States, and the Philippines. *Journal of Psychology, 121,* 199–202.

Cameron, J., & Lalonde, R. (1994). Self, eth-nicity and social group memberships in two generations of Italian Canadians. *Per-sonality and Social Psychology Bulletin, 20,* 514–520.

Camilleri, C. (1993). Les conditions structurel-les de l'interculturel. *Revue Française de Pédagogie, 103,* 43–50.

Camilleri, C., & Malewska-Peyre, H. (1997). Socialization and identity strategies. In J. W. Berry, P. R. Dasen, & T. S. Saras-wathi (Eds.), *Handbook of cross-cultural psychology,* Vol. 2, *Basic processes and human development* (pp. 41–68). Boston, MA: Allyn & Bacon.

Campbell, D. T. (1961). The mutual method-ological relevance of anthropology and psychology. In F. L. K. Hsu (Ed.), *Psychological anthropology* (pp. 333–352). Homewood, IL: Dorsey Press.

Campbell, D. T. (1964). Distinguishing differences in perception from failures of communication in cross-cultural studies. In F. S. C. Northrup & H. Livingston (Eds.), *Cross-cultural understanding: Epistemology in anthropology* (pp. 308–336). New York: Harper & Row.

Campbell, D. T. (1965a). Ethnocentric and other altruistic motives. In D. Levine (Ed.), *Nebraska symposium on motivation, 1965* (pp. 283–311). Lincoln: University of Nebraska Press.

Campbell, D. T. (1965b). Variation and selective retention in sociocultural evolution. In H. R. Barringer, G. I. Blanksten, & R. W. Mack (Eds.), *Social change in developing areas: A reinterpretation of evolutionary theory* (pp. 19–49). Cambridge, MA: Schenkmen.

Campbell, D. T. (1975). On the conflicts between biological and social evolution and between psychology and moral tradition. *American Psychologist, 30,* 1103–1126.

Campbell, D. T., & Naroll, R. (1972). The mutual methodological relevance of anthropology and psychology. In F. L. K. Hsu (Ed.), *Psychological anthropology* (rev. ed., pp. 435–463). Cambridge, MA: Schenkman.

Cann, R. L., Stoneking, M., & Wilson, A. C. (1987). Mitochondrial DNA and human evolution. *Nature, 325,* 31–36.

Capozza, D., & Volpato, C. (1990). Categorical differentiation and intergroup relationships. *British Journal of Social Psychology, 29,* 93–95.

Carballo, M. (1994). *Scientific consultation on the social and health impact of migration: Priorities for research.* Geneva: International Organization for Migration.

Carey, S. (1998). Knowledge of number: Its evolution and ontology. *Science, 282,* 641–642.

Carlson, M., & Miller, N. (1988). Bad experiences and aggression. *Social Science Research, 72,* 155–157.

Carraher, T. N., Carraher, D. W., & Schliemann, A. D. (1985). Mathematics in the streets and in schools. *British Journal of Developmental Psychology, 3,* 21–29.

Carraher, T. N., Carraher, D. W., & Schliemann, A. D. (1987). Written and oral mathematics. *Journal of Research in Mathematics Education, 18,* 83–97.

Casati, I., & Lézine, I. (1968). *Les étapes de l'intelligence sensori-motrice. Manuel.* Paris: Centre de Psychologie Appliquée.

Case, R. (1985). *Intellectual development: Birth to adulthood.* New York: Academic Press.

Cauthen, N. R., Robinson, I. E., & Krauss, H. H. (1971). Stereotypes: A review of the literature 1926–1968. *Journal of Social Psychology, 84,* 103–125.

Cavalli-Sforza, L. L. (1996). *Gènes, peuples et langues.* Paris: O. Jacob.

Cavalli-Sforza, L. L., & Bodmer, W. F. (1971). *The genetics of human populations.* New York: Freeman.

Cavalli-Sforza, L., Menozzi, & Piazza, A. (1994). *History and geography of human genes.* Princeton: Princeton University Press.

Chamoux, M. N. (1981). Les savoir-faire techniques et leur appropriation: Le cas des Nahuas du Mexique. *L'Homme, 21,* 71–94.

Chamoux, M. N. (1983). La division des savoir-faire textiles entre indiens et métis dans la Sierra de Puebla (Mexique). *Techniques & Culture, no 2,* 99–124.

Chamoux, M. N. (1986). Apprendre autrement: Aspects des pédagogies dites informelles chez les Indiens du Mexique. In P. Rossel (Ed.), *Demain l'artisanat?* (pp. 211–335). Paris: Presses Universitaires de France.

Chia, R. C., Moore, J. L., Lam, K. N., Chuang, C. J., & Cheng, B. S. (1994). Cultural differences in gender role attitudes between Chinese and American students. *Sex Roles, 31,* 23–30.

Child, I. L. (1954). Socialization. In G. Lindzey (Ed.), *Handbook of social psychology,* Vol. 2 (pp. 655–692). Cambridge, MA: Addison-Wesley.

Child, I., Storm, T., & Veroff, J. (1958). Achievement themes in folk tales related to socialization practices. In J. W. Atkinson (Ed.), *Motives in fantasy, action, and society* (pp. 479–492). Princeton, NJ: Van Nostrand.

Childs, C. P., & Greenfield, P. M. (1980). Informal modes of learning and teaching: The case of Zinacanteco weaving. In N. Warren (Ed.), *Studies in cross-cultural psychology,* vol. 2 (pp. 269–316). London: Academic Press.

Chinese Cultural Connection (1987). Chinese values and the search for culture-free dimensions of culture. *Journal of Cross-Cultural Psychology, 18,* 143–164.

Church, A. (1982). Sojourner adjustment. *Psychological Bulletin, 91,* 540–572.

Ciborowski, T. (1980). The role of context, skill and transfer in cross-cultural experimentation. In H. C. Triandis & J. W. Berry (Eds.), *Handbook of cross-cultural psychology,* Vol. 2, *Methodology* (pp. 279–296). Boston: Allyn & Bacon.

Clanet, R. (1990). *L'interculturel: Introduction aux approches interculturelles en éducation et en sciences.* Toulouse: Presses universitaires du Mirail.

Clément, R., & Noels, K. A. (1994). Langage et communication intergroupe. In R. Y. Bourhis & J.-P. Leyens (Eds.) *Stéréotypes, discrimination et relations intergroupes* (pp. 233–260). Liège: Mardaga.

Clément, R. (1984). Aspects socio-psychologiques de la communication interethnique et de l'identité sociale. *Recherches Sociologiques, 15,* 293–312.

Cohen-Emerique, M. (1991). Le modèle individualiste du sujet: Écran à la compréhension des personnes issues de sociétés non-occidentales. In M. Lavallée, F. Ouellet, & F. Larose (Eds.), *Identité, culture et changement social* (pp. 248–264). Paris: L'Harmattan.

Cole, M. (1978). Literacy without schooling: Testing for intellectual effects. *Harvard Educational Review, 48,* 448–460.

Cole, M. (1996). *Cultural psychology: A once and future discipline.* Cambridge, MA: Harvard University Press.

Cole, M., & Bruner, J. S. (1971). Cultural differences and inferences about psychological processes. *American Psychologist, 26,* 867–876. (Reprinted in J. W. Berry & P. R. Dasen, Eds., *Culture and Cognition,* pp. 231–246. London: Methuen, 1974.)

Cole, M., & Cole, S. R. (1996). *The development of children* (3rd ed.). New York: W. Freeman (Scientific American Books).

Cole, M., Gay, J., Glick, J. A., & Sharp, D. W. (1971). *The cultural context of learning and thinking: An exploration in experimental anthropology.* New York: Basic Books.

Cole, M., & Scribner, S. (1974). *Culture and thought: A psychological introduction.* New York: John Wiley.

Cole, M., & Scribner, S. (1977). Developmental theories applied to cross-cultural cognitive research. *Annals of the New York Academy of Sciences, 285,* 366–373.

Cole, M., Sharp, D. W., & Lave, C. (1976). The cognitive consequences of education: Some empirical evidence and theoretical misgivings. *Urban Review, 9,* 218–233.

Condon, J. C. (1984). *With respect to the Japanese.* Yarmouth, ME: Intercultural Press.

Conroy, M., Hess, R. D., Azuma, H., & Kashiwagi, K. (1980). Maternal strategies for regulating children's behavior: Japanese and American families. *Journal of Cross-Cultural Psychology, 11,* 153–172.

Constantino, J. N. (1993). Testosterone and aggression in children. *Journal of the American Academy of Child and Adolescent Psychiatry, 32,* 1217–122.

Corneille, O. (1994). Le contact comme mode de résolution du conflit intergroupes: Une hypothèse toujours très vivante. *Cahiers Internationaux de Psychologie Sociale, 23,* 40–60.

Côté, J. E. (1994). *Adolescent storm and stress. An evaluation of the Mead/Freeman controversy.* Hillside, NJ: Lawrence Erlbaum.

Coy, M. W. (Ed.). (1989). *Apprenticeship: From theory to method and back again.* Albany, NY: SUNY Press.

Cumming, P., Lee, E., & Oreopoulos, D. (1989). *Access to trades and professions.* Toronto: Ontario Ministry of Citizenship.

Daly, M., & Wilson, M. (1988). *Homicide.* New York: Aldine de Gruyter.

Danziger, K. (1983). Origins and basic principles of Wundt's *Völkerpsychologie. British Journal of Social Psychology, 22,* 303–313.

Darwin, C. (1859). *On the origins of species by means of natural selection, or the preservation of favoured races in the struggle for life.* London: John Murray.

Dasen, P. R. (1972). Cross-cultural Piagetian research: A Summary. *Journal of Cross-Cultural Psychology, 7,* 75–85.

Dasen, P. R. (1974). The influence of ecology, culture and European contact on cognitive development in Australian Aborigines. In J. W. Berry & P. R. Dasen (Eds.), *Culture and Cognition* (pp. 381–408). London: Methuen.

Dasen, P. R. (1975). Concrete operational development in three cultures. *Journal of Cross-Cultural Psychology, 6,* 156–172.

Dasen, P. R. (1980). Différences individuelles et différences culturelles. *Bulletin de Psychologie, 33,* 675–683.

Dasen, P. R. (1982). Cross-cultural data on operational development: Asymptotic development curves. In T. G. Bever (Ed.), *Dips in learning* (pp. 221–232). New York: Lawrence Erlbaum.

Dasen, P. R. (1983a). Apports de la psychologie à la compréhension interethnique. In G. Baer & P. Centlivres (Eds.), *L'ethnologie dans le dialogue interdisciplinaire* (pp. 47–66). Fribourg: Editions universitaires.

Dasen, P. R. (1983b). Aspects fonctionnels du développement opératoire: Les recherches intercuturelles. *Archives de Psychologie, 51,* 57–60.

Dasen, P. R. (1984). The cross-cultural study of intelligence: Piaget and the Baoulé. In P. S. Fry (Ed.), *Changing conceptions of intelligence and intellectual functioning: Current theory and research* (pp. 107–134). Amsterdam: North-Holland (*International Journal of Psychology, 19,* 407–434).

Dasen, P. R. (1988). Développement psychologique et activités quotidiennes chez des enfants africains. *Enfance, 41,* 3–24.

Dasen, P. R. (1993). Schlusswort. Les sciences cognitives: Do they shake hands in the middle? In J. Wassmann & P. R. Dasen (Eds.), *Savoirs quotidiens. Les sciences cognitives dans le dialogue interdisciplinaire* (pp. 331–349). Fribourg: Presses de l'Université de Fribourg.

Dasen, P. R. (1999). Rapid social change and the turmoil of adolescence: A cross-cultural perspective. *World Psychology, 5,* in press.

Dasen, P. R. (n.d.). Integration, assimilation et stress acculturatif. In P. R. Dasen, C. Perregaux, & Y. Leanza (Eds.), *L'intégration des migrants en Suisse,* forthcoming.

Dasen, P. R., Berry, J. W., Sartorius, N. (1988). (Eds). *Health and cross-cultural psychology: Towards applications.* Newbury Park, CA: Sage.

Dasen, P. R., Berry, J. W., & Witkin, H. A. (1979). The use of developmental theories cross-culturally. In L. Eckensberger, Y. Poortinga, & W. Lonner (Eds.), *Cross-cultural contributions to psychology* (pp. 69–82). Amsterdam: Swets & Zeitlinger.

Dasen, P. R., & Bossel-Lagos, M. (1989). L'étude interculturelle des savoirs quotidiens: revue de la littérature. In J. Retschitzki, M. Bossel-Lagos, & P. R. Dasen (Eds.), *La recherche interculturelle,* vol. 2 (pp. 98–114). Paris: L'Harmattan.

Dasen, P. R., Dembélé, B., Ettien, K., Kabran, K., Kamagaté, D., Koffi, D. A., & N'guessan, A. (1985). N'glouèlê, l'intelligence chez les Baoulé. *Archives de Psychologie, 53,* 293–324.

Dasen, P. R., & Heron, A. (1981). Cross-cultural tests of Piaget's theory. In H. C. Triandis & A. Heron (Eds.), *Handbook of cross-cultural psychology,* Vol. 4, *Developmental psychology* (pp. 295–342). Boston, MA: Allyn & Bacon.

Dasen, P. R., Inhelder, B., Lavallée, M., & Retschitzki, J. (1978). *Naissance de l'intelligence chez l'enfant Baoulé de Côte d'Ivoire.* Berne: Hans Huber.

Dasen, P. R., & Jahoda, G. (1986). Cross-cultural human development. Special issue. *International Journal of Behavioural Development, 9.*

Dasen, P. R., Lavallée, M., & Retschitzki, J. (1979). Training conservation of quantity (liquids) in West African (Baoulé) children. *International Journal of Psychology, 14,* 57–68.

Dasen, P. R., Ngini, L., & Lavallée, M. (1979). Cross-cultural training studies of concrete operations. In L. Eckensberger, Y. Poortinga, & W. Lonner (Eds.), *Cross-cultural contributions to psychology* (pp. 94–104). Amsterdam: Swets & Zeitlinger.

Dasen, P. R. & Ogay, T. (n.d.). Les stratégies identitaires, une théorie méritant un examen (inter)culturel comparatif. In M.-A. Hily, J. Costa-Lascoux, & G. Vermès (Eds.), *Hommage à C. Camilleri.* Paris: L'Harmattan.

Dasen, P. R., & de Ribaupierre, A. (1987). Neo-Piagetian theories: Cross-cultural and differential perspectives. *International Journal of Psychology, 22,* 793–832.

Dasen, P. R., & Super, C. M. (1988). The usefulness of a cross-cultural approach in studies of malnutrition and psychological development. In P. R. Dasen, J. W. Berry, & N. Sartorius (Eds.), *Health and cross-cultural psychology: Towards applications* (pp. 112–138). Newbury Park, CA: Sage.

Davies, E. (1969). This is the way Crete went: Not with a bang but a simper. *Psychology Today, 3,* 43–47.

Dawkins R. (1982). *The extended phenotype: The gene as the unit of selection.* Oxford: Freeman.

de Certeau, M. (1980). *L'invention du quotidien. Tome 1. Arts de faire.* Paris: Union Générale d' Editions (Collection 10/18).

de Lacey, P. R., & Poole, M. E. (Eds.). (1979). *Mosaic or melting pot: Cultural evolution in Australia.* Sydney: Harcourt Brace Jovanovich.

Delafosse, R. J. C., Fourasté, R. F., & Gbobouo, R. (1993). Entre hier et demain: Protocole d'étude des difficultés d'identité dans une population de jeunes ivoiriens. In F. Tanon & G. Vermes (Eds.), *L'individu et ses cultures* (pp. 156–164). Paris: L'Harmattan.

De la Rocha, O. (1985). The reorganization of arithmetic practice in the kitchen. *Anthropology and Education Quarterly, 16,* 193–198.

Delbos, G., & Jorion, P. (1984). *La transmission des savoirs.* Paris: Maison des Sciences de l'Homme.

Deregowski, J. B. (1980). *Illusions, patterns and pictures: A cross-cultural perspective.* London: Academic Press.

Deregowski, J. B. (1989). Real space and represented space: Cross-cultural perspectives. *Behavioral and Brain Sciences, 12,* 51–119.

Désalmand, P. (1983). *Histoire de l'éducation en Côte d'Ivoire,* Vol. 1. Abidjan, Côte d'Ivoire: CEDA (Paris: Hatier/Harmattan).

Detterman, D. K. (1994). The case for the prosecution: Transfer as an epiphenomenon. In D. K. Detterman & R. J. Sternberg (Eds.), *Transfer on trial: Intelligence, cognition, and instruction* (pp. 1–24). Norwood, NJ: Ablex.

Diaz-Guerrero, R. (1979). The development of coping style. *Human Development, 22,* 320–331.

Diaz-Loving, R., Diaz-Guerrero, R., Helmreich, R. L., & Spence, J. T. (1981). Cross-cultural comparison and psychometric analysis of masculine (instrumental) and feminine (expressive) traits. In Spanish. *Revista Associación Latinamericana Psicological Sociadad, 1,* 3–37.

Doise, W., & Mugny, G. (1981). *Le développement social de l'intelligence.* Paris: Inter-Editions. English Translation: (1984). *The social development of the intellect.* New York: Pergamon.

Doise, W., Mugny, G., & Perret-Clermont, A. N. (1975). Social interaction and the development of cognitive operations. *European Journal of Social Psychology, 5,* 367–383.

Doise, W., & Palmonari, A. (1984). *Social interaction in individual development.* Cambridge: Cambridge University Press.

Dollard, J., Doob, L., Miller, N., Mowrer, O., & Sears, R. (1939). *Frustration and aggression.* New Haven: Yale University Press.

Doob, L. W. (1962). From tribalism to nationalism in Africa. *Journal of International Affairs, 16,* 144–155.

Doob, L. W. (1981). *The pursuit of peace.* Westport, CT: Greenwood Press.

Dougherty, J. W. D. (Ed.). (1985). *Directions in cognitive anthropology.* Urbana, IL: University of Chicago Press.

Draper, P. (1976). Social and economic constraints on child life among the !Kung. In R. B. Lee & I. DeVore (Eds.), *Kalahari hunter-gatherers: Studies of the !Kung San and their neighbors* (pp. 199–217). Cambridge, MA: Harvard University Press.

Droz, R., & Rahmy, M. (1972). *Lire Piaget.* Bruxelles: Dessart.

Du Bois, C. (1944). *The people of Alor.* Minneapolis: University of Minnesota Press.

Dumont, L. (1983). *Essais sur l'individualisme: Une perspective anthropologique sur l'idéologie moderne.* Paris: Editions du Seuil.

Eagley, A. H. (1987). *Sex differences in social behavior: A social-role interpretation.* Hillsdale, NJ: Erlbaum.

Eagley, A. H. (1995). The science and politics of women and men. *American Psychologist, 50,* 145–158.

Eckhardt, W. (1973). Anthropological correlates of primitive militarism. *Peace Research, 5,* 5–10.

Edgerton, R. B., & Langness, L. L. (1974). *Methods and styles in the study of culture.* San Francisco: Chandler & Sharp.

Ekman, P. (1973). *Darwin and facial expression.* New York: Academic Press.

Eldering, L. & Kloprogge, J. (Eds.). (1989). *Different cultures, same school: Ethnic minority children in Europe.* Amsterdam: Swets & Zeitlinger.

Elkin, A. P. (1943). *The Australian Aborigines: How to understand them.* Sydney: Angus & Robertson.

Ellsworth, P. C., & Gross, S. R. (1994). Hardening of the attitudes: Americans' views on the death penalty. *Journal of Social Issues, 50,* 19–52.

Ember, C. R. (1973). Feminine task assignments and the social behavior of boys. *Ethos, 1,* 424–439.

Ember, M. (1974). Warfare, sex ratio, and polygyny. *Ethnology, 13,* 194–206.

Ember, C. R. (1981). A cross-cultural perspective on sex differences. In R. H. Munroe, R. L. Munroe, & B. B. Whiting (Eds.), *Handbook of cross-cultural human development* (pp. 531–580). New York: Garland.

Ember, C. R., & Ember, M. (1985). *Anthropology* (4th ed.). Englewood Cliffs, NJ: Prentice-Hall.

Ember, C. R., & Ember, M. (1992). Resource unpredictability, mistrust, and war: A cross-cultural study. *Journal of Conflict Resolution, 36,* 242–262.

Ember, C. R., & Ember, M. (1993). Issues in cross-cultural studies of interpersonal violence. *Violence and victims, 8,* 217–233.

Ember, C. R., & Ember, M. (1994b). War, socialization, and interpersonal violence: A cross-cultural study. *Journal of Conflict Resolution, 38,* 620–646.

Ember, C. R., & Ember, M. (1996). *Cultural anthropology* (8th ed.). Upper Saddle River, NJ: Prentice-Hall.

Ember, M., & Ember, C. R. (1994a). Prescriptions for peace: Policy implications of cross-cultural research on war and interpersonal violence. *Cross-Cultural Research, 28,* 343–350.

Endler, N., & Parker, J. (1990). Multidimensional assessment of coping. *Journal of Personality and Social Psychology, 58,* 844–854.

Erasmus, D. (1975/1514). Letter to Antoon van Bergen, Abbot of St. Bertin, Dated London, 14 March 1514. In R. A. Mynors & D. F. S. Thomson (Trans.) & W. K. Fergusen (Ed.), *The correspondence of Erasmus, Letters 142 to 297 (No. 288, p. 422).* Toronto: University of Toronto Press.

Erchak, G. M. (1994). Family violence. In C. R. Ember & M. Ember (Eds.), *Research frontiers in anthropology.* (pp. 37–51) Englewood Cliffs, NJ: Prentice-Hall.

Erchak, G. M., & Rosenfeld, R. (1994). Societal isolation, violent norms, and gender relations: A re-examination and extension of Levinson's model of wife beating. *Cross-Cultural Research, 28,* 11–133.

Erny, P. (1968). *L'enfant dans la pensée traditionnelle de l'Afrique Noire.* Paris: Le livre africain.

Erny, P. (1972a). *L'enfant et son milieu en Afrique noire.* Paris: Payot.

Erny, P. (1972b). *Les premiers pas dans la vie de l'enfant d'Afrique noire.* Paris: L'Ecole.

Erny, P. (1977). *L'enseignement dans les pays pauvres: Modèles et propositions.* Paris: L'Harmattan.

Erny, P. (1981). *The child and his environment in black Africa: An essay on traditional education.* (Translation of: *L'enfant et son milieu en Afrique noire;* original published 1972). New York: Oxford University Press.

Eron, L. D., & Heusmann, L. R. (1984). The control of aggressive behavior by changes in attitudes, values, and the conditions of learning. In R. J. Blanchard & D. C. Blanchard (Eds.), *Advances in the study of aggression* (Vol. 1, pp. 139–171). Orlando: Academic Press.

Esman, A. H. (1990). *Adolescence and culture.* New York: Columbia University Press.

Evans, J. L. (1975). Learning to classify by color and by class: A study of concept-discovery within Colombia, South America. *Journal of Social Psychology, 97,* 3–14.

Evans, J. L., & Segall, M. H. (1969). Learning to classify by color and by function: A study of concept-discovry by Ganda children. *Journal of Social Psychology, 77,* 35–55.

Evans-Pritchard, E. E. (1971). Introduction. In Lévy-Bruhl, L., *The soul of the primitive.* Chicago: Regnery.

Eysenck, H. J. (1971). *The IQ argument: Race, intelligence and education.* New York: Library Press.

Eysenck, H. J. (1988). The biological basis of intelligence. In S. H. Irvine & J. W. Berry (Eds.), *Human abilities in cultural context* (pp. 87–104). Cambridge: Cambridge University Press.

Feather, N. T. (1986). Cross-cultural studies with the Rokeach Value Survey: The Flinders program of research on values. *Australian Journal of Psychology, 38,* 269–283.

Feldman, R. E. (1971). Honesty toward compatriot and foreigner: Field experiments in Paris, Athens, and Boston. In W. W. Lambert & R. Weisbrod (Eds.), *Comparative perspectives on social psychology* (pp. 321–335). Boston, MA: Little, Brown.

Fernando, S. (1993). Racism and xenophobia. *Innovation in Social Sciences Research* (Special Issue on Migration and Health), *6,* 9–19.

Feuerstein, R. (1980). *Instrumental enrichment. An intervention program for cognitive modifiability.* Baltimore, MD: University Park Press.

Field, T. M., Sostek, A. M., Vietze, P., & Leiderman, P. H. (1981). *Culture and early interactions.* Hillside, NJ: Lawrence Erlbaum.

Finison, L. J. (1976). The application of McClelland's national development model to recent data. *Journal of Social Psychology, 98,* 55–59.

Fischer, K. W. (1980). A theory of cognitive development: The control and construction of hierarchies of skills. *Psychological Review, 87,* 477–531

Fischer, K. W., Knight, C. C., & Van Parys, M. (1993). Analyzing diversity in developmental pathways: Methods and concepts. In R. Case & W. Edelstein (Eds.), *The new structuralism in cognitive development: Theory and research on individual pathways* (pp. 33–56). Basel: Karger.

Fish, J. (1995). Mixed blood. *Psychology Today,* November/December, 1995, 52–58.

Fish, J. (1997). How psychologists think about "race." *General Anthropology, 4,* 1–4.

Fish, J. (1998). Psychologists and "race." *Anthropology Newsletter, 39,* 2.

Fleming, J. (1975). Fear of success imagery in urban Kenya. *Kenya Education Review, 2,* 121–129.

Fournier, M., Schurmans, M.-N., & Dasen, P. R. (1995). L'influence du contexte linguistique sur les representations sociales. *Papers on Social Représentations: Textes sur les Représentations Sociales, 3,* 152–165. (A paraître aussi dans: B. Bril, P. R. Dasen, B. Krewer, & C. Sabatier (Eds.). (n.d.). *Ethnothéories parentales et représentations de l'enfant et de l'adolescent: Une perspective culturelle comparative.* Paris: L'Harmattan.)

Fraczek, A. (1985). Moral approval of aggressive acts: A Polish-Finnish comparative study. *Journal of Cross-Cultural Psychology, 16,* 41–54.

Fraser, S. (Ed.). (1995). *The Bell curve wars: Race, intelligence, and the future of America.* New York: Basic Books.

Freeman, D. (1983). *Margaret Mead and Samoa: The making and unmaking of an anthropological myth.* Cambridge, MA: Harvard University Press.

Friedenberg, E. Z. (1973). The vanishing adolescent: Self-definition and conflict. In H. Silverstein (Ed.), *The sociology of youth: Evolution and revolution* (pp. 109–118). New York: Macmillan.

Frijda, N., & Jahoda, G. (1966). On the scope and methods of cross-cultural research. *International Journal of Psychology, 1,* 110–127.

Fuchs, I., Eisenberg, N., Herz-Lazarowitz, R., & Shrabany, R. (1986). Kibbutz, Israeli city and American children's moral reasoning about prosocial moral conflicts. *Merrill-Palmer Quarterly, 32,* 37–50.

Furnham, A., & Alibhai, N. (1985). The friendship networks of foreign students. *International Journal of Psychology, 9,* 365–375.

Furnham, A., & Bochner, S. (1986). *Culture shock: Psychological reactions to unfamiliar environments.* London: Methuen.

Furnham, A., & Karani, R. (1985). A cross-cultural study of attitudes to women, just world, and locus of control beliefs. *Psychologia, 28,* 11–20.

Furnham, A., & Shiekh, S. (1993). Gender, generation, and social support correlates of mental health in Asian immigrants. *International Journal of Social Psychiatry, 39,* 22–33.

Gabrenya, W. K., Latané, B., & Wang, Y. E. (1983). Social loafing in cross-cultural perspective: Chinese on Taiwan. *Journal of Cross-Cultural Psychology, 14,* 368–384.

Gabrenya, W. K., & Wang, Y. E. (1983, March). *Cultural differences in self schemata.* Paper presented at the Southeast Psychological Association, Atlanta, GA.

Gabrenya, W. K., Wang, Y. E., & Latané, B. (1985). Social loafing on an optimizing task: Cross-cultural differences among Chinese and Americans. *Journal of Cross-Cultural Psychology, 16,* 223–242.

Galland, O. (1991). *Sociologie de la jeunesse. L'entrée dans la vie.* Paris: Armand Colin.

Gallimore, R. (1981). Affiliation, social context, industriousness, and achievement. In R. H. Munroe, R. L. Munroe, & B. B. Whiting (Eds.), *Handbook of cross-cultural human development* (pp. 689–716). New York: Garland.

Gardiner, H., Mutter, J., & Kosmitzki, C. (1997). *Lives across cultures: Cross-cultural human development.* Boston: Allyn & Bacon.

Gardner, H. (1983). *Frames of mind: The theory of multiple intelligences.* New York: Basic Books.

Gardner, H. (1985). *The mind's new science: A history of the cognitive revolution.* New York: Basic Books.

Gardner, H. (1995). Cracking open the IQ box. In S. Fraser (Ed.), *The Bell curve wars: Race, intelligence, and the future of America* (pp. 23–35). New York: Basic Books.

Gay, J., & Cole, M. (1967). *The new mathematics in an old culture.* New York: Holt, Rinehart & Winston.

Geen, R. G. (1983). Aggression and television violence. In R. G. Geen & E. I. Donnerstein (Eds.), *Aggression: Theoretical and empirical reviews.* Vol. 2, *Issues in research* (pp. 103–125). New York: Academic Press.

Geertz, C. (1973). *The interpretation of cultures.* New York: Basic Books.

Gelfand, M. J., Triandis, H. C., & Chan, D. K.-S. (1996). Individualism versus collectivism or versus authoritarianism? *European Journal of Social Psychology, 26,* 397–410.

Gerdes, P. (1988a). On culture, geometical thinking and mathematics education. *Educational Studies in Mathematics, 19,* 137–162.

Gerdes, P. (1988b). On possible uses of traditional Angolan sand drawings in the mathematics classroom. *Educational Studies in Mathematics, 19,* 3–22.

Ghosh, E., & Huq, M. (1985). A study of social identity in two ethnic groups in India and Bangladesh. *Journal of Multilingual and Multicultural Development, 6,* 239–251.

Ghuman, P. A. S. (1991). Best or worst of two worlds? A study of Asian adolescents. *Educational Review, 33,* 121–132.

Giard, L. (1980). Faire la cuisine. In L. Giard & P. Mayol (Eds.), *L'invention du quotidien,* Tome 2, *Habiter, cuisiner.* Paris: Union Générale d'Editions (Collection 10/18).

Gibbons, J. L., Stiles, D. A., & Shkodriani, G. M. (1991). Adolescents' attitudes toward family and gender roles: An international comparison. *Sex Roles, 25,* 625–643.

Giles, H. (Ed.). (1977). *Language, ethnicity and intergroup relations.* London: Academic Press.

Giles, H., & Johnson, P. (1987). Ethnolinguistic identity theory: A social-psychological approach to language maintenance. *International Journal of the Sociology of Language, 68,* 69–99.

Giles, H., & Robinson, P. W. (1990). *Handbook of language and social psychology.* Chichester, England: Wiley.

Giliomee, H., & Gagiano, J. (1990). *The elusive search for peace.* Capetown: Oxford University Press.

Gill, R., & Keats, D. (1980). Elements of intellectual competence: Judgments by Australian and Malay university students. *Journal of Cross-Cultural Psychology, 11,* 233–243.

Gillet, B. (1976). Etudes comparatives sur l'influence de la scolarité. In M. Reuchlin (Ed.), *Cultures et conduites* (pp. 313–332). Paris: Presses Universitaires de France.

Gilligan, C. (1982). *In a different voice: Psychological theory and women's development.* Cambridge, MA: Harvard University Press.

Ginsburg, H. P. (Ed.). (1982). *The development of mathematical thinking.* New York: Academic Press.

Ginsburg, H. P., & Opper, S. (1969). *Piaget's theory of intellectual development: An introduction.* Englewood Cliffs, NJ: Prentice-Hall.

Ginsburg, H. P., Posner, J. K., & Russell, R. L. (1981). The development of mental addition as a function of schooling and culture. *Journal of Cross-Cultural Psychology, 12,* 163–178.

Ginsburg, H. P., & Russell, R. L. (1981). Social class and racial influences on early mathematical thinking. *Monographs of the Society for Research in Child Development, 46.*

Gladwin, T. (1970). *East is a Big Bird: Navigation and logic on Puluwat Atoll.* Cambridge, MA: Harvard University Press.

Glueck, S., & Glueck, E. (1950). *Unraveling juvenile delinquency.* New York: Commonwealth Fund.

Goldstein, A. P. (1983). U.S.: Causes, controls and alternatives to aggression. In A. P. Goldstein & M. H. Segall (Eds.), *Aggression in global perspective* (pp. 435–474). Elmsford, NY: Pergamon.

Goldstein, A. P., & Segall, M. H. (Eds.). (1983). *Aggression in global perspective.* Elmsford, NY: Pergamon.

Goldstein, S. B., & Ibaraki, T. (1983). Japan: Aggression and aggression control in Japanese society. In A. P. Goldstein & M. H. Segall (Eds.), *Aggression in global perspective* (pp. 313–324). Elmsford, NY: Pergamon.

Goodall-van Lawick, J. (1971). *In the shadow of man.* Boston: Houghton Mifflin.

Goodnow, J. J. (1981a). Everyday ideas about cognitive development. In J. P. Forgas (Ed.), *Social cognition: Perspectives on everyday understanding* (pp. 85–112). London: Academic Press.

Goodnow, J. J. (1981b). Parents' ideas about parenting and development: A review of issues and recent work. In M. Lamb, A. Brown, & B. Rogoff (Eds.), *Advances in developmental psychology* (pp. 193–242). Hillsdale, NJ: Lawrence Erlbaum.

Goodnow, J. J. (1985). *Change and variation in ideas about childhood and parenting.* Hillsdale, NJ: Erlbaum.

Goody, J. (1968). *Literacy in traditional societies.* Cambridge, England: Cambridge University Press.

Goody, J. (1977). *The domestication of the savage mind.* Cambridge, England: Cambridge University Press.

Goody, J. (1980). Thought and writing. In E. Gellner (Eds.), *Soviet and western anthropology* (pp. 119–133). New York: Columbia University Press.

Goody, J., Cole, M., & Scribner, S. (1977). Writing and formal operations. *Africa, 47,* 289–304.

Goody, J., & Watt, I. (1963). The consequences of literacy. *Comparative Studies in Society and History, 5,* 304–345.

Gordon, H. (1923). Mental and scholastic tests among retarded children. *Educational Pamphlet,* No. 44. London: Board of Education. (Reprinted in abridged form in I. Al-Issa & W. Dennis (Eds.), *Cross-cultural studies of behavior* (pp. 111–119). New York: Holt, Rinehart & Winston, 1970.)

Gordon, M. M. (1964). *Assimilation in American life.* New York: Oxford University Press.

Gottret, G. (1996). *Jeu et stratégies cognitives chez les enfants aymaras de la Bolivie.* Fribourg: Presses Universitaires de Fribourg.

Gough, H. G. (1952). Identifying psychological femininity. *Educational and Psychological Measurement, 12,* 427–439.

Gould, S. J. (1981). *The mismeasure of man.* New York: Norton.

Gould, S. J. (1995). Curveball. In S. Fraser (Ed.), *The Bell curve wars: Race, intelligence, and the future of America* (pp. 11–22). New York: Basic Books.

Graves, T. (1967). Psychological acculturation in a tri-ethnic community. *South-Western Journal of Anthropology, 23,* 337–350.

Greenfield, P. M. (1972). Oral and written language: The consequences for cognitive development in Africa, the United States, and England. *Language and Speech, 15,* 169–178.

Greenfield, P. M. (1976). Cross-cultural research and Piagetian theory: Paradox and progress. In K. F. Riegel & J. A. Meacham (Eds.), *The developing individual in a changing world,* Vol. 1 (pp. 322–333). The Hague: Mouton.

Greenfield, P. M. (1984). A theory of the teacher in the learning activities of everyday life. In B. Rogoff & J. Love (Eds.), *Everyday cognition* (pp. 117–138). Cambridge, MA: Harvard University Press.

Greenfield, P. M. (1994). Independence and interdependence as developmental scripts: Implications for theory, research, and practice. In P. Greenfield & R. Cocking

(Eds.), *Cross-cultural roots of minority child development* (pp. 1–37). Hillsdale, NJ: Lawrence Erlbaum.

Greenfield, P. M. (1996). Cultural change and human development. In *Book of abstracts. Centennial of Jean Piaget's birth conference "The Growing Mind"*, Geneva, Sept. 18.

Greenfield, P. M. (1997). Culture as process: Empirical methods for cultural psychology. In J. W. Berry, Y. H. Poortinga, & J. Pandey (Eds.), *Handbook of cross-cultural psychology*, 2 ed. Vol. 1, *Theory and method* (pp. 301–346). Boston, MA: Allyn & Bacon.

Greenfield, P. M. (1998). Cultural change and human development. In E. Turiel (Ed.), *New directions in child development* (n.d.). San Francisco, CA: Jossey-Bass.

Greenfield, P. M., & Bruner, J. S. (1969). Culture and cognitive growth. In D. A. Goslin (Ed.), *Handbook of socialization: Theory and research* (pp. 633–657). Chicago: Rand-McNally.

Greenfield, P. M., & Childs, C. P. (1977). Weaving skill, color terms and pattern representation: Cultural influences and cognitive development among the Zinacantecos of Southern Mexico. *Interamerican Journal of Psychology, 2,* 23–48.

Greenfield, P. M., & Cocking, R. R. (Eds.). (1994). *Cross-cultural roots of minority child development.* Hillsdale, NJ: Lawrence Erlbaum.

Greenfield, P. M., & Lave, J. (1979). Aspects cognitifs de l'éducation non scolaire. *Recherche, Pédagogie et Culture, 8,* 16–35.

Greenfield, P. M., & Lave, J. (1982). Cognitive aspects of informal education. In D. A. Wagner & H. W. Stevenson (Eds.), *Cultural perspectives on child development* (pp. 181–207). San Francisco: W. Freeman.

Greenfield, P. M., Maynard, A. E., & Childs, C. P. (1997). History, culture, learning, and development. In E. Turiel (Ed.), *Culture, development, and cognition.* Symposium presented at the biennial meetings of the Society for Research in Child Development. Washington, DC.

Greenfield, P. M., & Savage-Rumbaugh, E. S. (1990). Grammatical combination in Pan paniscus: Processes of learning and invention in the evolution and development of language. In S. T. Parker & K. R. Gibson (Eds.), *"Language" and intelligence in monkeys and apes: Comparative developmental perspectives* (pp. 540–578). Cambridge, England: Cambridge University Press.

Greeno, J. G., Smith, D. R., & Moore, J. L. (1994). Transfer of situated learning. In D. K. Detterman & R. J. Sternberg (Eds.), *Transfer on trial: Intelligence, cognition, and instruction* (pp. 99–167). Norwood, NJ: Ablex.

Gregor, A. J., & McPherson, D. A. (1965). A study of susceptibility to geometric illusion among cultural subgroups of Australian Aborigines. *Psychologia Africana, 11,* 1–13.

Gudykunst, W. B. (1995). Anxiety/Uncertainty management (AUM) theory: Current status. In R. L. Wiseman (Ed.), *Intercultural communication theory* (pp. 8–58). Thousand Oaks, CA: Sage.

Gudykunst, W. B., & Bond, M. H. (1997). Intergroup relations across cultures. In J. W. Berry, M. H. Segall, & C. Kagitçibasi (Eds.), *Handbook of cross-cultural psychology,* Vol. 3, *Social behavior and applications* (pp. 119–161). Boston, MA: Allyn & Bacon.

Gudykunst, W. B., Gao, G., Schmidt, K., Nishida, T., Bond, M. H., Leung, K., Wang, G., & Barraclough, R. (1992). The influence of individualism-collectivism on communication in ingroup and outgroup relationships. *Journal of Cross-Cultural Psychology, 23,* 196–213.

Gudykunst, W. B., & Nishida, T. (1994). *Bridging Japanese/North American differences* (2nd ed.). Newbury Park, CA: Sage.

Gurr, T. R. (1989). Historical trends in violent crime: Europe and the United States. In T. R. Gurr (Ed.), *Violence in America,* Vol. 1. *The history of crime* (pp. 21–49). Newbury Park, CA: Sage.

Gurr, T. R. (1993). *Minorities at risk: A global view of ethnopolitical conflicts.* Washington, DC: United States Institute of Peace.

Gurr, T. R., & Harff, B. (1994). *Ethnic conflict in world politics.* Boulder, CO: Westview.

Hall, G. S. (1916). *Adolescence.* New York: Appleton.

Halpern, D. (1993). Minorities and mental health. *Social Science and Medicine, 36,* 597–607.

Hamilton, A. (1981). *Nature and nurture: Aboriginal child-rearing in North-Central Arnhem Land.* Canberra: Australian Institute of Aboriginal Studies.

Hamilton, D. L., Sherman, S. J., & Ruvolo, C. M. (1990). Stereotype-based expectancies: Effects on information processing and social behavior. *Journal of Social Issues, 46,* 35–60.

Haque, A. (1973). Mirror image hypothesis in the context of Indo-Pakistan conflict. *Pakistan Journal of Psychology.* (Abstract in *Newsletter of the International Association of Cross-Cultural Psychology,* August, 1973, *7,* 6.)

Harkness, S., & Super, C. M. (1983). The cultural construction of child development. *Ethos, 11,* 221–231.

Harkness, S., & Super, C. M. (Eds.). (1996). *Parents' cultural belief systems: Their origins, expressions, and consequences.* New York: Guilford.

Harrington, C. (1968). Sexual differentiation in socialization and some male genital mutilations. *American Anthropologist, 70,* 952–956.

Harris, M. (1968). *The rise of anthropological theory.* New York: Thomas Crowell.

Harris, M. (1993). *Culture, people, nature: An introduction to general anthropology,* 6th ed. New York: HarperCollins.

Harris, P. (1991). *Mathematics in a cultural context: Aboriginal perspectives on space, time and money.* Geelong, Australia: Deakin University.

Harris, P., & Heelas, P. (1979). Cognitive processes and collective representations. *Archives Européennes de Sociologie, 20,* 211–241.

Harris, R. J., Schoen, L. M., & Hensley, D. L. (1992). A cross-cultural study of story memory. *Journal of Cross-Cultural Psychology, 23,* 133–147.

Hatano, G. (1982). Cognitive consequences of practice in culture: Specific procedural skills. *Quarterly Newsletter of the Laboratory of Comparative Human Cognition, 4,* 15–18.

Hauff, E., & Vaglum, P. (1993). Integration of Vietnamese refugees into the Norwegian labour market: The impact of war trauma. *International Migration Review, 27,* 388–405.

Hebb, D. O. (1949). *The organization of behaviour.* New York: Wiley.

Hebert, J. P. (1977). *Race et intelligence.* Paris: Copernic.

Heider, F. (1958). *The psychology of interpersonal relations.* New York: Wiley.

Heider, K. G. (1976). Dani sexuality: A low energy system. *Man (New Series), 11,* 188–201.

Hendrix, L. (1985). Economy and child training reexamined. *Ethos, 13,* 246–261.

Herrnstein, R. J., & Murray, C. (1994). *The bell curve: Intelligence and class structure in American life.* New York: Free Press.

Herskovits, M. J. (1927). *The Negro and intelligence tests.* Hanover, NH: Sociological Press.

Herskovits, M. J. (1948). *Man and his works: The science of cultural anthropology.* New York: Knopf.

Herskovits, M. J. (1955). *Cultural anthropology.* New York: Knopf.

Heusmann, L. R. (1983). Television violence and aggressive behavior. In L. B. D. Pearl & J. Lazar (Eds.), *Television and behavior: Ten years of scientific progress and implications for the 80's,* Vol. 2, *Technical Reviews* (pp. 126–137). Washington, DC: U. S. Government Printing Office.

Heusmann, L. R., Lagerspetz, K., & Eron, L. D. (1984). Intervening variables in the television violence-aggression relation: Evidence from two countries. *Developmental Psychology, 20,* 746–775.

Ho, D. Y. F. (1994). Cognitive socialization in Confucian heritage cultures. In P. Greenfield & R. Cocking (Eds.), *Cross-cultural roots of minority child development* (pp. 285–313). Hillsdale, NJ: Lawrence Erlbaum.

Hofstede, G. (1980). *Culture's consequences: International differences in work-related values.* Beverly Hills, CA: Sage.

Hofstede, G. (1983). Dimensions of national cultures in fifty countries and three regions. In J. B. Deregowski, S. Dziurawiec, & R. C. Annis (Eds.), *Expiscations in cross-cultural psychology* (pp. 335–355). Lisse, Netherlands: Swets-Zeitlinger.

Hofstede, G. (1991). *Cultures and organizations: Software of the mind.* London: McGraw-Hill.

Hollos, M., & Leis, P. E. (1989). *Becoming Nigerian in Ijo society.* New Brunswick, NJ: Rutgers University Press.

Horner, M. S. (1969). Fail: Bright women. *Psychology Today, 3,* 36–38, 62.

Horton, R. (1967a). African traditional thought and Western science, Part I. From tradition to science. *Africa, 37,* 50–71.

Horton, R. (1967b). African traditional thought and Western science. Part II. The "closed" and "open" predicaments. *Africa, 37,* 155–187.

Horton, R. (1982). Tradition and modernity revisited. In M. Hollis & S. Lukes (Eds.), *Rationality and relativism* (pp. 201–260). Oxford: Blackwell.

Howard, A., & Scott, R. A. (1981). The study of minority groups in complex societies. In R. H. Munroe, R. L. Munroe, & B. B. Whiting (Eds.), *Handbook of cross-cultural human development* (pp. 113–152). New York: Garland.

Hsu, F. L. K. (1981). *Americans and Chinese: Two ways of life.* Honolulu: University of Hawaii Press.

Huerre, P., Pagan-Reymond, M., & Reymond, J. M. (1990). *L'adolescence n'existe pas: Histoire des tribulations d'un artifice.* Paris: Editions universitaires.

Hui, C. H. (1984). *Individualism–collectivism: Theory, measurement, and its relation to reward allocation.* Unpublished doctoral dissertation, University of Illinois.

Hui, C. H., & Triandis, H. C. (1984). *What does individualism–collectivism mean: A study of social scientists.* Unpublished manuscript, University of Illinois Department of Psychology.

Hurh, W. M., & Kim, K. C. (1990). Adaptation stages and mental health of Korean male immigrants in the United States. *International Migration Review, 24,* 456–479.

Hutchins, E. (1980). *Culture and inference: A Trobriand case study.* Cambridge, MA: Harvard University Press.

Hutchins, E. (1983). Understanding Micronesian navigation. In D. Gentner & A. Stevens (Eds.), *Mental models* (pp 191–226). Hillsdale, NJ: Lawrence Erlbaum.

Hutchins, E. (1993). Learning to navigate. In S. Chaiklin & J. Lave (Eds.), *Understanding practice* (pp. 35–63). Cambridge, England: Cambridge University Press.

Hutchins, E. (1995). *Cognition in the wild.* Cambridge, MA: MIT Press.

Iannaccone, A., & Perret-Clermont, A.-N. (1993). Qu'est-ce qui s'apprend? Qu'est-ce qui se développe? In J. Wassmann & P. R. Dasen (Eds.), *Alltagswissen / Les savoirs quotidiens / Everyday cognition* (pp. 235–258). Fribourg: Editions Universitaires.

Ifrah, G. (1985). *Les chiffres ou l'histoire d'une grande invention.* Paris: Laffont.

Inglehart, R. (1995). Changing values, economic development and political change. *International Social Science Journal, 47,* 379–403.

Inhelder, B., Sinclair, H., & Bovet, M. (1974). *Apprentissage et structures de la connaissance.* Paris: Presses Universitaires de France.

Inkeles, A., & Smith, D. (1974). *Becoming modern.* Cambridge, MA: Harvard University Press.

Irvine, S. H. (1983). Cross-cultural conservation studies at the asymptote: Striking out against the curve. In S. Modgil (Ed.), *Jean Piaget: An interdisciplinary critique* (pp. 42–57). London: Routledge and Kegan Paul.

Ivic, I., & Marjanovic, A. (Eds.). (1986). *Traditional games and children of today.* Belgrade: OMEP & Institute of Psychology, University Belgrade.

Jacoby, R., & Glauberman, N. (Eds.). (1995). *The Bell curve debate: History, documents, opinions.* New York: Times Books/ Ramdom House.

Jacquard, A. (Ed.). (1978). *Eloge de la différence: la génétique et les hommes.* Paris: Seuil.

Jacquard, A. (1983). *Moi et les autres: Incitation à la génétique.* Paris: Seuil.

Jacquard, A. (1987). *Cinq milliards d'hommes dans un vaisseau.* Paris: Seuil.

Jahoda, G. (1980). Theoretical and systematic approaches in cross-cultural psychology. In H. C. Triandis & W. W. Lambert (Eds.), *Handbook of cross-cultural psychology,* Vol. 1, *Perspectives* (pp. 69–142). Boston, MA: Allyn & Bacon.

Jahoda, G. (1982). *Psychology and anthropology: A psychological perspective.* London: Academic Press.

Jahoda, G. (1990). Our forgotten ancestors. In R. A. Dienstbier & J. J. Berman (Eds.), *Nebraska Symposium on Motivation,* Vol.

37, *Cultural perspectives* (pp. 1–40). Lincoln: University of Nebraska Press.

Jahoda, G. (1992). *Crossroads between culture and mind.* New York: Harvester/Wheatsheaf.

Jahoda, G. (1995). The ancestry of a model. *Culture & Psychology, 1,* 11–24.

Jahoda, G., & Krewer, B. (1997). History of cross-cultural and cultural psychology. In J. W. Berry, Y. H. Poortinga, & J. Pandey (Eds.), *Handbook of cross-cultural psychology,* 2nd ed., Vol. 1, *Theory and method* (pp. 1–42). Boston, MA: Allyn & Bacon.

Jayasuriya, L., Sang, D., & Fielding, A. (1992). *Ethnicity, immigration and mental illness: A critical review of Australian research.* Canberra: Bureau of Immigration Research.

Jensen, A. R. (1969). How much can we boost IQ and scholastic achievement? *Harvard Educational Review, 39,* 1–123.

Jensen, A. R. (1981). *Straight talk about mental tests.* London: Methuen

Jensen, A. R. (1988). Speed of information processing and population differences. In S. H. Irvine & J. W. Berry (Eds.), *Human abilities in cultural context* (pp. 105–145). Cambridge, England: Cambridge University Press.

Jodelet, D. (Ed.). (1989). *Les représentations sociales.* Paris: Presses universitaires de France.

Kagitçibasi, C. (1978). Cross-national encounters: Turkish students in the United States. *International Journal of Intercultural Relations, 2,* 141–160.

Kagitçibasi, C. (1987). Individual and group loyalties: Are they compatible? In C. Kagitçibasi (Ed.), *Growth and progress in cross-cultural psychology* (pp. 94–103). Lisse: Swets & Zeitlinger.

Kagitçibasi, C. (1996). *Family and human development across cultures: A view from the other side.* Hillsdale, NJ: Lawrence Erlbaum.

Kagitçibasi, C. (1997). Individualism and collectivism. In J. W. Berry, M. H. Segall, & C. Kagitçibasi (Eds.), *Handbook of cross-cultural psychology,* Vol. 3, *Social behavior and applications* (pp. 1–49). Boston, MA: Allyn & Bacon.

Kagitçibasi, C. (1998). Human development: Cross-cultural perspectives. In J. Adair, D. Bélanger, & K. L. Dion (Eds.), *Advances in psychological science,* Vol. 2, *Developmental, personal, and social aspects* (pp. 474–494). London: Psychology Press.

Kahn, R. L. (1972). The justification of violence: Social problems and social solutions. *Journal of Social Issues, 28,* 155–175.

Kalin, R., & Berry, J. W. (1995). Ethnic and civic self-identity in Canada. *Canadian Ethnic Studies, 27,* 1–15.

Kalin, R., & Berry, J. W. (1996). Interethnic attitudes in Canada: Ethnocentrism, consensual hierarchy, and reciprocity. *Canadian Journal of Behavioral Science, 28,* 253–261.

Kalin, R., Heusser, C., & Edmonds, J. (1982). Cross-national equivalence of a sex-role ideology scale. *Journal of Social Psychology, 116,* 141–142.

Kalin, R., & Tilby, P. (1978). Development and validation of a sex-role ideology scale. *Psychological Reports, 42,* 731–738.

Kamara, A., & Easley, J. A. (1977). Is the rate of cognitive development uniform across cultures? A methodological critique with new evidence from Themne children. In P. R. Dasen (Ed.), *Piagetian psychology: Cross-cultural contributions* (pp. 26–63). New York: Gardner/Wiley.

Kaplan, H. B. (1980). *Deviant behavior in defense of self.* New York: Academic Press.

Kardiner, A. (1945). *The psychological frontiers of society.* New York: Columbia University Press.

Kaschak, E., & Sharrat, S. (1983). A Latin American sex role inventory. *Cross-Cultural Psychology Bulletin, 18,* 3–6.

Katz, D., & Braly, K. W. (1933). Racial stereotypes of 100 college students. *Journal of Abnormal and Social Psychology, 28,* 280–290.

Katz, P. A., & Taylor, D. A. (1988). *Eliminating racism: Profiles in controversy.* New York: Plenum.

Kealey, D. J. (1989). A study of cross-cultural effectiveness: Theoretical issues, practical applications. *International Journal of Intercultural Relations, 13,* 387–428.

Keats, D. M. (1982). Cultural bases of concepts of intelligence: A Chinese versus Australian comparison. In *Proceedings, Second*

Asian Workshop on Child and Adolescent Development (pp. 67–75). Bangkok: Behavioral Science Research Institute.

Keats, D. M. (1985). Strategies in formal operational thinking: Malaysia and Australia. In I. Reyes Lagunes & Y. H. Poortinga (Eds.), *From a different perspective: Studies of behavior across cultures* (pp. 304–318). Lisse: Swets & Zeitlinger.

Keenan, K. (1994). The development of aggression in toddlers: A study of low income families. *Journal of Abnormal Child Psychology, 22,* 53–77.

Keller, H. (1997). Evolutionary approaches. In J. W. Berry, Y. P. Poortinga, & J. Pandey (Eds.), *Handbook of cross-cultural psychology,* Vol. 1, *Theory and method* (pp. 215–255). Boston, MA: Allyn & Bacon.

Kelley, H. H. (1973). The processes of causal attribution. *American Psychologist, 28,* 107–128.

Kelly, M., & Philp, H. (1975). Vernacular test instructions in relation to cognitive task behavior among highland children of Papua New Guinea. *British Journal of Educational Psychology, 45,* 189–197.

Kelman, H. D. (Ed.). (1965). *International behavior: A social-psychological analysis.* New York: Holt, Rinehart and Winston.

Kelman, H. D. (1976). *Sources of attachment to the nation-state: An analysis of the social psychological dimensions of nationalism.* Paper presented at the Third Annual Floyd Allport Lecture, The Maxwell School, Syracuse University, Syracuse, NY.

Kim, U. (1988). *Acculturation of Korean Immigrants to Canada.* Unpublished Doctoral Dissertation, Queen's University, Canada.

King, M. C., & Wilson, A. C. (1975). Evolution at two levels in humans and chimpanzees. *Science, 188,* 107–116.

Klineberg, O. (1954). *Social psychology* (rev. ed.). New York: Holt. (Originally published 1940)

Klineberg, O. (1980). Stressful experiences of foreign students at various stages of sojourn: Counselling and policy implications. In G. V. Coelho & P. I. Ahmed (Eds.), *Uprooting and development dilemmas of coping with modernization.* (pp. 271–293) New York: Plenum.

Klineberg, O., & Hull, W. F. (1979). *At a foreign university: An international study of adaptation and coping.* New York: Praeger.

Kluckhohn, C. (1956). Toward a comparison of value emphases in different cultures. In L. D. White (Ed.), *The state of the social sciences* (pp. 116–132). Chicago: University of Chicago Press.

Kluckhohn, C., & Strodtbeck, F. L. (1961). *Variations in value orientations.* Evanston, IL: Row, Peterson.

Knudsen, J. (1991). Therapeutic strategies, and strategies for refugee coping. *Journal of Refugee Studies, 4,* 21–38.

Kohlberg, L. (1969a). Stage and sequence: The cognitive-development approach to socialization. In D. A. Goslin (Ed.), *Handbook of socialization theory and research* (pp. 347–480). Chicago: Rand-McNally.

Kohlberg, L. (1969b). *Stages in the development of moral thought and action.* New York: Holt, Rinehart & Winston.

Kohlberg, L. (1970). The child as a moral philosopher. In P. Cramer (Ed.), *Readings in developmental psychology today* (pp. 109–115). Del Mar, CA: CRM Books.

Kopp, C. B., & Kaslow, J. B. (1982). *The child.* Reading, MA: Addison-Wesley.

Kranau, E. J., Green, V., & Valencia-Weber, G. (1982). Acculturation and the Hispanic woman: Attitudes toward women, sex-role attribution, sex-role behavior, and demographics. *Hispanic Journal of Behavioral Science, 4,* 21–40.

Kriesberg, L. (1993). *Preventive conflict resolution of inter-communal conflicts.* Syracuse, NY: PARC.

Krishnan, A., & Berry, J. W. (1992). Acculturative stress and acculturation attitudes among Indian immigrants to the United States. *Psychology and Developing Societies, 4,* 187–212.

Kroeber, A. L. (1917). The superorganic. *American Anthropologist, 19,* 163–213.

Kurokawa, M. (1971). Mutual perceptions of racial images: White, black, and Japanese American. *Journal of Social Issues, 27,* 213–235.

Kurz, D. (1991). Corporal punishment and adult use of violence: A critique of "Discipline and deviance." *Social Problems, 38*, 155–161.

Laboratory of Comparative Human Cognition (LCHC). (1982). Culture and intelligence. In R. J. Sternberg (Ed.), *Handbook of human intelligence*. Cambridge, England: Cambridge University Press.

Laboratory of Comparative Human Cognition (LCHC). (1983). Culture and cognitive development. In W. Kessen (Ed.), *Handbook of child psychology*, vol. 1, *History, theory and methods* (pp. 295–356). New York: Wiley.

Labov, W. (1970). The logical non-standard English. In F. Williams (Ed.), *Language and poverty* (pp. 153–189). Chicago: Markham.

LaFromboise, T., Coleman, H., & Gerton, J. (1993). Psychological impact of biculturalism: Evidence and theory. *Psychological Bulletin, 114*, 395–412.

Lagerspetz, K., & Westman, M. (1980). Moral approval of aggressive acts: A preliminary investigation. *Aggressive Behavior, 6*, 119–130.

Lalonde, R. & Cameron, J. (1993). An intergroup perspective on immigrant acculturation with a focus on collective strategies. *International Journal of Psychology, 28*, 57–74.

Lamb, M. E., Sternberg, K. J., Hwang, C.-P., & Broberg, A. G. (Eds.). (1992). *Child care in context: Cross-cultural perspectives*. Hillsdale, NJ: Lawrence Erlbaum.

Lambert, W. E. (1987). The fate of old-country values in a new land: A cross-national study of child rearing. *Canadian Psychology, 28*, 9–20.

Lambley, P. (1973). Authoritarianism and prejudice in South African student samples. *Journal of Social Psychology, 91*, 341–342.

Lancy, D. F. (1996). *Playing on the motherground*. New York: Guilford.

Landau, S. F., & Beit-Hallahmi, B. (1983). Israel: Aggression in psychohistorical perspective. In A. P. Goldstein & M. H. Segall (Eds.), *Aggression in global perspective* (pp. 261–286). Elmsford, NY: Pergamon.

Langaney, A. (1988). *Les hommes: Passé, présent, conditionnel*. Paris: Armand Colin.

Langaney, A., Hubert van Blijenburgh, N., & Sanchez-Mazas. (1992). *Tous parents, tous différents*. Paris: Chabaud.

Latané, B. (1981). *Social loafing in Tailand in the sound production procedure*. (Unpublished manuscript.)

Latané, B., & Nida, S. (1981). Ten years of research on group size and helping. *Psychological Bulletin, 89*, 308–324.

Latané, B., Williams, K., & Harkins, S. (1979). Many hands make light the work: Causes and consequences of social loafing. *Journal of Personality and Social Psychology, 37*, 822–832.

Laurendeau, M., & Pinard, A. (1968). *Les premières notions spatiales de l'enfant*. Neuchâtel: Delachaux & Niestlé. English translation: *The development of the concept of space in the child*. New York: International Universities Press, 1970.

Laurendeau-Bendavid, M. (1977). Culture, schooling, and cognitive development: A comparative study of children in French Canada and Rwanda. In P. R. Dasen (Ed.), *Piagetian psychology: Cross-cultural contributions* (pp. 123–168). New York: Gardner/Wiley.

Lautrey, J., de Ribaupierre, A., & Rieben, L. (1986). Les différences dans la forme du développement cognitif évalué avec des épreuves piagétiennes: Une application de l'analyse des correspondances. *Cahiers de Psychologie Cognitive, 6*, 575–613.

Lave, J. (1977). Cognitive consequences of traditional apprenticeship in West Africa. *Anthropology and Education Quarterly, 8*, 177–180.

Lave, J. (1988). *Cognition in practice: Mind, mathematics and culture in everyday life*. Cambridge, England: Cambridge University Press.

Lave, J., Murtaugh, M., & de la Rocha, O. (1984). The dialectic of arithmetic in grocery shopping. In B. Rogoff & J. Lave (Eds.) *Everyday cognition* (pp. 67–94). Cambridge, MA: Harvard University Press.

Lave, J., & Wenger, E. (1991). *Situated learning: Legitimate peripheral participation*. Cambridge, England: Cambridge University Press.

Lazarus, R. S. (1990). Theory-based stress measurement. *Psychological Inquiry, 1*, 3–13.

Lazarus, R. S. (1991). Psychological stress in the workplace. *Journal of Social Behavior and Personality, 6,* 1–13.

Lazarus, R. S. (1993). From psychological stress to the emotions: A history of changing outlooks. *Annual Review of Psychology, 44,* 1–21.

Lazarus, R. S., & Folkman, S. (1984). *Stress, appraisal and coping.* New York: Springer.

Lecomte, J. (1998). Raisons de vivre, raisons d'agir. *Sciences Humaines, 79,* 30–33.

Leung, K. (1988). Theoretical advances in justice behavior: Some cross-cultural inputs. In M. H. Bond (Ed.), *The cross-cultural challenge to social psychology* (pp. 218–229). Newbury Park, CA: Sage.

Leung, K., & Bond, M. H. (1984). The impact of cultural collectivism on reward allocation. *Journal of Personality and Social Psychology, 47,* 793–804.

Leung, K., & Drasgow, F. (1986). Relation between self-esteem and delinquent behavior in three ethnic groups: An application of item response theory. *Journal of Cross-Cultural Psychology, 17,* 151–167.

LeVine, R. A. (1966). *Dreams and deeds.* Chicago: University of Chicago Press.

LeVine, R. A. (1970). Cross-cultural study in child psychology. In P. Mussen (Ed.), *Carmichael's manual of child psychology,* Vol. 2 (3rd ed.) (pp. 559–612). New York: Wiley.

LeVine, R. A., & Campbell, D. T. (1972). *Ethnocentrism: Theories of conflict, ethnic attitudes and group behavior.* New York: Wiley.

LeVine, R. A., & LeVine, B. B. (1966). *Nyansongo: A Gusii community in Kenya.* New York: Wiley.

LeVine, R. A., Miller, P., & West, M. (1988). Parental behavior in diverse societies. *New Directions for Child Development, 40,* 3–11.

Levinson, D. (1989). *Family violence in cross-cultural perspective.* Newbury Park, CA: Sage.

Lévi-Strauss, C. (1962). *La pensée sauvage.* Paris: Plon. English translation: *The savage mind.* Chicago: University of Chicago Press, 1966.

Lévy-Bruhl, L. (1910). *Les fonctions mentales dans les sociétés inférieures.* Paris: Alcan.

English translation: *How natives think.* London: Allen & Unwin, 1928.

Lévy-Bruhl, L. (1922). *Mentalité primitive.* Paris: Alcan. English translation: *Primitive mentality.* London: Allen & Unwin, 1926.

Lévy-Bruhl, L. (1949). *Les carnets de Lucien Lévy-Bruhl.* Paris: Presses Universitaires de France.

Lewin, K. (1936). *Principles of topological psychology.* New York: McGraw-Hill.

Lewis, O. (1966). The culture of poverty. *Scientific American, 215,* 19–25.

Lewis, O. (1969). Review of C. Valentine, Culture and poverty: A critique and counter-proposals. *Current Anthropology, 10,* 189–192.

Lewis, S. (1980). *We, the navigators. The ancient art of landfinding in the Pacific.* Canberra: Australian National University Press.

Liebing, U., & Ohler, P. (1993). Aspekte und Probleme des kognitionspsychologischen Kulturvergleichs. In A. Thomas (Ed.), *Kulturvergleichende Psychologie* (pp. 217–258). Göttingen: Hogrefe.

Lin, N., Dean, A., & Ensel, N. (1986). (Eds.). *Social support, life events and depression.* New York: Academic Press.

Lindgren, H. C., & Tebcherani, A. (1971). Arab and American auto- and heterosterotypes: A cross-cultural study of empathy. *Journal of Cross-Cultural Psychology, 2,* 173–180.

Lindzey, G. (1961). *Projective techniques and cross-cultural research.* New York: Appleton-Century-Crofts.

Linton, R. (1945). *The cultural background of personality.* New York: Appleton-Century-Crofts.

Lombard, C. (1978). *Les jouets des enfants baoulés.* Paris: Editions Quatre Vents.

Longeot, F. (1974). *L'échelle de développement de la pensée logique (EPL).* Issy-les-Moulineaux: Editions Scientifiques et Psychotechniques.

Longeot, F. (Ed.). (1978). *Les stades opératoires de Piaget et les facteurs de l'intelligence.* Grenoble: Presses Universitaires de Grenoble.

Lonner, W. J. (1980). The search for psychological universals. In H. C. Triandis & W. W. Lambert (Eds.), *Handbook of cross-cultural psychology,* Vol. 1, *Perspectives.* (pp. 143–204) Boston, MA: Allyn & Bacon.

Lonner, W. J., & Berry, J. W. (Eds.) (1986). *Field methods in cross-cultural research.* Boston: Allyn & Bacon.

Loosen, P. T. (1994). Effects on behavior of modulation of gonadal function in men with gonadotropin-releasing hormone antagonists. *American Journal of Psychiatry, 151,* 271–273.

Lore, R. K., & Schultz, L. A. (1993). Control of human aggression: A comparative perspective. *American Psychologist, 48,* 16–25.

Lorenz, K. (1963). *On aggression.* New York: Harcourt Brace Jovanovich.

Lorenzi-Cioldi, F., & Doise, W. (1994). Levels of analysis and social identity. In D. Abrams & M. A. Hogg (Eds.), *Social identity theory.* (pp. 71–88) London: Harvester & Wheatsheaf.

Low, B. S. (1989). Cross-cultural patterns in the training of children: An evolutionary perspective. *Journal of Comparative Psychology, 103,* 311–319.

Luce, R. D., & Raifa, H. (1957). *Games and decisions.* New York: Wiley.

Luria, A. R. (1976). *Cognitive development: Its cultural and social foundations.* Cambridge, MA: Harvard University Press.

Maccoby, E. E., & Jacklin, C. N. (1974). *The psychology of sex differences.* Stanford, CA: Stanford University Press.

Maccoby, E. E., & Jacklin, C. N. (1980). Sex differences in aggression: A rejoinder and reprise. *Child Development, 51,* 964–980.

Magnusson, D., & Stattin, H. (1978). A cross-cultural comparison of anxiety responses in an interactional frame of reference. *International Journal of Psychology, 13,* 317–332.

Maistriaux, R. (1955/1956). La sous-évolution des Noirs d'Afrique. *Revue de Psychologie des Peuples, 10,* 167–191, 397–456, *11,* 80–90, 134–173.

Majeed, A., & Ghosh, E. S. K. (1982). A study of social identity in three ethnic groups in India. *International Journal of Psychology, 17,* 455–463.

Malinowski, B. (1927). *Sex and repression in savage society.* London: Humanities Press.

Maloney, P., Wilkof, J., & Dambrot, F. (1981). Androgyny across two cultures: United States and Israel. *Journal of Cross-Cultural Psychology, 12,* 95–102.

Malzberg, B., & Lee, E. (1956). *Migration and mental disease.* New York: Social Science Research Council.

Markus, H. R. & Kitayama, S. (1991). Culture and the self: Implications for cognition, motivation, and emotion. *Psychological Review, 98,* 224–253.

Matsumoto, D. (1996). *People: Psychology from a cultural perspective.* Pacific Grove, CA: Brooks/Cole.

Mazrui, A. A. (1968). From social Darwinism to theories of modernization. *World Politics, 21,* 69–83.

Mazur, A. (1985). A biosocial model of status in face-to-face primate groups. *Social Forces, 64,* 377–402.

McClelland, D. C. (1958). The use of measures of human motivation in the study of society. In J. W. Atkinson (Ed.), *Motives in fantasy, action, and society* (pp. 518–554). Princeton, NJ: Van Nostrand.

McClelland, D. C. (1961). *The achieving society.* Princeton, NJ: Van Nostrand.

McClelland, D.C. (1965). N. Achievement and entrepreneurship. A longitudinal study. *Journal of Personality and Social Psychology, 1,* 389–392.

McClelland, D. C. (1971). *Motivational trends in society.* New York: General Learning Press.

McCord, J. (1991). Questioning the value of punishment. *Social Problems, 38,* 167–179.

McDougall, W. (1908). *Introduction to social psychology.* London: Methuen.

McGarry, J., & O'Leary, B. (1993). *The politics of ethnic conflict regulation.* London: Routledge.

McGrew, W. C. (1992). *Chimpanzee material culture: Implications for human evolution.* Cambridge, England: Cambridge University Press.

McLuhan, M. (1962). *The Gutenberg galaxy.* Toronto: University of Toronto Press.

McShane, D. A. (1983). Cognition, affect, and behavior in American Indian children: A developmental perspective of a transcultural situation. *Peabody Journal of Education, 61,* 34–48.

McShane, D. A., & Berry, J. W. (1988). Native North Ameri.cans: Indian and Inuit abilities. In S. H. Irvine & J. W. Berry (Eds.), *Human abilities in cultural context* (pp. 385–426). Cambridge, England: Cambridge University Press.

Mead, M. (1928). *Coming of age in Samoa.* New York: Morrow.

Mesquita, B., Frijda, N., & Scherer, K. (1997). Culture and emotion. In J. W. Berry, P. R. Dasen, & T. S. Saraswathi (Eds.), *Handbook of cross-cultural psychology,* 2nd ed., Vol. 2, *Basic processes and human development* (pp. 255–297). Boston, MA: Allyn & Bacon.

Miller, J. (1997). Theoretical issues in cultural psychology. In J. W. Berry, Y. H. Poortinga, & J. Pandey (Eds.), *Handbook of cross-cultural research,* Vol. 1, *Theory and method* (pp. 85–128). Boston, MA: Allyn & Bacon.

Minge-Klevana, W. (1986). Does labor time decrease with industrialization? A survey of time-allocation studies. *Current Anthropology, 21,* 279–298.

Minturn, L., & Lambert, W. W. (1964). *Mothers of six cultures: Antecedents of child rearing.* New York: John Wiley.

Minturn, L., & Shashak, J. (1982). Infanticide as a terminal abortion procedure. *Behavior Science Research, 17,* 70–90.

Mishra, R. (1997). Cognition and cognitive development. In J. W. Berry, P. R. Dasen, & T. S. Saraswathi (Eds.), *Handbook of cross-cultural psychology,* Vol. 2, *Basic processes and human development* (pp. 143–175). Boston, MA: Allyn & Bacon.

Mishra, R. C., Sinha, D., & Berry, J. W. (1996). *Ecology, acculturation and psychological adaptation: A study of Adivasi in Bihar.* New Delhi: Sage.

Moghaddam, F. M. (1988). Individualistic and collective integration strategies among immigrants. In J. W. Berry & R. C. Annis (Eds.), *Ethnic psychology* (pp. 69–79). Amsterdam: Swets & Zeitlinger.

Mohanty, A. K., & Perregaux, C. (1997). Language acquisition and bilingualism. In J. W. Berry, P. R. Dasen, & T. S. Saraswathi (Eds.), *Handbook of cross-cultural psychology,* Vol. 2, *Basic processes and human development* (pp. 217–254). Boston, MA: Allyn & Bacon.

Monahan, L., Kuhn, D., & Shaver, P. (1974). Intrapsychic versus cultural explanations of the "fear of success" motive. *Journal of Personality and Social Psychology, 29,* 60–64.

Montagu, A. (1976). *The nature of human aggression.* New York: Oxford University Press.

Moore, O. K., & Lewis, D. J. (1952). Learning theory and culture. *Psychological Review, 59,* 380–388.

Morelli, G. A., Rogoff, B., Oppenheim, D., & Goldsmith, D. (1992). Cultural variation in infants' sleeping arrangements: Questions of independence. *Developmental Psychology, 28,* 604–613.

Morgan, L. H. (1877). *Ancient society.* New York: Henry Holt.

Morin, E., & Kern., A. B. (1993). *Terre-patrie.* Paris: Seuil.

Morinaga, Y., Frieze, I. H., & Ferligoj, A. (1993). Career plans and gender-role attitudes of college students in the United States, Japan, and Slovenia. *Sex Roles, 29,* 317–334.

Moscovici, S. (1982). The phenomenon of social representations. In R. M. Farr & S. Moscovici (Eds.). *Social representations* (pp. 3–70). Cambridge, England: Cambridge University Press.

Mukene, P. (1988). *L'ouverture entre l'école et le milieu en Afrique noire.* Fribourg: Editions Universitaires.

Müller, H.-P. (1996). Kulturelle Gliederung der Entwicklungsländer [Cultural structuring of developing countries]. In H.-P. Müller (Ed.), Gliederung und Dynamik der Entwicklungsländer aus ethnologischer und soziologischer Sicht [Structure and dynamics of developing countries in anthropological and sociological perspective] (pp. 81–138). Berlin: Reimer.

Mundy-Castle, A. C. (1974). Social and technological intelligence in Western and non-Western cultures. *Universitas: University of Ghana, Legon, 4,* 42–56. Also in S. Pilowsky (Ed.), *Cultures in collision* (pp. 46–52). Adelaide: Australian National Association for Mental Health.

Mundy-Castle, A. C., & Bundy, R. (1988). Moral values in Nigeria. *Journal of African Psychology, 1,* 25–40.

Munroe, R. H., & Munroe, R. L. (1971). Household density and infant care in an East African society. *Journal of Social Psychology, 83,* 3–13.

Munroe, R. H., & Munroe, R. L. (1994a). Behavior across cultures: Results from observational studies. In W. J. Lonner & R. Malpass (Eds.), *Psychology and culture* (pp. 107–11). Boston, MA: Allyn & Bacon.

Munroe, R. H., Munroe, R. L., & Shimmin, H. S. (1984). Children's work in four cultures: Determinants and consequences. *American Anthropologist, 86,* 369–379.

Munroe, R. H., Munroe, R. L., & Whiting, B. B. (Eds.). (1981). *Handbook of cross-cultural human development.* New York: Garland.

Munroe, R. H., Munroe, R. L., Michelson, C., Koel, A., Bolton, R., & Bolton, C. (1983). Time allocation in four societies. *Ethnology, 22,* 355–370.

Munroe, R. H., Shimmin, H. S., & Munroe, R. L. (1984). Gender understanding and sex role preference in four cultures. *Developmental Psychology, 20,* 673–682.

Munroe, R. L., & Munroe, R. H. (1994b). *Cross-cultural human development.* Prospect Heights, IL: Waveland Press (1st edition, 1975).

Munroe, R. L., & Munroe, R. H. (1997). A comparative anthropological perspective. In J. W. Berry, Y. H. Poortinga, & J. Pandey (Eds.), *Handbook of cross-cultural psychology,* Vol. 1, *Theory and method* (pp. 171–213). Boston, MA: Allyn & Bacon.

Munroe, R. L., & Munroe, R. H. (1975). *Cross-cultural human development.* Monterey, CA: Brooks/Cole.

Munroe, R. L., & Munroe, R. H. (1988). *Further thoughts—and more evidence—on the couvade.* Paper presented at the meeting of the Society for Cross-Cultural Research, El Paso, Texas, February 19–21.

Munroe, R. L., & Munroe, R. H. (1980). Perspectives suggested by anthropological data. In H. C. Triandis & W. W. Lambert (Eds.), *Handbook of cross-cultural psychology* (Vol. 1, pp. 253–317). Boston, MA: Allyn & Bacon.

Munroe, R. L., Munroe, R. H., & Whiting, J. W. M. (1981). Male sex-role resolutions. In R. H. Munroe, R. L. Munroe, & B. B. Whiting (Eds.), *Handbook of cross-cultural human development* (pp. 611–632). New York: Garland.

Munroe, R. L., Munroe, R. H., & Winters, S. (1996). Cross-cultural correlates of the consonant–vowel (CV) syllable. *Cross-Cultural Research, 30,* 60–83.

Muralidharan, R., Khosla, R., Mian, G. M., & Kaur, B. (1981). *Children's games.* New Delhi: National Council of Educational Research and Training.

Murdock, G. P. (1937). Comparative data on the division of labor by sex. *Social Forces, 15,* 551–553.

Murdock, G. P. (1967). *Ethnographic atlas.* Pittsburgh, PA: University of Pittsburgh Press.

Murdock, G. P., & White, R. R. (1969). Standard cross-cultural sample. *Ethnology, 8,* 329–369.

Murphy, H. B. M. (1965). Migration and the major mental health disorders. In M. Kantor (Ed.), *Mobility and mental health* (pp. 221–249). Springfield: Thomas.

Murtaugh, M. (1985). The practice of arithmetic by American grocery shoppers. *Anthropology and Education Quarterly, 16,* 186–192.

Myerhoff, B. G., & Simic, A. (1978). *Life's career-aging. Cultural variations on growing old.* London: Sage.

Naidoo, J. C. (1992). The mental health of visible ethnic minorities in Canada. *Psychology and Developing Societies, 4,* 165–186.

Naidoo, J., & Davis, J. C. (1988). Canadian South Asian women in transition: A dualistic view of life. *Journal of Comparative Family Studies, 19,* 311–327.

Naroll, R. (1983). *The moral order: An introduction to the human situation.* Beverly Hills, CA: Sage.

Nerlove, S. B., & Snipper, A. S. (1981). Cognitive consequences of cultural opportunity. In R. Munroe, R. Munroe, & B. Whiting (Eds.), *Handbook of cross-cultural human development* (pp. 423–474). New York: Garland.

Newman, D., Griffin, P., & Cole, M. (1984). Social constraints in laboratory and classroom tasks. In B. Rogoff & J. Lave (Eds.), *Everyday cognition* (pp. 172–193). Cambridge, MA: Harvard University Press.

Newman, G. (1979). *Understanding violence.* New York: Lippincott.

N'guessan, A. G. (1989). Contribution du jeu dans l'insertion sociale de l'enfant ivoirien en milieu rural. In ARIC (Ed.), *Socialisations de cultures.* (pp. 143–152).

Toulouse: Presses Universitaires du Mirail.

N'guessan, A. G. (1992). *Mécanismes d'apprentissage de l'Awèlé.* Fribourg: Editions Universitaires.

Nichols, K. R., & McAndrew, F. T. (1984). Stereotyping and autostereotyping in Spanish, Malaysian, and American college students. *Journal of Social Psychology, 124,* 179–189.

Nsamenang, B. (1992). *Human development in cultural context.* Beverly Hills, CA: Sage.

Nsamenang, B., & Lamb, M. E. (1994). Socialization of Nso children in the Bamenda grassfields of Northwest Cameroon. In P. Greenfield & R. Cocking (Eds.), *Cross-cultural roots of minority child development* (pp. 133–146). Hillsdale, NJ: Lawrence Erlbaum.

Nugent, J. K., Lester, B. M., & Brazelton, T. B. (Eds.). (1989/1990). *The cultural context of infancy. Vol. 1: Biology, culture and infant development. Vol. 2: Multicultural and interdisciplinary approaches to parent-infant relations.* New York: Ablex.

Nunes, T., Schliemann, A. D., & Carraher, D. W. (1993). *Street mathematics and school mathematics.* Cambridge, England: Cambridge University Press.

Nyerere, J. M. (1967). *Education for self-reliance:* Dar es Salaam: Government Printer. Translated (1972) into French as *Indépendance et éducation.* Yaoundé: Clé.

Nyiti, R. M. (1982). The validity of "cultural differences explanations" for cross-cultural variation in the rate of Piagetian cognitive development. In D. A. Wagner & H. W. Stevenson (Eds.), *Cultural perspectives on child development* (pp. 146–165). San Francisco: Freeman.

Oberg, K. (1960). Culture shock: adjustment to new cultural environments. *Practical Anthropology, 7,* 177–182.

Offer, D., & Offer, J. B. (1975). *From teenage to young manhood.* New York: Basic Books.

Ogbu, J. U. (1994). From cultural differences to differences in cultural frame of reference. In P. Greenfield & R. Cocking (Eds.), *Cross-cultural roots of minority child development* (pp. 365–391). Hillsdale, NJ: Lawrence Erlbaum.

Ogunlade, J. A. (1971). National stereotypes of university students in Western Nigeria.

Journal of Cross-Cultural Psychology, 2, 173–180.

Okonji, O. M. (1971). The effects of familiarity on classification. *Journal of Cross-Cultural Psychology, 2,* 39–49.

Olmedo, E. L. (1979). Acculturation: A psychometric perspective. *American Psychologist, 34,* 1061–1070.

Olowu, A. A. (1985). Gender as a determinant of some Nigerian adolescents' self-concepts. *Journal of Adolescence, 8,* 347–355.

Olson, D. R. (1977). From utterance to text: The bias of language in speech and writing. *Harvard Educational Review, 47,* 257–281.

Orpen, C. (1971). Authoritarianism and racial attitudes among English-speaking South Africans. *Journal of Social Psychology, 84,* 301–302.

Orpen, C. (1972). The effect of race and similar attitudes on interpersonal attraction among White Rhodesians. *Journal of Social Psychology, 86,* 143–145.

Orpen, C., & Pors, H. (1972). Race and belief: A test of Rokeach's theory in an authoritarian culture. *International Journal of Psychology, 7,* 53–56.

Orpen, C., & Rookledge, Q. (1972). Dogmatism and prejudice in white South Africa. *Journal of Social Psychology, 86,* 151–153.

Oskamp, S., & Perlman, D. (1966). Effects of friendship and disliking on cooperation in a mixed-motive game. *Journal of Conflict Resolution, 10,* 221–226.

Otterbein, K., & Otterbein, C. S. (1965). An eye for an eye, a tooth for a tooth: A cross-cultural study of feuding. *American Anthropologist, 67,* 1470–1482.

Padilla, A. (1994). Bicultural develoment: A theoretical and conceptual examination. In R. Malgady, & H. Rodriguez (Eds.) *Theoretical and conceptual issues in Hispanic mental health.* (pp. 16–31). Thousand Oaks, CA: Sage.

Palmer, S. (1970). Aggression in fifty-eight nonliterate societies: An exploratory analysis. *Annales Internationales de Criminologie, 9,* 57–69.

Pareek, U. (1968). A motivational paradigm of development. *Journal of Social Issues, 24,* 115–122.

Parker, S. T. (1996). Apprenticeship in tool-mediated extraction foraging: The ontogenesis of imitation, teaching, and self-awareness in great apes. In A. Russon, K. Bard, & S. T. Parker (Eds.), *Reaching into thought* (pp. 348–370). Cambridge, England: Cambridge University Press.

Parker, S. T., & Mitchell, R. W. (1994). Evolving self-awareness. In S. T. Parker, R. W. Mitchell, & M. L. Boccia (Eds.), *Self-awareness in animals and humans. Developmental perspectives* (pp. 413–428). Cambridge, England: Cambridge University Press.

Pascual-Leone, J. (1980). *Constructive problems for constructive theories: The current relevance of Piaget's work and a critique of information-processing simulation psychology.* New York: Academic Press.

Pasternak, B., Ember, C. R., & Ember, M. (1997). *Sex, gender, and kinship: A cross-cultural perspective.* Upper Saddle River, NJ: Prentice-Hall.

Paulis, C. (1994). *L'adoption.* Thèse de doctorat non publiée. Université de Liège, Liège. (Cited in Bourhis and Leyens, 1994.)

Pellegrini, B. (1998). L'incertaine origine de l'Homme moderne. *Sciences Humaines, 79,* 12–17.

Pelto, P. J. (1968). The difference between "tight" and "loose" societies. *Transaction* (April), 37–40.

Perret-Clermont, A. N. (1979). *La construction de l'intelligence dans l'interaction sociale.* Bern: Peter Lang. English Translation: (1980). *Social interaction and cognitive development in children.* New York: Academic Press.

Petersen, A. C. (1993). Presidential address: Creating adolescents: The role of context and process in developmental theories. *Journal of Research on Adolescence, 3,* 1–18.

Peterson, B. E., Doty, R. M., & Winter, D. G. (1993). Authoritarianism and attitudes toward contemporary social issues. *Personality and Social Psychology Bulletin, 19,* 74–184.

Petitto, A. L., & Ginsburg, H. P. (1982). Mental arithmetic in Africa and America: Strategies, principles and explanations. *International Journal of Psychology, 17,* 81–102.

Pettigrew, T. F. (1959). Regional differences in anti-Negro prejudice. *Journal of Abnormal and Social Psychology, 59,* 28–36.

Pettigrew, T. F. (1960). Social distance attitudes of South African students. *Social Forces, 38,* 246–253.

Pettigrew, T. F. (1978). Three issues in ethnicity: Boundaries, deprivations, and perceptions. In J. M. Yinger & S. J. Cutler (Eds.), *Major social issues: A multidisciplinary view* (pp. 25–49). New York: Free Press.

Pettigrew, T. F. (1979). The ultimate attribution error: Extending Allport's cognitive analysis of prejudice. *Personality and Social Psychology Bulletin, 5,* 461–476.

Phinney, J. (1990). Ethnic identity in adolescents and adults: A review of research. *Psychological Bulletin, 108,* 499–514.

Piaget, J. (1932). *Le jugement moral chez l'enfant.* (M. Gabain, trans., *The moral judgment of the child.* London: Routledge & Kegan Paul (1965). Paris: Alcan.

Piaget, J. (1936). *La naissance de l'intelligence chez l'enfant.* Neuchâtel: Delachaux & Niestlé.

Piaget, J. (1947). *La psychologie de l'intelligence.* (A. Colin, trans., *The psychology of intelligence.* London: Routledge & Kegan Paul, 1950.) Paris: Alcan.

Piaget, J. (1956). Some impressions of a visit to Soviet psychologists. *American Psychologist, 11,* 343–345.

Piaget, J. (1965). *Etudes sociologiques.* Genève: Droz.

Piaget, J. (1966). Nécessité et signification des recherches comparatives en psychologie génétique. *Journal International de Psychologie, 1,* 3–13. English translation: Need and significance of cross-cultural studies in genetic psychology. In J. W. Berry & P. R. Dasen (Eds.), *Culture and cognition* (pp. 299–309). London: Methuen, 1974.

Piaget, J. (1969). *Mechanisms of perception.* London: Routledge.

Piaget, J. (1970a). *L'épistémologie génétique (4ème édition, 1988).* Paris: Presses Universitaires de France.

Piaget, J. (1970b). Piaget's theory. In P. H. Mussen (Ed.), *Carmichael's manual of child psychology, 3rd ed.,* Vol. 1 (pp. 703–732). New York: Wiley.

Piaget, J. (1972). Intellectual evolution from adolescence to adulthood. *Human Development, 15,* 1–12.

Piaget, J. (1975). *L'équilibration des structures cognitives.* Paris: Presses Universitaires de France.

Piaget, J., & Garcia, R. (1987). *Vers une logique des significations.* Genève: Murionde.

Piaget, J., & Inhelder, B. (1966). *La psychologie de l'enfant.* Paris: Presses Universitaires de France. English translation: *The psychology of the child.* London: Routledge & Kegan Paul, 1969.

Piéron, H. (1957). *Vocabulaire de la psychologie.* Paris: Presses Universitaires de France.

Pike, K. L. (1954). Emic and etic standpoints for the description of behavior. In K. L. Pike (Ed.), *Language in relation to a unified theory of the structure of human behavior,* Pt. 1 (preliminary edition) (pp. 8–28). Glendale, CA: Summer Instititute of Linguistics.

Pike, K. L. (1967). *Language in relation to a unified theory of the structure of human behavior.* The Hague: Mouton.

Pinto, A., Folkers, E., & Sines, J. O. (1991). Dimensions of behavior and home environment in school-age children: India and the United States. *Journal of Cross-Cultural Psychology, 22,* 491–508.

Pinxten, R., van Dooren, I., & Harvey, F. (1983). *The anthropology of space: Explorations into the natural philosophy and semantics of the Navajo.* Philadelphia, PA: University of Pennsylvania Press.

Pollnac, R. B. (1977). Illusion susceptibility and adaptation to the marine environment: Is the carpentered world hypothesis seaworthy? *Journal of Cross-Cultural Psychology, 8,* 425–433.

Porteus, S. D. (1937). *Intelligence and environment.* New York: Macmillan.

Posner, J. K., & Baroody, A. J. (1979). Number conservation in two West African societies. *Journal of Cross-Cultural Psychology, 10,* 479–496.

Preiswerk, R. (1976). Jean Piaget et l'étude des relations interculturelles. In G. Busino (Ed.), Les sciences sociales avec et après Jean Piaget. *Revue Européenne des Sciences Sociales, 14,* 495–511.

Preiswerk, R., & Perrot, D. (1975). *Ethnocentrisme et histoire. L'Afrique, l'Amérique indienne et l'Asie dans les manuels occidentaux.* Paris: Anthropos.

Price-Williams, D. R. (1962). Abstract and concrete modes of classification in a primitive society. *British Journal of Educational Psychology, 32,* 50–61.

Price-Williams, D. R. (1981). Concrete and formal operations. In R. H. Munroe, R. L. Munroe, & B. B. Whiting (Eds.), *Handbook of cross-cultural human development* (pp. 403–422). New York: Garland.

Rabain, J. (1979). *L'enfant du lignage.* Paris: Payot.

Rabain-Jamin, J. (1994). Language and socialization of the child in African families living in France. In P. Greenfield & R. Cocking (Eds.), *Cross-cultural roots of minority child development* (pp. 147–166). Hillsdale, NJ: Lawrence Erlbaum.

Rao, V. V. P., & Rao, V. N. (1985). Sex-role attitudes across two cultures: United States and India. *Sex Roles, 13,* 607–624.

Rapoport, T., Lomski-Feder, E., & Masalha, M. (1989). Female subordination in the Arab-Israeli community: The adolescent perspective of "social veil." *Sex Roles, 20,* 255–269.

Redfield, R., Linton, R., & Herskovits, M. (1936). Memorandum on the study of acculturation. *American Anthropologist, 38,* 149–152.

Reed, H. J., & Lave, J. (1979). Arithmetic as a tool for investigating relations between culture and cognition. *American Ethnologist, 6,* 568–582.

Reigrotski, E., & Anderson, N. (1959). National stereotypes and foreign contacts. *Public Opinion Quarterly, 23,* 515–528.

Reiss, I. (1986). *Journey into sexuality: An exploratory voyage.* Englewood Cliffs, NJ: Prentice-Hall.

Resnick, L., Levine, J., & Teasley, S. (Eds.). (1991). *Perspectives on socially shared cognition.* Washington, DC: American Psychological Association.

Retschitzki, J. (1990). *Stratégies des joueurs d'Awélé.* Paris: L'Harmattan.

Ribaupierre de, A., Rieben, L., & Lautrey, J. (1985). Horizontal decalages and individual differences in the development of concrete operations. In V. Restaino-Baumann, L. Shulman, & L. Butler (Eds.), *The future of Piagetian theory: The neo-*

Piagetians (pp. 175–197). New York: Plenum.

Richmond, A. (1993). Reactive migration: Sociological perspectives on refugee movements. *Journal of Refugee Studies, 6,* 7–24.

Rivers, W. H. R. (1901). Introduction and vision. In A. C. Haddon (Ed.), *Reports of the Cambridge anthropological expedition to the Torres Straits, Vol. 2, Pt. 1.* Cambridge, England: Cambridge University Press.

Rivers, W. H. R. (1905). Observations on the senses of the Todas. *British Journal of Psychology, 1,* 321–396.

Rogler, L. (1994). International migrations: A framework for directing research. *American Psychologist, 49,* 701–708.

Rogoff, B. (1981). Schooling and the development of cognitive skills. In H. Triandis & A. Heron (Eds.), *Handbook of cross-cultural psychology,* Vol. 4, *Developmental psychology* (pp. 233–294). Boston: Allyn & Bacon.

Rogoff, B. (1986). Adult assistance of children's learning. In T. E. Raphael (Ed.), *The contexts of school based literacy* (pp. 27–40). New York: Random House.

Rogoff, B. (1990). *Apprenticeship in thinking: Cognitive development in social context.* New York: Oxford University Press.

Rogoff, B. (1994). Developing understanding of the idea of communities of learners. *Mind, Culture, and Activity, 1,* 209–229.

Rogoff, B. (1995). Observing sociocultural activities on three planes: Participatory appropriation, guided participation, apprenticeship. In J. V. Wertsch, P. del Rio, & A. Alvarez (Eds.), *Sociocultural studies of mind* (pp. 139–164). Cambridge, England: Cambridge University Press.

Rogoff, B. (1996). Developmental transitions in children's participation in sociocultural activities. In A. Sameroff & M. Haith (Eds.), *The age of reason and responsibility* (pp. 273–294). Chicago: University of Chicago Press.

Rogoff, B., Baker-Sennett, J., Lacasa, P., & Goldsmith, D. (1995). Development through participation in sociocultural activity. In J. Goodnow, P. Miller, & F. Kessel (Eds.), *Cultural practices as contexts for development* (pp. 45–65). San Francisco: Jossey-Bass.

Rogoff, B., & Gardner, W. (1984). Adult guidance of cognitive development. In B. Rogoff & J. Lave (Eds.), *Everyday cognition* (pp. 95–116). Cambridge, MA: Harvard University Press

Rogoff, B., & Gauvain, M. (1984). The cognitive consequences of specific experiences: Weaving versus schooling among the Navajo. *Journal of Cross-Cultural Psychology, 15,* 453–475.

Rogoff, B., & Lave, J. (Eds.). (1984). *Everyday cognition: Its development in social context.* Cambridge, MA: Harvard University Press.

Rogoff, B., Mistry, J., Göncü, A., & Mosier, C. (1993). Guided participation in cultural activity by toddlers and caregivers. *Monographs of the Society for Research in Child Development, 58* (serial no. 236).

Rohner, R. P. (1975). *They love me, they love me not: A worldwide study of the effects of parental acceptance and rejection.* New Haven, CT: HRAF Press.

Rohner, R. P. (1976). Sex differences in aggression: Phylogenetic and enculturation perspectives. *Ethos, 4,* 57–72.

Rohrer, J. H., & Edmonson, M. E. (1960). *The eighth generation: Cultures and personalities of New Orleans Negroes.* New York: Harper & Row.

Rokeach, M. (Ed.). (1960). *The open and closed mind.* New York: Basic Books.

Rokeach, M. (1973). *The nature of human values.* New York: Free Press.

Rokeach, M., Smith, P. W., & Evans, R. I. (1960). Two kinds of prejudice or one? In M. Rokeach (Ed.), *The open and closed mind* (pp. 132–168). New York: Basic Books.

Rosch, E. (1977). *Human categorization.* London: Academic Press.

Rosen, B. C. (1962). Socialization and achievement motivation in Brazil. *American Sociological Review, 27,* 612–624.

Rosen, B. C., & D'Andrade, R. (1959). The psychological origins of achievement motivation. *Sociometry, 22,* 185–218.

Rosin, R. T. (1973). Gold medallions: The arithmetic calculations of an illiterate. *Council on Anthropology and Education Newsletter, 4,* 1–9.

Ross, B. M., & Millsom, C. (1970). Repeated memory of oral prose in Ghana and New

York. *International Journal of Psychology, 5,* 173–181.

Ross, L. (1977). The intuitive psychologist and his shortcomings: Distortions in the attribution process. In L. Berkowitz (Ed.), *Advances in experimental social psychology,* Vol. 10. (pp. 174–220). New York: Academic Press.

Ross, M. H. (1985). Internal and external conflict and violence: Cross-cultural evidence and a new analysis. *Journal of Conflict Resolution, 29,* 547–579.

Ross, M. H. (1993). *The culture of conflict: Interpretations and interests in comparative perspective.* New Haven, CT: Yale University Press.

Rothbart, M., & Taylor, M. (1992). Category labels and social reality: Do we view social categories as natural kinds? In G. Semin & K. Fiedler (Eds.), *Language, interaction and social organization* (pp. 11–36). London: Sage.

Rudmin, F. W. (1992). Cross-cultural correlates of the ownership of private property. *Social Science Research, 21,* 57–83.

Rushton, J. P. (1988). Race differences in behaviour: A review and evolutionary analysis. *Personality and Individual Differences, 9,* 1009–1024.

Rushton, J. P. (1995). *Race, evolution, and behavior: A life history perspective.* New Brunswick, NJ: Transaction.

Russell, E. W. (1972). Factors of human aggression: A cross-cultural factor analysis of characteristics related to warfare and crime. *Behavior Science Notes, 7,* 275–312.

Russell, P. A., Deregowski, J. B., & Kinnear, P. R. (1997). Perception and aesthetics. In J. W. Berry, P. R. Dasen, & T. S. Saraswathi (Eds.), *Handbook of cross-cultural psychology,* Vol. 2, *Basic processes and human development* (pp. 107–142). Boston: Allyn & Bacon.

Sabatier, C. & Berry, J. W. (1994). Immigration et acculturation. In R. Bourhis & J. P. Leyens (Eds.), *Stéréotypes, discrimination et relations intergroupes.* Liège: Mardaga.

Sahlins, M. (1972). *Stone age economics.* Chicago: Aldine.

Salomon, G. (Ed.). (1993). *Distributed cognitions: Psychological and educational considerations.* Cambridge, England: Cambridge University Press.

Sam, D. L., & Berry, J. W. (1995). Acculturative stress among young immigrants in Norway. *Scandinavian Journal of Psychology, 36,* 10–24.

Santerre, R. (1973). *Pédagogie musulmane d'Afrique noire.* Montréal: Presses de l'Université de Montréal.

Santerre, R., & Mercier-Tremblay, C. (Eds.). (1982). *La quête du savoir: Essais pour une anthropologie de l'éducation camérounaise.* Montréal: Presses de l'Université de Montréal.

Saraswathi, T. S., & Dutta, R. (Eds.). (1988). *Developmental psychology in India, 1975–1986.* New Delhi: Sage.

Saraswathi, T. S., & Kaur, B. (Eds.). (1993). *Human development and family studies in India.* New Delhi: Sage.

Savage-Rumbaugh, E. S., Murphy, J., Sevcik, R. A., Brakke, K. E., Williams, S. L., & Rumbaugh, D. M. (1993). Language comprehension in ape and child. *Monographs of the Society for Research in Child Development, 58,* serial no. 233.

Saxe, G. B. (1981). Body parts as numerals: A developmental analysis of numeration among remote Oksapmin village populations in Papua New Guinea. *Child Development, 52,* 306–316.

Saxe, G. B. (1982). Developing forms of arithmetical thought among the Oksapmin of Papua New Guinea. *Developmental Psychology, 18,* 583–594.

Saxe, G. B. (1991). *Culture and cognitive development: Studies in mathematical understanding.* Hillsdale, NJ: Lawrence Erlbaum.

Saxe, G. B. (1994). Studying cognitive development in sociocultural context: The development of a practice-based approach. *Mind, Culture, and Activity, 1,* 135–157.

Saxe, G. B., & Gearhart, M. (1990). The development of topological concepts in unschooled straw weavers. *British Journal of Developmental Psychology, 8,* 251–258.

Saxe, G. B., & Moylan, T. (1982). The development of measurement operations among the Oksapmin of Papua New Guinea. *Child Development, 53,* 1242–1248.

Scarr-Salapatek, S. (1971). Unknowns in the I.Q. equation. *Science, 174,* 1283–1288.

Scher, D., Nevo, B., & Beit-Hallahmi, B. (1979). Beliefs about equal rights for men and women among Israeli and American students. *Journal of Social Psychology, 109,* 11–15.

Schlegel, A. & Barry, H., III. (1986). The cultural consequences of female contribution to subsistence. *American Anthropologist, 88,* 142–150.

Schlegel, A., & Barry, H., III. (1991). *Adolescence: An anthropological enquiry.* New York: Free Press (Macmillan).

Schlemmer, B. (Ed.). (1996). *L'enfant exploité. Oppression, mise au travail, prolétarisation.* Paris: Karthala.

Schliemann, A., Carraher, D., & Ceci, S. (1997). Everyday cognition. In J. W. Berry, P. R. Dasen, & T. S. Saraswathi (Eds.), *Handbook of cross-cultural psychology,* Vol. 2, *Basic processes and human development* (pp. 177–216). Boston, MA: Allyn & Bacon.

Schmitz, P. (1992). Acculturation styles and health. In S. Iwawaki, Y. Kashima, and K. Leung (Eds.), *Innovations in cross-cultural psychology,* (pp. 360–370). Amsterdam: Swets and Zeitlinger.

Schmitz, P. G. (1994). Acculturation and adaptation processes among immigrants in Germany. In A-M. Bouvy, F. J. R. van de Vijver, & P. Schmitz (Eds.), *Journeys into cross-cultural psychology* (pp. 142–157). Amsterdam: Swets & Zeitlinger.

Schneuwly, B., & Bronckart, J.-P. (Eds.). (1985). *Vygotsky aujourd'hui.* Neuchâtel: Delachaux & Niestlé.

Schubauer-Leoni, M. L., Perret-Clermont, A.-N., & Grossen, M. (1992). The construction of adult child intersubjectivity in psychological research and in school. In M. von Cranach, W. Doise, & G. Mugny (Eds.), *Social representations and the social bases of knowledge* (pp. 69–77). Bern: Hogrefe & Huber.

Schurmans, M.-N., & Dasen, P. R. (1992). Social representations of intelligence: Côte d'Ivoire and Switzerland. In M. von Cranach, W. Doise, & G. Mugny (Eds.), *Social representations and the social bases of knowledge* (pp. 144–152). Bern: Hogrefe & Huber.

Schwartz, S. H. (1992). Universals in the structure and content of values: Theoretical advances and empirical tests in 20 countries. In M. P. Zanna (Ed.), *Advances in experimental social psychology* (Vol. 25, pp. 1–65). Orlando, FL: Academic Press.

Schwartz, S. H. (1994a). Beyond individualism/collectivism: New cultural dimensions of values. In U. Kim, H. C. Triandis, C. Kagitçibasi, S-C. Choi, & G. Yoon (Eds.), *Individualism and collectivism: Theory, method and applications* (pp. 85–119). Thousand Oaks, CA: Sage.

Schwartz, S. H. (1994b). Are there universal aspects in the structure and contents of human values? *Journal of Social Issues, 50,* 19–45.

Schwartz, S. H., & Bilsky, W. (1987). Towards a psychological structure of human values. *Journal of Personality and Social Psychology, 53,* 550–562.

Schwartz, S. H., & Bilsky, W. (1990). Toward a theory of the universal content and structure of values. *Journal of Personality and Social Psychology, 58,* 878–891.

Scribner, S. (1974). Developmental aspects of categorized recall in a West African society. *Cognitive Psychology, 6,* 475–494,

Scribner, S. (1979). Modes of thinking and ways of speaking: Culture and logic reconsidered. In R. O. Freedle (Ed.), *New directions in discourse processing* (pp. 223–243). Norwood, NJ: Ablex.

Scribner, S. (1984). *Studying working intelligence.* Cambridge, MA: Harvard University Press.

Scribner, S., & Cole, M. (1973). The cognitive consequences of formal and informal education. *Science, 182,* 553–559.

Scribner, S., & Cole, M. (1978). Unpacking literacy. *Social Science Information, 17,* 19–40.

Scribner, S., & Cole, M. (1981). *The psychology of literacy.* Cambridge, MA: Harvard University Press.

Searle, W., & Ward, C. (1990). The prediction of psychological and sociocultural adjustment during cross-cultural transitions. *International Journal of Intercultural Relations, 14,* 449–464.

Segall, M. H. (1976). *Human behavior and public policy: A political psychology.* New York: Pergamon.

Segall, M. H. (1984). More than we need to know about culture, but are afraid not to ask. *Journal of Cross-Cultural Psychology, 15,* 153–162.

Segall, M. H. (1988). Psychocultural antecedents of male aggression: Some implications involving gender, parenting, and adolescence. In J. W. Berry, P. R. Dasen, & N. Sartorius (Eds.), *Health and cross-cultural psychology: Towards applications* (pp. 71–92). Newbury Park, CA: Sage.

Segall, M. H., Campbell, D. T., & Herskovits, M. J. (1966). *The influence of culture on visual perception.* Indianapolis: Bobbs-Merrill.

Segall, M. H., Ember, C. R., & Ember, M. (1997). Aggression, crime, and warfare. In J. W. Berry, M. H. Segall, & C. Kagitçibasi (Eds.), *Handbook of cross-cultural psychology,* Vol. 3, *Social behavior and applications* (pp. 213–254). Boston, MA: Allyn & Bacon.

Segall, M. H., & Kagitçibasi, C. (1997). Introduction. In J. W. Berry, M. H. Segall, & C. Kagitçibasi (Eds.), *Handbook of cross-cultural psychology,* Vol. 3, *Social behavior and applications* (pp. xxv–xxxv). Boston, MA: Allyn & Bacon.

Segall, M. H., & Knaack, F. (1989). Un théorie de machisme compensatoire. In ARIC (Ed.), *Socialisation et cultures* (pp. 357–358). Toulouse: Presses Universitaires de Mirail.

Segall, M. H., Lonner, W. J., & Berry, J. W. (1998). Cross-cultural psychology as a scholarly discipline: On the flowering of culture in behavioral research. *American Psychologist, 53,* 1101–1110.

Seginer, R., Karayanni, M., & Mar'i, M. M. (1990). Adolescents' attitudes toward women's roles: A comparison between Israeli Jews and Arabs. *Psychology of Women Quarterly, 14,* 119–133.

Serpell, R. (1976). *Culture's influence on behaviour.* London: Methuen.

Serpell, R. (1977). Estimates of intelligence in a rural community of Eastern Zambia. In F. M. Okatcha (Ed.), *Modern psychology and cultural adaptation* (pp. 179–216). Nairobi: Swahili Language Consultants and Publishers.

Serpell, R. (1979). How specific are perceptual skills? A cross-cultural study of pattern reproduction. *British Journal of Psychology, 70,* 365–380.

Serpell, R. (1989). Dimensions endogènes de l'intelligence chez les A-chewa et autres peuples africains. In J. Retschitzki, M. Bossel-Lagos, & P. Dasen (Eds.), *La recherche interculturelle,* Vol. 2 (pp. 164–179). Paris: L'Harmattan.

Serpell, R. (1993). *The significance of schooling.* New York: Cambridge University Press.

Serpell, R., & Hatano, G. (1997). Education, schooling, and literacy. In J. W. Berry, P. R. Dasen, & T. S. Saraswathi (Eds.), *Handbook of cross-cultural psychology,* second edition. Vol. 2, *Basic processes and human development* (pp. 339–376). Boston, MA: Allyn & Bacon.

Sharp, D., Cole, M., & Lave, C. (1978). Education and cognitive development: The evidence from experimental research. *Monographs of the Society for Research in Child Development, 44,* 1–112.

Shayer, M., Demetriou, A., & Pervez, M. (1988). The structure and scaling of concrete operational thought: Three studies in four countries and only one story. *Genetic Psychology Monographs, 114,* 307–376.

Shea, J. D. (1985). Studies of cognitive development in Papua New Guinea. *International Journal of Psychology, 20,* 33–61.

Shweder, R. A. (1984). Anthropology's romantic rebellion against the enlightenment, or there's more to thinking than reason and evidence. In R. A. Shweder & R. A. LeVine (Eds.), *Culture theory: Essays on mind, self, and emotion* (pp. 27–66). New York: Cambridge University Press.

Shweder, R. A., & Sullivan, M. A. (1990). The semiotic subject of cultural psychology. In L. A. Pervin (Ed.), *Handbook of personality theory and research* (pp. 399–416). New York: Guilford.

Shweder, R. A., & Sullivan, M. A. (1993). Cultural psychology: Who needs it? *Annual Review of Psychology, 44,* 497–527.

Sigel, I. E. (Ed.). (1985). *Parental belief systems.* Hillsdale, NJ: Lawrence Erlbaum.

Sigel, I. E., McGillicuddy-DeLisi, V., & Goodnow, J. J. (Eds.). (1992). *Parental belief systems: The psychological consequences for children* (2nd ed.). Hillsdale, NJ: L. Erlbaum.

Silvar, S. D., & Pollack, R. H. (1967). Racial differences in pigmentation of the Fundus oculi. *Psychonomic Science, (7),* 159–160.

Singelis, T. M. (1994). The measurement of independent and interdependent self construals. *Personality and Social Psychology Bulletin, 20,* 580–591.

Singelis, T. M., & Brown, W. J. (1995). Culture, self, and collectivist communication: Linking culture to individual behavior. *Human Communication Research, 21,* 354–389.

Sinha, D. (1988). The family scenario in a developing country and its implications for mental health: The case of India. In P. R. Dasen, J. W. Berry, & N. Sartorius (Eds.), *Health and cross-cultural psychology: Towards applications* (pp. 48–70). Newbury Park, CA: Sage.

Sinha, D. (1997). Indigenising psychology. In J. W. Berry, Y. Poortinga, & J. Pandey (Eds.), *Handbook of cross-cultural psychology,* Vol. 1, *Theory and method* (pp. 129–169). Boston, MA: Allyn & Bacon.

Sipes, R. G. (1973). War, sports, and aggression: An empirical test of two rival theories. *American Anthropologist, 75,* 64–86.

Sipes, R. G., & Robertson, B. A. (1975). *Malevolent magic, mutilation, punishment, and aggression.* Paper presented at the annual meeting of the American Anthropological Association, San Francisco.

Skinner, B. F. (1971). *Beyond freedom and dignity.* New York: Knopf.

Skinner, B. F. (1974). *About behaviorism.* New York: Knopf.

Skinner, M. L. (1992). Linking economic hardship to adolescent aggression. *Journal of Youth and Adolescence, 21,* 259–276.

Smith, A. (1759). *The theory of moral sentiments.* London: A. Miller.

Smith, P. B., & Bond, M. H. (1993). *Social psychology across cultures: Analysis and perspectives.* Hemel Hempstead, England: Harvester/Wheatsheaf.

Smith, P. B., & Bond, M. H. (1994). *Social psychology across cultures.* Boston, MA: Allyn & Bacon.

Smith, P. B., & Schwartz, S. (1997). Values. In J. W. Berry, M. H. Segall, & C. Kagitçibasi (Eds.), *Handbook of cross-cultural psychology,* Vol. 3, *Social behavior and applications* (pp. 77–118). Boston, MA: Allyn & Bacon.

Snarey, J. R., Reimer, J., & Kohlberg, L. (1985). Development of social-moral reasoning among kibbutz adolescents: A longitudinal cross-cultural study. *Developmental Psychology, 21,* 3–11.

Soto, E., & Shaver, P. (1982). Sex-role traditionalism, assertiveness, and symptoms of Puerto Rican women living in the United States. *Hispanic Journal of Behavioral Science, 4,* 1–19.

Spearman, C. (1927). *The abilities of man.* London: Macmillan.

Spence, J. T., & Helmreich, R. L. (1978). *Masculinity and femininity: Their psychological dimensions, correlates, and antecedents.* Austin: University of Texas Press.

Spencer, H. (1876). *Principles of sociology.* New York: D. Appelton.

Spiro, M. E. (1961). Social systems, personality, and functional analysis. In B. Kaplan (Ed.), *Studying personality cross-culturally* (pp. 93–127). Evanston, IL: Row Peterson.

Spiro, M. E. (1965). *Children of the kibbutz.* New York: Schocken Books.

Spiro, M., & Swartz, L. (1994). Mothers' reports of behaviour problems in three groups of South African preschool children. *Journal of Cross-Cultural Psychology, 25,* 339–352.

Spock, B., & Rothenberg, M. B. (1992). *Dr. Spock's baby and child care.* New York: Pocket Books.

Stein, D. D., Hardyck, J. A., & Smith, M. B., (1965). Race and belief—an open and shut case. *Journal of Personality and Social Psychology, 1,* 281–289.

Sternberg, R. J. (1988). A triarchic view of intelligence in cross-cultural perspective. In S. H. Irvine & J. W. Berry (Eds.), *Human abilities in cultural context* (pp. 60–85). Cambridge, England: Cambridge University Press.

Sternberg, R. J. (1995). *In search of the human mind.* Fort Worth, TX: Harcourt-Brace.

Stevenson, H. (1994). Moving away from stereotypes and preconceptions: Students and their education in East Asia and the United States. In P. Greenfield & R. Cocking (Eds.), *Cross-cultural roots of minority child development* (pp. 315–322). Hillsdale, NJ: Lawrence Erlbaum.

Stevenson, H., Azuma, H., & Hakuta, K. (1986). *Child development and education in Japan.* London: W. Freeman.

Stewart van Leeuwen, M. (1973). Tests of the "carpentered world" hypothesis by race and environment in America and Zambia. *International Journal of Psychology, 8,* 83–94.

Stigler, J. W. (1984). "Mental abacus": The effect of abacus training on Chinese children's mental calculations. *Cognitive Psychology, 16,* 145–176.

Strauss, C. (1984). Beyond "formal" versus "informal" education: Uses of psychological theory in anthropological research. *Ethos, 12,* 195–222.

Stringer, C., & McKie, R. (1997). Neanderthals on the run. *New York Times,* OP-Ed, p. 7, July 27, 1997.

Sumner, W. G. (1906). *Folkways.* Boston: Ginn.

Super, C. M. (1981). Behavioral development in infancy. In R. H. Munroe, R. L. Munroe, & B. B. Whiting (Eds.), *Handbook of cross-cultural human development* (pp. 181–270). New York: Garland.

Super, C. M. (1983). Cultural variations in the meaning and uses of children's "intelligence." In J. B. Deregowski, S. Dziurawiec, & R. C. Annis (Eds.), *Expiscations in cross-cultural psychology* (pp. 199–212). Lisse: Swets & Zeitlinger.

Super, C. M. (1987). *The role of culture in developmental disorder.* New York: Academic Press.

Super, C. M., & Harkness, S. (1986). The developmental niche: A conceptualization at the interface of child and culture. *International Journal of Behavioral Development, 9,* 545–570.

Super, C. M., & Harkness, S. (1997). The cultural structuring of child development. In J. W. Berry, P. R. Dasen, & T. S. Saraswathi (Eds.), *Handbook of cross-cultural psychology,* 2nd ed., Vol. 2, *Basic processes and human development* (pp. 1–39). Boston, MA: Allyn & Bacon.

Super, C. M., Harkness, S., van Tijen, N., van der Vlugt, E., Fintelman, M., & Dijkstra, J. (1996). The three R's of Dutch childrearing and the socialization of infant arousal. In S. Harkness & C. M. Super (Eds.), *Parents' cultural belief systems: Their origins, expressions, and consequences* (pp. 447–466). New York: Guilford.

Sutton-Smith, B., & Roberts, J. M. (1981). Play, toys, games, and sports. In H. C. Triandis & A. Heron (Eds.), *Handbook of cross-cultural psychology,* vol. 4. *Developmental psychology* (pp. 425–471). Boston: Allyn & Bacon.

Suvannathat, C., Bhanthumnavin, D., Bhuapirom, L., & Keats, D. M. (1985). *Handbook of Asian child development and child rearing practices.* Bangkok: Behavioral Science Research Institute.

Suzuki, A. (1991a). Egalitarian sex role attitudes: Scale development and comparison of American and Japanese women. *Sex Roles, 24,* 245–259.

Suzuki, A. (1991b). Predictors of women's sex role attitudes across two cultures: United States and Japan. *Japanese Psychological Research, 33,* 126–133.

Szapocznik, J., & Kurtines, W. (1993). Family psychology and cultural diversity. *American Psychologist, 48,* 400–407.

Tajfel, H. (1978). *Differentiation between social groups: Studies in the social psychology of intergroup relations.* London and New York: Academic Press.

Tajfel, H. (1982). Social psychology of intergroup relations. *Annual Review of Psychology, 33,* 1–39.

Tajfel, H., Jaspers, J. M., & Fraser, C. (1984). The social dimensions in European social psychology. In H. Tajfel (Ed.), *The social dimension,* Vol. 1, (pp. 1–8). Cambridge, England: Cambridge University Press.

Tajfel, H. & Turner, J. C. (1979). An integrative theory of intergroup conflict. In W. G. Austin and S. Worchel (Eds.), *The social psychology of intergroup relations* (pp. 33–47). Monterey, CA: Brooks/Cole.

Tanaka-Matsumi, J., & Draguns, J. (1997). Culture and psychopathology. In J. W. Berry, M. H. Segall, & C. Kagitçibasi (Eds.), *Handbook of cross-cultural psychology,* Vol. 3, *Social behavior and applications* (pp. 449–491). Boston, MA.: Allyn & Bacon.

Tanon, F. (1994). *A cultural view on planning: The case of weaving in Ivory Coast.* Tilburg: Tilburg University Press.

Tapé, G. (1994). *L'intelligence en Afrique: Une étude du raisonnement expérimental.* Paris: L'Harmattan.

Tapia Uribe, F. M., LeVine, R. A., & LeVine, S. E. (1994). Maternal behavior in a Mexican community: The changing environments of children. In P. Greenfield & R. Cocking (Eds.), *Cross-cultural roots of minority child development* (pp. 41–54). Hillsdale, NJ: Lawrence Erlbaum.

Tavris, C. (1992) *The mismeasure of woman: Why women are not the better sex, the inferior sex, or the opposite sex.* New York: Simon & Schuster.

Tavris, C. (1996). Misreading the gender gap. *The New York Times,* September 17, p. A23.

Taylor, D. M., & Moghaddam, F. M. (1987). *Theories of intergroup relations: Social psychological perspectives.* New York: Praeger.

Teasdale, G. R. (1994). Education and the survival of small indigenous cultures. In L. F. B. Dubbeldam (Ed.), *International yearbook of education, 1994, Vol. 44, Development, culture and education* (pp. 197–224). Paris: UNESCO.

Tedeschi, J. T., Gaes, G. G., & Rivera, A. N. (1997). Aggression and the use of coercive power. *Journal of Social Issues, 33,* 101–125.

Tedeschi, J. T., & Melburg, V. (1983). Aggression and the illegitimate use of coercive power. In H. H. Blumberg, A. P. Hare, V. Kent, & M. Davies (Eds.), *Small groups and social interaction* (pp. 255–266). New York: John Wiley.

Tedeschi, J. T., Smith, R. B., & Brown, R. C. (1974). A reinterpretation of research on aggression. *Psychological Bulletin, 81,* 540–563.

Toelken, B. (1985). "Turkenrein" and "Turken, raus": Images of fear and aggression. In I. Basgoz & N. Furniss (Eds.), *Turkish workers in Europe* (pp. 151–164). Bloomington: Indiana University Press.

Tomasello, M., Kruger, A. C., & Ratner, H. H. (1993). Cultural learning. *Behavioral and Brain Sciences, 16,* 495–552.

Tonnies, F. (1887/1957). *Community and society.* (C. P. Loomis, trans.). East Lansing: Michigan State Press.

Tornblom, K., & Foa, U. (1983). Choice of a distribution principle: Cross-cultural evidence on the effects of resources. *Acta Sociologica, 2,* 161–173.

Triandis, H. C. (1961). A note on Rokeach's theory of prejudice. *Journal of Abnormal and Social Psychology, 62,* 184–186.

Triandis, H. C. (1972). *The analysis of subjective culture.* New York: Wiley.

Triandis, H. C. (1975). Social psychology and cultural analysis. *Journal for the Theory of Social Behavior, 5,* 81–106.

Triandis, H. C. (1983). *Allocentric vs. idiocentric social behavior: A major cultural difference between Hispanics and the Mainstream.* ONR Technical Report 16. Department of Psychology, University of Illinois at Champaign.

Triandis, H. C. (1990). Cross-cultural studies of individualism and collectivism. In J. Berman (Ed.), *Nebraska Symposium on Motivation, 1989* (pp. 41–133). Lincoln: Nebraska University Press.

Triandis, H. C. (1995). *Individualism and collectivism.* Boulder, CO: Westview.

Triandis, H. C., Leung, K., Villareal, M., & Clack, F. (1985). Allocentric versus idiocentric tendencies. *Journal of Research in Personality, 19,* 395–415.

Triandis, H. C., & Triandis, L. M. (1962). A cross-cultural study of social distance. *Psychological Monographs, 76* Whole No. 540.

Triandis, H. C., & Vassiliou, V. (1967). Frequency of contact and stereotyping. *Journal of Personality and Social Psychology, 7,* 316–328.

Triandis, H. C., Vassiliou, V., & Nassiakou, M. (1968). Three cross-cultural studies of subjective culture. *Journal of Personality and Social Psychology, 8* (Pt. 2 monograph supplement).

Triandis, H. C., Villareal, M., Asai, M., & Lucca, N. (1988). Individualism and collectivism: Cross-cultural perspectives on self-ingroup relationships. *Journal of Personality and Social Psychology, 54,* 323–338.

Trommsdorff, G. (1989). *Socialization im Kulturvergleich.* Stuttgart: Ferdinant Enke.

Trommsdorff, G., & Iwawaki, S. (1989). Students' perceptions of socialisation and gender role in Japan and Germany. *International Journal of Behavioral Development, 12,* 485–493.

Tryphon, A., & Vonèche, J. (1996). Introduction. In A. Tryphon & J. Vonèche (Eds.), *Piaget–Vygotsky: The social genesis of thought* (pp. 1–10). Hove, East Sussex: Psychology Press.

Tulviste, P. (1978). On the origins of theoretic syllogistic reasoning in culture and in the child. *Acta et Commentationes Universitatis Tartuensis, no. 474,* 3–22.

Turner, J. C., Shaver, I., & Hogg, M. (1983). Social categorization, interpersonal attraction, and group formation. *British Journal of Social Psychology, 22,* 227–239.

Tyler, S. A. (Ed.). (1969). *Cognitive anthropology.* New York: Holt, Rinehart & Winston.

Tylor, E. B. (1865). *Researches into the early history of mankind and development of civilization.* London: John Murray.

Vallerand, R. J. (Ed.) (1994). *Les fondements de la psychologie sociale.* Quebec: Gaetan Morin.

Valsiner, J. (1987). *Culture and the development of children's action: A cultural-historical theory of developmental psychology.* New York: Wiley. 2nd ed., 1997.

Valsiner, J. (1988). *Culture and developmental psychology.* Bern: Hogrefe.

Valsiner, J. (Ed.). (1989a). *Child development in cultural context.* Toronto: Hogrefe and Huber.

Valsiner, J. (1989b). *Human development and culture.* Toronto: Lexington Books.

Valsiner, J., & Lawrence, J. (1997). Human development in culture across the life span. In J. W. Berry, P. R. Dasen, & T. S. Saraswathi (Eds.), *Handbook of cross-cultural psychology,* Vol. 2, *Basic processes and human development* (pp. 69–106). Boston, MA: Allyn & Bacon.

van de Vijver, F. J. R., & Leung, K. (1997). Methods and data analysis of comparative research. In J. W. Berry, Y. H. Poortinga, & J. Pandey (Eds.), *Handbook of cross-cultural psychology,* Vol. 1, *Theory and method* (pp. 257–300). Boston, MA: Allyn & Bacon.

van Dongen-Melman, J. E.W. M., Koot, H. M., & Verhulst, F. C. (1993). Cross-cultural validation of Harter's self perception profile for children in a Dutch sample. *Educational and Psychological Measurement, 53,* 739–753.

Van Leeuwen, M. S. (1978). A cross-cultural examination of psychological differentiation in males and females. *International Journal of Psychology, 13,* 87–122.

Vasquez, A. (1984). Les implications idéologiques du concept d'acculturation. *Cahiers de Sociologie Economique et Culturelle, 1,* 83–121.

Vega, W., & Rumbaut, R. (1991). Ethnic minorities and mental health. *Annual Review of Sociology, 17,* 351–383.

Vega, W., Kolody, B., Valle, R., & Weir, J. (1991). Social networks, social support, and their relationship to depression among immigrant Mexican women. *Human Organization, 50,* 154–162.

Vernon, P. E. (1969). *Intelligence and cultural environment.* London: Methuen.

Viljoen, H. G. (1974). Relationship between stereotypes and social distance. *Journal of Social Psychology, 92,* 313–314.

Voland. E. (1993). *Grundriss der Soziobiologie.* Stuttgart, Jena: Fischer.

Vygotsky, L. A. (1962). *Thought and language.* Cambridge, MA: MIT Press.

Vygotsky, L. S. (1978). *Mind and society: The development of higher psychological processes.* Cambridge, MA: Harvard University Press.

Wade, C., & Tavris, C. (1996). *Psychology.* New York: HarperCollins.

Wagner, D. A. (1978). Memories of Morocco: The influence of age, schooling and environment on memory. *Cognitive Psychology, 10,* 1–28.

Wagner, D. A. (1981). Culture and memory development. In H. C. Triandis & A. Heron (Eds.), *Handbook of cross-cultural psychology,* Vol. 4, *Developmental psychology* (pp. 187–232). Boston, MA: Allyn & Bacon.

Wagner, D. A. (1983). Indigenous education and literacy in the third world. In D. A. Wagner (Ed.), *Child development and international development: Research–policy interfaces* (pp. 77–86). San Francisco: Jossey-Bass.

Wagner, D. A. (1988a). "Appropriate education" and literacy in the third world. In P. R. Dasen, J. W. Berry, & N. Sartorius (Eds.), *Health and cross-cultural psychology: Toward applications* (pp. 93–111). Newbury Park, CA: Sage.

Wagner, D. A. (1988b). L'acquisition du savoir et le "parcoeur": Passé et présent. In R. Bureau & D. de le Saivre (Eds.), *Apprentissages et cultures* (pp. 169–175). Paris: Karthala.

Wagner, D. A. (1993). *Literacy, culture & development: Becoming literate in Morocco.* Cambridge, England: Cambridge University Press.

Wagner, D. A., & Lofti, A. (1980). Traditional Islamic education in Morocco: Sociohistorical and psychological perspectives. *Comparative Education Review, 24,* 238–251.

Wagner, D. A., & Spratt, J. E. (1987). Cognitive consequences of contrasting pedagogies: The effects of Coranic preschooling in Morocco. *Child Development, 58,* 1207–1219.

Wallace, A. F. C. (1961). *Culture and personality.* New York: Random House.

Wallace, A. F. C., & Atkins, J. (1960). The meaning of kinship terms. *American Anthropologist, 62,* 58–80.

Ward, C. (1982). *Social loafing in Malaysia in the sound production procedure.* Unpublished manuscript.

Ward, C. (1995). Acculturation. In D. Landis & R. Bhagat (Eds.), *Handbook of intercultural training* (2nd Ed.) (pp. 124–147). Newbury Park, CA: Sage.

Ward, C., & Kennedy, A. (1992). Locus of control, mood disturbance and social difficulty during cross-cultural transitions. *International Journal of Intercultural Relations, 16,* 175–194.

Ward, C., & Kennedy, A. (1993a). Psychological and sociocultural adjustment during cross-cultural transitions: A comparison of secondary students overseas and at home. *International Journal of Psychology, 28,* 129–147.

Ward, C., Kennedy, A. (1993b). Where's the "culture" in cross-cultural transition? Comparative studies of sojourner adjustment. *Journal of Cross-Cultural Psychology, 24,* 221–249.

Ward, C., & Kennedy, A. (1995). Crossing cultures: The relationship between psychological and sociocultural dimensions of cross-cultural adjustment. In J. Pandey, D. Sinha, & P. Bhawuk (Eds.), *Asian contributions to cross-cultural psychology* (pp. 289–306). New Delhi: Sage.

Ward, C., & Searle, W. (1991). The impact of value discrepancies and cultural identity on psychological and sociocultural adjustment of sojourners. *International Journal of Intercultural Relations, 15,* 209–225.

Washburn, S. L. (1978). What we can't learn about people from apes. *Human Nature, 1,* 70–75.

Wassmann, J. (1993). Der kognitive Aufbruch in der Ethnologie. In J. Wassmann & P. R. Dasen (Eds.), *Alltagswissen / Les savoirs quotidiens / Everyday cognition* (pp. 95–133). Fribourg: Editions Universitaires.

Wassmann, J., & Dasen, P. R. (Eds.). (1993). *Alltagswissen / Les savoirs quotidiens / Everyday cognition.* Fribourg: Editions Universitaires.

Wassmann, J., & Dasen, P. R. (1994a). "Hot" and "cold": Classification and sorting among the Yupno of Papua New Guinea. *International Journal of Psychology, 29,* 19–38.

Wassmann, J., & Dasen, P. R. (1994b). Yupno number system and counting. *Journal of Cross-Cultural Psychology, 25,* 78–94.

Watkins, D., & Akande, A. (1992). The internal structure of the self-description questionnaire: A Nigerian investigation. *British Journal of Educational Psychology, 62,* 120–125.

Watkins, D., Hattie, J., & Regmi, M. (1994). The structure of self-esteem of Nepalese children. *Psychological Reports, 74,* 832–834.

Watkins, D., Lam, M. K., & Regmi, M. (1991). Cross-cultural assessment of self-esteem: A Nepalese investigation. *Psychologia, 34,* 98–108.

Weber, M. (1904). *The Protestant ethic and the spirit of capitalism.* New York: Scribner's.

Weiner, N., Pandey, J., & Latané, B. (1981). *Individual and group productivity in the United States and India.* Paper presented at the September, 1981 annual meeting of the American Psychological Association, Los Angeles, CA.

Weisner, T. S., & Gallimore, R. (1977). My brother's keeper: Child and sibling caretaking. *Current Anthropology, 18,* 169–190.

Weiss, B. (1992). Some consequences of early harsh discipline: Child aggression and a maladaptive social information processing style. *Child Development, 63,* 1321–1335.

Wertsch, J. V. (1985). *Vygotsky and the social formation of mind.* Cambridge, MA: Harvard University Press.

Wertsch, J. V., del Río, P., & Alvarez, A. (Eds.). (1995). *Sociocultural studies of mind.* Cambridge, England: Cambridge University Press.

Wertsch, J. V., Minick, N., & Arns, J. (1984). *The creation of context in joint problem-solving.* Cambridge, MA: Harvard University Press.

Westen, D. (1996). *Psychology: Mind, brain, and culture.* New York: Wiley.

Wetherell, M. (1982). Cross-cultural studies of minimal groups. In H. Tajfel (Ed.), *Social identity and intergroup relations* (pp. 207–238). Cambridge, England: Cambridge University Press.

Wheeler, L., Reis, H. T., & Bond, M. H. (1989). Collectivism/individualism in everyday social life: The middle kingdom and the melting pot. *Journal of Personality and Social Psychology, 57,* 79–86.

White, L. A. (1947). Culturological vs. psychological interpretations of human behavior. *American Sociological Review, 12,* 686–698.

Whiting, B. B. (Ed.) (1963). *Six cultures: Studies of child rearing.* Cambridge: Harvard University Press.

Whiting, B. B. (1965). Sex identity conflict and physical violence: A comparative study. *American Anthropologist, 67,* 123–140.

Whiting, B. B. (1980). Culture and social behavior: a model for the development of social behavior. *Ethos, 8,* 95–116.

Whiting, B. B., & Edwards, C. P. (1973). A cross-cultural analysis of sex differences in the behavior of children aged three through eleven. *Journal of Social Psychology, 91,* 171–188.

Whiting, B. B., & Edwards, C. P. (1988). *Children of different worlds: The formation of social behavior.* Cambridge, MA: Harvard University Press.

Whiting, B. B., & Whiting, J. W. M. (1971). Task assignment and personality: A consideration of the effects of herding on boys. In W. W. Lambert & R. Weisbrod (Eds.), *Comparative perspectives on social psychology* (pp. 33–45) Boston, MA: Little, Brown.

Whiting, B. B., & Whiting, J. W. M. (1975). *Children of six cultures: A psychocultural analysis.* Cambridge, MA: Harvard University Press.

Whiting, J. W. M. (1962). Comment. *American Journal of Sociology, 67,* 391–393.

Whiting, J. W. M. (1981). Environmental constraints on infant care practices. In R. H. Munroe, R. L. Munroe, & B. B. Whiting (Eds.), *Handbook of cross-cultural human development* (pp. 155–180). New York: Garland.

Whiting, J. W. M., & Child, I. L. (1953). *Child training and personality: A cross-cultural study.* New Haven, CT: Yale University Press.

Whiting, J. W. M., Kluckhohn, R., Anthony, A., & Hartley, E. L. (1958). The function of male initiation ceremonies at puberty. In E. E. Maccoby & T. Newcomb (Eds.), *Readings in social psychology* (3rd ed.) (pp. 359–370). New York: Holt.

Williams, J. E., & Best, D. L. (1989). *Sex and psyche: Self concept viewed cross-culturally.* Newbury Park, CA: Sage.

Williams, J. E., & Best, D. L. (1982/1990a). *Measuring sex stereotypes: A thirty nation study.* Beverly Hills, CA: Sage.

Williams, J. E., & Best, D. L. (1990b). *Sex and psyche: Gender and self viewed cross-culturally.* Newbury Park, CA: Sage.

Williams, K., Williams, K., Kawana, Y., & Latané, B. (1984). *Social loafing in Japan: A developmental cross-cultural study.* Paper presented at the May, 1984 annual meeting of the Midwestern Psychological Association, Chicago, IL.

Wilson, E. O. (1975). *Sociobiology.* Cambridge, MA: Harvard University Press.

Wilson, E. O., & Herrnstein, R. J. (1985). *Crime and human nature.* New York: Simon and Schuster.

Witkin, H. A. (1978). *Cognitive style in personal and cultural adaptation.* Worcester, MA: Clark University Press.

Witkin, H. A., & Berry, J. W. (1975). Psychological differentiation in cross-cultural perspective. *Journal of Cross-Cultural Psychology, 6,* 4–82.

Witkin, H. A., Dyk, R. B., Faterson, H. F., Goodenough, D. R., & Karp, S. A. (1962). *Psychological differentiation.* New York: Wiley.

Wober, M. (1974). Towards an understanding of the Kiganda concept of intelligence. In J. W. Berry & P. R. Dasen (Eds.), *Culture and cognition* (pp. 261–280). London: Methuen.

Wolf, A. W., Lozoff, B., Latz, S., & Paludetto, R. (1996). Parental theories in the management of young children's sleep in Japan, Italy, and the United States. In S. Harkness & C. M. Super (Eds.), *Parents' cultural belief systems: Their origins, expressions, and consequences* (pp. 364–384). New York: Guilford.

Wolfe, A. (1995). Has there been a cognitive revolution in America? The flawed sociology of The Bell Curve. In S. Fraser (Ed.), *The Bell curve wars: Race, intelligence, and the future of America* (pp. 109–123). New York: Basic Books.

Woodhouse, H. C. (1987). Inter- and intra-group aggression illustrated in the rock paintings of South Africa. *Ethnologie, 10,* 42–48.

Woodworth, R. S. (1938). *Experimental psychology.* New York: Holt.

World Health Organization (1991). *The mental health problems of migrants: Report from six European countries.* Geneva: WHO.

Worthman, C. M., & Whiting, J. W. M. (1987). Social change in adolescent sexual behavior, mate selection, and premarital pregnancy rates in a Kikuyu community. *Ethos, 15,* 145–165.

Wundt, W. (1910–1920). *Völkerpsychologie (10 vols.).* Leipzig: Englemann. English translation: *Elements of folk psychology.* London: Allen & Unwin, 1916.

Young, T. J. (1991). Poverty and aggression management among Native Americans. *Psychological Reports, 69,* 609–610.

Young, T. J. (1992). Myths about aggression and attitudes toward the death penalty. *Psychological Reports, 71,*1337–1338.

Zack, M., & Bril, B. (1989). Comment les mères françaises et bambara du Mali se représentent-elles le développement de leur enfant? In J. Retschitzki, M. Bossel-Lagos, & P. R. Dasen (Eds.), *La recherche interculturelle,* Vol. 2 (pp. 7–17). Paris: L'Harmattan.

Zempléni, A. (1972). Milieu africain et développement. In F. Duychaerts, C. B. Hindley, I. Lezine, M. Reuchlin, & A. Zempléni (Eds.), *Milieu et developpement* (pp. 151–213). Paris: Presses Universitaires de France.

Zheng, X., & Berry, J. W. (1991). Psychological adaptation of Chinese sojourners in Canada. *International Journal of Psychology, 26,* 451–470.

Zimet, S. G., Wiberg, J. L., & Blom, G. E. (1971). Attitudes and values in primers from the U. S. and twelve other countries. *Journal of Social Psychology, 84,* 167–174.

NAME INDEX

SUBJECT INDEX